Communications in Computer and Information Science 958

Commenced Publication in 2007
Founding and Former Series Editors:
Phoebe Chen, Alfredo Cuzzocrea, Xiaoyong Du, Orhun Kara, Ting Liu,
Dominik Ślęzak, and Xiaokang Yang

More information about this series at http://www.springer.com/series/7899

Pradeep Kumar Singh · Marcin Paprzycki
Bharat Bhargava · Jitender Kumar Chhabra
Narottam Chand Kaushal · Yugal Kumar (Eds.)

Futuristic Trends in Network and Communication Technologies

First International Conference, FTNCT 2018
Solan, India, February 9–10, 2018
Revised Selected Papers

 Springer

Editors
Pradeep Kumar Singh
Jaypee University of Information
Technology
Solan, India

Marcin Paprzycki
Systems Research Institute
Polish Academy of Sciences
Warsaw, Poland

Bharat Bhargava
Department of Computer Sciences
Purdue University
West Lafayette, IN, USA

Jitender Kumar Chhabra
National Institute of Technology
Kurukshetra
Kurukshetra, India

Narottam Chand Kaushal
National Institute of Technology Hamirpur
Hamirpur, India

Yugal Kumar
Jaypee University of Information
Technology
Solan, India

ISSN 1865-0929   ISSN 1865-0937 (electronic)
Communications in Computer and Information Science
ISBN 978-981-13-3803-8   ISBN 978-981-13-3804-5 (eBook)
https://doi.org/10.1007/978-981-13-3804-5

Library of Congress Control Number: 2018964612

This Springer imprint is published by the registered company Springer Nature Singapore Pte Ltd.
The registered company address is: 152 Beach Road, #21-01/04 Gateway East, Singapore 189721, Singapore

Preface

The International Conference on Futuristic Trends in Network and Communication Technologies (FTNCT 2018) targeted researchers from different domains of network and communication technologies with a single platform to showcase their research ideas. The main four technical tracks of conference were: Network Technologies, Wireless Networks, IoT, and Communication Technologies. The conference aims to be an annual ongoing event inviting researchers to exchange their ideas and thoughts. We hope that it will continue evolving and contributing to the field. The International Conference on Futuristic Trends in Network and Communication Technologies (FTNCT 2018) was hosted by Jaypee University of Information Technology, Waknaghat, Solan, India, during February 9–10, 2018, in association with the Southern Federal University, Russia, Sciences and Technologies of Image and Telecommunications (SETIT) of Sfax University, Tunisia, and technically sponsored by the CSI Chandigarh Chapter, India. We are thankful to our valuable authors for their contribution and our Technical Program Committee for their immense support and motivation toward making the first FTNCT a grand success. We are also grateful to our keynote speakers: Prof. Timothy A. Gonsalves, Director, IIT Mandi, India, Dr. Sanjay Sood, Jt. Director, CDAC Mohali, India, Dr. Pljonkin Anton, Southern Federal University, Russia, Dr. Jitender Kumar Chhabra, Professor, NIT Kurukshetra, India, and Dr. Mohd Helmy Abd Wahab, Faculty of Electrical and Electronic Engineering, Universiti Tun Hussein Onn, Malaysia, for sharing their technical talks and enlightening the delegates of the conference. We express our sincere gratitude to our publication partner, Springer, for believing in us.

February 2018

Pradeep Kumar Singh
Marcin Paprzycki
Bharat Bhargava
Jitender Kumar Chhabra
Narottam Chand Kaushal
Yugal Kumar

Organization

Technical Program Committee

TPC Chairs

Bharat Bhargava   Purdue University, USA
Wei-Chiang Hong   Jiangsu Normal University, China
Jitender Kumar Chhabra   NIT Kurukshetra, India
Pao-Ann Hsiung   National Chung Cheng University, Taiwan
Abhijit Sen   Kwantlen Polytechnic University, Canada

TPC Committee

A. K. Saini	University School of Management Studies, Guru Gobind Singh Indraprastha University, New Delhi, India
A. K. Verma	Centre for Reliability Engineering, IIT Mumbai, Mumbai, India
A. Q. Ansari	Jamia Millia Islamia, New Delhi, India
Abdelmajid Khelil	Technische Universität Darmstadt, Germany
Ahmed Kadhim Hussein	Babylon University, HIILA, Iraq
Ajith Abraham	Machine Intelligence Research Labs (MIR Labs), USA
Ajmer Saini	DCRUST, Sonipat, India
Alak Majumdar	National Institute of Technology, NIT-Arunchal Pradesh, India
Alessandro Brawerman	Positivo University, Brazil
Alex Kwang Leng Goh	Curtin University, Australia
Alexey Vinel	Saint-Petersburg Institute for Informatics and Automation, Russia
Alok Singh	University of Hyderabad, India
Amay Kumar Rath	DRIEMS, Cuttack, India
Amit Prakash Singh	GGSIPU, Delhi, India
Amit Prakash Singh	IP University, Delhi, India
Ammar Almomani	Al- Balqa Applied University, Jordan
Amrit Kumar Agrawal	Apollo Institute of Technology, Kanpur, India
Anand Kumar	M.S. Engineering College, Bangalore, India
Andera Stern	University of Sydney, Australia
Andy Adamatzky	University of the West of England, UK
Anil Panghal	HCTM Technical Campus, Kaithal, India

Animesh Dutta	National Institute of Technology, NIT-Durgapur, India
Ankit Mundra	Manipal University, Jaipur, India
Anmol Ratna Saxena	National Institute of Technology, NIT-Delhi, India
Anurag Jain	GGSIPU, Delhi, India
Anurag Seetha	CV Raman University, Bhopal, India
Anurag Singh	National Institute of Technology, NIT-Delhi, India
Anurag Srivastava	IIIT, Gwalior, M.P., India
Arti Noor	CDAC, Noida, India
Ashutosh Kumar Singh	NIT Kurukshetra, India
Atta ur Rehman Khan	University of Malaya, Kuala Lumpur, Malaysia
Augusto Neto	Universidade Federal do Ceará, Brazil
Awadhesh Kumar Singh	NIT Kurukshetra, India
B. B. Gupta	NIT Kurukshetra Haryana, India
B. B. Sagar	Birla Institute of Technology, BITS- Ranchi, India
Babita Pandey	Lovely Professional University, Punjab, India
Basant Kumar	MNIT Allahabad, India
C. K. Jha	Banasthali University, Rajasthan, India
C. S. Rai	USIT, GGSIPU, Delhi, India
Carsten Gremzow	University of Wuppertal, Germany
Christos Kartsaklis	Oak Ridge National Laboratory, USA
D. K. Lobiyal	Jawaharlal Nehru University, Delhi, India
David Eduardo Pinto Avendano	Benemérita Universidad Autónoma de Puebla (BUAP), Mexico
Debanjan Mahata	Infosys Innovation Labs, San Francisco, USA
Deeapak Garg	IEEE Delhi Section, India
Dheeraj Chahal	IBM Research Lab, India
Dheeraj Kaushik	Intel, USA
Dhiraj K. Pradhan	University of Bristol, UK
Dietmar Tutsch	University of Wuppertal, Germany
Dilbag Singh	National Institute of Technology, NIT-Jalandhar, India
Dilip Singh Sisodia	National Institute of Technology, NIT-Raipur, India
Eduard Babulak	University of Maryland University College, USA
Emmanuel Jeannot	Inria Bordeaux Sud-Ouest, France
Esraa Alomari	Universiti Sains Malaysia, Malaysia
Gaurav Bathla	Chandigarh University, India
Gaurav Bhatnagar	Indian Institute of Technology Jodhpur, Rajasthan, India
Ghulam Abbas	Liverpool Hope University, UK
Gilbert Babin	HEC Montreal, Canada
G. S. Badrinath	R&D Group, Samsung Electronics Noida, India
Gurvinder Singh Baicher	University of Wales, UK
Hamid Ali Abed Al-asadi	Basra University, Iraq
Hanen Idoudi	ENSI-Manouba University, Tunisia
J. Amudhavel	KL University, Andhra Pradesh, India
Jaisankar N.	SCSE, VIT, Vellore, Tamil Nadu, India
Jamuna Kanta Sing	Jadavpur University, West Bengal, India

Jean Frédéric Myoupo	The University of Picardie-Jules Verne, France
Jimson Mathew	University of Bristol, UK
Jinjun Chen	University of Technology Sydney, Australia
Jorge A. Cobb	University of Texas at Dallas, USA
K. N. Mishra	Birla Institute of Technology, BITS-Ranchi, India
Kanad Kishore Biswas	Indian Institute of Technology-Delhi, India
Kanwal Garg	Kurukshertra University, Haryana, India
Karan Singh	JNU, Delhi, India
Khalid Al-Begain	University of Glamorgan, UK
Lalit K. Awasthi	National Institute of Technology, NIT-Hamirpur, India
Lau Siong Hoe	Multimedia University, Malaysia
Lei Shu	Osaka University, Japan
Lillie Dewan	National Institute of Technology, NIT-KUK, India
Linsey Pang	Researcher at IBM, Sydney, Australia
Lukasz Andrzej Glinka	Poland
Lydia Manikonda	Arizona State University, USA
M. P. S. Bhatia	NSIT, Delhi, India
M. N. Doja	Jamia Millia Islamia, New Delhi, India
M. N. Hoda	BVICAM, New Delhi, India
M. P. Gupta	IIT Delhi, New Delhi, India
M. Karthikeyan	Tamilnadu College of Engineering, Coimbatore, India
M. P. S. Bhatia	Netaji Subhash Institute of Technology, India
M. U. Kharat	MET's Institute of Engineering, Adgaon, Nashik, India
Madhu	National Institute of Technology, NIT-Hamirpur, India
Manik Sharma	DAV University, Jalandhar, India
Manish Dixit	MITS Gwalior, India
Manish Khare	Shri Ramswaroop Memorial University, Lucknow, India
Manoj Diwakar	Babasaheb Bhimrao Ambedkar University, Lucknow, India
Manu Sood (Director)	UIIT, HPU, Shimla, India
Marcin Paprzycki	Systems Research Institute, Polish Academy of Sciences, Poland
Maria Engracia Gomez	Universidad Politecnica de Valencia, Spain
Matadeen Bansal	IIITDM Jabalpur, India
Mayank Dave	NIT Kurukshetra, India
Mayank Aggarwal	Gurukul Kangri University, Haridwar, India
Mikulas Alexik	University of Zilina, Slovakia
Mohammad Wazid	CSTAR, IIIT Hyderabad, India
Mohammed Al-Faiz	Nahrain University, Iraq
Mohand Lagha	Saad Dahlab University of Blida, Algeria
Mohd Helmy Abd Wahab	Universiti Tun Hussein Onn Malaysia, Malaysia
Mohit Mittal	Gurukul Kangri University, Haridwar, India
Mohsen Askari	University of Technology, Australia
Munish Kumar	CDAC-Noida, India
Nabanita Das	Indian Statistical Institute, India

Sandeep Saini	The LNM Institute of Information Technology, Jaipur, India
Sanjay Kumar Singh	IIT BHU, Varanasi, India
Sanjay Sood (Joint Director)	C-DAC Mohali, India
Sanjeev Patel	JIIT Noida, India
Santosh Kumar	IIT (BHU) Varanasi, India
Satish Chandra Tiwari	Cadence Design Systems, Noida, India
Satish Kumar Singh	IIIT Allahabad, India
Sattar Sadkhan	University of Babylon, Iraq
Shailendra Narayan	Amity School of Engineering and Technology, Noida, India
Shashidhar G. Koolagudi	National Institute of Technology, NIT-Surathkal, India
Siba Kumar Udgata	University of Hyderabad, Hyderabad, India
Siddharth Ghosh	Keshav Memorial Institute of Technology, Hyderabad, India
Siddharth Singh	NIT Delhi, India
Sunil Kaushik	HCTM Technical Campus, Kaithal, India
Sunil Kumar Vasistha	Mody University, Sikar, India
Sunil Kumar Pandey	ITS Ghaziabad, India
Surender Kumar	HCTM Technical Campus, Kaithal, India
Surendra Rahmatkar	Shree Rayeshwar Institute of Engineering and Information Technology, Goa, India
Sushila Madan	LSR University of Delhi, India
Taimoor Khan	National Institute of Technology, NIT-Silchar, India
Triloki Pant	Doon University Dehradun, India
Umesh Sisodia	CircuitSutra Technologies, India
Upendra	Government Polytechnic, Mirzapur, U.P., India
V. B. Singh	Delhi University, New Delhi, India
V. R. Singh	IEEE-Delhi Section, India
Vibhakar Mansotra	University of Jammu, Jammu, India
Victor Govindaswamy	Texas A&M University, USA
Vidushi Sharma	Gautam Buddha University, India
Vijay Kumar Semwal	NIT Jamshedpur, India
Vijay Saini	Alstom India Ltd., New Delhi, India
Vijay Singh Rathore (Chairman)	CSI, Jaipur-Chapter, India
Vikram Goyal	IIIT Delhi, India
Vincent Emeakaroha	Vienna University of Technology, Austria
Vipin Arora	University of Nebraska at Omaha, USA
Virender Kadyan	Chitkara University, Chandigarh, India
Virender Ranga	National Institute of Technology, Kurukshetra, India
Vishal Kesari	MTRDC DRDO Bangalore, India
Vivek Singh	BHU, Varanasi, India
Wlodek Zuberek	Memorial University, Canada
Yogendra Narain Singh	IET, Lucknow, India
Yogesh Singh	Delhi Technological University (DTU), Delhi, India

Yudhveer Singh	UIET, Maharishi Dayanand University, Rohtak, India
S. S. Dubey	IBM India, India
Zhihan Lv	SIAT, Chinese Academy of Science, China
Zhihui Du	Tsinghua University, China
Mohamed Salim Bouhlel	Sfax University, Tunisia
Hicham Berkouk	University of Bejaia, Algeria
Gwo-Jen Hwang	National Taiwan University of Science and Technology, Taiwan
Mahesh Bundele	Poornima University, Jaipur, Rajasthan, India
Joy Christian	Wolfson College, University of Oxford, UK
Arpan Kumar Kar	IIT Delhi, India
Joong Hoon Kim	Korea University, South Korea
Kazumi Nakamatsu	University of Hyogo, Japan
Zdzislaw Polkowski	Jan Wyzykowski University, Poland
Hammad Shafqat	MEDENGG, Pakistan
Hussain Falih Mahdi	National University of Malaysia, Malaysia
José António C. Santos	University of the Algarve, Portugal
Raghvendra Kumar	LNCT Group of College, Jabalpur, MP, India
Nilanjan Dey	Techno India College of Technology, Kolkata, India
Vishnu Narayan Mishra	Indira Gandhi National Tribal University, Madhya Pradesh, India
Wassila Issaadi	University of Bejaia, Algeria
P. B. Barman	Jaypee University of Information Technology, India
Sunil Kumar Khah	Jaypee University of Information Technology, India
Vineet Sharma	Jaypee University of Information Technology, India
Dheeraj Sharma	Jaypee University of Information Technology, India
Pankaj Sharma	Jaypee University of Information Technology, India
Ragini Raj Singh	Jaypee University of Information Technology, India
Rajesh Kumar	Jaypee University of Information Technology, India
Surajit Kumar Hazra	Jaypee University of Information Technology, India
Rajiv Kumar	Jaypee University of Information Technology, India
Shruti Jain	Jaypee University of Information Technology, India
Ashwani Sharma	Jaypee University of Information Technology, India
Emjee Puthooran	Jaypee University of Information Technology, India
Harsh Sohal	Jaypee University of Information Technology, India
Meenakshi Sood	Jaypee University of Information Technology, India
Nafis uddin Khan	Jaypee University of Information Technology, India
Neeru Sharma	Jaypee University of Information Technology, India
Shweta Pandit	Jaypee University of Information Technology, India
SunilDatt Sharma	Jaypee University of Information Technology, India
Vikas Baghel	Jaypee University of Information Technology, India
Abd El Rahman Shabayek	University of Luxembourg, Luxembourg
Ha Huy Cuong Nguyen	Quang Nam University, Vietnam
Ashish Kumar Luhach	CT Group of Institution, Jalandhar, Punjab, India
Abhishek Bhattacharya	Institute of Engineering and Management, Kolkata, India

Pljonkin Anton	Institute of Computer Technologies and Information Security, Southern Federal University, Russia
Sudeep Tanwar	Institute of Technology, Nirma University, Ahmedabad, Gujarat, India
Adityapratap Singh	AKGEC Ghaziabad, India
Samayveer Singh	Bennett University, Greater Noida, India
Ioan-Cosmin Mihai	Alexandru Ioan Cuza, Police Academy, Romania
Neha Choudhary	Manipal University, Jaipur, Rajasthan, India
Naveen Jaglan	JUIT, Waknaghat, Solan, India
Aruna Malik	Galgotias University, Greater Noida, India
Rajdeev Tiwari	ABESIT, Ghaziabad, India
Sakshi Babbar	BML Munjal University, Gurugram, India
Kaimrul Hawari	Universiti Malaysia Pahang, Malaysia
Anil Arora	Thapar University, Punjab, India
Rosilah Hassan	Universiti Kebangsaan Malaysia
Vinay Kumar	Thapar University, Punjab, India
Suresh Shanmugasundaram	Botho University, Botswana
Pradeep Chauhan	University of KwaZulu-Natal, South Africa
Arvind Selwal	Central University, Jammu, India
Baijmath Kaushik	SMVDU, Jammu, India
Yashwant Singh	Central University Jammu, India
Yugal Kumar	JUIT Waknaghat, Solan, India
Shailendra Shukla	Jaypee University of IT, Waknaghat, Solan, HP, India
Rajinder Sandhu	JUIT, Waknaghat, Solan, India
M. U. Bokhari	Aligarh Muslim University, India
Konstantin Rumyantsev	Southern Federal University, Russia
Sudhanshu Tyagi	GB Pant University, India
S. P Ghrera	JUIT, Solan, H.P, India
Ravindra Bhat	JUIT, Solan, H.P, India
Mohammad Ayoub Khan	Taibah University, Kingdom of Saudi Arabia
Vivek Shegal	JUIT, Solan, H.P, India
Nitin Rakesh	Amity University, Noida, India
Rajeev Kumar	NSIT Delhi, India
Rajesh Tyagi	SRM University, Modinagar Campus, UP, India

Organizing Committee

Chief Patrons

Shri Jaiprakash Gaur Ji   Jaypee Group, India
Shri Manoj Gaur Ji   Jaypee Group JUIT, India

Patron

Vinod Kumar   Jaypee University of Information Technology, India

Co-patron

Samir Dev Gupta   Jaypee University of Information Technology, India

Advisory Committee

Abhijit Sen   Computer Science and Information Technology,
    Kwantlen Polytechnic University, Canada
Ioan-Cosmin Mihai   Alexandru Ioan Cuza Police Academy, Romania
Pljonkin Anton   Institute of Computer Technologies and Information
    Security, Southern Federal University, Russia
Marcin Paprzycki   Systems Research Institute, Polish Academy
    of Sciences, Warsaw, Poland
Sanjay Sood   C-DAC Mohali, India
Arti Noor   C-DAC Noida, India

Principal General Chairs

Satya Prakash Ghrera   Jaypee University of Information Technology, India
Bharat Bhargava   Purdue University, USA

Honorary Chairs

Pao-Ann Hsiung   National Chung Cheng University, Taiwan
Wei-Chiang Hong   School of Education Intelligent Technology,
    Jiangsu Normal University, China

Program Chairs

Jitender Kumar Chhabra   Department of Computer Engineering, NIT
    Kurukshetra, India
Narottam Chand Kaushal   NIT Hamirpur, India

Executive General Chairs

Pradeep Kumar Singh   Jaypee University of Information Technology, India
Pelin Angin   Purdue University, USA

Finance Chair

Maj Gen Rakesh Bassi   Jaypee University of Information Technology, India
  (Retd.)

Organizing Secretariat

Yugal Kumar   Jaypee University of Information Technology, India
Amit Kumar   Jaypee University of Information Technology, India

Technical Program Committee Co-ordinators

Vivek Kumar Sehgal   Jaypee University of Information Technology, India
Amit Kumar Singh   Jaypee University of Information Technology, India

Academic Partner

Southern Federal University, Russia

Technically Associated with

Computer Society of India, Chandigarh Chapter

Sciences and Technologies of Image and Telecommunications (SETIT) of Sfax University, (Tunisia)

Sponsors

JUIT, Waknaghat, HP, India (Host Institute)

CSI JUIT STUDENT CHAPTER

ACM JUIT STUDENT CHAPTER

Contents

Network Technologies

Wireless Networks

Communication Technologies

Implementation of AES-128 Using Multiple Cipher Keys

Shivani Sachdeva$^{(\boxtimes)}$ and Ajay Kakkar

Thapar Institute of Engineering and Technology, Patiala, Punjab, India
shvschdv@gmail.com, ajay.kakkar@thapar.edu

Abstract. The growth in communication technology has connected billions of people all over the globe. The frequent sharing of data among individuals, organizations and even countries has raised concerns over the security and privacy of the communication process. A successful solution to this problem is Encryption, which converts the data to an unintelligible form. The keys for encrypting and decrypting the data are known only to authorised users. Thus, encryption can efficiently secure the communication process. The technique presented here is a modified form of Advanced Encryption Standard (AES) with multiple cipher keys of length 128 bits. AES uses symmetric cryptography which means that same keys are used for encryption and decryption. AES is known to be resistant against any known cryptanalytic attacks. Although it is known to be secure, various improvements have been suggested previously to further enhance the security of AES. The proposed technique enhances the security by using three cipher keys. By increasing the no. of keys, the encryption and decryption times are increased. Trading off with the increase in encryption time, advantage is gained because the attempt to hack the data will require drastic efforts and thus security is increased.

Keywords: Encryption · Decryption · Cipher · Security · Ciphertext
AES

1 Introduction

Cryptography is the science of imparting security to the means of communication. It helps to save critical information or communicate across channels so that contents can't be known by anybody except the desired receiver [1]. Cryptanalysis is the technique which aims to defeat the efforts of cryptography. The goal of cryptanalysis is to find some weakness or vulnerabilities in the cryptographic algorithm so that security can be breached. Ethically used, cryptanalysis helps to find certain vulnerabilities in the scheme which can be overcome to make the system secure without any underlying weakness in algorithmic implementation.

With the exponential growth in internet usage, people are sharing data more often than ever before. The data exchanged ranges from textual documents to images, audio and video. Huge amounts of data sets are collected, analyzed and shared by various governmental agencies and private sector organizations. There are always groups or individuals present who try to illegally access the secret communication between multiple parties, and may cause harm to both, in the form of information loss, financial loss, leakage of secret information etc. This raises security concerns all over the world.

© Springer Nature Singapore Pte Ltd. 2019
P. K. Singh et al. (Eds.): FTNCT 2018, CCIS 958, pp. 3–16, 2019.
https://doi.org/10.1007/978-981-13-3804-5_1

Thus, researchers are devoted to develop new techniques to cope up with these attacks. New techniques are being devised which are highly secured, reliable and computationally efficient. Existing communication techniques are being updated to minimise their vulnerability to attacks [1].

2 Advanced Encryption Standard (AES)

In 1997, US National Institute of Standards and Technology (NIST) called for proposals for Advanced Encryption Standard [2]. Fifteen proposals were submitted, out of which five were finalised for further analysis in 1999. In 2000, Rijndael algorithm was selected by NIST as AES. On 26 November 2001, AES was adopted as a formal US standard. It was published as Federal Information Processing Standard 197 (FIPS 197) in the Federal Register in 2001 [3]. AES is derived from Rijndael Algorithm, which was designed by two cryptographers - Jon Daemen and Vincent Rijmen. Rijndael has many sub-parts with different data block length and key lengths [4].

2.1 Description of Cipher

AES is a symmetric block cipher i.e. it uses same cipher key both for encrypting and decrypting. It encrypts a data block of 16 bytes in single iteration. It uses keys having different key lengths- 128, 192 or 256 bits. Therefore, depending upon key length used, different versions of AES are referred to as AES-128, AES-192, AES-256. Depending on the key size, the no. of round functions are 10, 12 and 14 respectively [2]. Figure 1 describes the basic input and output parameters for AES encryption.

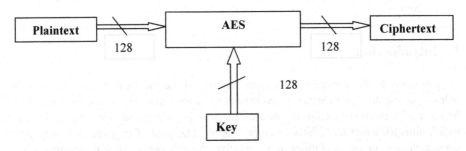

Fig. 1. Various parameters in AES-128

2.2 Byte

The main entity of data which is manipulated in AES is a byte, i.e. a group of 8 bits is considered as a basic single unit. Plaintext, Cipher key and Ciphertext are dealt with as collection of bytes [5].

Block length = 128 bits (128/8 = 16 bytes)   Key Length = 128 bits (128/8 = 16 bytes)
Key Length = 192 bits (192/8 = 24 bytes)
Key Length = 256 bits (256/8 = 32 bytes)

Here, the discussion is limited to AES-128 only as the proposed technique attempts at modifying it by increasing the no. of keys.

2.3 State of the Algorithm

The various operations in AES algorithm are operated upon a 4 × 4 array where each element represents a byte. This 4x4 array is called state of the algorithm. Initially, all the data bytes are input into the state array as shown:

B0	B4	B8	B12
B1	B5	B9	B13
B2	B6	B10	B14
B3	B7	B11	B15

Constituent bytes in each column of the array form 32 bit words. Therefore, state is signified as 1 × 4 matrix of four 32-bit words [5].

2.4 Galois Field Arithmetic

Galois field refers to a set with finite number of elements. The operations like addition, subtraction, multiplication and inversion are applicable to the elements of Galois fields. Smallest Galois field is a field with only two elements 0 and 1. This field is referred to as GF(2). The operations of addition and multiplication in GF(2) are equivalent to logical XOR and logical AND. For the purpose of encryption in AES, a Galois field with 256 elements i.e. $GF(2^8)$ was selected. This was done so because each element in this field is represented by 8 bits and 8 bits together constitute one byte. Since this field is derived from the basic Galois field with two elements, therefore all the operations in AES follow the basic rules of GF(2) [5].

2.5 Internal Structure of AES

AES consists of layers which manipulate the 128-bit block of data. These layers are briefly described as follows. Figure 2 describes the basic block diagram for AES-128 encryption.

- Key Addition layer: A cipher key or subkey of length 128 bits, that is sequentially extracted from the original key in the key schedule, is logically XORed with state matrix.
- Byte Substitution layer: Every element of the state matrix is transformed in a non-linear fashion with the help of tables called substitution boxes or S-Boxes [2].
- Diffusion layer: This layer helps in diffusing the information of one bit on all other bits. It comprises of two sublayers. ShiftRows sublayer operates upon the data in byte form. The MixColumn sublayer helps to mix the columns in state matrix each of which has four bytes [2].

The manipulation performed on individual bytes in AES is described in detail as follows.

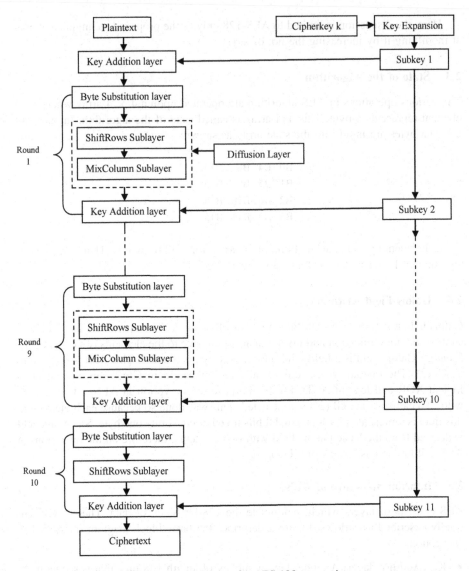

Fig. 2. Block diagram for AES-128 encryption

Byte Substitution Layer. The initial layer of every round is byte substitution layer. This is a byte substitution that operates in a non-linear fashion independently on every element of the State matrix using a Substitution-box. Each element from the state matrix is substituted by a byte from the substitution-box [2].

ShiftRows Sublayer. This operation performs shifting on the second row in state matrix cyclically by one position in left, the third row by two positions in the left and the fourth row by three positions to the left. No change is done to the first row. The main motive behind the operation of ShiftRows is to diffuse each element over the whole matrix [2]. Let us assume that the input for this operation is state matrix $E = (E_0, E_1,..., E_{15})$:

E_0	E_4	E_8	E_{12}
E_1	E_5	E_9	E_{13}
E_2	E_6	E_{10}	E_{14}
E_3	E_7	E_{11}	E_{15}

The result of the operation as a new state matrix is shown below:

E_0	E_4	E_8	E_{12}	← Elements not shifted
E_5	E_9	E_{13}	E_1	← Cyclic left Shift by 1 byte
E_{10}	E_{14}	E_2	E_6	← Cyclic left shift by 2 bytes
E_{15}	E_3	E_7	E_{11}	← Cyclic left shift by 3 bytes

MixColumn Sublayer. This operation is a linear operation which operates by mixing every column in the state matrix. MixColumn operation affects the AES in such a way that every input element changes the properties of four other bytes, therefore, most of the diffusion in AES occurs by this step. A column of state matrix is considered as a vector which has four bytes. Multiplication is performed on this vector using a static 4-by-4 matrix. GF(2^8) influences the rules followed in every subsequent operation [2]. For example, we can consider the calculation of first four output bytes as follows:

$$\begin{bmatrix} C0 \\ C1 \\ C2 \\ C3 \end{bmatrix} = \begin{bmatrix} 02\,03\,01\,01 \\ 01\,02\,03\,01 \\ 01\,01\,02\,03 \\ 03\,01\,01\,02 \end{bmatrix} \begin{bmatrix} B0 \\ B5 \\ B10 \\ B15 \end{bmatrix}$$

The next four bytes for the next column can be calculated by multiplication of the input bytes (B_4, B_9, B_{14}, B_3) by the same matrix given above.

Key Addition Layer. This layer in AES has two inputs – the state matrix which has 16 elements or 16 bytes, and the cipher key which also has byte length of 16 bytes. The inputs are added, which is equal to a logical XOR in Galois field having two elements. The subkeys for subsequent rounds are extracted by iterating the same operations in key schedule.

Key Schedule. Key Schedule extracts the subkeys from cipher key, which are subsequently used in further rounds of AES. The no. of subkeys required is equal to one more than the total no. of rounds. Therefore, in case of AES-128, the required no. of are 11 since there are total 10 rounds, as discussed previously. The subkeys are derived recursively in AES i.e. in order to extract 2nd key, 1st key must be known and for 3rd subkey, 2nd subkey must be known and so on [2].

2.6 AES Decryption

For the purpose of decryption in AES, all the rounds of encryption should be inverted. An inverse substitution box is used to perform inverse substitution. Inverse Shift Rows and Inverse Mix Columns are the other two constituent operations to remove the diffusion from AES. The constituent operations follow a similar order from encryption, just in a reverse fashion as shown in Fig. 5. The number of rounds in AES decryption remain the same as in encryption, i.e. 10 rounds.

For 10 rounds, 11 subkeys are needed in a recursion fashion. First round should have the last subkey, second round should have the second-to-last subkey. It is done by calculating the all subkeys initially and then storing them and retrieving as and when required. This aspect leads to a small delay in performing the decryption [2].

Since, the last encryption round does not perform the MixColumn operation, the first decryption round also does not contain the corresponding inverse layer. All other decryption rounds, however, contain all AES layers as described previously.

3 Literature Review

Tankard [6] discussed that in a big data set, it is impossible to find every piece of confidential information and tracking the users which have the access to sensitive data. Confidential data is to be encrypted which can include information in data bases, spread sheets, word documents and archives etc. Garfinkel [7] referenced the problem of securing financial transactions and other critical applications through the use of cryptography. Tomhave [8] introduced the main facets in key management. For coping up with key loss, it seemed befitting to establish an extra key that could be used in retrieving data for an emergent scenario. Parker [9] stressed upon the judicious usage of cryptography in various applications. The dangers and vulnerabilities posed to the system by cryptography were highlighted. Transmission errors, lost keys etc. can lead to critical information loss and harm an organisation greatly. Yang et al. [10] described the general theoretical ideas, algorithms, and standards for encryption of data, images and MPEG video. Comparisons were drawn between the various cryptographic algorithms based on various parameters like complexity, speed, memory requirement, key length etc. Patil et al. [11] discussed the basic standards for symmetric and asymmetric cryptography like DES, 3DES, AES, RSA and Blowfish. Nadeem et al. [12] highlighted the performance degradation of encryption algorithms when implemented in hardware across various applications. DES, TDES, AES and Blowfish were the algorithms which were used to encrypt same data files across various hardware platforms and performance was compared. Buchanan et al. [13] researched about the varying servers used across various industry sectors in today's scenario. In TLS Protocol, ECDHE-RSA-AES256-GCM-SHA384 is described to be the most popular cipher suite, which uses AES-256 for data encryption along with other schemes for key sharing and authentication. Rachh et al. [14] described the efficient implementation of

AES encryption and decryption in FPGA and ASIC using fully pipelined structures. Integrated circuits were designed by implementing block architectures of different layers in AES which minimized the delay in implementation. Osvik *et al.* [15] implemented AES-128 encryption technique in software targeting both low speed microcontrollers and microprocessors, and the high-speed Cell broadband engine and NVIDIA graphics processing units (GPUs). Jingmei *et al.* [16] discussed that the simple S-box of AES with only 9 terms can pose a vulnerability. A new S-box with 255 terms was presented which increase the security against attacks like linear and differential cryptanalysis. Gong *et al.* [17] discussed the AES Encryption Algorithm based on multiple look up tables. The main advantage was to reduce the encryption time. The mathematical preliminaries for generating the look-up tables were discussed. Dara *et al.* [18] discussed that the S-box used in standard AES algorithm is static. Generating the S-Box dynamically presents an important advantage of increasing the security of AES cipher system. Kumar *et al.* [19] suggested modification in AES by using a key of 320 bits from Polybius square and increasing the no. of rounds to 16 from 10, for encryption and decryption of data. Wahaballa *et al.* [20] discussed providing multiple layers of security to data communication by employing encryption and steganography, which is the technique to hide confidential data in a cover file so that data communication becomes undetectable to an intruder.

4   Proposed Methodology

From literature review, it was observed that the research done in field of AES was to improve performance and enhance the security by modifying the parameters and basic algorithm for AES. The changes were done either in by increasing the length of keys or improving S-Box implementation etc.

The proposed technique does not change the basic nature of AES-128 algorithm. The basic parameters are kept same as listed below.

- Data Block (Plaintext) Length: 128 bits (16 bytes)
- Cipher Key Length: 128 bits (16 bytes)
- Number of Rounds: 10
- State matrix: 4 × 4
- S-Box: Same as prescribed in the standard FIPS-197

In the proposed technique, an attempt is made to increase the security of the algorithm threefold by increasing the number of keys, which are used in encryption of the data or plaintext. A basic approach for a GUI is programmed in which user is prompted to enter the data or plaintext and three keys which are to be used for the purpose of encryption. The same keys shall be used for decrypting the ciphertext otherwise the result will not be the true plaintext. The increase in number of keys increases the effective key space. This drastically increases the number of permutations and combinations which will be required by the intruder to breach the security. Therefore, this approach enhances the security of algorithm in terms of encryption time as compared to security model proposed by Kakkar et al. [21].

Flowchart for encryption

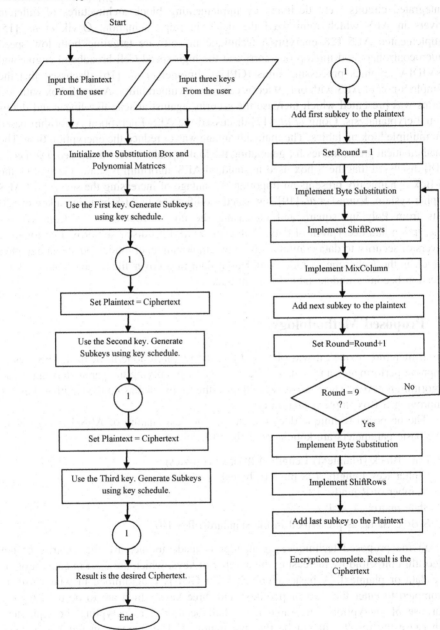

Fig. 3. Flowchart for encryption

Flowchart for Decryption

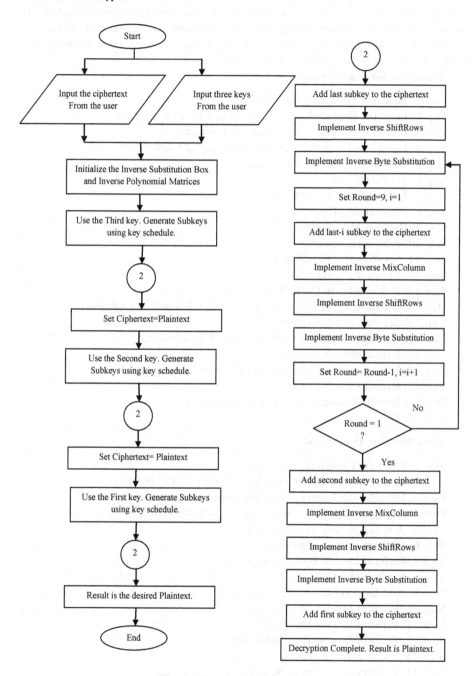

Fig. 4. Flowchart for decryption

It is to be kept in mind that increasing the number of keys also increases the corresponding execution time. A trade-off exists between number of keys which a user desires and the maximum allowable execution time which an application permits.

The basic algorithms and flowcharts which are followed for encryption and decryption of text are described in Figs. 3 and 4 respectively.

Algorithm for Encryption

Step 1: Input the Plaintext from user.
Step 2: Input the three cipher keys k1, k2 and k3 from the user.
Step 3: Initialize the S-box and polynomial matrices.
Step 4: Use k1 and generate subkeys using key schedule.
Step 5: Add first subkey to the plaintext.
Step 6: Set Round = 1.
Step 7: Perform Byte Substitution.
Step 8: Perform ShiftRows.
Step 9: Perform Mixcolumn.
Step 10: Add the next subkey.
Step 11: Set Round = Round + 1.
Step 12: Check if Round = 9.
Step 13: If Round! = 9, Go to Step 7.
Step 14: If Round == 9, repeat steps 7, 8 and 10. Result is Ciphertext.
Step 15: Set Plaintext = Ciphertext.
Step 16: Use k2 and generate subkeys from key schedule.
Step 17: Repeat steps 5 to 15.
Step 18: Use k3 and generate subkeys from key schedule.
Step 19: Repeat steps 5 to 14.
Step 20: Result obtained is the desired Ciphertext.
Step 21: End.

Algorithm for Decryption

Step 1: Input the Ciphertext from user.
Step 2: Input the three cipher keys k1, k2 and k3 from the user.
Step 3: Initialize the Inverse S-box and Inverse polynomial matrices.
Step 4: Use k1 and generate subkeys using key schedule.
Step 5: Add last subkey to the ciphertext.
Step 6: Perform Inverse ShiftRows.
Step 7: Perform Inverse Byte Substitution.
Step 8: Set Round = 9, i = 1.
Step 9: Add last-i subkey to the ciphertext.
Step 10: Perform Inverse MixColumn.
Step 11: Perform Inverse ShiftRows.
Step 12: Perform Inverse Byte Substitution.
Step 13: Set Round = Round-1, i = i+1
Step 14: If Round! = 1, Go to Step 9.
Step 15: If Round == 1, repeat steps 9 to 12.
Step 16: Add first subkey to the ciphertext. Result is plaintext.

Step 17: Set Ciphertext = Plaintext.
Step 18: Use k2 and generate subkeys from key schedule.
Step 19: Repeat steps 5 to 17.
Step 20: Use k3 and generate subkeys from key schedule.
Step 21: Repeat steps 5 to 16.
Step 22: Result obtained is the desired plaintext.
Step 23: End.

5 Results

The program code is implemented in MATLAB R2017a. The steps followed in implementing the code for AES-128 are explained as follows:

5.1 Encryption

User is required to input the data which has to be encrypted. As the code is implemented for AES-128, therefore, keys with only 16 letters are allowed. User has to input three cipher keys in order to securely encrypt the data. The necessary initializations of that of S-box and Polynomial Matrices has been done. The initial encryption on plaintext is performed using the 1st cipher key. The resulting ciphertext from the first round acts as the input plaintext for second round. Another round of encryption is implemented using the second cipher key. The ciphertext from the second round is made as final plaintext for the third and the final round. The output of the third round is final ciphertext. The screenshot of the whole encryption process is depicted in Fig. 5.

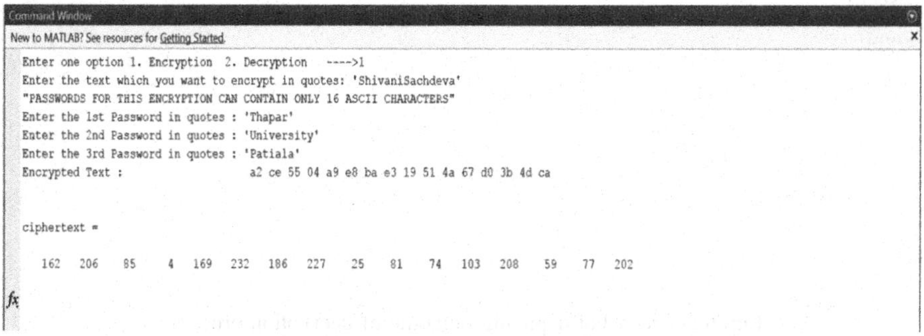

```
Command Window

New to MATLAB? See resources for Getting Started.

    Enter one option 1. Encryption 2. Decryption    ---->1
    Enter the text which you want to encrypt in quotes: 'ShivaniSachdeva'
    "PASSWORDS FOR THIS ENCRYPTION CAN CONTAIN ONLY 16 ASCII CHARACTERS"
    Enter the 1st Password in quotes : 'Thapar'
    Enter the 2nd Password in quotes : 'University'
    Enter the 3rd Password in quotes : 'Patiala'
    Encrypted Text :              a2 ce 55 04 a9 e8 ba e3 19 51 4a 67 d0 3b 4d ca


    ciphertext =

      162   206    85     4   169   232   186   227    25    81    74   103   208    59    77   202

fx
```

Fig. 5. Screenshot depicting outcome of encryption process

The process of encryption provides security to the data. A further enhancement in the security is provided by employing multiple cipher keys. Proposed scheme aims to enhance the security threefold by employing three keys. Some minor changes in the program code can provide with more or less keys, as required according to the application. The program can be used for personal applications in encrypting the data for some small level applications. Some further improvements in the code can be done by modifying the algorithm to decrease execution time.

5.2 Decryption

The process of decrypting the data is exact inverse of the process of encryption as shown in Fig. 6. User is required to enter the decimal equivalents of the ciphertext. The exact keys which are used for encryption must be known for the successful decryption of the data. The necessary initializations for inverse S-box and inverse polynomial matrices is done. The cipher keys are expanded. The addition of keys is done in a reverse order. Firstly, the third cipher key is utilized. The process of decryption is followed to generate the plaintext which will act as ciphertext for the next round. This ciphertext is input to the next round which also has second cipher key as the input. Following this the final round is performed in a similar way with the first cipher key as the input. The proposed model outperforms well in terms of execution time as compared to [22].

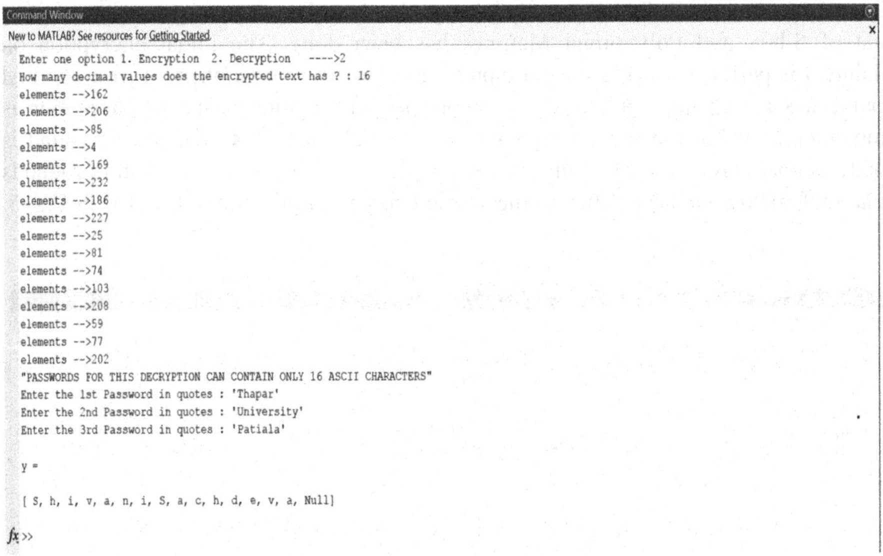

```
Command Window
New to MATLAB? See resources for Getting Started.
 Enter one option 1. Encryption  2. Decryption   ---->2
 How many decimal values does the encrypted text has ? : 16
 elements -->162
 elements -->206
 elements -->85
 elements -->4
 elements -->169
 elements -->232
 elements -->186
 elements -->227
 elements -->25
 elements -->81
 elements -->74
 elements -->103
 elements -->208
 elements -->59
 elements -->77
 elements -->202
 "PASSWORDS FOR THIS DECRYPTION CAN CONTAIN ONLY 16 ASCII CHARACTERS"
 Enter the 1st Password in quotes : 'Thapar'
 Enter the 2nd Password in quotes : 'University'
 Enter the 3rd Password in quotes : 'Patiala'

 y =

 [ S, h, i, v, a, n, i, S, a, c, h, d, e, v, a, Null]
fx >>
```

Fig. 6. Screenshot depicting outcome of decryption process

5.3 Encryption and Decryption Time

As stated previously, increasing the number of keys increases the effective execution times for Encryption and Decryption. Tests conducted to measure the encryption and decryption time using different number of keys gave following results.

Table 1. Execution time for encryption using different number of keys

No. of keys	Execution time (seconds)
1	13.88
2	22.31
3	32.55

As it is clear from Table 1, increasing the number of keys increases the effective execution time for encryption. This increase is due to increase in number of iterations and rounds with each additional key.

Table 2. Execution time for decryption using different number of keys

No. of keys	Execution time (seconds)
1	93.21
2	105.67
3	117.93

Table 2 indicates that increase in no. of keys increases the time for decryption. The reason being the same as in case of encryption. This execution time only exists when correct keys are input. If any intruder wants to attack the security system even by trying all the possible permutation and combination of keys, the effective key space (in case of multiple keys) makes it hugely complex and almost impossible to decrypt the data at an ordinary machine.

Thus, it is made clear that an increase in number of keys makes the system more secure by increasing the effective key space which makes it impossible for an intruder to guess the correct combination even by a brute-force attack. The encryption and decryption time increase only nominally, which will not be a big issue in case authenticated and intended parties with knowledge about keys, are accessing the system.

6 Conclusion and Future Scope

The advent of information technology and millions of bytes of data shared among the users all over the globe has made security and confidentiality a necessity in today's life. Cryptography is a really effective media to secure the data from the potential attacks by eaves-droppers. It fulfils the necessary goals of information security and hence is an indispensible tool in today's scenario. Keeping in mind the developments in the field of cryptography and that of AES-128, literature review has been carried out. The proposed scheme for AES-128 is designed using multiple cipher keys to enhance the security. The scheme increases the key space so that it becomes impossible for an eaves-dropper to guess the correct keys. Increase in execution times are only nominal. Results are presented in Sect. 5. Some improvisations in the code can be carried out in order to optimize the performance and increase the speed in execution.

References

1. PGP Corporation: An Introduction to Cryptography. Version 8.0, October 2002
2. Paar, C., Pelzl, J.: Understanding Cryptography: A Textbook for Students and Practitioners. Springer, Heidelberg (2010). https://doi.org/10.1007/978-3-642-04101-3
3. Forouzan, B.A., Mukhopadhyay, D.: Cryptography and Network Security. 2nd edn. McGraw Hill Publication (2013)
4. Daemen, J., Rijmen, V.: The Design of Rijndael Cipher. Springer, Heidelberg (2002). ISBN 978-3-662-04722-4
5. Announcing the Advanced Encryption Standard (AES). FIPS 197, 26 November 2001
6. Tankard, C.: Encryption as the corner stone of big data security. J. Netw. Secur. **2017**(3), 5–7 (2017)
7. Garfinkel, S.L.: Public key cryptography. Computer **29**(6), 101–104 (1996)
8. Tomhave, B.L.: Key management: the key to encryption. EDPACS J. **38**(4), 12–19 (2009)
9. Parker, D.B.: Cryptographic threat analysis. J. Inf. Syst. Secur. **2**(3), 13–17 (2008)
10. Yang, M., Bourbakis, N., Li, S.: Data-image-video encryption. IEEE Potentials **23**(3), 28–34 (2004)
11. Patil, P., Narayankar, P., Narayan, D.G., Meena, S.M.: A comprehensive evaluation of cryptographic algorithms: DES, 3DES, AES, RSA and Blowfish. In: International Conference on Information Security & Privacy (ICISP2015), 11–12 December 2015, Nagpur, India, pp. 617–624 (2015)
12. Nadeem, A., Javed, M.Y.: A performance comparison of data encryption algorithms. In: First International Conference on Information and Communication Technologies, ICICT-2005, Karachi, Pakistan, August 2005
13. Buchanan, W.J., Woodward, A., Helme, S.: Cryptography across industry sectors. J. Cyber Secur. Technol. **1**, 1–18 (2017)
14. Rachh, R.R., Ananda Mohan, P.V., Anami, B.S.: Efficient implementations for AES encryption and decryption. J. Circuits Syst. Signal Process. **31**(5), 1765–1785 (2012)
15. Osvik, D.A., Bos, J.W., Stefan, D., Canright, D.: Fast software AES encryption. In: Foundations of Software Engineering (FSE) (2010)
16. Jingmei, L., Baodian, W., Xinmei, W.: One AES S-box to increase complexity and its cryptanalysis. J. Syst. Eng. Electron. **18**(2), 427–433 (2007)
17. Gong, J., Liu, W., Zhang, H.: Multiple lookup table-based AES encryption algorithm implementation. In: International Conference on Solid State Devices and Materials Science (2012). Phys. Procedia **25**, 842–847 (2012)
18. Dara, M., Manochehri, K.: Using RC4 and AES key schedule to generate dynamic S-Box in AES. Inf. Secur. J.: Glob. Perspect. **23**(1–2), 1–9 (2014)
19. Kumar, P., Rana, S.B.: Development of modified AES algorithm for data security. Int. J. Light. Electron Opt. **127**(4), 2341–2345 (2016)
20. Wahaballa, A., Wahballa, O., Li, F., Ramadan, M., Qin, Z.: Multiple-layered securities using steganography and cryptography. Int. J. Comput. Appl. **36**(3), 93–100 (2015)
21. Kakkar, A., Singh, M.L., Bansal, P.K.: Mathematical analysis and simulation of multiple keys and S-Boxes in a multimode network for secure transmission. Int. J. Comput. Math. **89**(16), 2123–2142 (2012)
22. Kaur, L., Kakkar, A.: Data Security in Wireless Communication using Multiple Keys. http://dspace.thapar.edu:8080/jspui/handle/10266/4876

S-BOX Architecture

Abhishek Kumar and Sokat Tejani[⊠]

School of Electronics Engineering, Lovely Professional University,
Phagwara, Punjab, India
abkvjti@gmail.com, ssmtejani2@gmail.com

Abstract. Substitution-Box (S-BOX) is the most critical block in the Advanced Encryption Standard (AES) algorithm, consumes 75% of total power during encryption. The primary idea to implement S-BOX is to have a unique byte substitution. In this paper 4 different architecture of SBOX discussed; (a) look-up table or ROM based S-BOX contains a pre-computed value stored at defined address (b) modified look-up table based approach which uses decoders and multiplexer makes overall substitution faster (c) computational method has composite field architecture to compute the substitution byte (d) blend of computational method and look up table method where pre-computed multiplicative inverse values are stored in lookup table to reduce power consumption. Look up table based method requires a fetching circuit from a certain location, suffers from area overhead; to overcome that to be substituted values are divided into groups and using decoders and multiplexer that values will be fetched. The computational method requires complex computation result in high power consumption. To overcome that one particular module is pre-computed and stored in a look-up table in the last method. The overall objective of this paper is to implement S-box using different methods and to come up with method which is optimum as far as the area, power, delay parameters are concerned and security wise robust. In this work a comparative study of all these methods has been explored with CMOS 180 nm, 90 nm, and 45 nm technology node.

Keywords: S-BOX · Look up table · GF · RTL compiler · AES

1 Introduction

Modern day communication involves many kinds of security threat, though communications have increased significantly and also become sophisticated security issues are always present. Over the time, many techniques were developed to address this grey area; a technique devised to solve any issue, of communication must confirm three norms confidentiality, integrity, and availability. Confidentiality of communication said to be maintained when data which was to be communicated reaches to the desired recipient only and no one except that end user is able to gain any substantial information devising any illicit method. For any communication to take place it is must that end users get access to available medium which has been devised to establish the communication. Integrity presents only authorized parties should able to access to the medium, it should be taken care that recipient should get exactly what was desired to be communicated and not anything else.

© Springer Nature Singapore Pte Ltd. 2019
P. K. Singh et al. (Eds.): FTNCT 2018, CCIS 958, pp. 17–27, 2019.
https://doi.org/10.1007/978-981-13-3804-5_2

AES is adopted as the standard for cryptography by NSIT in the year 2001. Encryption is a method to include security while communication, plain text scrambled with a secret key generated from key generation center into ciphertext. Encryption is iterative process contains 4 steps AddRoundkey, SubByte, ShiftRow, and MixColumn [1], AES is iterative process it repeats substitution byte, shift row, mix column multiple time in the loop. AES-128, AES-192, and AES-256 execute in loop 10, 12 and 16 respectively. To get back original text from cipher similar key required; decryption is a reverse method of encryption contains AddRoundKey, InverseShiftRow, Inverse-SubByte, and InverseMixColumn. Substitution byte is a most complex bock and consumes 75% of the computation power of complete process; a byte is substituted for the output of add round key stage. Substitution is the implementation of Shannon's confusion-diffusion principles [1, 7–10].

Confusion: Creating confusion is one of the basic requirements of any cryptographic algorithm, Relationship between plain text and cipher-text with respect to the key. A strong confusion property is required to maintain the text secured in the ciphertext.
Diffusion: Diffusion is an element of randomness required to be present in substitution, for change in one bit of input, the substituted output should be changed by at least half of bits. This makes it unpredictable and the key gets difficult to predict in this case. It limits overall range available for substitution though or makes it difficult to make the table.

Substitution Box (S-Box) in AES takes care of confusion and diffusion; 256 different bytes are arranged as 16 * 16 matrix presented in Fig. 1. To read S-BOX output stages of add round key is grouped as first nibble select row (x) and the second nibble selects a column (y); respective -value fetched for substitution. In this work 4 different architectures of S-Box has been analyzed, SBOX with a lookup table (LUT), a modified lookup table with decoder and multiplexer, SBOX using goalies filed (GF) computation and modified GF based S-box using a look-up table. Section 2 contains the principle of mentioned 4 architectures implement with Cadence NCSIM using Verilog HDL and the result has been analyzed RTL compiler based CMOS 180 nm, 90 nm and 45 nm slow & fast library. Section 3 insights comparative analysis of SBOX in term of area, power and delay.

		y														
		0	1	2	3	4	5	6	7	8	9	a	b	c	d	e	f
	0	63	7c	77	7b	f2	6b	6f	c5	30	01	67	2b	fe	d7	ab	76
	1	ca	82	c9	7d	fa	59	47	f0	ad	d4	a2	af	9c	a4	72	c0
	2	b7	fd	93	26	36	3f	f7	cc	34	a5	e5	f1	71	d8	31	15
	3	04	c7	23	c3	18	96	05	9a	07	12	80	e2	eb	27	b2	75
	4	09	83	2c	1a	1b	6e	5a	a0	52	3b	d6	b3	29	e3	2f	84
	5	53	d1	00	ed	20	fc	b1	5b	6a	cb	be	39	4a	4c	58	cf
	6	d0	ef	aa	fb	43	4d	33	85	45	f9	02	7f	50	3c	9f	a8
x	7	51	a3	40	8f	92	9d	38	f5	bc	b6	da	21	10	ff	f3	d2
	8	cd	0c	13	ec	5f	97	44	17	c4	a7	7e	3d	64	5d	19	73
	9	60	81	4f	dc	22	2a	90	88	46	ee	b8	14	de	5e	0b	db
	a	e0	32	3a	0a	49	06	24	5c	c2	d3	ac	62	91	95	e4	79
	b	e7	c8	37	6d	8d	d5	4e	a9	6c	56	f4	ea	65	7a	ae	08
	c	ba	78	25	2e	1c	a6	b4	c6	e8	dd	74	1f	4b	bd	8b	8a
	d	70	3e	b5	66	48	03	f6	0e	61	35	57	b9	86	c1	1d	9e
	e	e1	f8	98	11	69	d9	8e	94	9b	1e	87	e9	ce	55	28	df
	f	8c	a1	89	0d	bf	e6	42	68	41	99	2d	0f	b0	54	bb	16

Fig. 1. S-BOX

2   Implementation Method of S-BOX

2.1   Look-Up-Table

Look up table (LUT) based realization of S-BOX it requires vast space of memory implemented with ROM or EPROM [1, 5]. Memory will be used to hold the values and scanning will be done across rows and columns to fetch the desired value shown in Fig. 2. 8 bits data which is to be substituted will be used to get the appropriate "to be substituted" value from the table. For this, 8 bits data as a combination of two nibbles. First of which, will give the number of the row from where data is to be fetched and second of which will give the number of the column from where data is to be fetched. The intersection point of these two entries will give the data to be substituted. [2] On the receiver side, the similar table will be there and the same method will be used there as well to get the desired outcome. LUT based S-BOX implementation is simple requires bulk memory. TheLUT S-BOX has rigid structure and suffers from unavoidable delay since LUT have predefined access time. Figure 2 presents a method to access a byte from LUT with multiplexing circuit; 8-bit input acts as address select a particular byte to be substituted from LUT. Simulation result of this architecture presents in Fig. 3, Table 1 shows the implementation with gpdk 180 nm, 90 nm, and 45 nm; slow library requires large number of cells and large delay compare to fast library while fast library results in more power consumption.

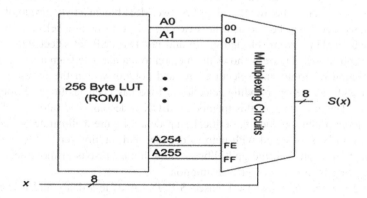

Fig. 2. Lookup table-based SBOX

It can be seen here from Table 1, for same technology node, faster library cells, gives improved delay but higher power consumption against slow library cells. Reason for this is power supply difference in faster and slower library. In the faster library, redundant cells also get removed result in a reduction in a total number of cell.

2.2   Modified Look-Up Table Using Decoders and Multiplexer

A unique method to read a byte from SBOX have been implemented using decoder and multiplexer, to make the ROM based implementation faster by reducing the number of

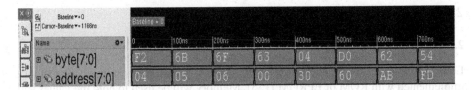

Fig. 3. Shows the simulation result of LUT based SBOX

Table 1. Implementation result of LUT based SBOX

LUT Based SBOX							
Technology		180 nm		90 nm		45 nm	
Library		Fast	Slow	Fast	Slow	Fast	Slow
Cell		414	415	409	441	443	460
Power (nw)	Static	54.747	124.588	14124.729	5670	135.414	37.608
	Dynamic	220603.21	131495.25	56032.9	39308.083	40715.29	22312.514
	Total	220658	131619.8	70157.63	44978.08	40850.7	22350.12
Delay (ps)		1702	4477	809	3070	1035	3320

LUT. An S-BOX is decomposed into 4 group of 64-byte further divided into 2×2 byte, Here 8 bits data which was divided in nibbles get further divided into a group of 2-bit which is explained below. Based on first two MSB bits in a byte, group of the "to be substituted data" will be decided, next two bit select a row in a selected row, next two-bit select column from selected group and last two LSB bit select the particular byte to be substituted. Figure 4 shows the method to fetch a byte from a 2×2 lookup table. Selection of group and selecting row and column within the group has been simplified with 2:4 decoders while selecting a byte has been facilitated through 4:1 multiplexer. The advantage of this method is SBOX is decomposed into a smaller size of 2×2 lookup table, reduce the critical path delay. Figure 4 illustrate a method to fetch a byte to be substituted with help of decoder and multiplexer. Table 2 presents implementation result with the gpdk library, slow library results in more delay while fast library results in high power consumption.

Table 2 presents modified LUT based S-BOX, gives less delay and hence faster design compare to earlier conventional Look-Up table based S-box. Area too gets somewhat reduced but at the cost of power. These two methods though suffer from cache memory attack where just observing access of cache key can be extracted except pre-fetching for each and every access is made a rule.

2.3 Galois Field

S-BOX can implement with composite field algorithm, contains two sub-module multiplicative inversions and the affine transformation. Byte substitution starts with mapping the field of input into composite filed by using isomorphic mapping, isomorphic mapped output applied to multiplicative inverse in Galois field followed

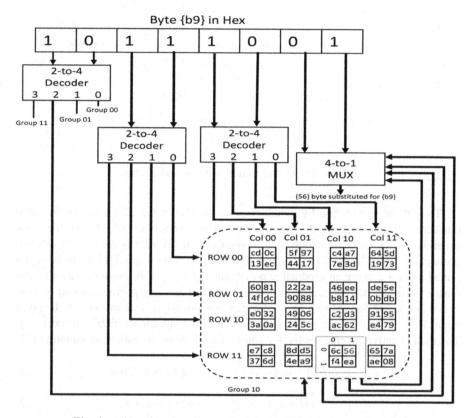

Fig. 4. Addressing decoding method for modified look-up table [4]

Table 2. Implementation result of modified LUT based SBOX

Modified LUT SBOX							
Technology		180 nm		90 nm		45 nm	
Library		Fast	Slow	Fast	Slow	Fast	Slow
No. of Cell		411	410	405	405	428	437
Power (nw)	Static	43.161	111.212	12384.882	4955.267	91.277	27.477
	Dynamic	367766.08	208492.91	73248.256	49448.729	43059.273	28590.554
	Total	367809.2	208604.1	85633.14	54404	43150.55	28618.03
Delay (ps)		1757	3961	728	2301	625	1845

finally re-map the result by inverse isomorphic function followed by an affine transform. Multiplicative inverse is a most expensive module, here number of hardware block greatly reduce by GF filed arithmetic shown in Fig. 5. Complete architecture has implemented with XOR and AND gate.

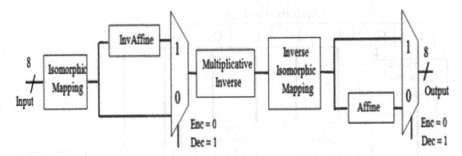

Fig. 5. SBOX architecture with GF mathematics

To find the substitution byte multiplicative inverse of GF (2^8) followed by affine transformation is calculated. The multiplicative inverse of GF (2^8) is the most expensive block in computation; here complexity of GF (2^8) is reduced by decomposing into GF (2^4) and GF (2^2). Any arbitrary polynomial in GF (2^8) can be represented as bx + c using an irreducible polynomial x2 + Ax + B. From the fact that any binary value can be represented in polynomial form and any polynomial can be converted into lesser power using bx + c we can find a multiplicative inverse for the given input. Here 'b' and 'c' are most significant and least significant nibbles respectively. The multiplicative inverse for bx + c can be found using the following equation [5]

$$(bx+c)^{-1} = b(b^2B+bcA+c^2)^{-1}x+(c+bA)(b^2B+bcA+c^2)^{-1} \qquad (1)$$

$$= b(b^2\lambda+c(b+c))^{-1}x+(c+b)(b^2\lambda+c(b+c))^{-1} \qquad (2)$$

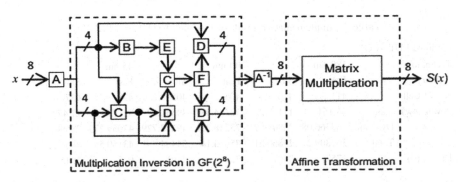

Fig. 6. Multiplication inversion and affine transformation in SBOX [3]

Figure 6 presents the different block in architecture of Eq. (1) where B = lamda (constant = 1100 in binary) and A is taken as 1; A presents isomorphic mapping, which maps the data of GF (2^8) to GF (2^4), B is squarer in GF (2^4) [first term in the Eq. (1) inside bracket], C is sum in GF (2^4) [which gives b + c of equation], D is multiplication in GF (2^4) [which gives multiplication of b + c with c], E is multiplication with constant in GF (2^4) [gives multiplication with constant lamda], F is inverse operation in GF (2^4) and A − 1 is inverse isomorphic mapping. Where, A = 1, B = λ, as the irreducible polynomial used is x2 + x + λ. The mapping structure in different fields along with the irreducible polynomials is as follows (2). Table 3 presents a composite method of SBOX implementation with CMOS90 nm require maximum cell, slow library based delay is thrice than fast library [6].

$$GF(2^2) \rightarrow GF(2) \qquad\qquad : x2 + x + 1 \qquad\qquad (3)$$

$$GF((2^2)^2) \rightarrow GF(2^2) \qquad\qquad : x2 + x + \varphi \qquad\qquad (4)$$

$$GF(((2^2)^2)^2) \rightarrow GF((2^2)^2) \qquad : x2 + x + \lambda \qquad\qquad (5)$$

Table 3. Implementation result of GF (2^8) based SBOX

GF(2^8) based SBOX							
Technology		180 nm		90 nm		45 nm	
Library		Fast	Slow	Fast	Slow	Fast	Slow
No. of Cell		170	170	182	182	165	170
Power (nw)	Static	119.49	138.42	13600.86	7169.91	77.817	28.832
	Dynamic	517036.99	312859.51	119434.17	75096.6	85664.846	55749.182
	Total	517156.5	312997.9	133035	82266.51	85742.66	55778.01
Delay (ps)		3656.6	9205.1	1567.8	5787.6	1440	4710

Table 3 present GF based S-BOX, compare to earlier methods area reduction here is significant so hardware becomes less bulky only to cause higher power consumption. Here higher power consumption is mainly because of computation required in the multiplicative inverse module. To address that, in next method, we have used the pre-computed multiplicative inverse module.

2.4 Modified GF Using Look-Up Table

Blend of look-up table method and GF method. It can be concluded that, In GF method, almost all the power is consumed by MI module. The 4th architecture includes multiplicative inverse implemented with a lookup table and affine transformation with a computational method. The multiplicative inverse of an individual byte is calculated and stored into a lookup table, computational complexity replaced by static block, While affine transformation implements with matrix multiplication. the matrix version of the transformation $b'_i = b_i \oplus b_{(i+4) \bmod 8} \oplus b_{(i+5) \bmod 8} \oplus b_{(i+6) \bmod 8} \oplus b_{(i+7) \bmod 8} \oplus$ ci for $0 \leq i \leq 8$, where b_i is the ith bit of the byte and c_i is the ith bit of a byte c. The affine transformation is calculated by multiple rotations of multiplicative inverse (MI) output where sum are implemented with XOR gate [8]. Figure 7 shows that affine transformation is computed by series of XOR applied with MI output. If MI output is

{01100011} of the XOR gate circuits produce the affine transformation outputs 00, 01, 06 and 06. Table 4 present CMOS library based result implementation; power consumption of slow library is thrice than the fast library and high power consumption.

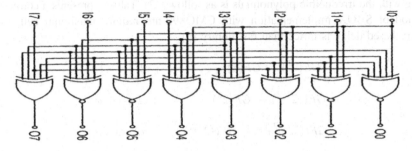

Fig. 7. Affine transformation of 63H

Table 4. Implementation result of modified GF (2^8) based SBOX

Modified GF based SBOX							
Technology		180 nm		90 nm		45 nm	
Library		Fast	Slow	Fast	Slow	Fast	Slow
No. of Cell		515	515	526	526	509	508
Power (nw)	Static	56.913	150.884	17721.43	7188.96	172.198	52.56
	Dynamic	373557.54	224814.83	83858.05	56383.37	54428.21	32373.08
		373614.5	224965.7	101579.5	63572.33	54600.41	32425.64
Delay (ps)		1840	4462	883	3312	1426	4468

Table 4 presents the RTL compiler based implementation result based on slow and fast library, power consumption is less compared to earlier method but again at cost of the area which is tradition trade-off in CMOS.

3 Result and Discussion

In this work, 4 different architecture of SBOX is implemented with Verilog HDL and their result has been analyzed with Cadence RTL compiler at technology node on 180 nm, 90 nm, and 45 nm with the slow and fast library. Figure 8 show that presence of lookup table greatly increases the cell count while GF architecture cells are below half of the others irrespective of technology node, GF calculation reduces area significantly. It will take a quarter of area from the LUT or Modified LUT for GF. SBOX implementation with LUT at 45 nm technology requires large area while minimum with GF calculation. GF architecture has possessed complex computation result in high power consumption shown in Fig. 9. Modified LUT gives faster substitution than LUT but the cost for that is a power which can be seen here. Modified GF method improves GF method and makes it in line with Modified LUT and LUT method which is boosting result. Figure 10 presents that Modified LUT method is fastest possible at 45 nm fast library followed by LUT then comes Modified GF and slowest is GF method. Reason being computation is slower than scanning. It is important to point out that Modified GF method's delay is very much close to LUT's and Modified LUT's delay. From Tables 1, 2, 3 and 4 it is analyzed that implementation with faster library consume high power with low delay while slow library low power and more delay. Primary reason for it; faster library power supply 1.98 V is higher than slower library 1.62 V causing less critical delay result in higher power consumption. Second is a reduction in a number of cells and reduction in redundant cells count.

SBOX implementation presents

Area requirement ➜ Modified GF → LUT → Modified LUT → GF
Power dissipation ➜ GF → Modified GF → Modified LUT → LUT
Speed requirement ➜ Modified LUT → LUT → Modified GF → GF

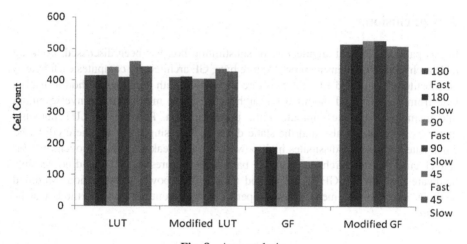

Fig. 8. Area analysis

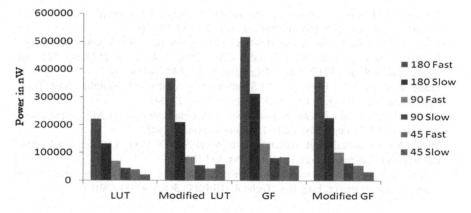

Fig. 9. Power comparison analysis

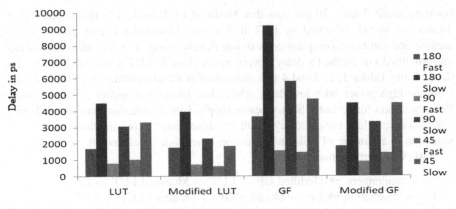

Fig. 10. Delay analysis

4 Conclusion

In this paper 4 different architecture of substitution box has been discussed. Look up table architecture contains memory to store byte, GF architecture computes each byte to be substituted, modified LUT architecture implement with a unique method to fetch a byte from memory and modified GF architecture store multiplicative inverse output into memory space and compute affine transformation. Presence of LUT not only increases the area but also add the static delay in accessing the byte where GF based composite architecture dissipates high power with low leakage value. It opens eye for side channel resistant architecture. LUT based architectures are bulky and not feasible hardware wise. While GF based method takes higher power consumption. Modified methods improve this method and as per application one of these methods can be devised.

References

1. Standard, NIST-FIPS: Announcing the advanced encryption standard (AES). Federal Information Processing Standards Publication 197, pp. 1–51 (2001)
2. Morioka, S., Satoh, A.: An optimized S-box circuit architecture for low power AES design. In: Kaliski, B.S., Koç, K., Paar, C. (eds.) CHES 2002. LNCS, vol. 2523, pp. 172–186. Springer, Heidelberg (2003). https://doi.org/10.1007/3-540-36400-5_14
3. Zhang, X., Parhi, K.K.: High-speed VLSI architectures for the AES algorithm. IEEE Trans. Very Large Scale Integr. (VLSI) Syst. **12**(9), 957–967 (2004)
4. Hossain, F.S., Ali, M.L.: A novel byte-substitution architecture for the AES cryptosystem. PlosOne J. (2015). https://doi.org/10.1371/journal.pone.0138457
5. Mui, E.N.C.: Practical Implementation of Rijndael S-BOX Using Combinational Logic. Custom R&D Engineer Texco Enterprise Pvt. Ltd (2007)
6. Krishna, C.V., et al.: Design implementation of composite field S-Box using AES 256 algorithm. Int. J. Emerg. Eng. Res. Technol. (IJEERT) **3**(12), 43–51 (2016)

7. Pammu, A.A., Chong, K.-S., Gwee, B.-H.: Secured low power overhead compensator Look-Up-Table (LUT) Substitution Box (S-Box) Architecture. In: IEEE International Conference on Networking, Architecture, and Storage (NAS), August 2016, pp. 1–7 (2016)
8. Van Buer, D.: Method and apparatus for high-speed implementation of data encryption and decryption utilizing, e.g. Rijndael or its subset AES, or other encryption/decryption algorithms having similar key expansion data flow. US 20030198345 A1 (2003)
9. Khan, F.A., Ahmed, J., Khan, J.S., Ahmad, J., Khan, M.A., Hwang, S.O.: A new technique for designing 8×8 substitution box for image encryption applications. In: IEEE International Conference on Computer Science and Electronic Engineering (CEEC), September 2017
10. Prathiba, A., Kanchana Bhaaskaran, V.S.: Lightweight S-Box architecture for the secure internet of things. Information **9**(1), 1–14 (2018)

Nonlinear Impairments in Fiber Optic Communication Systems: Analytical Review

Payal[(⊠)] and Suresh Kumar

ECE Department, University Institute of Engineering and Technology (UIET),
MDU, Rohtak, Haryana, India
payalarora325@gmail.com, skvashist_16@yahoo.com

Abstract. Fiber optic communications provides an enormous bandwidth for high speed data transmission. Optical fiber is an excellent transmission medium due to its robustness and low losses. However, the dispersive and nonlinear effects of an optical fiber may lead to signal distortions. In long haul communication systems, transmission impairments accumulate over the fiber distance and utterly distort the signal. By compensating for dispersive and nonlinear impairments the transmission performance can be significantly improved. In the present work, a theoretical analysis of various kinds of optical fiber nonlinearities, their thresholds and managements is carried out. Also, it focusses on various digital and optical methods to compensate for dispersive and nonlinear distortions, which significantly enhance transmission performance and system capacity. All over the paper, current applications dealing with these effects have been referred. The present paper will help the researchers in this field to find the aggregate material on the subject and further narrowing the topic selection for research work.

Keywords: Wavelength Division Multiplexing (WDM)
Erbium Doped Fiber Amplifier (EDFA)
Amplified Spontaneous Emission (ASE) · Conservation of Energy (COE)
Mach Zehender Modulator (MZM) · Optical Phase Modulator (OPM)
Refractive Index (RI) · Phase Modulation (PM) · Higher Order Terms (HOD)
Fiber Bragg Grating (FBG)

1 Introduction

An optical signal during propagation through an optical fiber gets distorted due to losses, dispersion and non-linearity. The transmission losses as low as 0.2 dB/km can be achieved. But for long distance transmissions, signal attenuation is of great importance which needs to be compensated in order to recover high quality signal. EDFA's can be used to compensate for fiber losses by adding ASE noise.

Optical fiber is a dispersive medium, the RI of which depends on frequency. As a result, dissimilar frequency components of an optical pulse disseminate at different speeds leading to pulse broadening and inter-symbol interference (ISI). Dispersion in fiber is a linear effect and is well-characterized by the dispersion coefficient and the transfer function. Another origin of signal impairments is fiber nonlinear effects [1]. Figure 1 shows the categorization of Non-linear Impairments in fiber optic communication systems.

© Springer Nature Singapore Pte Ltd. 2019
P. K. Singh et al. (Eds.): FTNCT 2018, CCIS 958, pp. 28–44, 2019.
https://doi.org/10.1007/978-981-13-3804-5_3

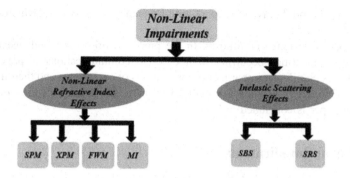

Fig. 1. Categorization of nonlinear impairments

The main fiber nonlinear effect in fiber-optic communication systems is the Kerr effect in which RI depends on the optical pulse intensity. For the case of single channel fiber-optic link, the Kerr effect results in Intra-channel Cross-Phase Modulation (IXPM), Self-Phase Modulation (SPM) and Intra-channel Four Wave Mixing (IFWM) [1].

SPM and IXPM are the addition of intensity reliant phase shifts to an optical pulse due to the existence of the same pulse and a neighboring pulse, respectively. When a nonlinear interaction occurs among signal pulses centered at 1Ts, m Ts and n Ts, it leads to a ghost pulse which is positioned at $(1 + m - n)$Ts. Figure 2 shows the intra-channel effects due to the nonlinear interactions of optical pulses of Channel 3.

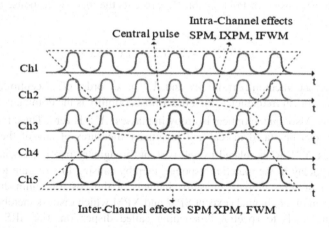

Fig. 2. Nonlinear interactions in a WDM fiber optic communication system

In a WDM system, the Kerr effect results in SPM, Cross-Phase Modulation (XPM), and Four Wave Mixing (FWM) [1]. As shown in Fig. 2, SPM, XPM and FWM correspond to the nonlinear interactions of one, two and three WDM channels, respectively. SPM brings a phase shift to the optical pulse itself due to power variation. This phase change also changes the pulse frequency spectrum. When multiple signal channels co-propagate in a single fiber, the power fluctuating in one signal channel produces a phase shift in another channel, which is the XPM effect [2, 3]. Due to the scattering of the incident photons, nonlinear interaction among channels centered at frequencies f_1, f_2 and f_3 gives rise to a fourth frequency $(f_1 + f_2 - f_3)$ which is known as FWM effect [4, 5].

The paper is designed as follows. In the present work, a comprehensive review regarding Non-linearities occurring in fiber optic communications is presented. In Sect. 2, various Non-linear impairments, their causes of occurrence and their thresholds are explained in detail. Section 3 describes various methods used for their mitigation. Finally, the paper is concluded in Sect. 4.

2 Nonlinear Impairments

The occurrence of Nonlinearities is due to the simultaneous interaction among numerous optical fields of the fiber. They may also include molecular vibrations or acoustic waves. There are two classes of nonlinearities [6, 7]:

- Stimulated Brillouin Scattering (SBS) and Stimulated Raman Scattering (SRS) which occur due to rigid scattering phenomena;
- The nonlinearities occurring due to RI changes that are brought up optically thereby resulting in two different outcomes: SPM and XPM belonging to Phase Modulation or Modulation Instability (MI) and FWM caused by wave mixing and generation of new frequencies.

Enormous optical field modifies the material response for both these forms of nonlinearities. Expansion of Polarization P represents the material response as given in equation below [8]:

$$P = \varepsilon_0 \mathcal{X}^{(1)} E + \varepsilon_0 \mathcal{X}^{(2)} E2 + \varepsilon_0 \mathcal{X}^{(3)} E3 + \ldots \tag{1}$$

Here ε_0 denote vacuum permittivity and $\mathcal{X}^{(k)}$ is k^{th} order of susceptibility for $k = (1, 2, 3, \ldots)$ at optical frequencies. First order Susceptibility is the dominant contributor in polarization. Also, due to optical isotropy in glasses, $\mathcal{X}^{(2)}$ is zero. Thus, from Eq. (1) nonlinearities can be stated in real and imaginary measures of any of the nonlinear susceptibilities $\mathcal{X}^{(k)}$. RI is related to real part and imaginary part is associated with a phase or time delay in the material response, thereby causing loss or gain to increase.

These impairments deliver gains to channels at the cost of diminishing power originating from other channels except SPM and XPM which distress merely the phase of signals and leads to spectral broadening called dispersion. For SRS and SBS, contribution is stated in measures of imaginary part of third order susceptibility [9, 10] while FWM subsidizes to the real part of the same [11].

For an optical fiber, Polarization vector P is always in direction of Electric field vector E. Accordingly, scalar notations may be used as an alternative of vector notations. For E given in Eq. (2)

$$E = E_0 \cos(\omega t - kz) \tag{2}$$

P is written as

$$P = \varepsilon_0 \mathcal{X}^{(1)} E_0 \cos(\omega t - kz) + \varepsilon_0 \mathcal{X}^{(2)} E_0^2 \cos^2(\omega t - kz) + \varepsilon_0 \mathcal{X}^{(3)} E_0^3 \cos^3(\omega t - kz) + \ldots$$

(3)

By using trigonometric relations, the above equation is expanded as

$$P = \frac{1}{2} \varepsilon_0 \mathcal{X}^{(2)} E_0^2 + \varepsilon_0 \mathcal{X}^{(1)} + \frac{3}{4} \varepsilon_0 \mathcal{X}^{(3)} E_0^2 E_0 \cos(\omega t - kz) + \frac{1}{2} \varepsilon_0 \mathcal{X}^{(2)} E_0^2 \cos 2(\omega t - kz)$$
$$+ \frac{1}{4} \varepsilon_0 \mathcal{X}^{(3)} E_0^3 \cos 3(\omega t - kz) + \ldots$$

(4)

$\mathcal{X}^{(2)}$ Vanishes for the case of optical fibers and the Eq. (4) becomes

$$P = \varepsilon_0 \mathcal{X}^{(1)} + \frac{1}{4} \varepsilon_0 \mathcal{X}^{(3)} E_0^3 \cos 3(\omega t - kz) + \frac{3}{4} \varepsilon_0 \mathcal{X}^{(3)} E_0^2 E_0 \cos(\omega t - kz)$$

(5)

As the contribution of higher order terms is negligible, they are neglected. Because of RI variations, there is a phase lacking between ω and 3ω frequencies. The second term of Eq. (5) can thus be neglected due to phase mismatch and P can be written as

$$P = \varepsilon_0 \mathcal{X}^{(1)} + \frac{3}{4} \varepsilon_0 \mathcal{X}^{(3)} E_0^3 \cos(\omega t - kz)$$

(6)

In above equation, first term is the linear polarization and second term is the nonlinear polarization. For Eq. (2) representing plane wave, the Intensity can defined as

$$I = \frac{1}{2} c \varepsilon_0 n_0 E_0^2$$

(7)

Here c and n_0 denote the velocity of light and the linear RI of the medium at low fields respectively. Hence, P in terms of I can be written as

$$P = \varepsilon_0 \mathcal{X}^{(1)} + \frac{3}{2} \frac{\mathcal{X}^{(3)}}{c n_0} I E_0 \cos(\omega t - kz)$$

(8)

2.1 Scattering Nonlinearities

SBS and SRS involve the lattice or molecular vibrations of the glass. They must satisfy the two laws: Conservation of momentum of the light and COE.

$$\Omega = \omega_L - \omega_S \cdots \vec{q} = \vec{k}_L - \vec{k}_S$$

(9)

Here symbol L stands for laser and S for stokes, ω is the frequency and k represents the wave vector of light. q, Ω denote lattice phonon.

For SBS, the acoustic phonon having an approximate frequency (~ 10 GHz) downshifts the scattered light, while for SRS the action is done by optic phonon frequency. The SRS gain has a maximum value at $\Omega = 13.2$ THz in silica [12]. SBS happens at low power levels. In backward direction, it is maximum while in forward direction, it reduces to zero. This makes SBS destructive in optic networks and therefore commonly eluded by taking the individual channel power beneath threshold. And phase modulation of the laser is used when powers greater than threshold are needed.

In SRS for glass being an isotropic medium, the cross-section unveils a smaller angular dependency. In both the directions, scattering can be perceived but more proficiently in forward direction [13]. For stimulated processes, the threshold is the input power at which phonons are generated at a higher rate than their annihilating rate expressed as given below [14].

$$P_{th} = \frac{CA_{eff}}{gL_{eff}} \tag{10}$$

Here A_{eff}, is effective modal area, L_{eff} is effective length, g signifies the gain coefficient and C denote that constant that is process-dependent. The variations of core size of fiber along with inhomogeneities likely increases the SBS threshold ranging 5–10 dBm for powers ranging 3–10 mW and 28–32 dBm for 0.7–1.17 W for SRS.

2.1.1   SBS

SBS occurs due to thermal molecular vibrations within the fiber. Due to these vibrations, the modulation of light takes place. Scattered light seems as two sidebands that are alienated from incident light by modulation frequency. The Stokes wave is scattered backward and the photo generated acoustic wave is transmitted collinearly with the pump beam that is incident [15]. The frequency of sound wave varies with acoustic wavelength. Due to higher gain coefficient, the SBS threshold is predominantly low when compared with SRS. The gain coefficient for SBS is given below.

$$\tilde{g}_B = \frac{\Delta v_B}{\Delta v_B + \Delta v_s} g_B(v_B) \tag{11}$$

For a perfect monotone signal, the maximum Brillouin gain i.e. $g_B(v_B)$ is $\sim 5 \times 10$–11 m/W. Δv_B and Δv_s Denote the Brillouin and signal spectral width.

2.1.2   SRS

In case of SRS, an optical phenon is generated while the acoustic scattering process. SRS is different from SBS in three means. Firstly, the Raman-gain coefficient g_R for SRS is $\sim 1 \times 10$–13 m/W, which is lower. Thus SRS occurs at considerably high power than SBS [16]. Secondly, the Raman shift is larger than SBS shift. Thirdly, SRS produces a beam in both directions, however in forward direction more efficiently.

For designing fiber amplifiers, the SRS gain can be harmful for WDM systems because of the fact that part of the pulse energy is transferred to neighboring channels when high frequency channel acts a pump for low frequency channels. This results in

Raman induced crosstalk among channels. It highly affects the high frequency channels. Vanholsbeeck et al. [17] explained that Raman phenomena tilts the spectral power distribution of several channels thereby inducing inter-channel crosstalk. MZM eradicates problem of frequency chirp but suffers from DC bias drift. Chi and Yao [18] investigated OPM as the problem's solution. Thus it endows with superior performance as compared to DE-MZM. Performance of WDM systems have been evaluated using different modulators to investigate the impact of Raman crosstalk [19]. By selecting least value of Raman crosstalk, system performance can be optimized at a given transmission distance and modulation frequency. The characteristics of scattering Nonlinearities (SBS and SRS) are compared in Table 1. The merits and demerits are compared using characteristics such as source, direction of occurrence, shift, gain bandwidth, power threshold and strength.

Table 1. Characteristics comparison of scattering non-linearities

Characteristic comparison	Scattering non-linearities	
	SBS	SRS
Source	Due to thermal molecular agitations within the fiber	It is the consequence of individual molecular motion
Direction of occurrence	It takes place in backward direction only	Occurs in both forward as well as backward directions
Shift	The Brillouin shift is due to interaction of photon-acoustic phonon	The reason for Raman shift is interaction of photon-optical phonon
Gain bandwidth	Narrow when compared to Raman gain bandwidth	Large gain bandwidth
Power threshold	Quite low	About three times greater threshold than SBS
Strength	Depends on material disorder	Independent of material disorder

2.2 Third Order ($\mathcal{X}^{(3)}$) Nonlinearities

These impairments occur due to changes induced in the RI by means of light thus resulting in Kerr effect or parametric collaborations. The expression for RI is given below.

$$n = n_0 + n_2 I \tag{12}$$

Here n_0 denote linear index, n_2 signifies nonlinear coefficient, and I denote light Intensity. The magnitude of non-linear effects is governed by the coefficient given below.

$$\gamma = \frac{2\pi}{\lambda} \frac{n_2}{A_{\text{eff}}} \tag{13}$$

Here A_{eff} is the effective core area and λ is the free-space wavelength. The phase shift introduced by non-linearities is given below.

$$\varphi_{NL}(z) = \gamma P_0 z \qquad (14)$$

P_0 Represents the peak input power. The nonlinear phase change in nonlinear length measure $L_{NL} = (\gamma P_0)^{-1}$ can be written as

$$\varphi_{NL} = \frac{z}{L_{NL}} \qquad (15)$$

This demonstrates the significance of impairments in optical signal transmission [20]. In case of numerous channels, when power incorporated over channels extend up to 15 dBm or further (~ 30 mW) at a point, the influence can be primarily significant [21, 22]. Due to spatial and time dependency of the optical power, third order impairments contribute to numerous variations in time as well as in frequency domain and alter the mode-field distribution.

2.2.1 SPM

When an optical pulse travels through a fiber, a high refractive index is encountered over higher intensity portions as compared with portions of lower intensity. Variation of signal intensity in time domain yields in the intensity-dependent RI medium, a time varying RI. Figure 3 shows the phenomenon of pulse broadening due to SPM. A positive RI gradient (+dn/dt) is experienced by the leading edge and a negative RI gradient (−dn/dt) by the trailing edge. The second pulse demonstrates a change in phase due to change in index. This non-linear PM is called as SPM.

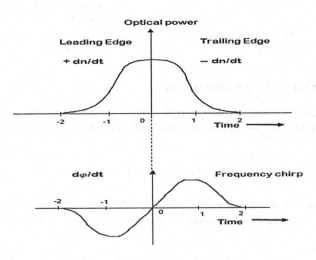

Fig. 3. Pulse broadening due to SPM

From the figure, different phase shifts are encountered by both the rising as well as the trailing edge as the phase fluctuations are intensity dependent. This results in Frequency Chirping (FC) [23]. As chirping is proportional to signal power, the SPM effects are more prominent in high-power systems. The phase that the field E induces over L fiber length is shown below.

$$\varphi = \frac{2\pi}{\lambda} nL \tag{16}$$

Here nL signifies the path length and λ signifies the optical wavelength of pulse in fiber having RI n. FC causes penalty in dispersion. These consequences would be minor if input power is smaller than the threshold one. SPM effects can also be reduced by proper chirping of the pulses by using Chirped RZ modulation. The impact of SPM depends on the power of nonlinear phase constant [24]. The necessary condition for reducing this impact is to have $\varphi_{nl} \ll 1$. The expression for φ_{nl} is given below.

$$\varphi_{nl} = k_{nl} P_{in} L_{eff} \tag{17}$$

Where nonlinear propagation constant is given as

$$k_{nl} = \frac{2\pi}{\lambda} \frac{n_{nl}}{A_{eff}} \tag{18}$$

$$\text{So, with } L_{eff} \approx \frac{1}{\alpha}, \ P_{in} \ll \frac{\alpha}{k_{nl}} \tag{19}$$

Therefore, to have $\varphi_{nl} \ll 1$ is equivalent to $P_{in} \ll \frac{\alpha}{k_{nl}}$.

The chirp that SPM produces depends on the shape of input pulse as well as on the prompt level of power within the pulse thereby causing broadening. The chirp is different for different pulse shapes i.e. even and gradual for Gaussian and the amount of chirp is greater for a square pulse that includes a sudden change in the power level. Therefore, an appropriate pulse shape must be chosen that can moderate the chirp and hence broadening. SPM is used for formation of optical solitons and used for fast optical switching and passive mode locking. However, it also degrades system performance by inducing spectral broadening.

Nain et al. [25] investigated and compared MZM and OPM together with the SPM effects for a single channel RoF system and analyzed the same for different dispersion and input channel power ranges. Results conclude that pulse broadening is increased as the dispersion modulus and channel input power increase. As the channel power increases from 10–17.5 dBm, SPM effects are better suppressed by OPM rather than MZM.

2.2.2 XPM

In a single channel system, SPM is a major nonlinear limitation. The intensity dependent RI causes another nonlinear phenomena called XPM. For simultaneous propagation of optical pulses, XPM accompanies SPM. It occurs due to nonlinearities in RI because of interference caused by adjacent beams.

Random modulation of the signal phase is done by the neighboring channels and then Group Velocity Dispersion (GVD) of the fiber converts it into Intensity Noise (IN) [26]. Subramaniam et al. [27] studied the performance of XPM crosstalk and its variation with transmission distance. Kumar et al. [28] investigated the XPM crosstalk due to dispersion. Arya and Sharma [29] studied XPM crosstalk because of Walk-Off Parameters (WOP). Yang et al. [30] examined the combination of XPM crosstalk and GVD and recommended a countermeasure for reducing crosstalk. Nain et al. [31] assessed XPM-induced crosstalk due to spreading using HOD and WOP.

XPM transforms the power fluctuations in one channel to phase fluctuations in co-propagating channels. It may result in irregular spectral broadening and pulse shaping. For a nonlinear medium, RI in input power and effective core area measures is given below.

$$n_{eff} = n_l + n_{nl}\frac{P}{A_{eff}} \tag{20}$$

The nonlinear effects are governed by the ratio of power to the fiber cross-sectional area. XPM hampers the performance of system greater than SPM through FC and chromatic Dispersion (CD). The impact of XPM can be minimized by increasing the channel spacing. Due to dispersion, the channel propagation constants become fully different causing pulses to move away from each other. Owing to this phenomena, the temporally coincident pulses stop to be the same after propagating some distance and no further interaction takes place thereby reducing the effect of XPM.

2.2.3   FWM

The nonlinearities in the movement of bound electrons creates the phenomenon of FWM. The magnitudes of linear and non-linear terms is governed by the $\mathcal{X}^{(k)}$. Two or additional light waves on interacting result in a kind of $\mathcal{X}^{(3)}$ nonlinearities which involve not only the index modulation but also the transfer of energy between waves [32]. These interactions are called parametric.

Simultaneous propagation of three optical fields having ω_1, ω_2 and ω_3 frequencies creates a fourth field having ω_4 frequency expressed as

$$\omega_4 = \omega_1 \pm \omega_2 \pm \omega_3$$

SPM and XPM are substantial mainly for systems with high bit rate, while the FWM effect is free of the bit rate and depends on the dispersion and channel spacing. FWM effect is increased by decreasing the channel spacing and so does decreasing the dispersion. Mixing two waves at ω_1 and ω_2 generate two sidebands as shown in Fig. 4. Equation (21) shows the optical side bands with three co-propagating waves.

$$\omega_{pqr} = \omega_p + \omega_q - \omega_r \quad \text{With} \quad p, q \neq r \tag{21}$$

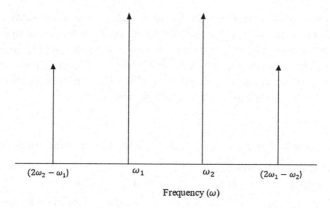

$(2\omega_2 - \omega_1)$ ω_1 ω_2 $(2\omega_1 - \omega_2)$

Frequency (ω)

Fig. 4. Mixing of two waves

Using dispersion-shifted fibers (DSF), FWM presents a severe problem in WDM systems. If slight CD is present, the waves propagate with dissimilar group velocities, thereby minimizing the FWM impact. This reduces the FWM efficiency and its penalty as well. If the created wavelengths overlap the wavelength of original signal, it causes interference thereby degrading SNR which can be improved by using unevenly spaced channels [33].

The major applications of FWM such as parametric amplification in WDM systems are explored [34, 35]. FWM has been used for optical regeneration of pulses [36]. The authors have presented an innovative dispersion monitoring mechanism based on FWM [37]. Dispersion has an important role in FWM than in other impairments due to the phase-matching condition. The fluctuations in dispersion reduces the FWM efficiency because of λ_{ZDW} fluctuations [38]. In [39], authors have confined the power in order to increase the efficiency of FWM using Dispersion-Decreasing Fibers (DDF). Course idea of parametric amplification and polarization effects on FWM is explored [40].

2.2.4 MI

When a continuos light wave undergoes small perturbation with frequency Ω and wave vector k, MI arises. It divides a continuous wave into a narrow pulse train [41]. From the Non-linear Schrödinger Equation (NLSE) covering SPM term, for perturbation frequencies $\Omega < \Omega_c$ the wave vector becomes imaginary and β_2 is the GVD. GVD effect introduces a periodic chirp and self-phase shift which leads to the breakup of CW. Maximum MI gain happens for $\Omega_{max} = \frac{\Omega_c}{\sqrt{2}}$

$$\Omega_c^2 = \frac{4\gamma P_0}{|\beta_2|} = \frac{4}{|\beta_2|L_{NL}} \tag{22}$$

MI gain is modified by different dispersion profiles considerably. Gain spectrum of MI is shown much broader in DDF than conventional fibers [42]. MI can be originated by noise likewise SBS and SRS. Modulation instability often enhances system noise. Although MI can produce ultra-short pulses at high repetition rates yet enhances system noise.

For the case, noise component at frequency Ω_{max} grows favorably. In Optical communication systems with ASE noise, MI generated due to noise damage the system performance in the presence of improper dispersion compensation [43]. Apart from β_2, MI is influenced by the even order dispersions [44] and odd order dispersions as well in the presence of wavelength dependent loss [45]. The Third-order Non-linearities explained above are compared in Table 2 given below.

Table 2. Characteristics comparison of third-order nonlinearities

Characteristic comparison	Third order non-linearities			
	SPM	XPM	FWM	MI
Cause	Third-order susceptibility $\chi^{(3)}$	Third-order susceptibility $\chi^{(3)}$	Third-order susceptibility $\chi^{(3)}$	Originated by noise likewise SBS and SRS
Bit-rate dependency	Dependent	Dependent	Independent	Independent
Effect	Phase shift due to pulse itself only	Phase shift is alone due to co-propagating signals	New waves are generated	Divides a continuous wave into a narrow pulse train
Channel spacing	No effect	Increases on decreasing the spacing	Increases on decreasing the spacing	FWM and MI interaction results in modulation of channel power due to channel spacing

3 Compensation Methods for Fiber Dispersive and Nonlinear Effects

The transmission capacity of fiber-optic communication systems is mainly restricted by the Kerr nonlinear effect [46]. Transmission performance is narrowed by ASE noise at low signal power. At high signal power, however, fiber nonlinear effects dominate and make it impossible to enhance transmission performance by simply increasing signal power. Various optical and digital compensation techniques have been investigated to partially or fully compensate for fiber nonlinear effects, or the combined effect of fiber dispersion and nonlinearities.

3.1 Optical Dispersion Compensation

A dispersion compensating fiber (DCF) with a large negative waveguide dispersion has been designed and fabricated for compensating dispersion [47]. The length of the DCF is chosen such that the net pulse broadening is zero. Hill *et al.* [48] employed FBG for compensating dispersion. FBGs reveal large dispersion in reflection mode and the sign of dispersion is easily controlled. A comparatively short Bragg grating is used to compensate dispersion of an optical fiber that is 10 km long.

3.2 Mid-point Optical Phase Conjugation (OPC)

The interaction of dispersion and nonlinearity lead to signal distortions in an optical fiber. Signal propagation distortions can be compensated by the use of a phase conjugation mirror [49]. Watanabe and Chikama [50] validated the FWM compensation using mid-point OPC in WDM systems. Martelli *et al.* [51] demonstrated OPC for polarization multiplexed signals. Mid-point OPC can undo the distortions using symmetric dispersion and power profiles. For EDFA which is a system with lumped amplification, with respect to OPC the power profile is not symmetric. This limits the compensation performance of OPC. In fiber-optic systems, better symmetry of power profile is offered by Raman amplification. Martelli *et al.* [52] presented that in a WDM system mid-point OPC brings about a substantial improvement in performance using dispersion-flattened Non-Zero Dispersion-Shifted Fibers (NZDSFs) and bidirectional Raman pumping amplification.

3.3 Optical Back Propagation (OBP)

Kumar *et al.* [53–55] has proposed OBP for compensating fiber dispersive and Non-linear impairments. An OBP module consisting of DCFs and nonlinearity compensators undo the distortions by reversing propagation of signal and is positioned at the receiver end [53]. Although OBP offers a better transmission performance, but network complexity increases due to use of various pumping sources. An improved OBP scheme without pump is obtainable, in which the module comprises of HNLFs and High-Dispersion Fibers (HDFs) preceded by an OPC. OBP scheme is better when compared with mid-point OPC in case of lumped amplifiers [54]. The scheme is further improved by optimizing various parameters of FBGs and HNLFs. Minimal Area Mismatch (MAM) procedure leads to substantial improvement up to some extent compared to uniform spacing for a given step size [55].

3.4 Digital Dispersion Compensation

The fiber nonlinearities can be compensated by using Digital signal processing (DSP) techniques. These techniques are generally complex and are capable in dealing with inter-channel and intra-channel non-linearities. They include perturbation solutions to the Coupled NLSE, Digital Back Propagation (DBP), Pulse shaping, Volterra Series Non-linear Equalizers and Advanced Modulation Formats [56]. Recent progresses in DSP have enabled the digital compensation of signal impairments [57]. CD is minimized using coherent detection, Finite Impulse Response (FIR) filter and Infinite Impulse Response (IIR) filter without Optical Phase Locked Loop (OPLL) [58–60]. IIR filters are more efficient as compared to FIR filters but requires buffering. The use of fast Fourier transforms (FFTs) minimizes the large accumulated dispersion. Ip and Kahn [61] explored a digital equalizer for CD compensation and PMD for polarization multiplexed coherent fiber-optic systems.

3.5 DBP

This method of compensation consists in processing the received signals after being launched with opposite-sign values into a virtual fiber [62]. Among all non-linear compensation techniques, Multi-Channel DBP (MC-DBP) is hopeful for compensating inter-channel and intra-channel fiber nonlinearities in WDM systems [63]. DBP mitigates non-linearities in multi-channel systems [64]. The propagating electric field E using NLSE is given below.

$$\frac{\partial E(z,t)}{\partial z} + j\frac{\beta_2}{2}\frac{\partial^2 E(z,t)}{\partial t^2} + \frac{\alpha}{2}E(z,t) = j\gamma|E(z,t)|^2 E(z,t) \tag{23}$$

The DBP and Kerr nonlinearity can be mitigated using inverse of Eq. (23)

$$\begin{cases} \alpha = -\alpha \\ \beta_2 = -\beta_2 \\ \gamma = -\gamma \end{cases} \frac{\partial E(z,t)}{\partial z} - j\frac{\beta_2}{2}\frac{\partial^2 E(z,t)}{\partial t^2} - \frac{\alpha}{2}E(z,t) = -j\gamma|E(z,t)|^2 E(z,t) \tag{24}$$

The transmitted signal can be recovered using DBP either by applying it at the transmitter or at the receiver. The authors in [65–67] discussed the various constraints such as ASE noise and PMD in reconstruction of entire signal. The authors in [68, 69] have discussed the impact of amplifier noise in transmitter that reduces the gain using DBP.

A Tabular comparison of Kerr nonlinearities and Scattering nonlinearities is explained in Table 3 given below.

Table 3. Comparison of Kerr nonlinearities and scattering nonlinearities

Characteristics comparison	Nonlinear impairments	
	Kerr nonlinearities	Scattering nonlinearities
Cause	Due to intensity dependence of RI	Due to the simultaneous interaction among numerous optical fields of the fiber
Sense	Elastic in nature	Inelastic in nature
Energy transference	They involve no energy transference	They involve energy transfer between pump wave and Stokes wave
Population inversion	No population inversion is needed	Requires population inversion

4 Conclusion

This paper presents a comprehensive review of non-linear impairments occurring in fiber optic communications and the techniques used for their mitigation. Also, it focusses on the origination of these nonlinearities, their advantages and disadvantages. These Non-linearities produces Spontaneous Raman Noise, SPM, XPM, MI, SBS, XPM and FWM. These non-linearities are widely used in designing Amplifiers,

Wavelength Converters and de-multiplexers. From the tabular comparison, it is evident that SRS is better in all aspects in terms of Gain bandwidth and power threshold while SBS on the other hand restricts the amount of optical power that can be transmitted. The nature of Kerr Nonlinearities is elastic requiring no energy transference. These impairments will be of great importance in Future Generation networks with enhanced Capacity. This paper will provide a base for the researchers to carry out their research in the field of evaluation and mitigating non-linearities in an effective and efficient manner.

References

1. Agrawal, G.P.: Nonlinear Fiber Optics, 5th edn. Academic Press, Cambridge (2007)
2. Mollenauer, L.F., Evangelides, S.G., Gordon, J.P.: Wavelength division multiplexing with solitons in ultra-long distance transmission using lumped amplifiers. J. Light. Technol. **9**(3), 362–367 (1991). (ISSN 1558-2213)
3. Hasegawa, A., Kodama, Y., Kumar, S.: Reduction of collision-induced time jitters in dispersion-managed soliton transmission systems. Opt. Lett. **21**(1), 39–41 (1996). https://doi.org/10.1364/OL.21.000039. (ISSN 1539-4794)
4. Inoue, K.: Four wave mixing in an optical fiber in the zero-dispersion wavelength region. J. Light. Technol. **10**(11), 1553–1561 (1992). https://doi.org/10.1109/50.184893. (ISSN 1558-2213)
5. Tkach, R., Chraplyvy, A., Forghieri, F., Gnauck, A., Derosier, R.: Four photon mixing and high-speed WDM systems. J. Light. Technol. **13**(5), 841–849 (1995)
6. Agrawal, G.P.: Nonlinear Fiber Optics, 2nd edn. Academic Press, San Diego (1995)
7. Agrawal, G.P.: Nonlinear Fiber Optics, 3rd edn. Academic Press, San Diego (2001)
8. Boyd, R.: Nonlinear Optics. Academic Press, San Diego (1992)
9. Hellwarth, R.W., Cherlow, J., Yang, T.T.: Origin and frequency dependence of nonlinear optical susceptibilities of glasses. Phys. Rev. B **11**(2), 964 (1975). (ISSN 1943-8206)
10. Hellwarth, R.W.: Third-order optical susceptibilities of liquids and solids. Prog. Quantum Electron. **5**(1-A), 1–68 (1977). https://doi.org/10.1364/JOSAB.2.000649. (ISSN 1520-8540)
11. Shen, Y.R.: Principles of Nonlinear Optics. Wiley, New York (1984)
12. Stolen, R.H., Ippen, E.P.: Raman gain in glass optical waveguides. Appl. Phys. Lett. **22**(6), 276 (1973). https://doi.org/10.1063/1.1654637
13. Vilhelmsson, K.: Simultaneous forward and backward Raman scattering in low-attenuation single-mode fibers. J. Lightw. Technol. **LT-4**(4), 400–404 (1986). (ISSN 1558-2213)
14. Smith, R.G.: Optical power handling capacity of low loss optical fibers as determined by stimulated Raman and Brillouin scattering. Appl. Opt. **11**(11), 2489 (1972). https://doi.org/10.1364/AO.11.002489. (ISSN 2155-3165)
15. Ippen, E.P., Stolen, R.H.: Stimulated Brillouin scattering in optical fibers. Appl. Phys. Lett. **21**(11), 539 (1972). https://doi.org/10.1063/1.1654249
16. Stolen, R.H., Ippen, E.P., Tynes, A.R.: Raman oscillations in glass optical waveguides. Appl. Phys. Lett. **20**(2), 62 (1972)
17. Vanholsbeeck, F., Coen, S., Emplit, P., Haelterman, M., Thibaut, S.: Raman induced power tilt in arbitrarily large wavelength-division-multiplexed systems. IEEE Photon. Technol. Lett. **17**(1), 88–90 (2005)
18. Chi, H., Zou, X., Yao, J.: Analytical models for phase-modulation-based microwave photonic systems with phase modulation to intensity modulation conversion using a dispersive device. J. Light. Technol. **27**(5), 511–521 (2009). (ISSN 1558-2213)

19. Kumar, S., Nain, A.: Simulative Investigation of WDM RoF systems including the effect of the raman crosstalk using different modulators. Telecommun. Radio Eng. **75**(14), 1243–1254 (2016)
20. Wegener, L.G.L., Povinelli, M.L., Green, A.G., Mitra, P.P., Stark, J.B., Littlewood, P.B.: The effect of propagating nonlinearities on the information capacity of WDM optical fiber systems: cross-phase modulation and four-wave mixing. Physica D **189**(1–2), 81–99 (2004)
21. Wu, M., Way, W.I.: Fiber nonlinearity limitations in ultra-dense WDM systems. J. Lightw. Technol. **22**(6), 1483–1498 (2004)
22. Chraplyvy, A.R.: Limitations on lightwave communications imposed by fiber optic nonlinearities. J. Lightw. Technol. **8**(10), 1548 (1990). (ISSN 1558-2213)
23. Singh, S.P., Singh, N.: Non-linear effects in optical fibers: origin, management and applications. Prog. Electromagn. Res., PIER **73**, 249–275 (2007). https://doi.org/10.2528/PIER07040201
24. Mandal, B., Chowdhary, A.R.: Spatial soliton scattering in a quasi phase matched quadratic media in presence of cubic nonlinearity. J. Electromagn. Waves Appl. **21**(1), 123–135 (2007)
25. Nain, A., Kumar, S.: Performance investigation of different modulation schemes in RoF systems under the influence of self phase modulation. J. Opt. Commun. (2017). https://doi.org/10.1515/joc-2016-0155. DG Gruyter, (ISSN 2191-6322, ISSN (Print) 0173-4911)
26. Jiang, Z., Fan, C.: A comprehensive study on XPM and SRS induced noise in cascaded IM-DD optical fiber transmission systems. J. Light. Technol. **21**(4), 953–960 (2003)
27. Subramaniam, S., Abbou, F.M., Chuah, H.T., Dambul, K.D.: Performance evaluation of SCM-WDM microcellular communication system in the presence of XPM. IEICE Electron. Express **2**, 192–197 (2005). https://doi.org/10.1587/elex.2.192
28. Kumar, N., Sharma, A.K., Kapoor, V.: Improved XPM-induced crosstalk with higher order dispersion in SCM–WDM optical transmission link. Optik **124**, 941–944 (2014). https://doi.org/10.1016/j.ijleo.2012.02.040. (ISSN 0030-4026)
29. Sharma, A.K., Arya, S.K.: Improved analysis for SRS and XPM induced crosstalk in SCM-WDM transmission link in the presence of HOD. Optik **120**, 773–781 (2009)
30. Yang, F.S., Marhic, M.E., Kazovsky, L.G.: Nonlinear crosstalk and two countermeasures in SCM–WDM optical communication systems. J. Light. Technol. **18**(4), 512–520 (2000)
31. Nain, A., Kumar, S., Singla, S.: Impact of XPM crosstalk on SCM-based RoF systems. J. Opt. Commun. (2016). https://doi.org/10.1515/joc-2016-0045. (ISSN 0173-4911)
32. Toulouse, J.: Optical nonlinearities in fibers: review, recent examples, and systems applications. J. Light. Technol. **23**(11), 3625 (2005)
33. Singh, S.P., Kar, S., Jain, V.K.: Novel strategies for reducing FWM using modified repeated unequally spaced channel allocation. Fiber Integr. Opt. **6**, 415–437 (2004)
34. Hedekvist, P.O., Karlsson, M., Andrekson, P.A.: Fiber fourwave mixing demultiplexing with inherent parametric amplification. J. Light. Technol. **15**(11), 2051–2058 (1997)
35. Hansryd, J., Andrekson, P.A., Westlund, M., Li, J., Hedekvist, P.O.: Fiber-based optical parametric amplifiers and their applications. IEEE J. Sel. Top. Quantum Electron. **8**(3), 506–520 (2002)
36. Ciaramella, E., Curti, F., Trillo, S.: All-optical signal reshaping by means of four-wave mixing in optical fibers. IEEE Photon. Technol. Lett. **13**(2), 142–144 (2001)
37. Li, S., Kuksenkov, D.V.: A novel dispersion monitoring technique based on four-wave mixing in optical fiber. IEEE Photon. Technol. Lett. **16**(3), 942–944 (2004)
38. Tsuji, K., Yokota, H., Saruwatari, A.M.: Influence of dispersion fluctuations on four-wave mixing efficiency in optical fibers. Electron. Commun. Jpn. (Part II: Electron.) **85**(8), 16–24 (2002)

39. Agrawal, G.P., Lin, Q.: Impact of polarization-mode dispersion on measurement of zero-dispersion wavelength through four-wave mixing. IEEE Photon. Technol. Lett. **15**(12), 1719–1721 (2003)

40. Lin, Q., Agrawal, G.P.: Vector theory of four-wave mixing: polarization effects in fiber-optic parametric amplifiers. J. Opt. Soc. Amer., B, Opt. Phys. **21**(6), 1216–1224 (2004)

41. Tomlinson, W.J., Stolen, R.H., Johnson, A.M.: Optical wave breaking of pulses in nonlinear optical fibers. Opt. Lett. **10**(9), 457 (1985)

42. Xu, W., Zhang, S., Chen, W., Luo, A., Liu, S.: Modulation instability of femtosecond pulses in dispersion-decreasing fibers. Opt. Commun. **199**(5–6), 355–360 (2001)

43. Hui, R., Sullivan, M.O., Robinson, A., Taylor, M.: Modulation instability and its impact in multi span optical amplified IMDD systems: theory and experiments. J. Lightw. Technol. **15** (7), 1071–1082 (1997)

44. Zhang, H., Wen, S., Han, W., Wu, J.: Generic features of modulation instability in optical fibers. In: Proceedings of SPIE—International Society for Optical Engineering, Wuhan, China, vol. 5279, no. 1, pp. 443–449 (2004)

45. Tanemura, T., Ozeki, Y., Kikuchi, K.: Modulational instability and parametric amplification induced by loss dispersion in optical fibers. Phys. Rev. Lett. **93**(16), 163902-1–163902-4 (2004)

46. Semrau, D., et al.: Achievable information rates estimates in optically amplified transmission systems using nonlinearity compensation and probabilistic shaping. Opt. Lett. **42**(1), 121–124 (2017)

47. Antos, A.J., Smith, D.K.: Design and characterization of dispersion compensating fiber based on the LP_{01} mode. J. Light. Technol. **12**(10), 1739–1745 (1994)

48. Hill, K., et al.: Chirped in-fiber Bragg gratings for compensation of optical fiber dispersion. Opt. Lett. **19**(17), 1314–1316 (1994)

49. Pepper, D.M., Yariv, A.: Compensation for phase distortions in nonlinear media by phase conjugation. Opt. Lett. **5**(2), 59–60 (1980). https://doi.org/10.1364/OL.5.000059. (ISSN 1539-4794)

50. Watanabe, S., Chikama, T.: Cancellation of four-wave mixing in multichannel fiber transmission by midway optical phase conjugation. Electron. Lett. **30**(14), 1156–1157 (1994)

51. Martelli, P., et al.: All-optical wavelength conversion of a 100-Gb/s polarization-multiplexed signal. Opt. Express **17**(20), 17758–17763 (2009)

52. Trapala, K.S., Inoue, T., Namiki, S.: Nearly-ideal optical phase conjugation based nonlinear compensation system. In: Optical Fiber Communication Conference, p. W3F.8. Optical Society of America (2014)

53. Kumar, S., Yang, D.: Optical backpropagation for fiber-optic communications using highly nonlinear fibers. Opt. Lett. **36**(7), 1038–1040 (2011)

54. Shao, J., Kumar, S.: Optical backpropagation for fiber-optic communications using optical phase conjugation at the receiver. Opt. Lett. **37**(15), 3012–3014 (2012)

55. Kumar, S., Shao, J.: Optical back propagation with optimal step size for fiber optic transmission systems. IEEE Photon. Technol. Lett. **25**, 523–526 (2013)

56. Cartledge, J.C., Guiomar, F.P., Kschischang, F.R., Liga, G., Yankov, M.P.: Digital signal processing for fiber nonlinearities. Opt. Express **25**(3), 1916 (2017). https://doi.org/10.1364/OE.25.001916

57. Li, G.: Recent advances in coherent optical communication. Adv. Opt. Photonics **1**(2), 279–307 (2009)

58. Taylor, M.G.: Coherent detection method using DSP for demodulation of signal and subsequent equalization of propagation impairments. IEEE Photon. Technol. Lett. **16**(2), 674–676 (2004). (ISSN 1041-1135)

59. Savory, S.J.: Digital filters for coherent optical receivers. Opt. Express **16**(2), 804–817 (2008)
60. Goldfarb, G., Li, G.: Chromatic dispersion compensation using digital IIR filtering with coherent detection. IEEE Photon. Technol. Lett. **19**(13), 969–971 (2007). (ISSN 1041-1135)
61. Ip, E., Kahn, J.M.: Digital equalization of chromatic dispersion and polarization mode dispersion. J. Light. Technol. **25**(8), 2033–2043 (2007)
62. Rafique, D., Mussolin, M., Forzati, M., Martensson, J., Chugtai, M.N., Ellis, A.D.: Compensation of intra-channel nonlinear fiber impairments using simplified digital backpropagation algorithm. Opt. Express **19**(10), 9453 (2011)
63. Xu, T., et al.: Modulation format dependence of digital nonlinearity compensation performance in optical fiber communication systems. Opt. Express **25**(4), 3311 (2017)
64. Bayvel, P., et al.: Maximizing the optical network capacity. Phil. Trans. R. Soc. A **374**, 20140440 (2016). https://doi.org/10.1098/rsta.2014.0440
65. Rafique, D., Ellis, A.D.: Impact of signal-ASE four-wave mixing on the effectiveness of digital back-propagation in 112 Gb/s PM-QPSK systems. Opt. Express **19**, 3449–3454 (2011). https://doi.org/10.1364/oe.19.003449
66. Gao, G., Chen, X., Shieh, W.: Influence of PMD on fiber nonlinearity compensation using digital back propagation. Opt. Express **20**, 14406–14418 (2012). https://doi.org/10.1364/oe.20.014406
67. Liga, G., Xu, T., Alvarado, A., Killey, R.I., Bayvel, P.: On the performance of multichannel digital backpropagation in high-capacity long-haul optical transmission. Opt. Express **22**, 30053–30062 (2014). https://doi.org/10.1364/oe.22.030053
68. Temprana, E., et al.: Twofold transmission reach enhancement enabled by transmitter-side digital backpropagation and optical frequency comb-derived information carriers. Opt. Express **23**, 20774–20783 (2015). https://doi.org/10.1364/oe.23.020774
69. Lavery, D., Ives, D., Liga, G., Alvarado, A., Savory, S.J., Bayvel, P.: The benefit of split nonlinearity compensation for optical fiber communications (2015). (http://arxiv.org/abs/1511.04028)

Hybrid Wavelet Transformation and Improved Wavelet Shrinkage Algorithm Method for Reduction of Speckle Noise

Mandeep Kaur$^{(\boxtimes)}$, Neeraj Julka, and Satish Saini

Asra College of Engineering and Technology, Sangrur, Punjab, India
Mandeepsaini17591@gmail.com, asraecef3@gmail.com,
Satishsaini@gmail.com

Abstract. Speckle noise weakens the visual quality of the image thereby limiting the accuracy of Computer aided diagnostic techniques for ultrasound image. An improved method for reduction of multiplicative speckle noise based on Wavelet Shrinkage Guided filter has been proposed in this paper. The Daubechies20 wavelet transformation has been used for the decomposition of the ultrasound images and then an improved wavelet shrinkage algorithm has been utilized for filtering the high-frequency component. The improved quantitative results show the effectiveness of the technique.

Keywords: Speckle noise · Ultrasound images · Guided filter
Edge preservation factor (EPF) · Wavelet transform

1 Introduction

Multiplicative Speckle noise reduction has been proposed in the paper using Wavelet Shrinkage Guided Filter. Input image has been corrupted with speckle noise from level 1 to 7 Wavelet has been used for the decomposition of input image into different spatial bands. and then Daubechies20 wavelet transformation has been used for the decomposition of the ultrasound images for the present study. After decomposition the Guided filters have been applied on different spatial bands for noise removal. In this way the noise is removed and important information like edges are preserved exactly.

1.1 Speckle Noise

Speckle is a multiplicative noise which is the prime factor that bounds the contrast resolution while diagnosing the ultrasound images restricting the detectability of low-contrast, small wounds and making the ultrasound images difficult to understand [1, 2, 6]. The actual implementation of image processing and the analysis algorithms have also been limited by the speckle noise. Therefore, the speckle is the main source of noise in ultrasound imaging and should be removed without disturbing essential characteristics of the image.

© Springer Nature Singapore Pte Ltd. 2019
P. K. Singh et al. (Eds.): FTNCT 2018, CCIS 958, pp. 45–56, 2019.
https://doi.org/10.1007/978-981-13-3804-5_4

1.2 Filters for De-speckling

Although various speckle reduction techniques and filters have been introduced, enhanced and studied by the researchers, but till now there is no perfect method that can consider all the constraints such as smoothing, details and edge preservation. The lee filter [3, 4] has been used based on minimum mean square error (MMSE) that produces a speckle free image. The kuanfilter based on minimum mean square error has also been introduced for speckle reduction [16]. Frost filter has been proposed by Frost et al. [5] which is an adaptive filter designed to de-speckle images based on local statistics similarly to Lee filter. The gf4d filter [9] has been introduced which has used a non-linear noise reduction method. The median filter [8, 15] is a simple nonlinear operator that replaces the central pixel of the window with the median-value of the neighborhood pixels. The hybrid median filter increases the optical perception and also preserves the edges. This filter is therefore utilized to maintain as well as enhance the edges in ultrasound images [19]. Wiener filter which uses the first order statistics such as the mean and the variance of the neighborhood has also been used for speckle noise reduction [11, 14]. Bilateral filter which is a non-linear filter that depends on spatial weighted middling has also been utilized for the reduction of speckle noise [10, 17]. Kuwahara filter considers the most homogenous neighborhood around every pixel [7] and has been widely used. The Kuwahara filter is able to smooth the image as well as it preserves the edges [20]. Speckle Reducing Anisotropic Diffusion filter (SRAD) is based on diffusion based technique for speckle reduction is introduced by Yu and Acton [12]. Buades [13] proposed Nonlocal means (NLM) filter. In the NLM filter the intensity values of the pixels can be related to the pixel intensity of the entire image. A comparative study is definitely needed to compare filters in terms of conserving the edges, features and the efficiency of different filters.

2 Performance Evaluation Metrics

There are many performance evaluation metrics found in literature. We will use some from the following to evaluate performance of the proposed algorithm.

2.1 Figure of Merit (FoM)

This parameter measures the performance of filter to preserve the edges of the image.

$$FoM\left(I_{filt}, I_{ref}\right) = \frac{1}{\max\left(E_{filt}, E_{ref}\right)} \sum_{i=1}^{N} \frac{1}{1 + d_i^2 \alpha} \tag{1}$$

Here E_{filt} and E_{ref} represents the number of the edge pixels in edge maps of the images I_{filt} and I_{ref}. α is $\frac{1}{9}$, d_i denotes the Euclidean distance between the detected ith edge pixel and the nearest ideal edge pixel of the reference image. The value of FoM lies between 0 and 1 where 1 represents perfect edge preservation of image.

2.2 Structural Similarity (SSIM) Index

SSIM is used to compare structure, contrast and luminance between the original and filtered image.

$$SSIM = \frac{1}{M} \frac{(2\mu_X\mu_Y + C_1)(2\sigma_{12} + C_2)}{(\mu_X^2 + \mu_Y^2 + C_1)(\sigma_1^2 + \sigma_2^2 + C_2)} \tag{2}$$

Here μ_X, μ_Y and σ_1, σ_2 are the means and standard deviations of the images that are compared. σ_{12} is the covariance between the images. $C_1, C_2 \ll 1$ Indicate stability. The values of SSIM lie between 0 and 1.

2.3 Peak Signal to Noise Ratio (PSNR)

This parameter provides the quality of image in terms of powers of the original and filtered images.

$$PSNR = 10log_{10}\frac{(2^n - 1)^n}{MSE} = 10log_{10}\left(\frac{255^2}{MSE}\right) \tag{3}$$

Here MSE is mean square error value.

3 Proposed Method

An efficient algorithm has been proposed for speckle noise reduction using wavelet transform and improved guided filter which gives better results when compared with existing methods. As wavelet transform can decompose the input images up to several levels, there is different value of noise reduction when we use different levels of wavelet decomposition, their fore approximation coefficients need to be filtered out depending upon the level of Wavelet decomposition level. In this work the de-noising step has been made level dependent which has improved the performance and hence can be selected for de-noising purposes. The steps in proposed algorithm have been shown in Fig. 1.

From the previously stated, an enhanced noise de-speckling strategy in view of wavelet and guided filter has been suggested and explained as under:

(1) The multiplicative noise model is converted into additive noise model by compressing the ultrasonic envelope signal with logarithmic transformation.

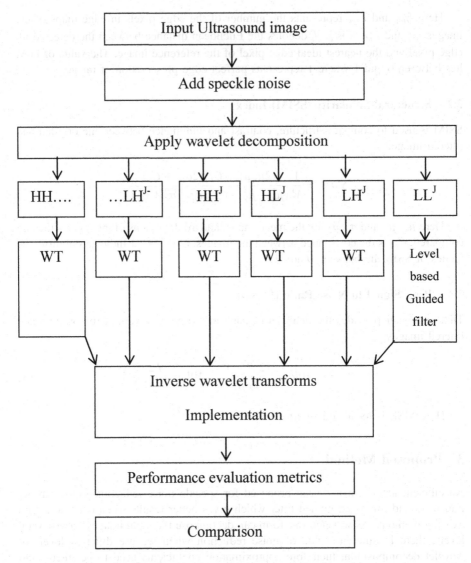

Fig. 1. Flowchart of the proposed algorithm

(2) The 2-D discrete wavelet change (DWT) is connected for the log-transforming images, and acquires four frequency domains (LL^1; LH^1; HL1 and HH^1). To proceed with the procedure of wavelet decomposition for the low frequency space LL1, four frequency areas (LL^2; LH^2; HL^2 and HH^2) are gotten.

(3) According to the factual properties of speckle noise and noise free sign in step 1, an enhanced wavelet threshold shrinkage calculation (WT) is outlined (Eq. (8)), which is utilized to handle the wavelet coefficients of the high frequency subbands in every layer (LH^j; HL^j and HH^j; j = 1; 2;...; J).

(4) Considering the way that the low frequency sub-band of the last layer (LL^j) still exists a great deal of huge spackle noise, therefore the guided filter is utilized to filter LL^j in which its wpsilon parameter has been used.

(5) Inverse wavelet transformation (IDWT) is utilized to prepare the de-noised wavelet coefficients and get the de-noised medicinal ultrasonic images.

4 Results and Discussions

Medical ultrasound images used for the purpose of experimentation have been acquired from www.ultrasoundcases.info. This site contains large number of general ultrasound images obtained from the GelderseVallei Hospital in Ede, the Netherlands. MATLAB has been used for the experimentation.

The experiments have been conducted on the ultrasound images taken from the above mentioned data set. These noise free images are corrupted with speckle noise with noise level of 1 to 7. Figures 2, 3, 4, 5, 6, 7 and 8 shows the image 1 after adding speckle noise of level 1 to 7 and comparison of the visual quality of an ultrasound image resulting from previous and proposed techniques.

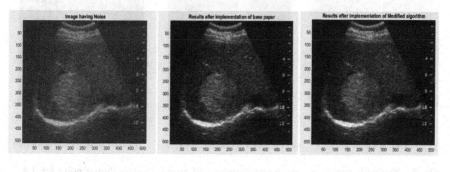

(a) Noise at Level 1   (b) Figure of previous technique   (c) Figure of proposed algorithm

Fig. 2. Noise filtering using previous technique and proposed algorithm at noise level 1

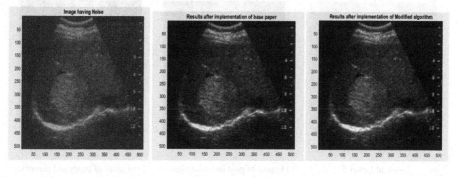

(d)   Noise at Level 2   (e) Figure of previous technique   (f) Figure of proposed algorithm

Fig. 3. Noise filtering using previous technique and proposed algorithm at noise level 2

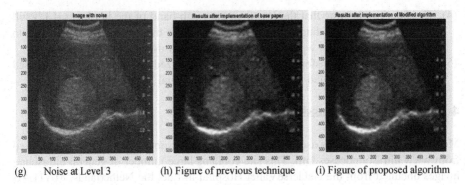

(g)   Noise at Level 3   (h) Figure of previous technique   (i) Figure of proposed algorithm

Fig. 4. Noise filtering using previous technique and proposed algorithm at noise level 3

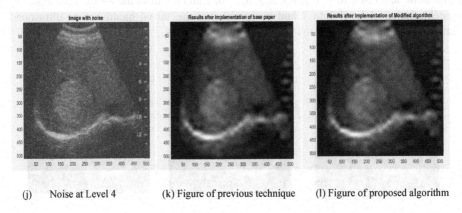

(j)   Noise at Level 4   (k) Figure of previous technique   (l) Figure of proposed algorithm

Fig. 5. Noise filtering using previous technique and proposed algorithm at noise level 4

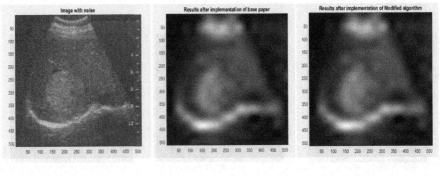

(m)   Noise at Level 5   (n) Figure of previous technique   (o) Figure of proposed algorithm

Fig. 6. Noise filtering using previous technique and proposed algorithm at noise level 5

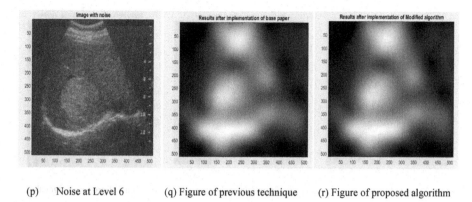

(p)   Noise at Level 6   (q) Figure of previous technique   (r) Figure of proposed algorithm

Fig. 7. Noise filtering using previous technique and proposed algorithm at noise level 6

Table 1 shows the comparison of the performance of the proposed system and existing method. The input image 1 has been added with noise starting from noise level 1 to noise level 7 and performance measures obtained i.e. FOM, SSIM and PSNR for the proposed method has been compared with the existing method (Figs. 9, 10, 11 and 12).

Table 1. Quantitative results of simulated ultrasound image experiment for image 1

	Noise level = 1			Noise level = 2		
	FOM	SSIM	PSNR	FOM	SSIM	PSNR
Base	0.5937	0.4509	19.1684	0.6884	0.6308	19.5549
Proposed	0.5876	0.4125	18.9964	0.6707	0.6331	19.5658
	Noise level = 3			Noise level = 4		
	FOM	SSIM	PSNR	FOM	SSIM	PSNR
Base	0.5218	0.6032	19.2679	0.2241	0.5348	18.6371
Proposed	0.5244	0.6027	19.2988	0.2179	0.5330	18.6475
	Noise level = 5			Noise level = 6		
	FOM	SSIM	PSNR	FOM	SSIM	PSNR
Base	0.1189	0.5027	17.8334	0.1701	0.4829	16.8922
Proposed	0.1327	0.5017	17.8803	0.2561	0.4803	16.7904
	Noise level = 7					
	FOM		SSIM		PSNR	
Base	0.3271		0.4609		16.0620	
Proposed	0.3099		0.4616		16.1066	

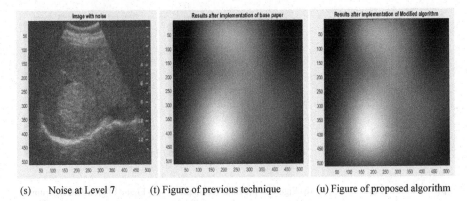

(s)   Noise at Level 7   (t) Figure of previous technique   (u) Figure of proposed algorithm

Fig. 8. Noise filtering using previous technique and proposed algorithm at noise level 7

Table 2. Quantitative results of simulated ultrasound image experiment for image 2

	Noise level = 1			Noise level = 2		
	FOM	SSIM	PSNR	FOM	SSIM	PSNR
Base	0.7680	0.5218	19.0816	0.8099	0.5894	19.3834
Proposed	0.7470	0.4973	18.9340	0.8198	0.5988	19.4045
	Noise level = 3			Noise level = 4		
	FOM	SSIM	PSNR	FOM	SSIM	PSNR
Base	0.4366	0.5045	19.1846	0.1762	0.4496	18.8997
Proposed	0.4117	0.5068	19.2167	0.1641	0.4485	18.9065
	Noise level = 5			Noise level = 6		
	FOM	SSIM	PSNR	FOM	SSIM	PSNR
Base	0.1641	0.4485	18.9065	0.1491	0.4185	18.1195
Proposed	0.1141	0.4279	18.5583	0.1715	0.4178	18.0797
	Noise level = 7					
	FOM		SSIM		PSNR	
Base	0.2746		0.4101		17.5819	
Proposed	0.2480		0.4102		17.6962	

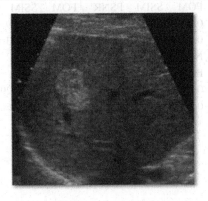

Fig. 9. Input Image-2

Table 3. Quantitative results of simulated ultrasound image experiment for image 3

	Noise level = 1			Noise level = 2		
	FOM	SSIM	PSNR	FOM	SSIM	PSNR
Base	0.7977	0.4505	19.0589	0.8124	0.4574	19.2318
Proposed	0.7848	0.4376	18.9147	0.8067	0.4646	19.2589
	Noise level = 3			Noise level = 4		
	FOM	SSIM	PSNR	FOM	SSIM	PSNR
Base	0.3860	0.3575	18.9920	0.1568	0.3116	18.6344
Proposed	0.3958	0.3605	19.0283	0.1661	0.3128	18.6945
	Noise level = 5			Noise level = 6		
	FOM	SSIM	PSNR	FOM	SSIM	PSNR
Base	0.0808	0.2912	18.1634	0.1423	0.2757	17.2135
Proposed	0.0954	0.2913	18.1813	0.1514	0.2763	17.3148
	Noise level = 7					
	FOM		SSIM		PSNR	
Base	0.2841		0.2622		16.4907	
Proposed	0.3550		0.2637		16.5661	

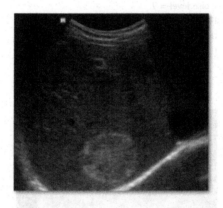

Fig. 10. Input image-3

As seen from above tables the output of previous and proposed method output has been shown. In the above tables distinguish the filtering of FOM, SSIM, and PSNR values of a selected image after the adding a specific noise in the image. As seen in the table we add some level of noises in the image. The noise level added to image has been shown like value which is 1, 2, 3, 4, 5, 6, and 7 respectively. By adding this noise level into the image then we filter the selected image using both previous and proposed techniques. As shown in the table at all level of noise our proposed algorithm is obtaining the better results of noise filtering. At each level FOM, SSIM, and PSNR values of the proposed method have been improved as compared to previous method which in turn shows the capability of the proposed method to filter the images from the speckle noise effectively (Tables 2, 3, 4 and 5).

Table 4. Quantitative results of simulated ultrasound image experiment for image 4

	Noise level = 1			Noise level = 2		
	FOM	SSIM	PSNR	FOM	SSIM	PSNR
Base	0.7791	0.4340	18.9940	0.7893	0.4609	19.0388
Proposed	0.6866	0.4179	18.8506	0.8089	0.4677	19.0682
	Noise level = 3			Noise level = 4		
	FOM	SSIM	PSNR	FOM	SSIM	PSNR
Base	0.3964	0.3641	18.6130	0.1923	0.3088	18.0581
Proposed	0.4215	0.3637	18.6505	0.1800	0.3082	18.1014
	Noise level = 5			Noise level = 6		
	FOM	SSIM	PSNR	FOM	SSIM	PSNR
Base	0.1135	0.2883	17.4808	0.1238	0.2786	16.9554
Proposed	0.1135	0.2883	17.4808	0.1682	0.2774	16.9549
	Noise level = 7					
	FOM		SSIM		PSNR	
Base	0.2970		0.2719		16.1098	
Proposed	0.2334		0.2702		16.0474	

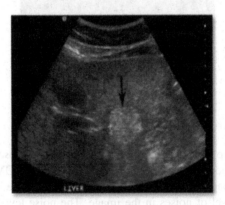

Fig. 11. Input image-4

Table 5. Quantitative results of simulated ultrasound image experiment for image 5

	Noise level = 1			Noise level = 2		
	FOM	SSIM	PSNR	FOM	SSIM	PSNR
Base	0.7178	0.4436	19.0912	0.7370	0.5271	19.3180
Proposed	0.6723	0.4176	18.9024	0.7533	0.5347	19.3804
	Noise level = 3			Noise level = 4		
	FOM	SSIM	PSNR	FOM	SSIM	PSNR
Base	0.3946	0.4709	19.2345	0.1674	0.4305	18.9188
Proposed	0.4023	0.4703	19.1987	0.1644	0.4318	18.9426
	Noise level = 5			Noise level = 6		
	FOM	SSIM	PSNR	FOM	SSIM	PSNR
Base	0.1041	0.4162	18.6040	0.1487	0.3998	17.5548
Proposed	0.1041	0.4162	18.6040	0.1941	0.3983	17.5518
	Noise level = 7					
	FOM		SSIM		PSNR	
Base	0.1779		0.3923		16.9211	
Proposed	0.2248		0.3919		16.7383	

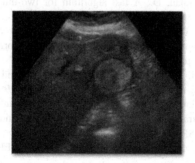

Fig. 12. Input image-5

5   Conclusion

Medical ultrasound images are usually corrupted with different kinds of noises in its attainment and transmission. The medical ultrasound images are corrupted by a type of locally interrelated multiplicative noise Speckle, therefore making visual observation challenging. In our proposed work we use different level for speckle noise filtering. For noise filtering wavelet and Guided filters are used. First of all we select an ultrasound image to filter. Then converted to gray scale and noise is added in the selected image. The noise filtering levels are used from 1 to 7 and then apply the filters to de-speckling the selected image. For evaluation of the results we perform our algorithm on various ultrasound images and calculate the FOM, PSNR, and SSIM values of the images. The proposed algorithm has shown the better results as compared to previous work. More performance evaluation criterion can be used to compare the de-speckling performance and new filters can be applied to de-speckle the ultrasound images as a scope of future extension.

References

1. Goodman, J.W.: Some fundamental properties of speckle. J. Opt. Soc. Am. **66**(11), 1145–1149 (1976)
2. Burckhardt, C.B.: Speckle in ultrasound B-mode scans. IEEE Trans. Sonic Ultrason. **SU-25** (1), 1–6 (1978)
3. Lee, J.S.: Digital image enhancement and noise filtering by use of local statistics. IEEE Trans. Pattern Anal. Mach. Intell. **PAMI-2**(2), 165–168 (1980)
4. Lee, J.S.: Refined Filtering of Image Noise using Local Statistics. Computer Graphics and Image Processing **15**, 380–389 (1981)
5. Frost, V., Stiles, J., Shanmugan, K., Holtzman, J.: A model for radar images and its application to adaptive digital filtering of multiplicative noise. IEEE Trans. Pattern Anal. Mach. Intell. **4**, 157–166 (1982)
6. Wagner, R.F., Smith, S.W., Sandrik, J.M., Lopez, H.: Statistics of speckle in ultrasound B-scans. IEEE Trans. Sonic Ultrason. **30**, 156–163 (1983)
7. Kuan, D.T., Sawchuk, A.A., Strand, T.C., Chavel, P.: Adaptive restoration of images with speckle. IEEE Trans. Acoust., Speech Signal Process. **ASSP-35**(3), 373–383 (1987)
8. Ahmad, M.O., Sundararajan, D.: A fast algorithm for two-dimensional median filtering. IEEE Trans. Circuits Syst. **CAS-3**(11), 1364–1374 (1987)
9. Busse, L., Crimmins, T.R., Fienup, J.R.: A model based approach to improve the performance of the geometric filtering speckle reduction algorithm. In: Processing IEEE Ultrasonic Symposium, pp. 1353–1356 (1995)
10. Tomasi, C., Manduchi, R.: Bilateral filtering for gray and color images. In IEEE International Conference on Computer Vision, pp. 839–846 (1998)
11. Loizou, C., Christodoulou, C., Pattichis, C., Istepanian, R. Pantziaris, M., Nicolaides, A.: Speckle reduction in ultrasound images of atherosclerotic carotid plaque. In: Proceeding of IEEE Conference on DSP, pp. 525–528 (2002)
12. Yu, Y., Acton, S.T.: Speckle reducing anisotropic diffusion. IEEE Trans. Image Process. **11** (11), 1260–1270 (2002)
13. Buades, A., Coll, B., Morel, J.M.: A review of image de-noising algorithms, with a new one. Multi-Scale Model. Simul. **4**, 490–530 (2005)
14. Loizou, C.P., Pattichis, C.S., Christodoulou, C.I., Istepanian, R.S., Pantziaris, M., Nicolaides, A.: Comparative evaluation of de-speckle filtering in ultrasound imaging of the carotid artery. IEEE Trans. Ultrason. Ferroelectr. Freq. Control. **52**(10), 1653–1669 (2005)
15. Gonzalez, R.C., Woods, R.E.: Digital Image Processing. Pearson Education, India (2008)
16. Sivakumar, R., Gayathri, M.K., Nedumaran, D.: Speckle filtering of ultrasound B-scan images–a comparative study between spatial and diffusion filters. In: 2010 IEEE Conference on Open System (ICOS 2010), pp. 80–85 (2010)
17. Vanithamani, R., Umamaheswari, G.: Wavelet based de-speckling of medical ultrasound images with bilateral filter. In: TENCON 2011 IEEE Region 10 Conference. IEEE (2011)
18. Sarode, M.V., Deshmukh, P.R.: Reduction of speckle noise and image enhancement of images using filtering technique. Int. J. Adv. Technol. **2**(1), 30–38 (2011)
19. Zhang, J., Wang, C., Cheng, Y.: Comparison of de-speckle filters for breast ultrasound images. Circuits Syst. Signal Process. **34**, 185–208 (2014)

Signal Processing Methods for Identification of Sudden Cardiac Death

Reeta Devi[1(✉)], Hitender Kumar Tyagi[2], and Dinesh Kumar[3]

[1] Department of Electronics and Communication Engineering,
University Institute of Engineering and Technology, Kurukshetra University,
Kurukshetra, Haryana, India
reetakuk@gmail.com
[2] Department of Electronics, University College, Kurukshetra University,
Kurukshetra, Haryana, India
hitender.tyagi@gmail.com
[3] YMCA University of Science and Technology, Faridabad, Haryana, India
dineshelectronics@gmail.com

Abstract. Sudden cardiac death (SCD) is defined as sudden natural death occurring within few minutes to an hour from the onset of symptoms due to known or unknown cardiac cause. An early stage prediction or identification of SCD has become a major challenge among the medical fraternity to save the life of SCD affected person. For prediction of sudden cardiac death, three distinct kinds of markers viz. markers of structural heart disease, markers of electrical instability and markers of abnormal autonomic balance have been devised. Based on these markers, many signal processing techniques like signal averaged electrocardiography, extraction of longer QRS duration, identification of QT-dispersion, and feature extraction from T-wave alternans, heart rate variability (HRV), and heart rate turbulence (HRT) with data mining, statistical and machine learning algorithms are fused together to validate the SCD prediction accuracy. But despite significant advances in the engineering research and medical science, there is no standard technique adopted to identify the SCD at an early stage which limits the fusion of any method into a medical product due to its own limitations. This paper is therefore, designed to discuss different signal processing methods based on these three markers in order to predict sudden cardiac death at an early and alarming stage. The contents embodied in this paper would benefit the community of the research groups designing signal processing algorithms for early prediction of SCD which will help the clinicians to save the precious life of the SCD affected patients.

Keywords: SCD · Signal processing · Structural heart disease
Electrical instability · Autonomic system

1 Introduction

Death is that certainty in everyone's life which can only be postponed, not denied. As per the estimates of World Health Organization (WHO), among all causes of death non- communicable diseases (NCD) are the number 1 killers contributing to 40 million

© Springer Nature Singapore Pte Ltd. 2019
P. K. Singh et al. (Eds.): FTNCT 2018, CCIS 958, pp. 57–72, 2019.
https://doi.org/10.1007/978-981-13-3804-5_5

of the 56 million global deaths in 2015 where 17.7 million lives a year are lost due to cardiac causes only. Table 1 shows annual NCD death estimates by WHO for the year of 2015 in different countries. Khor GL [1] in 2001 projected that in the year 2020, deaths due to non-communicable diseases including cardiac diseases would be accounting for 7 out of 10 deaths in India and other developing countries. *Sudden cardiac death (SCD)*, a growing concern among the non-communicable cardiovascular diseases particularly put a large burden because it cuts short the potential years of contribution of the affected persons to their family and the society [2]. SCD is defined by W.H.O criteria as the natural sudden death due to cardiac causes occurring within 24 h. But of witnessed deaths nearly 80% occurred within 2 h of the symptoms onset [3]. In the context of time, sudden is defined for most clinical purposes as 1 h between a change in clinical status announcing the onset of the life threatening cardiac arrest [4]. Prevention of SCD from this life threatening cardiac arrest, Implantable cardioverter defibrillator (ICD) presents the main primary solution [5]. But despite significant advances in the engineering research and medical science, evaluation of a patient at the high risk of SCD who would benefit from ICD still remains a daunting problem [6]. This issue is of particular importance from the view point of device cost in ICD therapy. The device cost lies between USD $ 25300 to USD $ 50700 per life year [7].

Table 1. Annual NCD death rates (both sexes)

Country	NCD death rates per 100,000 population per year
Japan	248
Australia	289
Canada	292
United Kingdom	351
United States of America	395
Thailand	442
Sri Lanka	511
China	550
India	600
Pakistan	710

Therefore, ICD therapy will be more cost-effective when patients at high risk of SCD are screened out using additional non-invasive markers of sudden cardiac death. There are three different markers for the prediction of SCD. It includes markers of structural heart disease, markers of electrical instability and markers of autonomic balance. This paper will describe the available signal processing methods for identification of sudden cardiac death based on these markers.

2 Materials and Methods

2.1 Dataset

To make easy understanding of different kinds of markers, we simulated the ECG signals of SCD affected patients. The ECG signals were downloaded from MIT/BIH database for normal control subjects (Normal Sinus Rhythm Database) and sudden cardiac death patients (Sudden Cardiac Death Holter Database) [8]. The dataset consists of 2 lead ECG signals of about 24 h duration for each of 23 SCD patients. Similarly, for each of 15 normal control subjects, it consists of 2 lead ECG signals of approximately 2 h duration. To describe the different kinds of markers, ECG waveform of lead MLII were preprocessed and plotted here. The preprocessing steps are outlined as follows.

2.2 Preprocessing of ECG Signals

The sampling frequency used for the ECG signals under study was 250 Hz for SCD patients and 128 Hz for normal control subjects. Both kinds of signals were subjected to filtering process as suggested by Wu et al. [9] for the removal of baseline wandering noise and power line interference. To remove the baseline wandering noise we have chosen two-stage moving average filter. The first and second stage averaging window lengths are set to 1/3 and 2/3 of the number of samples in the input signal. To remove the power-line interference, an IIR comb notch filter with the impulse response function as generated by FDATool in MATLAB 8.1 is given below in Eq. (1) was chosen:

$$H(z) = 0.9230 \frac{1 - Z^{-8}}{1 + Z^{-1} - 0.8451Z^{-8}} \tag{1}$$

A plot of magnitude response and phase response of the selected comb notch filter are shown in Figs. 1 and 2 respectively. A filtered labeled plot of ECG signal of a normal control subject is shown in Fig. 3. This way preprocessed ECG signals of the SCD patients associated with different markers were simulated and plotted here to explain the various signal processing methods for identification of sudden cardiac death at an early and alarming stage.

3 Markers of Structural Heart Disease

Among different kinds of markers for identification of sudden cardiac death, markers of structural heart disease are placed at the first position. The heart disease acquired through wear and tear or heart diseases that people are born with are referred to structural heart diseases [10]. An example of structural heart disease acquired through wear and tear would be a tight or leaky heart valve. A hole within the chambers of the heart is an example of structural heart disease people are born with. To predict or identify SCD, markers of structural heart disease are categorized into 4 categories i.e. depressed left ventricular ejection fraction, non sustained ventricular tachycardia, frequent ventricular ectopy and QRS duration [11, 12].

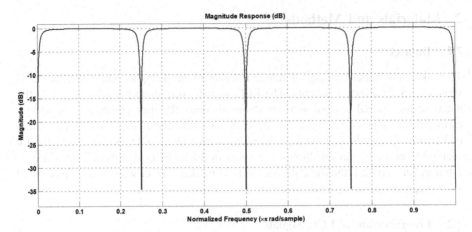

Fig. 1. Magnitude response of the IIR comb notch filter

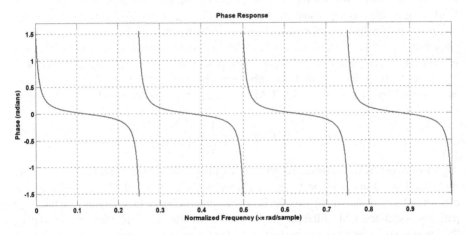

Fig. 2. Phase response of the IIR comb notch filter

3.1 Depressed Left Ventricular Ejection Fraction (Depressed LVEF)

With each heart beat, the fraction of blood ejected from a ventricle of the heart is termed as ejection fraction (EF). It therefore, measures the pumping efficiency of the heart. The efficiency of the heart pumping blood into the systematic circulation of the body is called Left Ventricular ejection fraction (LVEF) [12]. The LVEF affected subjects can be diagnosed with certain markers on standard 12-lead ECG. These markers include presence of prolonged QRS duration, bundle branch block and QT dispersion etc. indicating LVEF and may act as the significant markers of SCD. A depressed value of LVEF $\leq$ 30% screens out the SCD patient for implantation of cardioverter defibrillator to save the precious life [12]. If LVEF is only moderately depressed (30% $\leq$ LVEF $\leq$ 40%), the electro-physiologic testing can screen out the

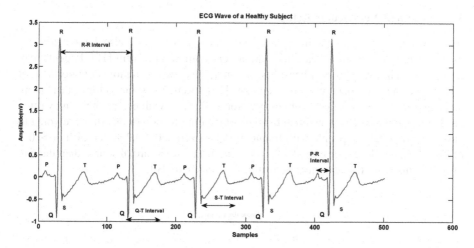

Fig. 3. ECG waveform of a healthy subject (record no. 16265)

patients with non-sustained ventricular- tachycardia and inducible ventricular arrhythmia who would be benefitting from an ICD [13].

3.2 Non Sustained Ventricular Tachycardia

The regular and fast heart rate as shown in Fig. 4 arising from inappropriate electrical activity in ventricles of the heart is termed as Ventricular Tachycardia (VT) [13]. Although, changes in heart rate for a shorter period may not result into problems, but heart rate changing for a longer period may turn into ventricular fibrillation or cardiac arrest causing SCD. According to Baldzizhar et al. [14] about 7% people in cardiac arrest are found suffering from ventricular techicardia.

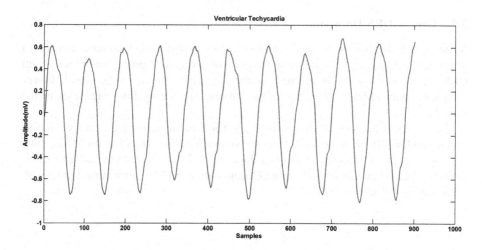

Fig. 4. Ventricular tachycardia (record no. 41)

3.3 Frequent Ventricular Ectopy

As shown in Fig. 5, premature ventricular contractions (PVC) also known as ventricular ectopics or ectopic heart beats are a very common problem [15]. Patients may suffer with skipped or missed beats but they may also have symptoms of shortness of breath, dizziness or poor exercise capacity [16]. Sometimes the ectopic beat is an incidental finding in a patient with no symptoms. Patients with ectopic beats may often be very anxious and concerned that there heart is going to stop or that they are going to have a heart attack. In people with frequent PVCs (>10,000–20,000 per 24 h or >10% of the QRS complexes) or if the PVCs originate from an epicardial source then the risk of SCD caused by the abnormal activation is increased [16].

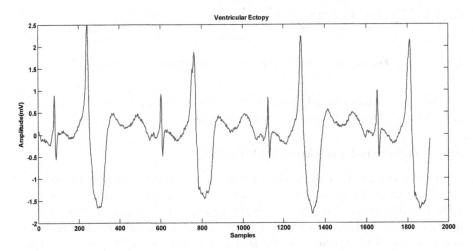

Fig. 5. Ventricular ectopic beats (record no. 47)

3.4 Longer QRS Duration

Normal QRS duration in healthy subjects is 70–100 ms. This duration is utilized to determine the origin of QRS complexes. For example narrow complexes with QRS < 100 ms originate from superaventicular origin. On the other hand, longer complexes with QRS > 100 ms have been found originating from ventricles in the heart [17].

Longer QRS duration as shown in Fig. 6 has been demonstrated as a risk stratification tool for SCD. Kurl et al. [17] has shown that 27% increased risk for SCD results with an increase of 10-ms in each QRS duration. A 2.50-fold risk for sudden cardiac death had been shown in subjects with QRS duration of >110 ms comparing those with QRS duration of <96 ms [17].

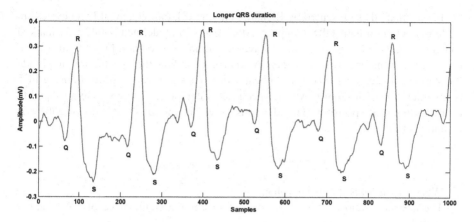

Fig. 6. Longer QRS duration (record no. 41)

4 Markers of Electrical Instability

4.1 Electrical Alternans of the T-waveform

On the standard 12-lead ECG recording, alternating amplitude of the T wave from beat to beat as shown in Fig. 7 is referred to as T-wave alternans [18]. It appears due to repolarization dispersion and has been demonstrated as a strong predictor of SCD [19, 20]. Microvolt T-wave electrical alternans (MTWA) may be measured by spectral methods or using Holter-based recordings with modified moving average analysis [18].

4.1.1 Spectral Method
The spectral method to assess the TWA is based on fast fourier transform (FFT) [20].

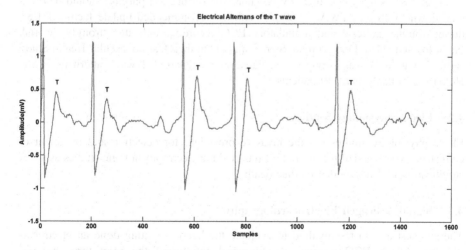

Fig. 7. Electrical alternans of the T-wave (record no. 34)

In this method as presented by Richard et al. in [18], the sequential ECG cycles are made to align with their QRS complex. After then 128 predefined points t are marked and at each t, the ST-segments and T-waves amplitude as shown in Fig. 1 is measured. Fast fourier transform (FFT) is then computed to obtain the spectra for amplitude fluctuations of each measured beat-to beat series. Thus a separate spectrum using FFT is generated for each point t. All the spectra of different time points t are averaged to form a composite spectrum. The alternans power in microvolt at 0.5 cycles/beat is computed as:

$$= \left(\text{the overall } \mu_v - \mu_{v \text{ of even or odd beats}}\right)^2 \tag{2}$$

Where μ_v denotes the mean voltage.

The alternans ratio known as K score expresses the significance of TWA and is calculated as:

$$\frac{\text{alternans power at 0.5 cycles per beat}}{\text{standard deviation of the spectral noise}} \tag{3}$$

4.1.2 Modified Moving Average Method (MMA)

The modified moving average method works on principle of recursive averaging algorithm for noise rejection [18]. The methodology presented here is described by the authors in reference number [18]. This algorithm keeps streaming the even and odd beats into different bins. The median of even and odd beats are then created as the median complexes and superimposed for each bin. Every 10 to 15 s the TWA value is reported. It is computed at any point between the junction T segments by taking the average of the largest difference in the two even and odd median complexes. With an adjustable update factor, this method controls the effect of incoming new beats on the computed median templates. To detect the transients with greater sensitivity, an update factor of $1/8^{th}$ is recommended. TWA values for verification purpose should be over-read down to 20 μV. TWA $\geq$ 60 μV with the recommended update factor of $1/8^{th}$ during routine exercise and ambulatory ECG recording indicates strongly the risk factor for SCD [18]. For example, Sten et al. [21] in their Cardiovascular Health Study showed that SCD was strongly associated with increased T-wave alternans in the Holter signal analysis of 49 patients.

4.2 Electrophysiology Studies

Electrophysiology studies are the invasive procedure for detection and treatment of cardiac arrhythmias. Hilfiker et al. [22] reported the electrophysiologic studies as a risk stratification tool for sudden cardiac death.

4.3 Signal Averaged Electrocardiography

The simplest and fastest method to evaluate the heart is getting done an electrocardiogram (ECG). ECG acquires the electrical activity of the heart through some electrodes placed at well designed sites of the body. A signal averaged electrocardiography (SAECG) is a detailed version of ECG. In this technique, a number of ECG signals are acquired usually over a period of approximately 20 min from different sites on the heart and then averaged to remove interference and analyze the small variations in the QRS complexes. These small variations in QRS complexes are called late potentials which are not visible in a simple and single ECG signal. Late potentials are an indicator of the fragmented or delayed depolarization of ventricular myocardium which may act as the substrate of fibrosis or a scar. These late potentials if not identified and treated in time may develop into dangerous ventricular techyarrhythmias. The presence of this type of ventricular late potentials in signal averaged electrocardiogram along with T wave alternans have been demonstrated as strong predictors of SCD [21].

4.4 QT-Dispersion

The term QT-dispersion stands for the difference between longest and shortest QT-interval on the standard 12-lead electrocardiography [23]. Research studies examining the possible relation between QT-dispersion (considering particularly QTc: corrected heart rate QT interval) and all cause sudden death published results contradicting with each other due to variation in the measurement methods for QT-interval [23, 24]. The potential trend between QT interval and sudden cardiac death is yet to be explored more taking into consideration the other factors like genetics, age, sex, certain medications and race etc.

5 Markers of Abnormal Autonomic Balance

5.1 Abnormalities in Resting Heart Rate

SCD in resting hearts indicate towards the genetic factors. For example risk stratification for SCD in young athletes having healthy, normal and resting heart is always associated with personal and family health history of the athlete with particular focus on blood pressure levels, chest pain and early sudden death of any family member [25].

5.2 Heart Rate Variability

A plot of consecutive RR intervals is called Heart rate variability (HRV) signal. It can be derived from short period of 2–30 min or longer period of 24 h ECG recordings. There are different features of HRV that are derived and analysed for specific purpose. The mathematical descriptions of some important features are given as under:

Time domain features:

$$\text{Mean RR:} \frac{1}{N} \sum RR(i) \tag{4}$$

$$\text{Median:} \begin{cases} \left(\frac{N+1}{2}\right)^{th} term; & \text{if } N \text{ is odd} \\ \left(\frac{N}{2}\right)^{th} term; & \text{if } N \text{ is even} \end{cases} \tag{5}$$

$$\text{SDRR:} \sqrt{\frac{1}{N}\sum (RR(i) - Mean\ RR)^2} \tag{6}$$

$$\text{SDRR}_i : \frac{1}{N}\sum_{i=1}^{N-1} SDRR_{ind} \tag{7}$$

$$\text{pNN50:} \frac{[(RR(i+1) - RR(i)) > 50\,\text{ms}]}{[\text{total}(RR(\text{diff}))]} \tag{8}$$

Frequency domain features:

$$\text{aVLF(ms}^2) = \text{Absolute power in very low frequency region i.e. } 0.003 \\ - 0.04\,\text{Hz of HRV} \tag{9}$$

$$\text{aLF(ms}^2) = \text{Absolute power in low frequency region i.e. } 0.04 - 0.15\,\text{Hz of HRV} \tag{10}$$

$$\text{aHF(ms}^2) = \text{Absolute power in high frequency region i.e. } 0.15 - 0.4\,\text{Hz of HRV} \tag{11}$$

$$\text{aTotal(ms}^2) = \text{aVLF(ms}^2) + \text{aLF(ms}^2) + \text{aHF(ms}^2) \tag{12}$$

$$\text{pVLF(\%)} = \text{aVLF/aTotal} \tag{13}$$

$$pLF(\%) = aLF/aTotal \tag{14}$$

$$pHF(\%) = aHF/aTotal \tag{15}$$

$$nLF(\%) = aLF/aTotal - aVLF \tag{16}$$

$$nHF(\%) = aHF/aTotal - aVLF \tag{17}$$

$$LF/HF \text{ Ratio} = nLF/nHF. \tag{18}$$

Plots of HRV for normal control subject and SCD patient at the moment of SCD and few minutes earlier are plotted in Figs. 8 and 9 respectively. Decreased values of the various statistical features of HRV described in Eqs. 4–18 have been associated with SCD by various research groups [26–34] and the results obtained were validated with different machine learning algorithms. Patil et al. [35] and Jilani et al. [36] developed data mining methods based on HRV parameters considering certain factors like effects of age, gender, race, smoking habits and illness level of the subject for modeling of an SCD pattern so that future prediction of SCD can be related to that particular pattern. From the other hand, Lammert et al. [37] developed methods based on feature extraction techniques from a patient's HRV signal.

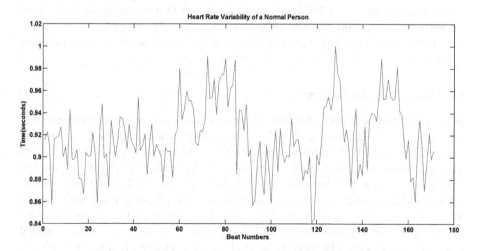

Fig. 8. HRV of a normal person (record no. 16265)

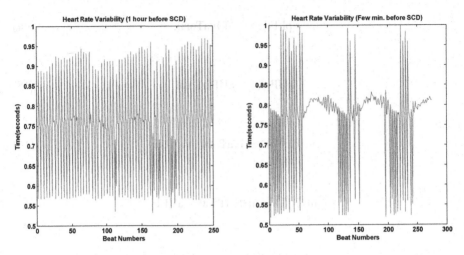

Fig. 9. HRV of an SCD patient (record no. 34)

5.3 Baro-Receptor Sensitivity

Varying blood pressure has a significant effect on sinus rhythm. The blood pressure is regulated by regulating the heart rate with the baro-reflex mechanism of the body. A negative feedback loop provided by this mechanism decreases the heart rate reflexively by an elevated blood pressure. The decreased heart rate causes the blood pressure to decrease which further decreases the baro-reflex activation and hence the heart rate increases restoring the level of blood pressure. The action of baro-reflex can begin to act in small fractions of time in seconds which may be smaller than a cardiac cycle. Thus the mechanism of baro-reflex adjusting levels of blood pressure via heart rate and vice-versa is considered an important factor in studies on SCD based on blood pressure and HRV as the baro-reflex mechanism of the body generates the low frequency component of the HRV which is a key indicator of the sympathetic activities of the nervous system [38]. Baro-receptors remain active at regular blood pressures as well so that any change in the level of blood pressure would be immediately informed to the brain.

5.4 Heart Rate Turbulence

Heart rate turbulence (HRT) provides information on activities of the autonomic nervous system of the human body [39]. This phenomenon was captured and explained by George Schmidt in 1990. Schmidt explained that HRT reflects the heart rate return to its equilibrium at a decreased speed after a premature ventricular contraction (VPC) [39]. After a VPC heart rate increases for 1–2 beats and then decreases slowly. To assess HRT, Holter recordings of 24-h duration are acquired. From these recordings, only those sinus rhythm R-R interval sequences are selected which surrounds the isolated VPCs [39]. A satisfactory number of pre and post sinus rhythm R-R interval sequences surrounding VPC must be selected. This includes two R-R intervals prior to

VPC, the in-between interval coupling R-R and VPC and 15 post VPC R-R intervals including the compensatory pause. These sequences are aligned and averaged together to construct the VPCs techogram. The VPCs techogram includes a sufficient and reliable number of VPCs > 5. The quantification of HRT is based on two clinical relevant features i.e. turbulence onset (increase in heart rate), and turbulence slope (slow decay of heart rate to its equilibrium). Turbulence Onset [39] is defined and measured as given in Eq. 19:

$$TO = \frac{(RR_1 + RR_2) - (RR_{-2} + RR_{-1})}{(RR_{-2} + RR_{-1})} \times 100[\%] \tag{19}$$

Where RR_{-2} and RR_{-1} are the two pre-VPC R-R intervals and RR_1 and RR_2 are two post R-R intervals. The turbulence slope (TS) is defined as the maximum positive regression slope computed over any 5 normal R-R intervals from the first 15 post VPC R-R intervals [39]. For clinical applications of HRT the mean values reported for normal healthy subjects of TO and TS are −2.7% to −2.3% and 11.0 to 19.0 ms per R-R interval [39] respectively. Research studies have demonstrated the practical use of HRT as a powerful and independent marker of sudden cardiac death [40–42].

6 Conclusion

Sudden cardiac death can't be identified with a single factor or a single test. Rather the prediction mechanism may include a variety of factors from three described markers viz. markers of structural heart disease, markers of electrical in-stability and markers of autonomic balance. Therefore, it would be unlikely that a single test would be able to screen out the patients at high risk of SCD and warrant the ICD implantation. For more accurate early identification of SCD, an integration of two or more than two methods as described above should be used as they are directly or indirectly related to each other. The signal processing methods discussed in this paper provide useful information on the kind of non-invasive markers of sudden cardiac death and the associated techniques to identify the SCD at an early and alarming stage. However, the current clinical use of many of these non-invasive techniques is still questioned due to their doubtful ability for risk identification and screening of patients for ICD therapy, especially if used alone. Therefore, fusion of a combination of some selected markers into a medical device would be possible only which would help the clinicians attending the SCD patient to take necessary actions at an early stage to save the precious life. Moreover, these tests are of much information to researchers searching for SCD risk stratification techniques to develop more accurate SCD identification algorithms based on these markers.

Acknowledgments. This present work is carried out with the help of library and research resource facilities provided by Kurukshetra University, Kurukshetra, Haryana, India.

Disclosure
The authors do not have any conflict of interest to declare.

Statement

Ethical approval: This article does not contain any studies with human participants or animals performed by any of the authors.

References

1. Khor, G.L.: Cardiovascular epidemiology in Asia-Pacific region. Asia Pac. J. Clin. Nutr. **10**, 76–80 (2001)
2. Stecker, E.C., et al.: Public health burden of sudden cardiac death in the United States. Circ. Arrhythm. Electrophysiol. **7**, 212e7 (2014)
3. Ladich, E., Virmani, R., Burke, A.: Sudden cardiac death not related to coronary atherosclerosis. Toxicol. Pathol. **34**, 52 (2006)
4. Chug, S.S.: Early identification of risk factors for sudden cardiac death. Nat. Rev. Cardiol. **7**, 318–326 (2010)
5. Hua, W., et al.: Preventive effectiveness of implantable cardioverter defibrillator in reducing sudden cardiac death in the Chinese population: a multicenter trial of ICD therapy versus non-ICD therapy. J. Cardiovasc. Electrophysiol. **23**, S5–S9 (2012)
6. Fam, J.M., Ching, C.K.: Review on non-invasive risk stratification of sudden cardiac death. Proc. Singapore Healthc. **20**(4), 263–278 (2011)
7. Sanders, G.D., Hlatky, M.A., Owens, D.K.: Cost- effectiveness of implantable cardioverter-defibrillators. N. Engl. J. Med. **353**, 1471–1480 (2005)
8. Goldberger, A.L., et al.: PhysioBank, PhysioToolkit and PhysioNet: components of a new research resource for complex physiologic signals. Circulation **101**, e215–e220 (2000)
9. Yunfeng, W., Rangayyan, R.M., Zhou, Y., Ng, S.-C.: Filtering electrocardiographic signals using an unbiased and normalized adaptive noise reduction system. Med. Eng. Phys. **31**(1), 17–26 (2009)
10. Ahmed, M.: https://myheart.net/heart-disease/heart-valves/
11. Goldberger, J.J., et al.: American Heart Association/American College of Cardiology Foundation/Heart Rhythm Society scientific statement on noninvasive risk stratification techniques for identifying patients at risk for sudden cardiac death: a scientific statement from the American Heart Association Council on Clinical Cardiology Committee on Electrocardiography and Arrhythmias and Council on Epidemiology and Prevention. Circulation **118**(14), 1497–1518 (2008)
12. Foley, T.A., et al.: Measuring left ventricular ejection fraction-techniques and potential pitfalls. Eur. Cardiol. **8**(2), 108–114 (2012)
13. John, R.M., et al.: Ventricular arrhythmias and sudden cardiac death. Lancet **380**(9852), 1520–1529 (2012)
14. Baldzizhar, A., Manuylova, E., Marchenko, R., Kryvalap, Y., Carey, M.G.: Ventricular tachycardias: characteristics and management. Crit. Care Nurs. Clin. North Am. **28**(3), 317–329 (2016)
15. Zareba, W., Moss, A.J., Le, C.S.: Dispersion of ventricular repolarization and arrhythmic cardiac death in coronary artery disease. Am. J. Cardiol. **74**, 550–553 (1994)
16. Ng, G.A.: Treating patients with ventricular ectopic beats. Heart **92**(11), 1707–1712 (2006)
17. Kurl, S., et al.: Duration of QRS complex in resting electrocardiogram is a predictor of sudden cardiac death in men. Circulation **125**(21), 12588–12594 (2012)

18. Verrier, R.L., et al.: Microvolt T-wave alternans: physiological basis, methods of measurement, and clinical utility—consensus guideline by International Society for Holter and Noninvasive Electrocardiology. J. Am. Coll. Cardiol. **58**(13), 1309–1324 (2011)
19. El-Menyar, A., Asaad, N.: T-wave alternans and sudden cardiac death. Crit. Pathways Cardiol. **7**, 21–28 (2008)
20. Pham, Q., Quan, K.J., Rosenbaum, D.S.: T-wave alternans: marker, mechanism, and methodology for predicting sudden cardiac death. J. Electrocardiol. **36**(1), 75–81 (2003)
21. Stein, P.K., Sanghavi, D., Sotoodehnia, N., et al.: Association of Holter-based measures including T-wave alternans with risk of sudden cardiac death in the community-dwelling elderly: the Cardiovascular Health Study. J. Electrocardiol. **43**, 251–259 (2010)
22. Hilfiker, G., Schoenenberger, A.W., Erne, P., Kobza, R.: Utility of electrophysiological studies to predict arrhythmic events. World J. Cardiol. **7**, 344–350 (2015)
23. Malik, M., Batchvarov, V.N.: Measurement, interpretation and clinical potential of QT dispersion. J. Am. Coll. Cardiol. **36**(6), 1749–1766 (2000)
24. Spargias, K.S., Lindsay, S.J., et al.: QT dispersion as a predictor of long-term mortality in patients with acute myocardial infarction and clinical evidence of heart failure. Eur. Heart J. **20**, 1158–1165 (1999)
25. Maron, B.J., Doerer, J.J., Haas, T.S., Tierney, D.M., Mueller, F.O.: Sudden deaths in young competitive athletes: analysis of 1866 deaths in the United States, 1980–2006. Circulation **119**(8), 1085–1092 (2009)
26. Acharya, U.R., Fujita, H., Sudarshan, V.K., Ghista, D.N., Lim, W.J.E., Koh, J.E.W.: Automated prediction of sudden cardiac death risk using Kolmogorov complexity and recurrence quantification analysis features extracted from HRV signals. In: SMC 2015 Hong Kong, pp. 1110–1115. IEEE (2015)
27. Ebrahimzadeh, E., Pooyan, M.: Early detection of sudden cardiac death by using classical linear techniques and time-frequency methods on electrocardiogram signals. J. Biomed. Sci. Eng. **4**, 699–706 (2011)
28. Ebrahimzadeh, E., Mohammad, P., Ahmad, B.: A novel approach to predict sudden cardiac death (SCD) using non-linear and time-frequency analysis from HRV signals. PLoS ONE **9**(2), e81896 (2014)
29. Fujita, H., et al.: Sudden cardiac death (SCD) prediction based on non-linear heart rate variability features and SCD index. Appl. Soft Comput. **43**(510), 519 (2016)
30. Murukesan, L., Murugappan, M., Omar, I., Khatun, S., Murugappan, S.: Time domain features based sudden cardiac arrest prediction using machine learning algorithms. J. Med. Imaging Health Inf. **5**, 1267–1271 (2015)
31. Murukesan, L., Murugappan, M., Iqbal, M., Saravanan, M.: Machine learning approach for sudden cardiac arrest prediction based on optimal heart rate variability features. J. Med. Imaging Health Inf. **4**, 1–12 (2014)
32. Devi, R., Tyagi, H.K., Kumar, D.: Early stage prediction of sudden cardiac death. In: Proceedings of the IEEE International Conference WiSPNET 2017 Held on 22–24 March 2017. SSN College of Engineering and Technology, Chennai (2017)
33. Devi, R., Tyagi, H.K., Kumar, D.: Early stage prediction of sudden cardiac death using linear and non-linear features of heart rate variability. Int. J. Electron. Electr. Comput. Syst. **6**(9), 742–754 (2017)
34. Devi, R., Tyagi, H.K., Kumar, D.: Heart rate variability analysis for early stage prediction of sudden cardiac death. World Acad. Sci. Eng. Technol. Int. J. Electr. Comput. Energ. Electron. Commun. Eng. **10**(3) (2016). PISSN: 2010-376X, EISSN: 2010-3778
35. Patil, S., et al.: Intelligent and effective heart attack prediction system using data mining and artificial neural network. Eur. J. Sci. Res. **31**(4), 642–656 (2009)

36. Jilani, T., et al.: Acute coronary syndrome prediction using data mining techniques - an application. Int. J. Inf. Math. Sci. 5(4), 295–299 (2009)
37. Lammert, M.E., et al.: Electrocardiographic predictors of out-of hospital sudden cardiac arrest in patients with coronary artery disease. Am. J. Cardiol. 109(9), 1278–1282 (2012)
38. Billman, G.E., Schwartz, P.J., Stone, H.L.: Baroreceptor reflex control of heart rate: a predictor of sudden cardiac death. Circulation 66(4), 874–880 (1982)
39. Bauer, A., et al.: Heart rate turbulence: standards of measurement, physiological interpretation, and clinical use: International Society for Holter and Noninvasive Electrophysiology consensus. J. Am. Coll. Cardiol. 52(17), 1353–1365 (2008)
40. Schmidt, G., Malik, M., Barthel, P., et al.: Heart-rate turbulence after ventricular premature beats as a predictor of mortality after acute myocardial infarction. Lancet 353, 1390–1396 (1999)
41. Baur, A., Zurn, C.S., Schmidt, G.: Heart rate turbulence to guide treatment for prevention of sudden death. J. Cardiovasc. Pharmacol. 55(6), 531–538 (2010)
42. Francis, J., Watanabe, M.A., Schmidt, G.: Heart rate turbulence: a new predictor for risk of sudden cardiac death. Ann. Noninvasive Electrocardiol. 10(1), 102–109 (2005)

Hybrid Technique to Reduce PAPR in OFDM

Hardeep Singh[✉], Harbinder Singh, and Dinesh Arora

Chandigarh Engineering College, Landran, Mohali, India
hardeepsingh711@ymail.com,
{harbinder.ece,dinesharora.ece}@cgc.edu.in

Abstract. Orthogonal Frequency Division Multiplexing (OFDM) is typically a system used in encoding digital data. It has huge benefits among which primary are high spectral efficiency upon Inter Symbol Interference (ISI) and robustness. It also has some drawbacks, the main hitch in OFDM system is High Peak to Average Power Ratio (PAPR). In order to minimize PAPR, many techniques are available among which some common and efficient are Partial Transmit Sequence (PTS), Selected Mapping (SLM), Coding, Interleaving, Companding, Peak windowing, Peak reduction, Envelope Scaling. Every method has both edge and snag. The simplest is clipping. There are also some complex techniques like PTS, SLM. In this paper the proposed method is a hybrid combination of Repeated Frequency Domain Filtering and Clipping (RFDFC) and Absolute Exponential Companding (AEC). This method not only bring PAPR to 3.5 dB as compared to 10.5 dB in original, but is also easy to implement.

Keywords: Domain filtering · Clipping · OFDM · PAPR · Bit error rate Companding

1 Introduction

In last few years there is a huge rise in field of wireless communication. This is due to use of internet browsing, social networking, online shopping, online banking, music, videos especially on YouTube and that too without buffering especially in video calling. Moreover in field of mobile communication this demand arises to unique level due to the increasing number of users day by day.

As advance technology especially in field of electronics makes it possible for almost everyone to own mobile handset. Hence there arises an immediate need of new standards which are capable of handling large number of users with high data rates.

In nutshell there is a need of a flexible system with huge coverage and potential which is simple by nature, has ability to carry huge data with less requirement of power at a reasonable price and that too with proper safety [1, 2].

The standard or the system which meets most of the above mentioned demands is Orthogonal Frequency Division Multiplexing system, commonly known as OFDM system as it not only meets present requirements but is efficient for long term use in future. But as one system does not carry whole lead with it, it also has some snags.

The OFDM system also has it in the form of Peak to Average Power Ratio, i.e. OFDM system has high PAPR [3]. This is so because in order to enlarge the efficiency

© Springer Nature Singapore Pte Ltd. 2019
P. K. Singh et al. (Eds.): FTNCT 2018, CCIS 958, pp. 73–84, 2019.
https://doi.org/10.1007/978-981-13-3804-5_6

of amplifier which is high powered in this case there is need to shift the focus on PAPR also, as both of these are interlinked. Due to this the condition become deteriorated in case of OFDM due to its multicarrier nature [4, 5]. There is a necessity to reduce high PAPR because generally OFDM is used as a 3GPP, LTE A. Which means one is using this system for our handsets, now as handsets have constrained battery life due to the size and bulkiness of batteries, these ranges to about 2000 mAh to 4000 mAh in most cases, and high PAPR consumes much battery. Hence it requires to be brought down to minimal level [6].

For reducing PAPR lot of techniques are available and work is under process to reduce PAPR to minimal level by developing more simple and efficient techniques which meets most of the requirements and which helps to implement the system easily and rapidly. The block diagram in Fig. 1 shows the basic techniques and their categories in which they are divided into.

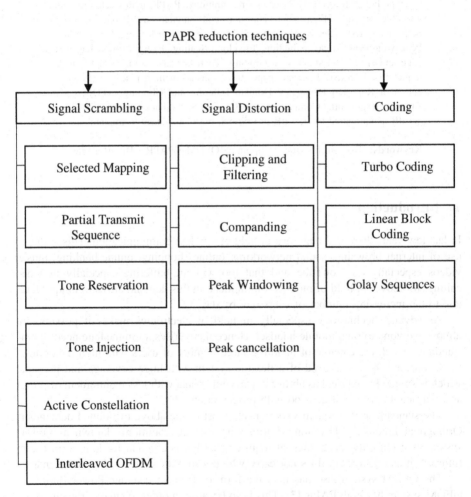

Fig. 1. Block Diagram of PAPR reduction techniques

1.1   Orthogonal Frequency Division Multiplexing (OFDM)

Orthogonal Frequency Division Multiplexing is a system which is an advancement of Frequency Division Multiplexing (FDM), i.e. the basic difference between OFDM and FDM is the orthogonality of subcarriers in OFDM which prevents ISI.

The basic concept of OFDM is dissection of streams with huge data rate into streams with shorter data rate. Further these strings are dispatched in parallel form. The basic idea behind this parallel dispatch is to enlarge the symbol duration, thus reducing dispersion [7].

In nutshell two signals are called orthogonal when they do not depend upon each other under any circumstances. This very property paves a way for many signals to be transferred in a single go without any inconvenience, it also makes process at receiver end during detection and correction which is prime requirement for getting correct message [8].

When coming to gaps in subcarriers they are implemented in such way, although they imbricate in frequency but are independent in time. This is done by making coexistence of peak of every signal with null of another, as an output is desirable and well gapped for preventing any merge [9].

The advantageous aspect of using OFDM system is that it do not rely upon extension in number of symbol rates which was basically done before, in order to gain extended data rates. This process defines the reason how ISI is kept at an optimum level [10].

1.2   Applications of OFDM

OFDM is considered to be a pilot technology of next-generation. Its applications includes HDSL, ADSL, VHDSL, HIPERLAN/2, HDTV, BWAS, DAB, DVB, WLAN, WiMAX, MBWA, 3GPP, IMT-A, LTE A etc. [11–16].

1.3   Peak to Average Power Ratio (PAPR)

The paramount concern in using OFDM system is high PAPR. It arises when large number of discrete data symbols of an OFDM signal are being modulated on large number of subcarriers which are orthogonal in nature, these signals are summed up while the phase remains alike. This process results in amplitude with peaks greater than average peak, thus giving rise to a term known as high PAPR.

If a signal is continuous time baseband signal, then Peak to Average Power Ratio is defined as the ratio of extreme power present at a given time of a signal to mean power.

On taking $x(t)$ as baseband signal PAPR is

$$\text{PAPR}[x(t)] = \frac{0 \leq t \leq T_s^{max}[|x(t)|]^2}{P_{avg}} \tag{1}$$

Here P_{avg} is average power and T_S is needful duration of symbol [17].

When discrete signal is taken then

$$PAPR\,[x\,(n)] = \frac{0 \le n \le NL^{max}[\|x(n)\|]^2}{E[\|x(n)\|]^2} \tag{2}$$

Here PAPR is determined from L time signal which is oversampled by nature, $E\,[\,]$ represents desired operator, and N denotes number of subcarriers. Further when value of PAPR is taken in decibels (dB), then it is expressed as [17].

$$PAPR[x\,(n)] = 10\log_{10}\frac{0 \le n \le NL^{max}\left[|x(n)|^2\right]}{E\left[|x(n)|^2\right]} \tag{3}$$

2 Repeated Frequency Domain Filtering and Clipping (RFDFC)

Repeated Frequency Domain Filtering and Clipping is a kind of modification of Repeated Clipping and Frequency Domain filtering technique. The basic difference is implementing filtering before clipping. It is done for a special purpose as in RFDFC the filtering improves the BER of OFDM system followed by clipping which improves PAPR.

If one go in detail then clipping is basically used to limits the amplitude of a given signal (OFDM in this case) to any specific or it can be said to a predefined level which is a threshold level as per the requirement i.e. in clipping the signal is usually clipped having high peak.

Clipping is performed on transmitting end, hence there arises need on the receiving end for at least having an approximation of the clipping performed at the transmitter in order to compensate the losses. As when the signal travels from one side to another it does not remains same due to added disturbances during its journey.

For this two parameters are taken into account at the receiving end, these are size and location of the clip. This process seems to be easy but is a tough task to perform, as a result In band as well as Out band distortions arises [18–20].

Here comes the filtering which minimizes out of band distortions thus increasing the system's performance in case of BER as well as spectral efficiency which gets degraded by clipping. This is the basic reason for using filtering in the beginning followed by the clipping.

Hence interchanging clipping and filtering makes a reliable and efficient technique which can be used to reduce high PAPR.

3 Absolute Exponential Companding (AEC)

Companding is composed of two different words Compress and Expand. The operation of the technique lies in these words i.e. compressing on transmitting end followed by expanding on receiving end. Companding is a special case of clipping, here the increasing function is strictly monotonic in nature with the help of which signal is recovered easily. It is due to the fact that modification of signal in companding is done by taking the help of firm monotone function which is increasing by nature.

Hence decompanding makes the task easy. In addition, this technique is lesser complex and gives better BER performance with no bandwidth expansion.

Then comes exponential companding in which calibration of both small and large signals is carried out in order to maintain the mean power on equal level.

AEC is a special case of Exponential companding. As in Exponential Companding signals of larger as well as shorter lengths are adjusted in a way which maintains the average power at equal level. Further transforming these signals into uniformly distributed form, the value of PAPR was considerably reduced.

Thus one get companding function.

$$H(x) = sgn(x)^d \sqrt{a\left[1 - exp\left(-\frac{|x|^2}{\sigma^2}\right)\right]} \qquad (4)$$

Here $H(x)$ represents Companding function, $Sgn(x)$ represents Sign function, σ^2 is input signal variance, exp denotes exponential and d is Companding degree.

Here α is a constant which is positive in nature and is known as degree of companding (Exponential). It basically helps to know the mean power of output signal and maintains mean power level of both input as well as output signal. It is kept as [21].

$$\alpha = \left[\frac{E\left\{|x|^2\right\}}{E\left\{\sqrt[d]{\left[1 - exp\left(-\frac{|x|^2}{\sigma^2}\right)\right]^2}\right\}}\right]^{\frac{d}{2}} \qquad (5)$$

Now as in Eq. 5 the square root portion will be either complex number or imaginary in nature, this is due to the fact that the received signal will be distorted in nature.

Hence in order to eliminate this possibility and for gaining a proper value, absolute value of the above mentioned part is taken. This modification will cancel possibility of potential phase distortions [22, 23]. This modification further will form a technique known as Absolute Exponential Companding technique known by a common name, AEC technique.

This technique is better than both Companding and Exponential Companding technique as not only it helps to reduce PAPR value to minimum possible level but is also simple as absolute value is taken in this case.

4 Proposed Technique

The proposed technique is a hybrid combination of Repeated Frequency Domain Filtering and Clipping (RFDFC) technique with Absolute Exponential Companding (AEC) technique. Here two different techniques are used together as a single technique i.e. two different techniques works in a combination for attaining a single or common goal.

The benefit of using hybrid technique is to use the advantageous aspects of both the techniques to get desired result. Although it slightly increases the complexity of the system as implementing two techniques instead of a single is always a difficult task to perform but this complexity is acceptable in a way of obtaining desirable result. Overall the benefits overrule its demerits.

Hybrid technique is explained using block diagram in Fig. 2, in which input is given to Signal mapper as shown by a downward arrow.

The signal mapper portrays the message bits. This results into a sequence of QAM, PSK, QPSK, etc. These are different modulation techniques used during carrying data from source to destination, followed by serial to parallel converter which converts the output of signal mapper from serial to parallel form, in other words De-multiplexing of data takes place here, followed by joining of pilot symbol block.

IDFT, IIFT is done for implementation of orthogonal signal in an effective manner at the transmitting part. Both IDFT and IIFT are inverse in nature.

Then comes implementation of first technique known as RFDFC, in which frequency domain filtering of the signal is performed followed by clipping which is set to be performed at a threshold level, i.e. here the high peak is clipped in accordance with threshold value, which is further followed by parallel to serial conversion i.e. the data is converted into serial form for next operation to be successful.

Finally, AEC comes into play whose main aim is to make signal efficient for transporting to destination and also to work on demerits of first technique i.e. it adjusts symbols to keep the average power at fixed or same level. After which Cyclic prefix is attached which meliorate the inter symbol interference (ISI) across the space separating OFDM symbols.

Cyclic prefix is actually a method for implementing guard band or simply it can be said as a method for inserting guard band at the starting and ending of a symbol. The Cyclic prefix inserted at the beginning is an exact copy of the cyclic prefix which is inserted at the ending of a symbol or vice versa.

At last digital to analog converter is added for conversion of digital signal into analog form for transmission, the channel through which signal has to be transmitted adds noise to the signal along with other disturbances and also multipath fading takes place.

Then coming on the receiver side, the incoming signal is converted back to digital form in order to recover or decode original information or data efficiently, after which the cyclic prefix which was added at the receiver is removed.

Further AEC decompanding is done which is further followed by conversion of serial data to parallel form. Then DFT or FFT operation is performed. This operation is performed to cancel the effect of IDFT or IFFT which were performed during transmission as it works opposite to IDFT/IFFT.

After the above operation pilot symbol which was added at receiver is finally removed to recover only required or original data. This operation is further led by process of one tap equalizer, which is further followed by conversion into serial form again and at last demapping of the signal is done which is actually a demodulation used to recover the original signal. Finally output is obtained from signal demapper which is shown by an upward arrow in Fig. 2.

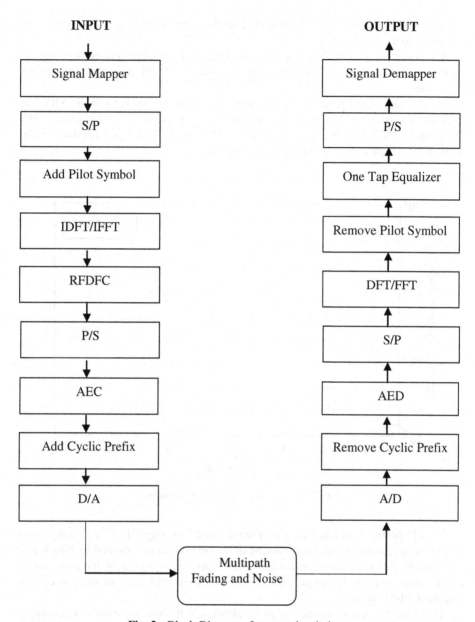

Fig. 2. Block Diagram of proposed technique

5 Simulation and Results

Taking a target of reducing PAPR to maximum possible level, keeping certain parameters in mind like Bit Error rate and maintaining simplicity in implementation of the technique, first OFDM signal or original signal is taken and with the help of

Complementary Cumulative Distribution Function also known as CCDF curve the value of PAPR in dB is shown.

The benefit of using CCDF over CDF is that one clearly able to notice the original value of PAPR in curve diagram and change in values of PAPR after applying various techniques.

For this same specifications or parameters for each technique is taken like QPSK is used with data point of 128 in number and spacing in frequency is been kept at 15000. Then using MATLAB simulation the value of Original OFDM signal obtained out to be 10.5 dB which is clearly shown in the Fig. 3.

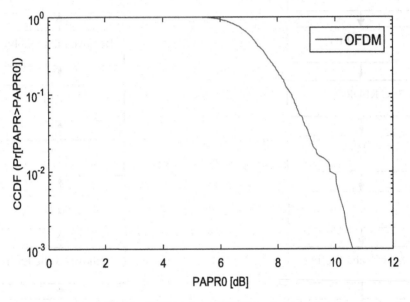

Fig. 3. CCDF curve of OFDM technique

Next Repeated Frequency Domain Filtering and Clipping (RFDFC) technique was taken in which frequency domain filtering of the signal is done followed by clipping of the peaks by taking threshold value and CCDF curve is used to know the reduction in PAPR value. For this technique also specifications are kept same as were in case of original OFDM signal.

This time the value comes out to be about 4.3 dB which means this technique reduces value of PAPR to about 6.2 dB as shown in Fig. 4.

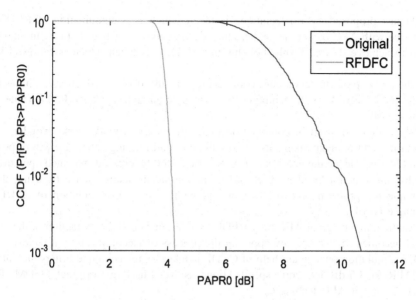

Fig. 4. CCDF curve of RFDFC technique

Then taking Absolute Exponential Companding (AEC) technique. The value of PAPR is taken using CCDF curve. This time also the specifications were same as for OFDM. This technique reduces the value of PAPR to 4.2 dB as shown in Fig. 5.

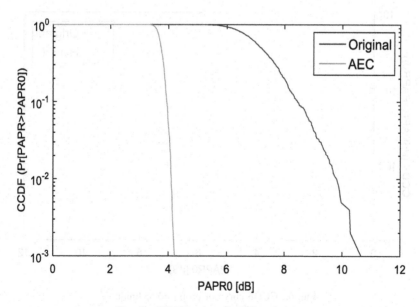

Fig. 5. CCDF curve of AEC technique

At last proposed hybrid technique is taken which is a combination of RFDFC technique with AEC technique i.e. here the advantageous aspects of both techniques is taken to achieve desired result. For this first RFDFC is taken which is followed by AEC.

The purpose of this technique was to achieve result to our satisfaction i.e. it has to be less than 4 dB. As both techniques were capable enough to reduce PAPR value to about 4.2 dB.

When they are used in combination their simultaneous work works wonder. As growth in spectral again takes place after clipping, and filtering causes growth of peak again [24–26]. Hence the necessity of AEC arises after the previous repeated operation. In AEC the function used is strict and is monotonic in nature, hence by using this technique the problem of expansion of bandwidth after implementation of RFDFC technique is solved.

Another advantage of AEC after RFDFC technique is that the extraction of the real signal becomes easy simply by applying the process of Decompanding at reciever.

For simulation once again help of CCDF is taken. This technique brings the value of PAPR to 3.5 dB for same specifications as were used for original OFDM, for RFDFC, and for AEC technique.

The result is shown in Fig. 6 in which the value of PAPR is reduced from 10.5 dB in original to 3.5 dB with hybrid technique.

The results also confirms that hybrid whether a combination of two or greater is more edged than single technique.

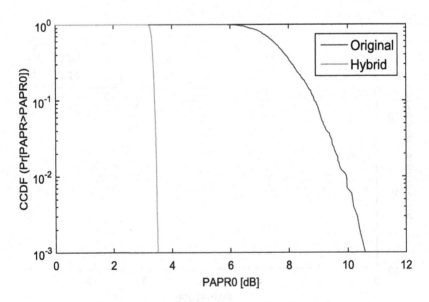

Fig. 6. CCDF curve of proposed technique

Table 1 is a comparison table of all techniques used along with their values obtained in decibels using CCDF curves, it also includes the reduction in values of PAPR after implementing respective techniques.

Here OFDM is original signal, hence reduction in PAPR value is not applicable in this case.

Table 1. Comparison of used techniques

Method	PAPR obtained in dB using CCDF	Reduced PAPR in dB using CCDF
OFDM	10.5	Not applicable
RFDFC	4.3	6.2
AEC	4.2	6.3
Hybrid	3.5	7

6 Conclusion

Our main aim in this work was to reduce PAPR to maximum possible level keeping the intricacy to minimum possible level. For this we begin with using simple techniques.

We perform operation on many techniques and compare their outputs using CCDF graphs and ultimately we end up on Repeated Frequency Domain Filtering and Clipping (RFDFC) technique which gives us value of reduced PAPR to about 4.3 dB as compared to 10.5 dB in original OFDM, and Absolute Exponential Companding (AEC) technique which gives us reduced value of PAPR about 4.2 dB.

We choose these two techniques because both techniques were simple and their implementation was easier as compared to another techniques. As results of both techniques were good but not to our satisfaction, now as each technique has its snag with it, but we found that they were perfect enough to work in a hybrid combination as one technique was fulfilling the snags created by another technique.

So ultimately we make hybrid combination of both these techniques and finally we implement the hybrid technique using MATLAB R2015a, and are able to bring the value of PAPR to 3.5 dB from 10.5 dB as in original OFDM system.

References

1. Fazel, K., Kaiser, S.: Multi-Carrier and Spread Spectrum Systems. From OFDM and MC CDMA to LTE and WiMAX, 2nd edn. Wiley, Chichester (2008)
2. Wunder, G., Fischer, R.F.H., Boche, H., Litsyn, S.: The PAPR problem in OFDM transmission. New directions for a long lasting problem. IEEE Signal Process. Mag. **20**(6), 130–144 (2013)
3. Jiang, T., Wu, Y.: An overview. Peak-to-average power ratio reduction techniques for OFDM signals. IEEE Trans. Wireless Commun. **54**(2), 257–268 (2008)
4. Correia, L.M., et al.: Challenges and enabling technologies for energy aware mobile radio networks. IEEE Commun. Mag. **48**, 66–72 (2010)

5. Litsyn, S.: Peak Power Control in Multicarrier Communications. Cambridge University Press, New York (2007)
6. Han, S.H., Lee, J.H.: An overview of peak-to-average power ratio reduction techniques for multicarrier transmission. IEEE Wirel. Commun. **12**(2), 56–65 (2005)
7. Joshi, H.D.: Performance augmentation of OFDM system. Ph.D. dissertation, Jaypee Univ. of engineering and Technology, India (2012)
8. Lathi, B.P.: Modern Digital and Analog Communication Systems. Oxford University Press, New York (1998)
9. Tariq, F.: Impact of PAPR on Link Adaptation Strategies of OFDM Based Systems. M.A. thesis, Chalmers University of Technology (2007)
10. Zyren, J.: Overview of the 3GPP Long Term Evolution Physical Layer. White Paper, freescale semiconductor (2007)
11. Goel, A.: Improved PAPR Reduction in OFDM Systems. Ph.D. dissertation, JAYPEE Institute of Information Technology, India (2013)
12. Chow, P.S., Dhahir, N.A.L., Cioffi, J., Bingham, M.: A multicarrier E1-HDSL transceiver system with coded modulation. J. Eur. Trans. Telecom. Rel. Tech. (ETT) (Spec. Issue: Appl. Coded Modulation Tech.) **4**(3), 257–266 (1993)
13. Chow, P.S., Tu, J.C., Cioffi, J.M.: Performance Evaluation of a Multichannel Transceiver System for ADSL and VHDSL services. IEEE J. Sel. Areas Commun. **9**(6), 909–919 (1991)
14. ETSI: Radio broadcasting systems. Digital Audio Broadcasting (DAB) to mobile, portable and fixed receivers. European Telecommunication Standard, Standard EN-300-401 (1997)
15. ETSI: Digital Video Broadcast (DVB). Framing Structure, Channel Coding and Modulation for Digital Terrestrial Television. ETSI EN 300 744 v1.1.2 (1997)
16. ETSI: BroadBand Radio Access Networks (BRAN). Hiperlan Type 2. Technical Specification Part 1-Physical Layer. DTS/BRAN 030003-1 (1999)
17. Choudhary, C., Gupta, V.: A study of performance enhancement schemes for multicarrier transmission. Int. J. Comput. Appl. **68**(5), 50–54 (2013)
18. ITU-R: Report M.2134. Requirements related to technical performance for IMT-Advance Radio Interface (2008)
19. Prasad, R.: OFDM for Wireless Communications Systems. Artech House Publishers, August (2004)
20. Schmidt, B., et al.: Efficient algorithms for PAPR reduction in OFDM transmitters implemented using fixed-point DSPs. In: IEEE 63rd Vehicular Technology Conference, vol. 4, pp. 2023–2027 (2006)
21. AL-Hashmi, Z.S.H.: An Overview Peak to Average Power Ratio (PAPR) in OFDM system using some new PAPR techniques (2015)
22. Jiang, Y.Y., Song, Y.: Companding technique for PAPR reduction in OFDM systems based on an exponential function. In: Global Telecommunications Conference. GLOBECOM 2005, vol. 05, pp. 2798–2801. IEEE (2005)
23. Jiang, T., Yang, Y., Song, Y.: Exponential companding technique for PAPR reduction in OFDM systems. IEEE Trans. Broadcast. **51**(2), 244–247 (2005)
24. Thompson, S.C., Proakis, J.G., Zeidler, J.R.: The effectiveness of signal clipping for PAPR and total degradation reduction in OFDM systems. In: IEEE Global Telecommunication Conference on St. Louis, MO, USA, pp. 2807–2811 (2005)
25. Wang, L., Tellambura, C.: A simplified clipping and filtering technique for PAPR reduction in OFDM systems. IEEE Signal Process. Lett. **12**, 453–456 (2005)
26. Chen, H., Haimovich, A.M.: Iterative estimation and cancellation of clipping noise for OFDM signals. IEEE Commun. Lett. **7**, 305–307 (2003)

Detection of Signals by the Frequency-Time Contrast Method

Konstantin Rumyantsev[✉], Aatoliy Zikiy[✉], and Pavel Zlaman[✉]

Southern Federal University, Taganrog, Rostov Region, Russian Federation
{rke2004, zikiy50, fmymail}@mail.ru

Abstract. A detection algorithm and a detector structure based on the time-frequency contrast method are proposed. The analysis of the detection characteristics for the case of a linear detector and distribution of the signal- interference mixture according to the Rayleigh-Rice law is carried out. It is shown that the detector ensures a constant false alarm rate when the interference dispersion is changed. A block diagram of the detector that implements the proposed algorithm is presented. The carried out research shows the expediency of using the method when detecting single radio pulses with an inaccurately known carrier frequency. It is shown that the use of an increased reference sample of interference with $N = 1$ to $N = 5$ makes it possible to reduce (at $L = 1$) the probability of false alarm with $P_F = 0.166$ to $P_F = 0.015$.

Keywords: Detector · Contrast · Algorithm · Reference sample of interference
Frequency and time separation of the process
Probabilistic detection characteristics

1 Introduction

When constructing optimal detectors, it is necessary to know the statistical characteristics of signals and interference. In practice, these characteristics are only partially known. In this case, non-optimal detectors that are invariant to unknown interference characteristics are often used. It is often assumed that the interference distribution law is known to within one or more parameters. When the unknown parameter is the dispersion of the interference, the detectors constructed using the contrast method found wide application.

The most frequently studied detectors using methods of time [1] or frequency contrast [2]. Moreover, the detectors have better detection characteristics with an increase in the volume of the reference interference sample. Therefore, it seems advisable to analyze the contrast detector, in which both the time separation of processes and the frequency one are used simultaneously to form the reference interference sample.

The article presents the results of the investigation of the proposed algorithm for detecting pulsed signals with a known minimum duration and an unknown repetition period.

© Springer Nature Singapore Pte Ltd. 2019
P. K. Singh et al. (Eds.): FTNCT 2018, CCIS 958, pp. 85–94, 2019.
https://doi.org/10.1007/978-981-13-3804-5_7

2 Overview of Known Works

The contrast detection algorithm was first proposed in [1] in 1965. A number of other papers [10–15], etc., are also devoted to the contrast method. This method can be attributed to the class which is invariant with respect to the unknown interference. At present, works devoted to spatial contrast [10, 18], frequency contrast [2], time contrast [1] are known. The detector, based on the contrast method, maintains a constant false alarm probability with a change in the dispersion of the interference and a constant distribution of the interference. The algorithm of operation of the contrast detector in the time domain has the form:

$$\left\{ \begin{array}{l} \prod_{i=1}^{N} U[x_0 - Lx_i] = 1 \ under \ the \ hypothesis \ H_1 \\ \prod_{i=1}^{N} U[x_0 - Lx_i] = 0 \ under \ the \ hypothesis \ H_0 \end{array} \right\} \tag{1}$$

here N – size of noise sampling;
x_i – independently identically distributed elements of the interference sample
U – Step function;
L – the ratio of the gain of the reference channel to the gain of the signal channel;
x_0 – signal sampling element;
I – element number of the interference sample.

In (1), the function U(x) represents a step (asymmetric unit) function

$$U(x) = \begin{cases} 1, x \geq 0; \\ 0, x < 0. \end{cases}$$

The functional scheme of the detector that implements the algorithm (1) is shown in Fig. 1.

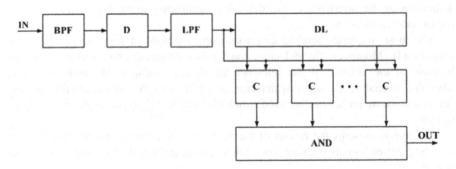

Fig. 1. Block diagram of the detector in time domain

The analysis of the algorithm (1) was carried out in numerous papers, for example, in [10, 15].

The method of contrast in the frequency domain assumes simultaneous reception of three statistically independent values of the envelopes of the process under study at the output of three frequency-adjacent channels ξ_1, ξ_2, ξ_3.

The decisive rule for checking statistical hypotheses about the absence or presence of a signal in the central filter of the detector is [2]

$$H_0 : \left\{ \begin{array}{c} (\xi_2 \gtrless L\xi_1) \wedge (\xi_2 < L\xi_3) \\ (\xi_2 < L\xi_1) \wedge (\xi_2 > L\xi_3) \end{array} \right\}$$

(2)

$$H_1 : \{(\xi_2 \geq L\xi_1) \wedge (\xi_2 \geq L\xi_3)\}.$$

Here Λ - the sign of logical multiplication;

L - the ratio of the gain of the side channel to the gain of the central channel by voltage.

The functional scheme of the detector that implements the algorithm (2) is shown in Fig. 2. The spacing of the central frequencies of the bandpass filters should ensure that the envelope values on their outputs are independent. The bandwidths of the bandpass filters are the same. The bandwidth of video filters is also equal.

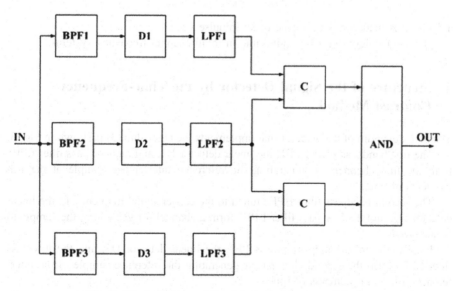

Fig. 2. Block diagram of the detector in frequency domain

3 The Detecting Signals Algorithm

Samples are used at different time points in three channels, differing in frequency setting, for generate a reference sample of the interference.

In the proposed detection algorithm, the decision to receive an impulse signal is taken when there is the condition

$$\prod_{i=1}^{N} U(x_s - L_{n1}x_{1ni}) \cdot U(x_s - L_{n2}x_{n2i}) = 1. \tag{3}$$

Here $x_{n1i}, i = \overline{1,N}$ - a sample of the output voltage at the i-th time in the 1st reference interference channel with a bandpass filter (BPF1);

x_s - a sample of the output voltage in the signal channel with a bandpass filter (BPF2), tuned to the frequency of the signal f_s;

$x_{n2i}, i = \overline{1,N}$ - a sample of the output voltage at the i-th time moment in the 2nd reference interference channel with a bandpass filter (BPF3);

L_{n1}, L_{n2} - the ratio of the gain of the voltage of the reference interference channels to the signal channel gain.

We note that if condition

$$\prod_{i=1}^{N} U(x_s - L_{n1}x_{1ni}) \cdot U(x_s - L_{n2}x_{n2i}) = 0$$

a decision is made on the absence of an impulse signal.

The use of algorithm (3) is advisable in multi-channel frequency systems.

4 Structure of the Signal Detector by the Time-Frequency Contrast Method

The block diagram of the detector that implements the algorithm (3) is shown in Fig. 3.

The first bandpass filter BPF1, the linear detector D1, and the low-pass filter LPF1 form the first channel for generating the reference interference sample at the i-th moments of time.

The second bandpass filter BPF2 tuned to the carrier signal frequency f_s, the linear detector D2, and the low-pass filter LPF2 form a channel for generating the sample to be analyzed.

Finally, the third bandpass filterB PF3, the linear detector D3, and the low-pass filter LPF3 form the second channel for generating the reference sample of the interference at the i-th moments of time.

The diagram in Fig. 1 shows the delay lines for N outputs of DL1 and DL2, 2N comparators and an AND element with 2N inputs.

The difference of the central frequencies of the bandpass filters BPF1-BPF3 ensures the independence of the processes at their outputs. It is assumed that the bandwidth of the filters BPF1-BPF3 in all channels are equal to each other. A similar condition is

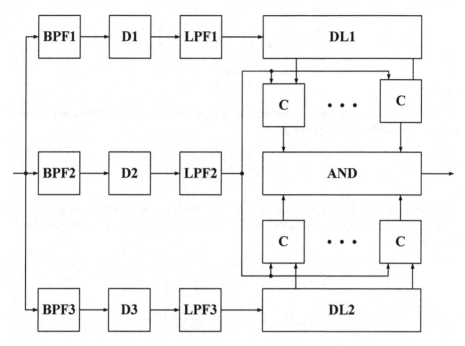

Fig. 3. Block diagram of the detector that implements the algorithm (3)

superimposed on the passband of low-pass filters. The delay interval between the branching points DL is selected more than the noise correlation interval, to obtain independent samples of the voltage x_s и $x_{n1i}, x_{n2i}, i = \overline{1, N}$.

5 Detector Efficiency

Suppose that at the input of the frequency-time contrast method detector, there is the process $\eta(t)$, representing a mixture of $\eta(t)$ of a harmonic radio signal $S(t) = A \cdot cos(\omega_0 t)$ with constant amplitude A with center frequency ω_0 and normal stationary interference $n(t)$ with zero mathematical expectation and unknown dispersion σ^2 [3]:

$$\eta(t) = C \cdot S(t) + n(t). \tag{4}$$

The coefficient C takes values 0 in the absence and 1 if there is a signal in the analyzed input process.

It is shown in [3, 4] that in the analyzed case the distributions of the samples at the output of the reference interference channels obey the Rayleigh law

$$W_1(x) = \frac{x}{L_{n1}^2 \sigma^2} exp\left(-\frac{x^2}{2L_{n1}^2 \sigma^2}\right);$$

$$W_3(x) = \frac{x}{L_{n2}^2 \sigma^2} exp\left(-\frac{x^2}{2L_{n2}^2 \sigma^2}\right).$$

(5)

At the output of the signal channel, the sample distribution is subject to the generalized Rayleigh law (Rayleigh-Rice)

$$W_2(x) = \frac{x}{\sigma^2} exp\left[-\frac{(x^2 + A^2)}{2\sigma^2}\right] I_0\left[\frac{xA}{\sigma^2}\right],$$

(6)

Here $I_0(z)$ - the Bessel function of order zero from the imaginary argument.

In this case, the integral distribution laws at the outputs of the reference channels take the form

$$P_1(x) = 1 - exp\left(-\frac{x^2}{2L_{n1}^2 \sigma^2}\right);$$

$$P_3(x) = 1 - exp\left(-\frac{x^2}{2L_{n2}^2 \sigma^2}\right).$$

(7)

In accordance with the detection algorithm (3), the probability of correct detection can be calculated by the formula

$$P_D = \int_0^\infty W_2(x) P_1^N(x) P_3^N(x) dx$$

(8)

Substituting (6) and (7) into (8), we obtain

$$P_D = \int_0^\infty \frac{x}{\sigma^2} \cdot exp\left[-\frac{(x^2 + A^2)}{2\sigma^2}\right] \cdot I_0\left[\frac{xA}{\sigma^2}\right] \times$$
$$\times \left[1 - exp\left(-\frac{x^2}{2L_{n1}^2 \sigma^2}\right)\right]^N$$
$$\left[1 - exp\left(-\frac{x^2}{2L_{n2}^2 \sigma^2}\right)\right]^N dx.$$

(9)

Using the expansion of the binomial in a series [5], we find

$$P_D = \int_0^\infty \frac{x}{\sigma^2} \cdot exp\left[-\frac{(x^2 + A^2)}{2\sigma^2}\right] \cdot I_0\left[\frac{xA}{\sigma^2}\right] \times$$
$$\times \sum_{r=0}^N \sum_{k=0}^N C_N^k \cdot C_N^r \cdot (-1)^{k+r} \cdot exp\left[-\left(\frac{kx^2}{2L_{n1}^2 \sigma^2} + \frac{rx^2}{2L_{n2}^2 \sigma^2}\right)\right] dx,$$

(10)

Here C_N^i - number of combinations from N to i.

Changing the order of summation and integration, we transform (10) to the form

$$
P_D = \frac{1}{\sigma^2} \sum_{r=0}^{N} \sum_{k=0}^{N} C_N^k \cdot C_N^r \cdot (-1)^{k+r} \times
$$
$$
\times \int_0^\infty x \cdot exp \left[-\frac{kx^2}{2L_{n1}^2 \sigma^2} - \frac{rx^2}{2L_{n2}^2 \sigma^2} - \frac{x^2}{2\sigma^2} - \frac{A^2}{2\sigma^2} \right] \cdot I_0 \left[\frac{xA}{\sigma^2} \right] \cdot dx.
$$

(11)

Expanding the Bessel function in a series [5] and using the tabular integral [6]

$$
\int_0^\infty x^{2a+1} e^{-b^2 x^2} dx = \frac{a}{2b^{2a+2}},
$$

after simple transformations we obtain

$$
P_D = exp(-q) \sum_{r=0}^{N} \sum_{k=0}^{N} \frac{C_N^k \cdot C_N^r \cdot (-1)^{k+r}}{\frac{k}{L_{n1}^2} + \frac{r}{L_{n2}^2} + 1} exp \left(-\frac{q}{\frac{k}{L_{n1}^2} + \frac{r}{L_{n2}^2} + 1} \right),
$$

(12)

Here $q = \frac{A^2}{2\sigma^2}$ - signal-to-interference ratio.

The probability of a false alarm can be determined from (12), with $q = 0$:

$$
P_F = \sum_{r=0}^{N} \sum_{k=0}^{N} \frac{C_N^k \cdot C_N^r \cdot (-1)^{k+r}}{\frac{k}{L_{n1}^2} + \frac{r}{L_{n2}^2} + 1}.
$$

(13)

It is seen that the probability of a false alarm depends only on the size of the reference sample and the relative gain factors of the reference channels, but does not depend on the a priori unknown dispersion of the interference.

Table 1 shows the results of the calculation of the detection characteristics for the signal-to-noise ratio q from 0 to 6.4 and the sample size of the interference from 1 to 5. Table 2 shows the results of calculating the probability of false alarms from the L coefficient for the sample size of the interference from 1 to 5.

Table 1. Detection characteristics

N	q					
	6.4	3.2	1.6	0.8	0.4	0
1	0.86	0.64	0.44	0.31	0.24	0.17
2	0.78	0.49	0.29	0.17	0.12	0.067
3	0.71	0.41	0.21	0.12	0.073	0.036
4	0.67	0.35	0.16	0.085	0.051	0.022
5	0.63	0.30	0.13	0.066	0.038	0.015

Table 2. Dependence of the probability of false alarm on the coefficient L1 = L3 = L

N	L						
	0.85	0.90	0.95	1.00	1.05	1.10	1.15
1	$2.3744 \cdot 10^{-1}$	$2.1087 \cdot 10^{-1}$	$1.8738 \cdot 10^{-1}$	$1.6666 \cdot 10^{-1}$	$1.484 \cdot 10^{-1}$	$1.323 \cdot 10^{-1}$	$1.181 \cdot 10^{-1}$
	0.624	0.676	0.727	0.778	0.829	0.878	0.928
2	$1.17 \cdot 10^{-1}$	$9.746 \cdot 10^{-2}$	$8.062 \cdot 10^{-2}$	$6.607 \cdot 10^{-2}$	$5.514 \cdot 10^{-2}$	$4.563 \cdot 10^{-2}$	$3.779 \cdot 10^{-2}$
	0.929	1.011	1.094	1.176	1.259	1.341	1.423
3	$7.361 \cdot 10^{-2}$	$5.796 \cdot 10^{-2}$	$4.553 \cdot 10^{-2}$	$3.572 \cdot 10^{-2}$	$2.798 \cdot 10^{-2}$	$2.191 \cdot 10^{-2}$	$1.715 \cdot 10^{-2}$
	1.133	1.237	1.342	1.447	1.553	1.959	1.766
4	$5.168 \cdot 10^{-2}$	$3.915 \cdot 10^{-2}$	$2.953 \cdot 10^{-2}$	$2.223 \cdot 10^{-2}$	$1.668 \cdot 10^{-2}$	$1.25 \cdot 10^{-2}$	$9.355 \cdot 10^{-3}$
	1.287	1.407	1.530	1.653	1.778	1.903	2.029
5	$3.891 \cdot 10^{-2}$	$2.856 \cdot 10^{-2}$	$2.081 \cdot 10^{-2}$	$1.513 \cdot 10^{-2}$	$1.095 \cdot 10^{-2}$	$7.927 \cdot 10^{-3}$	$5.737 \cdot 10^{-3}$
	1.410	1.544	1.682	1.820	1.961	2.101	2.241

Figure 4 shows the detection curves for a different number of samples N (sample size) and $L_{n1} = L_{n2} = 1$. Note that the curve $N = 1$ corresponds to the probability of false alarms $P_F = 1.67 \cdot 10^{-2}, N = 2 - P_F = 6.67 \cdot 10^{-2}, N = 3 - P_F = 3.57 \cdot 10^{-2}$, $N = 4 - P_F = 2.22 \cdot 10^{-2}, N = 5 - P_F = 1.51 \cdot 10^{-2}$.

The analysis of the curves in Fig. 4 shows that the proposed detector for $N > 1$ is useful when it is necessary to obtain lower values of the false alarm probability in comparison with the probability of false alarm obtained using the frequency contrast detector ($N = 1$).

It is seen that to ensure the probability of a correct detection of at least 0.5 it is required to provide a signal-to-noise ratio of at least 2.4 with a sample size $N \geq 1$. The threshold signal q is in the range of 2 to 5 for $P_D = 0.5, L = L_3 = 1$.

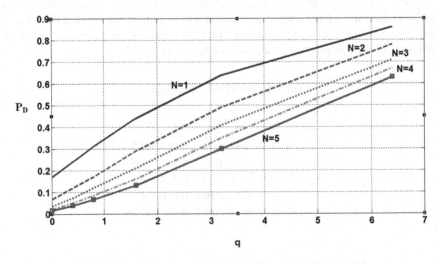

Fig. 4. Detection characteristics for different sample sizes N

6 Evaluation of the Effect of Channel Identity on the Parameters of the Detector

By changing the values of the parameters L_{n1} and L_{n2}, it is possible to estimate the effect of channel identity on stabilizing the probability of false alarm.

Figure 5 shows a plot of the probability of false alarm P_F from the ratio of the gains of the voltage of the reference interference channels to the signaling channel gain under the condition $L = L_{n1} = L_{n2}$.

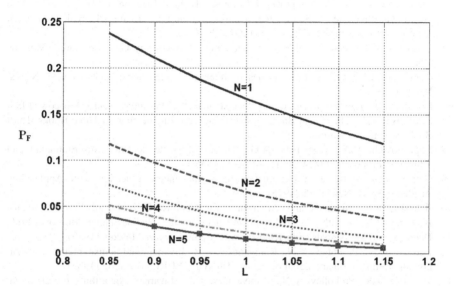

Fig. 5. Dependence of the probability of false alarm on the coefficient L

7 Conclusions

A detection algorithm and a detector structure are proposed in which both time and frequency separation of processes is used to generate a reference sample of interference. Here, a sample of interference from two side frequency channels is used. The algorithm is resistant to external influences (change in interference power), keeping the required level of false triggering. A block diagram of the detector that implements the proposed algorithm is presented.

Analytic expressions are derived for calculating probabilistic characteristics of the detector based on the frequency-time contrast method. The relationships allow us to formulate the requirements for the identity of the reference and analyzed channels. The carried out research shows the expediency of using the method when detecting single radio pulses with an inaccurately known carrier frequency. It is shown that the use of an increased reference sample of interference with $N = 1$ to $N = 5$ makes it possible to reduce (at $L = 1$) the probability of false alarm with $P_F = 0.166$ to $P_F = 0.015$.

When writing the article, works in the field of signal detection [7–11], as well as the results of author's studies [12–17] were used.

References

1. Nesteruk, V.F., Porfiryeva, I.N.: Contrast reception of a pulsed signal with a random phase against a background of correlated noise. Radiotekhnika **5**(12), 53–59 (1965)
2. Beletsky, Y.S., Skrebnev, G.K.: Algorithm for detecting a fluctuating signal in noise with an energy spectrum of unknown power. J. Commun. Technol. Electron. **1**(12), 172–175 (1976)
3. Picardi, G., Ragonese, P.: Su un circuito anti-interferenca per sistemi radar realizato linee di ritardo. Alta Frequenca **12**(12), 1147–1160 (1968)
4. Questions of the statistical theory of radar. Edn. Tartakovskiy G.P. Sov. radio, Moscow (1963)
5. Gradshtein, I.S., Ryzhik, I.M.: Tables of Integrals, Sums, Series and Products. Nauka, Moscow (1971)
6. Dwight, G.B.: Tables of Integrals and other Mathematical Formulas. Nauka, Moscow (1983)
7. Levin, B.R.: The Theoretical Basis of Statistical Radio Engineering. In Three Books. Third Book. Sov. radio, Moscow (1976)
8. Bogdanovich, V.A., Vostretsov, A.G.: Theory of stable detection, discrimination and estimation of signals. FIZMATLIT, Moscow (2004)
9. Gibson, J.D., Melsa, J.L.: Introduction to Nonparametric Detection with Application. Academic Press, New York (1975)
10. Beletsky, Y.S.: Methods and Algorithms for Contrast Detection of Signals Against Background Noise with a Priori Unknown Characteristics. Radiotekhnika, Moscow (2011)
11. Detection of radio signals. Edn Kolosov A.A. Radio i svyaz, Moscow (1989)
12. Denisov, O.N., Prokofiev, V.N., Rumyantsev, K.E.: Invariant and nonparametric quantization algorithms in binary signal detectors. Tutorial. TSURE, Taganrog (1983)
13. Denisov, O.N., Prokofiev, V.N., Rumyantsev, K.E.: Invariant Algorithms for Detecting Signals in Noise of Unknown Power. Tutorial. TSURE, Taganrog (1984)
14. Rumyantsev, K.E., Prokofiev, V.N.: Invariant Algorithms of Signal Detection in a Priori Unknown Noise. Tutorial. TSURE, Taganrog (1991)
15. Zikiy, A.N.: Detection of single pulses by contrast. Radioelectron. Commun. Syst. **7**(12), 80–81 (1980)
16. Zikiy, A.N., Zlaman, P.N.: Rank detector of dingle pulses. Izvestiya SFedU. Eng. Sci. **9**(12), 113–121 (2016)
17. Zikiy, A.N., Zlaman, P.N.: Resolving power of a rank detector. Inzhenernyy vestnik Dona (2017). http://www.ivdon.ru/ru/magazine/archive/N3y2017/4357
18. Mazor, Y.L., et al.: Noise immunity of detection of a noise signal operating in a two-way spatial contrast method. Izvestiya VUZov USSR, Radioelectron. **9**(12), 110–113 (1978)

Single Photon Algorithm of Search of a Pulse Radiation Source

K. Y. Rumyantsev$^{(\boxtimes)}$, K. B. Bamatgireeva$^{(\boxtimes)}$, and Y. K. Mironov$^{(\boxtimes)}$

Southern Federal University, Rostov-on-Don, Russian Federation
{rke2004, Puma-i}@mail.ru, tmiyapll7@gmail.com

Abstract. A new spatiotemporal search for pulsed radiation with a single-channel processing of the photon flux is proposed. The algorithm allows up to two device activations during the observation of the decomposition element. Reasons for activation of the amplitude discriminator (AD) during the analysis of the time frame are analyzed at repeated survey in the next time frame. The search algorithm provides an extension of the permissible range of changes in the intensity of background radiation on 25...50%. Thus the probability of the signal skip decreases more than in 4 times in comparison with an analog that allows only one activation of the search equipment. For the correct detection of the useful radiation with probability more than 90% the median number of signal photoelectrons in pulse shall be more than three. Implementation of an algorithm allows to reduce emissive power of the transmitter by 5 times.

Keywords: Spatiotemporal search · Single photon pulse · Channel registration Scanning · Single-photon photoemissive device

1 Introduction

Laser communication can significantly increase the speed of information transfer, increase the noise immunity of transmitted messages. This is especially important for applied and scientific tasks with the spacecraft use.

The creation of optical communication systems with spacecrafts demands the solution of complex problems. It is especially important to provide spatial search, acquisition and alignment of the correspondent [1]. Indeed, the high directivity of laser radiation requires mutual targeting of the complexes antennas.

Space optical communication systems (COSS) are known, which include equipment for the spatial search of a correspondent.

The actuality of establishing two-way optical communication between remote transceivers is noted in patents 3566126 [2] and 3511998 [3] US. In patent 3566126 US, one of the terminals is proposed to be equipped with an angle reflector, by which the optical antenna is aimed at the correspondent. In patent 3511998 proposes using a separate set of frequencies to distinguish between the surveillance mode and the call mode.

In patent 3504182 [4] suggests a method for targeting radiation patterns of two spaced transceivers. Here, the laser beam of the transceiver of the first AES is fixed in a predetermined direction for a certain period of time. The laser beam of the transmitter

P. K. Singh et al. (Eds.): FTNCT 2018, CCIS 958, pp. 95–108, 2019.
https://doi.org/10.1007/978-981-13-3804-5_8

of the second satellite scans the space. When the laser beams are mutually directed towards each other, the targeting stops. It is proposed to use the radiation of transceivers with different optical wavelengths. Similarly, in patent 4867560 [5], each satellite transceiver transmits beams having a different length of the optical wave.

In patent 3658426 [6], it is proposed to use a reflector in the opposite direction to target the directional patterns of the separated transceivers.

The method of targeting in patents 5060304 US [7] and 5142400 US [8] is based on the use of a ray reflection. In contrast to the patent 3504182 the US proposes to use a set of modulation frequencies, rather than radiation with different optical wavelengths.

In patents 3504979 US [9] and US 3942894 [10] use reflectors in the opposite direction.

The targeting method, in which the beamwidth of the radiation pattern changes during the targeting process, is proposed in patents 5282073 [11] and 5475520 US [12].

The described cosmic optical systems do not provide a continuous connection between objects in the case of their rotation. In patents 2106749 RU [13], 2275743 RU [14] and 2276836 RU [15], technical solutions for providing continuous optical communication between rotating objects are proposed.

The most promising in laser communication systems is the use of sources of optical pulsed radiation. In the mode of entering into communication, the moment of appearance of the impulse signal at the receiving end is considered unknown. The organization of space-time search for the purpose of detecting and isolating the moment of appearance of an optical pulse is a necessary condition for entering into the communication (synchronism) of the receiving-transmitting complex [16].

The limiting parameters of the photodetector equipment are realized with the use of single-photon photodetectors (single-photon dissector), which allow recording the acts of photon conversion into a photoelectron (FE), the primary electron. This is especially actual for secure communication systems, in space communications systems with interplanetary ships, in analyzing the retrieval of information from quantum channels in quantum key distribution systems [16, 17].

At present, there is an apparatus for spatial search and detection of optical radiation sources. However, the question of the specifications optimizing to equipment based on scanning single-photon photoemissive device (SPD) for long-distance space communication systems is still topical.

In [16] the methods for processing information in the search equipment with the SPD are described, algorithms for a pulse radiation searching are synthesised, parameters are optimised and the procedure of equipment designing is given.

In the [18], an algorithm for spatially-temporal search of pulsed signals is described in the single-channel registration mode of single-photon pulses (SPP). In [19, 20], formulas were obtained for calculating the temporal and probabilistic parameters of a complex for searching pulsed optical sources using a scanning device SPD with a limited bandwidth.

Application area of the described algorithm is limited to the search for radiation sources for a background radiation with a weak intensity on the photodetector. Indeed, for a reliable detection of the signal, the pulse recurrence frequency must be commensurate with the maximum realized for the exchange of information between moving correspondents (units is megahertz). In addition, if there is no excess of the level of discrimination in the repeated analysis, the equipment stops viewing the decomposition element. Therefore, in order to increase the probability of correct detection, it is necessary to continue the survey until a multiple of the optical pulses recurrence period.

The research purpose is directional on expansion of the successful search range and detection of pulse signals by one-photon equipment under the influence of intensive background radiation at the expense of magnifying of the observation time of the decomposition element.

2   Research Objective

An algorithm for the search for pulsed radiation is proposed, which presupposes up to two activations of the equipment during the observation of the decomposition element. Spatio-temporal search with the determination of the arrival time of optical signals is based on the fact that in the receiver are known the duration τ_s and the optical pulses repetition period T_s. In the interval $[0, T_s]$, the instant t_{AD1} of the first exceeding of the threshold level U_{AD} of the amplitude discriminator is fixed, the cause of which is analyzed in the subsequent interval $[T_s, 2T_s]$. The received optical radiation is converted by a photocathode into a flux of photoelectrons (PE). The use of an electronic multiplier system with N_d dynodes allows one to obtain a response in the form of a single-photon pulse (SPP) on each photoelectron. The SPP amplitude significantly exceeds the thermal noises level of load. To limit the supply of dark current pulses (DCP) from the collector, amplitude discrimination is applied.

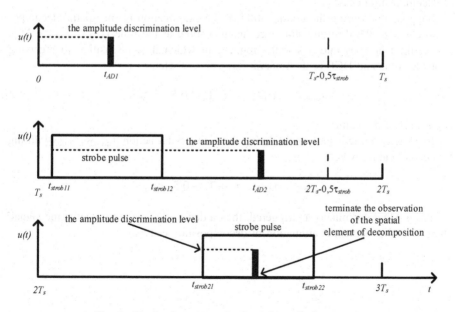

Fig. 1. Single photon search of a pulse radiation source

Let the equipment has registered a photoelectron (or DCP) at the moment of at the review of the spatial decomposition element (Fig. 1). At the same time, the equipment becomes insensitive to receiving photoelectrons and DCPs in the interval $[t_{AD1}, t_{strob11}]$. Here

$$t_{strob11} = t_{AD1} - \tau_1 + T_s - 0.5 \cdot \tau_{strob}$$

corresponds to the moment when the gating pulse starts to act upon at repeated survey.

The delay time between the moment of operation of the discriminator and the instant of generation of the first photoelectron is

$$\tau_1 = 7 \cdot \tau_d + 5.8 \cdot \tau_d \cdot U_{AD.n}.$$

The delay depends on propagation time of electron between two neighboring dynodes τ_d and standardized of respect to the SPP amplitude of level of the amplitude discrimination $U_{AD.n}$.

Repeated polling is performed in the interval $[t_{strob11}, t_{strob12}]$. Here

$$t_{strob12} = t_{AD1} - \tau_1 + T_s + 0.5 \cdot \tau_{strob}$$

is a moment of the termination of action of strobe pulse.

If discrimination level at the repeated analysis is not exceeded, the equipment continues time interval inspection. If in the range of $[t_{strob12}, 2T_s]$ the discrimination threshold is exceeded, the equipment transfers in an expectation regime. Repeated polling is made during action of the second gating pulse. If the discrimination threshold is again exceeded, that the signal is received. Otherwise, the examination of the element of decomposition ceases.

Suppose that during the continuation of the examination of the spatial decomposition element, the discriminator once again worked at the time $t_{AD2} \in [t_{strob12}, 2T_s]$. The equipment goes into a standby regime, in which it is insensitive to receiving photoelectrons and DCP in the interval $[t_{AD2}, t_{strob21}]$. Here

$$t_{strob21} = t_{AD2} - \tau_1 + T_s - 0.5 \cdot \tau_{strob}$$

is the start of the gating.

Repeated polling is performed during the gating pulse action $[t_{strob21}, t_{strob22}]$ during the second gating, where

$$t_{strob22} = t_{AD2} - \tau_1 + T_s + 0.5 \cdot \tau_{strob}.$$

If the AD discriminator is triggered, then a decision is made to receive the signal. Otherwise, the element examination of decomposition ceases.

3 Calculation of Probability of False Alarm

For the description of statistical properties of a flow of photons the Poisson law is used. At the same time the probability of reception of the given number of photons depends only on observation time.

False operations of an equipment of search of a pulse radiation in the mode of registration of background photoelectrons and DCP are possible in two situations. We will consider these situations applicable in case of the known arrival rates of background photoelectrons ξ_b and DCP ξ_{DCP}.

Situation 1. For false operation of an equipment of search of a pulse radiation there shall be sequentially two events.

The conditional probability of registration of one and more background FE and/or ITT on an interval $[0, T_s]$ will be (the first event).

$$P_{FA11} = 1 - exp(-\xi_n T_s),$$

where $\xi_n = \xi_b + \xi_{DCP}$ − frequency of appearance of noise pulses.

It is necessary for false operation to accept noise pulse in an interval $[t_{strob11}, t_{strob12}]$. The conditional probability of an event is equal:

$$P_{FA12} = 1 - exp(-\xi_n \tau_{strob}).$$

We will mark that the conditional probability of false alarm for the first situation does not depend on the accidental moment of detection of the first background photoelectron or DCP on an interval $[0, T_s]$:

$$P_{FA1} = P_{FA11} \cdot P_{FA12} = [1 - exp(-\xi_n T_s)] \cdot [1 - exp(-\xi_n \tau_{strob})].$$

Situation 2. Here for false operation of an equipment there shall be sequentially four events.

Firstly, it is necessary to accept at least one background photoelectron and/or DCP in an interval $[0, T_s]$. The conditional probability of this first event is equal:

$$P_{FA21} = 1 - \exp(-\xi_n T_s).$$

At strobing of an equipment there shall not be noise pulses. The probability of this second event is equal

$$P_{FA22} = \exp(-\xi_n \tau_{strob}).$$

From the moment of the termination of a strobe-pulse $t_{strob12}$ the equipment continues viewing of time slot $[t_{strob12}, 2T_s]$. The moment of $t_{strob12}$ is defined by the accidental moment of t_{AD1} of reception of the first noise pulse on an interval $[0, T_s]$.

The search equipment shall accept noise pulse in the range of time again $[t_{strob12}, 2T_s]$. The probability of the third event is equal

$$P_{FA23}\{t_{AD1}\} = 1 - \exp(-\xi_n T_s + 0.5\xi_n \tau_{srob} - \xi_n \tau_1 + \xi_n t_{AD1}).$$

For false operation it is necessary to accept noise pulse on an interval $[t_{strob21}, t_{strob22}]$. The conditional probability of this 4th event is equal:

$$P_{FS24} = 1 - \exp(-\xi_n \tau_{strob}).$$

It is necessary to mark that probability P_{FA54} does not depend on the moment of reception of noise pulse on an interval $[t_{strob12}, 2T_s]$.

The conditional probability of false alarm in case of a situation 2:

$$P_{FA2}\{t_{AD1}\} = P_{FA21} \cdot P_{FA22} \cdot P_{FA23}\{t_{AD1}\} \cdot P_{FA24}$$
$$= [1 - \exp(-\xi_n T_s)] \cdot \exp(-\xi_n \tau_{strob}) \cdot \rightarrow$$
$$[1 - \exp(-\xi_n T_s + 0.5\xi_n \tau_{strob} - \xi_n \tau_1 + \xi_n t_{AD1})] \cdot [1 - \exp(-\xi_n \tau_{storb})].$$

Unlike the conditional probability of P_{FA1} the probability of $P_{FA2}\{t_{AD1}\}$ depends on the accidental moment of reception of the first noise pulse of t_{AD1}. It will demand the subsequent averaging according to the distribution law of a random variable t_{AD1}.

The conditional probability of false alarm in case of the given moment of actuating AD t_{AD1} can be determined by a formula

$$P_{FA}\{t_{AD1}\} = P_{FA1} + P_{FA2}\{t_{AD1}\}.$$

The absolute probability of false alarm P_{FA} (further – probability of false alarm) is averaging of probability $P_{FA}\{t_{AD1}\}$ on distribution of a random variable t_{AD1}.

Let the generation frequency of noise pulses ξ_n (background photoelectrons and DCP) be known. Then the average number of noise pulses generated during the recurrence period of the optical pulses is $\overline{n_{n.T}} = \xi_n \cdot T_s$, and during of the gating pulse – $\overline{n_{n.strob}} = \xi_n \cdot \tau_{strob}$.

The probability of false activation during gating is

$$P_{strob} = 1 - exp(-\overline{n_{n.strob}}), \tag{1}$$

and the probability of AD activation in the interval $[0, T_s]$

$$P_T = 1 - exp(-\overline{n_{n.T}}). \tag{2}$$

The probability of false alarm can be calculated by the formula

$$P_{FA} = a_{FA} - \frac{b_{FA}}{\overline{n_{n.T}}} \cdot \frac{P_T}{1 - P_T} = a_{FA} - c_{FA}, \tag{3}$$

where

$$a_{FA} = P_T P_{strob}(2 - P_{strob}); \qquad (4)$$

$$b_{FA} = P_T P_{strob} \sqrt{1 - P_{strob}}(1 - P_T)\exp(-\xi_n \tau_1). \qquad (5)$$

Evident that for reduction of probability of false alarm it is necessary to generate duration optical pulses of nanosecond and picosecond with high frequency stability of following.

Follows from formulas (1)–(5) that the probability of false alarm depends on the period of following and duration of optical pulse, the OPPI parameters (number of dynodes, bandpass range), instability of the period of optical pulses, level of amplitude discrimination, frequency of generation of noise pulses.

Figure 2 shows the dependence of the probability of false alarm on the generating frequency of noise pulses at $N_d = 14$; $U_{AD.n} = 0.5$; $\tau_s = 10$ ns; $\tau_d = 0.36$ ns.

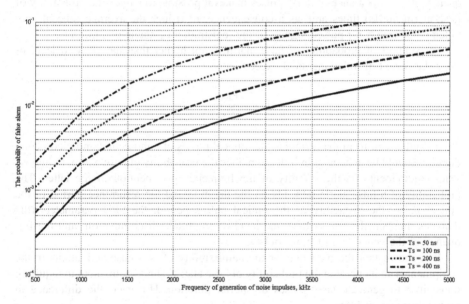

Fig. 2. Dependences of the probability of false alarms on the generating frequency of noise pulses

As expected, with increasing generating frequency of noise pulses, the probability of false alarm increases. And the nonlinear law of this change is obvious. For example, at a period of $T_s = 200$ ns, an increase in the generating frequency of noise pulses from 500 to 1000 kHz (by a factor of 2) leads to an increase in the probability of false alarm by 3.94 times. The probability increases with increasing frequency from 1 to 2 MHz in 3.85 times.

We will note, in case of $x \ll 1$ for exponential function approximation of exp $(-x) \approx 1 - x$ is fair. As arguments $\overline{n_{n.T}}$ and $\overline{n_{n.strob}}$ in exponential functions much less 1, it is possible to receive approximate formulas

$$P_{strob} \approx \overline{n_{n.strob}};$$
$$P_T \approx \overline{n_{n.T}}.$$

Then

$$a_{FA} \approx 2 \cdot \overline{n_{n.T}} \cdot \overline{n_{n.strob}};$$
$$b_{FA} = \overline{n_{n.T}} \cdot \overline{n_{n.strob}}.$$

We have obtained the formula

$$P_{FA0} \approx \overline{n_{n.T}} \cdot \overline{n_{n.strob}} \approx \xi_n^2 \cdot T_s \cdot \tau_s$$

for an approximate estimate of the false alarm probability for $\overline{n_{n.T}} << 1$.

The formula proves the quadratic nature of the change in the probability of false alarm from the generating frequency of noise pulses. A 10-fold decrease in the frequency of the appearance of noise pulses makes it possible to reduce the probability of false alarm in 100 times and, as a consequence, to reduce the average time of spatiotemporal search for pulsed signals at the registration of single-photon pulses.

For support of probability of false alarm is not higher than the allowed level of $P_{FA.p}$ the period of following shall exceed value

$$T_s > \frac{P_{FA.p}}{\xi_n^2 \cdot \tau_s}.$$

It can be seen from the formulas that optical pulses of nanosecond and picosecond duration should be generated in order to reduce the probability of false alarm, to impose strict requirements on the stability of the frequency of repetition of the latter. The probability of a false alarm depends on the duration and the recurrence period of the optical pulse, the instability of the optical pulses period, the SPD parameters (the dynodes number, the bandwidth), the level of amplitude discrimination, and the frequency of the generation of noise pulses.

It is shown that the payment for the admissibility of two false activations in the equipment is an increase in the probability of false alarm. This is equivalent to requiring transmitter to generate laser pulses of shorter duration. However, the difference in probabilities is not large.

4 Calculation of Probability of the Correct Detection

Let us assume, in a spatial element of expansion there is the useful radiation at an interval

$$[t_s + (j - 1)T_s, t_s + (j - 1)T_s + \tau_s], \ j \geq 1.$$

The probability of the correct detection of the useful radiation is possible in two cases. We will consider these cases with the known frequencies of reception of noise pulses and in case of the known median number of signal photoelectrons for duration of optical pulse $\bar{n}_s$.

In the first case the moment of appearance of optical pulse in the first temporal frame meets a condition $t_s \in [0, T_s]$.

The conditional probability of the correct detection of the useful radiation is defined by three probabilities:

- probability of absence of noise pulses by the time of reception of pulse of the useful radiation;
- probability of registration at least one noise pulse in the analysis of the time slot containing the useful radiation;
- probability of registration at least one pulse during action of a strobing pulse.

For Poisson flows of photoelectrons and DCP it is found

$$P_{D1}\{t_c\} = \exp(-\xi_n t_s) \cdot [1 - \exp(-\xi_n \tau_s - \bar{n}_s)] \cdot [1 - \exp(-\overline{n_{n.strob}} - \bar{n}_s)].$$

The conditional probability of the correct detection of the useful radiation for the second case is defined by probabilities:

- appearances of background FE and/or DCP by the time of arrival of pulse of the useful radiation;
- absence of FE or DCP during action of a strobing pulse;
- absence of background FE or DCP between the moments of the end of action of the first of time strobing pulse and arrival of pulse of the useful radiation;
- registration at least one FE or DCP when viewing the time slot containing the useful radiation;
- registration at least one photoelectron or DCP during action of the second time of strobing pulse.

For Poisson flows of photons and DCP it is found

$$P_{D2}\{t_s, t_{AD1}\} = [1 - exp(-\xi_n t_s)] \cdot exp(-\overline{n_{n.strob}}) \cdot \rightarrow$$
$$exp[-\xi_n(t_s + T_s - t_{strob12})] \cdot \rightarrow$$
$$[1 - exp(-\xi_n \tau_1 - \bar{n}_s)] \cdot [1 - exp(-\overline{n_{n.strob}} - \bar{n}_s)].$$

The resultant conditional probability of the correct detection in case of the moment of appearance of optical pulse of t_s is calculated by a formula

$$P_D\{t_s, t_{AD1}\} = P_{D1}\{t_s\} + P_{D2}\{t_s, t_{AD1}\}.$$

After averaging, we find probability of the correct detection

$$P_D = \frac{A}{\bar{n}_{n.T}}[1 - \exp(-\overline{n_{n.T}})] + \frac{B}{\bar{n}_{n.T}} \cdot \sum_{k=2}^{\infty} \frac{(-\overline{n_{n.T}})^k}{k! \cdot k}(2^k - 2). \qquad (6)$$

Here,

$$A = [1 - \exp(-\xi_n \tau_s - \overline{n}_s)] \cdot [1 - \exp(-\overline{n}_{n.strob} - \overline{n}_s)]$$

represents the probability at least one pulse at a time of successive reception of the optical pulse and the action of the gating pulse, and

$$B = A \cdot \exp(-\xi_n \cdot \tau_1 - 0.5 \cdot \overline{n}_{n.strob}).$$

Figure 3 shows the dependences of the probability of skipping signal $P_{ND} = 1 - P_D$ on the average number of signal photoelectrons over the duration of optical pulse of 10 ns for repetition period of the optical pulse 50, 100, 200 and 400 ns. The generating frequency of noise pulses, DCP and photoelectrons of background radiation, is 5 MHz. The calculations were carried out for a single-photon dissector with a number of dynodes 14, multiplication coefficients 71 dB, a bandwidth of 100 MHz, and a quantum efficiency of the photocathode of 20%. The amplitude of the produced SPP pulse at a load of 100 Ω is 62.8 mV with duration of 3.3 ns at 0.5 level. The threshold level of amplitude discrimination is 31.4 mV. The delay time between the moments of reception of a single photoelectron and the activation of an discriminator is 3.55 ns.

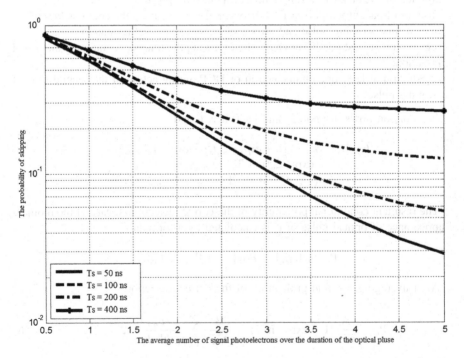

Fig. 3. Dependence of the skipping probability on the average number of signal photoelectrons over the duration of the optical pulse for the generating frequencies of noise pulses 5 MHz

It can be seen from the Fig. 3 that, in order to ensure a skipping probability of no more than 10%, an average of more than three signal photoelectrons over the duration of optical pulse at $T_s = 50$ ns and a change in the frequency of generation of noise pulses in the range $\xi_n = 1...5$ MHz band will be required.

Note that for correct detection, it is necessary to register at least one pulse during the analysis of the time interval containing useful radiation, and also during the action of the strobe pulse. The joint probability of these two events under the assumption that there are no background radiation and DCP is

$$P_{D.\lim} = [1 - exp(-\overline{n_s})]^2.$$

This is the lower estimate of the probability of correct detection, because always because of the presence of background radiation and DCP

$$P_D \geq P_{D.\lim} = [1 - \exp(-\overline{n_s})]^2.$$

Therefore, in order to ensure a given probability P_D, the average number of signal photoelectrons over the duration of optical pulse should exceed the limit level:

$$\overline{n_s} \geq \overline{n_{s.\lim}} = -ln\left[1 - \sqrt{P_D}\right].$$

It follows from the formula that in order to provide $P_D \geq 0.9$ it is necessary in the transmitter to provide the pulse energy, guaranteeing an average reception of at least 2.97 photoelectrons. When the probability $P_D \geq 99\%$ is required, it is necessary to provide $\overline{n_s} \geq 5.30$.

Calculations show that the main contribution to the probability of correct detection with a weak background is given by the first term in formula (6). The contribution of the second term corresponds to 2.4% at $T_s = 50$ ns and $\xi_n = 1$ MHz. It increases to 10% with an increase in the frequency of generation of noise pulses by 5 times to $\xi_n = 5$ MHz.

Note that in order to provide a $P_D \geq 90\%$ probability of the absence of background photoelectrons and DCP in the interval preceding the moment of arrival of the optical pulse,

$$Pr_n = \frac{1 - exp(-\overline{n_{n.T}})}{\overline{n_{n.T}}}.$$

should strictly exceed 0.9. This condition is satisfied for $\overline{n_{n.T}} < 0.2$.

The latter indicates the necessity of choosing the optical pulses repetition period, proceeding from the inequality

$$T_s > 1/(5\xi_n).$$

Figure 4 shows the family of dependences of the probability of skipping signal from the average number of signal photoelectrons over the duration of optical pulse for the proposed algorithm and analog for $\xi_n = 5$ MHz.

When $\overline{n}_s = 5$, $\xi_n = 1$ MHz and $T_s = 100$ ns, the probability of skipping is 4 times lower in the proposed algorithm. With a decrease in the average number of signal photoelectrons over the duration of the optical pulse, the difference in probabilities disappears (does not exceed about 1% for $\overline{n}_s = 0.5$).

Note that in the analog of algorithm

$$P_{D.an} = [1 - \exp(-\xi_n \tau_s - \overline{n}_s)] \cdot [1 - \exp(-\overline{n}_{n.strob} - \overline{n}_s)] \cdot \frac{[1 - \exp(-\overline{n}_{n.T})]}{\overline{n}_{n.T}}.$$

coincides with the first term in formula (6).

Figure 4 shows that when fixing the probability of skipping signal, the implementation of the proposed algorithm guarantees an extension of the permissible power range of noise pulses of 25...50%.

It is established that in order to obtain high probabilities of correct detection, the average number of background photoelectrons and DCP during the optical pulse period should not exceed 1. Moreover, the probability of stopping the review of the spatial decomposition element without analyzing the signal time interval does not exceed 0.1.

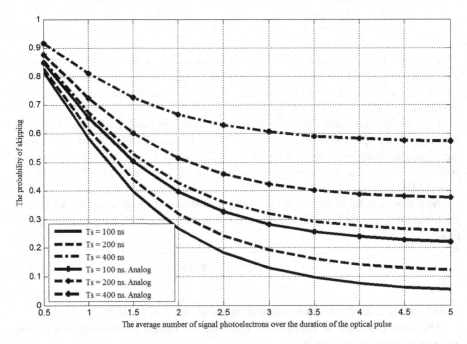

Fig. 4. Dependences of the probability of skipping signal on the average number of signal photoelectrons over the duration of the optical pulse duration for the proposed algorithm and analog for $\xi_n = 5$ MHz

Investigation of the search algorithm shows that even in the case of complete exclusion of background radiation and dark current, the average number of photoelectrons (energy) in the pulse should be more than three for a correct detection of useful radiation with a probability of more than 90%. Under these conditions, the probability of receiving more than one signal photoelectron during the duration of the light pulse is very close to 1. At the same time, the probability of registration two or more background photoelectrons during the duration of the optical pulse is negligible.

5 Conclusion

For the proposed search algorithm, the admissibility of two false alarm activations allows a 5-fold reduction in the requirements for the recurrence frequency of optical pulse signals. Due to the fact that the energy requirements in the pulse are the same, the implementation of the algorithm makes it possible to reduce the transmitter power by a factor of 5.

References

1. Gagliardi, R.M., Karp, S.: Optical Communications. Wiley, New York (1976). Translated to Russian (1978); translated to Japanese (1979). 2nd edn. (1995)
2. Acquisition and tracking laser communication system. Patent 3566126 US, 23 February 1971. https://www.google.com/patents/US3566126
3. Acquisition system. Patent 3511998 US, 12 May 1970. https://www.google.com/patents/US3511998
4. Optical communication system. Patent 3504182 US, 31 March 1970. https://www.google.com/patents/US3504182
5. Optical alignment system. Patent 4867560 US, 19 September 1989. http://www.google.com/patents/US4867560
6. Alignment telescope. Patent 3658426 US, 25 April 1972. https://www.google.com/patents/US3658426
7. Alignment acquiring, optical beam communication link. Patent 5060304 US, 22 October 1991. http://www.google.com/patents/US5060304
8. Solinsky, J.C.: Method and apparatus for automatic acquisition and alignment of an optical beam communication link. La Jolla – Patent 5142400 US. IPC H04B 10/00, 25 August 1992. http://www.google.si/patents/US5142400
9. Pizzurro et al.: Patent 3504182 US. 455/606, March 1970
10. Optical communication system. Patent 3504979 US, 7 April 1970. http://www.google.com/patents/US3504979
11. Self referencing retransmitting alignment sensor for a collimated light beam. Patent 3942894 US, 9 March 1976. http://www.google.com/patents/US3942894
12. System of optical communications between moving stations and corresponding communications method. Patent 5282073 US. http://www.google.ch/patents/US5282073
13. Satellite communications system. Patent 5475520 US, 12 December 1995. http://www.google.si/patents/US5475520
14. Space optical communication line between two objects. Patent 2106749 RU, 10 March 1998. http://www.freepatent.ru/patents/2106749

15. System for space optical communication between cooperated object and correspondent object. Patent 2275743 RU, 10 July 2005. http://www.freepatent.ru/images/patents/193/2275743/patent-2275743.pdf

16. Space optical system for communication between affiliated and sending objects. Patent 2276836 RU, 10 July 2005. http://www.freepatent.ru/images/patents/192/2276836/patent-2276836.pdf

17. Bichkov, S.I., Rumyantsev, K.E.: Scanning and detection of optical signals. In: Rumyantsev, K.E. (ed.) Radio and Communication, Moscow, 282 p. (2000)

18. Rumyantsev, K.Y.: Quantum Key Distribution Systems, p. 264. SFedU, Taganrog (2011)

19. Rumyantsev, K.E., Albogchieva, L.A., Bamatgireeva, K.B.: Algorithm of existential search of pulse signals in a single-channel registration mode of single-photon pulses. Electr. Data Process. Facil. Syst. **8**(4), 3–11 (2012)

20. Rumyantsev, K.E., Bamatgireeva, K.B.: Probabilistic characteristics algorithm spatiotemporal search pulsed radiation with single-channel information processing. XXI century: resumes of the past and challenges of the present plus. Sci. Periodical **3**(19), 70–77 (2014)

21. Rumyantsev, K.E., Albogchieva, L.A.: Time characteristics algorithm single-channel spatiotemporal search pulsed radiation. XXI century: resumes of the past and challenges of the present plus. Sci. Periodical **3**(19), 62–69 (2014)

A Robust Approach of Copyright Protection for Digital Videos Using Zero Padding Algorithm Technique

Jabir Ali[✉] and Satya Prakash Ghrera

Computer Science and Engineering, Jaypee University of Information
Technology, Solan, HP, India
jabirali.cse@gmail.com, sp.ghrera@juit.ac.in

Abstract. Copyright protections of the multimedia is become most highlighted area for the researchers because of velocity of multimedia data. Every day a huge amount of data is generating and to prove the ownership of data, it is a basic need of certain security programs. In this paper, a new approach of copyright protection for digital videos, SWEA (Split watermark embedding algorithm) with Zero Padding Algorithm (ZPA) is proposed. With the help of this algorithm, it is hard to know the original pattern of watermark because of SWEA and minimizing the perceptual degradation of watermarked video because of ZPA. Here in this paper 'db1' wavelet domain is used for embedding the watermark in the low frequency sub-band of the original identical frame (I-frame), based on the energy of high-frequency sub-band in an adaptive manner. SCD (Scene changed detection) is used to find out the identical frame (I-frame). The proposed algorithm has undergone various attacks, such as compression, uniform noise, Gaussian noise frame repetition and frame averaging attacks. The proposed algorithm, sustain all the above attacks and offers improved performance compared with the other methods from the literature.

Keywords: SWEA · ZPA · SCD · DWT · I-frame · Low frequency

1 Introduction

The term of copyright belongs to a branch of law that grants the protection to an author, (A writer, artist, musicians or another creator) for their work [1]. Under the law of copyright, authors are entitled to protection against illegal or unauthorized use of their original contribution. Digital watermarking techniques have been studied extensively. In this era, extensive use of video-based applications is growing which include the internet, multimedia, video recorder, video conferencing, etc. which increases the need to secure the videos. The video watermark technique is far more complicated than the image watermark technique [2–5]. Some of the impactful video watermarking characteristics include:

- Successive frames have a high correlation, so embedding, independent watermarks on each frame, an attacker could not remove significant portions of inserting watermarks by performing frame averaging.

© Springer Nature Singapore Pte Ltd. 2019
P. K. Singh et al. (Eds.): FTNCT 2018, CCIS 958, pp. 109–122, 2019.
https://doi.org/10.1007/978-981-13-3804-5_9

- Some of the applications require a real time processing like broadcasting, monitoring etc. and that's why they have low complexity.
- The susceptibility of watermarked video sequences is very high to pirate attacks.

To prove the ownership of a video is a great challenge. If a video becomes popular all of a sudden and people like to watch it over and over again or a video which may be useful to claim, offense or innocence of a person. The price/cost of these videos hikes a lot. In this case, many people claim the ownership of the video. To find out the authorized/legal owner out of all multiple people claiming the ownership, we perform the Digital Video Copyright Protection and this whole process is named as ownership proof. In Fig. 1 we have shown the block diagram of video copyright protection. In Table 1 we have shown the classifications of watermark system.

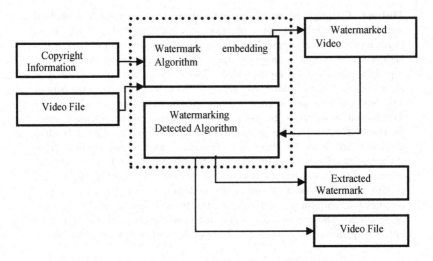

Fig. 1. Block diagram of video watermarking.

In this paper, we are using the ZERO PADDING with SWEA technique to ensure the authorized owner of the video. For the quality assurance of the algorithm, we have performed many attacks on it, to ensure that the video can bear it in order to maintain its originality and authorization. These attack techniques comprise of Spatial attack (Gaussian noise, uniform noise), compression attacks and temporal attacks (Frame repetition, frame averaging and frame swapping) etc. Out of all these attacks, the technique provides better results as compared with the literature.

The remaining part of the paper is organized as follows. In section *Related work*, we have discussed various digital video copyright protection techniques. In section *Proposed Method and Algorithm*, we have proposed an algorithm for providing the copyright protection for digital videos. In section *Result and Discussion*, the results are discussed. Finally, *the Conclusion section* provides the conclusion of this paper.

Table 1. Font sizes of headings.

Domain type		Watermark type		Information type
Spatial	Transform	Visual	PRNS	Blind
Manipulate the pixels values to embed the watermark	Modified the coefficients of Transform Domain to embed the watermark These are the some popular Transform:- Discrete Cosine Transform (DCT) Discrete Wavelet Transform (DWT) Discrete Fourier Transform (DFT)	The visual quality of embedded watermark is evaluated	Detecting the presence or absence of a watermark statistically. A PRN Sequence is generated by feeding the generator with a secret seed	Only secret key required

2 Related Work

In December 2013 Khalilian [6] proposed an algorithm for video watermarking. The encoding of watermark was in the wavelet domain, but he decoded the watermark with the help of PCA. He also used a scene changed detection algorithm so that he can select the target frame where the watermark is to be embedded. But this algorithm also was not suitable for the protection of watermark pattern and quality of extracted watermark.

In the literature review [2–13], we have studied that an attacker may crack or damage or detect watermark with the help of some possible algorithms. But in SWEA, it is very difficult to detect the original pattern of inserted watermark. In this paper, we also improved the robustness & security of inserted digital watermark and transparency of watermarked media using ZPA. For many years, researchers are doing their work in this field to protect the copyright of any multimedia document and they have succeeded in achieving the same, but on the other hand, many hackers or attackers are also finding out the way to crack or break the copyright technique. For the decoding process of the watermark, Data hiding techniques can be divided into three categories: Blind, Semi-blind, and non-blind.

3 Proposed Method

In the proposed method, a gray level image (256 × 256) is used as a watermark signal. As a gray image has 256 levels so 8 bits can represent each pixel. For embedding the watermark we have taken two video sequences first is 'Foreman' and the second is

'Car_race.mp4' video sequence. After applying scene changed algorithm on these video sequences, we obtain 77 and 97 scenes changed frames respectively. Before embedding the watermark inside the original media (original video), we have to pre-process the watermark and input video.

3.1 SWEA

With the help of SWEA (split watermark embedding algorithm), we split the watermark. In the process of watermark embedding, at first we scale the watermark to a particular size with the help of this equation.

$$(4^n \le m; n > 0) \tag{1}$$

In the above equation, m is the total no. of the scene changed frames of video and 4^n is the total number of split watermark in which n is an integer. In Fig. 2 we have an original watermark juit.jpg (256 × 256). Now apply the proposed algorithm SWEA on juit.jpg and we obtain small pieces of watermark (32 × 32) in Fig. 2(c). In this case, the watermark will be divided into 4^n small images.

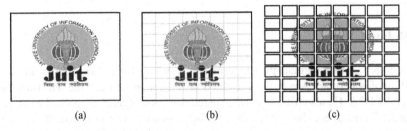

(a)   (b)   (c)

Fig. 2. Block diagram of video watermarking. (a) Original Watermark (b) split of watermark $(4^n \le m; n > 0)$ using proposed algorithm (c) 64 small pieces of original watermark after implementation of the proposed algorithm. Here m = 77 for Formen video and m = 97 for Car_race video. So n = 3 for both the cases

In Fig. 3, a scene changed detection algorithm is applied to input video sequence and get the non-overlapping GOP [10]. Select the identical frame (I-frame) with the help of the identical frame selection scheme. After getting the I-frames, apply 2-level DWT and find out the 2nd level coefficients [ca2, ch2, cv2, cd2]. In Fig. 3 we have used 2-level 'db1' wavelet transform on both video sequence and watermark, to obtain the higher (HH, HL) and lower frequency band (LL LH) [11, 12]. After performing 2-DWT on each I-frame (Identical Frame) of video, we get LL-2 (2nd Level low frequency band), which is named as Lf_2.

We are also applying the 2-DWT technique on each split watermark block and obtain LL-2, which is named as Wm_2 and multiplied by a scaling factor β. After getting scaled Wm_2 and Lf_2 we add them with the help of ZPA (Zero Padding Algorithm) then apply IDWT (Inverse discrete wavelet transform) on video frame Lf_2 and the result gets stored in Wml_i.

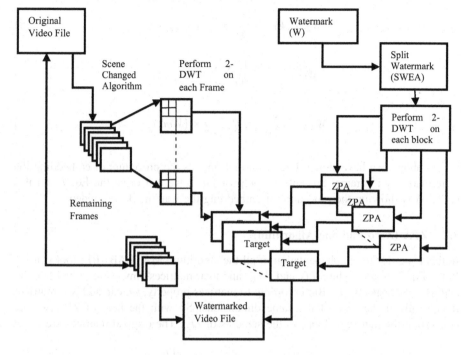

Fig. 3. Video pre-process

$$WmI_i = (Lf_{2_i}) + \beta \times (Wm_{2_i}) \tag{2}$$

Wavelets are a more general way to represent and analyze multi-resolution images and it can also be applied to 1D signals. Wavelets are very useful for image compression and removing noise. We don't need to calculate wavelet coefficients at every possible scale. It can choose scales based on powers of two, and get equivalent accuracy.

$$\psi_{j,k}(x) = 2^{j/2}\psi(2^j x - k) \tag{3}$$

We can represent a discrete function $f(n)$ as a weighted summation of wavelets $\psi(n)$, plus a coarse approximation $\varphi(n)$

$$f(n) = \frac{1}{\sqrt{M}}\sum_k W_\varphi(j_0,k)\varphi_{j_0,k}(n) + \frac{1}{\sqrt{M}}\sum_{j=j_0}^{\infty}\sum_k W_\psi(j,k)\psi_{j,k}(n) \tag{4}$$

Where j_0 is an arbitrary starting scale, and $n = 0,1,2,\ldots M$.

Now to find out the approximation coefficients we used Eq. 3. Approximation coefficients are those coefficients where we have to embed our watermark information. But the embedding process should not distort the original approximate coefficients. So we are using the concept of ZPA (Zero Padding Algorithm).

$$W_\Phi(j_0, k) = \frac{1}{\sqrt{M}} \sum_x f(x) \varphi_{j_0,k}(x) \tag{5}$$

$$W_\Psi(j, k) = \frac{1}{\sqrt{M}} \sum_x f(x) \psi_{j,k}(x) \tag{6}$$

$$W_{video} = \sum_{i=1}^{m} \left[(Lf_2^i) + q \times (Wm_2^i) \right] \tag{7}$$

As above, we have shown Eq. 2 and that implies the procedure of embedding the watermark for i^{th} frame. So with the help of Eq. 2 we can drive the Eq. 7 and this equation is showing the procedure of embedding the watermark in a video.

3.2   ZPA (Zero Padding Algorithm)

In this paper for the implementation of all the algorithm, MATLAB 2012 tool is used. In the Eq. 2 we are adding, Lf_{2i} and Wm_{2i} and their matrices dimensions are (72×88) and (8×8) respectively. But according to matrices property, we can add two matrices if and only if they are of the same dimensions. So with the help of ZPA we are converting the matrix of Wm_{2i} as the same as of Lf_{2i}. The original matrices are

$$\left(Lf_{2_i}\right) = \begin{bmatrix} a_{1,1} \ a_{1,2} \dots a_{1,88} \\ a_{2,1} \ a_{2,2} \dots a_{2,88} \\ \cdot \quad \cdot \quad \cdot \\ a_{72,1} \ a_{72,2} \dots a_{72,88} \end{bmatrix}, \left(Wm_{2_i}\right) = \begin{bmatrix} b_{1,1} \cdot \ \cdot \ b_{1,8} \\ \cdot \quad \cdot \quad \cdot \\ \cdot \quad \cdot \quad \cdot \\ b_{8,1} \cdot \ \cdot \ b_{8,2} \end{bmatrix} \tag{8}$$

$$\left(Lf_{2_i}\right) = \begin{bmatrix} a_{1,1} \ a_{1,2} \cdot \quad \cdot \quad \cdot \quad \cdot \ a_{1,87} \ a_{1,88} \\ \cdot \quad \cdot \quad \cdot \quad \cdot \quad \cdot \quad \cdot \quad \cdot \\ a_{36,1} \ a_{36,2} \cdot \cdot \ a_{36,44} \ a_{36,45} \cdot \cdot \ a_{36,87} \ a_{36,88} \\ a_{37,1} \ a_{37,2} \cdot \cdot \ a_{37,44} \ a_{37,45} \cdot \cdot \ a_{37,87} \ a_{37,88} \\ \cdot \quad \cdot \quad \cdot \quad \cdot \quad \cdot \quad \cdot \quad \cdot \\ a_{72,1} \ a_{72,2} \quad \cdot \quad \cdot \quad \cdot \ a_{72,87} \ a_{72,88} \end{bmatrix} \tag{9}$$

$$\left(Wm_{2_i}\right) = \begin{bmatrix} 0_{1,1} \ 0_{1,2} \quad \cdot \quad \cdot \quad \cdot \quad \cdot \quad 0_{1,87} \ 0_{1,88} \\ \cdot \quad \cdot \quad \cdot \quad \cdot \quad \cdot \quad \cdot \quad \cdot \\ 0_{33,1} \ 0_{33,2} \dots b_{33,41} \cdot \ \cdot \ b_{33,48} \cdot \cdot \ 0_{36,87} \ 0_{36,88} \\ \cdot \quad \cdot \quad \cdot \quad \cdot \quad \cdot \quad \cdot \quad \cdot \\ 0_{40,1} \ 0_{40,2} \dots b_{40,41} \cdot \ \cdot \ b_{40,48} \cdot \cdot \ 0_{37,87} \ 0_{37,88} \\ \cdot \quad \cdot \quad \cdot \quad \cdot \quad \cdot \quad \cdot \\ 0_{72,1} \ 0_{72,2} \quad \cdot \quad \cdot \quad \cdot \quad \cdot \ 0_{72,87} \ 0_{72,88} \end{bmatrix} \tag{10}$$

In Eq. 8, matrix dimensions of Wm_{2i} being 8×8. But after applying ZPA on Wm_{2i} the matrix dimensions will be changed in respect of Lf_{2i} as in Eq. 9.

3.3 Embedding Algorithm

1. **Input** Original video sequence (O_{video})

$$\text{Watermark } (W) \ [256, 256]$$

2. Extract scene changed frame (I) Total number of scenes changed frames = m
3. **SWEA**
   while $m \geq 4^n$
4. size of watermark blocks $Wb(x, y) = \left[\frac{256}{\sqrt{4^n}} \times \frac{256}{\sqrt{4^n}} \right]$
5. Take 2-level 2-dimensional DWT of I_i for i = 1 : m
   $[Ca_i, Ch_i, Cv_i, Cd_i] = DWT2(I_i, \text{"haar"})$ j = i + 1
   $[Ca_j, Ch_j, Cv_j, Cd_j] = DWT2(Ca_i, \text{"haar"})$
6. Calculate size of $Ca_j[p\,q] = size(Ca_j)$
7. Zero Padding in watermark block Z = zeros(p, q), size of Wb = [x y]
   Insert the values of Wb in Z
   Row value insertion at $Z\left(\frac{q-y}{2} + 1 : \frac{q+y}{2} \right)$
   Column value insertion at $Z\left(\frac{p-x}{2} + 1 : \frac{p-x}{2} + x \right)$
   Now, Zero padded watermark = ZW
8. Insert the zero padded watermark ZW into Ca_j
   Now new coefficients will be mod $Ca_{i,}$ mod Ca_j
   Take IDWT of modified coefficients
9. Finally get the zero padded watermarked frame (EW_f) and watermarked video (EW_{video})

3.4 Detection Algorithm

1. **Input** watermarked video (EW_{video}), Original Video (O_{video})
2. Take watermarked frame (EW_f) from (EW_{video}) Original frame (I_i) from (O_{video})
3. Subtract 1-level approximate coefficients of watermarked image (EW_f) from the 1-level approximate coefficients of I-frame (I_i) Now, $NewCa_i = mod\ Ca_i - Ca_i$
4. Calculate cross correlation between $NewCa_i$ and original watermark block if correlation = = high
   Then, Stop the execution. The detected watermark block is similar to original watermark block.
   else if
   Take 2-level approximate coefficients and repeat from step 3 until the detected watermark will get similarity with original watermark.
   else
   Watermark not found.

4   Experimental Results

In this section we have taken two parameters, transparency and robustness for the result analysis. To implement this technique we have used original videos 'foreman. yuv' and 'car_race. mp4' at the dimension of 288×352 and 640×360 respectively, and the size of the original watermark image is 256×256. For comparison and analysis we have taken two references [6] and [7]. Figures 4 and 5 shows original video frames (foreman.yuv and car_race.mp4 respectively), watermarked frames and extracted watermark.

4 (a) Original gray foreman video

4 (b) 2-Level De-composition of foreman video frame.

Fig. 4. Original frames and their decomposition.

5 (a) Original car_race video frame.

5 (b) 2-Level De-composition of car_race video frame.

Fig. 5. Original frames and their decomposition

In Fig. 4(b) we can see there are two types of rectangle blocks, the first one is (144×176) named as [LL-1 LH-1 HL-1 HH-1] and second (72×88) named as [LL-2 LH-2 HL-2 HH-2] starting from upper left corner. LL-2 is known as the approximate coefficient of 2nd level where we have to embed the watermark information and rest of this known as detailed coefficients of 2nd level. Same as in Fig. 5(b).

After embedding the first block of the watermark from Fig. 2(c) in LL-2 of Fig. 4(b), we have taken IDWT (Inverse discrete wavelet transform) of Fig. 4(b) that become Fig. 6.

Fig. 6. Watermarked frames (after embedding first block of watermark).

4.1   Merging Small Pieces Extracted Watermark Images

Applied watermark detection algorithm on all the watermarked I frames e.g. Figure 6 (a) and (b) and collect all the small pieces of watermark picture. When one picture stops, a new picture always starts. It means that these pictures are not having over-end points. Vertical and horizontal axes of final matrix picture have the same rule.

Now Scan xy Where x = number of rows, y = number of columns. We have the pictures in Fig. 2 of an object with the help of a proposed watermark split algorithm. These pictures are stored in the program folder with the same name given by the proposed watermark split algorithm. This algorithm creates a new empty image frame. With the help of 'for' loop all grayscale images are used. In Matlab, 'imread' function is used to read images.

These empty image frames are composed of the read images & finally, the output image is created.

In Eq. 11, it has been shown in the form of a matrix.

$$\begin{pmatrix} img[1] & \cdots & img[n] \\ \vdots & \ddots & \vdots \\ img[n] & \cdots & img[n] \end{pmatrix} = \begin{pmatrix} n[k]\,m[l] & \cdots & n[k]\,m[l] \\ \vdots & \ddots & \vdots \\ n[k]\,m[l] & \cdots & n[k]\,m[l] \end{pmatrix} \qquad (11)$$

$$= \left[\sum_{i=1}^{n} n_i[k] \ \sum_{i=1}^{n} m_i[k] \right]$$

In our example we have taken a watermark image that has the dimension of 256×256 and we obtain total no of scene changed frames 77 and 97 for Foreman video and Car race video respectively. Here we have been extracted all the watermark blocks from foreman video and car race video with the help of the watermark detection algorithm. After getting all the watermark blocks, we have been merged them with the help of Eq. 11.

Table 2. Video PSNR (In dB) after watermarking

Sequence	Average PSNR	Maximum PSNR	Minimum PSNR
Foreman	53.29	59.14	50.31
Car_Race	50.09	56.64	49.85

The PSNR (Peak Signal to Noise Ratio) is known for distinguishing between the original and watermarked video. If the PSNR of watermarked video is high, it means the original and watermarked videos are same (Fig. 7).

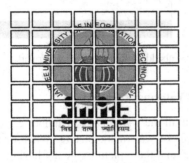

Fig. 7. Extracted watermark blocks and merged watermark.

So we can say that the watermark is not visible. In Table 2 we calculate the average, maximum and minimum PSNR of foreman video after embedding (8 × 8) watermark in all identical frames.

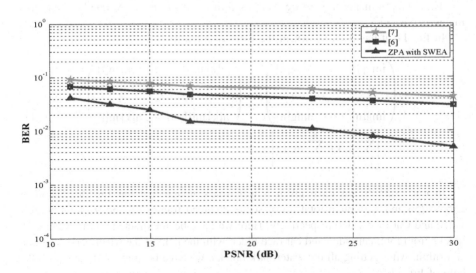

Fig. 8. BER (log scale) under spatial attack (Uniform noise)

In the Figs. 8, 9, 10 and 11, we have shown the robustness against spatial attack (Uniform Noise & Gaussian Noise) and temporal attacks (Frame swapping & Frame repetition) and compared our results with [6] and [7].

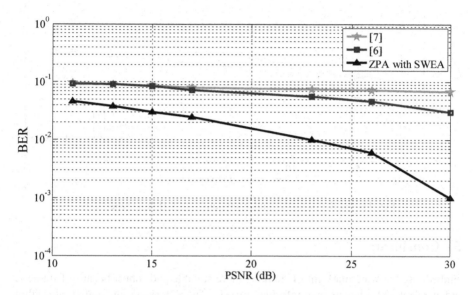

Fig. 9. BER (log scale) under spatial attack (Gaussian noise)

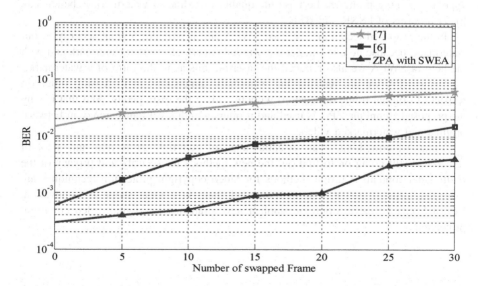

Fig. 10. BER (log scale) under temporal attack (Frame Swapping)

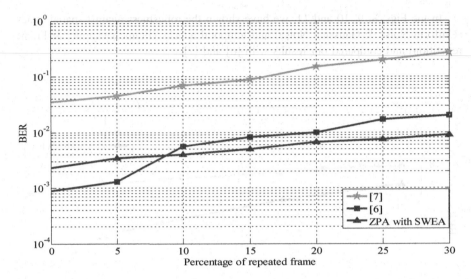

Fig. 11. BER (log scale) under temporal attack (Frame repetition)

5   Conclusion

Embedding the watermark into I-frame is more suitable and robust because I frame is independent and it has its own information only. The watermark embedding algorithm based on I-frame, entrenches watermark only in I-frame but simultaneously it guarantees the knowledge of the embedded watermark to each GOP. The proposed approach is more proficient because the quality of extracted watermark is better than [6, 7] in terms of PSNR and BER.

In the proposed technique we used SWEA and it provides a great security to our watermark, because no one can get the original pattern of inserted watermark and with the help of SWEA we also reduced the inserting bits as in the form of a watermark.

Using ZPA we are resizing the watermark dimensions in increasing order (in respect of original frame dimension) without adding the extra pixels. And that is why the proposed technique ZPA is used and it offers a high level transparency in between original and watermarked video.

Video watermarking is an essential need of copyright protection and a lot of research is still going on to find out the new methods for security and privacy of the multimedia contents. Current methods for video copyright protection techniques are extended form of image watermarking and there is a great scope of innovation. Research can be carried out to establish new strategies for digital video copyright protection.

References

1. Totcharova, P., et al.: The ABC of copyright. In: International Copyright and Related Right Protection by United Nation Educational Scientific and Cultural Organization
2. Langlaar, C., et al.: Watermarking digital image and video data. IEEE Signal Process. Mag. **17**, 20–46 (2000)
3. Cox, I.J., et al.: Digital Watermarking and Steganography, 2nd edn. Morgan Kauffman, San Mateo (2008)
4. Bhattacharya, S., et al.: A survey on different video watermarking techniques and comparative analysis with reference to H.264/AVC. In: IEEE Tenth International Symposium on Consumer Electronics, ISCE 2006, pp. 1–6. IEEE (2006)
5. Murshid, A., et al.: Blind compressed video watermarking in DCT domain robust against global geometric attacks. In: Proceeding of the International Cryptology Workshop and Conference (2008)
6. Khalilian, H., et al.: Video watermarking with empirical PCA-based decoding. IEEE Trans. Image Process. **22**(12), 4825–4840 (2013)
7. Huang, H., et al.: A video watermarking technique based on pseudo-3D DCT and quantization index modulation. IEEE Trans. Inf. Forensics Secur. **5**(4), 625–637 (2010)
8. Khalilian, H., et al.: Digital video watermarking in 3D ridgelet domain. In: Proceedings of the 11th ICACT, vol. 3, pp. 1643–1646, February 2009
9. Gandhe, S., et al.: Dual watermarking in video using discrete wavelet transform. In: Second International Conference on Machine Vision, ICMV 2009, pp. 216 –219, December 2009
10. Shahraray, B.: Scene change detection and content-based sampling of video sequences. In: SPIE 2419 (Digital Video Compression: Algorithms and Technologies), pp. 2–13 (1995)
11. Campisi, P., Neri, A.: Perceptual video watermarking in the 3D-DWT domain using a multiplicative approach. In: Barni, M., Cox, I., Kalker, T., Kim, H.-J. (eds.) IWDW 2005. LNCS, vol. 3710, pp. 432–443. Springer, Heidelberg (2005). https://doi.org/10.1007/11551492_33
12. Chan, P.-W., Lyu, M.R.: A DWT-based digital video watermarking scheme with error correcting code. In: Qing, S., Gollmann, D., Zhou, J. (eds.) ICICS 2003. LNCS, vol. 2836, pp. 202–213. Springer, Heidelberg (2003). https://doi.org/10.1007/978-3-540-39927-8_19
13. Yeo, B., et al.: Rapid scene change detection on compressed video. IEEE Trans. Circuits Syst. Video Technol. **5**(6), 533–544 (1995)
14. Hartung, F., et al.: Watermarking of uncompressed and compressed video. Signal Process. **66**(3), 283–301 (1998)
15. Hampapur, A., et al.: Digital video segmentation. In: Limb, J., Blattner, M. (eds.) Proceedings of the Second Annual ACM Multimedia Conference and Exposition, pp 357–364. ACM, New York (1994)
16. Akhaee, M.A., et al.: Contourlet based image watermarking using optimum detector in a noisy environment. IEEE Trans. Image Process. **19**(4), 967–980 (2010)
17. Yeung, M.M., Liu, B.: Efficient matching and clustering of video. In: IEEE International Conference on Image Processing, Piscataway, NJ, USA, vol. 1, pp. 338–341, October 1995
18. Park, J.Y., et al.: Invertible semi-fragile watermarking algorithm distinguishing MPEG-2 compression from malicious manipulation. In: International Conference on Consumer Electronics, pp. 18–19, June 2002
19. Shieh, J., et al.: A semi-blind digital watermarking scheme based on singular value decomposition. Comput. Stand. Interfaces **28**(4), 428–440 (2006)
20. Al-Khatib, T., et al.: A robust video watermarking algorithm. J. Comput. Sci. **4**(11), 6–9 (2004)

21. Ming, B.: Digital watermarking embedding and attacking. Sci. Technol. Inf. (8), 50–51 (2008)
22. Wang, Y., et al.: A wavelet-based watermarking algorithm for ownership verification of digital images. IEEE Trans. Image Process. 11(2), 77–88 (2002)
23. Wang, Y., et al.: A blind MPEG-2 video watermarking robust against geometric attacks: a set of approaches in DCT domain. IEEE Trans. Image Process. 15(6), 1536–1543 (2006)
24. Lin, et al.: An embedded watermark technique in video for copyright protection. In: Proceedings of the International Conference on Pattern Recognition, vol. 4, pp. 795–798 (2006)
25. Ganic, E., et al.: Robust DWT-SVD domain image watermarking: embedding data in all frequencies. In: Proceedings of the ACM Multimedia and Security Workshop, pp. 166–174 (2004)
26. Niu, X., et al.: A new wavelet-based digital watermarking for video. In: Proceedings of the IEEE Digital Signal Processing Workshop, Texas, pp. 1–6 (2000)

Optimal Camera Placement for Multimodal Video Summarization

Vishal Parikh[✉], Priyanka Sharma, Vedang Shah, and Vijay Ukani

Institute of Technology, Nirma University, Ahmedabad, India
{vishalparikh,priyanka.sharma,15mcei26,
vijay.ukani}@nirmauni.ac.in

Abstract. Video Surveillance systems are used to monitor, observe and intercept the changes in activities, features and behavior of objects, people or places. A multimodal surveillance system incorporates a network of video cameras, acoustic sensors, pressure sensors, IR sensors and thermal sensors to capture the features of the entity under surveillance, and send the recorded data to a base station for further processing. Multimodal surveillance systems are utilized to capture the required features and use them for pattern recognition, object identification, traffic management, object tracking, and so on. The proposal is to develop an efficient camera placement algorithm for deciding placement of multiple video cameras at junctions and intersections in a multimodal surveillance system which will be capable of providing maximum coverage of the area under surveillance, which will leads to complete elimination or reduction of blind zones in a surveillance area, maximizing the view of subjects, and minimizing occlusions in high vehicular traffic areas. Furthermore, the proposal is to develop a video summarization algorithm which can be used to create summaries of the videos captured in a multi-view surveillance system. Such a video summarization algorithm can be used further for object detection, motion tracking, traffic segmentation, etc. in a multi-view surveillance system.

Keywords: Multimodal surveillance · Multiview video summarization
Camera placement

1 Introduction

Video surveillance systems deal with monitoring, intercepting or observing activities, behavior, or any other changing information related to people, places or things. Video surveillance systems have evolved over three generations of surveillance systems namely, analog surveillance systems, digital surveillance systems, and smart/intelligent surveillance systems. Nowadays network of various surveillance video sensors/cameras are everywhere. Figure 1 shows an example of a video sensor/camera network, with overlapping as well as non-overlapping fields of view. Multimodal surveillance systems in intelligent transportation systems have a wide application area and has been an emerging field of research. A multimodal surveillance system normally consists of a wireless sensor network of video/image sensors, audio sensors, pressure sensors, thermal sensors and position sensors. Apart from these, some recent advances in sensor hardware includes, an embedded data processing algorithm which is used to process the

© Springer Nature Singapore Pte Ltd. 2019
P. K. Singh et al. (Eds.): FTNCT 2018, CCIS 958, pp. 123–134, 2019.
https://doi.org/10.1007/978-981-13-3804-5_10

data captured by the sensor and send it to a base station. The placement of different video sensors/cameras are very important. The main idea in multimodal scenario is: weather we get an idea of which camera/sensor has captured an important video content without watching all the videos of all sensors/cameras entirely.

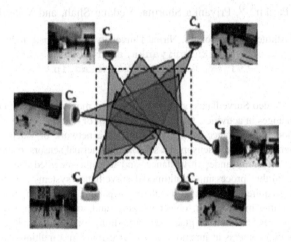

Fig. 1. Illustration of multi-view camera network [3]

Sufficient progress has been made in summarizing a single video. Comprehensive reviews in video summarization can be found in [1] and [2]. Truong et al. in [1] gives two ways in which video can be summarized, a key-frame sequence and a video skim. Nowadays multiview video summarization is gaining popularity as there are number of video sensors/cameras deployed which covers overlapping region. The contribution of our work can be summarized as a video sensor/camera placement strategy for surveillance in intelligent transport system, and also we propose a key-frame based summarization technique to preserve both intra and inter view correlation for MPEG-4 or H.264(AVC) videos for generating video summaries.

2   Related Works

While the goal of many optimal camera placement strategies has been to minimize the overlapping views; with respect to the objective of the proposed system, overlapping views were necessary so as to track the complete path of motion of the subjects under surveillance from multiple views, maximize their visibility and maximize the degree of coverage of the surveillance perimeter. Most summarization algorithms work on single-view video, due to redundancy in multi-view video, multiview video summarization is much more comprehensive.

Zouaoui et al. in [4] have proposed a multimodal system composed of two microphones and one camera integrated on-board for video and audio analytic for surveillance. The system relies on the fusion of unusual audio events detection and/or object detection from the captured video sequences. The audio analysis consists of modeling the normal ambience and detecting deviation from the trained models during testing, while the video analysis involves classification according to geometric shape and size. However, even though the system succeeds in detecting robust 3D position of objects, it employs only a single camera for surveillance which does not provide a robust multi-dimensional view of the object of interest.

Wang et al. in [5] have presented a system for detecting and classifying moving vehicles. The system uses video sensors along with Laser Doppler Vibrometer (LDVs) a kind of acoustic sensor for detecting the motion, appearance and acoustic features of the moving vehicles - and later on using the data to classify them.

Magno et al. in [6] have proposed a multimodal low power and low cost video surveillance system based on a CMOS video sensor and a PyroelectricInfraRed (PIR) sensor. In order to control the power consumption, instead of transmitting full image, the sensors only transmit very limited amount of information such as number of objects, trajectory, position, size, etc., thus saving a large amount of energy in wireless transmission and extending the life of the batteries. However nothing is done from the point of view of data transmission and power consumption if the targeted object is not detected. In addition to this, this system is used only for detecting an abandoned or removed object from the perimeter under surveillance and hence there is no proper evidence of its usage in a large-scale, dynamically changing environment.

Gupta et al. in [7] have designed a distributed visual surveillance system for military perimeter surveillance. The system is used to detect potential threats and create actionable intelligence to support expeditionary war fighting for the military base camp by using multimodal wireless sensor network. The system employs certain rule-based algorithms for detection of atomic actions from video. Some of the atomic actions that are automatically detected by the system are: a person appearing in a restricted area, tripwire crossing, a person disappearing from a protected perimeter, a person entering or exiting, leave behind action, loiters, take away action, etc. A geodetic coordinate system is used which provides metric information such as size, distance, speed, and heading of the detected objects for high level inference and inter-sensor object tracking.

Prati et al. in [8] have proposed a PIR sensor based multimodal video surveillance system. In this system PIR sensors are used to bring down the cost of deployment of the surveillance systems and at the same time they are combined with vision systems for precisely detecting the speed and direction of the vehicles along with other complex events.

Rios-Cabrera et al. in [9] have presented an efficient multi-camera vehicle identification, detection and tracking system inside a tunnel. In this system a network of non-overlapping video cameras are used to detect and track the vehicles inside a tunnel by creating a vehicle-fingerprint using the haar features of the vehicles despite poor illumination inside tunnel and low quality images.

Lopatka et al. in [10] have proposed a system for detecting the traffic events which uses special acoustic sensors, pressure sensors and video sensors to record the occurrence of audio-visual events. A use-case of detection of collision of the two cars is demonstrated in this paper. The data collected by the multimodal sensors is sent to a computational cluster in real time for analysis of the traffic events. For this purpose a Real Time Streaming Protocol (RTSP) is used in the system.

Wang et al. in [11] have proposed a large scale video surveillance system for wide area monitoring which has capability of monitoring and tracking a moving object in a widely open area using an embedded component on the camera for detailed visualization of objects on a 2D/3D interface. In addition to this, it is also capable of detecting illegal parking and identifies the drivers face from the illegal parking event.

van den Hengel et al. in [12] have proposed a genetic algorithm for automatic placement of multiple surveillance cameras which is used to optimize the coverage of cameras in large-scale surveillance systems and at the same find overlapping views between cameras if necessary. Yildiz et al. in [13] have presented a bilevel algorithm to determine an optimal camera placement with maximum angular coverage for a WSN of homogeneous and heterogeneous cameras. Zhao et al. in [14] have presented two binary integer programming (BIP) algorithms for finding optimal camera placement and network configuration. Moreover they have extended the proposed framework to include visual tagging of subjects in the surveillance environments. Liu et al. in [15] have presented a Multi-Modal Particle Filter technique to track vehicles from different views (frontal, rear and side view). In addition to this they have also discussed a technique for occlusion handling in surveillance systems.

Denman et al. in [16] have presented a system for automatic monitoring and tracking of vehicles in real time using optical flow modules and motion detection from videos captures by four video cameras. Wang et al. in [17] have proposed an effective foreground object detection technique for surveillance systems by estimating the conditional probability densities for both the foreground and background objects using feature extraction techniques and temporal video filtering. Zheng et al. in [18] have proposed a key-frame selection technique based on motion-feature based approach in which motion information for each key-frame from the traffic surveillance video stream is computed in a GPU based system and key-frames with motion information greater than their neighbors are selected. By implementing GPU based processing capabilities, the authors have shown a significant increase in the accuracy and processing speed of the algorithm.

Panda et al. in [19] have proposed a novel sparse representative selection method for summarizing multi-view videos, that is videos captured from multiple cameras. They have used inter-view and intra-view similarities between the feature descriptors of each view for modelling multi-view correlations. Kuanar et al. in [20] have proposed a bipartite matching method for multi-view correlation of features like visual bag of words, texture, color, etc. and extracting frames for summarization of multi-view videos. In this method the authors have used Optimum-Path Forest algorithm for clustering the intra-view dependencies and removing intra-view redundancies. Liu et al. in [21] have proposed a unique method for visualizing object trajectories in multi-camera videos and creating video summaries of suspicious movements in a building.

3   Optimal Camera Placement in Multimodal Surveillance System

Many large-scale multimodal surveillance systems have used human experts for camera selection and placement, however such a technique is not capable to effectively design a system while considering the multitude of factors. Also a straightforward method to deploy the video cameras would be to deploy them uniformly around the surveillance area. However, in real-world deployment scenarios, such a method of uniform placement is not practical, since the placement of cameras is restricted by many constraints like costs, availability, visibility, applicability, feasibility, and other factors. This study has investigated the effect of all the factors listed above, and an optimal camera placement strategy has been designed which satisfies all these factors.

Figure 2 gives the coverage of a video camera C in three-dimensional space. With reference to the Fig. 2, point V is the position of the video camera V(x, y, z) and point G indicates the centre of gravity for the video camera V. The four points A, B, C and D are the extreme points in the FOV of V and can be computed using horizontal AOV, vertical AOV and position of the video camera. These points also form the base plane of the rectangular pyramid. Point X is an arbitrary point present in the FOV of video camera V which is to be observed using V.

The volume of the rectangular pyramid formed by the points {V, A, B, C, D} (that is the volume of the coverage area of the camera C) is given by the Eq. 1,

$$V_c = \frac{l * b * h}{3} \tag{1}$$

where h is height of apex from the base.

Now since X is an arbitrary point inside the FOV of V, it forms four tetrahedrons with the four sides of the pyramid and point V as the apex. Volume of each such tetrahedron is given by the Eq. 2,

$$V_i = \frac{\sqrt{2} * Area_{base} * h}{12} \tag{2}$$

where h is height of apex from the base and i = 1 to 4.

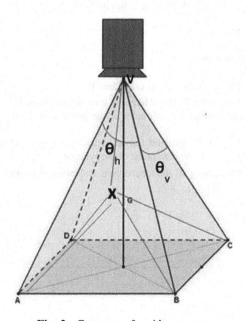

Fig. 2. Coverage of a video camera

Consider V_{total} as the total volume computed by adding volumes of all the four tetrahedrons and pyramid created with X as the apex. V_{total} is given by the Eq. 3,

$$V_{total}^X = V_{base} + \sum V_i \tag{3}$$

for all i = 1 to 4 in Eq. 3, V_{base} is the volume of pyramid with point X as apex and points A, B, C, D as the base plane. The Eq. 4 is used to test the presence of a point X within the FOV of a video camera C whose coverage area can be modelled as a rectangular pyramid of volume V, and returns true or false accordingly.

$$FOV(C,X) = \begin{pmatrix} true, & if\ V_c = V_{total}^X \\ false & \end{pmatrix} \tag{4}$$

Algorithm 1 depicts systematic steps for calculating optimal camera placement in a multimodal surveillance system. This algorithm can be used to decide the placement of multiple cameras at intersections, junctions and crossroads and achieve the best possible coverage of the surveillance area.

Algorithm 1 Optimal Camera Placement

$C_i(x,y,z)$

Require: Surveillance area P of size LxBxH

                 Cameras C_i, where i = 1 to 4

1: Initialization

2: Find midpoint M_j for each side of the region LxB of P and divide the region LxB of P into four equal regions R_i; where i = 1 to 4

3: **for** i = 1 to 4 **do**

4:      For region R_i, midpoints M_j on the adjacent edges of R_i and camera C_i, find $C_i(x,y,z)$ using **function** FOV(C_i,M_j) such that $C_i(x,y,z)$ lies inside $R_i(x,y,z)$

5: **end for**

6: **function:** FOV(C_i,M_j)

7:      **Input:** $C_i(x,y,z), M_j$

8:      **Output:** TRUE/FALSE

9:      $result$ = FALSE

10:      For camera C_i find volume of its coverage area V_i

11:      For point M_j find individually volume of four tetrahedrons $V_n^{M_j}$ formed by M_j with $C_i(x,y,z)$ as apex and each of the four sides of the coverage area of $C_i(x,y,z)$, where n =1 to 4

12:      Find volume $V_{base}^{M_j}$ of the pyramid formed with M_j as apex and the base plane of the coverage area of $C_i(x,y,z)$ as the base plane of the pyramid

13:      Find the total volumes of all the tetrahedrons and pyramid created with M_j as: $V_{total}^{M_j} = V_{base}^{M_j} + \sum V_n^{M_j}$, where n = 1 to 4

14:      **if** $V_{total} == V_i$

15:          $result = TRUE$

16:      **end if**

17:      **return** $result$

18: **end function**

---

4   Experimental Results and Discussion

4.1   Simulation Environment and Parameters

The optimal camera placement Algorithm discussed previously was simulated in OMNET++ Network Simulator. Table 1 lists the simulation parameters that were considered while checking the results and validity of the algorithm.

The network topology was configured in a way that each video camera would be placed randomly inside or on the edges of the one-fourth part of the surveillance area as shown in the Fig. 3, since the surveillance area is divided into four equal parts. Also as mentioned in the algorithm, each camera needed to have two midpoints of adjacent sides in their FOV to have the best possible coverage of the surveillance area.

Table 1. Simulation parameters for optimal camera placement algorithm

Parameter	Value
Simulation time	300 s
Surveillance area	25 m × 20 m × Depth of surveillance area (mentioned below)
Depth of surveillance area	10 m to 15 m
Number of video cameras	4
Focal length	4.0 mm
AOV of each camera	90 to 120
Camera deployment (co-ordinates in three dimensional space)	Random

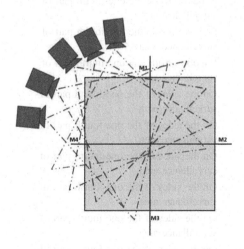

Fig. 3. Surveillance area with various possible camera placements

4.2   Results

During the simulation, the cameras were placed randomly inside each one-fourth part of the surveillance area, near the midpoints and on the vertex joining the two edges. At any moment of time, the AOV and Depth of Field of each camera was fixed and identical, though it was selected randomly from the range specified in Table 1.

The results of the simulation are presented in Table 2. From the results, it can be inferred that the best placement for all the cameras in a multimodal surveillance system is near the vertex joining any two edges of the surveillance area. It can also be derived that higher depth of field and wider angle of view produces better region coverage for a surveillance camera leaving less than 5% of area uncovered. However, since all the cameras have overlapping views, it is possible to achieve better coverage of the whole area leaving very less to zero blind spots. The Fig. 4, shows the best placement for video cameras in a multimodal surveillance system from the result derived using the optimal placement algorithm discussed in Algorithm 1.

Table 2.   Simulation results for optimal camera placement algorithm

AOV (degree)	DOF (m)	Camera placement	Area covered (%)
90	10	Random-inside the one-fourth part of surveillance area	29
90	11	Random-inside the one-fourth part of surveillance area	34
100	12	Random-inside the one-fourth part of surveillance area	45
100	13	Random-inside the one-fourth part of surveillance area	50
105	14	Random-inside the one-fourth part of surveillance area	48
100	15	Random-inside the one-fourth part of surveillance area	53
90	10	On the sides of the one-fourth part of surveillance area	43
95	11	On the sides of the one-fourth part of surveillance area	50
110	12	On the sides of the one-fourth part of surveillance area	61
100	13	On the sides of the one-fourth part of surveillance area	70
105	14	On the sides of the one-fourth part of surveillance area	73
120	15	On the sides of the one-fourth part of surveillance area	74
95	10	Near the midpoints	23

(continued)

Table 2. (*continued*)

AOV (degree)	DOF (m)	Camera placement	Area covered (%)
110	11	Near the midpoints	28
120	12	Near the midpoints	39
100	13	Near the midpoints	38
100	14	Near the midpoints	27
95	15	Near the midpoints	24
95	10	At the vertices joining the two edges	94
110	11	At the vertices joining the two edges	97
105	12	At the vertices joining the two edges	95
120	13	At the vertices joining the two edges	98
105	14	At the vertices joining the two edges	95
120	15	At the vertices joining the two edges	97

4.3 Video Summarization

The Ko-PER Intersection Dataset [22] that comprises of highly accurate reference trajectories of cars, raw laser scanner measurements, undistorted monochrome camera images has being used. From this dataset, four videos were generated of varying GOP size N = 8, 16, 24 and 30 with a constant frame rate of 30 fps and were encoded using

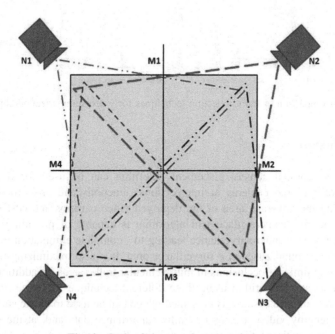

Fig. 4. Optimal camera placement design

the H.264 or MPEG-4 Part 10, Advanced Video Coding (AVC) standard. These different videos were used to check the performance of each frame selection technique individually. The graph presented in Fig. 5 shows the comparison of the total execution times of the proposed three frame selection techniques for video summarization. It is evident from the graph that, with increase in GOP size, the execution time of the algorithms increases. By using any of the technique of frame selection for video summarization, the duration of the final summarized video is same, since no key-frames have been dropped in the process, and hence all the three techniques are suitable to create video summaries without the loss of important contextual information from the video.

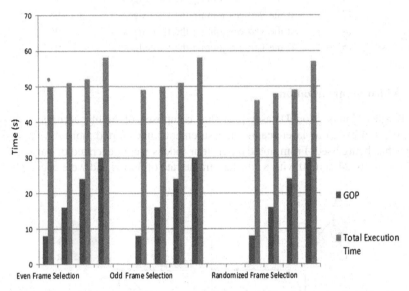

Fig. 5. Comparison of frame selection techniques for video summarization algorithm

5   Conclusion

The proposed optimal camera placement algorithm can be used for deciding the placement of multiple cameras at intersections, junctions and cross-roads without compromising the coverage area of the deployed video cameras and cost of deployment. This optimal camera placement algorithm is capable of providing maximum coverage of the area under surveillance leading to - complete elimination or reduction of the number of blind zones in a surveillance area. It is also maximizing the view of subjects and minimizing occlusions in high vehicular traffic areas. In addition to this, a video summarization algorithm using three different techniques of frame selection for multi-view surveillance systems is presented which can be used to create summaries of large-sized, lengthy video streams of traffic surveillance data and, at the same time reduce the computational processing for creating the video summaries. Collectively, both the proposed algorithms will be able to reduce the cost of camera deployment, computational cost, power consumption and, provide efficient performance in a multi-view, as well as multimodal surveillance system.

References

1. Truong, B.T., Venkatesh, S.: Video abstraction: a systematic review and classification. ACM Trans. Multimed. Comput. Commun. Appl. (TOMM) **3**(1), 3 (2007)
2. Money, A.G., Agius, H.: Video summarisation: a conceptual framework and survey of the state of the art. J. Vis. Commun. Image Represent. **19**(2), 121–143 (2008)
3. Panda, R., Roy-Chowdhury, A.K.: Multi-view surveillance video summarization via joint embedding and sparse optimization. IEEE Trans. Multimed. **19**, 2010–2021 (2017)
4. Zouaoui, R., et al.: Embedded security system for multi-modal surveillance in a railway carriage. In: Proceedings of SPIE, January 2016
5. Wang, T., Zhu, Z.: Multimodal and multi-task audio-visual vehicle detection and classification. In: 2012 IEEE Ninth International Conference on Advanced Video and Signal-Based Surveillance (AVSS), pp. 440–446, September 2012
6. Magno, M., Tombari, F., Brunelli, D., Stefano, L.D., Benini, L.: Multimodal abandoned/removed object detection for low power video surveillance systems. In: Sixth IEEE International Conference on Advanced Video and Signal Based Surveillance, AVSS 2009, pp. 188–193, September 2009
7. Gupta, H., Yu, L., Hakeem, A., Choe, T.E., Haering, N.: Multimodal complex event detection framework for wide area surveillance. In: CVPR 2011 Workshops, pp. 47–54, June 2011
8. Prati, A., Vezzani, R., Benini, L., Farella, E., Zappi, P.: An integrated multi-modal sensor network for video surveillance. In: Proceedings of the Third ACM International Workshop on Video Surveillance & Sensor Networks, pp. 95–102 (2005)
9. Rios-Cabrera, R., Tuytelaars, T., Gool, L.V.: Efficient multi-camera vehicle detection, tracking, and identification in a tunnel surveillance application. Comput. Vis. Image Underst. **116**, 742–753 (2012)
10. Lopatka, K., Kotus, J., Szczodrak, M., Marcinkowski, P., Korzeniewski, A., Czyzewski, A.: Multimodal audio-visual recognition of traffic events. In: 2011 22nd International Workshop on Database and Expert Systems Applications, pp. 376–380, August 2011
11. Wang, Y.K., Fan, C.T., Huang, C.R.: A large scale video surveillance system with heterogeneous information fusion and visualization for wide area monitoring. In: 2012 Eighth International Conference on Intelligent Information Hiding and Multimedia Signal Processing (IIH-MSP), pp. 178–181, July 2012
12. van den Hengel, A., et al.: Automatic camera placement for large scale surveillance networks. In: 2009 Workshop on Applications of Computer Vision (WACV), pp. 1–6, December 2009
13. Yildiz, E., Akkaya, K., Sisikoglu, E., Sir, M.Y.: Optimal camera placement for providing angular coverage in wireless video sensor networks. IEEE Trans. Comput. **63**, 1812–1825 (2014)
14. Zhao, J., Cheung, S.C., Nguyen, T.: Optimal camera network configurations for visual tagging. IEEE J. Sel. Top. Signal Process. **2**, 464–479 (2008)
15. Liu, L., Xing, J., Ai, H.: Multi-view vehicle detection and tracking in crossroads. In: The First Asian Conference on Pattern Recognition, pp. 608–612, November 2011

16. Denman, S., et al.: Multi-view intelligent vehicle surveillance system. In: 2006 IEEE International Conference on Video and Signal Based Surveillance, p. 26, November 2006
17. Wang, K., Liu, Y., Gou, C., Wang, F.Y.: A multi-view learning approach to foreground detection for traffic surveillance applications. IEEE Trans. Veh. Technol. **65**, 4144–4158 (2016)
18. Zheng, R., Yao, C., Jin, H., Zhu, L., Zhang, Q., Deng, W.: Parallel key frame extraction for surveillance video service in a smart city, vol. 10, pp. 1–8, August 2015
19. Panda, R., Dasy, A., Roy-Chowdhury, A.K.: Video summarization in a multi-view camera network. In: 2016 23rd International Conference on Pattern Recognition (ICPR), pp. 2971–2976, December 2016
20. Kuanar, S.K., Ranga, K.B., Chowdhury, A.S.: Multi-view video summarization using bipartite matching constrained optimum-path forest clustering. IEEE Trans. Multimed. **17**, 1166–1173 (2015)
21. Liu, S., Lai, S.: Schematic visualization of object trajectories across multiple cameras for indoor surveillances. In: 2009 Fifth International Conference on Image and Graphics, pp. 406–411, September 2009
22. Krause, J., Stark, M., Deng, J., Fei-Fei, L.: The ko-per intersection laserscanner and video dataset. In: 17th International IEEE Conference on Intelligent Transportation Systems (ITSC), pp. 1900–1901, October 2014

Internet of Things (IoT)

Future Perspectives in Elastic Optical Networks

Suresh Kumar[(✉)] and Deepak Sharma

Department of Electronics and Communication Engineering,
University Institute of Engineering and Technology,
Maharshi Dayanand University, Rohtak, Haryana, India
skvashist_16@yahoo.com, d.29deepak@gmail.com

Abstract. The new generation Elastic Optical Networks (EONs) based on Orthogonal Frequency Division Multiplexing (OFDM) can accommodate exponentially increasing heterogeneous data traffic efficiently and economically. In EONs, the optimum channel spacing between various subcarriers is very crucial for its efficient performance. The use of Sub-Carrier Multiplexing (SCM) in EONs is visualized as an evolving field. This paper present the evaluation of SCM based EONs for both mathematical and simulative model. The designed SCM-EON network is analytically evaluated for its performance with different modulation techniques (Direct Modulation and External Modulation). The performance of system is also evaluated for amplification using Semiconductor Optical Amplifier (SOA) and Erbium Doped Fiber Amplifier (EDFA). Simulative results show that Optical Phase Modulation (OPM) along with EDFA offers enhanced performance for the proposed model. It has also been observed that OPM is a better technique for SCM and hence it can be deduced that the combination will boost EONs efficiency in handling network resources.

Keywords: Elastic Optical Networks · OFDM
Quadrature Amplitude Modulation (QAM) · SCM · EDFA · OPM
Mach-Zehnder modulator (MZM)
Bandwidth variable-wavelength cross-connects (BV-WXC)
Coherent Optical Orthogonal Frequency Division Multiplexing (CO-OFDM)

1 Introduction

The recent growth in digital multimedia applications has triggered the growth of internet data traffic volume at an exponential rate. The traditional WDM technique allocates entire wavelength to a connection even if the traffic demand is low and entire grid is not necessary [1, 2]. WDM networks have mainly been used in optical backbone and are not found capable of accommodating heterogeneous traffic [3, 4]. To accommodate heterogeneous traffic volume, recently OFDM based EONs have been proposed. EONs make the spectrum flexible and offers improved spectral efficiency when compared with WDM networks [5, 6]. SCM based system provides optimal use of entire bandwidth of the fiber, provides flexibility in the optical network design while

© Springer Nature Singapore Pte Ltd. 2019
P. K. Singh et al. (Eds.): FTNCT 2018, CCIS 958, pp. 137–151, 2019.
https://doi.org/10.1007/978-981-13-3804-5_11

enhancing the transmission capacity. SCM provides various advantages and is used extensively in applications like RoF networks & microwave photonic systems.

In this paper, a designed network model of SCM based EONs along with detailed description of its various enabling components has been presented. Further, using mathematical and simulative models the performance of the proposed model has been analyzed on the basis of received output power with different amplifiers, modulation schemes and increased spacing between channels frequency and also with variation in input modulating frequency. Section 2 provides a brief description of EONs, their design and related work. The mathematical modeling of SCM based optical network for different modulation scheme is described in Sect. 3. Section 4 demonstrates the design and simulation setup followed by results and discussion in Sect. 5.

2   EON

EONs are OFDM-based networks and have been proposed recently as an alternative to traditional networks. EONs are spectrum efficient networks, composed of flexible trans-receiver with adaptable network elements [7, 8]. Unlike WDM system, the use of OFDM allows subcarrier of the same light-path to overlap. Thereby leads to high spectrum efficiency. The authors in [1] have presented a detailed description of EONs and its various enabling components. The authors have also highlighted various advantages of EONs over traditional optical networks. The term elastic in EONs refers to three key properties of the optical networks.

(1) Flexible optical spectrum
(2) Bandwidth variable Transponder (BVT)
(3) BV-WXC.

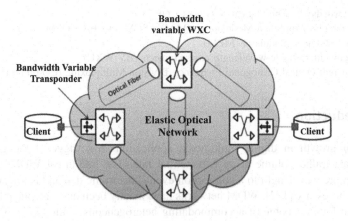

Fig. 1. Basic architecture of EON [8]

Figure 1 shows the basic architecture of EONs. OFDM together with BVT and BV-WXC paved the way for elastic allocation of spectral resources. BV-WXC at each node uses bandwidth variable wavelength select switches (BV-WSS). Figure 2 shows the basic functions of BV-WSS. BV-WSS is a flexible spectrum selective switch and uses an integrated spatial optics such as a diffraction grating which performs multiplexing and de-multiplexing.

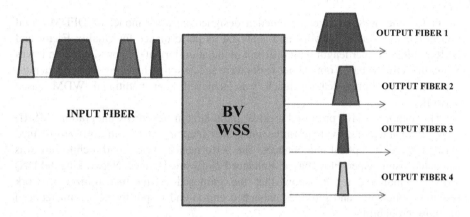

Fig. 2. A bandwidth variable–wavelength select switch

BVT generates optical signal with optimum spectrum usage. Various subcarrier channels are combined into a single super-channel using OFDM and transported as an individual OFDM channel, hence making these networks more efficient.

Figure 3 depicts various characteristics of EONs over traditional optical networks. EONs support flexible bandwidth granularity, fractional data rates and variable traffic by enabling the concept of sub-wavelength & super wavelength.

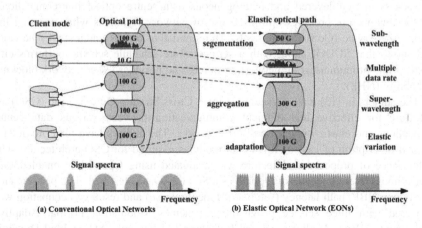

Fig. 3. Spectrum assignment over (a) conventional optical networks with rigid frequency grid (b) EONs

In traditional WDM networks, the optical bandwidth is wasted due to frequency spacing for guards bands even for low bit rate signals. EONs support multiple data rates and thereby have the ability to provide high spectrum efficiency through flexible spectrum allocation and hence improve spectrum utilization over WDM networks. EONs have a unique property to save power consumption as it turns off unused OFDM subcarriers.

In [9], the authors have presented a designed network model of OFDM based optical communication network and analyzed its performance for Quality Factor and BER at different fiber length with different modulation formats. Upon simulation it was found that OFDM based optical networks were successful in handling higher data rates and extended communication reach was achieved over traditional WDM based networks.

The authors in [10] proposed a novel multi-stratum resources integration (MSRI) architecture integrated with resource integrated mapping (RIM) in software defined elastic data center optical interconnect. The performance of proposed architecture was evaluated using Open-Flow-based Enhanced Software Defined Networking (eSDN) testbed. Simulative results show that the proposed architecture utilizes network resources efficiently and provides enhanced end-to-end responsiveness with reduced blocking probability.

In [11], the authors have presented novel strategies for project IDEALIST to remove data plane bandwidth constraints for efficient handling of exponentially increasing data traffic. The authors used BVT, BV-WSS and novel node architecture for creating flexibility in handling network resources. The performance of proposed model was analyzed using DSP technique and advanced power saving modulation formats using open flow optical module. Upon simulation, results shows that the proposed design can handle dynamic traffic with improved flexibility and scalability.

The author in [12] have presented a novel Software Defined Networking for Ubiquitous Data Center Optical Interconnection (SUDOI) architecture for widespread user access in multilayered and heterogeneous data centre optical interconnections. SUDOI architecture provides optimized use of network resources while meeting the Quality of Service (QoS) requirements. The simulative results under heavy network load shows that SUDOI along with a service-aware schedule scheme performs efficiently with optimum usage of network resources and provides lesser network blocking probability (NBP).

The authors in [13] have presented a novel Cross Stratum Optimization (CSO) architecture for effective and efficient communication between various data center applications and elastic optical transport networks. The authors have also provided a detailed description of various functional modules required for CSO architecture. The performance of proposed architecture was evaluated using Open-Flow enabled four optical nodes over Objective of Optical as a Service (OaaS) test-bed. The performance based upon NBP, path latency (setup/adjustment/release) and resource occupation was compared with three service provisioning schemes Modulation Format Adaptive Adjustment (MFA), Application Load Balancing (ALB), and CSO-enabled Dynamic Global Load Balancing (CSO-DGLB). Simulative result shows that CSO with CSO-DGLB performs efficiently with optimum usage of network resources.

The authors in [14] have proposed a new generation optical network based upon CO-OFDM. CO-OFDM based network uses bandwidth variable ROADMs for optical channel filtering. The authors have done a comprehensive literature survey on CO-OFDM based optical networks and also provided a detailed description of various key issues in design of CO-OFDM such as traffic grooming, routing and spectrum assignment (RSA), control plane management, impact of channel modulation, network survivability and reconfiguration.

In [15], authors have compared the performance of traditional WDM based networks with EONs in multimode dynamic environment for inter data centre environment for communication requiring higher bandwidth. From numerical results it was concluded that WDM technology and EONs outperforms other optical communication technologies. The authors also proposed a Client-Server Assignment based RSA algorithm to assign light paths to clients based upon light path occupancy.

The authors in [16] have presented a comprehensive literature review of sate of art survivable EONs. The paper covers all the related aspects such as spectrum sharing among light paths, sharing of high speed optical transponders, spectrum conversion, bandwidth squeezed restoration multiple sub-band optical channels and energy efficiency related issues. This paper also covers impact of spectrum conversion, elastic optical transponder configuration, impact of physical layer impairments and network availability and path based network defragmentation.

In [17], the authors have presented spectrum allocation algorithm to reduce NBP and node cost for spatially and spectrally all optical networks. The authors classify the spectrum slots into several prioritized areas for connection alignment in dynamic environment. Simulative results show that the proposed algorithm provides better performance with reduced network blocking probability and fragmentation of spectral resources.

Thus, the EONs provide an efficient mechanism to handle the ever increasing traffic demand. Various enabling network architectures and spectrum assignment techniques have been reported in literature to tap benefits of EONs. However, this paper adopts a different approach of using SCM for enhancing bandwidth and transmission efficiency while minimizing non-linear distortions in EONs by using various types of amplifiers, modulation schemes and increased spacing between channels frequency and modulating frequency.

3 SCM: Mathematical Modeling

SCM based system provides optimal use of entire bandwidth of fiber and provides flexibility in the optical network design with enhanced transmission capacity. SCM involves multiplexing of multiple signals which are to be transmitted over a single wavelength in RF domain [18]. However, SCM also suffers from inherent impairments such as dispersion, nonlinear effects such as cross-phase modulation (XPM), four-wave mixing (FWM) and stimulated Raman scattering (SRS).

As shown in Fig. 4(a) to (c), three different block diagrams with different modulation schemes in which different frequencies are combined and modulated through DM, MZM and OPM modulators.

Different wavelengths are combined together using a multiplexer at the transmitter and are split apart at receiver using de-multiplexer. SCM offers various advantages and is used extensively in applications such as RoF networks and microwave photonic systems.

The external modulation technique involves the use of external modulators such as MZM and OPM. External modulation has an advantage over direct modulation as it minimizes the chirp effect and provides better modulated output. However in external modulation using MZM, the DC bias shift problem degrades the stability of output signal.

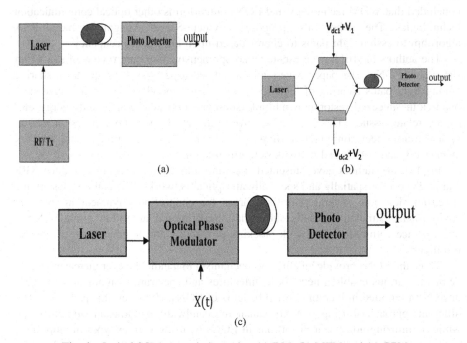

Fig. 4. Optical SCM transmission using (a) DM, (b) MZM and (c) OPM

The received signal can be expressed as

$$X_{DM}(t) = \hat{e}(-\tilde{a}\acute{L}) v_R \dot{c}os(u_R t) \tag{1}$$

Where, amplitude of input signal v_R, u_R is frequency, $\acute{L}$ distance of transmission and $\tilde{a}$ is loss inherent to fiber.

At receiver, resulting photo current given by as

$$\iota_{DM}(t) = R|X_{DM}(t)|^2 \tag{2}$$

Where, R is photo-detector responsivity.

The output signal from MZM modulator is given as:

$$X_d(t) = P_0 \, \hat{e}(jw_d t) \tag{3}$$

Where, P_0 and w_d is the amplitude and angular frequency of laser signal. The RF signal can be expressed as

$$X(t) = v_0[\dot{c}os(w_1 t) + \dot{c}os(w_2 t) + \dot{c}os(w_3 t)] \tag{4}$$

Where, v_0 represent the amplitude.
The modulated signal using MZM modulator can be expressed as

$$\dot{E}_{mzm}(0,t) = \frac{1}{2}\sqrt{2P_{in}}e^{jw_c t}\left\{\hat{e}_J\left[\frac{\pi V_{dc1}}{V_\pi} + \frac{\pi V_1}{V_\pi}\right] + \hat{e}_J\left[\frac{\pi V_{dc2}}{V_\pi} + \frac{\pi V_2}{V_\pi}\right]\right\} \tag{5}$$

Where, w_c represents the carrier frequency, P_{in} is Laser power, v_π represents switching voltage, and the bias voltage at v_{dc1} & v_{dc2} is given by $v_{bias} = v_{dc1} - v_{dc2}$.
On further simplification of Eq. 5 we get

$$\dot{E}_{mzm}(0,t) = \sqrt{2P_{in}}e^{jw_c t}\left\{\hat{e}_J\left[\frac{\pi(v_{dc1}+V_{dc2})}{2v_\pi} + \frac{\pi(v_1+v_2)}{2v_\pi}\right] + \dot{c}os\left[\frac{\pi v_{bias}}{2v_\pi} + \frac{\pi v}{2v_\pi}\right]\right\} \tag{6}$$

The output photocurrent using square law model can be expressed as

$$\iota_{MZM}(t) = R\left|E_{mzm}(\dot{L},t)\right|^2 + 'n(t) \tag{7}$$

Where additive noise is given by $'n(t)$.
The various current components of output current can be expressed as

$$\iota_{MZM}(t) = \iota_{mzm.F}(t) + \iota_{mzm.Im2}(t) + \iota_{mzm.Im3}(t) + 'n(t) \tag{8}$$

$\iota_{mzm.F}(t)$ is the fundamental, $\iota_{mzm.Im2}(t)$ 2nd order, $\iota_{mzm.Im3}(t)$ 3rd order terms respectively.
This signal current after phase shift can be expressed as

$$\iota_{PM}(t) = \Re.\left[\dot{E}_{PM}(t).\dot{E}_{PM}^*(t)\right] \tag{9}$$

Higher orders harmonics can be expressed as

$$\begin{aligned}\iota_{k_1,k_2,k_3} = &\, R(-1)^{k_1+k_2+k_3}\,\hat{e}(jk_2\varphi)\,\hat{e}(j2k_3\varphi)\,\hat{e}[j(k_1 w_1 + k_2 w_2 + k_3 w_3)t] \times\\ &\, J_{k_1}\left(2m\,\dot{s}in\frac{\theta_1}{2}\right) \times J_{k_2}\left(2m\,\dot{s}in\frac{\theta_2}{2}\right) \times J_{k_3}\left(2m\,\dot{s}in\frac{\theta_3}{2}\right)\end{aligned} \tag{10}$$

Where,

$$\theta_1 = \beta_2\dot{L}\,(k_1 w_1^2 + k_2 w_1 w_2 + k_3 w_1 w_3), \quad \theta_2 = \beta_2\dot{L}\,(k_2 w_2^2 + k_1 w_1 w_2 + k_3 w_2 w_3)$$

and

$$\theta_3 = \beta_2 \acute{L} \left(k_3 \mathrm{u}_3{}^2 + k_2 \mathrm{u}_3 \mathrm{u}_2 + k_1 \mathrm{u}_1 \mathrm{u}_3\right).$$

The received k^{th} order harmonic component of optical output signal from three different modulating tones (signals) along the dispersive fiber is represented by Eq. (10). In case of OPM, in order to minimize the unwanted harmonics and IM distortions, the modulation index of OPM modulator is kept at lower values.

4 Design and Simulation

The EONs use OFDM subcarriers to serve variable demands in effective manner. But the use of multiple subcarriers have inherent disadvantage of inter-symbol interference, dispersion and induced non-linear distortions. Till recent times, the SPM effects have been analyzed only for single wavelength links only. In single channel optical system, the energy exchange and impact of presence of dispersion determines the impact of channel power on the maximum transmittable distance, which further depends upon amplitude modulation and phase modulation used.

In this present work, a simulative and mathematical model of SCM-EON model using OFDM modulation is designed and analyzed using Opti-system simulator and MATLAB. The impact of SCM on three independent input sources has been evaluated using three different modulators DM, MZM and OPM.

The transmitter section and receiver sections of designed model are shown in the Fig. 5.

In transmitter section, three input sources are first OFDM modulated and then applied to a power splitter. The power splitter splits the signal in three different signals of equal power. Each splitted signal is then modulated separately using DM, MZM and OPM modulators with individual optical source. The output of different modulators is optically combined and amplified before transmission.

At the receiver, three different optical filters are used for separating individual components of DM, MZM and OPM modulating signal. The three different received signals are splitted into two signals of equal power and are individually amplified using EDFA and SOA. The photo-detector in each branch converts the optical signal into electrical signal. The electrical signal gets analyzed at the receiving end.

The designed model is simulated using optisystem simulator for various values of subcarrier spacing for the input signals. The modulating frequency is varied from 20 to 21 GHz. The inherent MZM and OPM losses are kept at 0 dB and the extinction ratio of MZM is taken as 15 dB. The noise figure, responsivity and channel frequency spacing is 4.5 dB, 09A/W and 1, 2, 3 GHz respectively. The parameters used for simulation are given in Table 1.

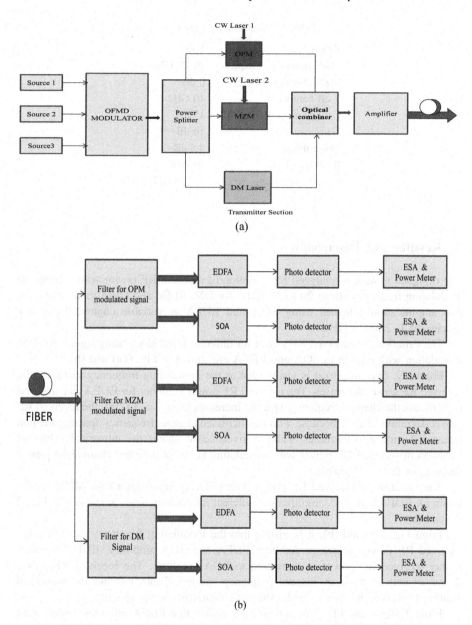

Fig. 5. Proposed designed system transmitter section and receiver section

Table 1. Simulation parameters

Parameter	Value
Modulating tone frequency	20–21 GHz
MZM, OPM losses	0 dB
3 dB bandwidth	40 GHz
Extinction ratio of MZM	15 dB
Gain	16 dB
Noise figure	4.5 dB
Responsivity	09 A/W
Channel spacing	1, 2, 3 GHz

5 Results and Discussion

The designed system is analyzed for variation of received RF power with increase in modulating frequency (from 20 to 21 GHz) for DM, MZM and OPM modulators, for two amplification schemes using SOA and EDFA at variable channel frequency spacing of 1, 2 and 3 GHz.

The variations of received RF power for different input modulating signals for DM modulation with respect to SOA and EDFA are shown in Fig. 6(a) and (b).

From Fig. 6(a) and (b) it is visible that as the modulating frequency increases the received RF power decreases. The received RF power is higher for EDFA as compared to SOA. As the channel frequency spacing increases from 1 to 3 GHz, the received RF power decreases. This is because with the increased channel frequency spacing, the non linear distortion also increases. Table 2 given below shows the numerical values of variation of received RF power with modulating signal at different channel frequency spacing for Direct Modulation.

The variation of received RF power with different input signals for MZM modulation for EDFA and SOA amplifier for different modulating tones are shown in Fig. 7 (a) and (b).

From Fig. 7(a) and (b), it is visible that the modulating frequency increases, the received RF power decreases for both EDFA and SOA amplifier. EDFA provides higher received RF power as compared to SOA amplifier. The received RF power decreases with increase in channel frequency spacing. Table 3 shows the numerical values of received RF power with different channel frequency spacing.

From Table 3 and Fig. 7(a) and (b), it's visible that EDFA provides a significant improvement in the received RF power as compared to SOA. Figure 8 shows variation of the received RF power for OPM modulated signal. As the channel frequency spacing is increased from 1 to 3 GHz, it is observed that the received RF power decreases for both EDFA & SOA.

Table 4 shows the numerical values of received RF power with different channel frequency spacing.

From Tables 2, 3 and 4 and Figs. 6, 7 and 8, with increase in spacing between channel frequencies, there is a reduction in received RF power due to increased non

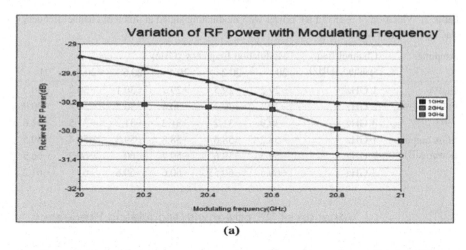

(a)

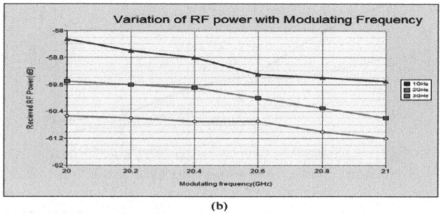

(b)

Fig. 6. Variation of received RF power for DM modulated signal with modulating RF for (a) EDFA and (b) SOA

linear distortions. It is also evident that both external modulation schemes using MZM and OPM provide considerable improvement in received RF power while mitigating non-linear distortions.

In the designed EON model, OPM provides higher received RF power as compared to MZM and Direct Modulation formats. It also achieves suppression of distortions for long-haul optical communication networks. There is a difference of upto 20 dB in the received RF power from EDFA and SOA amplifiers hence it can also be concluded that use of EDFA in EONs outperforms SOA.

Table 2. Variation of received RF power with modulating signal at different channel frequency spacing for Direct Modulation.

Amplifier	Channel freq. spacing (GHz)	Modulation frequency (GHz)					
		20	20.2	20.4	20.6	20.8	21
EDFA output power (dB)	1 GHz	−29.2	−29.5	−29.7	−30.1	−30.2	−30.3
	2 GHz	−30.3	−30.3	−30.4	−30.5	−30.8	−30.9
	3 GHz	−30.9	−31.2	−31.2	−31.2	−31.5	−31.6
SOA output power (dB)	1 GHz	−58.2	−58.6	−58.8	−59.3	−59.4	−59.5
	2 GHz	−59.5	−59.6	−59.7	−60	−60.3	−60.5
	3 GHz	−60.5	−60.53	−60.6	−60.6	−61	−61.2

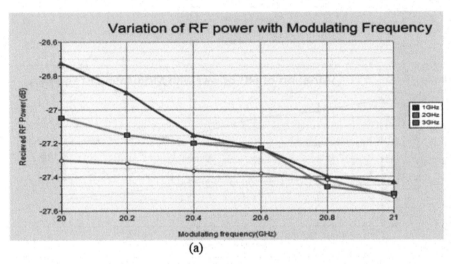

(a)

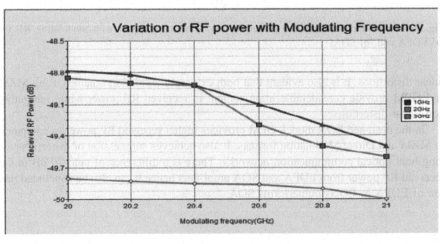

(b)

Fig. 7. Variation of received RF power for MZM modulated signal with modulating RF (a) EDFA and (b) SOA

Table 3. Variation of received RF power with modulating signal at different channel frequency spacing for MZM modulated signal

Amplifier	Channel freq. spacing (GHz)	Modulation frequency (GHz)					
		20	20.2	20.4	20.6	20.8	21
EDFA output power (dB)	1 GHz	−50.5	−50.8	−51.5	−51.8	−52	−52.2
	2 GHz	−52	−52.2	−52.5	−52.8	−53.2	−53.5
	3 GHz	−53.5	−53.7	−53.8	−54	−54.2	−54.5
SOA output power (dB)	1 GHz	−76.8	−77	−77.4	−77.7	−78	−78.2
	2 GHz	−78.2	−78.25	−78.5	−78.9	−79.14	−79.5
	3 GHz	−79.5	−79.8	−79.82	−79.95	−80.1	−80.5

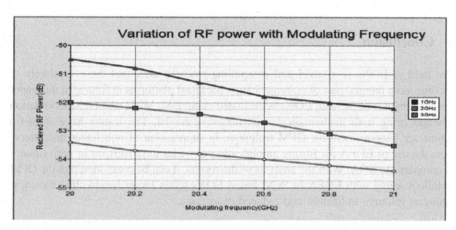

(a)

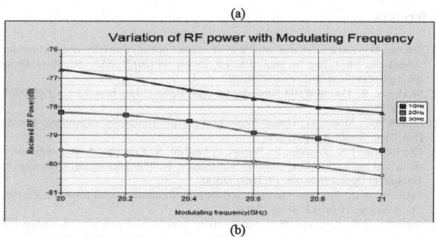

(b)

Fig. 8. Variation of received RF power for OPM modulated signal with modulating RF for (a) EDFA and (b) SOA

Table 4. Variation of received RF power with modulating signal at different channel frequency spacing for OPM modulated signal

Amplifier	Channel freq. spacing (GHz)	Modulation frequency (GHz)					
		20	20.2	20.4	20.6	20.8	21
EDFA output power (dB)	1 GHz	−26.72	−26.9	−27.15	−27.23	−27.4	−27.48
	2 GHz	−27.05	−27.15	−27.2	−27.23	−27.48	−27.5
	3 GHz	−27.3	−27.33	−27.37	−27.39	−27.42	−27.52
SOA output power (dB)	1 GHz	−48.8	−48.82	−49	−49.1	−49.38	−49.5
	2 GHz	−48.83	−48.88	−49	−49.38	−49.5	−49.62
	3 GHz	−49.8	−49.85	−49.87	−49.9	−49.93	−50

6   Conclusion

The field of EONs is a novel and compelling research area, and these are likely to become more integral part of communication backhaul platforms in future. In this paper the performance of SCM in EONs is evaluated using DM, MZM and OPM modulation schemes using both mathematical and simulative model. The results have shown a significant improvement for OPM technique in suppression of non linear distortions. Also the use of EDFA for further amplification provides improvement in performance as compared to SOA. With the analysis of the results, it can be concluded that the OPM technique along with EDFA in SCM based EONs offers larger bandwidth efficiency, optimum resource utilization and reduced distortions.

References

1. Sharma, D., Kumar, S.: An overview of elastic optical networks and its enabling technologies. Int. J. Eng. Technol. (IJET) **9**, 1643–1649 (2017). ISSN 0975-4024. https://doi.org/10.21817/ijet/2017/v9i3/170903022
2. Mukherjee, B.: Optical WDM Networks. Springer, Berlin (2006). https://doi.org/10.1007/0-387-29188-1
3. Siva, R.M.C., Mohan, G.: Optical Networks: Concepts, Design and Algorithms. Prentice-Hall, Upper Saddle River (2003)
4. Khodashenas, P.S., Pomares, P., Perello, J., Spadaro, S., Comellas, J.: A comparison of elastic and multi-rate optical networks performance. In: 16th International Conference on Transparent Optical Networks (ICTON) (2014)
5. Talebi, S., et al.: Spectrum management techniques for elastic optical networks: a survey. Opt. Switching Netw. **13**, 34–48 (2014)
6. Jinno, M., et al.: Spectrum-efficient and scalable elastic optical path network: architecture, benefits, and enabling technologies. IEEE Commun. Mag. **47**(11), 66–73 (2009)
7. Gerstel, O., Jinno, M., Lord, A., Yoo, S.B.: Elastic optical networking: a new dawn for the optical layer? IEEE Commun. Mag. **50**(2), s12–s20 (2012)

8. Punia, S., Kumar, S.: Reduction of congestion in optical networks. CiiT Int. J. Netw. Commun. Eng. **3**, 276–279 (2011). ISSN 0974-9713

9. Sharma, D., Kumar, S.: Design and evaluation of OFDM based optical communication network. J. Eng. Appl. Sci. (JEAS) **12**, 6227–6233 (2017). https://doi.org/10.3923/jeasci.2017.6227.6233. ISSN 1818-7803

10. Yang, H., Zhang, J., Ji, Y., Tian, R., Han, J., Lee, Y.: Performance evaluation of multi stratum resources integration based on network function virtualization in software defined elastic data center optical interconnect. Opt. Express **23**(24), 31192–31205 (2015). https://doi.org/10.1364/oe.23.031192

11. Napoli, A., et al.: Next generation elastic optical networks: the vision of the European research project IDEALIST. IEEE Commun. Mag. **53**(2), 152–162 (2015). https://doi.org/10.1109/MCOM.2015.7045404

12. Yang, H., et al.: SUDOI: software defined networking for ubiquitous data center optical interconnection. IEEE Commun. Mag. **54**(2), 86–95 (2016)

13. Yang, H., Zhang, J., Ji, Y., Tian, R., Han, J., Lee, Y.: CSO: cross stratum optimization for optical as a service. IEEE Commun. Mag. **53**(8), 130–139 (2015)

14. Shen, G., Zukerman, M.: Spectrum-efficient and agile CO-OFDM optical transport networks: architecture, design, and operation. IEEE Commun. Mag. **50**(5), 82–89 (2012). https://doi.org/10.1109/MCOM.2012.6194386

15. Bulira, D., Walkowiak, K.: Performance of dynamic many-to-many routing in WDM and Elastic Optical Networks. In: 2015 17th International Conference on Transparent Optical Networks (ICTON), Budapest, pp. 1–4 (2015). https://doi.org/10.1109/icton.2015.7193433

16. Shen, G., Guo, H., Bose, S.K.: Survivable elastic optical networks: survey and perspective (invited). Photonic Netw. Commun. **31** (2015). https://doi.org/10.1007/s11107-015-0532-0

17. Hirota, Y., Hatada, Y., Watanabe, T., Tode, H.: Dynamic spectrum allocation based on connection alignment for elastic optical networks. In: 2015 10th Asia-Pacific Symposium on Information and Telecommunication Technologies (APSITT), Colombo, pp. 1–3 (2015). https://doi.org/10.1109/apsitt.2015.7217117

18. Sheetal, A., Sharma, A.K., Kaler, R.S.: Impact of optical modulation formats on SPM-limited fiber transmission in 10 and 40 Gb/s optimum dispersion-managed lightwave systems. Optik **121**, 246–252 (2010)

Intelligent Traffic Management System
for Smart Cities

Abhirup Khanna[1(✉)], Rohit Goyal[2], Manju Verma[2],
and Deepika Joshi[2]

[1] The University of Melbourne, Melbourne, Australia
abhirupkhanna@yahoo.com
[2] Himgiri ZEE University, Dehradun, India
rohitgoyalhzu@gmail.com, mv.verma2007@gmail.com,
deepika.joshi0401@gmail.com

Abstract. In present-day times, the number of vehicles has increased drasti-cally, but in contrast, the capabilities of our roads and transportation systems still remain underdeveloped and as a result, fail to cope with this upsurge in the number of vehicles. As a consequence, traffic jamming, road accidents, increase in pollution levels are some of the common traits that can be observed in our new age cities. With the emergence of the Internet of Things and its applicability in Smart Cities, creates a perfect platform for addressing traffic-related issues, thus leading to the establishment of Intelligent Traffic Management Systems (ITMS). The work presented in this paper talks about an intelligent traffic management system that lays its foundation on Cloud computing, Internet of Things and Data Analytics. Our proposed system helps to resolve the numerous challenges being faced by traffic management authorities, in terms of predicting an optimum route, reducing average waiting time, traffic congestion, travel cost and the extent of air pollution. The system aims at using machine learning algorithms for predicting optimum routes based upon traffic mobilization pat-terns, vehicle categorization, accident occurrences and levels of precipitation. Finally, the system comes up with the concept of a green corridor, wherein emergency services are allowed to travel without facing any kinds of traffic congestion.

Keywords: Smart Cities · Internet of Things · Traffic management system
Machine learning

1 Introduction

In today's times, traffic management has become one of the core concerns for an urban city. The constant increase in the number of vehicles has led to the recurring problem of traffic management. An increase in the infrastructure growth is a possible solution but turns out to be costly in terms of both time and effort. Countries all over the world are looking forward to developing efficient traffic management systems by making use of ICT technologies. The recent advancements in Wireless Sensor Networks (WSN) and

© Springer Nature Singapore Pte Ltd. 2019
P. K. Singh et al. (Eds.): FTNCT 2018, CCIS 958, pp. 152–164, 2019.
https://doi.org/10.1007/978-981-13-3804-5_12

low-cost low power consuming sensors have strengthened the regime towards creating an intelligent traffic management system [2]. Governments are trying to capitalize the power of present-day computing, networking and communication technologies for building systems that are able to improve the efficiency of current roads and traffic conditions. The advent of the Internet of Things and high availability of Cloud resources are helping us create mechanisms that can automate the transportation systems and enhance utilization of existing infrastructures [4].

The tiny sensors which we have today have their applicability across various fields such as health, surveillance, home automation and industrial practices. A network of such sensors is able to map an entire city and collect minutest of the details with minimum time and cost overhead. With IPv6 becoming more and more popular it becomes easy to allocate a sensor node with an IP address for its tracking and localization purposes [12]. Traffic systems can make use of such sensor nodes for gathering real-time information regarding traffic conditions like traffic flow, traffic congestion, etc. These sensors are also capable of vehicle classification, speed calculation and vehicle count [5]. The data being collected from these sensor nodes is diverse in nature and humongous in size. We are fortunate to live in times where we have efficient data analytics through machine learning algorithms for extracting information or say knowledge from these huge chunks of data. Machine learning algorithms are capable of making predictions regarding the levels of traffic congestion in a particular area of a city. They can very well depict patterns with respect to traffic flow and suggest measures that authorities can take to curb traffic-related problems. A traffic management system can only be successful when all of its actors work and communicate in sync with another. Talking about our work, we present an Intelligent Traffic Management System that caters to all traffic related issues of a smart city. Our model suggests an optimum route which it takes into consideration parameters like, travel time, travel cost (fuel consumption) and travel distance. Our system in use of machine learning algorithms predicts levels of traffic congestion at various time intervals. It also comes up with the concept of a green corridor catering to emergency vehicles.

The rest of the paper is categorized as follows: Sect. 2 elucidates the algorithm that depicts the workflow of the entire system, whereas its complete layered architecture and mathematical model are discussed in Sect. 3. Finally, Sect. 4 exhibits the implementation and simulation of our proposed system.

2 Algorithm

The working of our Intelligent Traffic Management System could be explained through the illustration of the algorithm that forms the core for it. The algorithm depicts the workflow of the system by representing the relationship between various actors and the information that they share in form of parameters among themselves.

Step 1: Start()

Step 2: Traffic_Management_Controller()   Initialization Block

Step 3: Traffic_Moinitoring_Unit ()

Step 4: ORS()

Step 5: On Road Sensors collect information from every road and intersection

Step 6: Vehicle Nodes transmit there location information

Step 7: All information is sent to the respective Gateways. The entire city is divided into areas and each are has a gateway assigned to it.

Step 8: Gateways transmits all the information to respective TMU and TMC.

Step 9: Data is stored and processed at the Cloud end. KNN based anomaly detection algorithm is used for categorizing incidents as an accident or not. Features such as traffic density, moving traffic velocity, vehicle presence, average waiting time and levels of precipitation are taken into consideration. Levels of precipitation have been divided into three categories: 0 -10 cm; 10 - 20cm and above 20cm.

Step 10: Random Forest algorithm is used for traffic estimation and predicts traffic congestion levels across various time intervals.

Step 11: End user enters Source and Destination.

Step 12: Optimum Route is computed considering factors like, average waiting time, total travel time, travel distance, moving traffic velocity, number of intersections and intended fuel consumption. A vector space model is constructed based on all of these parameters for all routes leading to the desired destination. A route whose vector lies in the region of optimization is considered as optimum route.

Step 13: Results are communicated to the specific Vehicle Node

Step 14: End()

3   Proposed Work

In this section, we discuss our proposed Intelligent Traffic Management System and all the various actors that constitute it. We present a layered architecture that depicts the functionalities of our traffic management system and showcases all the different entities which it comprises. The core of our proposed system is based upon presenting an optimum route followed by traffic estimation.

3.1   Design Objectives

In this subsection, we elucidate some of the prominent objectives which we intend to achieve through our proposed work. These objectives can also be considered as driving forces for designing our proposed intelligent traffic management system.

- **Traffic Monitoring:** It can be considered as one of the key components of a smart city. Traffic monitoring allows the local authorities to monitor the flow of traffic pertaining to a particular area, route or street. It helps in keeping track of the inflow of traffic from other neighboring cities during specific days or a particular time of the year. Historical data of traffic monitoring can be very useful in smart city planning and city infrastructure development.
- **Pollution Avoidance:** Rising pollution levels pose a threat to the environment as along with having adverse impacts on human health and wellbeing. The extent of air and noise pollution are directly proportionally to the intensity of traffic congestion in a city. Long-standing queues of vehicles result in the exorbitant emission of pollutants resulting in an increase in temperatures, a decrease in rainfall, respiratory problems, etc.
- **Route Optimization:** In recent times, it has been observed that the shortest route doesn't seem to work well in terms of total travel time, fuel consumption and average waiting time. In such scenarios, an optimum route is the best option for travel as it considers factors such as traffic congestion, distance traveled, total travel time and fuel consumption. An optimum route comprises of a tradeoff between all these parameters and sits well for a traveler in context to its time and money being spent on travel.
- **Green Corridor:** It's been a couple of years since the concept of a green corridor has seen the light of the day. It is a corridor which in reality is a route from a source to the destination comprising of various traffic signals all of which having a green signal. The green corridor is used to cater to the emergency vehicles by allowing them to reach their desired destination without any waiting time and at maximum speed.
- **Accident Detection:** The overcrowded streets of present-day roads have given rise to the number of accidents. Accident detection is a crucial part of a traffic management system as it not only informs the medical services to attend to the accident hit personnel's but also has an impact on the traffic flow and congestion levels of a particular region.
- **Jamming:** Prevention of traffic jams and reduction in average waiting time are the two most important functionalities of an efficient traffic management system.

- **Vehicle Tracking:** It helps the local administration in keeping track of vehicles in terms of the areas they are traveling, time of travel, speed, places visited and vehicle type. All of these parameters prove to be fruitful when it comes to maintaining a state of law and order in the city.

3.2 Layered Architecture

In this subsection we would be discussing the layered architecture of our proposed intelligent traffic management system. We would also be talking about the various actors along with their functionalities that constitute the system. Following is the diagram that depicts the layered architecture for our proposed system (Fig. 1).

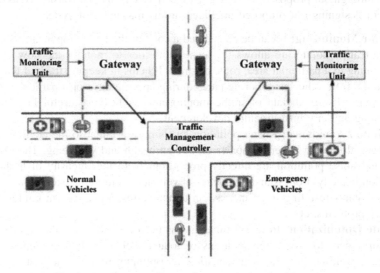

Fig. 1. Intelligent traffic management system architecture

- **Traffic Management Controller (TMC):** The purpose of the controller is to manage and govern the entire system [16]. It is the controller which orchestrates the functionalities of other application modules and entities within the system. The controller resides at the Cloud end and has detailed information regarding every vehicle, traffic signal, gateway, On Road Sensors and Traffic Management Unit. All of this information is stored and processed by the controller in order to generate optimized routes between the specified source and destination. The controller establishes a one to one connection with the middleware and circulates all of its orders through it. It is the controller which generates prediction data concerning with levels of traffic congestion at varying time intervals. The TMC is the one which uses a hop counter based flooding algorithm for broadcasting notifications regarding an accident, change of routes, road developmental activities and adverse climatic impact. The occurrence of an emergency vehicle and creating a green corridor for it is all done through the traffic management controller.

- **Gateways:** All the information that has been sensed and collected by the on-road sensors are transmitted to the gateways [6]. Gateways act as a common point of contact wherein diverse kinds of information coming from heterogeneous types of sensors gets collected. The gateways use greedy based data collection algorithm for collecting data from various data sources. It is the gateway which is responsible for the global addressing of Vehicle Nodes (V) by making use of IPv4 addresses [9]. Each gateway is allotted a coverage area, wherein each on-road sensor and vehicle node has been given an IP address thus facilitating efficient identification of objects within that area. Every gateway is allocated more than one area so as to enhance the granularity of vehicle identification. The gateway also keeps track of its neighboring gateways along with the total number of vehicle nodes traveling in its area. Finally, the gateway transmits all forms of unstructured information to its subsequent traffic management controller.

- **Traffic Monitoring Unit (TMU):** It acts as an intermediary node between On Road Sensors and Gateways. The purpose of adding a TMU is to enhance the response time of the system as communicating directly with the TMC could lead to increased latency cost. TMU provides a communication link between TMC and the rest of the system and also offers local processing and storage capabilities in order to boost the efficiency of the system [8]. Any information coming from an on-road sensor or vehicle node is addressed by the TMU which then subsequently informs the Controller and other devices on the network. All the instruction given by the Controller are communicated through the TMU to the respective vehicle nodes and local authorities. The traffic monitoring unit can also be considered as a Fog computing element as it resides at the edge of the network making its access both easy and efficient. It is the TMU which at regular intervals updates the traffic management controller about information regarding every entity involved in the system.

- **On Road Sensors (ORS):** Sensors are the eyes and ears of the system as they detect the occurrence of events, surrounding conditions and transmit the collected information. The work of the on-road sensors is to monitor and perceive events or phenomena that take place on road. Every ORS can be categorized on the basis of three parameters namely, sensor type, methodology, and sensing parameters. Sensor type defines which type of sensor it is i.e. whether it is a homogeneous or a heterogeneous sensor or it is a single dimensional or a multidimensional sensor. Methodology talks about the ways in which a sensor gathers information [16]. It can be either active or passive in nature. Sensing parameters are the number of parameters which a sensor can sense. A sensor might just sense one parameter like body temperature or many parameters like in the case of an ECG. Each sensor node is provided an IP address which helps in its unique identification. Every sensor node communicates all of its sensor data to its subsequent gateway. Entities starting with the letter "S" represent the On Road Sensors in the physical topology. In case of our work, we have used inductive loop sensor technology. The following are the functionalities that an On-Road Sensor provides.
  - Vehicle Count
  - Vehicle Presence
  - Vehicle Speed

- Vehicle Classification
- Low Bandwidth Consumption
- **Vehicle Node:** It is the vehicle for whom an entire transportation system is constructed in order to provide an effortless and convenient traveling experience. It can also be seen as a moving sensory node which continues to receive and transmit information while traveling. Each vehicle node is provided an IP address which helps in its unique identification. Every sensor node communicates all of its sensor data to its subsequent gateway. Entities starting with the letter "V" represent the Vehicle Node in the physical topology. Every transportation vehicle has an LED display installed that informs the pilot about the most optimum route and the constantly changing levels of traffic. All messages or notifications such as accident alert or prevention of entry in a particular area from the TMC can be seen on the LED display.

3.3 Mathematical Model

In this subsection we would be discussing the mathematical model for our proposed system. Following is the nomenclature table that describes all the various entities that have been used in this mathematical model (Table 1).

$$V = \{\Psi, \delta, E\} \tag{1}$$

Table 1. Nomelclature table

Symbol	Meaning
Γ	On road sensors
V	Vehicle node
r	Road
R	Route
A	Fuel consumption
ß	Traffic density
Φ	Moving traffic velocity
T	Average waiting time
H	Total waiting time
Ψ	Vehicle type
Δ	Vehicle state
N	Number of intersections
E	Vehicle priority
Θ	Optimum vehicle speed
RC	Road capacity
RS	Route selection function
F	Travel cost function
W	Traffic management controller
X	Traffic signal
Ω	Traffic flow percentage

$\Psi \in (0, 1)$: Vehicle type i.e. 0 for light vehicle and 1 for heavy vehicles
$\delta \in (0, 1)$: Vehicle state i.e. 0 for stationary and 1 for moving
$E \in (0, 1)$: Vehicle priority i.e. 0 for normal vehicles and 1 for emergency vehicles

$$H = T/N \tag{2}$$

$$\Phi = \sum(D/t) - (\sum D)/T \tag{3}$$

$$\text{Total Distance} = \sum D \tag{4}$$

$\beta \propto 1/\Phi$
$\beta = K/\Phi$

$$\Phi = (K/D)\,X\,t \tag{5}$$

$$t = (\Phi\,X\,D)/K \tag{6}$$

$$\tau = \sum t + T \tag{7}$$

$$\alpha = (\text{mileage}\,X\,(t)2\,X\,(\text{speed})2)/\text{Total Distance} \tag{8}$$

$\left.\begin{array}{l}\alpha \propto \text{speed} \\ \alpha \propto \text{time}\end{array}\right\}$ Vehicle Speed $> \theta$

$\left.\begin{array}{l}\alpha \propto 1/\text{speed} \\ \alpha \propto \text{time}\end{array}\right\}$ Vehicle Speed $<= \theta$

$$F \leftarrow (\alpha, t, D) \tag{9}$$

RC > threshold value

$$W \rightarrow V\{\text{speed} = 0\} \tag{10}$$

$$\Psi = 1$$

In case the road capacity exceeds the threshold value, the traffic management controller will prevent entry of all heavy vehicles into that zone. Any such vehicle in the affected zone will be directed to stop until further directions from the central controller.

$X = 3$: Traffic light goes green 10 s prior to arrival of emergency vehicle at the intersection

$V(E) = 1$

$$\omega = ((D/\text{Speed} - T)X\,100)/(D/\text{Speed}) \tag{11}$$

4   Implementation and Simulation

The above mentioned algorithm is implemented on iFogSim framework. In iFogSim [17] there are various predefined classes that provide a simulation environment for Internet of Things combined with the benefits of cloud computing. It is a java based simulation toolkit and can be implemented either using Eclipse or NetBeans IDE. In our case we would be using the eclipse IDE. To run iFogSim on eclipse, we first need to download the eclipse IDE and install it. After successful installation of eclipse IDE, download the latest iFogSim package, extract it and import it in eclipse. Talking of our proposed work we have created our own classes in iFogSim and have portrayed our algorithm in form of java code.

In terms of implementing machine learning algorithms, we have made use of Weka [15], which is a popular open source tool for executing machine learning algorithms.

The following tables depict the simulation environment for our paper along with the improvements that can be seen after successful implementation of our model (Tables 2, 3 and 4).

Table 2. Vechile count per road

Road 1	Road 2	Road 3	Road 4
45	92	70	60
53	75	4	78
90	12	80	77
103	13	95	66
13	20	78	82
9	54	20	95
33	88	28	86

Table 3. Average waiting time per road

Road 1	Road 2	Road 3	Road 4
602.76	460.94	526.07	561.25
531.72	473.87	712.51	443.89
446.38	717.13	487.73	511.73
463.87	664.86	483.43	557.89
689.59	622.82	457.14	412.45
664.12	524.49	618.45	332.98
658.03	464.25	629.67	458.07

Table 4. Improved average waiting time per road

Road 1	Road 2	Road 3	Road 4
552.72	422.84	507.13	522.15
501.76	433.77	695.16	417.09
408.35	687.11	452.03	486.43
403.57	614.74	428.53	559.39
669.47	612.32	462.03	402.15
644.14	501.42	602.05	311.08
628.15	424.17	611.07	419.17

It is very much evident that the average waiting time has reduced for each road over all time intervals. Although, the degree of reduction in average waiting time varies from road to road but the predominant trend over the entire data set remains the same i.e. a decrease in the average waiting time.

As earlier as discussed in Sect. 2, our traffic estimation is based upon the Random Forest algorithm and below is a graph illustrating the correctness of our feature selection along with the algorithm that we have chosen. The graph depicts the comparison between the actual and estimated values of traffic in terms of vehicle count. As inferred from the graph below, the estimated traffic count may not be the same as that in actual but in a larger prospective the increase and decrease in the levels of traffic over all time intervals turnout to be the same for both estimated and actual values. Figure 2, 3 and 4 represents findings at different roads.

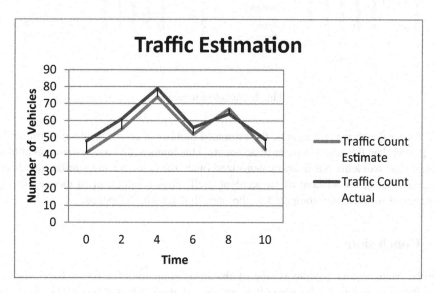

Fig. 2. Traffic estimation

Till now we have discussed how our proposed intelligent traffic management system turns out to be beneficial in terms of reducing the average waiting time for a given road along with making correct predictions with respect to varying levels of traffic. The following graphs present an analysis of our accident detection mechanism and presents a comparison between the estimates and actual number of accidents occurred for a particular road at different time intervals.

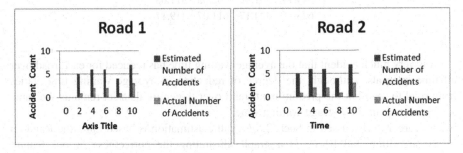

Fig. 3. Accident detection

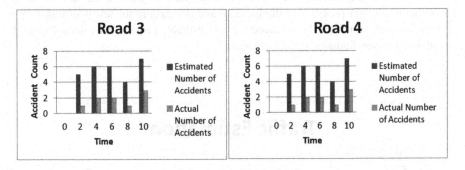

Fig. 4. Accident detection

As per the above two figures, the estimated number of accidents always turn out to be greater than the actual number of accidents. This implies, that our system was able to detect real accidents but it also categorized other scenarios having similar characteristics as that of an accident as an accident itself. Thus resulting in an increase in the number of accidents as compared to the ones that actually happened.

5 Conclusion

Traffic Management System is one of the many domains of a Smart City wherein significant research can be seen. It is an area of work which has answers to many current day problems pertaining to traffic management of smart cities. We propose a novel Intelligent Traffic Management System for Smart Cities which facilitates Wireless Sensor Networks, Internet of Things, Cloud Computing and Data analytics. The work discusses the ways in an optimum route is suggested to the end user. The optimum route turns out to be beneficial than the shortest route in most cases in terms of fuel cost and total travel time. Through our research, we were successful in generating an optimum route along with making predictions regarding traffic congestion levels. The system also talks about events of accidents and how they may have an impact on the traffic flow of a region. Levels of precipitation, an occurrence of an accident, concept of a green corridor, the rate of fuel consumption, % flow of traffic and use of machine learning algorithms are some of the novel features of our work. In future, we intend to introduce the vehicle to vehicle communication and impact of speed breakers on traffic flow and congestion.

References

1. Miz, V., Hahanov, V.: Smart traffic light in terms of the cognitive road traffic management system (CTMS) based on the internet of things. In: 2014 East-West Design & Test Symposium (EWDTS), pp. 1–5. IEEE, September 2014
2. Gubbi, J., Buyya, R., Marusic, S., Palaniswami, M.: Internet of things (IoT): a vision, architectural elements, and future directions. Future Gener. Comput. Syst. **29**(7), 1645–1660 (2013)
3. Foschini, L., Taleb, T., Corradi, A., Bottazzi, D.: M2M-based metropolitan platform for IMS-enabled road traffic management in IoT. IEEE Commun. Mag. **49**(11), 50–57 (2011)
4. Yu, M., Zhang, D., Cheng, Y., Wang, M.: An RFID electronic tag based automatic vehicle identification system for traffic IOT applications. In: 2011 Chinese Control and Decision Conference (CCDC), pp. 4192–4197. IEEE, May 2011
5. Zhou, H., Liu, B., Wang, D.: Design and research of urban intelligent transportation system based on the internet of things. In: Wang, Y., Zhang, X. (eds.) IOT 2012. CCIS, vol. 312, pp. 572–580. Springer, Heidelberg (2012). https://doi.org/10.1007/978-3-642-32427-7_82
6. Khanna, A., Anand, R.: IoT based smart parking system. In: International Conference on Internet of Things and Applications (IOTA), pp. 266–270. IEEE, January 2016
7. Lingling, H., Haifeng, L., Xu, X., Jian, L.: An intelligent vehicle monitoring system based on internet of things. In: 2011 Seventh International Conference on Computational Intelligence and Security (CIS), pp. 231–233. IEEE, December 2011
8. Kyriazis, D., Varvarigou, T., White, D., Rossi, A., Cooper, J.: Sustainable smart city IoT applications: heat and electricity management & eco-conscious cruise control for public transportation. In: 2013 IEEE 14th International Symposium and Workshops on World of Wireless, Mobile and Multimedia Networks (WoWMoM), pp. 1–5. IEEE, June 2013
9. Khanna, A., Tomar, R.: IoT based interactive shopping ecosystem. In: 2016 2nd International Conference on Next Generation Computing Technologies (NGCT), pp. 40–45. IEEE, October 2016
10. Tarapiah, S., Atalla, S., AbuHania, R.: Smart on-board transportation management system using GPS/GSM/GPRS technologies to reduce traffic violation in developing countries. Int. J. Digital Inf. Wirel. Commun. (IJDIWC) **3**(4), 430–439 (2013)
11. Parwekar, P.: From internet of things towards cloud of things. In: 2011 2nd International Conference on Computer and Communication Technology (ICCCT), pp. 329–333. IEEE, September 2011

12. Zhou, J., et al.: CloudThings: a common architecture for integrating the internet of things with cloud computing. In: 2013 IEEE 17th International Conference on Computer Supported Cooperative Work in Design (CSCWD), pp. 651–657. IEEE, June 2013

13. Rajan, M.A., Balamuralidhar, P., Chethan, K.P., Swarnahpriyaah, M.: A self-reconfigurable sensor network management system for internet of things paradigm. In: 2011 International Conference on Devices and Communications (ICDeCom), pp. 1–5. IEEE, February 2011

14. Tomar, R., Khanna, A., Bansal, A., Fore, V.: An architectural view towards autonomic cloud computing. In: Satapathy, S.C., Bhateja, V., Raju, K.Srujan, Janakiramaiah, B. (eds.) Data Engineering and Intelligent Computing. AISC, vol. 542, pp. 573–582. Springer, Singapore (2018). https://doi.org/10.1007/978-981-10-3223-3_55

15. Hall, M., Frank, E., Holmes, G., Pfahringer, B., Reutemann, P., Witten, I.H.: The WEKA data mining software: an update. ACM SIGKDD Explor. Newsl. 11(1), 10–18 (2009)

16. Fore, V., Khanna, A., Tomar, R., Mishra, A.: Intelligent supply chain management system. In: 2016 International Conference on Advances in Computing and Communication Engineering (ICACCE), pp. 296–302. IEEE, November 2016

17. Gupta, H., Vahid Dastjerdi, A., Ghosh, S.K., Buyya, R.: iFogSim: a toolkit for modeling and simulation of resource management techniques in the internet of things, Edge and Fog computing. Softw.: Pract. Exp. 47(9), 1275–1296 (2017)

A Hybrid Query Recommendation Technique in Information Retrieval

Neelanshi Wadhwa[✉], Rajesh Kumar Pateriya,
and Sonika Shrivastava

Department of Computer Science and Engineering,
Maulana Azad National Institute of Technology, Bhopal, India
neelanshiwadhwa@gmail.com, pateriyark@gmail.com,
ms271104@gmail.com

Abstract. As the amount of information available online is enormous, search engines continue to be the best tools to find relevant and required information in the least amount of time. However, with this growth of internet, the number of pages indexed in search engines is also increasing rapidly. The major concern at present is no more having enough information or not; it is rather having too much information which is in numerous different formats, languages and without any measure of precision. Therefore, it is essential to devise techniques that can benefit the process of extracting useful information suitable for users' demands. Several mechanisms have been developed and some methods have been enhanced by researchers from all over the world to generate better or more relevant query that can be provided as suggestion to the user for enriched Information Retrieval. The objective of this paper is to summarize and analyze the various techniques adopted to optimize the Web Search process to support the user. The existing strategies developed in this scenario are also compared using standard IR metrics to evaluate the relevance of results.

Keywords: Query recommendation · Query logs · Information retrieval

1 Introduction

1.1 Fundamental Information Retrieval Process

The basic Information Retrieval process in a search engine is depicted as:

- Data is available in form of documents or Webpages. These are organized in a specific format and an index is created.
- As the query is fired to the search engine, best matching entries from the index are selected.
- Simultaneously, a learning algorithm is developed that guides the rank updation of results.
- Finally, the results are displayed to the user in descending order of ranks.

This process is displayed in Fig. 1.

© Springer Nature Singapore Pte Ltd. 2019
P. K. Singh et al. (Eds.): FTNCT 2018, CCIS 958, pp. 165–175, 2019.
https://doi.org/10.1007/978-981-13-3804-5_13

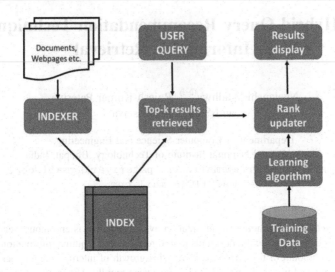

Fig. 1. Basic IR process

1.2 Motivation Behind Query Recommendation

With such huge volume of information available, it is a challenging task to find relevant information that meets the needs of the user using simple search queries. This problem arises mainly because the queries submitted by the user to the search engine are usually very short and turn out to be ambiguous. These queries fail to convey the user's requirements precisely. Consequently, lots of results retrieved by the search engine might be irrelevant with respect to the users' needs due to the implicit ambiguity in queries. Also, most of the users go through only the first one or two pages of the retrieved results, there is a possibility that they would fail to notice many relevant results obtained in successive pages that are left unread. Hence, Web Search becomes an iterative trial and error process by changing queries each time so as to fulfill the information need. Alternatively, the users may not want to reformulate their queries in order to avoid the additional efforts while searching.

The compulsive need to extract useful piece of information for the user from such voluminous store of web pages leads to various issues such as the ranked list problem, ambiguous query problem, obtaining results semantically dissimilar to what the user desires and so on.

To overcome all the above discussed limitations of search engines, research is directed towards generating clear and more efficient queries as suggestions to users. These newly generated queries tend to retrieve more relevant results as per the users' requirements. There are number of strategies proposed in this direction, each of them involves a unique yet effective method of query recommendation. Some of these strategies exploit various kinds of background knowledge or data available to study users' behavior in order to yield focused results.

1.3   Terminology

Query recommendation can be defined as the process of reconstructing queries entered by the user so as to provide the user with better results which are more relatable to user context or domain.

   Query Log – The search engine records an entry for each user (each query) which contains entries such as

- Query q given by the user
- User or session ID
- The URLs which the users clicked from the displayed results
- Rank of the web page accessed etc.

   The rest of the paper is organized as follows: Sect. 2 gives a detailed review of related work in query recommendation and various proposed models. A comparison chart based on advantages, shortcomings and performance metrics has also been described. Section 3 describes a unique strategy proposed to increase the efficiency of existing query suggestion process. In the end, there is the conclusion and a brief discussion of future work.

2   Literature Survey

Most approaches of query recommendation focus on users' previously submitted queries which are analogous to the current query either in terms of content or in click context. Liu et al. [2] propose a framework very different from its preceding methods, which attempts to obtain user's information need by means of click-through logs as shown in Fig. 2. It is observed that although the clicked documents may not always be relevant to user but the snippets that make the users click on the links better represent users' need. Therefore, two snippet click models are built according to this finding and corresponding algorithms are described. These methods do enhance the query recommendation process, but the users' context (or background) cannot be ignored as it provides a good insight to understand the domain of the query. Hence, users' context features should be added to create a universal model.

   In paper [3], author aims on an eminent problem of Web searches, known as the ranked list problem, which has emerged as a consequence of two major activities; the first being the fact that search engines mostly present the results in the form of ranked lists, and the second being the semantic ambiguity of users' queries put in to the search engines. Search engines usually retrieve and rank documents irrespective of the probable different semantics of query terms due to short and ambiguous queries. Moreover, since it is a general notion amongst most users to explore only the few pages of ranked results, the possibility that users might miss many relevant documents retrieved in subsequent and unread pages is quite huge. To overcome these weaknesses, users perform iterative cycles based on hit and trial to reformulate their query. In the attempt to capture new and more relevant documents in the top p (assumed) ranked positions, users submit minor variants of the original query at each step which may express their needs in a better way. However, this behavior leads to the retrieval of almost the same documents in the first

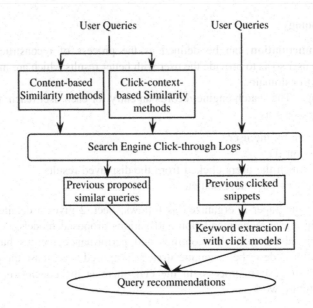

Fig. 2. Snippet click model [2]

positions of the ranked list, thereby vanishing the efforts of users. They propose an iterative query disambiguation procedure that attempts to create and suggest disambiguated queries, which potentially may retrieve both new and relevant documents [3].

Baeza-Yates et al. [5] propose a technique to suggest a list of queries related to the query that is submitted. These new queries are can be used by the users' to redirect the search process. Their method consists of a query clustering process which identifies queries that are similar in meaning or definition and groups them to form a cluster. The clustering procedure is based on the historical activities of users recorded in the query log of the search engine. After finding a set of related queries, they are ranked as per certain relevance criteria. The two measures used in this method to calculate rank of a query are:

1. Similarity – That defines how much the new query is alike to the input query. This is calculated using term-weight vector quantities for each query.
2. Support – That is the fraction of the documents returned by the query that are clicked by the user. This is obtained using query logs.

Although this technique yields good results in terms of precision of suggested queries as compared to the original query, but the overall performance of this technique may not prove to be good enough for huge number of users and queries with corresponding query logs. Also, there might be sets of similar queries that have common words but do not have same set of clicked URLs (or vice versa), which is not captured in this technique.

Bordogna et al. address the ranked list problem that arises in internet search whenever a user puts in a very short request or query. It is because the entered words generate ambiguity and convey many different meanings at the same time pertaining to many different scenarios. Hence they have devised an iterative mechanism for disambiguation of queries that contains following major steps and depicted in Fig. 3:

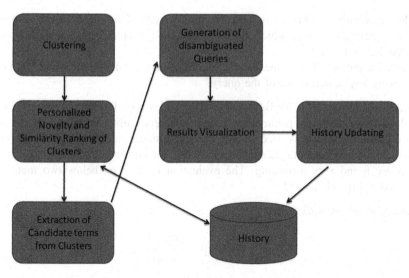

Fig. 3. Query disambiguation scheme [3]

1. Clustering – This is the very first step where the results obtained from a web search made by a user are grouped together into different clusters.
2. Personalized novelty and similarity ranking – In this step, each cluster is assigned a score which is calculated from two parameters, similarity of cluster content to query and originality of cluster with respect to user's past behavior.
3. Extraction of cluster candidate terms – From each cluster, a certain no of set of weighted terms along with their weights is selected. These will be used further in creating new query.
4. Disambiguated query creation – Now, first n number of highest weighted candidate terms are used to form the new query.
5. Displays of results – The clusters are shown according to the ranking and one disambiguated query for every cluster is also shown to the user.
6. History updating – Finally, when user selects one of the new queries, that query is taken as more relevant to repeat the entire process until the user stops submitting further queries [3].

This technique is unique and would considerably achieve good results in desired time, but the idea of displaying clusters to the users is that appropriate as the user is only interested in getting the required information in form of documents or web pages. Also, the process is time consuming as it contains complex computations at each step of each iteration.

Zhu et al. [8] claim that instead of just looking for higher relevance value of queries, it is more advantageous to directly recommend queries with greater utility. They define query utility as "The information gain that a user can get from the search results of the query as per the user's original search objective." For this a Query Utility Model (QUM) has been proposed by them to obtain query utility. This parameter, Query Utility, is calculated by studying users' query reformulation and their click activity in a particular search process. Query utility is said to contain two components:

1. Perceived utility – This is based on the attractiveness of the search results displayed for a particular query, which further increases the chance that a URL will be accessed by the user.
2. Posterior utility – This is the satisfaction that a user obtains as information gain by clicking any search result of the query.

Further, a unique dynamic Bayesian network is developed to compute Query Utility based on above discussed parameters, known as Query Utility Model (QUM). A publicly released query log is used to test the performance and compare it with other already renowned methods available for query recommendation and experimental results are found very promising. The evaluation is done on below two metrics as described in Eqs. (1) and (2):

1. Query Relevant Ratio (QRR)

$$QRR\,(q) = \frac{RQ(q)}{N\,(q)} \qquad (1)$$

Where
RQ(q) is the total frequency of query q with relevant results clicked by users,
And N(q) is the total frequency of query q issued by users.
2. Mean Relevant Document (MRD)

$$MRD\,(q) = \frac{RD\,(q)}{N\,(q)} \qquad (2)$$

Where
RD(q) is the total frequency of relevant results clicked by users when they use query q for their search tasks,
and N(q) is the total frequency of query q issued by users.

Many other different ways and models have been proposed to improve the process of query recommendation. He et al. [6] focus more on the ordering of queries within a search session, as they have high degree of correlation. These queries should be analyzed sequentially so as to know the information need of the user in a better way. However, to set up this kind of model on huge data set (i.e. query log of all users available) might require training the data. Nguyen et al. [7] present a different view to some extent. They say that Web-page recommendation can be more efficient by integrating the Web usage knowledge as well as the domain knowledge related to the key concepts of the query. They have proposed models to establish relation between the two and use them to provide better recommendation to the user.

Song et al. [1] propose to integrate all essential features that enhance the query recommendation process by creating a hybrid recommendation strategy. To begin with, a concept extraction method is efficiently modified to find queries similar in terms of concept. These concepts are mined using the web-snippets of the original query. To better represent co-related queries, a bipartite graph (between query and concept) is created that helps in finding similarity. Secondly, it is also observed that many times

URLs contain significant tokens that may depict the actual webpage contents. URLs are separated into tokens using the TF-IQF model. Further, three vital similarity features are exploited to develop a hybrid sematic similarity model for query recommendation. These aspects are defined below:

1. Clicked document – The set of URLs clicked or set of documents accessed for a particular query can be assumed to have alike content in terms of concept.
2. Associated Query – It is natural that queries that contain more number of identical terms (with respect to meaning i.e. synonyms), they will have a higher value of similarity.
3. Reverse Query – Two or more queries that cause the users to click on the same URL are obviously similar and relevant queries. They are called as reverse queries.

Finally, the unique approach suggested takes into account all the above measures in weighted form as any one of them is not sufficient. This hybrid approach is formulated as:

$$sim(p, q) = \alpha * sim_{doc}(p, q) + \beta * sim_{ass}(p, q) + \gamma * sim_{rev}(p, q)$$

Where
$sim_{doc}(p, q)$ is the clicked document similarity,
$sim_{ass}(p, q)$ is the associated query similarity
And $sim_{rev}(p, q)$ is the reverse query similarity.
α, β, and Υ are three real constants between 0 and 1, and they satisfy the restriction of $\alpha + \beta + \Upsilon = 1$.

Now, to find the optimal weights of these real constants, experiments are done by randomly adjusting their values. The results are evaluated using the standard IR metrics Precision, Recall and F-Measure. It has been shown via experimental analysis that the hybrid scheme achieves better Precision and Recall simultaneously as compared to applying each individual similarity measure separately.

Table 1 shows the comparison of various query recommendation methods.

Table 1. Comparative analysis of existing techniques

Author	Problem addressed	Technique	Advantage	Disadvantage	Metrics
Liu et al. [2]	Getting users' exact information need	Snippet click model	More efficient than current practical search engines	Users' prior search context not taken into account	No standard metrics used for performance evaluation
Gloria et al. [3]	Ranked List problem	Query disambiguation	Retrieves new documents	Unnecessary display of cluster along with best query suggested	No standard metrics used for performance evaluation
Zhu et al. [8]	Reformulating Queries	Query Utility Model (Bayesian Network)	Achieves useful recommendation of queries	Automated procedure not formed	Query Relevant Ratio (QRR)
Song et al. [1]	Ambiguous and Short Queries	Hybrid query similarity model	Considers all major similarity measures and gives good results	Purely experimental method of parameter evaluation	Precision, Recall, F-Measure

3 Proposed Model

In this section, we propose a collaborative query recommendation model which incorporates all major similarity measures in a weighted scheme to generate a resultant similarity score for queries. This resultant score will be the deciding factor to select the best query (or set of queries) to be provided as a suggestion to the users so as to narrow down their search process and retrieve the most relevant information.

In the proposed scheme we attempt to calculate the weight of different similarity measures by using Genetic Algorithm as the learning algorithm. Initially random weights can be assigned to create a set of chromosomes and then on applying genetic algorithm to these chromosomes, we can obtain optimal values. The set of weights that would yield the highest similarity score can be taken as the best chromosome or the best solution to the problem. Further, we will generate an alternate query based on achieved similarity measure and the optimal weights. The set of queries obtained can be provided to the user as suggestions. The working flowchart of the proposed methodology is given below in Fig. 4 and the detail working of Genetic algorithm is described in Fig. 5.

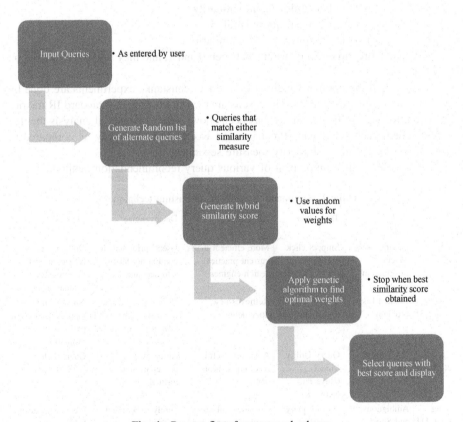

Fig. 4. Process flow for proposed scheme

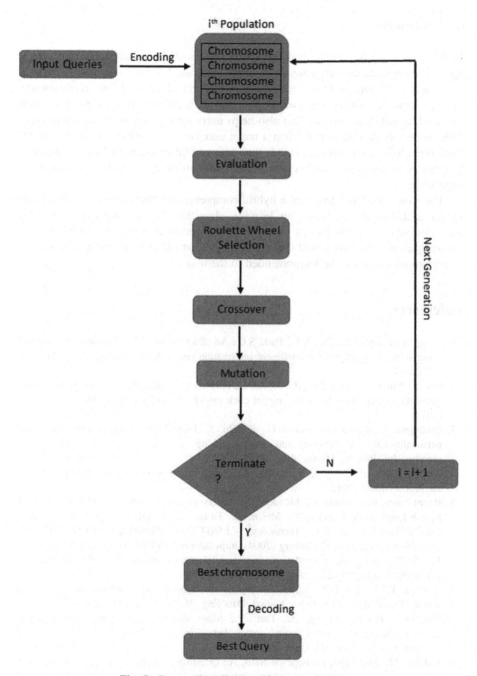

Fig. 5. Proposed application of genetic algorithm

4 Conclusion

In this paper, we have described the Query recommendation strategies that can be applied to improve the performance of search engines. We have also discussed what issues led to the idea of Query reformulation/Recommendation. Query recommendation has now become an inseparable part of search process as it saves users' time involved in rephrasing queries and also helps users satisfy their need for information. This process is also beneficial when a naïve user enters an ambiguous query. At the same time, it guides the users towards their ultimate information goal even when they themselves are unable to clearly express their requirements due to lack of knowledge or experience.

Thereafter, we have proposed a hybrid comprehensive strategy for effective query recommendation that is based on learning algorithm. By making use of Genetic algorithm significant results can be achieved for optimized values of the weights of similarity measures. This would lead to the generation of better and more relevant and unambiguous queries to be recommended to the user.

References

1. Song, W., Liang, J.Z., Cao, X.L., Park, S.C.: An effective query recommendation approach using semantic strategies for intelligent information retrieval. Expert Syst. Appl. **41**, 366–372 (2014)
2. Liu, Y., Miao, J., Zhang, M., Ma, S., Ru, L.: How do users describe their information need: query recommendation based on snippet click model. Expert Syst. Appl. **38**, 13847–13856 (2011)
3. Bordogna, G., Campi, A., Psaila, G., Ronchi, S.: Disambiguated query suggestions and personalized content-similarity and novelty ranking of clustered results to optimize web searches. Inf. Process. Manag. **48**, 419–437 (2012)
4. Zahera, H.M., El Haddy, G.F., Keshk, A.E.: Optimizing Search Engine Result using an Intelligent Model (2012)
5. Baeza-Yates, R., Hurtado, C., Mendoza, M.: Query Recommendation Using Query Logs in Search Engines. In: Lindner, W., Mesiti, M., Türker, C., Tzitzikas, Y., Vakali, A.I. (eds.) Current Trends in Database Technology - EDBT 2004 Workshops. LNCS, vol. 3268, pp. 588–596. Springer, Heidelberg (2004). https://doi.org/10.1007/978-3-540-30192-9_58
6. He, Q.: Web query recommendation via sequential query prediction. In: IEEE International Conference on Data Engineering, 1084–4627/09 (2009)
7. Nguyen, T.T.S., Lu, H.Y., Lu, J.: Web-page recommendation based on web usage and domain knowledge. IEEE Trans. Knowl. Data Eng. **26**(10), 2574–2587 (2014)
8. Zhu, X., Guo, J., Cheng, X., Lan, Y.: More than relevance: high utility query recommendation by mining users' search behaviors, In: CIKM 2012, 29 October–2 November 2012, Maui, HI, USA (2012)
9. Habibia, M., Mahdabib, P., Popescu-Belis, A.: Question answering in conversations: query refinement using contextual and semantic information. Data Knowl. Eng. **106**, 38–51 (2016)
10. Shanna, A.K., Aggarwal, N., Duhan, N., Gupta, R.: Web search result optimization by mining the search engine query logs. In: International Conference on Methods and Models in Computer Science (2010)

11. Anagnostopoulos, A., Becchetti, L., Castillo, C., Gionis, A.: An optimization framework for query recommendation. In: WSDM, pp. 161–170 (2010)
12. Beeferman, D., Berger, A.: Agglomerative clustering of a search engine query log. In: SIGKDD, pp. 407–416 (2000)
13. Yadav, U., Duhan, N., Kaushik, B.: Relevant page retrieval and query recommendation using semantic analysis of queries. Int. J. Sci. Eng. Res. **4**(7), 694 (2013)
14. Deepak, G., Priyadarshini, J.S., Hareesh Babu, M.S.: A differential semantic algorithm for query relevant web page recommendation. In: IEEE International Conference on Advances in Computer Applications (ICACA) (2016)
15. Sahu, S.K., Mahapatra, D.P., Balabantaray, R.C.: Analytical study on intelligent information retrieval system using semantic network. In: ICCCA (2016)

Predicting the Risk Factors Influencing the Behavioral Intention to Adopt Mobile Banking Services: An Exploratory Analysis

Nitin Nayak[1], Vikas Nath[2(✉)], and Nancy Singhal[2(✉)]

[1] Bharati Vidhyapeeth Institute of Management and Research, Kolhapur, India
drnayaknitin007@gmail.com
[2] Bharati Vidhyapeeth Institute of Management and Research, New Delhi, India
{vikas.nath,nancy.goel}@bharatividhyapeeth.edu

Abstract. Mobile Banking is a next big challenge in the technologically dependent era after Mobile Commerce and there are many factors that are influencing the use of M-banking Services, perceived Risk is one of them. Although perceived Risk as a single construct has been studied by many researchers but in this paper, empirical research has been done to find out the actual characteristics of Perceived Risk and the reason for refusing the use of m-banking services by the users in the technologically advanced era. In order to study the reason behind the reluctance in using m-banking services, a more detailed study of attributes of Perceived Risk has been conducted. This research work is intended to examine the six components of Perceived Risk. In this study EFA was applied on various measures of Risk to ascertain the different underlying variables affecting the individual's Behavioral Intention to adopt m-banking services. After applying EFA researcher has applied SEM in order to investigate the association between the factors. The results of this empirical testing found that out of all the six variables only four variables i.e. Social Risk, Psychological Risk, Time Risk and Financial Risk were statistically significant as per results of this study and these are the main factors affecting the influence of Behavioral Intention towards using m-banking services in the Indian context.

Keywords: Perceived Risk · Factors · Adoption of mobile banking
Factor analysis · SEM

1 Introduction

According to Juniper Research 2014, more than 1.75 billion Cellular phone users will prefer to use their cellular phones for conducting financial and non-financial banking transactions by the year 2019 as compared to 800 million in the Year 2016. So, with the advancement in the technology number of users are also increasing day by day, especially in the banking industry which has undergone a rapid change. Major change in the banking sector is that banks have changed from paper-based banking system to the most recent and advanced technologies like online-banking, mobile-banking, etc.

But sometimes, Consumers are avoiding using m-banking services because of security issues, Risk involved, lack of awareness etc. As studied by Hoffman [1],

P. K. Singh et al. (Eds.): FTNCT 2018, CCIS 958, pp. 176–191, 2019.
https://doi.org/10.1007/978-981-13-3804-5_14

consumers are facing problems in completing the online transactions because of involvement of Risk. Hence, Perceived Risk is an important attribute and it has been hypothesized as a salient obstruction of user acceptance in the online banking environment [2, 3]. According to Cox [4], perceived Risk factor is initially modelled as the single factor then it was decomposed into its various sub facets. In this way, perceptivity may be gained as to which all different facets of Risks are important for the users of m-banking services. This present study emphasized on the role of Perceived Risk in affecting the Behavioral Intention for using m-banking services.

The state of banking industry is not admirable in India. In 2011, 65% of India's population did not have admittance to a bank account [5]. Till date lots of Indian population do not have their own personal bank accounts. Reserve Bank of India also appealing to the masses of the country that each person should have at least one saving account in any of the bank of India. But still the population is not much aware. So, mobile banking is a good opportunity for the banking sector to build their customer base. With the assistance of mobile telecommunication technology, the clients can make various transactions in the bank anytime. There are various researches which illustrated that India is moving fast in terms of mobile phone users as well as mobile phone internet users which is also a great push to the banking industry to support the mobile banking.

To summarize, this research work presented the in depth analysis of the factors influencing m-banking services adoption process by modelling the Perceived Risk variable within Behavioral Intention. The main research questions of this research work are:

- How much essential are the different Risk facets to the m-banking adoption intention?
- What is the association between different Risk facets and Behavioral Intention to use m-banking services?

This research work proceeded with the following main sections and sub sections. Primarily, a concise assessment has been performed for various Perceived Risk variables and Behavior Intention to use m-banking services then exploratory factor analysis (EFA) was applied in order to explore the variables from the different items. Secondly, Structural Equation Modelling (SEM) technique was applied to check the associations and relationships between the various factors. Then finally this paper has been concluded with limitations and possible topics for further research.

2 Literature Review

M-banking services gives many services to the financial institutions like generating an additional income, expanding the consumer base, reduce costs, and improve operations. M-banking services applications are accessed via smartphones, cell phones, and tablets for performing financial transactions like transfer of funds and other non-financial transactions like enquiry of balance [6].

In the recent mobile technological advancements among the latest advancements; one is m-banking. Although ATM, Internet banking and telephone also offers provision for conventional banking products, but retail banking sector and microfinance banks in many developing and developed countries has established as a latest delivery channels; one is m-banking that has an important impact on the market [7].

Since 1960s, Perceived Risk has verified to be the important predictor of users' behavior. According to Lin [8], significant research and surveys has been studied by various researchers to verify the effect of Risk on customary consumer decision making. Perceived Risk is characterized as a "form of subjective expected loss" [9]. Cunningham [10] also distinguished that Perceived Risk comprised of the "extent of the potential loss if the outcomes of the act were not satisfactory and the entity's subjective feelings of certainty that the outcomes will be unfavorable". Maximum of the research academics also stated that users' Perceived Risk is a many-fold concept. So majorly, Six types of Risk has been classified as Financial, Social, Performance, Privacy, physical, and Time-loss [11–13]. Researcher has also explained Perceived Risk in m-banking as the "personally ascertained anticipation of loss by m-banking users". Details has been mentioned in Table 1.

Table 1. Definitions of perceived risk dimensions in the literature

Factors	Description	Research
Performance Risk	"The possibility of the product malfunctioning and not performing as it was designed and advertised and therefore failing to deliver the desired benefits. (Grewal et al. [39])"	[9–11, 14]
Financial Risk	"The potential monetary outlay associated with the initial purchase price as well as the subsequent maintenance cost of the product. (ibid)."	[9–11, 13, 14]
Time Risk	"Consumers may lose Time when making a bad purchasing decision by wasting Time researching and making the purchase, learning how to use a product or service only to have to replace it if it does not perform to expectations."	[9, 10, 13, 14]
Psychological Risk	"Potential loss of self-esteem (ego loss) and ego frustration based on feelings about oneself. Consumers feel unwise if they experience a non-performing product and may experience feelings of harm to their self-image from the frustration of not achieving their buying goals."	[9–11, 13, 14]
Social Risk	"Potential loss of status in one's Social group as a result of adopting a product or service, looking foolish or untrendy."	[9–11, 14]
Privacy Risk	"Potential loss of control over personal information, such as when information about you is used without your knowledge or permission. The extreme case is where a consumer is 'spoofed' meaning a criminal uses their identity to perform fraudulent transactions."	[15–18]

Source: [17]

Perceived Risk is still considered as the foremost important element that influences the user Behavior Intention towards the adoption of any new technological applications such as m-banking. Soroor [19] in his research perceived the security issues in m-banking and also tried propose few methods and techniques to improve this system. Privacy Risk is influenced to the extent by which a user is ready to provide any personal information on the online platform, users are ready to sacrifice their privacy [15, 20, 21]. According to Cox and Rich [4], when conducting any kind of retail transactions, Performance Risk is one which can cause users' to feel insecure about "not getting what they want".

Performance Risk referred to the losses that has experienced because of malfunctioning of the m-banking applications. Consumers are generally concerned about the situations while doing transactions through mobile banking technological failures tends to occur [22]. So the hypothesis framed was:

H1: Performance Risk has negative relationship with Behavioral Intention for using m-banking services.

Time Risk

Time Risk is also important in influencing the Behavioral Intention to adopt services of mobile banking. Delays in the payment may lead to loss of convenience while using mobile banking services. So Time – conscious users usually safeguard themselves by not adopting mobile banking service [17]. Therefore, it was hypothesized that:

H2: Time Risk has negative relationship with Behavioral Intention for using m-banking services.

Social Risk

Lee [23] described Social Risk as "the possibility that use of mobile banking may result in condemnation by one's friends, family and work group". Five aspects of Perceived Risks: Time Risk, Security Risk, Financial Risk, Social Risk and Performance Risk, has negative association with intention in adopting online banking services as found out by Lee [23, 24]. After reviewing the concerned literature following hypothesis was developed.

H3: Social Risk has negative relationship with Behavioral Intention for using m-banking services.

Psychological Risk

According to Fain [25], Risk is not the characteristics of any product or service but it is present in the mind of the user. Some author also claims that Risk is the factor that changes the mind of the consumer towards the usability of the technology [26]. The Risk of image is generally refer to as the psychological Risk that is causing conflicts within the beliefs of the consumers [27]. So following the literature reviewed the following hypothesis was framed:

H4: Psychological Risk has negative relationship with Behavioral Intention for using m-banking services.

Privacy Risk

According to Bestavros [28], there has always been a Privacy issue with the customers as they always try to avoid sharing their personal information online. Some researchers also stated that consumer has a Privacy as a major concern while adopting online services [29–31]. To ensure security and Privacy, banks has to develop trust with the consumers, which will lead to increase in customer satisfaction. So it can be hypothesized that.

H5: Privacy Risk has negative relationship with Behavioral Intention for using m-banking services.

Financial Risk

As using mobile banking services involves money, so there exists a type of Risk which is known as Financial Risk. Financial Risk may be due to the non-refund of money when by mistake user enters the wrong account number or amount. According to Luarn [32], Financial cost negatively influence the Behavioral Intention of the user to use mobile banking services. According to Kuisma [22], many of the users are not using internet banking because they are afraid of losing money because of transaction error or bank account misuse. Cudjoe [33] also suggested that financial cost is a vital inhibitor in adopting m-banking services. So from the reviewed literature following hypotheses was suggested:

H6: Financial Risk has negative relationship with Behavioral Intention for using m-banking services.

The intention of this study is to investigate the chief attributes that are developed from the various studies related to Perceived Risk including the Behavioral Intention to adopt m-banking services. After critically reviewing the literature, few important points have been gathered by the researcher, which is the main framework of this research. The factor Behavioral Intention was added to the different facets of perceived Risk in order to extract the factors associated with different types of Risk. And finally SEM was used to check the relationship between the multiple constructs effecting Behavioral Intention to use M-Banking Services.

3 Objectives of the Study

This main aim of the researcher was to get in-depth knowledge of the different facets of Risk which have not been studied earlier. So from the gap identified while reviewing the literature these three objectives have been framed by the researcher which are:

- To identify the different types of Risk affecting the Behavioral Intention of mobile banking service users.
- To identify the relationship between the different facets of Perceived Risk and Behavioral Intention.
- To develop the model linking these factors and test the same.

4 Research Methodology

In this study the researcher has used both types of sources of data collection i.e. the primary as well as secondary sources. First hand data i.e. the Primary data was collected through questionnaire using offline as well as online mode.

4.1 Sample and Sampling Technique

For the interpretation of SEM results the determination of sample size is important, as it provides an important base for the estimation of errors while selecting the samples. In this study sample size of 250 respondents is taken. According to Hair et al. [38], in applying SEM, the size of the sample is important and should be within 200 to 500. As per Sekaran [34], there is no possibility of sampling frame error unless there are non-response errors. Hence, after the final questionnaire, researcher was able to collect data from 250 respondents out of which 220 were the usable responses to fulfil the above objectives.

Sampling technique that was used for this study was snowball sampling also known as chain-referral sampling method, and it is a kind of non-probability sampling technique. This type of sampling method involves primary data sources that nominates another probable bases that can be used in the research work. Snowball sampling technique is centered on referrals from initial subjects to generate further subjects. Therefore, while applying this sampling technique participants of the sample group were enlisted via chain referral.

The respondent's demographic profile depicted that male respondents were marginally more than the female respondents i.e. 65% male and 45% female. As per the analysis of demographic profile of the respondents 60% of the respondents belong to the age group of 21–30 Years. Education also played an important role as majority of the respondents were highly educated or professionally qualified. One major limitation of this research work was that the selection of the respondents is inclined towards the educated respondents.

4.2 Collection of Data

For the present research work the data was collected from Mobile banking services users in Delhi and NCR. For collecting data from different customers reference from the family and friends was taken.

Questionnaire survey was used for this research. Hair [35] suggested that questionnaire is the most effective way for a well-educated target population and normally generates a large amount of response rate.

For collection of primary data, schedule/questionnaire was an essential tool that was developed for reliable and first hand data collection. The questionnaire is "mainly accumulation of inquiries that suits the study area and its targets, and the solutions to which will give the information necessary to check the assumptions made for the research" [36]. Researcher has used structured schedule/questionnaire for this purpose.

5 Analysis

In this research work Exploratory Factor Analysis (EFA) and SEM was applied to perform data analysis using SPSS version 21 and AMOS version 21.

5.1   Factor Analysis

In this research paper, EFA technique was applied. Factor loading is an important statistical measure that indicated that the factor loading must be at least .50 before an item is allocated to a factor and according to rule it requires a minimum sample size of 100 [36]. In the present study, 220 sample size was taken for EFA. The data for the analysis is examined using Principle component Axis (PCA) matrix methods. A total of 7 factors were identified for PCA with varimax rotation and Eigen value more than 1. The result confirmed that there were 7 factors that accounted for 68.21% percent of total variance explained in this analysis. By using cronbach alpha, the reliability of the questionnaire was also checked. Alpha (α) the reliability coefficient of each construct are depicted in Table 2.

Table 2. Reliability coefficient - cronbach alpha value of factors

S.No.	Factors	Cronbach alpha
1	Performance Risk	0.851
2	Financial Risk	0.922
3	Time Risk	0.862
4	Social Risk	0.902
5	Privacy Risk	0.789
6	Psychological Risk	0.883
7	Behavioral Intention towards adopting mobile banking	0.883
8	Overall reliability	0.795

After checking the individual reliability of factors and overall reliability, Barlett's test for sphericity and Kaiser-Meyer-Olkin (KMO) which measure the adequacy of the samples, was run refer Table 3. Barlett's test for sphericity indicates that whether there is enough correlation between the factors or not to run the factor analysis. KMO measures the adequacy of the data to run the factor analysis. In this study the KMO shows the measure of 0.867 which is above the lower limit of 0.5 [36]. The value of Barlett's test is $\chi 2 = 4654.539$ (p-value < .001), which is also acceptable. This confirms that data is appropriate for conducting EFA.

Table 3. KMO and Barlett's test

Kaiser-Meyer-Olkin measure of sampling adequacy		.867
Bartlett's test of sphericity	Approx. Chi-Square	4654.539
	df	595
	Sig.	.000

Factor extraction technique which is also known as factor analysis was conducted using Varimax factor rotation. It has been used to categorize the Perceived Risk related variables that has an influence on the user's Behavioral Intention to adopt m-banking services. Researcher has considered 35 items for seven factors in this research paper, which was examined by using PCA. Total variance explained showed "the extent to which total variance of the observed variable is explained by each of the principle component". Initial factor extraction reveled seven important Risk related factors with Eigen value greater than one. The first principle element, which is related to Financial Risk (FR) of m-banking services which makes the principal and major part of the total variance explained, has an Eigen value of 8.890 which amounts to 25.39% of the total variance explained as shown in Table 4.

Table 4. Total variance explained for all the factors

S.No.	Factors	Total variance explained
1	Financial Risk	25.399
2	Behavioral Intention towards adopting Mobile banking	12.990
3	Social Risk	8.162
4	Psychological Risk	7.463
5	Performance Risk	5.513
6	Privacy Risk	4.507
7	Time Risk	4.179

However, all the seven factors have identified from 35 statements accounted for 68.21% percent of total variance explained.

Table 5 shows the number of items measuring the respective variables with factor loading values. The table of factor loading shows that all the items are loaded fairly on to each of the corresponding factor. These are seven factors that have been identified from 35 variables.

5.2 Structural Equation Modelling

It was applied to check the relationship amongst the multiple factors in the research model. It was applied in two parts; first part is the measurement model and second part is the structural model. Measurement model was used to verify the relation between the constructs and their indicators while structural model was used to check the relationship between the factors. Measurement model is validated via CFA and the estimation of structural model is through Path analysis.

First of all, the model was analyzed as a CFA model that provides an assessment of Reliability, Convergent Validly and Discriminant validity and then secondly, to understand the causal relationship, path analysis was executed.

Table 5. Measurement propertied for multi-item construct (factor loadings)

Rotated component matrix[a]

	Component						
	1	2	3	4	5	6	7
FR9	.904						
FR8	.879						
FR10	.874						
FR11	.872						
FR7	.807						
BI36		.808					
BI35		.777					
BI37		.739					
BI40		.698					
BI38		.650					
BI39		.636					
SR19			.799				
SR22			.797				
SR20			.768				
SR21			.754				
SR18			.691				
PSY33				.830			
PSY30				.824			
PSY31				.821			
PSY32				.808			
PSY34				.718			
PER4					.833		
PER3					.814		
PER1					.810		
PER2					.789		
PER5					.694		
PR25						.763	
PR23						.762	
PR24						.668	
PR27						.666	
PR26						.636	
TR17							.832
TR15							.799
TR14							.740
TR13							.679

[a]Rotation Converged in 6 Iterations.

5.3 Conducting CFA to Validate the Measurement Model

As discussed, Measurement model was analyzed by checking the Reliability, Convergent Validly and Discriminant validity.

Cranach alpha value was used to check the Reliability, which should be below 0.7 according to Nunnally [37]. In this research paper this condition is satisfied by the data. To check the convergent validity and Discriminant validity the condition that should be satisfied is mentioned below:

- Convergent validity = cronbach's Alpha > Average Varaince explained.
- Discriminant validity = Maximum Shared Variance < Average Varaince explained.

In this research paper convergent validity and discriminant validity was satisfied by the data as shown in Tables 6 and 7.

Table 6. Convergent validity for all the factors

S.No.	Factors	Cronbach alpha	Average variance explained
1	Performance Risk	0.851	0.517
2	Financial Risk	0.922	0.703
3	Time Risk	0.862	0.596
4	Social Risk	0.902	0.642
5	Privacy Risk	0.789	0.519
6	Psychological Risk	0.883	0.600
7	Behavioral Intention towards adopting mobile banking	0.883	0.542

Table 7. Discriminant validity for all the factors

S.No.	Factors	Average variance explained	Maximum shared variance
1	Performance Risk	0.517	0.058
2	Financial Risk	0.703	0.058
3	Time Risk	0.596	0.291
4	Social Risk	0.642	0.387
5	Privacy Risk	0.519	0.256
6	Psychological Risk	0.600	0.134
7	Behavioral Intention towards adopting mobile banking	0.542	0.387

In order to check the zero order model in CFA, P-value of all Individual constructs was checked that is below 0.05 and model fit is shown in Table 8 and model fit for the first order measurement model was also checked and is satisfying all the condition for goodness of fit.

Table 8. Model fit indices for zero order

Summary of zero order model fit indices				
Constructs	CFI	GFI	RMSEA	CMIN/df
Performance Risk	1	.994	.017	1.063
Financial Risk	.996	.988	.058	1.735
Time Risk	.997	.995	.068	2.022
Social Risk	.994	.986	.067	1.971
Privacy Risk	1	.993	0	0.956
Psychological Risk	1	. 998	0	0.280
Behavioral Intention towards adopting mobile banking	.982	.970	.093	2.880

The value of GFI was 0.906 above 0.90, the required cut off criterion. The CFI was also 0.936, above the acceptable guideline of 0.90. Additionally, the RMSEA was 0.039, below the 0.08 guideline of acceptability. Therefore the model was determined to be acceptable enough to proceed with further analysis (Fig. 1).

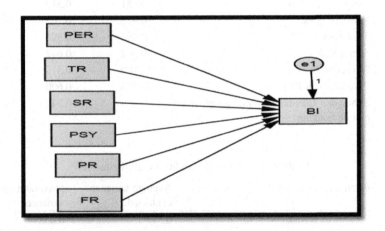

Fig. 1. Proposed research model (Source: Self)

After conducting the path analysis, researcher would examine the selected overall fit measures as discussed in the preceding section, how the path model fits the data. Analysis of path model yielded a reasonable fit to the data. The value of GFI was 0.995 above 0.90, the required cut off criterion. The CFI was also 0.992, above the acceptable guideline of 0.90. Additionally, the RMSEA was 0.043, below the 0.08 guideline of acceptability.

The establishment of an identified path model then allows the researcher for testing the postulated relationship of the factors as outlined in the proposed research model.

Table 9 shows the result of the path analysis that was executed to check the relationship between the multiple factors that were identified in the EFA. So as per the

Table 9. Testing the proposed model with regression weight

			Estimate	S.E.	C.R.	P	Relationship
BI	←	PER	−.015	.070	−.214	.830	Not significant
BI	←	TR	−.273	.064	−4.240	***	Significant
BI	←	SR	−.373	.061	−6.073	***	Significant
BI	←	PSY	−.142	.063	−2.261	***	Significant
BI	←	PR	−.080	.058	−1.375	.169	Not significant
BI	←	FR	−.098	.040	−2.447	***	Significant

result Social Risk, Time Risk, Psychological Risk and Financial Risk were found to be statistically significant and can affect the Behavioral Intention in adoption of m-banking services in the Indian context. So the hypotheses H2, H3, H4, and H6 are accepted and H1 and H5 are rejected.

6 Major Results and Findings

The findings of this research work support the four hypotheses out of six. Social Risk, Time Risk, Psychological Risk and Financial Risk was found to have statistically significant negative relationship with the Behavioral Intention in adopting m-banking services. The interpretation of the each finding is discussed in detail below.

Financial Risk was found to be the utmost significant factor that influence Behavioral Intention in adopting m-banking services. This implies that all those users who perceives mobile banking as vulnerable platform when doing the financial transaction and who have concern about the non-refund of the money because to careless mistakes of the users' like wrong entry of own account number or amount of the money to be transferred or withdrawn were liable to have negative intentions towards adopting mobile banking services.

Social Risk has also come out to be the second important factor influencing consumer intention in adopting m-banking services and it is also the powerful inhibitor to the Behavioral Intention in adopting m-banking services. This implies that the Indian consumer do not have very favorable attitude towards its adoption and they care about the Social pressure from their peer group. And it also implies that they have their friends, family, relatives who also do not have positive attitude towards mobile banking services.

Time Risk has also emerged as a negative factor influencing the Behavioral Intention in adopting m-banking services. The significant impact of Time Risk implies that consumers in the Indian market do not like to wait if there is a delay in the transaction to get completed or delay in the payment. It may be due to network problem or an error occurred with the site or application.

The result also indicated that the Psychological Risk was also the important inhibiting factor in influencing the behavioral adoption of m-banking services. This may be due to the fact that consumers do not want unnecessary tension due to involvement of money and Risk while using mobile banking services. The stress of the consumers may also increase when response Time in completing the transaction increases.

Indian consumers are not giving much importance to Performance Risk and Privacy Risk. This may be due to the fact that they are not much concerned about the expectations and level of benefits received while using mobile banking services. They also do not worry about the sharing of their personal details with others because they trust the mobile banking services that they will not fraud but they doubt the technical error that may occur anytime.

7   Implications of the Research

This study is useful for the banking sector to implement the strategies for adoption of mobile baking services which will enable them to increase the customer base and provide them with better services. The implications of this research work are discussed below.

This study provides new information related to the different facets of Perceived Risk and Behavioral Intention in adopting m-banking services which have not been covered in the Indian context. Thus this study supplements to the existing body of knowledge.

Most of the previous researches have studied perceived Risk as a single construct but in this study researcher tried to bring out the different facets of perceived Risk. So detailed and in-depth analysis of different types of Risk by the researcher can help the banks to take care of all the Risk variables while designing the mobile banking services applications and to develop the Risk reducing strategies so as to give assurance to the user and it will help in increasing the customer base.

This study is also contributing in deciding which factor is the most influential and as per the result of the empirical analysis, Financial Risk affects the adoption intention the most. So banks should give surety to the consumers regarding their finance. And banks should also have a proper refund facility, in case of any wrong transaction occurred or it may be due to carelessness of the consumer that the consumer may have entered the wrong account number or wrong amount.

This study also helps the bank to understand the effect of different types of Risk; out of all i.e. Social Risk, Privacy Risk, Psychological Risk, Performance Risk, Time Risk and Financial Risk only two came out to be statistically non-significant in the Indian context i.e. Privacy Risk and Performance Risk.

This study also provides important strategic guidelines to the banks. For instance, this study revealed that Financial Risk is the most influential Risk factor affecting the adoption intention of the user. Findings of this research work also helps the bank to provide the better customer service through M-banking by overcoming the Risk factors and providing surety to the customers about their security.

8 Conclusion

This research paper aimed at extracting the factors to predict the different facets of perceived Risk in Mobile banking. This study incorporated six components of perceived Risk to investigate in detail the positives and negatives of adopting mobile banking services.

So some of the suggestions by the researcher is also discussed. Banks should also give various offers to the customers to lure them to shift from traditional way of banking to mobile banking. Banks, should provide important information to the customers regarding phishing, hacking and fraud.

Many of the user's shows reluctance in using the online base for financial transaction, to overcome these banks should organize awareness programs for the public to increase the adoption towards mobile banking services. Security is the major concern in the customers towards nominal banking services usage, so banks should provide trials to use M-banking services on their mobile phone.

In all, banks should use alternative ways of motivating customers to adopt mobile as a medium to do financial transactions online and to use different modes of advertisement to create awareness among the customers. All these suggestions and implications may help banks and government to increase the financial inclusion in India.

In future research it is important to generalize the result through in-depth investigations ion the various developed and developing countries. This may be because the Behavioral Intention varies with the population and the country as well. The future research may also incorporate other factors in the model such as Perceived Cost, Trust, and Culture in order to examine their influence on Behavioral Intention towards adopting m-banking services.

References

1. Hoffman, D.L., Novak, T.P., Peralta, M.: Building consumer trust online. Commun. ACM **42**, 1–5 (1999)
2. Jarvenpaa, S., Tractinsky, N.: Consumer trust in an internet store: a cross-cultural validation. J. Comput. Mediat. Commun. **5**, 1–35 (1999)
3. Pavlou, P.A.: Consumer acceptance of electronic commerce—integrating trust and risk with the technology acceptance model. Int. J. E-Commer. **7**, 69–103 (2003)
4. Cox, D.F., Rich, S.U.: Perceived risk and consumer decision making the case of telephone shopping. J. Mark. Res. **1**, 32–39 (1964)
5. Global Findex Report. http://www.worldbank.org/en/programs/globalfindex
6. Shaikh, A., Karjaluoto, H., Chinje, N.B.: Continuous mobile banking usage and relationship commitment – a multi-country assessment. J. Financ. Serv. Mark. **20**, 208–219 (2015)
7. Safeena, R., Date, H., Hundewale, N., Kammani, A.: Combination of TAM and TPB in internet banking adoption. Int. J. Comput. Theory Eng. **5**, 146–150 (2013). https://doi.org/10.7763/IJCTE.2013.V5.665
8. Lin, Y.H., Hu, S.Y., Chen, M.S.: Managerial optimism and corporate investment: some empirical evidence from Taiwan. Pac.-Basin Financ. J. **13**(5), 523–546 (2005)
9. Peter, J., Ryan, M.: An investigation of perceived risk at the brand level. J. Mark. Res. **13**, 184–188 (1976)

10. Cunningham, S.: The major dimensions of perceived risk. In: Cox, D. (ed.) Risk Taking and Information Handling in Consumer Behaviour. Harvard University Press (1967)
11. Jacoby, J., Kaplan, L.B.: The components of perceived risk. Adv. Consum. Res. **3**, 382–383 (1972)
12. Kaplan, L.B., Szybillo, G.J., Jacoby, J.: Components of perceived risk in product purchase: a crossvalidation. J. Appl. Psychol. **59**(3), 287 (1974)
13. Roselius, T.: Consumer rankings of risk reduction methods. J. Mark. **35**, 56–61 (1971)
14. Stone, R.N., Gronhaug, K.: Perceived risk: further considerations for the marketing discipline. Eur. J. Mark. **27**, 39–50 (1993)
15. Jarvenpaa, S.L., Todd, P.A.: Consumer reactions to electronic shopping on the World Wide Web. Int. J. E-Commer. **1**, 59–88 (1996)
16. Comegys, C., Hannula, M., Vaisanen, J.: Effects of consumer trust and risk on online purchase decision-making. Int. J. Manag. **26**, 295–308 (2009)
17. Featherman, P.: Predicting e-services adoption: a perceived risk facets perspective. Int. J. Hum.-Comput. Stud. **59**, 451–474 (2003)
18. Scott, N., Batchelor, S., Ridley, J., Jorgensen, B.: The Impact of Mobile Phones in Africa. Prepared for the Commission for Africa (2004)
19. Soroor, J.: Implementation of a secure internet/mobile banking system in Iran. J. Internet Bank. Commer. **10** (2005)
20. Bhatnagar, A., Misra, S., Rao, H.R.: On risk, convenience, and internet shopping behaviour. Commun. ACM **43**, 98–105 (2000)
21. Vijayasarathy, L.R.: Internet taxation, privacy and security: opinions of the taxed and legislated. Q. J. Electron. Commer. **3**, 53–71 (2002)
22. Kuisma, T., Laukkanen, T., Hiltunen, M.: Mapping the reasons for resistance to Internet banking: a means-end approach. Int. J. Inf. Manag. **27**, 75–85 (2007)
23. Lee, M.C.: Factors influencing the adoption of internet banking: an integration of TAM and TPB with perceived risk and perceived benefit. E-Commer. Res. Appl. **8**, 130–141 (2009)
24. Lee, M.C.: Predicting behavioral intention to use online banking. In: Proceedings of the 19th International Conference on Information Management (2008)
25. Fain, D., Roberts, M.L.: Technology vs. consumer behaviour: the battle for the financial services customer. J. Direct Mark. **11**, 44–54 (1997)
26. Laforet, S., Li, X.Y.: Consumers' attitudes towards online and mobile banking in China. Int. J. Bank Mark. **23**, 362–380 (2005)
27. Ram, S., Sheth, J.N.: Consumer resistance to innovations: the marketing problem and its solutions. J. Consum. Mark. **6**, 5–14 (1989)
28. Bestavros, A.: Banking industry walks 'Tightrope' in personalization of web services. Bank Syst. Technol. **37**, 54–56 (2000)
29. Daniel, E.: Provision of electronic banking in the UK and the Republic of Ireland. Int. J. Bank Mark. **17**, 72–82 (1999)
30. Sathye, M.: Adoption of internet banking by Australian consumers: an empirical investigation. Int. J. Bank Mark. **17**, 324–334 (1999)
31. Chiou, J.S., Shen, C.C.: The antecedents of online financial service adoption: the impact of physical banking services on Internet banking acceptance. Behav. Inf. Technol. **31**, 859–871 (2012)
32. Luarn, P., Lin, H.H.: Toward an understanding of the behavioral intention to use mobile banking. Comput. Hum. Behav. **21**, 873–891 (2005)
33. Cudjoe, A.G., Anim, P.A., Nyanyofio, J.G.N.T.: Determinants of mobile banking adoption in the Ghanaian banking industry: a case of Access Bank Ghana Limited. J. Comput. Commun. **3**, 1–19 (2015)

34. Sekaran, U.: Research Methods For Business A Skill Building Approach, 4th edn. Wiley-India Pvt. Ltd., New Delhi (2006)
35. Hair, J.F., Anderson, R.E., Tatham, L., Black, W.: Multivariate Data Analysis, 5th edn. Prentice Hall, Upper Saddle River (2003)
36. Kothari, C.R.: Research Methodology-Methods and Techniques. New Delhi, Wiley Eastern Limited (1985)
37. Nunnally, J.C.: Psychometric Theory, 2nd edn. McGraw-Hill, New York (1978)
38. Hair Jr., J.F., Anderson, R.E., Tatham, R.L., Black, W.C.: Multivariate Data Analysis, 3rd edn. Macmillan Publishing Company, New York (1995)
39. Grewal, D., Gotlieb, J., Marmorstein, H.: The moderating effects of message framing and source credibility on the price perceived risk relationship. J. Consum. Res. 21(1), 145–153 (1994)

An Online Monitoring System for Measuring Human Attention Level Based on Brain Activities

Haitham Mohammed Al Balushi[✉]
and Satish Masthenahally Nachappa

Middle East College, Muscat, Sultanate of Oman
haitham.m.7007@gmail.com, satish@mec.edu.om

Abstract. One of the major organ and resource in human is brain which is interconnected with millions of neurons, these neurons can be used to know the attention of human at different time intervals. The human brain waves plays a vital role in controlling and monitoring the devices and environment. The EEG sensor is used to transfer brain waves using Bluetooth and automated through a microcontroller for knowing the attention of the Human brain. The major system in the designed work is with Arduino Mega Microcontroller which is programmed to monitor the attention of the brain activities. All the readings helps in predicting the status of the human brain Activity. The quality of the work is defined by recording the mental states of human brain by different frequencies of brain waves. The different frequencies are detected are alpha, beta, gamma and delta patterns. In the carried work real time simulation and testing is done on breadboard. The implementation results are clearly shown by signifying each step importance. The outcomes of the carried work are monitored in real time and checked through Internet of things (IOT). The carried work is tested on different participants and they were advised to analyze and think on various tasks such as left, right, forward and back. The data is although collected from various participants for correlation and deviation values. In general the analysis is performed with the thinking data and computed in terms of attention levels. Further to this it can be used for Alzheimer's disease and cognitive impaired people to know the exact thinking of the people and their needs or requirements.

Keywords: EEG · Arduino · IOT · Brain · Attention · Alpha

1 Introduction

Mind Machine Interface is the one which connects brain with computer. It creates a path between human and external device for assisting and knowing the cognitive behavior of human brain. The Brain computer Interface (BCI) is much focused on neuro prosthetics and dreadful diseases like Alzheimer and Bipolar disorder diseases. These interfaces gives a direct correspondence to the human movement and influence on its execution. Brain attention is very important measurement in psychology for many decades [2]. According to chih-Ming (2017) recognizing the attention levels provide higher potential and timely alert for feedback and online monitoring. However

© Springer Nature Singapore Pte Ltd. 2019
P. K. Singh et al. (Eds.): FTNCT 2018, CCIS 958, pp. 192–206, 2019.
https://doi.org/10.1007/978-981-13-3804-5_15

the attention level determines the learning performance and easily prediction of the effects from distraction of the work. Moreover this study attains importance for sustained attention level with respect learning activity and evaluation of performance. The attention level from human brain are recorded as Delta, theta, alpha, beta, Mu, lambda and vertex for different users and are placed in different locations of brain [1]. These waves determine sleep, coma, stress and intention towards tasks etc. The psychological process gives a better analyzing and understanding of any human in terms of concentration and focus. This helps in enhancing the speed and accuracy of human [6] (Fig. 1).

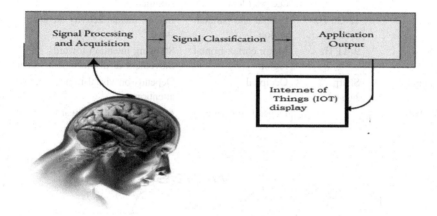

Fig. 1. Shows the human Brain computer Interface (BCI)

The Brain waves are used to produce synchronized electrical pulses with neurons to communicate with each other. These EEG sensors are placed on the scalp and divided for each sections of bandwidths for its respective functions. The best spectrum determined is for consciousness and complex situations [13]. The waves produced from brain are measured in Hertz (Cycles/Second) for determining the bands of fast, slow and moderate frequencies. However the problems associated in our life are from all sorts of emotional and neurological conditions [12]. The below table gives the various levels of frequency through the Table 1.

The first type of waves are with a frequency of <0.5 Hz known as Infra low used for slow and cortical potentials. They are very difficult to measure and underlie to higher brain functions. The other frequency type is from 0.5 to 3 Hz known as delta waves which are like drum beat and generated from meditation and dreamless sleep. The third type of brain waves are from 3 to 8 Hz frequency band which are known as theta waves for learning and intuition with external world. Next waves are about Alpha waves which are from a frequency of 8 to 12 Hz. These waves come from the flowing thoughts and meditative states. Beta waves are other type of waves from 12 to 38 Hz and they work for waking state of consciousness and these waves are fast and usually appear during the judgement and mental activity state [11] (Fig. 2).

Table 1. Shows the frequency bands and its relative use [2]

Different types of signals	Frequency (cut off)	Location-brain position	Purpose
Delta	<4 Hz	Can be placed anywhere on the brain	This information is useful during coma or sleep
Theta	4–7 Hz	Parietal and temporal lobe	Frustration, disappointment and emotional stress can be in relation
Alpha	8–12 Hz	Parietal and occipital lobe	Mental imaging or sensor stimulation
Beta	12–36 Hz	Frontal and parietal region	Intense mental activity advance stage
Mu	9–11 Hz	Motor cortex-frontal region	Showing intention towards movement or displacement related
Lambda	Sharp Jagged	Occipital	Depends on visual movement and attention
Vertex		Depends on patient	Monitored mostly towards patients affected with epilepsy

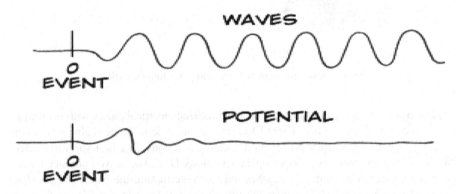

Fig. 2. Shows how the waves are interpreted in real time with potential

Lastly Gamma waves are highest frequency waves from 38 to 42 Hz for representing the love and virtues of human.

2 Literature Survey

In order to thoroughly understand and find the related literature, a comparison study has been defined to the earlier works. Besides this work has been compared with two papers which are more close to the novel attention awareness system (Table 2).

These comparison of results show the recording and attention level of human and the various components used for recording the brain activity and learning design for the

Table 2. Shows the survey of literature studied

Se. No.	Title of the paper	Hardware and software used	Methods and related results	Measurement of response and its results
1	Chen et al. assessing the attention levels of students by using a novel attention aware system based on brainwave signals [1]	Headset for mind wave measurements, classifier of support vector machine and genetic algorithm	Measurement of EEG with data of beta, alpha and gamma waves Able to determine the attention level	Validation by recall and precision rates
2	Frey et al. framework for electroencephalography-based evaluation of user experience [2]	Signals or waves from EEG sensors for a frequency of 512 Hz, anova tools for graphical measurement, virtual keyboard and its LCD interface	To define the states of brain like relaxed, emotional, motivational, mental	Ranges have been defined as hard and easy and ultra for different classifications. LDA or fish analysis for predicting the reaction time 0.93 s

user modelling systems. All the literature studied gives a broad experience in understanding human response. The mind wave head set sends the data through Bluetooth for graphical representation on the computer through microcontroller. The processing software of Arduino sketch is used to define brain Grapher with python programming. All the details are observed in Internet of things (IOT) from anywhere and anytime. Arduino board supports the python programming with IDE for measuring the brain activity. The system detects the brain activities and initiate control for assessing the human brain [1–6].

2.1 Existing Drawbacks

1. Proper safety steps should be followed while connecting the sensor on the scalp and its reference contacts should be grounded as needed but not on the head Sections.
2. Choosing appropriate sensor is required as often the complaints are through low battery power and hair disturbing or not kept suitably on the head [3].
3. From the literature studied it is seen that environmental noise, manmade noise too have more effect on electric signals strongly.
4. Moving the head improperly and not following instructions and clamor is unavoidable for the sensor.

3 System Design

Neurosky mindwave sensor provides EEG sensor values and these waves are carried out wirelessly through Bluetooth and Arduino is programmed in Sketch IDE to determine the values of Alpha, theta and gamma. These values are sent through a channel using things speak software which enables the user to verify and monitor the values from anywhere which is much useful for any user. These values are updated online and monitored as per the need (Fig. 3).

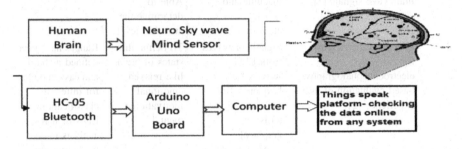

Fig. 3. Block diagram for detecting brain activity.

3.1 Flow Chart and Design Steps

System Flow Chart: The work carried out is defined in steps with a flowchart where the total process of the work defined is shown below and the coding for this work has been carried out with Arduino sketch. The implementation work is described in two steps as shown in Fig. 4.

Arduino IDE is the environmental framework used for coding and its results were checked out in Arduino sketch. This software is user friendly and it is inbuilt to carry out any activity on the web and it is quite easy for understanding. The baud rate used in communication is 9600. The steps followed in the process is defined as follows

1. Adruino IDE install in your system
2. Use the board with drivers installed through USB cable
3. Launch the application of Adruino and involve the use of Blink Example
4. Use the serial port to connect the board and define the values
5. Register online in things speak and create a channel
6. Use the Channel ID for updating the values
7. Appropriately check the connection and refresh it as required
8. The graphs plotted are considered and check the numerically to correlate the graph and information
9. Understand the values and check at different intervals to know the difference
10. Calculate the values and analyze the readings as required
11. Perform this operation at different ages and find the relevancy and percentage of matching.

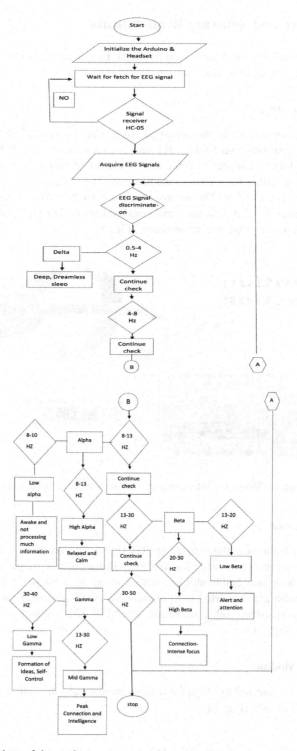

Fig. 4. Flowchart of the total system output with appropriate implementation procedure

4 Hardware and Software Requirements

The proposed work designed uses Arduino Mega, EEG sensor and HC-05 Module and a PC for display or LCD screen.

4.1 Arduino Mega

It is the major component in the proposed work. This microcontroller board has 54 digital input/output pins and four UART and crystal oscillator of 16 MHz this has a USB cable to directly connect to computer or adapter of power. This microcontroller support and compatible to Arduino duemilanove. The voltage recommended for the Microcontroller is 7 to 12 V. The memory used is 8 Kb SRAM and Arduino software uses serial monitor for text data and serial communication. The bootloader of 1280 has STK500 protocol for programming incircuit (Fig. 5).

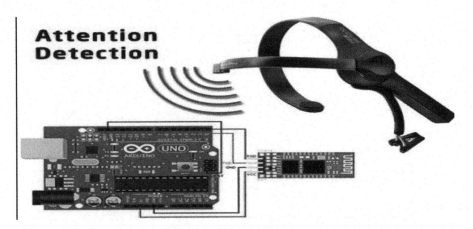

Fig. 5. Shows the interfacing of Arduino with Mindwave headset

4.2 EEG Sensor

In this work Electroencephalography (EEG) signals are recorder using this sensor. These sensors are placed on scalp and electrical signals of low frequency are recorded from brain. The signal bandwidth are with a range of 1 Hz to 50 Hz. The analog signals from brain are converted in to digital with ASIC processor inbuilt and passed through Bluetooth or any other hardware. The MSP 430 is major processor in Neurosky module (Fig. 6).

4.3 HC-05 Module

This module is connected to Mega for reading the data and uploading and sending the information wirelessly (Fig. 7).

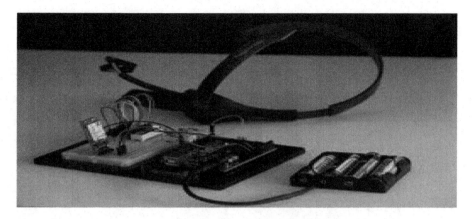

Fig. 6. Prototype design and testing with all hardware

Fig. 7. Bluetooth (Hc-05 Module)

5   Experimental Results

The following steps are to be followed for installing and configuring the proposed work and the steps are detailed enough to explain the operation

1. First take the Mind wave kit and switch it on and unpair the last connections and then switch it off
2. Use the program of Arduino as uploaded in the sketch IDE and use source code to Arduino Board using Arduino compiler.
3. The serial monitor should be opened with Arduino compiler for 9600 baudrate.
4. Define all the connections as represented then switch ON the Arduino Board.
5. After the 7 s, switch ON the Mindwave device.
6. Now the Mindwave device and Arduino Board will pair automatically.
7. Wear the Mindwave device in Head, and give the attention.
8. Check the LED variation with respect your attention level.
9. After obtaining the data on serial port, our target is send the data over THING-SPEAK, to make the sensor data as public using IOT
10. See the below images and follow the steps according for establishing the channel output from anywhere (Figs. 8, 9, 10, 11, 12, 13, 14, 15, 16, 17, 18 and 19).

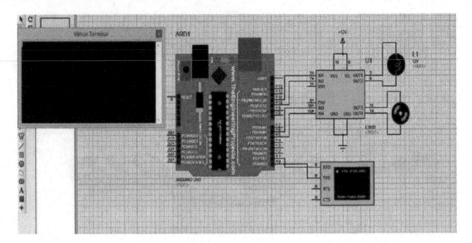

Fig. 8. Shows the simulation testing done in proteus software

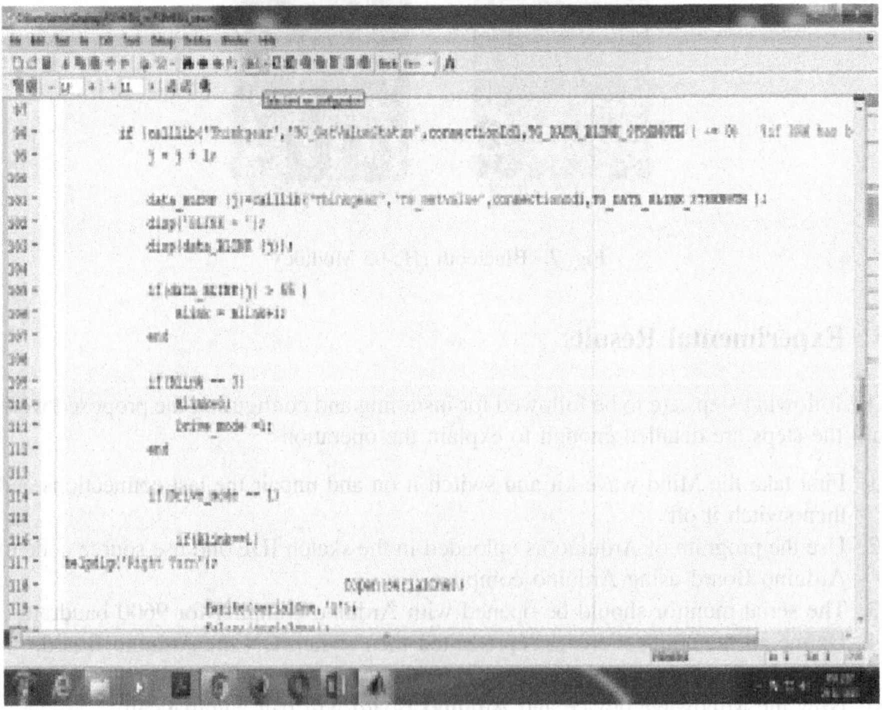

Fig. 9. Shows the simulation testing done in proteus software

Fig. 10. Shows the hardware components used in design of the proposed work

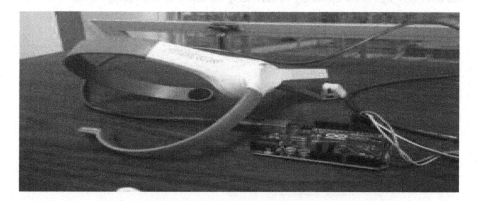

Fig. 11. Shows the prototype design and output verification

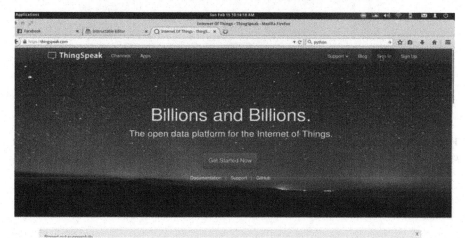

Fig. 12. It is a application that acts as an interface to internet of things and any input data to monitor

Fig. 13. It shows an interface with user login this can be done by having account in mathworks and can easily sign in for uploading or interfacing the data into IOT (Things Speak)

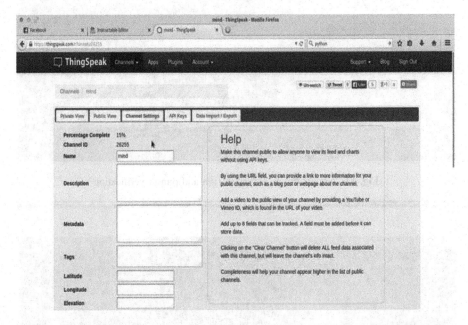

Fig. 14. After establishing account with things speak it will provide a channel with ID and you can give the name for the account and can define what sensor data is used to in internet

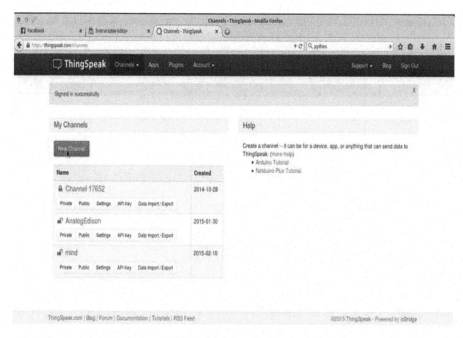

Fig. 15. Shows how you establish a new channel to upload the data of Mind wave sensor

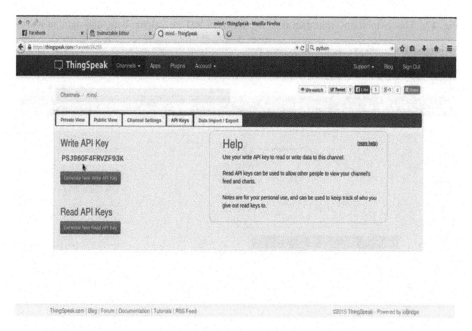

Fig. 16. You can see an application peripheral interface key to link the data obtained from sensor through microcontroller

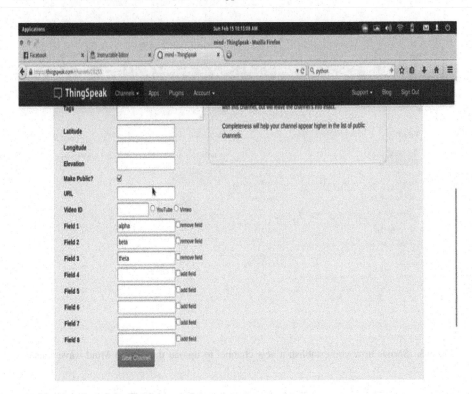

Fig. 17. This is to show what data is to be shown in IOT i.e., alpha, beta, and gamma waves

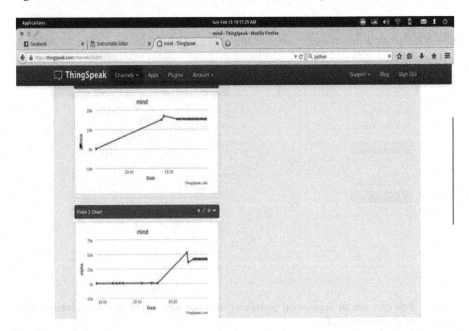

Fig. 18. You can see the result of alpha, beta in the above which describes how the data has been presented through IOT (anytime and anywhere)

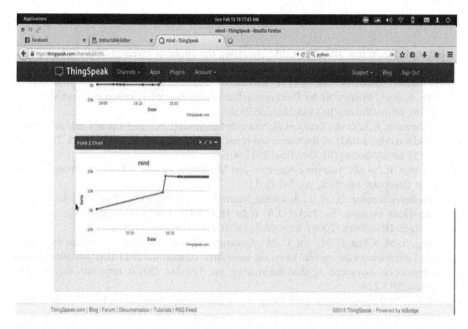

Fig. 19. Shows the gamma result with mind wave sensor through IOT to observe and monitor the situation.

6 Conclusion

This is how the sensor data which is provided by the Mind wave about the status of the person is uploaded to the IOT which is a public domain. Anyone can open and observe the readings. The main Aim of this project is make the brain data accessible by the doctor at any point, as such the necessary treatments can be planned from anywhere and expert doctors can reach the patients at all the respective different locations. Brain attention is measured in the form of meditation and concentration values as alpha, gamma, beta and delta waves. The graphical view can be seen through Things speak from a valid login channel. The EEG signals are optimal to record the status of the human brain Activity. This biofeedback is defined as neurofeedback for teaching and understanding the activities through brain. The Human status and his brain activity can be monitored through IOT and is a public domain. These readings from brain activity are analyzed and can be useful for a doctor for accurate treatment. The treatments can be planned and human attention can be monitored from anywhere and anytime.

Acknowledgment. I am very much thankful to Middle East College, Muscat for providing me lab facilities and also creating an environment of renowned professors who helped me at every step during contribution to my work and defining me new research findings related to the work proposed.

References

1. Chen, C.M., Wang, J.Y., Yu, C.M.: Assessing the attention levels of students by using a novel attention aware system based on brainwave signals. Br. J. Educ. Technol. **48**(2), 348–369 (2017). https://doi.org/10.1111/bjet.12359
2. Frey, J., et al.: Framework for Electroencephalography-Based Evaluation of User Experience (2016). https://doi.org/10.1145/2858036.2858525
3. Mathewson, K.J., et al.: Regional electroencephalogram (EEG) alpha power and asymmetry in older adults: a study of short-term test-retest reliability. Front. Aging Neurosci. **7**(9), 1–10 (2015). https://doi.org/10.3389/fnagi.2015.00177
4. Mokhtar, R., et al.: Assessing Attention and Meditation Levels in Learning Process Using Brain Computer Interface, pp. 3–7 (n.d.)
5. Rebolledo-Mendez, G., et al.: Assessing NeuroSky's usability to detect attention levels in an assessment exercise. In: Jacko, J.A. (ed.) HCI 2009. LNCS, vol. 5610, pp. 149–158. Springer, Heidelberg (2009). https://doi.org/10.1007/978-3-642-02574-7_17
6. Yang, S.-M., Chen, C.-M., Yu, C.-M.: Assessing the attention levels of students by using a novel attention aware system based on brainwave signals. In: 2015 IIAI 4th International Congress on Advanced Applied Informatics, pp. 379–384 (2015). https://doi.org/10.1109/iiai-aai.2015.224
7. Li, K.: P300 Based Single Trial Independent Component Analysis on EEG Signal (2009). http://dl.acm.org/citation.cfm?id=1611130. Accessed 19 July 2009
8. Campisi, P.: Brain waves for automatic biometric-based user recognition (2014). http://dl.acm.org/citation.cfm?id=2714006. Accessed May 2014
9. Clodoaldo A.M.: Kernel Machines for Epilepsy Diagnosis via EEG Signal Classification (2011). http://dl.acm.org/citation.cfm?id=2031305. Accessed 2 Oct 2011
10. Robbins, R.: Investigating the Neurosky Mindwave EEG Headset. http://dl.acm.org/citation.cfm?id=2031305. Accessed 2 Oct 2014
11. Asif Hussain, S., Giri Prasad, M.N., Ramaiah, C.: An intelligent frame work system for finger touch association on planar surfaces. In: Attele, K.R., Kumar, A., Sankar, V., Rao, N.V., Sarma, T.H. (eds.) Emerging Trends in Electrical, Communications and Information Technologies. LNEE, vol. 394, pp. 185–191. Springer, Singapore (2017). https://doi.org/10.1007/978-981-10-1540-3_19
12. Campisi, P., La Rocca, D.: Brain waves for automatic biometric-based user recognition. IEEE Trans. Inf. Forens. Secur. **9**(5), 782–800 (2014)
13. Abbas, A., Lee, C.J., Kim, K.-I.: Delay bounded Spray and wait in delay tolerant networks. In: Proceedings of the 9th International Conference on Ubiquitos Information Management and communication, Bali, Indonesia, 08–10 January 2015. ACM, New York (2015)

Privacy Preserving Ranked Multi Keyword Context Sensitive Fuzzy Search Over Encrypted Cloud Data

Anu Khurana[1(✉)], Rama Krishna Challa[2], and Navdeep Kaur[3]

[1] I.K. Gujral Punjab Technical University, Kapurthala, Punjab, India
annu_khurana@yahoo.com
[2] Department of Computer Science and Engineering, NITTTR,
Chandigarh, India
rkc_97@yahoo.com
[3] Department of Computer Science and Engineering,
Sri Guru Granth Sahib World University, Fatehgarh Sahib, Punjab, India
drnavdeep.iitr@gmail.com

Abstract. The privacy preserving search feature is very useful for a cloud user to retrieve the desired encrypted documents easily, securely and cost effectively in the cloud. However, a search query issued by the user may sometimes have mis-typos i.e. wrongly typed words. The mis-typos could occur because of the addition or drop of letter(s) from the word or by swapping of characters in a word. At times such mis-typos may have many spelling suggestions against them within a given threshold, of which only a few makes sense as per the context of the query. Also the mistyped word may sometimes result in another valid word from the dictionary or the word list and hence the mis-spelt word may go unnoticed. Recent works in cloud address the issue of fuzzy search. However, these approaches do not suggest a word suitable as per the context and co-occurrence with other words of the query for such mis-typos. This paper presents a privacy preserving scheme 'Context Sensitive Fuzzy Search' (CSFS) in a cloud computing environment that address these issues. CSFS uses Levenshtein distance and neighbor co-occurrence statistics computed from encrypted query click logs and suggest(s) word(s) from the generated suggestions and set distance as per their co-occurring frequency with other words of the query. The results achieved show that the spelling suggestions listed are as per the context of the query and have high recall value.

Keywords: Mis-typos · Fuzzy · Cloud computing · Encrypted query click logs
Co-occurrence

1 Introduction

Cloud computing has become prevalent because of the enormous benefits it provides. People now rely on cloud for the various services it offers, including storage as a service [1] resulting in remarkable increase in the volume of data stored on the cloud. Cloud Service Providers (CSP) need to keep the user data in encrypted format as it may

P. K. Singh et al. (Eds.): FTNCT 2018, CCIS 958, pp. 207–220, 2019.
https://doi.org/10.1007/978-981-13-3804-5_16

contain sensitive and crucial data [2]. Encryption though needed makes searching on the encrypted data difficult. However, for enhancing user experience and for retrieving desired documents quickly and economically from the encrypted cloud data, a suitable search mechanism is desired.

The practical solution to the problem of searchable encryption has been given by Song et al. in the year 2000 [3] for the first time. Thereafter, many [4–9] solutions from different perspectives towards improving the techniques and ways of searchable encryption have been proposed. These techniques, however, are not directly applicable in the cloud computing environment as they lack in providing a good user search experience. Many researchers in [10–16] have given schemes for privacy preserving multi keyword search in the cloud. These schemes provide invaluable insight in the area of keyword search over encrypted data in cloud computing. Thereafter researchers in [19–22] provided schemes for fuzzy search over encrypted cloud data, towards enhancing search capability. Fuzzy search refers to a search process in which the search is carried out against the keywords that does not match the search query completely, but approximately. One reason for this, could be introduction of spelling errors (due to typing errors i.e. mis-typos) in the search query.

2   Related Work

Li et al. in [17] have given a fuzzy search using the wild card method. They use 'edit distance' and their scheme returns the matched files if the user query exactly matches the pre-set keywords and in case there are typos or format inconsistencies then the server returns the closest possible results based on the pre-specified similarity semantics. Later, Ahsan et al. in [18] have given a fuzzy based scheme in which they use monograms and give relevance to the position of the character in a word and find the correct word for the mis-typo with maximum similarity. They use 'Jaccard similarity' with a variation to compute the similarity. Ding et al. in [19] proposed a scheme wherein they reduced the index size in order to incur low storage costs. They use k-grams and 'Jaccard distance' for construction of fuzzy keyword sets and produce fuzzy results. Chen et al. in [20] gives a scheme, in which they give a two-stage index structure, Locality-Sensitive Hashing, and a Bloom filter and assures that the search time is linearly independent of the file size. Their multi-keyword fuzzy search function is implemented based on the Gram Counting Order, the Bloom filter, and Locality-Sensitive Hashing. In the research by Khan et al. [21], the objective proffered is to make the index and trapdoor more secure hence 'Vernam cipher' is used and for finding the near correct spelling 'Levenshtein distance' is used. The focus in [22] relates to enhancing user search experience. They use tree based index, expand the query locally with correction for wrong spelling and sends it to the server. They also expand their query for synonyms.

These fuzzy schemes available in literature as well as our previous work [21] addresses the problem of fuzzy search but none of these deal with the issue of choosing the best available suggestion as per the context of the query.

3   Proposed Scheme CSFS

3.1   Problem Formulation

For a given mistyped word under the set distance of adding, removing or substituting a character there could be many spelling suggestions. Out of these, the best suggestions could be further shortlisted as per its context and relevance. For example, if a query issued is "world pece day" where the "pece" is wrongly typed. If we consider the distance of 1 the correct word suggestions for it could be "pace", "peck", "piece", "pence" and "peace". Accordingly the confusion set will be "world pece day", "world pace day", "world piece day" and "world peace day". From among these, if the context is checked, the correct word suggestion "peace" is most appropriate. Considering another scenario the misspelled word because of insertion, deletion or swapping of characters may generate another valid word. For example, the character 's' missed from the word 'sword' generates 'word', 'tent' gives 'rent' because of wrong key press and 'cat' gives 'act' because of swapping of letters. Here all three mistyped words are valid word that makes it difficult to identify that a spelling error has occurred. So a mechanism is needed for suggesting correct spelling suggestion(s) by considering the context of the query.

3.2   System Model

To address the issue of shortlisting the suggestions of correct spellings as per the context of the query, we propose a scheme Context Sensitive Fuzzy Search (CSFS). We address the issue for both cases i.e. where mistypos does not generate a valid word and a case where they generate a valid word. The proposed scheme CSFS consider cloud storage system to consist of four entities namely data owner, data user, private cloud server (a trusted entity) and the public cloud server. Data owner is responsible for uploading the encrypted document collection $C = Enc (D1, D2... Dn)$ along with its encrypted index file $\hat{I}(M)$. We assume that the data owner authorizes the data user to perform search and access the document collection C. The private cloud server holds cipher table IVV and spell table. Public cloud server is a rented commodity where

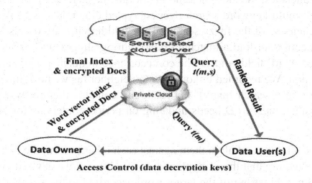

Fig. 1. Architecture of CSFS system model

document collection C is uploaded along with its index file $\hat{I}(M, S)$, it maintains the master encrypted query click log $\bar{Q}$, collocation dictionary $\mathcal{CD}$ and returns relevant documents mapped against the user's search query. Figure 1 shows the architecture of CSFS system model.

3.3 Threat Model

In this paper, we consider private cloud server to be a fully trusted entity whereas for the public cloud server we consider it as honest-but-curious server. So despite keeping all the documents in encrypted format we need to assure that the search is performed in a secure manner and prevents information leak from which statistical inferences could be drawn.

3.4 Notation

- $\hat{I}(M)$: Index of unique words encrypted with key M
- $\hat{I}(M, S)$: Index of unique words encrypted with key M further encrypted with key S
- $t(M)$: Query unique words encrypted with key M
- $t(M, S)$: Query unique words encrypted with key M further encrypted with key S
- $\cancel{WV}$: Table containing all ciphers of the word vectors
- $\mathcal{CD}$: Collocation Dictionary
- $\bar{Q}$: Master Encrypted Query Click Log

3.5 Preliminaries

Collocation Dictionary ($\mathcal{CD}$)
Collocation dictionary $\mathcal{CD}$ is formed by aligning the queries (from $\bar{Q}$) against each other. The queries picked for alignment are from same cluster. This cluster is formed by keeping all queries that have clicked the same document in search results, and further adds all the queries, linked to the shortlisted document in the cluster. The queries selected for alignment have equal number of keywords with only one dissimilar term in them, which then becomes the aligned word. The $\mathcal{CD}$ formed contains, the aligned words (as *mainword* and *alignedword*) and the neighboring terms with their co-occurrence frequencies. We designed the $\mathcal{CD}$ in this manner, as we plan to use $\mathcal{CD}$ for synonym based multi keyword search over encrypted cloud data as well. However, to increase the efficiency of the fuzzy search, while building up $\mathcal{CD}$, we also included the queries which could not find a matching query during alignment. For such entries we left the 'aligned word' field empty. The co-occurrence frequencies are encrypted using Paillier encryption. We recorded up to the tenth neighbor (as we have limited our study to 10 keywords in a search query). $\mathcal{CD}$ randomly contains dummy words to prevent keyword guessing attacks. $\mathcal{CD}$ needs updating on periodic intervals for efficiency.

Word Vectors
We use query click logs and align them against each other to form the $\mathcal{CD}$. For aligning the queries, we require that the encryption is term-wise. So, we devised "word vector", wherein we form a bit string of the target word according to the key M (length 167 in

our experiments) and then shift the formed bit string by shifting factor (mid-point in this paper). The key M is an array of characters 'a–z' repeated multi-time, but all randomly arranged. We then set the bits of the target word by referring this array. We strictly set the bit in the order of the occurrence of characters as in the target word. For e.g. if the part of the key M is (a, b, s, e, b, r, a, e, b, d, a, d...) then the bit strings for the word 'bed' is 010100000100, for the word 'bread' it is 010001010011, for the word 'bead' it is 010100100100. We then shift these bit strings around the midpoint (shift factor) so the final bit string for the word 'bed' will become 000100010100. These bit strings are different for every word and even for the word with same characters but in different order of occurrence.

Cipher Table (WV)
We encrypt the received word vectors (bit string formed above) in the private cloud. This encryption is done by lookup method in WV. WV is formed in the offline stage. It contains the bit string and its equivalent cipher. The equivalent cipher are obtained by recording any one occurrence of the random cipher obtained by using a non- deterministic cipher. We used Advanced Encryption Standard (AES) in CSFS.

4 Proposed Solution CSFS Scheme

The proposed solution CSFS scheme makes following assumptions regarding the typing errors that a user make:

1. A user can miss or add an extra character in one of the query word.
2. The characters in a word may also be swapped due to wrong key press order.
3. Mistyped words due to any reason i.e. characters missed, swapped or added normally are invalid words; where invalid words mean they are not found in the dictionary/word list.
4. At times the mistypos due to any reason i.e. characters missed, swapped or added may result in another valid word; where valid words mean they are found in the dictionary/word list.
5. We also assume that in a multi-keyword query the user makes spelling errors; and in proposed CSFS scheme we consider that only one of the keyword is misspelled.

4.1 Index Construction

Unique Keywords
The data owner in CSFS extracts the unique words from the documents, unique keywords of the filename and the file description keywords and add some dummy keywords. File description keywords act as metadata for the file, explaining the intent of the file. Data owner adds the file description keywords while uploading a document. For example for a document 'The tempest' or 'Julius Caesar' he may enter 'Tales of Shakespeare' as file description. Now it may be possible, that nowhere in the document 'Julius Caesar' the keyword 'Shakespeare' is present. But, if the user issues a query 'tales of Shakespeare' all such documents become relevant due to the file description

keywords and are listed in search results. Dummy keywords are added to provide protection against guessing of keywords [23]. He/She then generates an index of the above extracted keyword set, followed by their term frequencies and their squares. For the dummy keywords it adds the term frequency as zero.

Encryption

In CSFS, the data owner encrypts the term frequency and its squares using Paillier encryption. We use Paillier encryption because of its additively homomorphic properties i.e. given $Enc(x1)$ and $Enc(x2)$ you can get $Enc(x1 + x2)$. Also Paillier encryption is used to multiply an encrypted number with a plain number i.e. given $Enc(x1)$ and $x3$, we can get $Enc(x1)*x3$. So, it secures the data and yet computes the similarity and find the most relevant documents. The keywords of the index file are encrypted with the word vectors to form $\hat{I}(M)$. He/She then uploads the index file $\hat{I}(M)$ along with the encrypted document collection C to the private cloud server. Here ~~WV~~ is referred to encrypt the unique keywords in the index file and finally form $\hat{I}(M, S)$.

Uploading

$\hat{I}(M, S)$ and the document *collection* C are uploaded from the private cloud server to the public cloud server.

4.2   Encrypted Search Query

Encryption and Spell Correction

In CSFS the data user is authorized by the data owner to perform search and can access the document collection C. A data user issues a search query. The keywords in the search query are checked within the set distance using Levenshtein distance. If a spelling suggestion is returned, then this is the case of the query having spelling mistakes that result in invalid words. In this case all correct spelling suggestions for the mis-spelled query keyword in the form $t(M)$ is sent to the private cloud server where it is encrypted to get $t(M, S)$. However, if no spelling suggestions are returned then all the keywords in the query are valid words. So, we assume that the query may have keywords that have spelling errors, but these spelling errors have generated another valid word. In this case, the original user query $t(M)$ is sent to the private cloud server. We do not expand the query $t(M)$ and it only contains the user's search query keywords. But the keywords in the query however may be misspelled and have resulted in another valid word, so with this assumption, CSFS checks all query keywords in the spell table in the private cloud. It picks suggestions for all query keywords to build the confusion set. Spell table is built during the offline stage and contains the spell suggestions for every valid word in the word list. For spelling errors that result in another valid word, we limited our work to the spelling errors occurring within the edit distance of 1 for insertion and deletion and edit distance of 2 for the swapping of characters. For e.g. if we consider, the word 'word' it checks all words within the given edit distance for substitution, deletion and addition of characters from a word. So, the suggestions within the set edit distance (i.e. edit distance of 1 for insertion and deletion of a character and 2 for swapped characters) that make up are 'work', 'wore', 'worm', 'worn', 'lord', 'wood', 'world', 'sword'. After running the algorithm code for finding the valid word suggestion set for every word we built the spell table. All words in the spell table are encrypted with key M and then with key S. Based on the suggestions given for a wrong spelling not in dictionary and for spelling error that generates a new valid word CSFS builds a confusion set. $t(M, S)$ is then sent to the public cloud server. In both cases $t(M,S)$ contains some dummy keywords as well to prevent keyword guessing attacks.

4.3   Refine Query

Check Collocation Dictionary
ϵD is checked on receiving the confusion set from the private cloud server.

Refining of Query
This step is basically for the pruning the correct suggestion list as per the context. For case 1 i.e. when the misspelled word does not generate a new valid word, spell correction suggestions contains valid words that could be formed in the given distance. These words are checked in ϵD for their co-occurrence statistics with neighbouring words of the query. For case 2 i.e. when the spelling error generates a new valid word, the spelling suggestions are picked for every keyword. Suppose the original query is 'word peace day', here we assumes that the word 'word' has been wrongly written instead of the word 'world'. But then 'word' is also a valid word. A suggestion list contains suggestion for all three keywords based on which a confusion set is received by the public cloud server. Now it refers ϵD to check the neighbouring words. According to ϵD the queries from confusion set for which the words are not found in neighbourhood are dropped. Rest are arranged as per the frequency of togetherness for user's selection.

Refinement Process
This process helps in shortlisting the spelling suggestion(s) by checking the co-occurrence frequency (from ϵD) of the spelling suggestion candidate with other keywords of the query. In ϵD we have the words, their co-occuring words and their co-oocurence frequencies. These frequencies are encrypted with Paillier encryption that is additively homomorphic. In refinement process we prune the suggestions that are not relevant or we can say that are never found as neighbour in user queries.

For the refinement process, we pick the query keywords and check their co-occurrence (as per neighbouring distance) with the listed spelling suggestions and arrange them in tabular form as shown in Table 1.

Table 1. Arrangement of query keywords and all spelling suggestions for refinement

	k_1	k_2	....	k_m
s_1				
s_2				
.				
.				
s_n				

We first calculate the sum of frequencies $sum1_i = \sum(f(S_i))$, $0 < i \leq n$ (n is the number of spelling suggestions) for every keyword K_i where S_i is the spelling suggestion received and K_i are the neighbouring keywords (as per their position i.e. first neighbor, second neighbor etc.). Then we find the sum of all $sum1_i$ as given in Eq. 1.

$$sum = \sum_{i=1}^{n} sum1_i \tag{1}$$

Now we calculate the sum of the co-occurrence frequencies of neighbouring keywords for every spelling suggestion to find its context relevance as $sum2_i = \sum(f(K_i))$, $0 < i \leq m, 0 < j \leq n$ (m is the number of neighbouring keywords including dummy keywords) for every spelling suggestion S_i. For every $sum2_j$ obtained, we now compute the $grandsum_j$ as per the Eq. 2.

$$grandsum_j = sum + \sum_{i=1}^{n} sum2j \tag{2}$$

For the calculation of final score we multiply the $grandsum$ of each spelling suggestion S_i with $count$ (the number of keywords the spelling suggestion is found to co-occur with and whose co-occurrence is not zero, to sweep out dummy keywords) as per Eq. 3.

$$finalscore_i = grandsum_i * count_i, 0 < i \leq n \tag{3}$$

This gives the final context relevance score for every spelling suggestion that was generated. All the spelling suggestions that were found to highly co-occur with the neighbouring keywords gets the highest score. For the spelling suggestions that co − occurred with lesser number of neighbouring keywords of the query gets comparatively lower scores. In all this calculation, the public cloud server only gets to know the $finalscore_i$, no other value or score is revealed to the cloud server as the frequencies in the ED were encrypted with Paillier encryption.

4.4   Search

The corrected query is now checked for the presence of its keywords in the index file. Suppose we have a query Q comprising of keywords $k1$, $k2$ and $k3$ and dummy words $d1$, $d2$ and $d3$. So now looks as $k1$ $k2$ $k3$ $d1$ $d2$ $d3$ (dummy keywords arranged randomly). The index file is checked for the presence of these keywords and cosine similarity is computed as per Eq. 4. The D refers to the document and Q refers to the query in Eq. 4. Dummy words are available in the index file and in the user query as well. But they do not hinder the search process and Q affect the search result as their term frequency is zero. So, when the final scores are calculated dummy keywords automatically sweep out. The top n ranked search result is returned to the user in order of the similarity scores.

$$similarity = \cos(\theta) = \frac{D.Q}{||D||_2 \cdot ||Q||_2} = \frac{\sum_{i=1}^{n} D_i Q_i}{\sqrt{\sum_{i=1}^{n} D_i^2} \cdot \sqrt{\sum_{i=1}^{n} Q_i^2}} \qquad (4)$$

5   Experiment

5.1   Experimental Setup

The experiments are done in python on a Linux server with Intel i7 processor with 8 GB RAM. For the experimentation purpose we picked the words from / usr/share/dict/british-english of Ubuntu 14.04 for creation of cipher dictionary and spell table. We ran different algorithms to introduce typos by inserting, deleting and swapping characters and check the valid words from it for the creation of the spell table. A training set of queries of different lengths was built by selecting and customizing the queries from AOL-user-ct-collection [24]. The dataset of documents was specially built to make the documents suitable to test and use the queries corpus from AOL-user-ct-collection.

5.2   Experiment Results

Index Generation

For the index, the unique words from the concerned document, document's name, the file descriptor text entered by the data owner and some dummy words are selected. Index contains the term frequency and their squares encrypted with Paillier encryption. Figure 2 shows the index construction time taken by CSFS for maximum of 12000 keywords in the index file. It shows that index construction time increases linearly with the increase in the number of keywords. The index construction time is computed as in Eq. 5.

$$\begin{aligned} Index\ Construction\ Time = \\ Time(Equivalent\ Cipher(Word\ Vector(Select\ Index\ Words))) + \\ Time(Enc(Compute\ Term\ Frequency\ and\ Squares)) \end{aligned} \qquad (5)$$

Correct Spelling Suggestion Efficiency

Case 1: When Spelling Mistakes are not Valid Words

These mistypos are identified locally. All the suggestions (considering deletion, insertion and swapping of characters) are expanded. During experimentation it is seen that the number of correct spelling suggestions generated here ranges from 5 to 12 that are further pruned. Experiments conducted show that when pruning of the suggestions was done by considering at least 30% of the query keywords as neighboring words, it helped in improving the final suggestions. So, after dropping the spelling suggestions whose frequency was below 30%, the number of spelling suggestions normally left are between 1 to 3. Experiments show that more the number of keywords in the search

Total Index Construction Time (in secs)

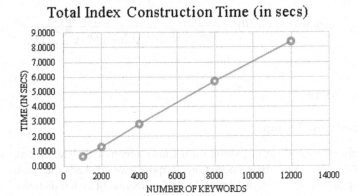

Fig. 2. Time taken for constructing index

query, more accurately, the collocates decide the correct spelling suggestions. The results of these experiments are shown in the Fig. 3.

Correct Spelling Suggestions Returned after Refinement Process

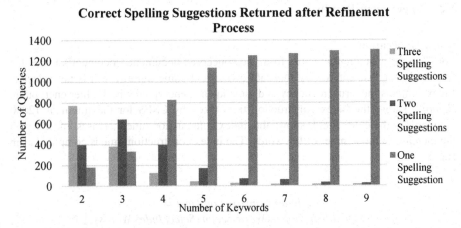

Fig. 3. Experiment results for number of correct spelling suggestions returned after refinement process (case 1)

In Fig. 4 we show precision and recall, where precision is percentage of actual the correct spelling suggestions (as selected by user) divided by the total spelling suggestions returned after the refinement process. The results show that the precision is high when the query keywords contains more keywords in it. This means it better understands the context when the number of query keywords is more. For getting the recall value, we divide the correct spellings selected by the actual correct spellings. We found that the recall is approximately 100%.

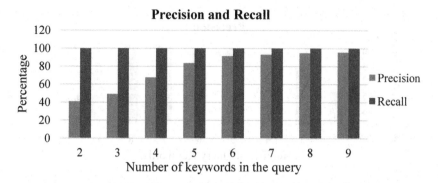

Fig. 4. Precision and recall of suggestion when mis typos are not valid words

Case 2: When Spelling Mistakes are Valid Words

These mistypos are not identified locally, their confusion set is built by looking up the spell table in the private cloud within the set edit distance. Since it is difficult to identify the keyword that may be a mis-typo. We build confusion set by picking suggestions for every keyword. So, the confusion set built in this case is larger.

Figure 5 shows the experiment results of the correct spelling suggestions returned after refinement process for the case where mistypos are valid words. The confusion set built in this case is larger than in case 1. After pruning, the number of suggestions returned is shown in Fig. 5. The number of correct spelling suggestions returned is comparatively more in this case. In our experiments, we included queries that had keywords with more choices of forming another valid word as a result of single letter deletion, substitution or deletion. Most of the queries after refinement process returned 3 to 5 correct spelling suggestions with a lesser number returning 1 or 2 spelling suggestions. The user can ignore or select the query with suggested spelling correction. Since the number of spelling suggestions returned after the refinement process in this

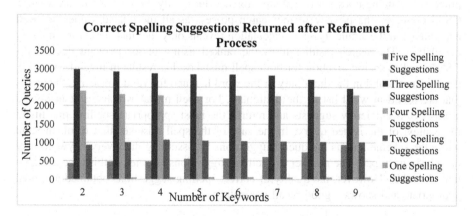

Fig. 5. Experiment results for number of correct spelling suggestions returned after refinement process (case 2)

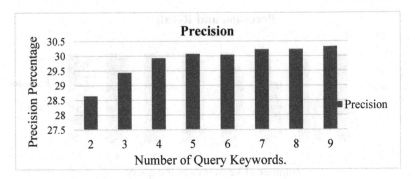

Fig. 6. Precision of suggestion when mis typos are valid words

case is more than in case 1 therefore precision percentage is comparatively low as shown in Fig. 6. Precision is calculated similarly by computing the percentage of the actual correct spelling suggestions (as selected by user) divided by the total spelling suggestions returned after the refinement process. However the recall is approximately 100%.

6   Conclusion

In this paper, CSFS has been proffered to address the problem of privacy preserving context sensitive fuzzy search in cloud computing. CSFS ensures privacy of the query and the search process. CSFS suggests a spelling correction for the mistyped words as per the context of the query. It exploits the capability of query click logs for the formation of the collocation dictionary. We used collocation dictionary to find the most appropriate spelling suggestion by checking out the co-occurrence frequency of the suggested correct spellings for the misspelled word with other neighbouring words of the query and later pruned the suggested spellings as per the scores obtained. The entire process of pruning does not reveal any stored values, only the final scores are visible. CSFS preserves the privacy of the search process as all the related values are well encrypted and the similarity score calculation reveals only the final sums for similarity calculation. The search result returns the ranked listing of the relevant documents. CSFS handles spell correction for both spell mistakes that results in invalid words i.e. the ones not found in the dictionary or the word list, and for valid words i.e. the words that are found in word list or the dictionary. For spell mistakes that result in invalid words CSFS efficiently suggests and returns the most appropriate spelling that fits in the context of the issued query. In the case of the spell mistakes that result in valid word, the scheme returns the query suggestions by assuming that every keyword may have been mistyped. The number of spelling suggestions returned in this case is higher than the other. However, the quality of correct spelling suggestions obtained are more appropriate and shows a good recall percentage.

References

1. White Paper Cisco Public: Cisco global cloud index: forecast and methodology, 2015–2020. Retrieved from https://www.cisco.com/c/dam/en/us/solutions/collateral/service-provider/global-cloud-index-gci/white-paper-c11-738085.pdf (2016)
2. https://www.skyhighnetworks.com/cloud-security-blog/9-stats-itshould-know-on-sensitive-data-stored-and-shared-in-the-cloud/. (2017)
3. Song, D., Wagner, D., Perrig, A.: Practical techniques for searches on encrypted data. In: Proceedings of IEEE Symposium on Security and Privacy (2000)
4. Goh, E.-J.: Secure Indexes*. Cryptology ePrint Archive: Report 2003/216 (2004)
5. Chang, Y.-C., Mitzenmacher, M.: Privacy preserving keyword searches on remote encrypted data. In: Ioannidis, J., Keromytis, A., Yung, M. (eds.) ACNS 2005. LNCS, vol. 3531, pp. 442–455. Springer, Heidelberg (2005). https://doi.org/10.1007/11496137_30
6. Boneh, D., Di Crescenzo, G., Ostrovsky, R., Persiano, G.: Public key encryption with keyword search. In: Cachin, C., Camenisch, Jan L. (eds.) EUROCRYPT 2004. LNCS, vol. 3027, pp. 506–522. Springer, Heidelberg (2004). https://doi.org/10.1007/978-3-540-24676-3_30
7. Bellare, M., Boldyreva, A., Desai, A., Pointcheval, D.: Key-privacy in public-key encryption. In: Boyd, C. (ed.) ASIACRYPT 2001. LNCS, vol. 2248, pp. 566–582. Springer, Heidelberg (2001). https://doi.org/10.1007/3-540-45682-1_33
8. Boneh, D., Franklin, M.: Identity-based encryption from the weil pairing. SIAM J. Comput. **32**(3), 586–615 (2003)
9. Curtmola, R., Garay, J.A., Kamara, S., Ostrovsky, R.: Searchable symmetric encryption: improved definitions and efficient constructions. In: Proceedings of ACM CC 2006 (2006)
10. Wang, C., Cao, N., Li, J., Ren, K., Lou, W.: Secure ranked keyword search over encrypted cloud data. In: Proceedings of ICDCS 2010 (2010)
11. Cao, N., Wang, C., Li, M.: Privacy- preserving multi-keyword ranked search over encrypted cloud data. In: Proceedings of IEEE INFOCOM, pp. 829–837 (2011)
12. Xu, Z., Kang, W., Li, R., Yow, K., Xu, C.Z.: Efficient multi-keyword ranked query on encrypted data in the cloud. In: Proceedings of ICPADS (2012)
13. Yang, C., Zhang, W., Xu, J., Xu, J., Yu, N.: A fast privacy-preserving multi-keyword search scheme on cloud data. In: Proceedings of International Conference on Computing and Processing (Hardware/Software), pp. 104–110 (2012)
14. Handa, R., Rama Krishna, C.: A cluster based multi-keyword search on outsourced encrypted cloud data. In: Proceedings of 2nd IEEE International Conference on Computing for Sustainable Global Development, pp. 115–120 (2015)
15. Handa, R., Rama Krishna, C.: An efficient cluster-based multi-keyword search on encrypted cloud data. CSI Commun. **39**(3), 20–27. CSI (2015)
16. Mangal, G., Rama Krishna, C., Handa, R.: Dynamic cluster based privacy-preserving multikeyword search over encrypted cloud data. In: Proceedings of 6th IEEE International Conference on Cloud System and Big Data Engineering, Noida, India, pp. 146–151 (2016)
17. Li, J., Wang, Q., Wang, C., Cao, N., Ren, K., Lou, W.: Fuzzy keyword search over encrypted data in cloud computing. In: Proceedings of IEEE INFOCOM, pp. 1–5 (2010)
18. Ahsan, M.A.M., Sabilah, M., Wahab, A.: An efficient fuzzy keyword matching technique for searching through encrypted cloud data. In: Proceedings of International Conference on Research and Innovation in Information Systems (ICRIIS) (2017)
19. Ding, S., Li, Y., Zhang, J., Chen, L., Wang, Z., Xu, Q.: An efficient and privacy preserving ranked fuzzy keywords search over encrypted cloud data. In: Proceedings of IEEE International Conference on Behavioral, Economic and Socio-cultural Computing (BESC), USA (2016)

20. Chen, J., et al.: EliMFS: achieving efficient, leakage-resilient, and multi-keyword fuzzy search on encrypted cloud data. IEEE Trans. Serv. Comput. **PP**(99) (2017)
21. Khan, N.S., Rama Krishna, C., Khurana, A.: Secure ranked fuzzy multikeyword search over outsourced encrypted cloud data. In: Proceedings of 5th IEEE International Conference on Computer and Communication Technology, Allahabad, pp. 241–249 (2014)
22. Saini, V., Challa, R.K., Khan, Neelam S.: An efficient multi-keyword synonym-based fuzzy ranked search over outsourced encrypted cloud data. In: Choudhary, Ramesh K., Mandal, J. K., Auluck, N., Nagarajaram, H.A. (eds.) Advanced Computing and Communication Technologies. AISC, vol. 452, pp. 433–441. Springer, Singapore (2016). https://doi.org/10.1007/978-981-10-1023-1_43
23. Liu, C., Zhu, L., Wang, M., Tan, Y.: Search pattern leakage in searchable encryption: attacks and new construction. J. Inf. Sci. Int. J. **265**, 176–188 (2014)
24. http://www.cim.mcgill.ca/~dudek/206/Logs/AOL-user-ctcollection/. (2017)

Blended Learning for Calculus Course: WebBLoC

Aslina Baharum[1(✉)], Nur Shahida Ab Fatah[2],
Nurhafizah Moziyana Mohd Yusop[3], Nurainna Ramli[4],
Noor Fzlinda Fabeil[2], and Song Teck Kang[1]

[1] Faculty of Computing and Informatics, Universiti Malaysia Sabah,
88400 Kota Kinabalu, Sabah, Malaysia
aslinabaharum@gmail.com
[2] Faculty of Business, Economics and Accountancy, Universiti Malaysia Sabah,
88400 Kota Kinabalu, Sabah, Malaysia
[3] Faculty of Defence Science and Technology,
National Defence University of Malaysia, 57000 Kuala Lumpur, Malaysia
[4] Faculty of Economics and Muamalat, Universiti Sains Islam Malaysia,
Bandar Baru Nilai, 71800 Nilai, Negeri Sembilan, Malaysia

Abstract. In this paper, the study of Blended Learning (BL) for Calculus Course is proposed. Based on the observation, most of first year students of Universiti Malaysia Sabah (UMS) that have taken calculus course failed due to unsuitable learning approach. The traditional classroom learning used for teaching makes students misunderstand the concept and lack of enthusiasm in learning calculus course, since their first impression is to consider the calculus a difficult course in university and college. In order to overcome the problem, three objectives were proposed in this project, which are to identify the suitable media for BL in calculus using quantitative method, to develop the web-based system, namely as WebBLoC, based on selected media using calculus syllabus and finally to evaluate the developed system. For the development, the Waterfall model is used as a system development method to study the BL system. In general, this project expected to decrease the number of students failed in calculus and provide them more understanding the concepts and formulas of calculus by using the developed BL system (WebBLoC).

Keywords: Calculus · WebBLoC · Blended learning system

1 Introduction

Not only mentioned as boring course, Calculus also was claimed by some students that had a complex mathematical formulas. Thus, identified as the key reason that makes student failed. According to [1], many students' measurement reasoning is superficial with poorly understood procedures or formulas substituting for deep understanding. This makes them misunderstanding and failed to apply formulas for solving problem. In addition, [2] mentioned that students enrolled in the traditional university calculus class (traditional instructor-led classroom learning approach) have a very superficial and

© Springer Nature Singapore Pte Ltd. 2019
P. K. Singh et al. (Eds.): FTNCT 2018, CCIS 958, pp. 221–236, 2019.
https://doi.org/10.1007/978-981-13-3804-5_17

incomplete understanding of many of the basic concepts in calculus. This was attributed to the rote and manipulative learning that takes place in an introductory course.

Tucker [3] stated that large numbers of repeat students take calculus on first semester in college and university, although they were taking it during high school. A survey by [4] found that only 25% of students received a good grade for calculus exam from 70% of students at colleges and universities, who had taken calculus in high school previously. Many of students failed their calculus course, which cause the increased in failure rates. Thus, many of students who earned calculus credit in high school never took a calculus in college and university. These situations tend to indicate phenomena of increasing student fail in calculus. Thus, teaching and learning approach plays as an important key to solve the problems. [5] mentioned that conceptions of effective teaching have been connected closely to understandings of how students learn. Learning can also be influenced by what the learners believe about college or university and about learning. In addition, [6] mentioned that the current populations of students are technology-savvy and they always considered that traditional methods of teaching is boring and have a short attention span. [7] highlighted that technology tools provide great opportunities to enhance student learning. According to [8] a teaching and learning method that mixed between technology and social support was thought to be the best solution to the problem of student failed in calculus. Therefore, courseware of teaching and learning could implements with animations, video, picture and other online resources. [9] also mentioned that high quality learning refers to learning that includes understanding concepts and mastery of content through multiple effective approaches, such as video and game.

This paper is organized as follows. In Sect. 2, related studies on BL system will be presented. Section 3 demonstrates the methods applied in developing WebBLoC system based on selected media. The data collection obtained is illustrated in Sect. 4 and followed by a conclusion.

2   Related Studies

According to the Oxford dictionary, blended learning (BL) defined as a formal education program which a student learns at least in part through content delivery and instruction via digital and online media with some elements of student control over time, place, pace or path. In a book of "*Towards a Definition and Methodology for Blended Learning*"; BL is a term gradually used to describe the way of e-learning that combines with traditional instructor-led classroom learning method and technology-based e-learning method to create a new hybrid teaching methodology [10]. BL provides multiple learning strategies that makes learning easier and tends to leverage the student interest [11]. Calculus is one of the most significant courses and fundamental tool for undergraduate students and as such is provided as a prerequisite course to other advanced mathematics courses who wish to pursue programs in Information Technology (IT), Science, Mathematics, Engineering, Medicine, Architecture, Business and many other fields [12]. The system will be created based on the following problems such as the increasing of student fails in calculus [13, 14], the students are not interested and feel boring in calculus course through traditional instructor-led classroom learning approach [6] and calculus consists of many complex mathematical formulas which cause the student hardly to understand it [1]. Three main objectives will be identified in order to solve the problems such as identify the suitable media for BL (WebBLoC) in calculus using quantitative method, develop the WebBLoC based on selected media using calculus syllabus and evaluate students' and instructors' perception towards the developed WebBLoC using quantitative method.

BL is most useful in learning approach since it is combining both traditional instructor-led classroom learning and technology-based e-learning that elaborate a hybrid learning methodology. In general, technology-based e-learning and traditional instructor-led classroom learning with conventional traditional learning classes, blended instruction has been more effective and providing a rationale for the effort required designing and implementing blended approaches. Based on the Table 1, BL is an all-round learning that more effective than another two learning. It contains characteristics of both learning. It is more effective in learning since it is mixed and united of a variety of learning approaches.

Table 1. Comparison of characteristics between learning approaches

Characteristics	Traditional instructor-led classroom learning approach	Technology-based e-learning approach	Hybrid or blended learning
Courseware	Textbook	Online materials (web-based application, video and audio, forum, blog, wikis)	Included both learning approach's courseware
Primary mode of communication/environment	Synchronous (face-to-face)	Asynchronous (e-mail, threaded discussion)	Combination of all modes
Interaction	Interaction between either lecturer and students or students themselves	Interaction with online materials	Combination of all interactions
Learning delivery methods	Lecturer only	Internet only- some use of videotapes	Combination
Collaboration in learning	Collaborate in the physical classroom	Collaborate online	Combination

BL as learning that mixing of face-to-face learning (traditional classroom learning) and online learning (e-learning). BL mixes various event-based activities such as face-to-face learning, live e-learning and Web-based learning [15]. It is the combinations of multiple approaches to learning. BL as hybrid learning describes a learning environment that is either combine teaching methods, delivery methods, media formats or a mixture of all these [16]. It is a combination of different training "media", there are technologies, activities and types of events. It combines media in order to create an optimum teaching and learning program for students [17]. Hybrid BL views online material as an extension of the learning and the traditional lectures may be linked with virtual tours of organizations being studied. The students can receive the benefit of face-to-face interaction with educator and other students through traditional instructor-led classroom learning while at the same time being exposed to web-based learning paradigms via technology-based learning as virtual real-time information, maps, pictures or images, streaming video and audio clips. Hence, a new hybrid learning and teaching method appear when it is combining traditional instructor-led learning approach and technology-based e-learning approach [18]. It applied a range of learning activities and resources to aid learners to achieve learning objectives. These activities, like visual material, face-to-face presentation, online research and paper-based assessments and group activities [19]. BL is really a combination of all of these approaches means that mixing teaching and learning methods from face-to-face and online learning means it is a mixture of technology-based e-learning and traditional instructor-led classroom learning.

The webpage or website acts as Learning Management System (LMS). Web-based application refers to any program or system that accessed over a network connection. By using theory technology-based, e-learning integrated of various media that may connect with traditional instructor-led classroom learning to extend a hybrid or BL [20]. For example, Modular Object Oriented Dynamic Leaning Environment system (MOODLE), MOOC and WebCT are popular open-source learning management system that using BL. Web-based BL is effective to combine multiple media in teaching and learning by online technology based on BL approach. WebBLoC focus on multiple media such as tutorial video, live drawing video, quiz and game, traditional courseware, online forums and chat. The following comparing the features between current systems and WebBLoC:

a. *Traditional Courseware*

Traditional courseware normally contains of power point slides and pdf documents for lecture class, such as textbook and example exercises. These documents are important to build and frame concept of the course. It also provides more details of the course information. Although it is less attractive compare with other media, but indispensable in learning [21].

b. *Video*

Video contains of the tutorial video and live drawing video. Tutorial video is real time learning video that explained by lecturer or professor. Whereas, live drawing video is one type of video that to continue showing a series of animated drawings for explaining something. Live drawing video learning approach is a kind of visual learning style. Therefore, this kind of video can display to the students in real time for learning through animated drawing. Student also can learn within asynchronous environment by using theory of technology-based e-learning.

c. *Game-based Learning*

Game Based Learning (GBL) broadly refers to use games or quizzes to support in teaching and learning method. It is one kind of game play that defined the learning outcome. Basically, it is designed to balance the subject matter with game play and the ability of the player to retain and apply subject matter to the real world. In other word, it refers to borrowing the certain gaming principles and applying it to real-life settings to engage users (learners). It describes a method to teaching, where students can explore relevant aspects of games in learning context designed by lecturer [22]. The motivational psychology is involved in GBL that enables students to participate with educational materials in a playful and dynamic way. It is not just creating to play for students while it is designed with learning activities that can incrementally introduce concepts and towards an end goal in teaching and learning field. The concepts to engage students in learning via incorporating competition, points, incentives and feedback loops [23].

d. *Forums and Chat*

The online forums and chats provide asynchronous communication outside of classroom learning. It gives the opportunity to more contribute their time to generate responses them and can master to more thoughtful discussion. Sharing information and remote communication will be carried out between groups of students or instructor to students. Through the communication, student can obtain the feedback from others, such as student or instructor [17].

Table 2 shows comparison features of current system using web-based BL approach.

Table 2. Comparison features of current system using web-based BL

Features and functionality	MOODLE	MOOC	WebCT
Video	Yes but lack	Yes but lack	Yes but lack
Live drawing video	None	None	None
Tutorial video	None	None	None
Game	None	None	None
Quiz	Lack	Lack	Lack
Traditional courseware	PDF and power point slides	PDF and power point slides	PDF and power point slides
Online forums and chat	Yes	Yes	Yes
Students can upload and share media	Disable	Disable	Disable

According to [22], web-based application (web page or website) with theory technology-based e-learning is integrated of various media that may connect with traditional instructor-led classroom learning to extend a hybrid or BL. The material knowledge that will be learned by the students prepared in accordance with the syllabus equipped with learning resources such as ebook, images, applications, games and video learning geometry. According to [18], the students can receive the benefit of face-to-face interaction with instructor while at the same time being exposed to web-based learning paradigms via technology-based learning as virtual real-time information, pictures or images, streaming video and audio clips. However, it contains many of media that required developing for teaching and learning approach. Thus, it is effective to combine multiple media in teaching and learning by online technology based on BL approach.

3 Methodology

A Waterfall model as a method to develop the system of UMS BL project for Calculus course. It consists phases of requirements, design, implementation (coding/prototyping), verification (testing) and evaluation. Waterfall Model also can know as Linear Sequential Model. Basically, Waterfall or linear sequential model is theoretically the best model for system and software development. Researcher considers that the Waterfall model is a theoretical way of developing system and software because it is not a practical model can be used in actual system and software development project. They choose this kind of model because all other life cycle models are essentially derived from Waterfall model. The life cycle of this model is broken down into an intuitive set of phases. The phases of this model are including requirement, design, implementation or coding, verification and maintenance (evaluation) [24] (Fig. 1).

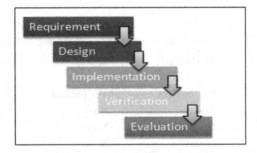

Fig. 1. Waterfall model for WebBLoC system.

3.1 Participants and Procedure

In this section, analysis requirements of media for applying in the WebBLoC system among UMS students and instructors are obtained. A set of questionnaires is prepared in order to realize the requirements from student and get the recommendations from them to identify the suitable media for BL using in calculus course in UMS. Participants involved in this project are comprised of a group of 112 students and 10 instructors who required taken a calculus course at Universiti Malaysia Sabah (UMS).

Based on the findings, being identified that the chapter of "application of derivatives", "integration" and "transcendental functions" are three main chapters that student considers it is difficult to learn in Calculus course. These three chapters (100, 100 and 80% participants) are act as suitable media that we require prepared in learning system. Besides, BL is a suitable learning approach that may need to use it in teaching and learning system for Calculus. In addition, student and instructors are agreed using multiple media such as video, game and power point slides in their learning and teaching.

4 Results and Discussion

Based on the Table 3, finding of Question 1 identified students consider that the chapter of "Application of Derivatives", "Integration" and "Transcendental Functions" are three main chapters that difficult to learn in Calculus course. These three chapters (85, 98 and 81% participants) are act as the suitable contents that required to be prepared in the learning system (Fig. 2). This is because of these three chapters contain complex calculus formulas. Figure 3 show that "blended learning" is highest type of learning preferred compare with the others two learning: "traditional classroom learning" and "e-learning". BL is the combination of various learning and this is in line with the response to Question 7, which the student also agreed to use learning system consists of multiple media such as video, game, power point slide and quiz (100% participants). This shows that students preferred the BL approach. Based on Questions 9 until 12, show that instructors agreed using BL in teaching and learning. Finally, instructor agreed to use BL with their students in their learning based (Questions 10 and 11). Based on Question 13, they are more preferred by using BL as a teaching approach in their Calculus course (80%). Results shown in Figs. 4 and 5.

Table 3. Result from data requirements.

Question (for student)	Answer	Score (%)
1. Which of the following chapters do you consider hardly to learn in calculus course?	Functions and their graphs	2
	Limits and continuity	9
	Applications of derivatives	85
	Integration	98
	Applications of definite integrals	27
	Transcendental functions	81
	Techniques of integration	8
	First-order differential equations	3
	Infinite sequences and series	2
	Inverse functions	3
2. Which type of learning does you or would you to prefer apply in calculus?	Blended learning/hybrid learning	92

(continued)

Table 3. (*continued*)

Question (for student)	Answer	Score (%)
3. What is your first reaction to blended learning?	Very positive	70
4. Do you own a computer?	Yes	98
5. Are you spending more time to use computer on one day?	Yes	96
6. Which type of style does you or would you to prefer for learning your course?	Through textbook	45
	Through video from E-learning website via computer	76
	Through game from E-learning website via computer	83
	Others	0
7. If you could use learning system consists multiple media such as video, game, power point slide and quiz, would you try to apply it?	Yes	100
8. Are you preferred using blended learning to learn calculus course?	Agree	100
9. How satisfied you have been with the blended learning courses?	Very satisfied and generally satisfied	90
10. Would you try to apply blended learning approach on you teaching?	Yes	90
11. Would you like to support your student uses this kind of learning (BL) from other source?	Yes	100
12. How satisfied you have been with traditional classroom teaching implements in online environment?	Very satisfied and generally satisfied	90
13. What kind of learning approaches that you will more prefer to apply in your teaching?	Blended learning	80

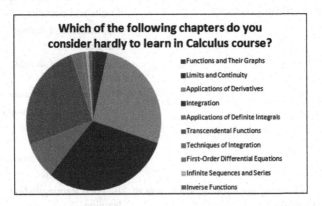

Fig. 2. Chapters that considered hardly learning in calculus

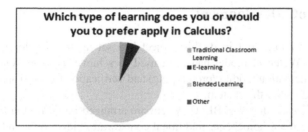

Fig. 3. Learning approach that student prefer apply in calculus

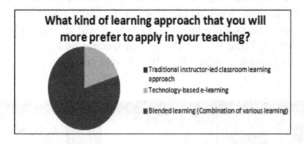

Fig. 4. Instructor preferred using BL in calculus

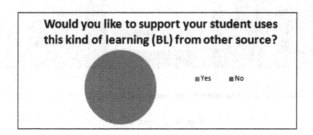

Fig. 5. Instructor supports student using BL

Based on the results, web page or website is the most satisfying to use by students learning the Calculus by using BL approach. Based on BL, web-based application allow combination of live drawing video and GBL in teaching and learning to achieve end goals with traditional learning simultaneously. It is also a type of learning by using the technology-based e-learning theory. Therefore, we could conclude that BL is a suitable learning approach to be used in teaching and learning system. Besides, the main three chapters of calculus also will be studied in learning system based on the standpoint of students. Web-based BL is more suitable used in this system since BL implements in web page or website. Many of media also will apply in the system for enhancing the learning system in order to improve student's learning skills in calculus.

5   WebBLoC Development

Based on the findings obtained, this project had set up the development phase for WebBLoC. A Waterfall model had been used to achieve its target. Only process of design, implementation (coding/prototyping) and verification (testing) are carried out in this phase to develop the system.

The interfaces of the WebBLoC system are arranged based on the six main modules. There are main homepage, traditional courseware, video, quiz and game, forum chat and user profile. Before shows out any pages of the system, user requires to login the system. This is because the system is protected with security to ensure only accessible by authorized users. Figure 6 indicates the login page of WebBLoC system. User is required to fill in the valid username and password to log into their account. In this system, there are two types of users, which is admin (lecturer) and normal user (student). After user successfully login the system, it will shift to welcome homepage of the system. Figures 7 and 8 show the several features and interfaces of WebBLoC system such as live drawing video (Fig. 7), quiz and game (Fig. 8).

Fig. 6. Login page

5.1   Satisfaction Towards the Developed WebBLoC

The evaluation on WebBLoC system participated among 64 randomly selected UMS student. During the procedures, participants are given a brief explanation about the system. After that, the participants are given some times to explore and test the WebBLoC system by themselves. Then, participants are required to fill in the evaluation form.

As depicted in Figs. 9 and 10, most of students satisfied with WebBLoC system used in Calculus course learning. In terms of WebBLoC system satisfiability, it provided multiple of media such as traditional courseware, video, forum and chat and quiz and game that help student to learn the Calculus via these multiple media. From Fig. 9, about 66% of students satisfied and 30% of students very satisfied with the WebBLoC system used in Calculus learning. Figure 10 shows 94% of students are satisfied with

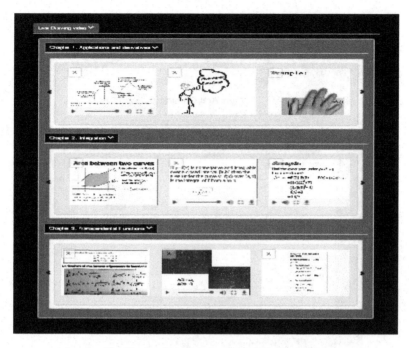

Fig. 7. Section "live drawing video" page

traditional courseware in system, 83% of students are satisfied with video in system, 88% of students are satisfied with forum and chat in system and 84% of students are satisfied with quiz and game in system.

In general, students' feedback on the WebBLoC system, most of the students truly enjoyed with WebBLoC and agreed that owning this system has been a good experience.

As depicted in Fig. 11, in term of WebBLoC system satisfiability from instructors, most of them are satisfied with WebBLoC system because the system provided multiple media for Calculus. About 67% of instructors are satisfied with the system and 22% of instructors are very satisfied. Only a few of the instructors feel neither dissatisfied nor satisfied. Figure 12 shows 89% of instructors are satisfied and 11% of instructors are very satisfied with traditional courseware and forum and chat in the system, 67% of instructors are satisfied and 33% of instructors are very satisfied with video. Whereas 78% of instructors are satisfied and 22% of instructors are very satisfied with quiz and game in the system. Instructors can easy to teach calculus through these multiple media.

As depicted in Figs. 13 and 14, in term of WebBLoC system with multiple media importance, most of instructors agreed that multiple media of system provided helpful, knowledgeable, detail information and value that is help student easily to learn in Calculus. About 44% of instructors consider very important and 56% of instructors feel important that multiple media within WebBLoC system.

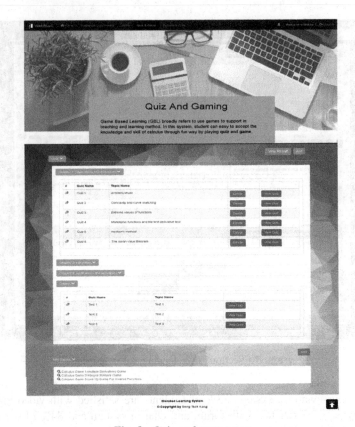

Fig. 8. Quiz and game page

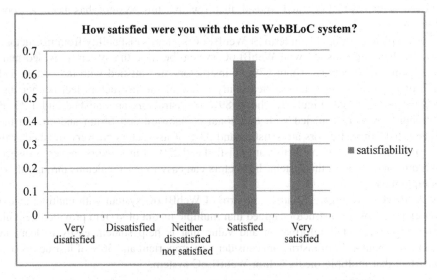

Fig. 9. Student's feedback on the WebBLoC system satisfiability

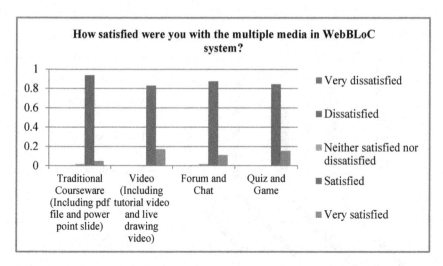

Fig. 10. Student's feedback on the WebBLoC system satisfiability (based on multiple media)

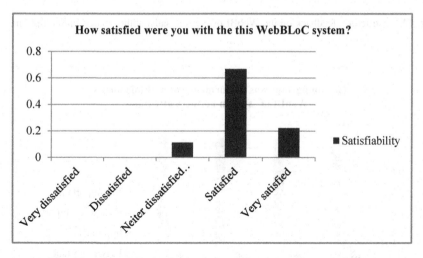

Fig. 11. Instructor's feedback on the WebBLoC system satisfiability

As overall, the result of findings analysed for multiple media within the WebBLoC system based on two categories such as satisfiability level and importance level. Besides, multiple media is also increasing the learning ability of calculus. This is to be concluded that the WebBLoC system is satisfied by users and multiple media is quite helpful and important in teaching and learning system for Calculus based on the evaluation.

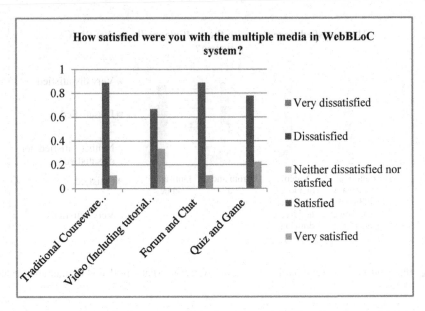

Fig. 12. Instructor's feedback on the WebBLoC system satisfiability (based on multiple media)

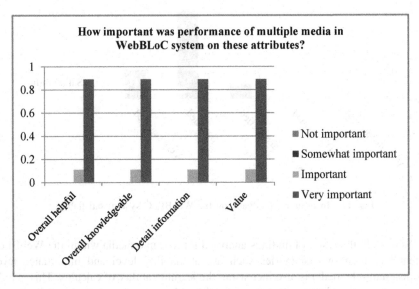

Fig. 13. Instructor's feedback on the WebBLoC system with performance of multiple media importance

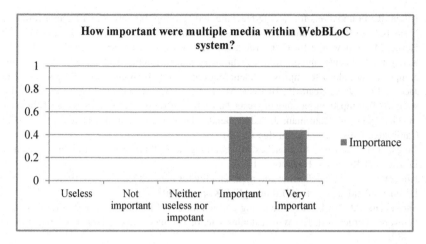

Fig. 14. Instructor's feedback on the WebBLoC system with multiple media importance

6 Conclusion

Through the literature review and findings, we obtained three of difficult chapters of calculus was applied in WebBLoC system by using BL method. In additions, media of traditional courseware, forum and chat, video and quiz and game are included in this system in order to support student learning calculus through multiple learning. Therefore, students can learn calculus through multiple media that provided in Web-BLoC system. Future works could be continued with this project by improving the system to be more efficient. The data collection based on people who will be using the system also should be done in future works. Since the user perception is important for evaluating the alignment of management and requirements of the user by estimate the rating that given by respondent in order to overall reaction to the system.

References

1. Battista, M.T.: The development of geometric and spatial thinking. In: Lester, F.K. (ed.) Second Handbook of Research on Mathematics Teaching and Learning, Charlotte, USA, pp. 843–908 (2007)
2. Naidoo, N., Naidoo, R.: Using blended learning to facilitate the mathematical thought processes of primary school learners in a computer laboratory: a case study in calculating simple areas. S. Afr. J. Coll. Teach. Learn. **4**(7), 2 (2007)
3. Tucker, A.: The history of the undergraduate program in mathematics in the United States. Am. Math. Mon. **120**(8), 689–705 (2013). http://www.maa.org/sites/default/files/pdf/CUPM/pdf/MAAUndergradHistory.pdf
4. Bressoud, D.M., Carlson, M.P., Mesa, V., Rasmussen, C.: The calculus student: insights from the Mathematical Association of America national study. Int. J. Math. Educ. Sci. Technol. **44**(5), 685–698 (2013). https://doi.org/10.1080/0020739x.2013.798874

5. Killen, R.: Foundations for quality teaching and learning. In: Effective Teaching Strategies: Lessons from Research and Practice, pp. 1–4, South Melbourne, Australia (2006)
6. Horne, M.: A new role for CTE. Tech. Connect. Educ. Careers **85**(4), 10–11 (2010)
7. Keengwe, J.: Faculty integration of technology into instruction and students' perception of computer technology to improve student learning. J. Inf. Technol. Educ. **6**, 169–180 (2007)
8. Jacobs, J.E., Davis-Kean, P., Bleeker, M., Eccles, J.S., Malanchuk, O.: 'I can, but i don't want to': the impact of parents, interests, and activities on gender differences in mathematics. In: Gallagher, A., Kaufman, J. (eds.) Gender Differences in Mathematics, pp. 246–263. Cambridge University, Cambridge (2005)
9. Biggs, J.B.: Student Approaches to Learning and Studying. Australian Council for Educational Research, Hawthorn (1987)
10. Kim, W.: Towards a definition and methodology for blended learning. In: Fong, J., Wang, F. L. (eds.) Blended Learning, Edinburgh, UK, p. 9 (2007)
11. Subramani, P.C.N.: Effective teaching and learning. J. Eff. Teach. **5**(2), 229 (2002)
12. Schwarzenberger, R.L.E.: Why calculus cannot be made easy. Math. Gaz. **64**, 158–166 (1980)
13. Ocken, S.: Why students fail calculus, pp. 1–2. Department of Mathematics, Bronx, New York (2001)
14. McMahon, D.: Calculus in Focus, p. 7. Preface, Raleign (2006)
15. Singh, H.: Building effective blended learning programs. Educ. Technol. **43**(6), 51–54 (2003)
16. Ahmad, F., Shafie, A., Janier, J.B.: Students' perceptions towards blended learning in teaching and learning mathematics: application of integration. Department of Computer & Information Sciences. Universiti Teknologi PETRONAS, Tronoh, Perak (2007)
17. Bersin, J.: The Blended Learning Book: Best Practices, Proven Methodologies, and Lessons Learned. Defining Blended Learning, pp. 1–53. Wiley, San Francisco (2004)
18. Black, G.: A comparison of traditional, online and hybrid methods of course delivery. J. Bus. Adm. Online **1**(1), 2 (2002)
19. Watterston, J.: Blended Learning: Department of Education and Training. What is Blended Learning, Melbourne, Australian, p. 5 (2012)
20. Cavus, N., Ibrahim, D.: Is blended learning the solution to web-based distant engineering education? Department of Computer Information Systems. Near East University, North Cyprus (2007)
21. Spence, D.J., Usher, E.L.: Engagement with mathematics courseware in traditional and online remedial learning environments: relationship to self efficacy and achievement. J. Educ. Comput. Res. **37**(3), 267–288 (2007)
22. Perrotta, C., Featherstone, G., Aston, H., Houghton, E.: Game-based learning: latest evidence and future directions, p. 1. National Foundation for Educational Research (NFER), Slough (2013)
23. Pho, A., Dinscore, A.: Tips and trends. Game-based learning: overview and definition, p. 1. ACRL/IS Instructional Technologies Committee, American, USA (2015)
24. Mall, R.: Fundamentals of Software Engineering. Software Life Cycle Models, p. 39. Prentice-Hall of India Private Limited, Delhi (2006)

Shared Folder Based Virtual Machine Migration in Cloud Computing

Yashveer Yadav[1(✉)] and C. Rama Krishna[2(✉)]

[1] I. K. Gujral Punjab Technical University, Kapurthala, Punjab, India
yadav.yashveer@gmail.com
[2] NITTTR, Chandigarh, India
ramakrishna.challa@gmail.com

Abstract. Virtual Machine Migration (VMM) is a process to migrate Virtual Machine (VM) from one physical host to another physical host. VMM is a complex task and can degrade the performance of overall cloud computing experience. VMM generates heavy network traffic that leads to network congestion. This network congestion further leads to packet loss and increases the total migration time. To handle such problem, we have proposed Shared Folder Based Migration (SFBM) approach to minimize the total migration time and network congestion. SFBM approach uses the modified pre-copy migration technique to relocate the data from source host to destination host. We have categorized the data into two categories: (1) working data set (2) data at rest. In proposed SFBM approach, we send the current working data set at the time of migration and resumes the VM at the destination host without sending data at rest. The data at rest reaches the destination from time to time according to the client request. This may increase the page fault but leads to less network congestion effectively speed up the transmission and making delay negligible to end user. We further analysed the proposed SFBM approach in different scenarios. The results show that proposed SFBM approach significantly reduces the total migration time and packet loss up to 91% and 32% respectively in scenario of no data requested after VM migration.

Keywords: Virtualization · Virtual machine · Pre-copy · Post-copy
Virtual machine migration · Shared folder based migration

1 Introduction

Cloud computing has become popular in the last few years as it provides new way of computing that has changed the traditional concept of computing. It has attracted business and IT industries because it enables utilizing huge computing power from the cloud servers as a utility, instead of owning it [1]. In cloud system, services are availed through Internet based on pay-per-use basis. Cloud computing is defined by different researchers in various perspectives, and few of them have been defined in a better way. National Institute of Standards and Technology (NIST) defines cloud computing as "Cloud computing is a model for enabling ubiquitous, convenient, on-demand network access to a shared pool of configurable computing resources (e.g., networks, servers, storage, applications, and services) that can be rapidly provisioned and released with

© Springer Nature Singapore Pte Ltd. 2019
P. K. Singh et al. (Eds.): FTNCT 2018, CCIS 958, pp. 237–250, 2019.
https://doi.org/10.1007/978-981-13-3804-5_18

minimal management effort or service provider interaction" [2, 3]. Computational power is available as a utility to clients. Virtual machines, virtual server and even virtual networks are available according to the customized requirement of client. Virtualization plays very important role in the growth of cloud computing. Virtualization offers the utility to expand or shrink computing power on demand.

Cloud computing leverages virtualization technology to form pools of computing resources from the physical infrastructure. Virtualization technology enables a physical machine to host multiple VMs. This is achieved with the help of a hypervisor which abstracts the underlying physical resources. Virtualization offers advantages such as server consolidation, dynamic resource management, hardware optimization, heterogeneous system operation, faster provisioning time, and dynamic load balancing. Furthermore, cloud computing inherits a key features provided by virtualization called VMM. VMM is defined as, "process of copying memory pages of a VM from one physical server to another physical server, in two phases called the iterative phase, and stop-and-copy phase" [4]. The physical server is termed as the host and the VMs that run on the host are termed as guests. The terms VMs and guests can be used interchangeably. Each VM is assigned its share of the host's physical resources (CPU, memory, disk, I/O, etc.) by a middleware called the hypervisor. VMM is a process used in cloud computing for load balancing, power saving, system maintenance, disaster recovery and green computing. The parameters to measure the VMM are Total Migration Time (TMT), Total Down Time (TDM), service interrupt time and network load. TMT is a time between initialization of migration at source host to resume services of VM at destination host. In traditional live VMM techniques [5, 6], the downtime is lesser than TMT. Downtime is termed as the state of VM where it is in non-responsive state. Network traffic is the traffic generated by the VMM process for migrating VM from source physical host to destination physical host. VMM generates overheads on cloud system so it becomes very important to develop an efficient technique to minimize the effect of migration on the cloud services.

Rest of the paper is structured as follows. In Sect. 2, we discuss the related work. In Sect. 3, we describe the background of virtual machine migration. In Sect. 4, we demonstrated the influence on TMT and network traffic for sending multiple VMs at a time. The detailed discussion of the proposed shared folder based migration framework is given in Sect. 5. In Sect. 6 we define the experimental setup for the proposed architecture. Results are discussed in Sect. 7. Section 8 gives the concluding remarks.

2 Related Work

Live migration of VM needs to be done without the user noticeable downtime. Several approaches are used to do so. Several authors have proposed to minimize downtime as Akoush et al. [7] computed the TMT and TDM using the mathematical model as shown in Eqs. (1) and (2) respectively. The *init* is the initialization phase in which detection of hotspot, selection of victim, copy of the current data set are performed. Commitment represents the time between when VM enter in non-responsive state and final data set is being saved at destination host and activation of VM at destination host. Authors had considered initialization and reservation phase as pre-migration overheads. Commitment and activation are considered as post migration overheads.

$$TotalMigrationTime = Init + Reservation + \sum_i Pre - Copy_i + Stop -$$
$$and - copy + Commitment + Activation \tag{1}$$

$$Total\,Downtime = Stop - and - Copy + Commitment + Activation \tag{2}$$

Jiao et al. [8] computed the TDM on the basis of VM size and allocated bandwidth. Authors had considered bandwidth for calculating TDM as shown in Eq. (3). In Eq. (3), T_{dwn} represents the TDM and T_{tot} represents the TMT. N represents the total number of pages of the virtual machine. B_p is the required bandwidth allocated in the channel. B_m is the maximum bandwidth and I is the total number of iterations during the stop and copy phase. One limitation with the model is, it is critical to compute the number of pages in each round N. This model does not differentiate high dirty and low dirty pages and keep sending pages to destination host.

$$T_{dwn} = \frac{N_{K+1}}{B_m} , \, T_{tot} = \sum_{i=1}^{K} N_i \frac{1}{Bp} + T_{dwn} \tag{3}$$

Auto-converge [9] is a tool developed and released under KVM/QEMU hypervisor. Auto-converge technique put some virtual CPU's (vCPU's) on sleep so that the dirty paging can be reduced. Less computing power leads to reduce the throughput of applications that further leads to low dirty paging in current RAM pages. It reduces the dirty paging, which reduces the TMT due to less number of iterative re-copied attempts. The draw back with auto-coverage is, it puts some vCPU's on sleep that degrades the performance of VM. It reduces the performance up to a level where client is able to detect the degradation in performance of VM. Deshpande et al. [10] introduced scatter and gather technique, which is based on scattering and gathering data. In this, they have two phases. In first phase they select the intermediate nodes between source host and destination host to scatter the data. In second phase, they gather the data and transfer to the destination host. They use the post-copy scheme for VM migration. Data was stored in between intermediator nodes and took less time to reach at destination. This scheme also helped to provide support to migrate the VM between fast source host and slow destination host and vice versa. The main drawback with the scatter and gather technique was, intermediate node failure may lead to data loss.

Raad et al. [11] proposed modified locator/identifier separation protocol (LISP) to handle resiliency and programmability issues in existing internet protocol architecture for handling Wide Area Network based VM migration process. They defined LISP control plane function to handle WAN VM migration process. Authors have defined LISP mapping system which gets updated whenever a VM change its physical location. In this, xTR register the VM's endpoint identifiers as a single/32 prefix before the migration process starts. In LISP based migration, source xTR and destination xTR are set in the initial state to authenticate the communication between them. Source host hypervisor and Destination host hypervisor communicate several times and set their change priority bit, hypervisor bit and update cache bits to communicate with each other. In the final stage the source host xTRs update their mapping cache data and redirect the upcoming packets to the new routing locator. In [12] authors proposed two-path routing algorithm for migrating VMs onto available servers which can satisfy the resource requirement while considering the amount of inter-VM traffic and network load. This algorithm finds multiple paths between source physical host to destination physical host. The goal of finding multiple path is to distribute the packets between multiple routes and partially saves the migration process from the link failures. In this approach for each communication between source host to destination host, two disjoint links are calculated. The selection of the links are based on congestion on the paths. The traffic flow on the network can be split at packet level. Some packets are sent through one path while other packets are sent through second path. One link failure do not affect the flow on the other disjoint link. The computation complexity of proposed algorithm is $O(w2)$, w represents the number of switches in the network. Authors clarify that the complexity of the proposed algorithm can be reduced if pre-computed set of alternative paths between different pair of switches are computed in advance.

On the basis of the literature survey we can conclude that VMM is a complex task and it requires further attention to improve the migration process by reducing the TMT and TDM.

3 Background

We begin the background work with the introduction of the pre-copy [5] and post-copy [13, 14] migration techniques.

Pre-copy Live Migration: In pre-copy migration, virtual machine remains in running state while migration process starts in background. In first step, the hypervisor copies all the data from source physical host to destination physical host. Virtual machine remain in running state. There are some pages which have been modified since the last copy to destination. These pages are called as dirty pages. They are re-copied and resent to destination until the rate of re-copy is not less than the dirty page rate. Once all of the dirty pages are copied, virtual machine is stopped at the source host. The most recent dirty pages are copied and control is transferred to destination host. The destination host generates an ARP request and assigns new IP address to the VM and resumes its functioning at the destination. When the VM is resumed at the destination then the VM is removed from the source. In pre-copy migration, VM first transfer all of the data to the destination host and then resume to the destination host as shown in Fig. 1. The time between pausing and resuming the virtual machine at destination is called down time. The time between starting the migration and ending the migration is called migration time.

Post-copy Live Migration: The drawback of the pre-copy migration is that it copies the data first and then resumes its functioning at the destination host. In cloud environment, migration is required because of lack of resources on physical host. In pre-copy, VM keeps running on source physical host which is in hotspot situation, this increases the TMT and also degrade the cloud service experience. To overcome this limitation in

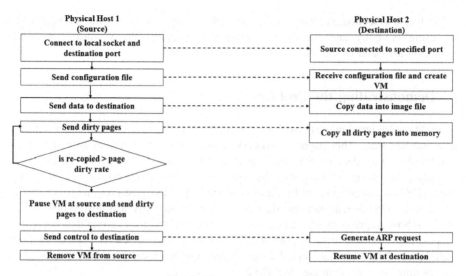

Fig. 1. Pre-copy migration

post-copy migration, it first copies the minimum pages and then resumes the VM at destination. Rest of the data is copied in later stage. Sometimes it happens that client requests for a page which is still in process to be copied to destination host. This condition is called as page fault. In post-copy migration, VM first resumes its work and rest of the data coping is done in later iterations as shown in Fig. 2. This method reduces the migration time but generates the risk that if source machine gets down before copying the complete data, the data may be lost for forever.

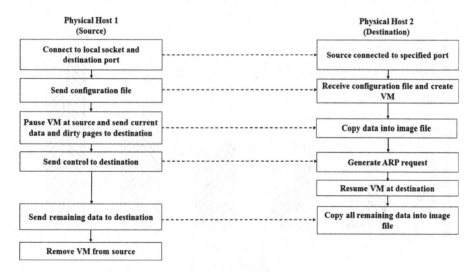

Fig. 2. Post-copy migration

In the next section we demonstrate the problem develop by sending multiple VMs by using pre-copy and post-copy migration techniques. We performed multiple migration tests and results show negative effect on TMT.

4 Demonstrating the Problem

In traditional migration systems, VM is migrated from source to destination with all data and VM state. This migration process includes transfer of current state of VM, or current data, i.e., data in use and data at rest (i.e., data which is not in process). Normally data at rest is more than the current data. VM image consists of Operating System (OS), current data and data at rest. Pre-copy and post-copy migration techniques copy OS, current data and data at rest from source physical host to destination physical host. In pre-copy, the data at rest is copied first and then current data is copied. In post-copy, current data is copied first and then data at rest is copied. In both techniques, data at rest is copied from source host to destination host which takes longer time and thus increases the TMT.

We conducted experiments using DELL OptiPlex 980 server connected to Cisco 2960x Ethernet switch for problem demonstration. All of the servers running Ubuntu 14.04 LTS as host OS and run KVM/QEMU as hypervisor. All VMs run Ubuntu 14.04 as guest OS, use Kernel Ver. 3.2, 1 to 2 vCPUs and have Virtio enabled for both the network adapter and hard disk. All of the host's uses Network File System (NFS) service to share the data between VM's. We keep the same load on all VM's. We use the standard implementation of pre-copy and post-copy live migration techniques. These migration techniques comes bundled with KVM/QEMU [9] and are publicly available.

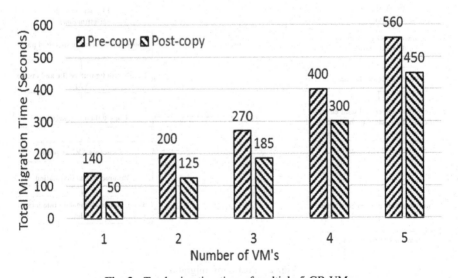

Fig. 3. Total migration time of multiple 5 GB VMs.

In our experimental setup we have considered the VM size of 8 to 15 GB depending upon the type of running guest OS. We have performed multiple VM migrations on which we transferred different VM's instances. These instances belongs to Ubuntu and Windows family. We have used *scp* Ubuntu command to copy data from one physical host to another physical host to generate heavy load on the network. We generate network load on same link on which the destination host is attached. To rectify the variation of results, the mean value of results is considered. As shown in Fig. 3, when we migrate multiple virtual machines, it generates heavy load on the network. Heavy network load leads to packet loss and it varies according to congestion in network. So we analyze the packets loss with moderate network congestion and high network congestion as shown in Table 1. These lost packets are resent that further increases the TMT. All data which we transfer is not always required but we transfer all of the data in a single shot at the same time, in both of the techniques (pre-copy and post-copy).

Table 1. Comparison of packet loss without network congestion and with network congestion.

S. No.	Packet loss without network congestion (in %)		Packet loss with network congestion (in %)	
	Pre-copy	Post-copy	Pre-copy	Post-copy
1	0.013	0.008	2.48	2.40
2	0.025	0.012	3.80	3.60
3	0.026	0.015	4.90	4.70
4	0.027	0.017	5.70	5.50
5	0.029	0.019	7.80	7.20

5   Proposed Shared Folder Based Migration (SFBM) Technique

In traditional migration systems, VM is migrated from source physical host to destination physical host with all data and VM state. This migration process includes transfer of current state of VM, current data, i.e., VM state, current data and data at rest (i.e., data which is not in process). Normally data at rest is much more than the current data and a VM image consists of OS and current data.

In implementation phase, we observed that VM migration is required due to the limited resources at physical machine. To avoid this temporary situation, we migrate the VM to another physical machine. This leads VM to non-responsive state and generates high network traffic. Non responsive state of VM is directly related to the amount of data which the VM required to resume its work at destination. More data leads to more delay in migration and less data leads to less delay. After the migration an image manager is required to keep track of running VM with their associated physical machine because VM's are continuously shuffling from one physical host to another physical host.

In proposed SFBM approach, only the current state of VM and current data is transmitted. Data at rest is stored in a shared folder in source host. We store the image file in place where it is accessible by the source as well as by the destination. We propose a modified pre-copy migration technique in which we first pause the VM at source and then resumes VM at destination with minimum system requirements and current data. We do not copy data at rest because data at rest is already stored in shared folder as shown in Fig. 4. Wherever data at rest is required, system copies only required block of data from source to destination. In initial stage, it copies only current data and the requested data is copied in later stages. The file which is not required will remain at the source. The working of our proposed technique under different scenarios depending on user requests for data is as shown in Fig. 4.

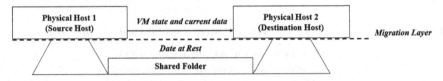

Fig. 4. Shared folder based migration approach

No Data Requested After VM Migration: In this scenario, it is assumed that the client will not request further data after the VM has been migrated from source to destination. In this scenario, our proposed approach copies the current data and VM state at the time of VM migration from source to destination. As the client makes no further request for the data from source host, hence no further network traffic is generated. Thus, it reduces load on the network. As fewer amounts of data are transferred during VM migration so the overall migration time is also reduced. In pre-copy and post-copy migration techniques, whole data, i.e. current data, VM state and data at rest are transferred from source physical host to destination physical host during the VM migration. Therefore, it generates heavy load on network and increases the overall time of the migration process.

Partial Data Requested After VM Migration: In this scenario, after VM migration, client makes further request for data from data at rest. In this, our approach copies only the requested files. The remaining data will be stored at the source only. It will not be migrated till the next request of client. Thus, it generates less load on network therefore reduces TMT. In both pre-copy and post-copy VM migration techniques, whole data, i.e., current data, VM state and data at rest are transferred from source to destination during VM migration.

Full Data Requested After VM Migration: In the third scenario, the client generates multiple requests to copy all of the remaining data after the VM has been migrated from source to destination. The requests by client are made one after the other at different times. Using our approach, the client makes multiple requests for files as per the requirement from source to destination. So, according to the request of the client file will be migrated from source to destination. In worst case scenario, all the files will be requested by client but at different time span. This will not overload the network and will lead to negligible loss of packets. In pre-copy and post-copy VM migration techniques, whole data (i.e., current data, VM state and data at rest) is transferred from source physical host to destination physical host during VM migration in one go. Thus, it generates heavy network traffic at the same time. This leads to network congestion and ultimately results in packet loss. The lost packets will have to be re-transmitted which further worsens the situation. Re-transmission of lost packets increases delay which further increases the TMT.

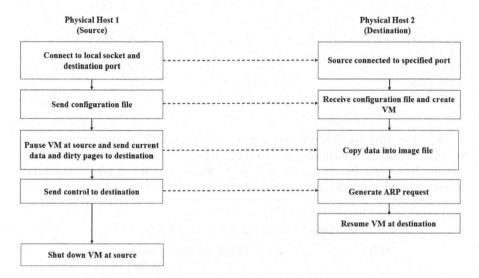

Fig. 5. Conceptual flow diagram for shared folder based migration approach

In this section we proposed the Shared Folder Based Migration (SFBM) Technique, which only transfers the state of VM with current data to destination as shown in Fig. 5. In our approach we do not transfer the whole data to destination host at single attempt. We transfer only part of data which is currently in use. Once the VM is shutdown, the data saves at the source physical host and copy of VM is deleted from the destination physical host. So the VM manager is not required to keep record of the running VM.

6   Experimental Setup

To validate the SFBM technique, to prove that it gives significant improvement over pre-copy and post-copy techniques in VM migration process, we have developed an experimental setup. In this, we have in total 28 physical hosts. We choose Dell

PowerEdge R520 server, Dell OptiPlex 980 and HP Compaq Elite 8300 as the host physical machines. All the hosting devices are equipped with 4 to 64 GB of RAM and have dedicated 320 GB to 1 TB of Hard Disk. We have used Cisco 2960x Ethernet switch to establish a connection between devices. Nodes run NFS server to share an image file of VM to other nodes. Further detail of the experimental setup is given in Table 2.

Table 2. Experimental setup details

Physical machine	Number of physical host	CPU type	Number of cores	CPU clock	RAM (in GB)
Dell OptiPlex 980	12	I5–650	4	3.2–3.46 GHz	4
HP Compaq Elite 8300	11	I7–3770	4	3.4–3.9 GHz	8
Dell PowerEdge R520	5	Xeon– E5-2420	24	2.2 GHz	64

We have used five different instances of virtual machines in our experiment. The running VMs have different configurations depending upon OS types. Salient details of running VM instances are shown in Table 3. We have followed type 2 hypervisor architecture, where we have considered Ubuntu 14.04 as the host OS.

Table 3. Salient features of running VMs

VM ID	OS	vCPU	vRAM (in MB)	Secondary storage (in GB)
VM1	Windows 7	1	2048	15
VM2	Windows 8	2	4096	15
VM3	Windows 10	2	4096	15
VM4	Ubuntu 16.04	1	1024	8
VM5	Ubuntu 14.04	1	512	8

We use KVM-Libvirt command for live migration of VM from source physical host to destination physical host. The commands first setup the connection with destination host. After getting the conformation call, we establish a Secure Socket Host (SSH) connection between source host to destination host. We use Wireshark [15] as network monitoring tool to monitor the network load. In our experiment, the internal time between two migration processes is deliberately set between 5 to 10 s. The workload on VMs remain same to evaluate the performance of proposed model.

7   Results and Discussion

As proposed SFBM uses the pre-copy migration technique so we have not implemented SFBM on post copy migration technique. In traditional VMM techniques, as shown in Fig. 3 takes long time for VMM and packet loss is also very high as shown in Table 1. In proposed SFBM as we do not send all the data at single attempt and keep the network traffic low which further reduces the packet loss. We test the proposed SFBM technique with moderate network congestion and heavy network congestion. We also found that load on the victim VM also affect the packet loss thus increases the TMT and TDM. So we further tested the proposed SFBM with the victim VM which is highly CPU and RAM stressed. We used *stress* [16] command to generate load on the CPU and RAM. The result of proposed SFBM is shown in Table 4. The packet loss in network congestion scenario goes down up to 5.3% as compared to 7.8% in the existing pre-copy migration technique as shown in Table 1.

Table 4. Packet loss with proposed SFBM technique.

VM	Packet loss without network congestion (in %)		Packet loss with network congestion (in %)	
	Ideal VM	Stressed VM	Ideal VM	Stressed VM
1	0.004	0.005	1.2	1.9
2	0.006	0.007	1.7	3.3
3	0.007	0.008	2.6	4.3
4	0.010	0.009	2.8	4.9
5	0.011	0.010	3.0	5.3

To check the effect of network load, VM stress on TMT and TDM, we have developed four different scenarios. In our first scenario we have taken the Ideal VMs with Moderated Network (IVM MN) traffic. In second scenario, we have considerd Stressed VMs (CPU and RAM stress) with Moderate Network (SVM MN) traffic. In third scenario, we have taken Ideal VMs with High Network Congestion (IVM HNC) and at last we have considered Stressed VMs with High Network Congestion (SVM HNC). We have calculated the TDM and TMT with above said scenarios and results are shown in Tables 5 and 6 respectively. The TMT goes down from 560 s as shown in Fig. 3 to 52 s in scenario of no data requested after VM migration.

Table 5. Total migration time (in seconds) with proposed SFBM in different scenarios

VM	IVM MN	SVM MN	IVM HNC	SVM HNC
1	7	11	14	17
2	7.5	12	19	25
3	9	13	30	37
4	9.5	15	38	43
5	10	16	46	52

Table 6. Total down time (in seconds) with proposed SFBM in different scenarios

VM	IVM MN	SVM MN	IVM HNC	SVM HNC
1	1.3	5	6	10
2	1.6	7	9	15
3	1.8	9	12	23
4	2	12	18	30
5	2.3	15	26	38

In Fig. 6, we have shown that TMT increases as we increase number of migration. More data leads to more packet loss and more time to transfer the lost packets. The load on the VM also an important role in downtime. The RAM stress on the VM leads to copy same pages again and again, network congestion makes the situation worst. The downtime is adequate when VM is in ideal and network also not in congestion as shown in Fig. 7. The network congestion makes the situation worse, thus increases the TMT and TDM. All of the techniques [8–12] use the scenario where they transfer all of the data in single shot and develop congestion in the network that leads to delay in migration process and also increase the performance of cloud platform. In SFBM technique we keep the network congestion low so that the transmission would be done in minimum time.

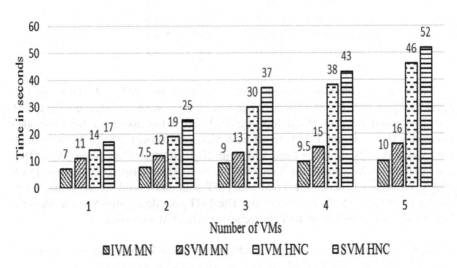

Fig. 6. Total migration time (in seconds) with proposed SFBM in different scenario

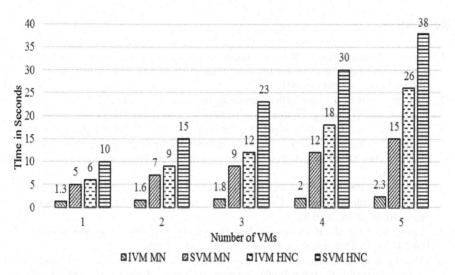

Fig. 7. Total down time (in seconds) with proposed SFBM in different scenario

8   Conclusion

In this paper, we have considered the VMM techniques which are essential for power saving, system maintenance, disaster recovery and green computing. In our problem demonstration, we have demonstrated that multiple VM migrations generates heavy load on the network that further increase the TMT and packet loss. The previous studies transferred all of the data in a single shot to the destination host. In proposed SFBM, data is logically shared between physical hosts which uses modified pre-copy migration technique. We first copy the current data of VM from source host to destination host and then resume VM at destination with minimum system requirements. Data at rest is not copied because it is already stored in logically shared folder. This data is accessible to both source and destination hosts. Thus, saving TDM and reducing network traffic. We found that the network congestion and resources utilization is a major factor that affect the TMT, TDM and packet loss. We further considered four different scenarios for evaluation of proposed SFBM approach. These scenarios are considered to validate the efficiency of the proposed approach. These scenarios are broadly divided into two parts first VMM with moderate network congestion and VMM with heavy network congestion. These two scenarios further divided into two parts (1) VMM with ideal victim VM and (2) VMM with resources stress victim VM. So we have considered four scenarios with different network traffic and load on victim VM. We have tested with respect to all of these cases and results show SFBM approach significantly reduces the TMT from 560 s to 52 s and thus saves the time up to 91%. Besides, the packet loss rate also went down from 7.8% to 5.2% in adequate conditions.

In this paper, we have consider the local area network topology to migrate VM from source host to destination host. In future, it will be interesting to investigate the problem of the VMM between two distinct data centres in wide area network topology architecture.

References

1. Gupta, P., Seetharaman, A., Raj, J.R.: The usage and adoption of cloud computing by small and medium businesses. Elsevier Int. J. Inf. Manag. **33**(5), 861–874 (2013). https://doi.org/10.1016/j.ijinfomgt.2013.07.001
2. Mell, P., Grance, T.: The NIST definition of cloud computing. National Institute of Standards and Technology, Information Technology Laboratory (2011)
3. Buyya, R., Yeo, C.S., Venugopal, S., Broberg, J., Brandic, I.: Cloud computing and emerging IT platforms: vision, hype, and reality for delivering computing as the 5th utility. Elsevier Future Gen. Comput. Syst. **25**(6), 599–616 (2009). https://doi.org/10.1016/j.future.2008.12.001
4. Sotiriadis, S., Bessis, N., Petrakis, E.G.M., Amza, C.: Virtual machine cluster mobility in inter-cloud platforms. Elsevier Future Gen. Comput. Syst. **10**(2), 1–11 (2016). https://doi.org/10.1016/j.future.2016.02.007
5. Nelson, M., Lim, B., Hutchins, G.: Fast transparent migration for virtual machines. In: USENIX Annual Technical Conference, pp. 391–394 (2005)
6. Clark, C., et al.: Live migration of virtual machines. In: 2nd Conference on Symposium on Networked Systems Design & Implementation, vol. 43, no. 3, pp. 14–26 (2009). https://doi.org/10.17485/ijst/2015/v8is9/65579
7. Akoush, S., Sohan, R., Rice, A., Moore, A.W., Hopper, A.: Predicting the performance of virtual machine migration. In: International Symposium on Modeling, Analysis and Simulation of Computer and Telecommunication Systems, pp. 37–46 (2010). https://doi.org/10.1109/mascots.2010.13
8. Zhang, J., Ren, F., Shu, R., Huang, T., Liu, Y.: Guaranteeing delay of live virtual machine migration by determining and provisioning appropriate bandwidth. IEEE Trans. Comput. **65**(9), 2910–2917 (2016). https://doi.org/10.1109/TC.2015.2500560
9. Shah, A.: Live Migrating QEMU-KVM Virtual Machines (2017). www.redhat.com. [Online]. https://developers.redhat.com/blog/2015/03/24/live-migrating-qemu-kvm-virtual-machines/. Accessed 24 Sept 2017
10. Deshpande, U., Chan, D., Chan, S., Gopalan, K., Bila, N.: Scatter-gather live migration of virtual machines. IEEE Trans. Cloud Comput. **PP**(99), 1–14 (2015). https://doi.org/10.1109/cloud.2014.58
11. Raad, P., Secci, S., Phung, D.C., Cianfrani, A., Gallard, P., Pujolle, G.: Achieving sub-second downtimes in large-scale virtual machine migrations with LISP. IEEE Trans. Netw. Serv. Manag. **11**(2), 133–143 (2014). https://doi.org/10.1109/TNSM.2014.012114.130517
12. Kanagavelu, R., Lee, B.S., Le, N.T.D., Mingjie, L.N., Aung, K.M.M.: Virtual machine placement with two-path traffic routing for reduced congestion in data center networks. Comput. Commun. **53**, 1–12 (2014). https://doi.org/10.1016/j.comcom.2014.07.009
13. Hirofuchi, T., Yamahata, I.: Yabusame: Postcopy Live Migration. KVM Forum (2011)
14. Hines, M.R., Deshpande, U., Gopalan, K.: Post-copy live migration of virtual machines. ACM SIGOPS Oper. Syst. Rev. **43**(3), 14 (2009). https://doi.org/10.1145/1618525.1618528
15. www.wireshark.org. "Wireshark" (2017). [Online]. https://www.wireshark.org/. Accessed 31 July 2017
16. Www.ubuntu.com. "Stress ubuntu manuals". [Online]. http://manpages.ubuntu.com/manpages/zesty/man1/stress.1.html. Accessed 10 Dec 2017

Network Technologies

Wideband Monopole Planar Antenna with Stepped Ground Plane for WLAN/WiMAX Applications

Rakesh N. Tiwari[1(✉)], Prabhakar Singh[2,3], Binod Kumar Kanaujia[4], and Partha Bir Barman[5]

[1] Department of Electronics and Communication Engineering,
Uttarakhand Technical University, Dehradun, Uttarakhand, India
srakeshnath@gmail.com
[2] Department of Physics, Galgotias University, Greater Noida,
Uttar Pradesh, India
prabhakarsingh3@gmail.com
[3] Department of Applied Sciences, Galgotias College of Engineering
and Technology, Greater Noida, Uttar Pradesh, India
[4] School of Computational and Integrative Sciences,
Jawaharlal Nehru University, New Delhi, India
bkkanaujia@yahoo.co.in
[5] Department of Physics and Materials Science,
Jaypee University of Information Technology, Solan, India
pb.barman@juit.ac.in

Abstract. A microstrip line fed compact monopole antenna is presented for the WLAN and WiMAX applications. The proposed antenna has a compact size of dimensions $34 \times 20 \times 1.6$ mm^3. A stepped shaped defected ground plane is used for the bandwidth enhancement. The parametric study is performed to obtain the best results for the design process of the antenna. The effect of asymmetric U-shaped strip and step slots in the ground plane provide an enhanced bandwidth. The antenna gives the measured impedance bandwidth of 105.21% (2.23–7.18 GHz). The simulated antenna gain is varying in the range of 2.39–4.68 dBi for the entire band of operation. Radiation efficiency is higher than 75.0% throughout the entire operating band. Measured radiation patterns are almost omnidirectional in H-plane and dumbbell shape pattern in E-plane. The antenna parameters are calculated using CST Microwave Studio and the simulated results are validated with the measured results.

Keywords: Asymmetric U-shaped patch · Stepped ground · Wideband antenna
Microstrip line · WLAN/WiMAX applications

1 Introduction

The assigned IEEE standards, IEEE 802.11 and IEEE 802.16, are WLAN (wireless local area network) and WiMAX (worldwide interoperability for microwave access), covering multiband (2.4–2.484, 5.15–5.35, and 5.725–5.85 GHz) and wideband (2.5–2.69, 3.3–3.7, and 5.25–5.85 GHz) operations respectively. Thus, WLAN and

© Springer Nature Singapore Pte Ltd. 2019
P. K. Singh et al. (Eds.): FTNCT 2018, CCIS 958, pp. 253–264, 2019.
https://doi.org/10.1007/978-981-13-3804-5_19

WiMAX are presently most popular areas of research. As these bands are commonly used in the same system simultaneously, a single antenna is required to cover both the bands. Therefore, a lot of research on the printed monopole antenna is going on to meet the need of a multi/wideband single radiator with a compact size, and easy fabrication [1–4]. In modern communication systems, monopole antennas are good candidates for wireless personal area as a network, body area network for medical applications etc. [5, 6]. Therefore, in the process of improvements, many efforts are still going on such as, to minimize the overall size, compactness of antenna and enhancement of impedance bandwidth. Several monopole antennas are designed by modifying the radiating patch such as E-shaped, Arc-shaped and modifying the ground plane as semi-elliptical shape [7–9]. M-shaped patch monopole antenna gives wideband response when a circular ground plane is implemented [10]. In [11] a microstrip line fed planar antenna with wide-slot is proposed which increases the bandwidth and improves the radiation pattern using the parasitic patch. Radiating patch with modified ground plane and curved slot loaded monopole antenna reports enhanced bandwidth [12]. Recently defected ground plane for both WLAN and WiMAX applications is designed [13]. Further, UTM-Logo shape monopole antenna is printed for wideband frequency operating from 1.98 to 6.48 GHz. This antenna is used for cognitive radio application [14]. The multiband antenna can also be realized using E-shaped and U-shaped strip in the ground plane [15] and using the tuning stub, square ring and T-shaped stub [16]. However, almost all these antennas are either bearing large size or complex in design.

In this paper, a compact monopole antenna consists of a U-shaped patch with unequal arms along with a stepped ground plane is proposed for Bluetooth, WLAN, WiMAX and ISM band applications. The dimensions of this antenna along with ground plane are 34 (L_s) × 20 (W_s) × 1.6 (h) mm^3 printed on a low cost FR4 material and fed by microstrip line. Further, this antenna is fabricated, measured and compared with the simulated results obtained by CST Microwave Studio. The design and measurement of monopole planar antenna is presented in Sect. 2. Results and discussion are described in Sect. 3. The radiation patterns of the antenna are described in Sect. 4 followed by the conclusion in Sect. 5.

2   Antenna Configuration and Measurement

Configuration of the antenna is depicted in Fig. 1. U-shaped patch having unequal arms along with a center strip is printed on the upper side of the FR4 dielectric material $(\varepsilon_r = 4.4)$. On the lower side of the substrate a stepped ground plane with a center slit is printed. The antenna is fed with microstrip line of dimensions $W_1 \times L_1$. The fabricated antenna design with its top and bottom view is shown in Fig. 2. The optimized antenna size is presented in Table 1. The designed antenna is measured using VNA (Model: Agilent N5230A). The simulated and measured return loss curve is plotted in Fig. 3 and the corresponding bandwidths are found to be 105.21% (2.23–7.18 GHz) and 100.10% (2.42–7.27 GHz) respectively which are in good agreement. A comparison of antenna performance is presented in Table 2 which comprises the earlier reported results with proposed antenna structure in terms of dimensions and frequency bands [11–13]. Surface current flowing on the radiator is calculated using CST microwave studio and depicted for 2.65, 2.86, 3.22 and 6.17 GHz (Fig. 4) respectively. From this figure it is clear that the 1st and 2nd resonances are produced due to surface current density developed on L_5 and L_3 respectively.

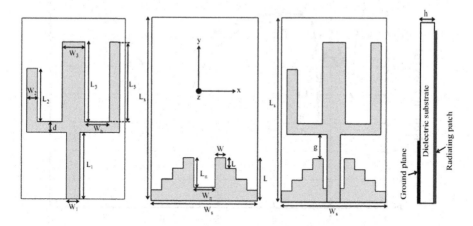

(a) Microstrip line   **(b)** Stepped ground metal   **(c)** Front design   **(d)** Side design

Fig. 1. Structure of antenna.

(a) Top structure   **(b)** Bottom structure

Fig. 2. Fabricated prototype antenna.

Table 1. Design specifications of the antenna.

Dimensions	Values (mm)	Dimensions	Values (mm)
$L_s \times W_s$	34 × 20	$L_1 \times W_1$	12.5 × 2.2
$L_2 \times W_2$	10 × 2	$L_3 \times W_3$	15 × 4.4
W_h	4.8	h	1.6
L_5	15	d	2
$L_g \times W_s$	8 × 20	$L_n \times W_n$	6 × 4.5
$L \times W$	2 × 2	g	4.5

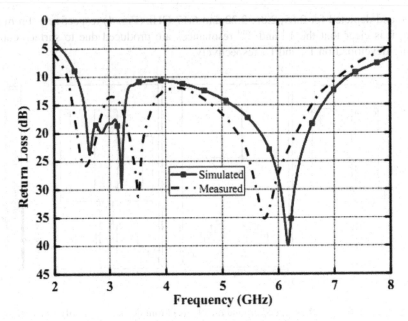

Fig. 3. Comparison of return loss for the designed antenna.

Table 2. Antenna comparison with earlier reported results.

Reference no.	Dimensions (mm³)	Frequency band (GHz)	Bandwidth (%)
[11]	37 × 37 × 1.6	2.23–5.36	80.0
[12]	50 × 55 × 1.5	2.0–6.8	109.0
[13]	38 × 25 × 1.6	2.4–6.0	86.71
Proposed Antenna	34 × 20 × 1.6	2.23–7.18	105.21

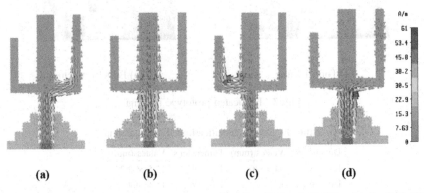

Fig. 4. Surface current distribution at (a) f = 2.65 GHz, (b) f = 2.86 GHz, (c) f = 3.22 GHz, and (d) f = 6.17 GHz.

The 3rd and 4th resonances are created due to current flowing on L$_2$ and microstrip line respectively. From the current distribution analysis the resonance frequencies of the proposed design can be formulated and tuned by varying the dimensions of the asymmetric U shaped radiator.

3   Antenna Results and Discussions

Figure 5 depicts the variation of return loss for different values of left arm of the asymmetric U shaped strip (L$_2$). The graph clearly shows that the third resonance is controlled by L$_2$ and it is shifted towards the lower side as the value of L$_2$ increases. Therefore, the third resonance is inversely proportional to L$_2$ and can be tuned by varying the values of L$_2$. It is also observed that the return loss value for 4th resonance is improved up to 40 dB as the value of L$_2$ increases. The maximum bandwidth is found to be 4.75 GHz (2.42–7.17 GHz) for L$_2$ = 8 mm.

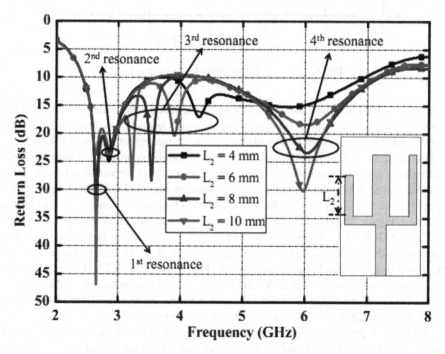

Fig. 5. Effect of L$_2$ on return loss of the antenna.

The return loss curve for different values of right arm of the asymmetric U shaped patch (L$_5$) is plotted in Fig. 6. This figure also illustrates that the first resonance frequency is controlled by varying the value of L$_5$. From this figure it is inferred that there is negligible effect of L$_5$ on the antenna matching. At the same time it is also noted that fourth resonance is inversely proportional to the value of L$_5$. Thus, L$_5$ is

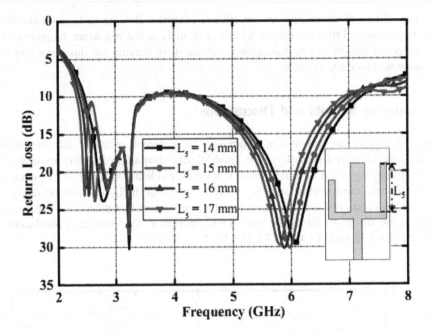

Fig. 6. Effect of L₅ on return loss of the antenna.

simultaneously controlling the first and fourth resonance frequencies. However, from the current distribution value, it is seen that the fourth resonance is also affected by the strip line. From the Fig. 6 it can be observed that the maximum bandwidth achieved is 4.90 GHz (2.33–7.23 GHz). The ground plane, in monopole antenna, generally works as a radiator and the dimensions of the ground plane controls the variation of return loss of the antenna. When a rectangular slot of dimensions $L_n \times W_n$ is incorporated in the ground plane, it is observed that the impedance matching performance of the antenna is modified. Figure 7 shows that the bandwidth of the antenna improves upto 4.85 GHz (2.42–7.27 GHz) as L_n increases. From the Fig. 8 it is clear that the fourth resonance shifts towards lower end with increasing values of W_n. At the optimum value of $W_n = 4.5$ mm, the maximum bandwidth of 4.88 GHz (2.39–7.27 GHz) is achieved. From this figure it is also noted that the matching condition improves as the value of W_n increases. If the value of W_n is less than 3.5 mm, antenna operates in dual band mode and the impedance matching condition is deteriorated.

Figure 9 depicts the graph for real and imaginary parts of the impedance of the proposed antenna. It is found that the real part of input impedance is varying approximately 50 Ω and the imaginary part is nearly 0 Ω respectively. Therefore, it can be concluded that the resultant input impedance is nearly matching with the characteristic impedance of the microstrip line which is equal to 50 Ω. Thus the good impedance matching condition of the present antenna design causes the improvement in the overall bandwidth.

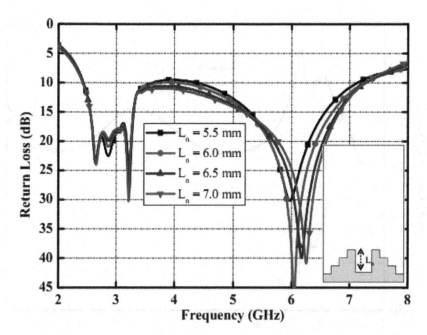

Fig. 7. Return loss versus frequency for different values of L_n.

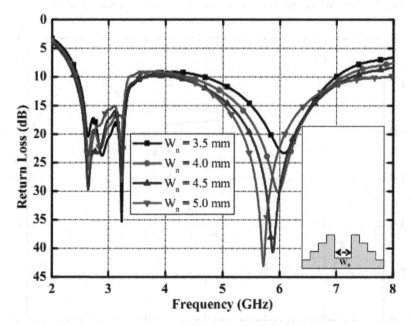

Fig. 8. Return loss versus frequency for different values of W_n.

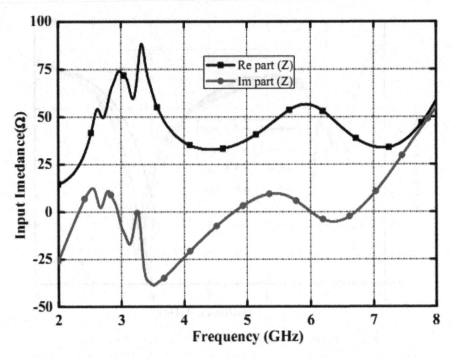

Fig. 9. Graph of Re. part (Z) and Im. part (Z) of input impedance with frequency.

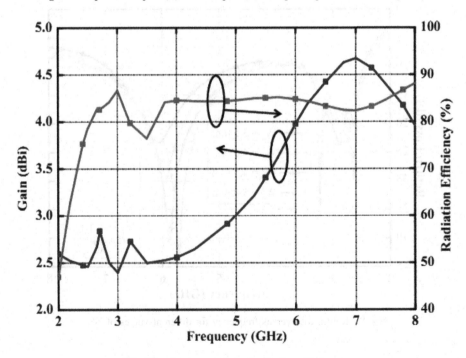

Fig. 10. Antenna gain and radiation efficiency.

The radiation efficiency and gain of the antenna are shown in Fig. 10. The simulated antenna radiation efficiency is always above 75.0% while the antenna gain varies between 2.39–4.68 dBi throughout the entire operating band. However, it is noted that the gain of the antenna is less than 3 dBi upto 4 GHz of frequency band. But the antenna gain increases as the frequency increases beyond 4 GHz while the antenna efficiency remains almost constant for the entire usable frequency band.

4   Radiation Pattern of the Antenna

The antenna radiation patterns are measured in a microwave shielded Anechoic chamber and shown in Fig. 11. The test antenna is placed at a distance 3.2 m from the horn antenna. The co and cross polarization patterns are plotted in Fig. 12 for frequencies 2.65, 4.85 and 6.17 GHz respectively. Co-polar plot for H-plane ($\varphi = 0°$) is almost omnidirectional for all the frequencies with low cross polarization level.

For E-plane ($\varphi = 90°$), co-polar pattern is bidirectional at two sampling frequencies 2.65 and 4.85 GHz while at 6.17 GHz it is slightly deteriorated due to high mode generation. The cross polar pattern in E-plane is lower than the co-polar pattern for all the frequencies. Thus, the far filled pattern of the proposed antenna is suitable to meet the necessary requirements for the broadband communication systems. Both the radiation patterns (calculated from CST and from the measurement) are showing quite acceptable results.

Fig. 11. Radiation pattern measurement setup.

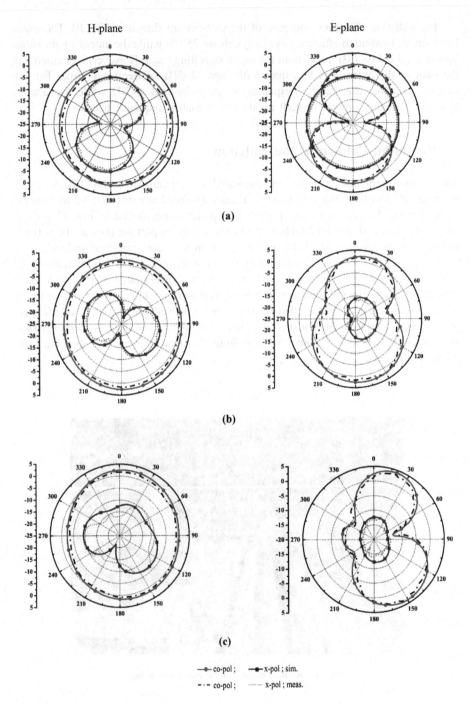

H-plane

E-plane

(a)

(b)

(c)

co-pol ;   x-pol ; sim.

co-pol ;   x-pol ; meas.

Fig. 12. Measured antenna radiation patterns at (a) 2.65 GHz, (b) 4.85 GHz, and (c) 6.17 GHz.

5 Conclusion

In the present paper, a compact, wideband monopole antenna is designed, fabricated and measured. Parametric study of the patch and ground plane shows that the impedance bandwidth and various resonance frequencies can be tuned by optimizing the values of L_2, L_5, L_n and W_n. The maximum bandwidth of 105.21% (2.23–7.18 GHz) is obtained by optimizing the patch and ground plane dimensions. H-plane patterns calculated at different frequencies are stable and omnidirectional while E-plane patterns are showing bidirectional radiation. Thus the designed antenna characteristics are appropriate for the LTE 2300 (2.305–2.40 GHz), LTE 2500 (2.50–2.690 GHz), Bluetooth, WLAN/WiMAX and other wireless applications.

References

1. Chen, I.F., Peng, C.M.: Printed broadband monopole antenna for WLAN/WiMAX applications. IEEE Antennas Wirel. Propag. Lett. **8**, 472–474 (2009)
2. Bod, M., Hassani, H.R., Taheri, M.M.S.: Compact UWB printed slot antenna with extra bluetooth, GSM, and GPS bands. IEEE Antennas Wirel. Propag. Lett. **11**, 531–534 (2012)
3. Moosazadeh, M., Kharkovsky, S.: Compact and small planar monopole antenna with symmetrical L- and U-shaped slots for WLAN/WiMAX applications. IEEE Antennas Wirel. Propag. Lett. **13**, 388–391 (2014)
4. Cui, Y., Yang, L., Liu, B., Li, R.L.: Multiband planar antenna for LTE/GSM/ UMTS and WLAN/WiMAX handsets. IET Microw. Antennas Propag. **10**(5), 502–506 (2016)
5. Li, H.B., Kohno, R.: Introduction of SG-BAN in IEEE 802.15 with related discussion. In: Proceedings of 2007 IEEE International Conference on Ultra-Wideband, Singapore, pp. 134–139 (2007)
6. Kohno, R., Hamaguchi, K., Li, H.B., Takizawa. K.: R & D and standardization of body area network (BAN) for medical healthcare. In: Proceedings of 2008 IEEE International Conference on Ultra-Wideband, vol. 3, pp. 5–8 (2008)
7. Kimouche, H., Abed, D., Atrouz, B., Aksas, R.: Bandwidth enhancement of rectangular monopole antenna using modified semi-elliptical ground plane and slots. Microw. Opt. Technol. Lett. **52**(1), 54–58 (2010)
8. Dastranj, A., Abiri, H.: Bandwidth enhancement of printed E-shaped slot antennas fed by CPW and microstrip line. IEEE Trans. Antennas Propag. **58**(4), 1402–1407 (2010)
9. Lu, J.H., Yeh, C.H.: Planar broadband arc-shaped monopole antenna for UWB system. IEEE Trans. Antennas Propag. **60**(7), 3091–3095 (2012)
10. Aghda, M.R., Kamarudin, M.R., Iddi, H.U.: M-shape surrounded with ring patch wideband monopole printed antenna. Microw. Opt. Technol. Lett. **54**(2), 482–486 (2012)
11. Sung, Y.: Bandwidth enhancement of a microstrip line-fed printed wide-slot antenna with a parasitic center patch. IEEE Trans. Antennas Propag. **60**(4), 1712–1716 (2012)
12. Baudha, S., Vishwakarma, D.K.: Bandwidth enhancement of a planar monopole microstrip patch antenna. Int. J. Microw. Wirel. Technol. **8**(2), 237–242 (2016)
13. Gautam, A.K., Bisht, A., Kanaujia, B.K.: A wideband antenna with defected ground plane for WLAN/WiMAX applications. Int. J. Electron. Commun. (AEÜ) **70**(3), 354–358 (2016)

14. Aghda, M.R., Kamarudin, M.R.: UTM-logo wideband printed monopole antenna surrounded with circular ring patch. Prog. Electromagnetics Res. C **15**, 157–164 (2010)
15. Wang, T., Yin, Y.Z., Yang, J., Zhang, Y.L., Xie, J.J.: Compact triple-band antenna using defected ground structure for WLAN/WIMAX applications. Prog. Electromagnetics Res. Lett. **35**, 155–164 (2012)
16. Huang, S.S., Li, J., Zhao, J.Z.: A novel compact planar triple-band monopole antenna for WLAN/WiMAX applications. Prog. Electromagnetics Res. Lett. **50**, 117–123 (2014)

Node Activity Based Routing in Opportunistic Networks

Prashant Kumar[✉], Naveen Chauhan, and Narottam Chand

Department of Computer Science and Engineering,
National Institute of Technology Hamirpur, Hamirpur, India
prashantkumar32@gmail.com, {naveen, nar}@nith.ac.in

Abstract. In mobile networks, the problem of intermittent and truncated connectivity leads to the growth of opportunistic networks. In opportunistic networks, the disconnected mobile nodes communicated whenever they get opportunity to share the information or their connectivity is resumed. Because of this intermittent connectivity, routing in this type of networks becomes very challenging. Efficient use of resources is extremely important in such conditions. In this work, we propose an innovative routing strategy for opportunistic networks based on the node's activities. In NABR, we consider node's past behavior and activities to maximize the message delivery ratio under opportunistic network environment. We also propose a buffer management scheme that efficiently use buffer storage of nodes to reduce message drop rate. To simulate and demonstrate the performance of the proposed NABR protocol the ONE simulator is used and results are compared with existing routing schemes.

Keywords: Opportunistic networks · Routing · Delay tolerant network
OppNets routing · History based routing

1 Introduction

Opportunistic Networks (OppNets) are the special class of wireless ad-hoc networks where connectivity is intermittent and a direct and complete route between source and destination is almost absent. Thus, opportunistic network falsify the statement about all the communication networks that they have been assumed to be connected at least most of the time [1]. Communication between the OppNets devices is based on the instantaneous response of the meeting among them. OppNets supports the concepts of "anywhere anytime computing".

OppNets remove the assumption of physical end-to-end connection while providing and extending the connectivity among the nodes. So connectivity can be extended to the point where direct access to the network is not available. Thus, OppNets provides the opportunity to pervasive devices that are repeatedly out of the range of the network, but comes in the range of other devices. In OppNets, carriers may be human, wildlife animals or the vehicles, this leads to a different kind of disconnection as in normal networks. Therefore, when source wants to transmit to the destination, the end-to-end connection may not exist between them at that time [2]. Intermittent connectivity, heterogeneity of the nodes decentralize nature, resource limitations, short range

© Springer Nature Singapore Pte Ltd. 2019
P. K. Singh et al. (Eds.): FTNCT 2018, CCIS 958, pp. 265–277, 2019.
https://doi.org/10.1007/978-981-13-3804-5_20

communication, opportunistic nature of contacts etc., make OppNets completely different sort of network. Therefore, routing strategies used in traditional wireless networks such as Mobile Ad-hoc Networks (MANETs) cannot be directly applied to OppNets. This leads to necessity to develop routing strategies for OppNets that would better acquire the nature of OppNets.

OppNets possess a different routing mechanism. Wang et al. [3] defined mechanism for OppNets routings. According to authors, OppNets use "receive-carry-forward" instead of "receive-forward". Upon receiving, packets are stored in node's buffer storage instead of being forwarded immediately. Nodes carry the packets until they get communication opportunity *i.e.* they meet other nodes during movement. Network division as well as nonexistent of end-to-end connectivity problem can be overcome with this mechanism [3]. Thus, OppNets nodes does not broadcast the information rather they exchange information in pairs. Further OppNets forward mechanism is unpredictable. In some OppNets routing strategies, data will be forwarded many times when they meet different nodes and multiple copies of forwarded data are kept in the network. This differs OppNets routing from traditional "one-time forward to the next finite hop". This is one of the two major routing approaches in OppNets and known as *replica-based* approach. The other is *forwarding based* approach in which only one copy of the forwarded data is kept and attempt to deliver data to destination using network dynamics and resources.

A typical OppNets routing scenario at time t is shown in Fig. 1. Let source node is S and destination node is D. Currently S and D are in different area and no path is existing between them. Hence, S send the message to neighbor nodes n_1 and n_4. Both n_1 and n_4 put message into their buffer until a communication opportunity is find. After some at time t_1, node n_1 meets to node n_6, and transfer the message to n_6 and n_4 meets to node n_2 and transfer the message to n_2. Finally, at time t_3, node n_2 meets destination node D and deliver message to D to complete message transmission.

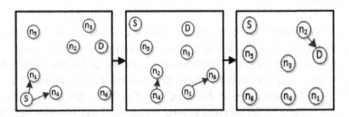

Fig. 1. Illustration of OppNets routing

A good OppNets routing algorithm should be able to discover the new nodes and ensure high data delivery ratio. It must distribute message evenly over entire network and reduces the resource consumption to deliver any single message. Spyropoulos et al. [4], point at some desirable design goals for a good OppNets routing strategy. The authors states: "OppNets routing scheme should perform significantly fewer transmissions the epidemic and other flooding-based routing schemes, under all conditions.

It should generate low contention, especially under high traffic loads. It must be highly scalable and adaptable to changes in network size or node density".

Jain et al. [5], gives performance and knowledge trade-offs, considering contacts, queuing and traffic demands as knowledge oracle. Figure 2(a) depicts a trade-off between performance and network knowledge. The x-axis depicts the amount of knowledge and y-axis depicts the expected achievable performance by using a certain amount of knowledge. Most of the OppNets routing algorithms in which network information used, mainly focus upon these knowledge oracles with "*interconnect time (ICT)*" and "*contact frequency*". ICT is defined as contact duration. In many of such approaches the delivery probability of the message is calculated by these oracles and mainly focus upon contact frequency of the sender nodes and the node sender meet most. Nothing taken account to previous meeting results as well as to messages, which are being transferred to frequent meeting node. However, all of these are important parameters to consider, but we argue that nodes past behavior must be considered while designing routing algorithms for OppNets. It will make massive impact on the routing performance in such networks. So, there should be another knowledge oracle called "Recent Activity" as shown in Fig. 2(b).

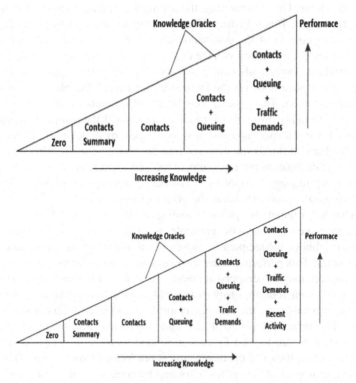

Fig. 2. (a) Performance vs. knowledge trade-off (b) Performance vs. knowledge trade-off (modified)

Considering the facts discussed above, in this paper, we propose a novel routing strategy for OppNets called *NABR*. In NABR we aim to maximize the message delivery ratio under OppNets resource constraints by utilizing network bandwidth and node's buffer storage. In NABR, node's past behavior and activities are considered, while forwarding a message to bundle carrier (*i.e.* neighbor node). Based on these activities, node's *confidence level*, is calculated and message is transfer to node with highest *confidence* level. To reduce resource consumption, we propose a buffer management scheme, which further improve the overall performance of NABR.

Rest of the paper is organized as follows. In Sect. 2, we describe the existing OppNets routing schemes. The system model is given in Sect. 3. The proposed node activity based routing protocol (NABR) for OppNets is described in Sect. 4. Simulation and results are discussed in Sect. 5. In Sect. 6 we conclude the paper.

2 Related Work

Routing has been widely discussed in opportunistic network over last decade. In *Direct Transmission* [6], the node stores message in its buffer until it directly encounters with the destination node. On such meeting, the intermediate carrier, transfer the message to the destination node. This scheme suffers from highly delay as source node may not come into direct contact of the destination node over a longer period. Further, if the carrier node does not encounter with the destination node, the message will never reach to the destination. Instead of waiting for meeting with the destination node, *First Contact* [5], the source node (or the intermediate carrier) forwards the message to the first encountered node. This scheme may be useful in multicast messages, but it also suffers from high delay. In *epidemic* routing protocol [7] the source node transfer the message to all nodes it encounter and process is repeat by nodes who receive a copy of the message. Thus, it floods the message into the entire network. Although, the message reaches its destination but this protocol has very high resource consumption, such as large memory requires to store large number of messages, high bandwidth utilization, high communication the drains the power of nodes etc.

An enhanced version of *epidemic* routing is *Meetings and Visits* (MV) [8]. It exchanges messages in pair-wise principle as in epidemic routing, but instead of flooding its neighbors, the recipient is chosen based on previous meetings and locations visit frequencies. This performs better than *epidemic*, suffer for its buffer management at nodes, packets may be dropped regularly, as it uses First-in-first-out (FIFO). An extension of *epidemic* routing, *spray and wait* [4] is proposed to reduce the overhead of flooding. In spray and wait, the message is forwarded to intermediate nodes with some probability. This protocol has two phases: spray phase and wait phase. In spray phase, L copies of message are formed for each generated message. In wait phase, the nodes wait for direct transmission if the destination is not found in spray phase. The protocol reduces adverse impact of the *epidemic* routing by controlling the amount of flooding, but it still suffers from delay and resource consumption issues. Moreover, the message delivery possibility highly depends on the number of copies (L) generated to spray.

A variation of *spray and wait* is proposed in [9] as *spray and focus*. This scheme again has two phases: *Spray phase*- When a new message is generated at a source node, it also creates L "forwarding tokens" for this message. Each node maintains a "summary vector" with IDs of all messages that it has stored. When two nodes meet, they exchange their SV and identifies common messages they have other message are which have n > 1 forwarding tokens handed over to each other with n/2 forwarding tokens. When n = 1, the decision taken as in *focus phase*, which uses a utility function to choose the next forwarding the node.

Adaptive Fuzzy Spray and Wait, yet another variation of *spray and wait* is proposed in [10]. This routing protocol also propose a buffer utilization policy based on the fuzzy decision making technique. This is use to classify and store the messages into levels inside the buffer and promotes high priority messages are transferred first during the meetings. However, the randomized buffer message dropping policy of the protocol, does not works well as large message may suffer long delays and if all messages are almost same size then message size become extraneous to priority.

Content Encounter Probability based Message Forwarding in Opportunistic Network (*CEPMF*) [11] is proposed to achieve an efficient *publisher/subscriber* service. Subscriber's interest of flow in network in the form of *predicates*. In CEPMF, nodes may receive some message(s), which they do not want, if predicates of these messages are similar to their demands. The History-Based Routing Protocol for Opportunistic Networks (HiBOp) proposed in [12] aims to utilize the context information of the nodes. *HiBOP* has three phases: emission phase, forwarding phase and delivery phase. The protocol is suits very much for human mobility patterns as they generally follow a particular pattern. Lindgren et al. proposed Probabilistic Routing Protocol using History of Encounters and Transitivity (*PRoPHET*) [13]. In *PRoPHET* the history of node transitivity and encounters is used to enhance performance. It assumes that movement patterns are repeated and they can be predicted. In *PRoPHET* each node calculates *Delivery Predictability*, before sending a message for each destination. A message is transferred to the other node if the *Delivery Predictability* of the destination of the message is higher at the other node, otherwise retains with the current node.

Context-Aware Routing (*CAR*), proposed in [14], assumes that nodes share their 'logical connectivity information' among them. Within the same cloud message delivered using proactive protocol like DSDV [15], otherwise node is chosen with the highest delivery probability calculated at every node from the context information. Instead of using context of a node as it is, this protocol predicts the future values to make the information more 'realistic'. However, messages may have lost in absence of proper buffer management. The message is encoded in another format before it transferred to neighbor node in *Network Coding* [16] protocol. Before forwarding intermediate nodes can also combine packets using a given invertible function to limit the message flooding. However, this protocol suffers overhead as encoding and decoding of messages requires extra processing power as well as memory.

TBR, proposed by Prodhan et al. [17], is a TTL based routing approach. TBR is a quota based routing protocol. TBR uses priority at both level i.e. at message forwarding as well as at message dropping from buffer. These priorities are based on massage time to live (TTL), hop count, replication count and size. Chen and Lou propose a group aware routing protocol GAR [18]. GAR is a cooperative message transfer scheme and authors also proposed a buffer management policy to reduce the message drop rate. However, GAR is limited to environment where nodes move in groups, which is very unlikely in opportunistic networks. Further nodes are highly dependable as cache message are regularly exchanged between the same group members and buffer management is inefficient as phantom messages occupy space in buffer. Table 1 shows the comparison among opportunistic network routing protocols based on the knowledge oracles discussed in introduction section.

Table 1. Comparison among OppNets routing protocols

	Zero knowledge	Contact summary	Contacts	Queuing	Prioritization	Node encounter	History based
First contact [5]	✓						
Direct transmission [6]	✓						
Epidemic routing [7]	✓						
Spray & Wait [4]	✓						
Spray & Focus [9]		✓				✓	
Adaptive spray & Wait [10]			✓	✓	✓		
PRoPHET [13]			✓	✓		✓	
PRoPHET + [19]			✓	✓		✓	✓
HiBOP [12]			✓	✓		✓	✓
CEPMF [11]	✓		✓				
RFP [20]	✓			✓			
RPRP [21]			✓			✓	✓
TBR [17]			✓	✓	✓		
GAR [18]	✓			✓	✓		
NABR (Proposed)			✓	✓	✓	✓	✓

3 System Model

This work assumes that an OppNets comprises a group of n mobile nodes moving within a finite region. The connectivity is intermittent and links are almost permanently absent. In our proposed model, we will use several statistics based on the nodes activities. For example, the contact information, such as meeting time and number of total encounters of two nodes, total message received by node and nature of action taken to those messages, message hop count etc. However, none of these as well as other network information is not known in advance. The Time-to-Live (TTL) value is associated with every message and message must be delivered within TTL time; otherwise, it will be removed from buffer. All nodes have a limited space storing the message, known as buffer storage. A message can be delivered to the destination either by source node or through the various bundle carriers. Message are assumed to be transmit as a whole *i.e.* no fragmentation is done. When a node transmits the message to the bundle carrier, it will increase the message hop count by one.

Each node will maintain two table. One is called *"Buffer Table* (BT)*"* and other is called *"Meeting Table* (MT)*"*. The BT will store the three entries related to each message. These entries are: size, TTL and hopcount of the message. Hopcount is defined as the total number of bundle carriers *i.e.* intermediate nodes through which this message is passed on in order to reach the destination.

The second table, MT, will maintain the record of the most frequent meetings of the node. In this table will maintain the information about last 10 such nodes. This table also has three entries: total number of meetings (MC_{xy}), total number of successful meetings (SM_{xy}), and the Meeting Counter Ratio (MCR_{xy}). Successful meetings refer to those meetings in which at least one message was exchanged between the nodes (x, y).

4 Proposed Routing Algorithm: NABR

The idea of our proposed algorithm is based on the node activities. We used recent behavior of nodes to determine the message delivery probability and select the next bundle carrier to forward the message.

4.1 Working of Proposed Algorithm

In the proposed model a message can be generated at the application layer of node itself or it can be arrived from any other neighboring node. When a message (m_k) is generated at the node, it will have tagged with its size ($S(m_k)$) and Time-to-live (TTL(m_k)). Initially, the hop count of message hopcout (m_k) is zero. When a node is received message from its neighbor then its hop count is increased by one. At every node, these three entries are saved in table BT for each message (Fig. 3).

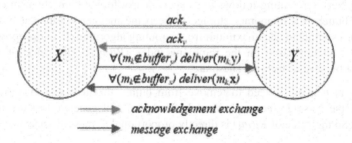

Fig. 3. Working of NABR, when two nodes X and Y comes

When nodes are in the meeting, then they will exchange the list of their acknowledged messages since their last meetings. If any node has such message(s) that has been delivered, the node will delete the message from its buffer. If the node has some message(s) that is destined for the meeting node(s), then those messages are transferred to the meeting node. The sender is acknowledged by the receiving node and then sender will delete those messages from its buffer and update the counter T_D. Now the nodes will attempt to deliver their buffered message to each other. While delivering a message to a node *confidence level* CL_x of each node is calculated according to Eq. 1 and message is delivered to a node with highest CL_x. After transferring the messages to each other, the sender and receiver will update their F_b and T_R counters respectively.

$$CL_x = \begin{cases} MCR_{xy} * (DDIndex_x + FBIndex_x), & SM_{xy} \geq 1 \\ DDIndex_x + FBIndex_x, & otherwise \end{cases} \tag{1}$$

Where, MCR_{xy} is Meeting Counter Ratio between node x & y. SM_{xy} is Successful Meeting counter of node x & y. $DDIndex_x$ (Eq. 2) is the percentage of messages that are directly delivered to destination by node x.

$$DDIndex_x = \frac{T_D}{T_m} * 100 \tag{2}$$

(T_D is total number of messages delivered to destination by node x and T_m is total message received by node x).

$FBIndex_x$ (Eq. 3) is the percentage of messages that are forwarded to bundle carrier by node x.

$$FBIndex_x = \frac{T_b}{T_m} * 100 \tag{3}$$

(T_b is total number of messages forwarded to bundle carrier by node x and T_m is total message received by node x).

4.2 Buffer Management

As in OppNets, the routing follows the "receive-carry-forward" mechanism, the nodes require a buffer as a temporary storage to keep the messages. Efficient buffer management is essential to take maximum from a routing algorithm. In our proposed model we select a victim based on the removing index ($RI(m_k)$). The value of $RI(m_k)$ is influenced by several factors. These are:

1. When an item is selected to remove from buffer, the item size matters, because bigger the message removed, more buffer space will generate to store new messages. So the value of $RI(m_k)$ is directly proportional to message size $S(m_k)$ (Eq. 4).

$$RI(m_k) \propto S(m_k) \tag{4}$$

2. An older message must be removed before a newer message, because the older one will be automatically removed from buffer as its TTL expires. So a message with lower TTL will be removed first. Thus $RI(m_k)$ is inversely proportional to TTL of message ($TTL(m_k)$) (Eq. 5).

$$RI(m_k) \propto \frac{1}{TTL(m_k)} \tag{5}$$

3. Selecting a message to remove by size and TTL value may impact adverse on its delivery probability. So there will be another factor that ensures delivery is least affected. During the process of message delivery, a message may will travel in the network through various bundle carrier. With the passage of time there are several copy of message will be buffered by the different nodes. So we will select a message to remove from the buffer with highest number of such copies *i.e.* the highest number of *hopcount* (Eq. 6). This will impact least on the message delivery.

$$RI(m_k) \propto hopcount(m_k) \tag{6}$$

By combining Eqs. 1, 2 and 3 we get

$$RI(m_k) \propto \frac{S(m_k) * hopcount(m_k)}{TTL(m_k)}$$

$$RI(m_k) = C\frac{S(m_k) * hopcount(m_k)}{TTL(m_k)} \tag{7}$$

Where C is proportionality constant.

Thus Eq. 7 gives us a formula to select a victim message. A message with highest value of $RI(m_k)$ will be removed from buffer first.

5   Simulation and Results

To evaluate our proposed NABR protocol, the Opportunistic Network Environment (ONE) simulator version 1.5.1 is used [22]. In order to analyze our proposed algorithm with other routing protocols, we use delivery ratio and latency as performance matrices.

Table 2. Simulation parameter

Parameter	Value
Simulation area	4000 m × 3000 m
Number of nodes	50–150
Transmission range	100 m
Transmission rate	250 KBps
Movement speed	0.5 m/s–1 m/s
Mobility model	Random Way Point
TTL of each message	30 min
Size of messages	500 KB–1 MB
Buffer size	10 MB
Message generation rate	2–3 message per min

5.1 Simulation Setup

Our simulation model is similar to the model used in [3, 17]. We use the Random Way Point as the mobility model. Movement speed of the nodes vary from 0.5 m/s–1 m/s, within the area of 4000 m × 3000 m. The transmission range of each node is 100 m and transmission rate is 250 KBps. Buffer size is kept 10 MB, however the performance of algorithm is tested by varying buffer size from 8 MB–30 MB. Message generation rate is 2–3 messages per minute. Simulation parameters are listed in Table 2.

5.2 Results and Discussion

We evaluate NABR with TBR [17] and GAR [18] OppNets routing protocols under different node density and buffer size.

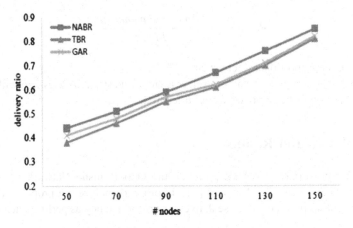

Fig. 4. Number of nodes vs. delivery ratio

First, we present the result of message delivery with varying node density in Fig. 4. It can have observed from figure that deliver ratio is increases as number of nodes increases and NABR outperform other routing protocols. This is due to fact that the forwarder node was choose on the basis of maximum involvement is successful destination deliveries. Figure 5 shows the plot of number of nodes vs. latency. This figure illustrates that, NABR achieves best latency among the protocols compared.

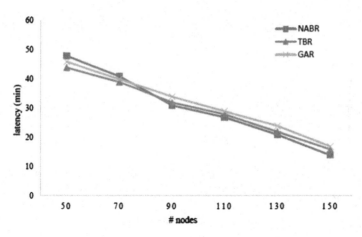

Fig. 5. Number of nodes vs. latency

Figure 6 illustrate the effect of buffer size on deliver ratio. Due to effective buffer management technique, NABR makes most efficient use of buffer storage and gives best delivery ration among the compared protocols. Effect of buffer size on the latency is plotted in Fig. 7. Latency is decreases as buffer size is increases, but still NABR manage to deliver message in minimum time results in less delay.

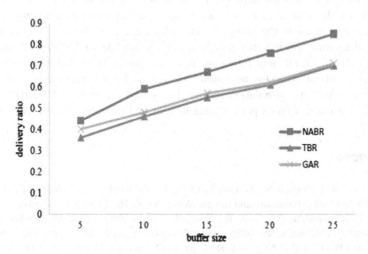

Fig. 6. Buffer size vs. delivery ratio

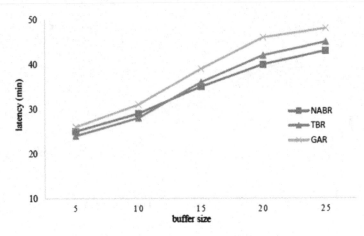

Fig. 7. Buffer size vs. latency

6   Conclusion

In this paper, we propose a novel routing protocol for OppNets. As OppNets are intermittently connected, the main aim of OppNets is to provide reliable commutations in such environment. While designing a routing protocol for OppNets, it is essential to make efficient use of resource and communications opportunities in order to achieve good performance from the network. In this paper, we consider all these issues and proposed NABR, a node activity based routing protocol. In this we consider nodes previous action taken to the messages and calculate the confidence level of node in order to determine the whether this is a good candidate to forward the particular message or not. An efficient buffer management policy is also proposed; as buffer storage is a critical issue for both node as well as for the performance of routing protocols in OppNets. Simulation results shows that the proposed NABR protocol performs well under various performance metrics and different network environment.

References

1. Spyropoulos, T., Rais, R.N., Turletti, T., Obraczka, K., Vasilakos, A.: Routing for disruption tolerant networks: taxonomy and design. Wirel. Netw. **16**, 2349–2370 (2010)
2. Hui, P., Chaintreau, A., Gass, R., Scott, J., Crowcroft, J., Diot, C.: Pocket switched networking: challenges, feasibility and implementation issues. In: Stavrakakis, I., Smirnov, M. (eds.) WAC 2005. LNCS, vol. 3854, pp. 1–12. Springer, Heidelberg (2006). https://doi.org/10.1007/11687818_1
3. Wang, W., Guo, F., Zheng, F., Tang, W., Wang, J.: Research on routing protocols and simulation analysis for opportunistic networks. Int. J. Multimed. Ubiquitous Eng. **10**, 181–202 (2015)
4. Spyropoulos, T., Psounis, K., Raghavendra, C.S.: Spray and wait: an efficient routing scheme for intermittently connected mobile networks. In: Proceedings of the 2005 ACM SIGCOMM Workshop on Delay-Tolerant Networking, pp. 252–259 (2005)

5. Jain, S., Fall, K., Patra, R.: Routing in a delay tolerant network. In: ACM SIGCOMM 2004, pp. 145–157 (2004)
6. Spyropoulos, T., Psounis, K., Raghavendra, C.S.: Single-copy routing in intermittently connected mobile networks. In: IEEE SECON 2004, Sensor and Ad Hoc Communications and Networks, pp. 235–244 (2004)
7. Vahdat, A., Becker, D.: Epidemic Routing for Partially-Connected Ad Hoc Networks (2000)
8. Burns, B., Brock, O., Levine, B.N., Burns, B., Levine, B.N.: MV routing and capacity building in disruption tolerant networks. In: Proceedings IEEE 24th Annual Joint Conference of the IEEE Computer and Communications Societies, pp. 398–408 (2005)
9. Spyropoulos, T., Psounis, K., Raghavendra, C.S.: Spray and focus : efficient mobility-assisted routing for heterogeneous and correlated mobility. In: IEEE International Conference on Pervasive Computing and Communications Workshops, pp. 79–85 (2007)
10. Makhlouta, J., Harkous, H., Hutayt, F., Artail, H.: Adaptive fuzzy spray and wait: efficient routing for opportunistic networks. In: International Conference on Selected Topics in Mobile and Wireless Networking (iCOST), pp. 64–69 (2011)
11. Yazhi, L.: Content encounter probability based message forwarding in opportunistic networks. In: International Conference on Information Science and Engineering (ICISE 2009), pp. 2589–2594 (2009)
12. Boldrini, C., Conti, M., Jacopini, J., Passarella, A.: HiBOp: a history based routing protocol for opportunistic networks. In: IEEE International Symposium on World of Wireless, Mobile and Multimedia Networks (WoWMoM 2007), pp. 1–12 (2007)
13. Lindgren, A., Doria, A.: Probabilistic routing in intermittently connected networks. ACM SIGMOBILE Mob. Comput. Commun. Rev. 7, 19–20 (2003)
14. Musolesi, M., Mascolo, C.: CAR: context-aware adaptive routing for delay-tolerant mobile networks. IEEE Trans. Mob. Comput. 8, 246–260 (2009)
15. Perkins, C.E., Bhagwat, P.: Highly dynamic (DSDV) for mobile computers routing. In: Proceedings of the ACM SIGCOMM94, London, UK, pp. 234–244 (1994)
16. Widmer, J., Le Boudec, J.: Network coding for efficient communication in extreme networks. In: ACM SIGCOMM (2005)
17. Prodhan, A.T., Das, R., Kabir, H., Shoja, G.C.: TTL based routing in opportunistic networks. J. Netw. Comput. Appl. 34, 1660–1670 (2011)
18. Chen, H., Lou, W.: GAR: group aware cooperative routing protocol for resource-constraint opportunistic networks. Comput. Commun. 48, 20–29 (2014)
19. Huang, T.K., Lee, C.K., Chen, L.J.: PRoPHET+: an adaptive PRoPHET-based routing protocol for opportunistic network. In: Proceedings of the International Conference on Advanced Information Networking and Applications, AINA, pp. 112–119 (2010)
20. Greede, A., Allen, S.M., Whitaker, R.M.: RFP: repository based forwarding protocol for opportunistic networks. In: Third International Conference on Next Generation Mobile Applications, Services and Technologies, pp. 329–334 (2009)
21. Kathiravelu, T., Ranasinghe, N., Pears, A.: A robust proactive routing protocol for intermittently connected opportunistic networks. In: Seventh International Conference on Wireless and Optical Communications Networks - (WOCN), pp. 1–6 (2010)
22. Keranen, A., Karkkainen, T., Ott, J.: Simulating mobility and DTNs with the ONE. J. Commun. 5, 92–105 (2010)

Taxonomy of DDoS Attacks in Software-Defined Networking Environment

Tushar Ubale and Ankit Kumar Jain[✉]

NIT Kurukshetra, Kurukshetra 136119, Haryana, India
ankitjain@nitkkr.ac.in

Abstract. Software Defined Networking brings in the concept of "Programmable Network" in the networking domain which in turn lends flexibility, simplicity for managing the network. The key idea behind this simplicity is decoupling of the control plane from the data plane. Nevertheless, such decoupling of the planes also acquaints SDN to the most critical type of attack, i.e., DDoS attack. Our goal is to showcase a concise survey of DDoS attacks in SDN and then present comparative solutions against these DDoS attacks. Firstly, we discuss the life cycle of DDoS attack in SDN. Then several taxonomies of DDoS attacks which affect SDN environment have been discussed, followed by which analysis is performed to cover the taxonomy of solutions for this severe type of attacks. Finally, we present, future research directions that will be a crucial idea to defend such attacks in near future.

Keywords: Software Defined Networking (SDN) · DDoS attack
Security · Authentication

1 Introduction

Current networks such as data centres, enterprise networks, and cloud networks are increasing in terms of size and complexity. This demand for computer systems has changed drastically since the early days of file sharing or hosting the servers of companies. Today's Organization are using advanced computing to meet their challenging needs which require more computing resources, planning, availability, and scalability. Existing network technologies are not designed to enable such complex systems. In order to design such complex networks which can satisfy these ongoing demands various approaches have been proposed and software defined networking (SDN) is one among them. SDN is a networking paradigm which makes the network programmable. The first advantage SDN provides is separation of control plane from the data plane, which currently are clustered inside the same networking device because of which innovation and evolution of each layer are hindered separating these planes provides much more flexibility. In rest of the paper, we will use plane and layer interchangeably. The second advantage using SDN is developers can program the network according to their use and convenience.

© Springer Nature Singapore Pte Ltd. 2019
P. K. Singh et al. (Eds.): FTNCT 2018, CCIS 958, pp. 278–291, 2019.
https://doi.org/10.1007/978-981-13-3804-5_21

1.1 Basics of SDN

Decoupling which is the most impingement feature of SDN innovate the architecture. Because of which the data plane devices become just packet forwarding devices and the entire logic of managing the network moves to the control plane. The idea behind the separation of these planes is to allow application programmers to program the networks accordingly. This feature also results in automatic reconfiguration of networking devices according to changing traffic demands which is not present in current networks. Figure 1 represents SDN Architecture. International telecommunication union telecommunication sector (ITU-T) [1] is a United Nation agency that started the standardization of SDN in its (SGs) study group 13. SG 13 is the leading study group that develops the framework of SDN. Another Study group SG 11 develops signals and protocols for SDN. In addition to this there are several Software development organizations (SDOs) and Open Source Software Projects working for standardization of SDN [1]. The communication interface between the controller which belongs to the control plane and the data plane switches is carried out with the help of OpenFlow protocol. OpenFlow is a standard Application Programming Interface (API) [2]. The detail bottom up layering specification is as follows.

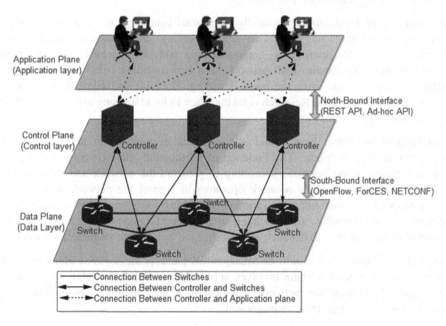

Fig. 1. SDN architecture.

Data Plane: Data plane includes forwarding devices such as routers, switches, wireless access point, virtual switches. In SDN terminology all these devices are named as switches or OpenFlow switches. Switches contain flow table which represents the packet forwarding rule. Switches forward the traffic to the corresponding destination according to the control plane logic.

Southbound Interface: Southbound protocols facilitate efficient control over the data plane. OpenFlow is the standardized and most well-known southbound protocol. Many vendors including Hp, NetGear, and IBM produce their own switches which support OpenFlow. The Open Networking Foundation is responsible for standardization of OpenFlow. The main characteristic of OpenFlow protocol is that it uses Flow table so that the entries can be added and removed in the flow table to handle the network traffic expeditiously. Besides OpenFlow there are several other protocols such as ForCES [3], OpFlex [3].

Control Plane: Control plane involves the controller which represents the brain of the entire network. Controller makes the packet forwarding decisions and installs the decisions in the switches. SDN represents physically distributed but the logically centralized controller. Logical centralization eases the jobs of the network operators to configure and contend the network. The functions or services the controller provides are notifications, device management, and security mechanisms. A physically centralized controller leads to a single point of failure as well as it is hard to manage a huge network with a single controller. Contrary to this distributed controller can meet any requirement from small scale to large scale network. There are various types of controllers NOX [3], Floodlight [3], POX [3].

Eastbound and Westbound: Physically distributed controllers use East-West bound interface to communicate. Also, two complementing entities use east-west bound interface (e.g., SDN controller is communicating with VPN network). As a single controller may only handle small network, so if one controller fails it can inform the other controller to take over the traffic handling. Onix [4] and Hyperflow [5] have suggested these strategies. Research is taking place to build a strong and robust API to handle controller traffic.

Northbound Interface: Northbound interface acts as middleware between control plane and application plane. The Function of northbound interface is to abstract the internal details of the network, permitting to program the network and to quest the services from it. This helps network operators to control the network accordingly. Since SDN can be configured for various applications using single API to meet these demands is not possible. So it is likely that different protocols can exist. Current controllers provide their APIs such as Rest API, ad hoc API to control the network.

Application Plane: Application or Management plane is the topmost plane in SDN architecture. Application plane involves applications which are written by software developers to manage the network. Application plane functionalities include fault monitoring and configuration management.

1.2   Basics of DDoS

DoS attack is a cyber attack where a malicious user sends excessive fake requests to network or server. Since the requests does not have valid return address when the server or network tires to serve the requests, it does not find the return address of the attacker which causes the server to wait before closing the connection. Thus the server keeps busy waiting closing the connection of fake requests. This causes legitimate users to get the denial of service leading to DoS attack. The primary targets of DoS attack are websites and servers making it unavailable to benign users. Sometime DoS attack may be on user too. The Aim of this type of attack is not theft or loss of information but to waste time, money and resources of the victim. When this attack comes from several hosts managed by a malicious user, it is called Distributed Denial of Service Attack (DDoS). In [6, 7] authors have discussed the countermeasures of these attacks. DDoS attack provides many advantages to the attacker:

- The location of attacker is difficult to identify due to randomly distributed attacking system.
- Attacker can use multiple systems to attack the victim unquietly.
- Affecting the victim for many days.

Several types of DoS attack affecting the victim or server are: Email Bombing, Ping of death, Smurf attack, Buffer Overflow attack, SYN Flood, UDP Flood, HTTP GET Flood, NTP Reflection Amplification attack, DNS Reflection Amplification attack, Zero-Day Attack.

1.3   Different Types of Attacks in SDN

Software Defined Networking provides strength and flexibility in networking. In addition to that, it also provides centralized control and brings down the deployment cost. This centralized control becomes vulnerable to some more attacks other than DDoS. Details about this attacks scenarios are discussed in the following subsections. Table 1 categorizes these attacks and different planes affected.

Network Manipulation: Once the controller is compromised the attacker can program the network and manipulate the resources.

Data Leakage: Different commands for handling the packets include drop, forward and send to the controller. The way packets are handling by the switch the attacker can determine by analyzing the packet processing time. If the attacker discovers the packets which are being sent to the controller the attacker can generate similar types of packets which would be redirected to controller causing the denial of service. In [8] explains how the DDoS attack can be launched through data leakage.

DDoS Attack: Separation of planes and protocols to communicate between different planes exploits the vulnerability of congestion. South-bound interface, North-bound interface, Switch hardware and Controller all can be the target of Denial of Service attack due to their limited capability.

Compromised Application: SDN allows third-party application to supervise the network. Writing malicious applications can manipulate and exhaust the networking resources. Also writing an ambiguous application by developers exposes to vulnerabilities in software application which the attacker can exploit to attack.

Man in the Middle Attack: The attacker modifies the communication between communicating entities making the entities believe as if they are communicating with each other. This attack happens if there is no security between the communicating protocols. In [9] author studies about this attack and presents the feasible solution.

In [10] authors have discussed various security solutions for the above attacks. Despite such attacks the easiest and devastating attack to launch is DDoS attack. The peculiarity of this attack is it is easy to launch but difficult to detect. In this paper a deeper analysis of this issue is provided.

Table 1. Categorization of attacks affecting SDN planes.

Attacks	Focus	Area
Network manipulation	Compromising controller	Control plane
Data leakage	Analysing packet processing time	Data plane
DDoS attack	Flooding the controller and flow table	Control plane, Data plane
Compromised application	Writing fraudulent software	Management plane
Man in the middle attack	Seizing the controller	Control plane

1.4   Lifecycle of DDoS Attack in SDN

Centralization of the controller makes it vulnerable to many types of attack. Compromising the controller can manipulate the entire network. If the attacker gets access to the controller, it can be used to control the networking devices. The attacker can then use those devices to launch some potential attacks towards the victim or in the network. SDN OpenFlow enabled switch handles the packet differently compared to traditional switches. When Packet comes for processing towards switch it checks the Flow Table which contains FlowRules for packet forwarding, matches the entry and forwards the packet. When a new packet arrives whose entry does not match FlowRules, then the switch saves part of packet except the header into the buffer and forwards the header as Packet_In message to the controller asking to install new FlowRule. Controller after processing the header installs a new FlowRule to handle the packet if the switch Flow Table is full switch sends an error message to the controller. This rule of FlowRule installation is known as Reactive FlowRule installation. There is another method of FlowRule installation known as Proactive FlowRule installation in which the rule are installed prior to traffic comes to the switch. The attacker can launch DDoS attack on buffer inside the switch, Flow Table, communication channel between controller and switch and controller too. Figure 2 shows different SDN modules exploited during DDoS attack.

The rest of the paper is structured as follows. In Sect. 2, we discuss the taxonomy of DDoS attack in SDN environment. In Sect. 3, taxonomy of defence mechanism is discussed. Open issues and challenges are discussed in Sect. 4. Finally, Sect. 5 concludes the paper.

2   Taxonomy of DDoS Attack in SDN

As described in Sect. 1.5, the way packet is processed by each module of the architecture attacker can exploit vulnerabilities of these modules for an attack. In the following sub-sections, we will discuss how attacker can make use of these modules to launch DoS attack in SDN architecture.

2.1   Buffer Saturation

The switch maintains a memory called as Ternary Content Addressable Memory (TCAM) which is scarce in resource. When there is missing FlowRule in the Flow Table, switch stores part of the packet into buffer memory and sends the header as Packet_In message. But when the buffer memory gets full switch sends the entire packet as Packet_In message. Thus the attacker can send numerous packets whose entry does not match in Flow Table, therefore, forcing the switch to send entire packet to the controller. A switch can send limited number of Packet_In messages to the controller, for example, Hp Procurve [11] generates 1000 Packet_In messages. Thus the limited capacity of buffer leads to buffer saturation.

2.2   Flow Table Overloading

SDN Switch characteristic is to send entry miss packet to the controller asking for new FlowRule. Each FlowRule has specific timeout value after which the entries will be replaced. The attacker takes advantage of this feature and generates new packets; controller sends new FlowRules to the switch for this packet. These new entries will replace the old entries, and within no time all entries will be replaced and the table gets filled up with fake entries. Therefore the legitimate entries find no space in the Flow Table and hence get dropped. Pronto pica8 3290 [11] switch can hold 2000 Flow Table entries at a time.

2.3   Congesting Data-Control Plane Channel

SDN switch holds part of the packet in the buffer when the packet is sent to the controller for processing. But the buffer also has limited capacity. So when the buffer gets full switch sends entire packet to the controller as a Packet_In message for processing. Sending entire packet towards the controller using the single bandwidth causes high constriction in the channel. Due to this legitimate users also face high bottleneck for their request to get served.

2.4   Saturating the Controller

Finally, as the flood requests arrive at controller, the controller gets busy satisfying the fake request thus these requests exhaust the throughput and processing capabilities of the controller. Infecting the controller downgrades the whole SDN architecture. To make this happen attacker only needs to generate some significant amount of anomalous packets.

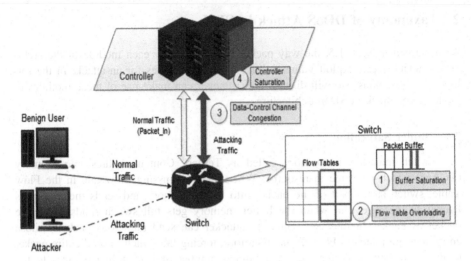

Fig. 2. DDoS attack in SDN

3 Taxonomy of DDoS Defence Mechanism in SDN

DDoS mitigation in SDN environment is an active area of research; several explorations are carried out in various areas of SDN. Following are the defence mechanism on the above discussed issues.

3.1 Defences for Buffer Saturation

Wang et al. [11] present Scotch a mesh of Open VSwitches that overlay the physical switches. When the physical switch gets overloaded because of new FlowRule the new flow rules are then forwarded to Open VSwitches. Open VSwitches then forward it to the controller as Packet_In message. The Controller then installs new FlowRule either in Physical Switch or Open Vswitch, which then forwards the packet to the destination. Thus Open VSwitches act as the buffer to store the new FlowRules. The main drawback of this technique is that it is unable to distinguish between regular traffic and DDoS traffic, thus after certain threshold VSwitches drops the packet too.

Wang et al. [12] presents an entropy based approach to defend against DDoS attack; it involves statistics and analysis of network traffic arriving to network. Authors deploy their algorithm in the edge switch (switch which is near to victim) for anomaly detection mechanism. The scheme calculates entropy based on IP and switch, when the entropy decreases beyond specific threshold attack is detected. But for this we need to modify a switch which is not feasible solution.

Another similar work is done by Mousavi et al. [13] where the randomness of the packet is measured. To detect the attack two components are used (1) window (2) entropy window represents the number of packets and entropy represents the randomness. Sample entropy of normal traffic is decided as threshold. If Traffic coming towards controller exceeds the threshold, it is declared as attack traffic. Traffic coming towards controller may vary in size this method fails to detect it. In Table 2, summary of solutions under Buffer Saturation Attack in SDN is provided.

Table 2. Categorization of solutions for buffer saturation attack

DDoS technique	Focus	Solution
Scotch [11]	Open VSwitches	Open VSwitch act as buffer for physical switches to store FlowTable
Entropy distribution [12]	Anomaly detection	Entropy of IP and switch is used as threshold to detect attack
Early detection [13]	Randomness of packet	Sample entropy of normal traffic is decided traffic exceeding baseline is declared as attack traffic

3.2 Defences for Flow Table Overflow

Kandoi et al. [14] proposed two methods Flow Aggregation and Optimal Flow Timeout value to control DDoS attack. Flow Aggregation is used for matching several incoming packets for one FlowRule and, Optimal Flow Timeout for replacing the FlowRule after a specific time interval to prevent flow table overflow. In short, they suggest having an optimal timeout. The drawback of this method is it is not suitable for large area networks and hence cannot be used for heavy load traffic.

Dao et al. [15] detects DDoS attack based on IP filtering. As per analysis an average user at least makes 'k' number of connections and it sends at least 'n' packets per connection. So when a new packet arrives its entry is made in the controller table. Then it is checked if the average number of packet counter 's' is less than then 'n', if it is then drop rule is installed in the Flow Table otherwise timeout value of particular source IP is increased indicating that it is a normal user. The disadvantage of this method is that it may install drop rule for false positive user also.

You et al. [16] proposed dynamic in/out balancing algorithm known as DIOB/LFU algorithm to defend against the Flow Table overflow attack. DIOB/LFU algorithm maintains the difference between rule-in and rule-out FlowRules. The difference between rule-in rule-out FlowRule must always be less than or equal to zero. Addition to that when 'table full error' message is received from switch algorithm evicts certain amount of rules from flow table whose idle timeout value is zero and counter value is zero. The algorithm tries to maintain the balance of FlowRules in the table. The drawback of this algorithm is as the attacks packet incoming rate is much higher than balancing rate it is difficult to deploy this algorithm in a real scenario.

Yuan et al. [17] execute a strategy known as Peer-Support strategy. This Quality of Service-Aware (QoS) peer support mitigation strategy is implemented as an application in the controller. This application monitors status of each switch. When the switch flow table gets full, this application guide's the traffic to other switches thus the traffic loads gets distributed across other switches. Peer switches support the targeted switch to manage the flow entries forwarded towards it. The disadvantage of this method is it does not distinguish between legitimate traffic and attack traffic. In Table 3, the summary of solutions under Flow Table Overflow in SDN is provided.

Table 3. Categorization of solution for flow table overflow

DDoS technique	Focus	Solution
DDoS in OpenFlow [14]	Protection rule handling	Flow aggregation for matching FlowRules and Timeout Value for FlowRule replacement
Feasible method to combat DDoS [15]	IP filtering	If user sends less than 'n' number of packets it is consider as attacker
SDN FlowTable over flow [16]	Dynamic in/out balancing algorithm	Difference between Rule-in and Rule-out must always be less than or equal to zero
Defending against FlowTable overloading [17]	Peer-support strategy	If flow table gets overloaded direct the traffic to other switches

3.3 Defences for Control-Data Channel Congestion

In networking when a client wants to communicate with the server or another client they have to follow specific networking rules they are TCP handshake rules. In normal TCP handshake whenever packet comes in the switch and if switch entry does not match packet switch directly forwards it to the controller and this is the cause of Flooding attack called as control plane saturation attack. In Avantguard [18] the problem is solved with the help 'Migration Module'. The migration module delays the handshake by making the switch work as a proxy server for TCP handshake and forwards only those connections to the controller who makes complete TCP handshake. The reason is whenever attacker tries for TCP handshake it will never do complete handshake means it never replies to packet sent by the server. Thus this complete TCP handshake policy prevents the DoS attack. However Avantguard can only defend TCP synch flood attacks.

Piedrahita et al. [19] proposed FlowFence mechanism to handle the network traffic. According to this scheme, the switches monitor their interfaces for congestion once congestion is detected the switch notifies this to the controller. The controller requests the flow statistics from all the switches, and then the controller sends commands to switch to rate limit. This mechanism only rate limits the flows but it does not stop the attack entirely.

FloodDefender [20] presents a switch sharing mechanism to defend the channel congestion attack. In this mechanism, four modules Table-miss engineering module, Packet filtering module, Flow rule management module and attack detection module work together to defend the attack. Attack detection module keeps monitoring the switch for attack detection. Once the attack is detected, it activates other three modules. When DDoS attack occurs Table-miss engineering module uses Protecting Rules to forward the traffic to neighbour switches. It uses average delay model to analyze how many neighbouring switches to involve in sharing. Table miss packets are forwarded to neighbouring switches to save bandwidth between controller and victim switch. Packet filtering module filters the packet in two steps. Further Flow Table management module installs the monitoring rules inside the victim switch to manage FlowRules by removing the useless entries.

Wang et al. proposed FloodGuard [21] a scalable efficient, lightweight and protocol-independent defence framework for SDN networks to prevent data-to-control plane saturation attack. It uses two techniques proactive flow rule analyzer module and packet migration module. The Proactive flow rule analyzer module sits in the controller as an application that generates flow rules based on the current status of the controller. Proactive flow rules are data plane flow rules. It represents the range of Packet_In messages which current control logic can handle at this moment. Proactive flow rule analyzer module uses symbolic execution engine, application tracker and flow rule dispatcher to install flow rules. The packet migration module has two functions First is to detect the saturation attack based on a particular threshold. The second task of the migration module is to migrate the table miss packets to data plane cache so that switch and controller does not get overloaded by packets. The data plane cache then sends flow requests as Packet_In message to the controller. The migration executes the symbolic engine and generates flow rule to stop further flow requests. The disadvantage of this techniques is symbolic execution cannot trace all execution paths.

In Flowsec [22] model the author proposed a rate limiting mechanism. Inside a switch, a meter is an element which measures the bandwidth utilization and number of packets passed through it. If packets rate exceeds the threshold, the meter band drops the packet. This packet drop mechanism filters out legitimate traffic too which is undesirable and hence it is a drawback of this model. In Table 4, the summary of solutions under Control-data Plane Congestion in SDN is provided.

Table 4. Categorization of solution for control-data channel congestion.

DDoS Technique	Focus	Solution
Avantguard [18]	Protection against southbound interface	Connection migration component reducing data-control plane congestion
FlowFence [19]	Handling network traffic	Rate limiting rules installed in switches
FloodDefender [20]	Switch sharing mechanism	Table miss packets are forwarded to neighbouring switches and further applying packet filtering
FloodGuard [21]	Data-to-control plane saturation attack	Proactive Flow Rule analyzer module installs FlowRules and Execution Engine trace to generate suppressing rules
Flowsec [22]	Rate limiting mechanism	Switch meter drops the packet if packet rate exceeds threshold

3.4 Defences for Controller Saturation

Avantguard [18] uses two modules 'Actuating Trigger' and 'Connection Migration' modules to overcome controller saturation. The Actuating trigger enables the data plane to asynchronously report network status and payload information to the control plane. In addition to that Actuating triggers can be used to activate flow rules under some predefined conditions to help control plane manage network flow without delays. Connection migration module as explained above delays the handshake by allowing switch work to as a proxy server for TCP handshakes and forwards only those connections to the controller who forms complete TCP handshakes. This mechanism fails because it defends only a particular type of DDoS attack in addition to that switch hardware needs to be changed which is undesirable.

Zhang et al. [23] proposed a queue management technique for resource saturation attack. The controller schedules among the switches using weighted round robin (WRR) to serve the request of these queues for processing. If the size of switches queues increases beyond a threshold, then the queue is expanded to per-port queues of the each switch. When the traffic serving is accomplished the queue size again becomes normal. The drawback of this technique is for massive attack multiple queues have to be maintained which becomes cumbersome.

Hsu et al. [24] proposed a solution based on hash value. A hash function operates in control plane which is used to assign incoming packets to queues in control plane. Round-Robin model is used to schedule the queues. Whenever new packet comes whose entry not match arrives to the controller the controller extracts the essential information from the packet and calculates its hashed value. Then from hash value packets are distributed to the queues, as a result sharing the services of the controller. However, this method does not detect the attacking traffic.

FlowRanger [25] proposed a novel solution to handle controller saturation attack. They proposed a buffer prioritizing solution. The mechanism derives the source identity based on the ranking algorithm and then it serves the requests using multiple priority buffers. FlowRanger has three components: Trust Management component, Queuing Management component, Requests Scheduling component. Trust management component computes trust value of new packet based on past requests. Queuing management components maps the request to the priority queue based on trust value. Request Scheduling component analyzes and serves the request based on length and priority

Table 5. Categorization of solutions for controller saturation attack

DDoS Technique	Focus	Solution
Avantguard [19]	Tcp-Syn flooding	Connection migration modules delays the handshake and actuating trigger sends switch statistics to controller
Denial of service in SDN [23]	Switch queue management	Weighted Round Robin strategy is used to schedule the switch queues to serve the request
Design hashed based control [24]	Hashed based rate limiting	New packets hashed value is calculated and assign to queue to get service from controller
FlowRanger [25]	Buffer prioritization	Derives source identity based on ranking algorithm and serve the request according to priority
Lightweight DDoS [26]	Self organizing maps mechanism	SOM technique is used to differentiate normal traffic from attacking traffic

level for this it uses Weighted Round-Robin strategy. There might be benign flows that may appear for the first time. So blocking this request is not a good way to differentiate the users.

Braga [26] presents Self-Organizing-Maps (SOM) a neural network mechanism to control the controller traffic. SOM mechanism is used to classify normal traffic from attack traffic. It has three modules Flow Collector, Feature Extractor, and Classifier. Flow collector requests flow table entries periodically. Feature Extractor modules collect these Flow entries extract the essential features and organizes them into six-tuples. To classify regular traffic from attacking traffic, the SOM is initially fed with the broad set of six-tuples of attack traffic and normal traffic. In Table 5, summary of solutions under Controller Saturation Attack in SDN is provided.

4 Open Issues and Challenges

As modern business communication systems are becoming more complex, the traditional network is unable to support this augmenting demand. SDN plays a vital role to satisfy these requirements along with speed and accuracy. SDN is still in its early adoption stage and security is the primary concern to make this transition to SDN. Centralization theme of Software Defined Networking exposes too many weaknesses which should be examined for the better evolution of architecture. Such weakness includes:

Policy Conflict Resolution: Third party applications must follow some policy rules to communicate with the controller this maintains the integrity of the system. In [27] authors have proposed policy conflict technique.

Mutual Authentication: Controller communicates with both north-bound and south-bound interface. Authentication mechanism with the controller results in trust management and secure identification between the communicating entities. A role-based access control (RBAC) and audits must be done to look for unauthorised access to the controllers.

Application Development: Current application developments are controller dependent which hinders the evolution of the architecture. Hence independent third-party application must be developed. Besides these applications must be authenticated because they have access to controllers [28].

Optimization of Flow Tables: Optimal timeout values must be asserted for FlowRules in switch Flow Tables [14]. As well as TLS policy must be deployed to prevent eavesdropping between the switches.

DDoS mitigation should not affect the legitimate users when the attack takes place. Hence preserving major functionality of network working at the time of attack is the main goal. Other countermeasure includes scanning the third party applications for buggy code and securing the communication channel between controllers and switches. Since controller is the central point of performance, efforts are being carried out to make it more scalable, reliable, programmer friendly and resilient. So it will be interesting to see how SDN centralization and programmability defends the DDoS attack.

5   Conclusion

In this paper, we surveyed the concept of Software Defined Networking (SDN). Particularly we described SDN architecture and functioning of each layer. We reviewed lifecycle of DDoS attack along with different classification of DDoS attacks that falls out and might take place in near future. Different solutions that are implemented at various modules of SDN architecture and their limitations to defend as well as to obstruct it from happening are discussed. In addition to that various potential security issues of these solutions that we might face to deploy it in large scale environment are also analyzed. Finally, we concluded with open issues, and challenges that need to be addressed to make SDN more influential.

References

1. ITU Telecommunication Standardization Sector's SDN Portal. www.itu.int/en/ITU-T/about/Pages/default.aspx
2. Open Networking Foundation. https://www.opennetworking.org
3. Kreutz, D., Ramos, F.M., Verissimo, P.E., Rothenberg, C.E., Azodolmolky, S., Uhlig, S.: Software-defined networking: a comprehensive survey. Proc. IEEE **103**(1), 14–76 (2015)
4. Koponen, T., et al.: Onix: a distributed control platform for large-scale production networks. In: OSDI, vol. 10, pp. 1–6, October 2010
5. Tootoonchian, A., Ganjali, Y.: HyperFlow: a distributed control plane for OpenFlow. In: Proceedings of the 2010 Internet Network Management Conference on Research on Enterprise Networking, p. 3, April 2010
6. Specht, S.M., Lee, R.B.: Distributed denial of service: taxonomies of attacks, tools, and countermeasures. In: ISCA PDCS, pp. 543–550, September 2004
7. Zargar, S.T., Joshi, J., Tipper, D.: A survey of defense mechanisms against distributed denial of service (DDoS) flooding attacks. IEEE Commun. Surv. Tutor. **15**(4), 2046–2069 (2013)
8. Shin, S., Gu, G.: Attacking software-defined networks: a first feasibility study. In Proceedings of the Second ACM SIGCOMM Workshop on Hot Topics in Software Defined Networking, pp. 165–166. ACM, August 2013
9. Brooks, M., Yang, B.: A man-in-the-middle attack against opendaylight SDN controller. In: Proceedings of the 4th Annual ACM Conference on Research in Information Technology, pp. 45–49. ACM, September 2015
10. Akhunzada, A., Ahmed, E., Gani, A., Khan, M.K., Imran, M., Guizani, S.: Securing software defined networks: taxonomy, requirements, and open issues. IEEE Commun. Mag. **53**(4), 36–44 (2015)
11. Wang, A., Guo, Y., Hao, F., Lakshman, T.V., Chen, S.: Scotch: elastically scaling up SDN control-plane using vswitch based overlay. In: Proceedings of the 10th ACM International on Conference on Emerging Networking Experiments and Technologies, pp. 403–414. ACM, December 2014
12. Wang, R., Jia, Z., Ju, L.: An entropy-based distributed DDoS detection mechanism in software-defined networking. In: 2015 IEEE Trustcom/BigDataSE/ISPA, vol. 1, pp. 310–317. IEEE, August 2015
13. Mousavi, S.M., St-Hilaire, M.: Early detection of DDoS attacks against SDN controllers. In: 2015 International Conference on Computing, Networking and Communications (ICNC), pp. 77–81. IEEE, February 2015

14. Kandoi, R., Antikainen, M.: Denial-of-service attacks in OpenFlow SDN networks. In: 2015 IFIP/IEEE International Symposium on Integrated Network Management (IM), pp. 1322–1326. IEEE, May 2015

15. Dao, N.N., Park, J., Park, M., Cho, S.: A feasible method to combat against DDoS attack in SDN network. In: 2015 International Conference on Information Networking (ICOIN), pp. 309–311. IEEE, January 2015

16. You, W., Qian, K., Qian, Y.: Software-defined network flow table overflow attacks and countermeasures. Int. J. Soft Comput. Netw. 1(1), 70–81 (2016)

17. Yuan, B., Zou, D., Yu, S., Jin, H., Qiang, W., Shen, J.: Defending against flow table overloading attack in software-defined networks. IEEE Trans. Serv. Comput. (2016)

18. Shin, S., Yegneswaran, V., Porras, P., Gu, G.: Avant-guard: scalable and vigilant switch flow management in software-defined networks. In: Proceedings of the 2013 ACM SIGSAC Conference on Computer & Communications Security, pp. 413–424. ACM, November 2013

19. Piedrahita, A.F.M., Rueda, S., Mattos, D.M., Duarte, O.C.M.: FlowFence: a denial of service defense system for software defined networking. In: 2015 Global Information Infrastructure and Networking Symposium (GIIS), pp. 1–6. IEEE, October 2015

20. Shang, G., Zhe, P., Bin, X., Aiqun, H., Kui, R.: FloodDefender: protecting data and control plane resources under SDN-aimed DoS attacks. In: INFOCOM 2017-IEEE Conference on Computer Communications, IEEE, pp. 1–9. IEEE, May 2017

21. Wang, H., Xu, L., Gu, G.: FloodGuard: a DoS attack prevention extension in software-defined networks. In: 2015 45th Annual IEEE/IFIP International Conference on Dependable Systems and Networks (DSN), pp. 239–250. IEEE, June 2015

22. Kuerban, M., Tian, Y., Yang, Q., Jia, Y., Huebert, B., Poss, D.: FlowSec: DOS attack mitigation strategy on SDN controller. In: 2016 IEEE International Conference on Networking, Architecture and Storage (NAS), pp. 1–2. IEEE, August 2016

23. Zhang, P., Wang, H., Hu, C., Lin, C.: On denial of service attacks in software defined networks. IEEE Netw. 30(6), 28–33 (2016)

24. Hsu, S.W., et al.: Design a hash-based control mechanism in vSwitch for software-defined networking environment. In: 2015 IEEE International Conference on Cluster Computing (CLUSTER), pp. 498–499. IEEE, September 2015

25. Wei, L., Fung, C.: FlowRanger: a request prioritizing algorithm for controller DoS attacks in software defined networks. In: 2015 IEEE International Conference on Communications (ICC), pp. 5254–5259. IEEE, June 2015

26. Braga, R., Mota, E., Passito, A.: Lightweight DDoS flooding attack detection using NOX/OpenFlow. In: 2010 IEEE 35th Conference on Local Computer Networks (LCN), pp. 408–415. IEEE, October 2010

27. He, B., Dong, L., Xu, T., Fei, S., Zhang, H., Wang, W.: Research on network programming language and policy conflicts for SDN. Concurr. Comput.: Pract. Exp. 29(19), e4218 (2017)

28. Shin, S., et al.: Rosemary: a robust, secure, and high-performance network operating system. In: Proceedings of the 2014 ACM SIGSAC Conference on Computer and Communications Security, pp. 78–89. ACM, November 2014

Organization and Protection on the Basis of a Multi-agent System of Distributed Computing in a Computer Network to Reduce the Time for Solving Large-Scale Tasks

Sergey Khovanskov[✉], Konstantin Rumyantsev,
and Vera Khovanskova

Southern Federal University, Rostov-on-Don, Russia
{Sah59, rke2004}@mail.ru, v.s.khovanskova@gmail.com

Abstract. Special compilers are often used to solve multivariate tasks with time constraints. However, in this case, the cost of solving the problem is significantly increased and the time required to organize access to such a computing environment is required. At present, the use of distributed computing organized in a computer network is one of the most accessible and widespread technologies for reducing the time for solving large-scale tasks. Many different approaches for organization of distributed computing in a computer network are grid technology, metacomputing (BOINC, PVM and others). The purpose of most of the existing approaches for creating centralized systems of distributed computing is their main disadvantage.

We propose to organize solutions to such a problem as multivariate modeling by creating distributed computing in a computer network based on a decentralized multi-agent system. A typical computer network is selected as a computing environment. A self-organizing distributed computing system based on a decentralized multi-agent system is proposed as a computer system. A system is a set of agents performing the same algorithm. We propose an agent algorithm for a decentralized multi-agent system. Agents working on this algorithm create a self-organizing distributed computing system and protect the results of calculations from such a thunderstorm as "denial of service".

Keywords: Distributed computing · Information protection
Computational process

1 Introduction

Nowadays special computers are often used to solve multivariant tasks with time constraints. However, this significantly increases the cost of solving the problem and requires time to organize access to such a computing environment.

Distributed computing is one of the most accessible and common technologies for reducing the time for solving complex multivariant problems [1–6].

Different computing environments are used to implement such calculations. The multiprocessor computer, cluster computing system, multi-computer system, or an

P. K. Singh et al. (Eds.): FTNCT 2018, CCIS 958, pp. 292–303, 2019.
https://doi.org/10.1007/978-981-13-3804-5_22

ordinary computer network can be used as a computing environment. The most accessible computing environment on which distributed computing is possible is a computer network that has a sufficient or excessive number of data centers (local, wide area networks). Most available computing environment where it is possible to perform distributed computing is a computer network having a sufficient or excessive number of data centers (LAN/WAN).

Currently, there are many different approaches for organization of the distributed calculations in computer network technology grid, metacomputing (BOINC, PVM and others). Most existing approaches are designed to create centralized distributed computing systems. This is their main drawback. In the global network there is a real threat to the operability of the distributed computational processes due to the extreme instability of the computing environment and the actions of intruders. We propose to use self-organizing distributed computing system based on a decentralized multi-agent system for the solution of large-task and to reducing the threats to the existence of distributed computing and the security of the obtained results [7–10] (see Fig. 1).

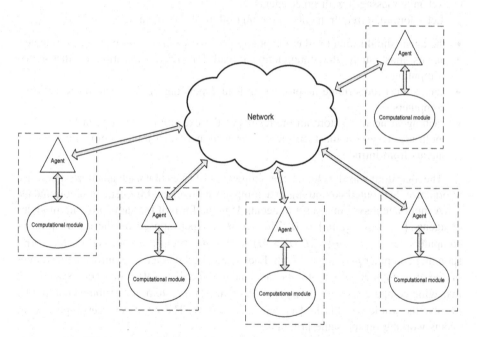

Fig. 1. Structure of the agent program of the multi-agent system

Multiagent system is a set of agents, each of which represents a software module and placed on a separate computer. The agent performs the office only of its computer and therefore its work is independent. It organizes the decision of tasks on your computer initiates the communication with the computers of other agents, performs processing of information provided by them and based on it make decisions.

Decentralized multi-agent system is a set of networked computers. Each computer is under the control of his agent. All agents execute the same algorithm. The result is a peer-to-peer computing system. Each agent works independently from the other agents, the exchange between agents is done using broadcast messages. It allows in the process of implementing distributed computing scaling a multi-agent system without affecting functionality of processes computing.

We the developed the multi-agent system algorithm for the realization and protection of distributed computations in computer networks. The algorithm allows organizing the distributed computing system based on the nodes of computer network [11–20].

2 Implementing a Multi-agent System

The system should be decentralized—each agent should have equal rights and be able to exchange messages with other agents.

Let's formulate requirements to the algorithm of the agent:

- the agent should monitor the computing processes running on managed computer;
- agents must share the computational load for the organization of distributed computing;
- agents must redistribute its processing load depending on the performance of their computers;
- each agent needs to store all the results of the execution of a large task;
- multi-agent system must ensure the protection of distributed computing against threats from intruders.

The algorithm was developed containing a set of rules that each agent must perform to organize distributed computing in a computer network and implement requirements.

A multi-agent system is a set of agents M in the form of the same program modules of agents $\{m_1, m_2, \ldots, m_n\} \in M$. The set M is superimposed on the set of network computers $\{p_1, p_2, \ldots, p_j\} \in P$ ($P > M$) so that the agent m_i is located on the corresponding computer p_i of the network. Each agent module (agent) controls the resources of the p_i computer and monitors the load on the W_i. All multi-agent system M, managing computers $\{p_1, p_2, \ldots, p_j\} \in P$, organizes a system of distributed computing to solve the whole set of tasks $\{w_1, w_2, \ldots, w_n\} \in W$. The set M is a peer-to-peer set of agents working on the same program.

At the beginning of the organization of distributed computing, the agents $\{m_1, m_2, \ldots, m_n\} \in M$ are operating in the computer network $\{p_1, p_2, \ldots, p_n\} \in P$ on M. At the first stage, the $m_i \in M$ agent receives the basic information for the organization of distributed computations in the set M. It includes the computational load W of the M system and indicating which part of w_i of the total volume W the agent must perform. To monitor the execution of the computational load, each agent has two tables for work. The first W_{nrez} table includes all outstanding tasks. The second W_{rez} table includes the completed tasks with the results of the execution $\{W_{nrez}, W_{rez}\} \in W$.

At the initial stage of organizing distributed computing in a computer network $w_i \subseteq W$.

After the agent receives the load $m_i \in M$ and general information about the system, he initiates on his computer p_1 a computational process to perform wi_1, performing the actions in accordance with the rule of computational load.

3 Algorithm of the Agent for Organizing Distributed Computing and Ensuring the Safety of the Results of Computing Processes

Each agent of a multi-agent system is located on its network computer. Each computer is an autonomous computing system, the work of which does not depend on other computers on the network.

The agent m_i monitors the state of the p_i computer and manages its operation in accordance with the "computational load" rule. If p_i does not perform calculations, then the agent m_i selects from the list of its computational load W_i the next order in the order and passes it for execution to the computing block of the computer p_i. The choice is made by sequentially viewing the list of computing load $Wi \in W_{nrez}$ by the agent.

The algorithm of actions of the agent m_i by the rule "computational load execution".

1°. The agent $m_i \in M$ checks whether the next task $w_j \in Wi$ is completed? If not then to point 7°.
2°. Agent m_i receives the result of the task $w_j \in Wi$.
3°. The m_i agent looks at the list of uncompleted Wi_{nrez} jobs.
4°. Load Wi completely fulfilled $Wi_{nrez} = 0$? If yes, go to item 7°.
5°. Selection by agent m_i of the next job $w_j + 1$ from the list of uncompleted computing load Wi_{nrez}.
6°. Transfer the selected job $wj + 1$ to the computer $p_i \in Pz$.
7°. Go to another rule.

Due to the "computational load" rule, each computation node p_i continuously performs computational load Wi. The process is performed completely under the control of the agent m_i. This allows you to optimally use the computing resources of each computer.

To implement the interaction between the agents $\{m_1, m_2, \ldots, m_n\} \in M$, during the execution of distributed calculations, agents exchange messages with results among themselves. Exchange between agents occurs against the background of computational load carrying out by computers controlled by the agents $\{m_1, m_2, \ldots, m_n\} \in M$. The agent m_i, having received the result from the other agent, writes $w_j \in W$ into its table of the results of the general computing load. At the end of the work, each agent stores all the results of the solutions to tasks W.

The algorithm of actions of m_i agent according to the rule "transfer the obtained results to the other agents".

1°. Verification is not passed to their computational load $w_j \in Wi$? If Yes, go to item 2°, if not then to paragraph 5°.

2°. To form a package for transmitting information agents $\{m_1, m_2, \ldots, m_n\} \in M$.

3°. Free medium? If Yes, go to item 4°, if not to the point 5°.

4°. To send a package with information about the result of the calculation $w_j \in Wi$ from all agents $\{m_1, m_2, \ldots, m_n\} \in M$.

5°. Go to the selection rules of behavior.

The execution time of the entire computing load W by the multi-agent system M is equal to the time for executing the average load Wi by the agent $m_i \in M$.

Incomplete or slow execution of computational load by agents of the distributed computing system can be caused not only by the low speed of individual computers, but also by the consequence of the implementation of a denial-of-service threat. A denial-of-service attack can lead to a disruption in the performance of some compute nodes and, as a consequence, the termination of the operation of the distributed computing system itself. To ensure the protection of distributed computing from this threat, each agent performs actions according to the rule of monitoring the completeness of the execution of the total computing load W.

The agent m_i performs the tracking of the completeness of the execution of W with each obtaining of results from both agents $m_j \in M$ and from the computer p_i and recording of the results obtained in the list. W_{rez}. If the entire Wi load is performed in full, then the agent scans and selects from W_{nrez}. The job and and passes it on to execution p_i.

The algorithm of actions of the agent m_i according to the rule of monitoring the completeness of execution of the general computing load.

1°. The agent $m_i \in M$ checks whether all tasks included in its computational load are executed $Wi_{nrez} = 0$? If yes then go to item 5°, if not to item 2°.

2°. The agent m_i selects from the table of the general computing load W_{nrez} the job w_j by which the result is not obtained.

3°. Does the agent m_i check that he performed w_j before? If yes then go to item 5°, if not then go to item 4°.

4°. The agent m_i transmits the selected task to its computer $p_i \in Pz$.

5°. Go to the next rule.

A graphical representation of the algorithm in Fig. 2

Due to the implementation of the rule for monitoring the completeness of the overall computing load, there is a redistribution of the load between the agents of the multi-agent system. When you attack "denial of service" and the failure of one or more of the agents, the load is redistributed among the remaining healthy compute nodes of the multi-agent system. This ensures high resiliency of the distributed computing system created on the basis of a multi-agent system in a computer network.

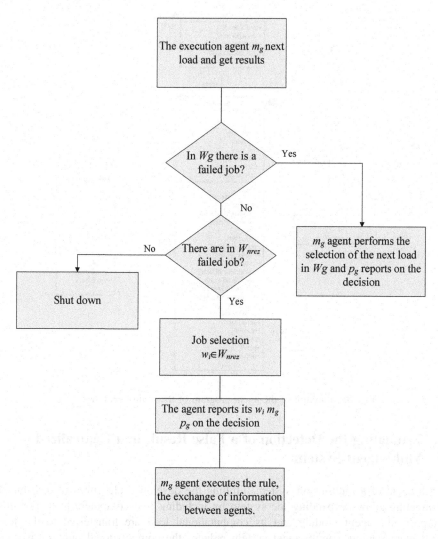

Fig. 2. Structure of the agent program of the multi-agent system

Based on the developed algorithm was written in Python and streamlined program of work agent multi-agent system. The program structure is shown in Fig. 3.

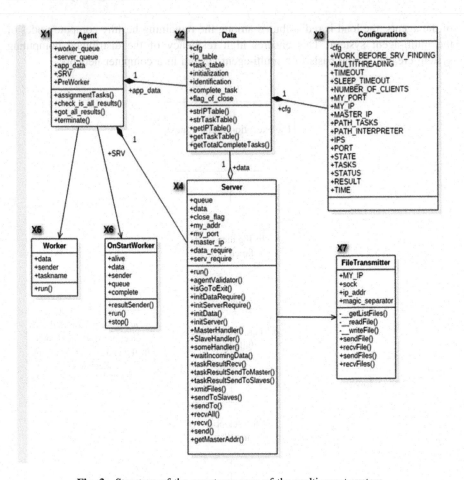

Fig. 3. Structure of the agent program of the multi-agent system

4   Estimating the Detection of a False Result in a Centralized Multi-agent System

Each agent of a multi-agent system fulfilling the developed algorithm of distributed computing allows expanding the system by including free computers in it. For this purpose, the agent module and its computational load are transferred to the free computer. Scaling a multi-agent system reduces the computational burden on each agent and reduces the execution time of a larger volume task. The agent module can be located on any network computer, including on the computers of the global Internet. This increases the degree of threat to the security of processes and the results of distributed computing. The management agents verify the correctness of the results obtained from the agents of a multi-child system for protecting distributed computing from the threat of receiving a false result.

Let's calculate on a concrete example the probability of finding a false result for a centralized multi-agent system. The calculation is feasible for a multi-agent system consisting of thousands of agents performing calculations and one managing agent. Assume that among the many agents that make up the multi-agent system, there are intruders, each of which transmits false results of calculations. The controlling agent from the results obtained from the agents selects some and checks their correctness by repeating the calculations. The results to be checked are randomly selected, since the managing agent, having limited computing resources, does not know exactly which agent is the attacker.

The probability of P_{olr} detecting one false result in a centralized multi-agent system, which is constantly formed by an attacker, is determined by the Bernoulli formula. The Bernoulli formula makes it possible to determine the probability of occurrence of a certain event under independent conditions. This suggests that the occurrence of an event in an experiment does not depend on the appearance or non-appearance of the same event in earlier or subsequent tests.

$$P_n(m) = \frac{n!}{m! * (n - m)!} * p^m * (1 - p)^{n-m} \tag{1}$$

where m is the number of times the event occurred;

p - probability that the event will occur;

n is the number of repetitions of the experiment.

For our case, the number of repetitions of the experiment n is the average computational load kr for each agent. It depends on the total amount of computational load W and the number of agents N in the multi-agent system M. Load kr is calculated by formula

$$n = kr = \frac{W}{N} \tag{2}$$

where N is the number of agents in the multi-agent system M;

W is the total amount of computational load.

The probability of occurrence of an event in one experiment is determined by the number of agents of the multi-agent system:

$$p = \frac{1}{N}; \tag{3}$$

To calculate the probability of finding a false result, we substitute in our formula (1) our data from formulas (2) and (3).

$$P_{olr} = \frac{\left(\frac{W}{N}\right)!}{m! * \left(\frac{W}{N} - m\right)!} * \left(\frac{1}{N}\right)^m * \left(1 - \frac{1}{N}\right)^{\frac{W}{N} - m} \tag{4}$$

where m is the number of false results found.

Since an attacker can generate false results for his entire computing load, the probability of generating a false result is $ko = 1$. If the probability of forming a false result is $ko = 0.5$, this means that it produces false results for only half of its computational load.

In accordance with the structure of the multi-agent system, formula (5) is used to calculate the probability of detecting a false result, reflecting the dependence of the probability on the number of control agents and the probability of creating false results by the attacker:

$$p = \frac{b}{N} * ko; \tag{5}$$

ko - probability of false results creation by an intruder;
b is the number of control agents.

Substituting in formula (4) instead of probability p, calculated from formula (3), the value of p calculated by formula (5), we will form the probability of detection of at least one false result ($m = 1$) from the attacker by the controlling agent ($b = 1$). Probabilities of detecting at least one false result in a centralized multi-agent system that are generated by an attacker with probabilities $ko = 1$, $ko = 0.8$ and $ko = 0.6$ (see Fig. 4).

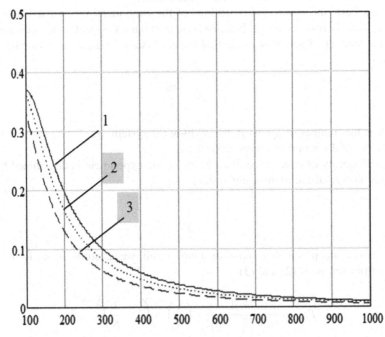

Fig. 4. The probability of detection of at least one false result when the probability of the formation of a "false result" (1) $ko = 1$ (2) $ko = 0.8$ and (3) $ko = 0.6$.

The calculation is performed for a centralized multi-agent system with one managing agent. The number of tasks for a large-volume problem $W = 10000$ for a different number of agents N of a multi-agent system from 100 to 1000. When analyzing the obtained graphs, it is seen that the probability of detecting at least one false result by the managing agent decreases with the increase in the number of system agents. With the number of agents $N = 1000$, the probability of detecting at least one false result is $P_{olr} = 0.005$. When N $\rightarrow \infty$ the probability $P_{olr} \rightarrow 0$. The reason for this is when scaling the multi-agent system the number of results you get a managing agent, increases. Managing agent is unable to verify all the results transferred to him by the agents of multi-agent system M.

Reducing the likelihood of false results is also affected by a decrease in the probability of false results from the attacker, since in this case the total number of false results in the multi-agent system decreases, which reduces the probability of detection of false results by the managing agent.

Similarly, the probability of detection by the managing agent of at least 2 false results for one intruder is calculated, similarly to 3 and 4 ($Polr2$, $Polr3$, $Polr4$). In the formula (4) we substitute $m = 2, 3, 4$.

The probabilities P_{olr2}, P_{olr3}, $_{Polr4}$ of the detection agent of false results are calculated with one attacker. Probabilities of detection of 2, 3 and 4 false results in a centralized multi-agent system of those that are formed by an attacker with probabilities $ko = 1$. are shown in Fig. 5.

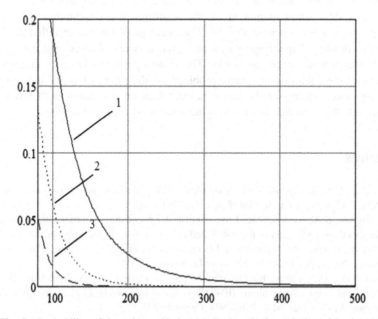

Fig. 5. Probability of detection with $ko = 1$ (1) 2x, (2) 3x and (3) 4 false results.

Comparing the graphs in Figs. 3 and 4, we can conclude that in the centralized multi-agent system the probability of finding false results decreases with the increase in the number of false results that the controlling agent should detect.

5 Conclusion

The algorithm was developed for the organization and protection of distributed computations in computer networks based on multi-agent system with the aim of reducing the solution time of large-scale problems. We developed the algorithm for decentralized multi-agent agent system, which allows securing distributed computing based on multi-agent systems in computer networks and reducing the solution time of large-scale problems. Decentralized computer system provides higher protection efficiency of the processes of distributed computing than centralized in an unstable computing environment of a computer network. Agents, working on information in the article, algorithm, perform their own distribution between a given computational load for the organization of distributed computing. In the process of implementing distributed computing, the agents communicate with multicast messages pass each other the results of the calculations and redistribute among themselves the given computational load depending on the performance of computers. It allows you to provide in addition to reducing the solution time of large-scale problems, the protection efficiency of computational processes and computing results from the substitution. It increases the degree of protection for distributed computing from the threat of "denial of service" and safety results of the decision from the threat of a "false" result compared to a centralized computing system. Implementation of the algorithm for decentralized multi-agent system program was written in Python. The agent program was installed on 3 computers. The results of multi-agent system in the network showed that an organized system of distributed computing works. The system performs integrity monitoring of the results of the solutions of a large problem. At the organization of the distributed computing system decreases the computational load on computers with low productivity through the redistribution of computational load among the agents.

References

1. Kureichik, V.V., Kureichik, V.M., Sorokoletov, P.V.: Analysis and a survey of evolutionary models. J. Comput. Syst. Sci. Int. **5**(46), 779–791 (2007)
2. Khovanskov, S.A., Norkin, O.R., Litvinenko, V.A.: Algorithm of optimization of computing loading of the organization of the distributed calculation. In: Proceedings of the Congress on Intelligent Systems and Information Technologies, IS-IT 2011, Scientific Publication in 4 Volumes, No. 4, pp. 142–145. Physmathlit, Moscow (2011)
3. Pljonkin, A., Rumyantsev, K.: Quantum-cryptographic network. In: 2016 IEEE East-West Design and Test Symposium (EWDTS). https://doi.org/10.1109/ewdts.2016.7807623. Electronic ISSN 2472-761X. ISBN 978-150900693-9
4. Khovanskova, V.S., Khovanskov, S.A., Litvinenko, V.A., Litvinenko, E.V.: Primenenie parametricheskoj adaptacii v algoritmah postroeniya ortogonal'nogo dereva SHtejnera. Informatika, vychislitel'naya tekhnika i inzhenernoe obrazovanie **4**(28), 9–16 (2016)

5. Khovanskov, S.A., Litvinenko, V.A., Litvinenko, E.V.: Gibridnyj metod upravleniya tochnost'yu resheniya ehkstremal'nyh zadach na grafah. Izvestiya YUFU. Tekhnicheskie nauki **7**(144), 112–116 (2013)
6. Kshemkalyani, A.D., Singhal, M.: Distributed Computing: Principles. Algorithms, and Systems. Cambridge University Press, Cambridge (2008)
7. Khovanskova, V.S., Khovanskov, S.A., Litvinenko, V.A.: Ocenka sokrashcheniya vremeni postroeniya svyazyvayushchih derev'ev cepej s pomoshch'yu raspredelyonnoj vychislitel'noj sistemy. Informatika, vychislitel'naya tekhnika i inzhenernoe obrazovanie **4**(28), 34–42 (2016)
8. Khovanskov, S.A., Norkin, O.R.: The approach to the implementation of the algorithm trace connections of electronic components in a distributed computer networks. Int. J. Innov. Inf. Manuf. Technol. **1**, 26–31 (2014)
9. Foster, I., Zhao, Y., Raicu, I., Lu, S.: Cloud Computing and Grid Computing 360-Degree Compared. http://arxiv.org/pdf/0901.0131.pdf. Accessed 14 Sept 2012
10. Kotenko, V.V., Rumyancev, K.E., Kotenko, S.V.: Identifikacionnyj analiz v informacionno-telekommutacionnyh sistemah. Monografiya. Rostov-na-Donu: Izd-vo YUFU (2014)
11. Madkour, A.M., Eassa, F.E., Ali, A.M., Qayyum, N.U.: Mobile-agent-based systems against malicious hosts. World Appl. Sci. J. **2**(29), 287–297 (2014)
12. Muñoz, A., Pablo, A., Maña, A: Multiagent systems protection. Adv. Softw. Eng. Article ID 281517, 9–12 (2011)
13. Guan, X., Yang, Y., You, J.: POM-a mobile model against malicious hosts. In: Proceedings of High Performance Computing in the Asia-Pacific Region, vol. 2, pp. 1165–1166 (2000)
14. Khovanskov, S.A., Khovanskova, V.S., Litvinenko, V.A., Norkin, O.R.: The algorithm for determining the direction of building relations in a distributed computing system. In: Proceedings of the Congress on Intelligent Systems and Information Technologies, IS&IT 2012, vol. 4, pp. 49–50. Physmathlit, Moscow (2012)
15. Khovanskova, V.S., Khovanskov, S.A., Litvinenko, V.A.: Algoritm organizacii bezopasnyh raspredelennyh vychislenij na osnove mnogoagentnoj sistemy.Izvestiya YUFU. Tekhnicheskie nauki **10**(183), 146–158 (2016)
16. Müller, J.P., Fischer, K.: Application impact of multi-agent systems and technologies: a survey. In: Shehory, O., Sturm, A. (eds.) Agent-Oriented Software Engineering, pp. 27–53. Springer, Heidelberg (2014). https://doi.org/10.1007/978-3-642-54432-3_3
17. Wooldridge, M.: An Introduction to Multiagent Systems, p. 484. Wiley, New Jersey (2012)
18. Khovanskov, S.A., Khovanskova, V.S.: Metody zashchity raspredelennykh vychisleniy. Modernizatsiya sovremennogo obshchestva: problemy. puti razvitiya i perspektivy: sbornik materialov VI Mezhdunarodnoy nauchno-prakticheskoy konferentsii, pp. 104–107. Logos, Stavropol (2015)
19. Khovanskov, S.A., Khovanskova, V.S.: Povysheniye stepeni zashchity raspredelennykh vychisleniy. Sovremennoye sostoyaniye estestvennykh i tekhnicheskikh nauk: Materialy XVIII Mezhdunarodnoy nauchno-prakticheskoy konferentsii (20.03.2015). M.: Izd-vo «Sputnik +», pp. 96–100 (2015)
20. Khovanskova, V., Khovanskov, S.: Mul'tiagentnye sistemy: koncepcii zashchity, Bezopasnost' mul'tiagentnyh sistem. – Technical and natural sciences: Theory and practice. In: Proceedings of Materials of International Scientific e-Symposium, Russia, Moscow, 27–28 March 2015, Kirov, pp. 167–175 (2015)

Mobility in MANET Using Robot: A Review

Farkhana Muchtar[1,2(✉)], Abdul Hanan Abdullah[1],
Siti Nor Zawani Ahmmad[3], and Yugal Kumar[4]

[1] Faculty of Computing, Universiti Teknologi Malaysia,
81310 Skudai, Johor, Malaysia
farkhana2@live.utm.my, farkhana@gmail.com,
hanan@utm.my
[2] School of Computer Sciences, Universiti Sains Malaysia,
11800 Gelugor, Penang, Malaysia
[3] Instrumentation and Control Engineering, University Kuala Lumpur, MITEC,
Persiaran Sinaran Ilmu, Bandar Seri Alam, 81750 Masai, Johor, Malaysia
sitinorzawani@unikl.edu.my
[4] Department of Science and Engineering and Information Technology,
Jaypee University of Information Technology, Waknaghat,
Solan 173234, Himachal Pradesh, India
yugal.kumar@juit.ac.in

Abstract. Recently, MANET (Mobile Ad Hoc Network) researchers have shown increased interest towards using mobile robot technology for their testbed platforms. Despite the existence of articles that discuss the usage of mobile robot technology pertaining to MANET testbed from the perspective of MANET researcher, the discussion provided in the papers are rather lacklustre as it is not the sole purpose of those articles. Hence, this review aims to discuss MANET testbeds that were facilitated with mobile robot technology from previous undertaken researches. With the wealth of information provided in this paper, it is hoped that this paper will be the ultimate source of reference for other MANET researchers who need to choose the most suitable mobile robots with real mobility in their MANET testbeds.

Keywords: Mobile Ad Hoc Network · MANET testbed · Mobile robot
Real mobility

1 Introduction

Recently, MANET (Mobile Ad Hoc Network) researchers have shown increased interest toward using mobile robot technology for their testbed platforms. As a result, many prior research papers have produced considerable amount of articles that encompasses myriad aspects of discussions on MANET testbed with real mobility as part of their review. Upon observation, similarities from all these previous articles can be deduced and it was found that all of these previous review articles comprised in their discussion section, the inclusion of either one or more of the issues mentioned below:

i. reported researches on MANET technology that was used as a backbone to a communication network of multiple mobile robots e.g. CENTIBOTS [1–5], Robomote [6–10] and Mobile Multirobot Systems [11, 23].

© Springer Nature Singapore Pte Ltd. 2019
P. K. Singh et al. (Eds.): FTNCT 2018, CCIS 958, pp. 304–324, 2019.
https://doi.org/10.1007/978-981-13-3804-5_23

ii. review papers on the use of mobile robot in the testbed that were more focused towards testbed for mobile sensor networks.

iii. brief statements on the use of the mobile robot in testbed as mere generalization without any specific focus on MANET testbed.

Of deplorable note however, is the fact that none of the previous review articles have adequately or thoroughly in an academic sense, vivisected and performed more assiduous in-depth holistic scrutiny from the perspective of MANET researcher on three areas of importance mention below:

i. detail discussion of MANET testbed using mobile robot technology

ii. technical review of MANET testbed using mobile robot technology

iii. critical review of MANET testbed using mobile robot technology

Acting as a preliminary introduction to educate MANET researcher on mobility issues in MANET using mobile robot technology, the main focus of this review article dwells only on the first issue from the three inadequately examined areas mentioned above. However, it is important to note that issues related to technical review and critical review are omitted from this paper as it is extended in our next papers [96, 97].

This review paper is organized as follows. Section 1 provides an introductory outline. In Sect. 2, prior researches that utilised robot for mobility in MANET testbed are detailed, and finally in Sect. 3, this research is summarized and the future goals of this works are outlined.

2 Prior Research that Utilised Robots for Mobility in MANET Testbeds

During the early stages of compiling this review, the choice of suitable robot-based MANET testbeds that were appropriate for discussion was difficult due to the fact that the definition on the scope of MANET-based research itself was rather vague. For example when we posed the question, were mobile sensor networks (MSNs), an opportunistic networks and delay tolerant networks (DTNs) a subsets of MANET? There has yet to be one existing and agreeable reference that discusses and defines these vague but bordering and closely knitted definitions of MANET. It was then decided that MSNs, opportunistic networks and DTNs were in fact a subset of MANET because all the mentioned wireless ad-hoc networks had mobility criteria and most importantly, wireless multi-hop ad-hoc communication.

Instead of discussing all existing MANET testbeds, the primary focus of this paper is to expound robot-based MANET testbeds that can be highlighted as a source of reference for other MANET researchers who are interested to use mobile robots for real mobility in their MANET testbeds. Thus for this paper, only selected articles relevant to this review were compiled, namely Mobile Emulab, MiNT-m, MiNT-2, Proteus, w-ilab.t, ARUM, Sensei-UU, Kansei, CONET-IT, CONE, Roomba MADNet, Explore-bots, SCORPION, MOTEL, iRobotSense, IoT-Lab, and NITOS.

2.1   Mobile Emulab Testbed (Also Known as TrueMobile)

Mobile Emulab, otherwise known as TrueMobile was developed and run by Flux Group, part of the School of Computing at the University of Utah. It was one of the first mobile sensor node network testbed facilities that provide registered users public access to mobile sensor network testbeds with real mobility using robots. Mobile Emulab was a continuation of the Netbed testbed, a testbed platform that used emulation method especially for wired network testbeds [13]. Mobile Emulab was among the most popular public WSN testbeds until its discontinuation in 2008 [14].

The L-shaped testbed was conducted indoors in an area that covered 60 m^2. There were 25 static sensor nodes Mica2 installed in the testbed arena and for the Mobile Emulab setup, 6 units of mobile robots based on the Acroname Garcia robot platform were developed and each mobile node was accompanied with a unit of 900 MHz Mica2 sensor node and Intel Stargates computer board with X-Scale 400MH CPU (running Linux) as a robot and mobile node controller. Each mobile node had two Wi-Fi interfaces, one with a wifi interface for sensor node (WSN) and the other Wi-Fi interface was for the testbed control network. Wi-Fi antenna for the sensor nodes were placed on top of a 1 m pole to represent the height of humans that carried mobile devices [15–19].

Visual based localisation was used by placing 6 units of ceiling-mounted cameras to trace the position of each mobile node in the testbed area. Each mobile node was placed with a colored card that had different patterns to represent different mobile nodes. The sensors on the Acroname Garcia robot platform were used for collision and obstacle avoidance in the testbed [15–19]. Mobile Emulab used a standard Emulab API and Interface that enabled the Mobile Emulab GUI to display the current status of the mobile nodes in the testbed using images when the testbed was in progress.

The main drawback of the Mobile Emulab was that, the developed mobile node did not have a self-recharging mechanism. As a result, the testbed operations were often a painstaking effort that limited the number of times and duration that it could be operated [20].

2.2   MiNT, MiNT-m and MiNT-2

MINT (miniaturized mobile multi-hop wireless network testbed), developed by Stony Brook University, was an indoor MANET testbed that emphasized on the miniaturization of testbeds where real multihop wireless network could be conducted in a small testbed area. The MINT testbed was used as an experimental platform in researches that were related to mobile ad-hoc network testbeds [20–26].

12 units of MINT-m (mobile) were developed to replace the initial prototype of mobile node that originally used LEGO Mindstorm based robot platform [27]. Mint-m was equipped with iRobot Roomba as its robot platform and Routerboard RN-230 as its robot controller and mobile node. At the same time, the Mint-m was a self-recharging mobile node that fully utilised self-charging docking facilities that were available on the iRobot Roomba [20, 28, 29]. Each unit of the MINT-m Wi-Fi was installed with 4 Wi-Fi interfaces where 3 of the Wi-Fi interfaces were used for the multi-channel ad hoc network testbed and the other Wi-Fi interface was used for the

testbed control network. Robot localisation was conducted in a centralized manner using visual localisation where the tracker software received input from 4 overhead cameras to determine the position of each mobile node [20].

To enable users to control the operation of the testbed, the MOVIE (Mint Control and Visualization Interface) software was developed. MOVIE functioned as the 'eyes' and 'hands' for the user to regulate and manage existing resources in the MINT. MOVIE also enabled the MiNT testbed to be accessed remotely by outside users [20].

Each of the MINT-m mobile nodes were equipped with a hybrid simulator, which was a modified ns simulator where the simulation model of the link layer, the MAC layer and the physical layer of the simulator were replaced with wireless card drivers, firmware, and real wireless channels respectively. In addition, MINT also suggested a distribution solution that was easy to deploy and test with the availability of the Fault Injection and Analysis Tool (FIAT) component [20].

A few years later, MINT-2 was developed as a continuation to the MINT project in a collaboration between the University of Binghamton and Stony Brook University. The main goal of the MINT-2 project was to reproduce the MINT testbed for research purposes on wireless networking in Binghamton University using methods and technologies that were more effective and up to date [30–32].

There were three notable and significant improvements to the MiNT-2 testbed when compared to the original MINT testbed namely:

i. The first improvement was in the use of iRobot Create instead of iRobot Roomba that was cheaper and more developer friendly. The iRobot Create was coupled with the Roomba Serial Console User Interface (SCI) to allow manipulation [30–32].

ii. The second visible improvement was the replacement of the visual based localisation with an RFID based localisation that was more robust, simple and cheap. The MINT-2 mobile node navigation system was a combination of an RFID based localisation and wheel odometry from a wheel encoder found on iRobot Create [30–32].

iii. The third improvement was the replacement of the Routerboard RB-230 to a Soekris net5501 board, a x86 processor-based computer board. The net5501 board was easier to use and could share a power source with the iRobot Create as compared with the old MINT-m, where the Routerboard RB-230 used a separate laptop battery [30–32].

2.3   Proteus Mobile Node in PHAROS Testbed

PHAROS Testbed was a project developed by a team of researchers from the Department of Electrical and Computer Engineering in collaboration with research teams from the Mobile and Pervasive Computing Group, the Laboratory for Informatics, Networks, and Communication (LINC) and the Wireless Network and Communications Group (WNCG). The Proteus mobile node on the other hand, was developed to meet the need for creating multiple mobile robots in PHAROS testbed facilities that were often used in other multidisciplinary research namely; robotics, MANET, VANET, WSN, mobile networks and wireless networks [33].

There are several design versions of the Proteus robots developed by PHAROS Testbed developers. Most of the testbeds involved pervasive computing and mobile networks that utilised the Proteus robot that used a Traxxas Stampede RC Car Chassis [33, 34].

The design layout of the Proteus robot components was arranged modularly where each component was placed in a staggered manner and the components were divided separately in different platform panels according to their respective functions. In general, the components of the Proteus robot consisted of three layers namely; the mobility plane, the computation plane and the application plane.

In Proteus, the combination of x86 embedded computer and microcontroller was used as the robot control module. The microcontroller was used for tasks that were related to real-time processing such as motor control and sensor data processing. The x86 computer on the other hand, was used to perform high-end and complex processes such as the robot control logic [34].

A player framework (in the latest version, an ROS framework) was selected as the main software platform to control the Proteus robot mobility when the testbed was running while several other software such as Jbot were used for the path coordination of the Proteus robot when the testbed was in use [33].

The Pharos testbed platform was used to experiment in various fields such as MANET [35] VANET [36], DTN [37–39], mobile cyber-physical systems [40] and Autonomous Intersection Management Policies [41].

2.4 An Approach for the Resilience of Ubiquitous Mobile Systems (ARUM) Mobility Platform

An Approach for the Resilience of Ubiquitous Mobile Systems (ARUM) Mobility is a testbed platform that was developed in collaboration with The Mosaic project, The Hidenets (highly dependable IP-based Networks and Services) project and The ReSIST organization. Mobile robot technology was chosen as the mobility platform for the ARUM testbed to enable the testbed to be carried out using a repeatable real mobility. The Lynxmotion 4WD Rover was the main robot platform as this particular robot chassis had the capacity and ability to carry loads weighing 2 kg at speeds of 1 m/s for several hours while it was in duration. This was a required feature for this particular experiment as it was similar to a person carrying a laptop. Robot control and localisation were implemented using the Lynxmotion Atom Bot Board, a robot control module that also included the Lynxmotion 4WD Rover. The robot control module communicated with the localisation server that also interacted with motion capture based facilities to ensure that each of the mobile robots knew their time and position exactly [42, 43].

Each mobile robot in the ARUM testbed moved according to the line track that was drawn on the floor surface while robot localisation and positioning used motion capture technology. Previously, researchers in the ARUM project used several localisation methods such as ultrasound beacon-based localisation and a Cricket Solution developed by MIT. However, noises captured from the ultrasound sensors severely reduced its accuracy. Ultimately, they resorted to the solution of motion capture based on localisation utilizing 3 different products for a motion capture solution, namely The

Cortex system, the Hagisonic Stargazer technology and the Ultra-Wide-Band-based localisation system (UWB) by Ubisense [42–44].

The ARUM testbed also utilised a miniaturization approach by reducing the Wi-Fi transmit power and at the same time, used a radio signal attenuator to reduce the radius signal range between each mobile node up to 4 meters in radius to enable the multihop wireless network to be conducted in a small space testbed [45].

2.5 Robotic Mobile Nodes in w-iLab.t Testbed Laboratory

w-iLab.t Zwijnaarde testbed laboratory in iMinds Research Institute is one of the GENI based wireless testbeds that has mobile nodes as part of their testbed assets. It is located in Zwijnaarde, Ghent, Belgium where it provided 20 units of mobile robots along with 60 other static sensor nodes. Mobile robots for the wireless network testbed were deployed in a second w-iLab.t (Zwijnaarde lab) in 2013 [46] as an extended mobility facility in the w-iLab.t testbed [46–49].

w-iLab.t is a heterogeneous wireless network testbed that supports IEEE 802.11 a/b/g for Wi-Fi, IEEE 802.15.4 (e.g. ZigBee) for WSN, IEEE802.15.1 for Bluetooth and cellular networks such as GSM, HSDPA and LTE platforms by using a software-defined radio platform (USRP) technology. W-iLab.t also allows the testbed to be conducted in a centralized mode (or infrastructured network) or in an ad hoc multihop wireless network (e.g. mesh network and MANET). A spectrum sensing component was also attached to conduct studies that included wireless signal spectrum analysis in their testbeds [46–49].

Mobile robots in the w-iLab.t Zwignaarde used iRobot Roomba as the robot platform and a Roomba Serial Console Interface (SCI) to control and utilize the sensors available in the Roomba. Each mobile robot was also equipped with the same facilities such as a fixed node that consisted of 1 unit of a sensor node (eZ430), 1 unit of powered embedded PC with an Intel Atom processor chip that was used as a mobile node, 1 unit of an emulator environment. In addition, an extra battery pack was required to supply power to the PC and the embedded in-house custom made board to control a mobile robot and to recharge both the iRobot Roomba and the mobile node (embedded PC) [46, 47, 50].

The integration between the control and coordination of the mobile robots with the testbed management system was based on an OMF framework whereby users used the OMF format testbed configuration file to determine the coordination of the mobile robots and how they were used in the testbed. The use of the OMF framework for the testbed configuration simplified the process in cases where users needed or were required to repeat their experiment repeatedly using mobile nodes [47].

Similar to other testbeds that used iRobot Roomba as their main robot platform for mobile nodes, w iLab.t also used a self-charging docking station that was available on Roomba to be part of its autonomous features in mobile nodes for the w-iLab.t testbed lab. Every time the mobile node spent one cycle of experimental task, the mobile node then will return to the docking station for self-charging while at the same time connecting itself back to testbed control network [47, 48].

In the early stage of testbed development, w-iLab.t used a dead reckoning approach for mobile robot localisation and positioning. This method was based on the assumption that the current position of the mobile robot was known and accurate. The current position of the mobile robot while moving was detected through a method known as odometry using a wheel encoder that was already available on the iRobot Roomba. To improve the position accuracy, the testbed area floor was marked with black and white lines both vertically and horizontally to allow mobile robots to recheck their current positions using cliff sensors that were also available on the iRobot Roomba each time it passed through the white and black line on the floor of testbed area [47].

However, it was found that the robot localisation approach also created many flaws and had many disadvantages particularly when the exact location of the mobile robot was missed. The accuracy of the mobile robot localisation greatly affected the quality of the experiments conducted and therefore new robot localisation methods needed to be developed to overcome robot localisation accuracy issues [48]. Hence, the latest method developed for mobile robots in the w-iLab.t was an RF-based indoor localisation system where Wi-Fi RSSI signals were processed using RSS-based multilateration algorithm to determine the exact current position of the mobile robot [50, 51].

w-iLab.t mobile node facilities can be used remotely via web based testbed interface by authorized users only. w-iLab.t is integrated with other testbed laboratories under the fed4fire federation and uses a GENI interface to allow integration on the experiment [47, 52].

One of the MANET experiments that utilised mobile node facilities in the w-iLab.t laboratory was a research conducted by Neumann et al. [53] that compared performance and resource consumption of three open source mesh routing protocols which were olsrd, babeld and bmx6 with real mobility on each of the MANET nodes. The facilities available in the w-iLab.t allowed Neuman et al. to carry out the experiment with ease on the testbed setup using real mobility as compared to their previously reported experiments [54, 55] which were conducted using only emulation-based node mobility. They found that the use of the testbed facilities that provided real mobility in the testbeds enabled results that were more accurate and realistic, most notably on issues related to interference and CPU consumption [53].

2.6 Sensei-UU

Sensei-UU is a WSN testbed that uses a group of small mobile robots for repeatable real mobility. It was developed by the Uppsala Vinn Excellence Center for Wireless Sensor Networks and was partly supported by VINNOVA. This testbed was run indoor and was integrated with static nodes and a central site manager of an existing WSN testbed lab [56–60].

Mobile nodes were built using LEGO NXT robots as their main platform and each mobile node was equipped with 1 unit of TelosB WSN nodes and 1 unit of a smartphone. TelosB was used as the sensor node for testbed purposes and the smartphone functioned as a testbed robot controller with Wi-Fi communication and as the central site manager. Therefore, there were two wireless network in the Sensei-UU, namely ZigBee WSN testbed for the network (IEEE 802.15.4) that was available in the TelosB sensor node and a Wi-Fi network for the testbed control network (IEEE 80.211b/g) that was available on a smartphone [56, 59, 60].

Sensei-UU utilised a simple robot positioning technique that used tracks and markers approach where each mobile robot would move according to track lines on the floor inside the testbed area. For mobile robot localisation, the TelosB sensor node would share the RSSI reading with the smartphone to estimate the individual mobile robot location through an RSSI based localisation approach. The usage of line tracking and positioning and the RSSI based localisation ensured that the same simple mobile node localisation could be easily adapted by various different types of mobile robots. The whole Sensei-UU testbed architecture used a centralized approach that provides modularity and flexibility in its design to fulfill the requirements from internal developers [56, 59, 60].

2.7 Kansei Testbed

The Kansei testbed is a testbed facility that was used as a research platform related to networked sensing applications that was conducted on a large scale. The Kansei testbed was designed to support a variety of WSN related research that would cover indoor or outdoor environments.

The testbed facilities developed consisted of one WSN with 210 static sensor nodes and multiple Acroname-based mobile robots. Each node in the WSN on the other hand, were combinations of Extreme Scale Mote (XSM) and Stargate board. Mobile nodes that used the Acroname robot were equipped with XSM to represent the mobile sensor nodes in the Kansei testbed and interacted with static sensor nodes available in the Kansei testbed [61, 62].

To ensure that the testbed was properly managed, the Kansei Director was developed as a centralized modular testbed management system that allowed customization and integration to be carried out according to the requirements of an experiment. The Kansei Director is a software component developed to manage complex multi-tier experiments. The Kansei testbed could be accessed remotely (open to public in 2005) and hybrid simulation method(s) could be performed simultaneously in both a simulator and the real hardware [61, 62].

The use of a mobile robot in the Kansei testbed was merely for the mobility of the sensor node purposes as robot localisation was centrally controlled through the Kansei Director. Interactions of the mobile robots did not fully occur on the sensor nodes carried in the mobile node but the interactions that took place were simply testbed instructions sent by the Kansei Director via the mobile robot controller [61, 62]. The same approach was also used in other testbeds such as ones that were developed by Rahimi et al. [7], Giordano et al. [63], Jayasingha et al. [64] and Forster et al. [65].

2.8 Mobile Robots in CONET-IT (Cooperating Objects Network of Excellence Integrated Testbed)

The Cooperating Object Network of Excellence (CONET) testbed is a generic remote testbed that supports various forms of experimentation and it provides a variety of applications for research purposes related to wireless networking. It was developed at the University of Seville under the Cooperating Objects Network of Excellence fund [66–68].

Two types of mobile robots were developed using two different robot platforms known as Pioneer 3AT and another custom robot platform that used a RC car chassis.

Each mobile robot unit was equipped with a laser range finder, Microsoft Kinect, GPS and IMU sensor nodes [69, 70].

The mobile robot operations were controlled via a Player/Stage modular software with commands from the testbed control center. Mobile nodes in CONET-IT could be accessed via an interactive web-based interface and it provided some basic functions such as user-controlled mobility for experiments in various fields such as mobile sensor networks and ubiquitous robotics [14, 66, 67, 69].

CONET-IT facilities have been used in several experimental fields including mobile robots, WSN, and integrations between WSN and mobile robots. Some of the experiments conducted in CONET testbed facilities were RSSI based WSN localisations, simultaneous multiple robot localisations, mobile robots and WSN cooperation for data collection, as well as robot guiding using WSN [14, 70].

CONET-IT facilities were designed in a flexible manner that enabled new experiments to be conducted whenever the need for new equipment and technology arose in the future. The main strength of CONET testbed facilities was that peer to peer integration of mobile nodes could be enabled without full intervention of the controller from the main testbed [70].

2.9 Mobile Nodes in Cooperation and Network Coding (CONE) Testbed

Mobile MANET testbeds were developed by the Cooperation and Network Coding (CONE) as a research project under Aalborg University to address issues related to network coding implementation in mesh networks of mobile devices. In particular, CONE researchers realized that data dissemination processes performed differently in dynamic networks as agile protocol was required to enable mobile nodes to interact with each other when they were within communication range [71].

CONE researchers used the LEGO Mainstorms NXT as their robot platform for mobile nodes and Nokia Mobile Phones (7 units Nokia N97 mini, 1 unit of Nokia 97 and 2 units Nokia 5800 XpressMusic) as mobile devices for the MANET testbeds with real mobility as its purpose. Previously, CONE researchers tried to reuse testbeds with a mobile robot method proposed by Reich [72] for the Roomba MADNet that utilised the Robot Create robot platform. However iRobot Create did not meet the criteria that they required in terms of speed and steering abilities and at the same time, it was also less suitable for outdoor testbeds [71, 73].

The CONE testbed design did not utilise robot localisation and merely provided simple logic to the LEGO NXT to perform random movements within the testbed arena. All the 10 units of mobile robots involved were placed in a circular formation in the middle of testbed arena before the testbed was initiated. The Standard LEGO Mindstorms ultrasonic and color sensors used equipped each mobile node with the ability for obstacle and collision avoidance and it moved inside the testbed area that was bordered and marked with green lines [71, 73].

LEGO NXT and the Nokia mobile phone on each mobile node had no direct interaction with each other. The robot platform served only to provide real mobility in the testbed. All the testbed processes and collection of testbed results were conducted in the Nokia mobile phones. Testbed autonomy was achieved by setting a coordinator node among the 10 mobile nodes in the testbed that would determine the start and stop mode of the testbed and at the same time, determine which testbed should be running. The coordinator node also monitored the status of each mobile node to ensure that the testbed performed effectively. During the testbed run time, some human interventions were required when the mobile robot stopped moving and after it failed to overcome a particular obstacle in the testbed area [73].

During the testbed operation, the results obtained were collected on each of the Nokia mobile phones and then analyzed based on several metrics such as bandwidth, throughput, completion time and energy consumption, each at different data dissemination strategies [73].

2.10   Roomba MADNet in SCAN (Spreadable Connected Autonomic Network) Research

MADNet (mobile, ad-hoc, delay tolerant network testbed) is a testbed setup with real mobility and it was developed as a testbed platform for Spreadable Connected Autonomic Network (SCAN) Research at Columbia University. The objective of SCAN research was to study ad hoc network connectivity and data collection. MADNet was designed to be a platform to implement mobile SCAN network designs.

iRobot Create robots were selected as the main platform, although Reich et al. [72, 74, 75] named the mobile node platform of the testbed as Roomba MADNet and the Linksys WRTSL54GS wireless router (installed with OpenWRT Linux OS) was chosen as the mobile wireless device. Roomba MADNet was equipped with multi peripherals such as webcam for generating image data in the network testbed and USB storage to save testbed log files. The router and the peripherals were supplied with power from the iRobot Create battery through a modified serial port that are connected to the iRobot Create serial interface.

The focus of SCAN research was on network connections and therefore, researchers have excluded the robot localisation method on Roomba MADNet. Simple algorithms were used to operate Roomba MADNet that prescribed each of the mobile nodes to move forward until an obstacle was detected, then the Roomba MADNet moved towards the opposite direction, away from the detected obstacle. To ensure the formation of a random network topology, each Roomba MADNet would change the polarity of its direction of rotation at random before it move forward again [76].

2.11   Explorebots

Explorebots is an indoor based mobile robot testbed designed for mobile multi-hop network research. It was constructed using Rogue ATV as its robot chassis, a Rabbit 3000 microprocessor as its main controller and Mica2 as its wireless communication module. In addition, Explorebots was also equipped with multisensors such as the ultrasonic range sensor, a magnetometer for heading and direction sensors, tactile sensors for obstacle avoidance and custom-made wheel encoders for odometry measurements. The combination of the ultrasonic range sensor, magnetometer and wheel encoder functioned as its robot localisation. In addition to the robot controller board, sensor nodes and various other sensors, Explorebots was also equipped with a wireless webcam for remote monitoring purposes on the GUI-based testbed controller [76].

2.12   SCORPION, Heterogeneous Wireless Networking Testbed

SCORPION (Santa Cruz Mobile Radio Platform for Indoor and Outdoor Networks) is a heterogeneous multihop wireless network testbed run by the Inter-Networking Research Group (i-NRG) at UC Santa Cruz University of California. The SCORPION project was created to study heterogeneous wireless networking environments that included MANET. The SCORPION testbed has many types of mobile nodes namely, airplane node, bus node, briefcase node (carried by people to reflect human mobility) and iRobot Create mobile node [77].

There were 4 units of airplane nodes, 40 mobile nodes installed on the bus, 20 nodes in the form of briefcase nodes and 20 nodes in the form of mobile robots. Each mobile node was equipped with a mini-ITX computer and used the Wi-Fi network for wireless communication. The iRobot based mobile node was used as the indoor mobile node where every movement of the mobile robot used a random waypoint mobility model [77].

2.13   MOTEL: Mobile Wireless Sensor Network Testbed

MOTEL testbed is a mobile sensor network testbed platform developed by the Networking Laboratory, ISIN-DTI, University of Applied Sciences of Southern Switzerland. The MOTEL testbed platform consisted of two main components namely, the MuRobA (MultiRobot Architecture for Coordinated Mobility) as its first component that was related to localisation and navigation of multiple mobile robots which allowed real mobility to be performed in mobile sensor network and a second component named FLEXOR (flexible sensor network architecture for enabling backchannel-free WSN experiments) that controlled and managed mobile sensor network experiments performed in the MOTEL testbed [65, 78, 79].

e-puck is chosen as the main robot platform for the MOTEL testbed and it did not interact with the piggybacked sensor node. Mobile robot (epuck) positioning and localisation was controlled through a MuRobA system via Bluetooth wireless communication. Testbed processes towards sensor nodes carried by each mobile robot was controlled by FLEXOR via IEEE 802.15.4 wireless communication. MOTEL used a visual localisation approach utilizing one fisheye camera unit that was mounted on the ceiling to recognize the position and movement of each mobile node and the information obtained was sent to MuRobA. After that, MuRobA would provide further instructions to each of the mobile nodes regarding the direction of movement and destination of each random waypoint from the information that was generated [78].

2.14   iRobotSense: A Mobile Sensing Platform Based on iRobot Create

iRobotSense is a mobile node for mobile sensor network testbeds that use iRobot Create as its robot platform. The main goal for the development of iRobotSense was to test the effectiveness of routing algorithms in the sensor node when it reconnect a disconnected wireless connection due to sensor node mobility [80]. iRobotSense mobility did not use a robot localisation method as the movement distance and destination was already known and fixed. The combination of compass sensors (HMC6352) and a wheel encoder on iRobot Create was used to help iRobotSense identify the direction and distance of movement according to the given movement instructions [80, 81].

The simplistic design of the Simple iRobotSense was intended to ensure that the cost of iRobotSense was kept low through the use of a simple mobility mechanism and straightforward operation as well as a simple mechanism of robot localisation [80, 81].

Among the experiments conducted using iRobotSense testbed was a research conducted by Senturk et al. [82] that involved real implementation of MSN connectivity based on a partition approach.

2.15 Mobile Nodes in FIT IoT Laboratory (IoT-Lab)

FIT (Future Internet of Things) IOT-lab is the largest IOT laboratory ever built to date and was developed by the Future Internet of Things (FIT) Consortium [83–85]. IOT-lab was a continuation to the SensLAB project [86, 87] (operated from 2010 to 2013) [88]. It consisted of 2728 wireless sensor nodes placed in 4 different lab facilities namely, Inria Grenoble (928 nodes), Inria Lille (640 nodes), ICube Strasbourg (400 nodes), Inria Rocquencourt (344 nodes), Inria Rennes (256 nodes) and Institute Mines-Télécom Paris (160 nodes) that included several mobile nodes in each lab facility.

IoT-Lab has two types of mobile robots, turtlebot2 and wifibot. IOT-lab turtlebot2 used a turtlebot2 robot platform and a low cost open source robotic platform that was powered by a Kobuki mobile robot. It was equipped with an Asus X200CA netbook as the robot controller, Microsoft Kinect, a gyroscope and a 4 hall encoder for robot localisation. IOT lab wifibot was a mobile robot that uses a 4 × 4 wheel RC car chassis. It was equipped with a dual core Intel Atom based single board computer (SBC) as its robot controller, Microsoft Kinect and a gyroscope for robot localisation [88].

IOT-Lab turtlebot2 was a COTS robot platform that was equipped with a self-recharging docking station. IOT-lab wifibot on the other hand, required an IOT-lab team to develop their own self docking station. A self- recharging mechanism was required on the IoT-Lab mobile robot to enable testbeds operate autonomously [88].

At present, the mobility method used for mobile robots in the IOT lab is a fixed circuit-based mobility and this method falls under the category of predictable uncontrolled mobility. In future, the IoT-Lab will add two more modes of mobility namely, model-based mobility such as random waypoint mobility and manhattan mobility and user controlled mobility [89].

2.16 Mobile Nodes at NITOS Testbed

The NITOS wireless testbed is one of testbed facilities offered by the Fed4Fire federated community. NITOS focuses on the provision of testbed facilities for experimenting with wireless communication research that includes mesh networks, cloud computing, cellular networks, WSN and computer wireless networks [90–94].

Mobile robot based testbed facilities developed by NITOS testbeds were based on the present need for mobile nodes with real mobility in their testbeds [91, 95] The NITOS team used iRobot Create as its robot platform equipped with an Alix motherboard and Arduino Uno as the robot controller. In addition, a webcam, a digital accelerometer and an ultrasonic range finder were also installed as sensors for mobile robot localisation purposes. The Alix motherboard was equipped with two Wi-Fi interfaces (Atheros AR5006), where the first controlled the robot and testbed while the second was utiised for wireless multi-hop networking [95].

The NITOS team believed that augmented reality-based localisation was the practical choice for the mobile robots that they developed whereby each waypoint destination of the mobile robot mobility path was placed with different specific pattern and the webcam was used to recognize the patterns to ensure that mobile robots were positioned at the desired waypoints in the testbed. A GUI-based application was developed to control and monitor the movements of each of the mobile nodes involved. Currently, mobile robots in NITOS testbeds are still in the prototype level and have not been optimised for general use [95].

To illustrate reader with the type of robot used in MANET testbed mentioned above, pictures of each robot are presented in Table 1.

Table 1. Picture of robots used in MANET testbeds

Robot Used in MANET Testbed				
Explorebots	MiNT-m	CONET-IT	CONET-IT	ARUM
NITOS	Roomba MADNet	MiNT-2	iRobotSense	w-ilab.t
CONE	Sensei-UU	Mobile Emulab	IoT-lab	IoT-lab
Kansei	Motel	Proteus		

3 Conclusions and Suggestions for Future Work

The targeted objective of this work was achieved, that is to provide an in depth discussion on the use of mobile robot usage in MANET testbeds. Armed with the wealth of relevant information provided in this paper, the content of this paper is expected to be the ultimate source of reference for MANET researchers who are at a crossroad when selecting the preferred mobile robot technology and approach to suit their own specific needs.

It was identified that one of the main reasons for the inadequate use of testbeds as a platform in the experimental implementation of MANET research is due to the various complexities and technical know-hows that the researchers need to confront in order to develop mobile robots as well as the high costs incurred to develop the facility. Hence, we dealt with those problems by providing detailed information on the mobility issue purely from the perspective of the robot technologies in MANET research through the use of easy-to-understand tabular form that we further presented as two additional extended papers in [96, 97]. Not only that, in our quest to increase the number of MANET researchers that choose testbeds as their choice of evaluation tool, we also provided guidelines that will help MANET researchers build their own robots for their future MANET testbeds and we presented this as an extended paper in [98]. The summary of our three extended papers can be referred as per following:

- *A Technical Review of MANET Testbed Using Mobile Robot Technology* [96], where the discussions of the article is divided into three parts, namely hardware, software as well as mobile robot positioning and localization.
- *A Critical Review of MANET Testbed Using Mobile Robot Technology* [97], where the discussions of the article are dwell into four aspect, namely (i) purpose, accessibility and scope of testbed facilities, (ii) usability and controllability of robot mobility in testbed facilities, (iii) repeatability and reproducibility of real mobility in testbeds, and (iv) tools for MANET implementation, deployment and debugging for experiments.
- *ToMRobot: A Low-Cost Robot for MANET Testbed* [98], where the discussion of the article include guidelines to enable technically limited MANET researchers with a design to develop their own low cost MANET robots from an ordinary remote control car that is capable of performing a real system MANET testbed with the addition of only a few low-cost electronic components e.g. Cubieboard2 and Arduino as its robot controller.

References

1. Ko, J., Stewart, B., Fox, D., Konolige, K., Limketkai, B.: A practical, decision-theoretic approach to multi-robot mapping and exploration. In: Proceedings of the 20003 IEEE/RSJ International Conference on Intelligent Robots and Systems, (IROS 2003), vol. 4, pp. 3232–3238 (2003). https://doi.org/10.1109/iros.2003.1249654
2. Konolige, K., et al.: CentiBOTS: large-scale robot teams. In: Proceedings from the 2003 International Workshop on Multi-robot Systems: From Swarms to Intelligent Autonoma, vol. 2, pp. 193–204. Springer, Berlin (2003)

3. Konolige, K., et al.: Centibots: very large scale distributed robotic teams. In: Ang, M.H., Khatib, O. (eds.) Experimental Robotics IX. STAR, vol. 21, pp. 131–140. Springer, Heidelberg (2006). https://doi.org/10.1007/11552246_13

4. Fox, D., Ko, J., Konolige, K., Limketkai, B., Schulz, D., Stewart, B.: Distributed multi-robot exploration and mapping. Proc. IEEE **94**(7), 1325–1339 (2006). https://doi.org/10.1109/JPROC.2006.876927

5. Stewart, B., Ko, J., Fox, D., Konolige, K.: The revisiting problem in mobile robot map building: a hierarchical bayesian approach. In: Uffe, K., Christopher, M. (eds.) Proceedings of the Nineteenth conference on Uncertainty in Artificial Intelligence (UAI'03), pp. 551–558. Morgan Kaufmann Publishers Inc., San Francisco (2002)

6. Sibley, G.T., Rahimi, M.H., Sukhatme, G.: Robomote: a tiny mobile robot platform for large-scale ad- hoc sensor networks. In: Proceedings of the 2002 IEEE International Conference on Robotics and Automation (ICRA 2002), vol. 2, pp. 1143–1148. IEEE (2002)

7. Rahimi, M., Shah, H., Sukhatme, G.S., Heideman, J., Estrin, D.: Studying the feasibility of energy harvesting in a mobile sensor network. In: Proceedings of the 2003 IEEE International Conference on Robotics and Automation (ICRA 2003), vol. 1, pp. 19–24 (2003). https://doi.org/10.1109/robot.2003.1241567

8. Dhariwal, A., Sukhatme, G.S., Requicha, A.A.G.: Bacterium-inspired robots for environmental monitoring. In: Proceedings of the 2004 IEEE International Conference on Robotics and Automation, (ICRA 2004), vol. 2, pp. 1436–1443 (2004). https://doi.org/10.1109/robot.2004.1308026

9. Dantu, K., Rahimi, M., Shah, H., Babel, S., Dhariwal, A., Sukhatme, G.: Robomote: enabling mobility in sensor networks. In: 4th International Symposium on Information Processing in Sensor Networks (IPSN 2005), pp. 404–409 (2005). https://doi.org/10.1109/ipsn.2005.1440957

10. Dantu, K., Sukhatme, G.S.: Detecting and tracking level sets of scalar fields using a robotic sensor network. In: Proceedings of the 2007 IEEE International Conference on Robotics and Automation (ICRA 2007), pp. 3665–3672 (2007). https://doi.org/10.1109/robot.2007.364040

11. Antonelli, G., Arrichiello, F., Caccavale, F., Marino, A.: Decentralized time-varying formation control for multi-robot systems. Int. J. Robot. Res. **33**(7), 1029–1043 (2014). https://doi.org/10.1177/0278364913519149

12. Li, W., Shen, W.: Swarm behavior control of mobile multi-robots with wireless sensor networks. J. Netw. Comput. Appl. **34**(4), 1398–1407 (2011). https://doi.org/10.1016/j.jnca.2011.03.023

13. White, B., Lepreau, J., Guruprasad, S.: Lowering the barrier to wireless and mobile experimentation. ACM SIGCOMM Comput. Commun. Rev. **33**(1), 47–52 (2003). https://doi.org/10.1145/774763.774770

14. Jiménez-González, A., Martinez-de Dios, J.R., Ollero, A.: Testbeds for ubiquitous robotics: a survey. Robot. Auton. Syst. **61**(12), 1487–1501 (2013). https://doi.org/10.1016/j.robot.2013.07.006

15. Johnson, D., Stack, T., Fish, R., Flickinger, D., Ricci, R., Lepreau, J.: TrueMobile: a mobile robotic wireless and sensor network testbed. In: Proceedings of the 25th Annual Joint Conference of the IEEE Computer and Communications Societies (INFOCOM 2006). IEEE Computer Society (2006)

16. Johnson, D., et al.: Mobile emulab: a robotic wireless and sensor network testbed. In: Proceedings of the 25th International Conference on Computer Communications (INFOCOM 2006), pp. 1–12. IEEE (2006). https://doi.org/10.1109/infocom.2006.182

17. Flickinger, D.M.: Motion planning and coordination of mobile robot behavior for medium scale distributed wireless network experiments. Master's thesis, The University of Utah (2007)
18. Johnson, D., et al.: Robot couriers: precise mobility in a wireless network testbed. In: Proceedings of the 3rd International Conference on Embedded Networked Sensor Systems (SenSys 2005), pp. 276–277. ACM, New York (2005). https://doi.org/10.1145/1098918. 1098952
19. Johnson, D.: Design and implementation of a mobile wireless sensor network testbed. Master thesis, University of Utah (2010)
20. De, P.: Mint: a reconfigurable mobile multi-hop wireless network testbed. Ph.D. thesis, State University of New York at Stony Brook, Stony Brook (2007)
21. Krishnan, R., Raniwala, A., Chiueh, T.C.: Design of a channel characteristics-aware routing protocol. In: Proceedings of the 27th Conference on Computer Communications (INFOCOM 2008). IEEE (2008). https://doi.org/10.1109/infocom.2008.314
22. Krishnan, R., Raniwala, A., Chiueh, T.C.: An empirical comparison of throughput-maximizing wireless mesh routing protocols. In: Proceedings of the 4th Annual International Conference in Wireless Internet (WICON 2008), pp. 40:1–40:9. ICST (Institute for Computer Sciences, Social-Informatics and Telecommunications Engineering). ICST, Brussels (2008)
23. Raniwala, A., Chiueh, T.C.: Evaluation of a wireless enterprise backbone network architecture. In: Proceedings of the 12th Annual IEEE Symposium on High Performance Interconnects (HOTI 2004), 22–24 August, pp. 98–104. IEEE Computer Society, Washington, DC (2004)
24. Raniwala, A., Chiueh, T.C.: Architecture and algorithms for an IEEE 802.11-based multi-channel wireless mesh network. In: Proceedings of the 24th Annual Joint Conference of the IEEE Computer and Communications Societies (INFOCOM 2005), vol. 3, pp. 2223–2234 (2005). https://doi.org/10.1109/infcom.2005.1498497
25. Raniwala, A., De, P., Sharma, S., Krishnan, R., Chiueh, T.C.: End-to-end flow fairness over IEEE based wireless mesh networks. In: Proceedings of the 26th Annual IEEE International Conference on Computer Communications (INFOCOM 2007). IEEE (2007). https://doi.org/ 10.1109/infcom.2007.281
26. Raniwala, A., Gopalan, K., Chiueh, T.C.: Centralized channel assignment and routing algorithms for multi-channel wireless mesh networks. ACM SIGMOBILE Mob. Comput. Commun. Rev. 8(2), 50–65 (2004). https://doi.org/10.1145/997122.997130
27. De, P., Raniwala, A., Sharma, S., Chiueh, T.C.: MiNT: a miniaturized network testbed for mobile wireless research. In: Proceedings of the 24th Annual Joint Conference of the IEEE Computer and Communications Societies (INFOCOM 2005), vol. 4, pp. 2731–2742 (2005). https://doi.org/10.1109/infcom.2005.1498556
28. De, P., Raniwala, A., Sharma, S., Chiueh, T.C.: Design considerations for a multihop wireless network testbed. IEEE Commun. Mag. 43(10), 102–109 (2005). https://doi.org/10. 1109/mcom.2005.1522132
29. De, P., et al.: MiNT-m: an autonomous mobile wireless experimentation platform. In: Proceedings of the 4th International Conference on Mobile Systems, Applications and Services (MobiSys 2006), pp. 124–137. ACM, New York (2006). https://doi.org/10.1145/ 1134680.1134694
30. Mitchell, C., Munishwar, V., Singh, S., Wang, X., Gopalan, K., Abu-Ghazaleh, N.: Testbed design and localization in MiNT-2: a miniaturized robotic platform for wireless protocol development and emulation. In: First International Communication Systems and Networks and Workshops (COMSNETS 2009), pp. 1–10 (2009). https://doi.org/10.1109/comsnets. 2009.4808866

31. Munishwar, V., Singh, S., Wang, X., Mitchell, C., Gopalan, K., Abu-Ghazaleh, N.: On the accuracy of RFID-based localization in a mobile wireless network testbed. In: IEEE International Conference on Pervasive Computing and Communications (PerCom 2009), pp. 1–6 (2009). https://doi.org/10.1109/percom.2009.4912872

32. Munishwar, V., Singh, S., Mitchell, C., Wang, X., Gopalan, K., Abu-Ghazaleh, N.: RFID based localization for a miniaturized robotic platform for wireless protocols evaluation. In: Proceedings of the 7th IEEE International Conference on Pervasive Computing and Communications (PerCom 2009), pp. 1–3 (2009). https://doi.org/10.1109/percom.2009.4912794

33. Paine, N.A.: Design and development of a modular robot for research use. Master thesis, The University of Texas at Austin, USA (2010)

34. Stovall, D., Paine, N., Petz, A., Enderle, J., Julien, C., Vishwanath, S.: Pharos: an application-oriented testbed for heterogeneous wireless networking environments. Technical report TR- UTEDGE-2009-006, The University of Texas at Austin (2009)

35. Petz, A., Jun, T., Roy, N., Fok, C.-L., Julien, C.: Passive network-awareness for dynamic resource-constrained networks. In: Felber, P., Rouvoy, R. (eds.) DAIS 2011. LNCS, vol. 6723, pp. 106–121. Springer, Heidelberg (2011). https://doi.org/10.1007/978-3-642-21387-8_9

36. Petz, A., Fok, C.L., Julien, C.: Experiences using a miniature vehicular network testbed. In: Proceedings of the Ninth ACM International Workshop on Vehicular Inter-networking, Systems, and Applications (VANET 2012), pp. 21–26. ACM, New York (2012). https://doi.org/10.1145/2307888.2307894

37. Petz, A., Bednarczyk, A., Paine, N., Stovall, D., Julien, C.: MaDMAN: a middleware for delay-tolerant mobile ad-hoc networks. Technical report TR-UTEDGE-2010-011, University of Texas at Austin (2010)

38. Petz, A., Fok, C.L., Julien, C., Walker, B., Ardi, C.: Network coded routing in delay tolerant networks: an experience report. In: Proceedings of the 3rd Extreme Conference on Communication: The Amazon Expedition (ExtremeCom 2011), pp. 4:1–4:6. ACM, New York (2011). https://doi.org/10.1145/2414393.2414397

39. Petz, A.: The Click Convergence Layer: Putting a Modular Router Under DTN2 (2010)

40. Fok, C., Petz, A., Stovall, D., Paine, N., Julien, C., Vishwanath, S.: Pharos: a testbed for mobile cyber-physical systems. Technical report TR-ARiSE-2011-001, University of Texas at Austin (2011)

41. Fok, C.L., et al.: A platform for evaluating autonomous intersection management policies. In: Proceedings of the IEEE/ACM Third International Conference on Cyber-Physical Systems (ICCPS 2012), pp. 87–96 (2012). https://doi.org/10.1109/iccps.2012.17

42. Killijian, M.O., Roy, M., Severac, G.: ARUM: a cooperative middleware and an experimentation platform for mobile systems. In: Proceedings of the IEEE 6th International Conference on Wireless and Mobile Computing, Networking and Communications (WiMob 2010), pp. 442–449 (2010). https://doi.org/10.1109/wimob.2010.5645030

43. Killijian, M.O., Roy, M., Severac, G.: The ARUM experimentation platform: an open tool to evaluate mobile systems applications. In: Rückert, U., Joaquin, S., Felix, W. (eds.) Advances in Autonomous Mini Robots, pp. 221–234. Springer, Heidelberg (2012). https://doi.org/10.1007/978-3-642-27482-4_22

44. Killijian, M.-O., Roy, M.: Data backup for mobile nodes: a cooperative middleware and an experimentation platform. In: Casimiro, A., de Lemos, R., Gacek, C. (eds.) WADS 2009. LNCS, vol. 6420, pp. 53–73. Springer, Heidelberg (2010). https://doi.org/10.1007/978-3-642-17245-8_3

45. Killijian, M.O., Powell, D., Roy, M., Sévérac, G.: Experimental evaluation of ubiquitous systems: why and how to reduce WiFi communication range. In: Proceedings of the 2nd International Conference on Distributed Event-Based Systems (DEBS 2008) (2008)

46. Federation for Future Internet Research and Experimentation (fed4fire): w-iLab.t - Fed4Fire (2015). http://www.fed4fire.eu/w-ilab-t/. Accessed 30 Nov 2015

47. Becue, P., Jooris, B., Sercu, V., Bouckaert, S., Moerman, I., Demeester, P.: Remote control of robots for setting up mobility scenarios during wireless experiments in the IBBT w-iLab.t. In: Korakis, T., Zink, M., Ott, M. (eds.) TridentCom 2012. LNICST, vol. 44, pp. 425–426. Springer, Heidelberg (2012). https://doi.org/10.1007/978-3-642-35576-9_51

48. Moerman, I., et al.: Toolkit for wireless mobility testbeds. Deliverable report Deliverable D3.5, OpenLab (2014)

49. Bouckaert, S., Jooris, B., Becue, P., Moerman, I., Demeester, P.: The IBBT w-iLab.t: a large-scale generic experimentation facility for heterogeneous wireless networks. In: Korakis, T., Zink, M., Ott, M. (eds.) TridentCom 2012. LNICST, vol. 44, pp. 7–8. Springer, Heidelberg (2012). https://doi.org/10.1007/978-3-642-35576-9_4

50. Abdelhadi, A., et al.: Position estimation of robotic mobile nodes in wireless testbed using GENI. In: Proceedings of the 2016 Annual IEEE Systems Conference (SysCon 2016), pp. 1–6. IEEE (2016)

51. Van Haute, T., et al.: Comparability of RF-based indoor localization solutions in heterogeneous environments: an experimental study. Int. J. Ad Hoc Ubiquit. Comput. 23 (1–2), 92–114 (2015)

52. Bouckaert, S., Vandenberghe, W., Jooris, B., Moerman, I., Demeester, P.: The w-iLab.t testbed. In: Magedanz, T., Gavras, A., Thanh, N.H., Chase, J.S. (eds.) TridentCom 2010. LNICST, vol. 46, pp. 145–154. Springer, Heidelberg (2011). https://doi.org/10.1007/978-3-642-17851-1_11

53. Neumann, A., López, E., Navarro, L.: Evaluation of mesh routing protocols for wireless community networks. Comput. Netw. Part 2 93, 308–323 (2015). https://doi.org/10.1016/j.comnet.2015.07.018

54. Viñas, R.B.: Evaluation of dynamic routing protocols on realistic wireless topologies. Ph.D. thesis, Autonomous University of Barcelona, Spain (2012)

55. Neumann, A., Lopez, E., Navarro, L.: An evaluation of BMX6 for community wireless networks. In: Proceedings of the 8th IEEE International Conference on Wireless and Mobile Computing, Networking and Communications (WiMob 2012), pp. 651–658 (2012). https://doi.org/10.1109/wimob.2012.6379145

56. Rensfelt, O., Hermans, F., Gunningberg, P., Larzon, L.Å., Björnemo, E.: Repeatable experiments with mobile nodes in a relocatable WSN testbed. Comput. J. 54(12), 1973–1986 (2011). https://doi.org/10.1093/comjnl/bxr052

57. Rensfelt, O., Ferm, F.H.C., Gunningberg, P., Larzon, L.Å.: Sensei-UU: a nomadic sensor network testbed supporting mobile nodes. Technical report 2009-025, Department of Information Technology, Uppsala University (2009)

58. Rensfelt, O., Hermans, F., Ferm, C., Larzon, L.A., Gunningberg, P.: Sensei - a flexible testbed for heterogeneous wireless sensor networks. In: Proceedings of the 5th International Conference on Testbeds and Research Infrastructures for the Development of Networks Communities and Workshops (TridentCom 2009), pp. 1–2 (2009). https://doi.org/10.1109/tridentcom.2009.4976218

59. Rensfelt, O., Hermans, F., Larzon, L.Å., Gunningberg, P.: Sensei-UU: a relocatable sensor network testbed. In: Proceedings of the Fifth ACM International Workshop on Wireless Network Testbeds, Experimental Evaluation and Characterization (WiNTECH 2010), pp. 63–70. ACM, New York (2010). https://doi.org/10.1145/1860079.1860091

60. Hermans, F., Rensfelt, O., Gunningberg, P., Larzon, L.-Å., Ngai, E.: Sensei-UU — a relocatable WSN testbed supporting repeatable node mobility. In: Magedanz, T., Gavras, A., Thanh, N.H., Chase, J.S. (eds.) TridentCom 2010. LNICST, vol. 46, pp. 612–614. Springer, Heidelberg (2011). https://doi.org/10.1007/978-3-642-17851-1_57
61. Arora, A., Ertin, E., Ramnath, R., Nesterenko, M., Leal, W.: Kansei: a high-fidelity sensing testbed. IEEE Internet Comput. **10**(2), 35–47 (2006). https://doi.org/10.1109/MIC.2006.37
62. Ertin, E., et al.: Kansei: a testbed for sensing at scale. In: The Fifth International Conference on Information Processing in Sensor Networks, IPSN 2006, pp. 399–406 (2006). https://doi.org/10.1109/ipsn.2006.243879
63. Giordano, V., Ballal, P., Lewis, F., Turchiano, B., Zhang, J.B.: Supervisory control of mobile sensor networks: math formulation, simulation, and implementation. IEEE Trans. Syst. Man Cybern. Part B Cybern. **36**(4), 806–819 (2006). https://doi.org/10.1109/TSMCB.2006.870647
64. Jayasingha, D., Jayawardhane, N., Karunanayake, P., Karunarathne, G., Dias, D.: Wireless sensor network testbed for mobile data communication. In: Proceedings of the 4th International Conference on Information and Automation for Sustainability (ICIAFS 2008), pp. 97–103 (2008). https://doi.org/10.1109/iciafs.2008.4783994
65. Forster, A., et al.: MOTEL: towards flexible mobile wireless sensor network testbeds. In: Proceedings of the 8th European Conference on Wireless Sensor Networks (EWSN 2011), Bonn, Germany, February 2011
66. Jiménez-González, A., Martínez-de Dios, J., Ollero, A.: An integrated testbed for heterogeneous mobile robots and other cooperating objects. In: Proceedings of the 2010 IEEE/RSJ International Conference on Intelligent Robots and Systems (IROS 2010), pp. 3327–3332 (2010). https://doi.org/10.1109/iros.2010.5650665
67. Jimenez-Gonzalez, A., Martinez-De Dios, J.R., Ollero, A.: An integrated testbed for cooperative perception with heterogeneous mobile and static sensors. Sensors **11**(12), 11516–11543 (2011). https://doi.org/10.3390/s111211516
68. Martinez-de Dios, J.R., Jimenez-Gonzalez, A., de San Bernabe, A., Ollero, A.: Introduction. In: Martinez-de Dios, J.R., Jimenez-Gonzalez, A., de San Bernabe, A., Ollero, A. (eds.) A Remote Integrated Testbed for Cooperating Objects. SpringerBriefs in Electrical and Computer Engineering, pp. 1–4. Springer, Cham (2014). https://doi.org/10.1007/978-3-319-01372-5_1
69. Martinez-de Dios, J.R., Jimenez-Gonzalez, A., de San Bernabe, A., Ollero, A.: CONET integrated testbed architecture. In: Martinez-de Dios, J.R., Jimenez-Gonzalez, A., de San Bernabe, A., Ollero, A. (eds.) A Remote Integrated Testbed for Cooperating Objects. SpringerBriefs in Electrical and Computer Engineering, pp. 23–39. Springer, Cham (2014). https://doi.org/10.1007/978-3-319-01372-5_3
70. Martinez-de Dios, J.R., Jimenez-Gonzalez, A., de San Bernabe, A., Ollero, A.: CONET integrated testbed experiments. In: Martinez-de Dios, J.R., Jimenez-Gonzalez, A., de San Bernabe, A., Ollero, A. (eds.) A Remote Integrated Testbed for Cooperating Objects, pp. 59–73. Springer, Cham (2014). https://doi.org/10.1007/978-3-319-01372-5_5
71. Vingelmann, P., Pedersen, M., Heide, J., Zhang, Q., Fitzek, F.: Data dissemination in the wild: a testbed for high-mobility MANETs. In: Proceedings of the 2012 IEEE International Conference on Communications (ICC 2012), pp. 291–296 (2012). https://doi.org/10.1109/icc.2012.6364123
72. Reich, J., Misra, V., Rubenstein, D.: Roomba MADNeT: a mobile ad-hoc delay tolerant network testbed. ACM SIGMOBILE Mob. Comput. Commun. Rev. **12**(1), 68–70 (2008). https://doi.org/10.1145/1374512.1374536

73. Vingelmann, P., Heide, J., Pedersen, M.V., Zhang, Q., Fitzek, F.H.P.: All-to-all data dissemination with network coding in dynamic MANETs. Comput. Netw. **74**(Part B), 34–47 (2014). https://doi.org/10.1016/j.comnet.2014.06.018

74. Reich, J., Misra, V., Rubenstein, D.S., Zussman, G.: Spreadable connected autonomic networks (SCAN). Technical report CUCS-016-08 (2008)

75. Reich, J., Misra, V., Rubenstein, D., Zussman, G.: Connectivity maintenance in mobile wireless networks via constrained mobility. IEEE J. Sel. Areas Commun. **30**(5), 935–950 (2012). https://doi.org/10.1109/JSAC.2012.120609

76. Dahlberg, T.A., Nasipuri, A., Taylor, C.: Explorebots: a mobile network experimentation testbed. In: Proceedings of the 2005 ACM SIGCOMM Workshop on Experimental Approaches to Wireless Network Design and Analysis (E-WIND 2005), pp. 76–81. ACM, New York (2005). https://doi.org/10.1145/1080148.108015

77. Bromage, S., et al.: SCORPION: a heterogeneous wireless networking testbed. ACM SIGMOBILE Mob. Comput. Commun. Rev. **13**(1), 65–68 (2009). https://doi.org/10.1145/1558590.1558604

78. Förster, A., Förster, A., Garg, K., Puccinelli, D., Giordano, S., Gambardella, L.M.: MOTEL-a mobile robotic-assisted wireless sensor networks testbed. In: Wireless Integration of Sensor Networks in Hybrid Architectures, p. 13 (2012)

79. Foerster, A., Foerster, A., Garg, K., Giordano, S., Gambardella, L.M.: MOTEL: mobility enabled wireless sensor network testbed. Adhoc Sensor Wirel. Netw. **24**(3) (2015)

80. Janansefat, S., Senturk, I., Akkaya, K., Gloff, M.: A mobile sensor network testbed using irobots. In: 37th Annual IEEE Conference on Local Computer Networks (LCN 2012), Clearwater, FL, 22–25 October 2012 (2012)

81. Janansefat, S., Akkaya, K., Senturk, I., Gloff, M.: Rethinking connectivity restoration in WSNs using feedback from a low-cost mobile sensor network testbed. In: IEEE 38th Conference on Local Computer Networks Workshops (LCN 2013), pp. 108–115 (2013). https://doi.org/10.1109/lcnw.2013.6758506

82. Senturk, I., Akkaya, K., Janansefat, S.: Towards realistic connectivity restoration in partitioned mobile sensor networks. Int. J. Commun. Syst. **29**(2), 230–250 (2016). https://doi.org/10.1002/dac.2819

83. Tonneau, A.S., Mitton, N., Vandaele, J.: How to choose an experimentation platform for wireless sensor networks? A survey on static and mobile wireless sensor network experimentation facilities. Ad Hoc Netw. **30**, 115–127 (2015). https://doi.org/10.1016/j.adhoc.2015.03.002

84. Tonneau, A.S., Mitton, N., Vandaele, J.: A Survey on (mobile) wireless sensor network experimentation testbeds. In: Proceedings of the 2014 IEEE International Conference on Distributed Computing in Sensor Systems (DCOSS 2014), pp. 263–268 (2014). https://doi.org/10.1109/dcoss.2014.41

85. Fleury, E., Mitton, N., Noel, T., Adjih, C.: FIT IoT-LAB: the largest IoT open experimental testbed. ERCIM News **101**(14) (2015)

86. Burin des Rosiers, C., et al.: SensLAB. In: Korakis, T., Li, H., Tran-Gia, P., Park, H.-S. (eds.) TridentCom 2011. LNICST, vol. 90, pp. 239–254. Springer, Heidelberg (2012). https://doi.org/10.1007/978-3-642-29273-6_19

87. Rosiers, C.B.D., et al.: SensLAB Very Large Scale Open Wireless Sensor Network Testbed (2011)

88. Quilez, R., Zeeman, A., Mitton, N., Vandaele, J.: Docking autonomous robots in passive docks with Infrared sensors and QR codes. In: Proceedings of the 10th International Conference on Testbeds and Research Infrastructures for the Development of Networks and Communities (TRIDENTCOM 2015), pp. 113–122 (2015)

89. IoT-LAB Team: IoT-LAB Mobile Robot (2015). https://www.iot-lab.info/robots/. Accessed 30 Nov 2015
90. Choumas, K., et al.: Optimization driven multi-hop network design and experimentation: the approach of the FP7 project OPNEX. IEEE Commun. Mag. **50**(6), 122–130 (2012). https://doi.org/10.1109/MCOM.2012.6211496
91. Giatsios, D., Apostolaras, A., Korakis, T., Tassiulas, L.: Methodology and tools for measurements on wireless testbeds: the NITOS approach. In: Fàbrega, L., Vilà, P., Careglio, D., Papadimitriou, D. (eds.) Measurement Methodology and Tools. LNCS, vol. 7586, pp. 61–80. Springer, Heidelberg (2013). https://doi.org/10.1007/978-3-642-41296-7_5
92. Keranidis, S., et al.: Experimentation on end-to-end performance aware algorithms in the federated en- vironment of the heterogeneous PlanetLab and NITOS testbeds. Comput. Netw. **63**, 48–67 (2014). https://doi.org/10.1016/j.bjp.2013.12.026
93. Keranidis, S., Kazdaridis, G., Passas, V., Korakis, T., Koutsopoulos, I., Tassiulas, L.: NITOS energy monitoring framework: real time power monitoring in experimental wireless network deployments. SIGMOBILE Mob. Comput. Commun. Rev. **18**(1), 64–74 (2014). https://doi.org/10.1145/2581555.2581566
94. Pechlivanidou, K., Katsalis, K., Igoumenos, I., Katsaros, D., Korakis, T., Tassiulas, L.: NITOS testbed: a cloud based wireless experimentation facility. In: Proceedings of the 26th International Teletraffic Congress (ITC 2014), pp. 1–6 (2014). https://doi.org/10.1109/itc.2014.6932976
95. Niavis, H., Kazdaridis, G., Korakis, T., Tassiulas, L.: Enabling sensing and mobility on wireless testbeds. In: Korakis, T., Zink, M., Ott, M. (eds.) TridentCom 2012. LNICST, vol. 44, pp. 421–424. Springer, Heidelberg (2012). https://doi.org/10.1007/978-3-642-35576-9_50
96. Muchtar, F., Abdullah, A.H., Latiff, M.S.A., Hassan, S., Wahab, M.H.A., Abdul-Salaam, G.: A technical review of MANET testbed using mobile robot technology. In: Journal of Physics: Conference Series (2018, manuscript submitted for publication)
97. Muchtar, F., Abdullah, A.H., Arshad, M.M., Wahab, M.H.A., Ahmmad, S.N.Z., Abdul-Salaam, G.: A critical review of MANET testbed using mobile robot technology. In: Journal of Physics: Conference Series (2018, manuscript submitted for publication)
98. Muchtar, F., Abdullah, A.H., Wahab, M.H.A., Ambar, R., Hanafi, H.F., Ahmmad, S.N.Z.: Mobile ad hoc network testbed using mobile robot technology. In: Journal of Physics: Conference Series (2018, manuscript submitted for publication)

Software Defined Network-Based Vehicular Adhoc Networks for Intelligent Transportation System: Recent Advances and Future Challenges

Hardik Trivedi, Sudeep Tanwar[✉], and Priyank Thakkar

Department of Computer Engineering, Institute of Technology,
Nirma University, Ahmedabad 382481, Gujarat, India
hardiktrivedi544@gmail.com,
{sudeep.tanwar,priyank.thakkar}@nirmauni.ac.in

Abstract. With the worldwide growth in vehicles due to the increase in population, Vehicular ad hoc networks (VANETs) have attracted researchers both from academia as well as the industry. It provides a smart and efficient driving experience for drivers. Traditional VANET suffers from various issues of security, QoS, and latency. To address these problems, software-defined network (SDN) based VANET is one of the key components in the field of transportation systems. It plays an important role in VANET and also provides features such as flexibility and programmability. It also deals with security, dynamism and heterogeneous features of the VANET environment. It helps the VANET in scalability and dynamic deciding the optimal path and aids the routing in situations of a congestion in VANET. In this paper, we have explored the suitability of SDN in VANET. We have also compared the various state-of-the-art approaches existing. These approaches are based on the concepts of clustering, geo broadcast, road side unit (RSU) based Geocast, fog and SDN based VANET, cloud-based VANET. It is evident from the literature that SDN based VANET provides better QoS, latency, and also efficiently handles heterogeneity. It also has good efficiency in comparison to a traditional network. Security is a crucial parameter in the SDN and hence has been explored in the paper. We have further highlight the open issues and challenges encountered while merging the VANET with SDN. This paper give insights to the researchers willing to start work in this domain.

Keywords: SDN · VANET · Heterogeneity · QoS · Latency
Security

1 Introduction

Nowadays in the field of vehicular adhoc network (VANET) many researchers are working on emerging challenges and applications which aid the development of Intelligent Transport System (ITS). VANET is similar to MANET in which, each and every vehicle behaves as a single node. Most of the vehicles use GPS and OBU (On Board Unit), equipped with sensors and communication hardware. Here, vehicles may

© Springer Nature Singapore Pte Ltd. 2019
P. K. Singh et al. (Eds.): FTNCT 2018, CCIS 958, pp. 325–337, 2019.
https://doi.org/10.1007/978-981-13-3804-5_24

communicate with other vehicles, vehicle communicates with RSU or directly to a controller. Traditional networks are unable to provide flexibility, scalability while managing high mobility [1].

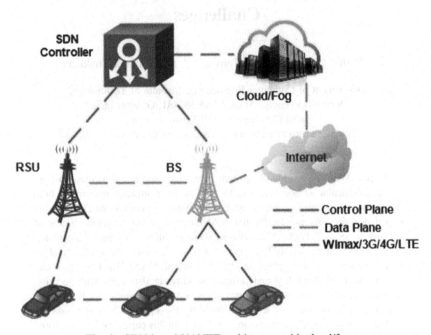

Fig. 1. SDN based VANET architecture with cloud/fog

Majority of these issues can be solved using the SDN paradigm. Here, the control plane and data plane are separated from each other. The north bound and south bound APIs provides a more secure communication. It also provides better QoS, better resource management, low latency and good packet delivery ratio (PDR) in VANET [2, 3]. To meet the different requirements of VANET, different SDN based architectures were exist in the literature. Out of theses architectures, SDN-based VANET architecture can be of three forms: centralized, distributed and hybrid. Some of the VANET use clustering approach to reduce the burden of RSU and BS and form a cluster number of the messages between V2V (vehicle to vehicle) are increased and the number of messages between V2I (vehicle to infrastructure) is decreased [4]. Basic SDN-based VANET architecture with cloud/fog computing is shown in Fig. 1.

1.1 Motivation

We have surveyed many research papers related to the domain to motivate the researchers in the direction of SDN-based Vehicular Adhoc network. SDN has brought new features in the field of VANET but at the same time it is vulnerable to new threats.

Security is one of the key feature for any system but only few papers have fully explored this parameter into details. VANET sometimes work on the multiple applications at a time like route optimization, track analysis, security-based applications, hazard notifications. For this multiple requirements like QoS, Latency, heterogeneity, and security should be taken in to consideration.

1.2 Research Contributions

Following are research contributions of our paper:

- In this paper, we have surveyed different approaches and provide parametric comparisons based on detailed taxonomy, which may help the researchers willing to start in SDN-based VANET.
- We also compared different architectures of SDN-based VANET involve QoS, latency, heterogeneity, and security.
- We have also provide the open issues and challenges.

The rest of the paper is organized as follows: Sect. 2 contains details of current approaches of SDN-based VANET and their comparisons with impact of each. Section 3 describes the open issues and challenges in SDN-based VANET. Section 4 concludes the paper with future scope.

2 Literature Review

We have extensively surveyed many research papers and identified the four main parameters used for the main taxonomy of our review paper. Integration of SDN with VANET mainly depends upon these four identified parameters. These four parameters are: QoS, Latency, Security, and Heterogeneity. Main taxonomy of SDN-based VANET is shown in Fig. 2. SDN can easily manage issues like congestion, resilience etc. The detailed description of each sub taxonomy is explained in next subsections.

2.1 QoS

Duan et al. [5] proposed a special architecture on VCPS (Vehicular Cyber Physical Systems). It work on the location-based routing protocol. The architecture is classified into three levels, the RSU, an OpenFlow switch, and a global SDN controller. Vehicle sends a request to the RSU, if the data is found a reply is given else the same request is forwarded to the switch by RSU. The same computation is performed at second level, if the data is found, a response is given to the RSU by switch or else the request is forwarded to the main global controller. Through simulation they claimed, when the vehicle speed was 180 km/h success ratio was 92%. This approach works better than multi-hop routing algorithm. QoS sub-taxonomy is shown in Fig. 3.

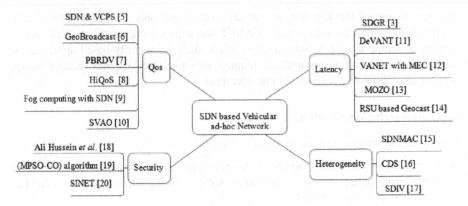

Fig. 2. Main taxonomy of SDN based VANET

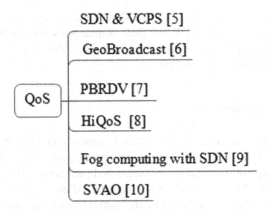

Fig. 3. Sub-taxonomy for QoS

Liu et al. [6] proposed the idea of GeoBroadcast in VANET. Here, the Floodlight was used as a controller. Mainly, there are two components in this architecture, switch management component with topology management and the routing component. They considered different scenarios like static event scenario and moving event scenario. The application of the idea is to notify a user about the emergency. User may request to locate the RSUs, which may get the results on a google map. The application administrator may select a particular area; to send the emergency notification and range of the Geodestination can be selected by admin; to notify the user in a particular area. The controller's overhead is reduced by 2 to 8% and the bandwidth consumption is reduced by 20 to 40% through this approach.

Khan et al. [7] improved the routing protocol proposed by Ian et al. for better performance. This algorithm assumes that all vehicles are equipped with GPS. They informs the speed and direction to the controller at a time interval *t*. Using these details, if required, the controller makes changes in the flow table after receiving the required information from the vehicles. Mainly two algorithms are used: update controller algorithm and topology prediction algorithm. In conventional algorithm, the SDN performance is degraded but in [7], the topology prediction is used. Which reduce the case of decrease in performance during an event of a controller miss. Researchers aim to extend the work in the SDN-based VANET architecture for an autonomous unmanned vehicle.

Jinyao et al. [8] proposed an approach of HIQoS to reduce the delay, increase the throughput, and the QoS of SDN-based VANET is increased. They used Content Delivery Network (CDN) to improve the QoS. HIQOS differentiation of requirements can be done on the bases of IP, MAC address, trac header, and type of service (TOS). When a request with more value appears, the amount of total bandwidth congestion take place in the network increases. Which reduces the QoS performance of the network. To overcome this problem, multipath components are used. To validate the results HIQoS was compared with LIQoS and MIQoS. This approach is better in resilience and recovery time of HIQoS much lesser then MIQoS. Truong et al. [9] proposed idea of using SDN in VANET with fog computing (FC) to optimize resource utility and latency. When the number of nodes are exponentially increased in the network then the QoS decreases. FC provides low latency, location awareness and mobility support which are useful in VANET. Here, the central data centers and edge devices share their resources. They also used hypervisors to virtualize the resource. BS and RSU use fog orchestration for forwarding rules and service hosting.

Dong et al. [10] proposed SDN-based on-demand routing protocol named as SVAO. It is a Map based protocol which used road topology and consider the road information into the account. This contains two level, where the first level is the global level (GL) and the second level is the local level (LL). LL computes the routes for vehicles and maintains link between resources, whereas the GL is responsible for finding the accurate location of the vehicle and also calculate the global route. When path request is received by RSU first it checks whether the requested node is in range or not. If node is not in the range then the LL sends a request to the second level for node's location. Parameters like vehicles velocity and density make a change in the throughput. It outperforms compared to other state-of-the-arts approaches in term of latency and PDR. Although, it is not suitable for sparse VANET.

2.2 Latency

Xiang et al. [3] proposed an SDN-based geographic based routing protocol (SDGR), where the central controller collects all the details and provides a global view. It further eliminates the problem of local maxima. It is the combination of optimal path forwarding algorithm and packet forwarding algorithm. Here, overhead is less because unlike topology based protocol nodes does not need to update link status. SDN controller takes the better decisions on the bases of combined information rather than details which are individually received from each node. It outperforms compared to traditional algorithms like AODV and GPSR in both PDR and delay. For a sparse network, it provides better result because of SDN controller's global view. Subtaxonomy diagram for latency is shown in Fig. 4.

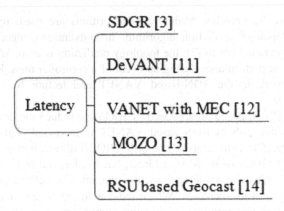

Fig. 4. Sub-taxonomy for latency

Kazmi et al. [11] claimed that SDN provides many features in VANET, but its performance degraded for large network. To address this issue, researchers proposed partitioning of VANET in distributed manner. The controller level is distributed in two level such as a domain controller (DC) and a root controller (RC) and both have a stable communication link. DC periodically send domain information to RC for a global view. When DC finds the faulty link it sends a message to RC for link update and also for change in flow tables. They performed simulation in VENIS with different traffic flow (TF) patterns were taken into consideration such as the number of the domain controllers and root controllers are increased or decreased. Liu et al. [12] proposed idea of using Mobile Edge Computing (MEC) with SDN in VANET. It achieved good responsiveness and scalability. They used 5G cellular network which provide speed of 7.5 Gb/s in a stable situation and can also provide speed of 1.2 Gb/s in a mobile environment where vehicle's speed is 100 km/h. This approach is useful in VANET applications like collision avoidance which requires better efficiency and also low latency. To keep details of vehicle's location, continuous messages to be sent, but it may over flow the capacity of single switch or distributed SDN controller, so prediction is the best solution. This can be overcomes using seamless handover, network partition and reliable communication in controller miss situation.

Lin et al. [13] proposed an idea of only using the V2V communication and clustering. They used self-organizing mobility based architecture, where cluster, captain vehicle (CV) is responsible for each area and other member's communication. The CV keeps information about other vehicles with the help of approaches such as combined location and velocity tree (CLV-tree). Which is a combination of B+ tree and hash table. Different activities like new captain selection, merging two zones, splitting zones is based on this CLV tree. Another algorithm they have used is MOZO which is compared with Beacon-less Routing Algorithm (BRAVE) for Vehicular Environments and Clustering-Based Directional Routing Protocol (CBDRP). Different scenarios like effect of message delivery distance, number of vehicles and number of messages to be sent were taken into consideration. Network traffic is less in MOZO then BRAVE and CBDRP, PDR of MOZO is also better. Peng et al. [14] used RSU assisted Geocast

(RAG) in SDN-based VANET to solve the issue of delivering the message using minimal cost. They have decomposed the network in a hierarchical manner and used the concept of election of optimal RSU for forwarding message. Geocast particularly targets some location and to make it easy quadtree model was used. The quadtree is a model in which root refers to the whole region and it has four children. They used different color representation to explain quadtree structure. When vehicle wants to communicate with the destination, first it checks that destination node exists in its communication range or not, if yes, then they directly communicate, otherwise, message is sent to nearest RSU. It finds out nearest RSU to the destination and also use quadtree concept, trajectory prediction concept and then forwards the packet to the most suitable optimal RSU. Finally, nearest RSU from destination sends the message to the destination. This approach was compared with other approaches of similar nature like flood and random and it outperform better in terms of delivery cost.

2.3   Heterogeneity

Luo et al. [15] proposed a hybrid architecture in VANET for managing physical resources and also to provide pre-warning collision as well as support topology change. It is based on TDMA and time is partitioned in the equal size of frames. If RSU detects collision then time slot is reallocated. A vehicle is not directly controlled by the controller because this architecture follows two-level hierarchy. In traditional VANET, all request were not served because of mobility, but in this approach scheduling is done on the bases of vehicle's velocity so most of the request is served. This approach was compared with other algorithms like STDMA and VeMAC. The number of packet loss and number of collisions were less in sdnMAC. Sub-taxonomy for heterogeneity is shown in Fig. 5.

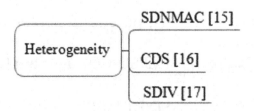

Fig. 5. Sub-taxonomy for heterogeneity

Liu et al. [16] proposed a novel idea of using Cooperative Data Scheduling (CDS) in hybrid SDN-based VANET. The ultimate goal is to serve the maximum number of request. Here, two service channel were used, one was for I2V communication and second was for V2V communication. Each vehicle has own record of requested items and vehicle can transmit or receive only one data item in one scheduling period. Some of the parameters which were taken into consideration in this algorithm are gain of scalability, broadcast productivity, distribution of gains, service ratio and service delay. It outperforms as compared to MRF and FCFS in areas of mean delay, service ratio, broadcast productivity and gain of scalability. They have not considered the coordination among RSUs which is required to support the concept of a logically centralized controller in a distributed network. Wang et al. [17] proposed an SDN-based IoV (SDIV). The main goal is to reduce number of rule installation without degrading performance. By using SDN and the centralized controller (global view), optimal path selection is achieved. It served real-time query service which is typical in IoV. It is three-layer architecture such as- physical layer, controller layer, and application layer. The vehicle can communicate with the controller using nearby access point (AP), controller installs rules in advance so when vehicle reach near to a particular AP issues are not raised. To serve multiple requests at once idea of one rule is defined for a rule which has the same destination, known as the multicast address for the last hop. It outperforms with simple rule installation in terms of latency and also less number of rule installation is required to implement it.

2.4 Security

Hussein et al. [18] proposed an integration between SDN, 5G, and VANET to provide mobility, performance, and security. This approach secured the system from attacks like Distributed Denial of Service (DDOS) and can also trace back the source of the attack. When vehicle wants to connect to the network for the first time, it sends a request to RSU. It is assisted by FC, so it can manage the normal operation and light weighted security module operations. RSU forwards the vehicle's request to the main controller. When vehicle sends connect request for the second time, a key can be generated by RSU or controller but the only controller can generate the certificate. IP/ID binding of the vehicle is done so that IP spoofing can be detected. This architecture prevents attacks and also have the capacity to track back the source of the attack. Sub-taxonomy for security is shown in Fig. 6.

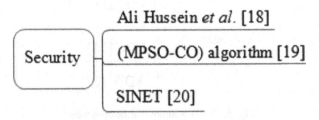

Fig. 6. Sub-taxonomy for security

Xiuli et al. [19] proposed an idea of using FC in SDN-based VANET to provide less latency and support mobility and location awareness. They proposed modified constrained optimization particle swarm optimization (MPSO-CO) algorithm. To reduce the burden of cloud computing (CC) researchers introduce the idea of using CC with FC and SDN. The architecture is divided into layers as cloud server, SDN server, RSU, and vehicles. Fog network is composed of fragmented network devices, so fog focus on load balancing and for that algorithm is proposed. They have used particle swarm optimization (PSO) algorithm has strong global search ability, but PSO cannot be used for constraint optimization thus PSO-CO was used. The latency of this algorithm is less than cloud and fog. Quan et al. [20] proposed a new approach of smart identifier networking (SINET) with crowd collaboration. Crowd collaborate adapt to different vehicle scenario and application and provides intra-slice and inter-slice collaborations. There is security slice also so when it detects attack it calls collaborative nodes and build the defensive line and then defend or counter attack it. This approach guarantees network security, supports the heterogeneous communication and the load balancing. It was compared with 4G-LTE and it has low RTT time then 4G-LTE. The comparative analysis of state-of-the-art approaches exist for SDN-based VANET is given in Table 1.

Table 1. Comparative analysis of various state-of-the-art approaches exist in the literature for SDN-based VANET

Approach	Objective	QoS	Latency	Security	Hete.	Pros	Cons
SDGR [3]	Remove local maxima and sparse connectivity issue from routing protocol	Moderate	Good	Low	Low	No local maxima and sparse connectivity issue in routing protocol	Heavy control overhead occurs while maintaining the network topology
SDN & VCPS [5]	Designing efficient and stable routing algorithm for VANET	Moderate	Moderate	Low	Low	Efficiency	Security
GeoBroadcast [6]	Reduce latency, network over-load	Good	Good	Low	Low	Low network overhead, Reduce latency, less network bandwidth consumption	Security
PBRDV [7]	Improved routing protocol	Moderate	Moderate	Low	Low	Good PDR in controller miss situation	Periodic update so more re-source utilization
HiQoS [8]	Improve the current QOS of networks	Good	Moderate	Low	Moderate	Reduced delay	Single point of failure
Fog computing with SDN [9]	Increase flexibility, scalability, programmability	Good	Good	Low	Moderate	Good resource utilization, openflow secure channel for communication	Cost
SVAO [10]	Improve data transmission efficiency in VANET	Moderate	Moderate	Low	Low	Improved communication efficiency	Considered only one way road, Not suitable for spars VANET

(continued)

Table 1. (continued)

Approach	Objective	QoS	Latency	Security	Hete.	Pros	Cons
DeVANET [11]	Performance gain then traditional network	Moderate	Good	Low	Low	Better performance than decentralized clustering based algorithm	Local maxima
VANET-MEC [12]	To meet dynamic application requirements	Moderate	Good	Low	Moderate	Low latency, high reliability, good scalability and responsiveness	No reliable communication in the controller-miss situation
MOZO [13]	Reduce communication over-head	Moderate	Moderate	Low	Low	Good PDR	Vehicle to vehicle communication only, local maxima
RSU-based Geocast [14]	Minimized forwarding cost, optimal forwarding	Moderate	Good	Moderate	Moderate	Scalability, flexibility, inter-operability	Local view only
sdnMAC [15]	Manage the physical resources in vehicular ad-hoc networks (VANETs)	Moderate	Low	Low	Moderate	Prewarning of collision. Ability to topology change	Security
CDS [16]	Maximize the number of vehicles that retrieve their requested data	Moderate	Moderate	Low	Moderate	Improved QOS	vehicles cannot transmit and receive a data item at the same time
SDIV [17]	Real time query service in SDN VANET	Moderate	Moderate	Low	Moderate	Less rule installation, good data plane data transmission	Security
Hussein et al. [18]	Good balance between network, mobility, performance and security	Good	Good	Moderate	Moderate	Improved security	Extra overhead of process ing Difficulty of time syn chronization
MPSO-CO [19]	Lighten the burden of the cloud and decrease task processing latency	Good	Good	Moderate	Moderate	Decreased latency, increased QOS, load balancing	Cost, single point of failure
SINET [20]	Improve VANET	Good	Good	Good	Moderate	Good PDR	Single point of failure

3   Open Issues and Challenges

Integrating the SDN with VANET is not an easy task. This integration have some issues such as heterogeneity, cost, security, performance in the controller miss situation as compared to the traditional network. Following are the open issues and challenges which needs to be addressed by the researchers:

- VANET consist of devices like RSU, BS, IOT enabled devices, etc. All the devices used different communication standards. Hence, it is difficult to maintain synchronization among the devices.
- During synchronization of all the devices, latency must be taken in to consideration.
- Some VANET architectures are centralized and can be the single point of failure. Moreover, sometimes controller suffers from overload and cannot give appropriate results. Decentralized architecture can be used to address this issue of a single controller. Further, issues like local-maxima, no idea of the global view are also taken into consideration.
- Integration of SDN with VANET includes other technologies like 5G, FC and CC which provides feature like low latency, good PDR. It also give high-performance but at the same time overall cost increases.
- Although SDN provides security, but it is vulnerable to new attacks. So security in VANET need to be considered. Also, the attacks on communication north bound and South bound API are also crucial to handle.
- IP spoofing, sending dummy request to the controller, ultimately controller is busy with communication and cannot perform its dedicated task.

4   Conclusions

SDN plays a key role in VANET. It overcomes the issue of traditional network such as-heterogeneity, cost, security and performance in connection loss and has brought the new scope of technology in VANET. It is flexible, programmable and also provides many other features like low latency, high throughput. Although many proposals exist in the literature which were focused on integration of SDN with VANET. Keeping the above mentioned issues into consideration, in this paper, we have provided a detailed survey of suitability of SDN in VANET. We have also highlighted the various issues and challenges encountered by the researchers while integrating the SDN with VANET. Some of them are using clustering, geographic routing, 5G as a communication, network slicing. To maintain the perfect balance between performance, security, and cost in VANET are challenging task.

References

1. Chahal, M., Harit, S., Mishra, K.K., Sangaiah, A.K., Zheng, Z.: A survey on software-defined networking in vehicular ad hoc networks: Challenges, applications and use cases, Sustainable Cities and Society (2017)

2. Ku, I., Lu, Y., Gerla, M., Ongaro, F., Gomes, R.L., Cerqueira, E.: Towards software-defined VANET: architecture and services. In: 2014 13th Annual Mediterranean Ad Hoc Networking Workshop (MED-HOC-NET), pp. 103–110. IEEE (2014)

3. Ji, X., Yu, H., Fan, G., Fu, W.: SDGR: an SDN-based geographic routing protocol for vanet. In: 2016 IEEE International Conference on Internet of Things (iThings) and IEEE Green Computing and Communications (GreenCom) and IEEE Cyber, Physical and Social Computing (CPSCom) and IEEE Smart Data (SmartData), pp. 276–281. IEEE (2016)

4. Duan, X., Liu, Y., Wang, X.: SDN enabled 5G-VANET: adaptive vehicle clustering and beamformed transmission for aggregated traffic. IEEE Commun. Mag. **55**(7), 120127 (2017)

5. Duan, P., Peng, C., Zhu, Q., Shi, J., Cai, H.: Design and analysis of software defined vehicular cyber physical systems. In: 2014 20th IEEE International Conference on Parallel and Distributed Systems (ICPADS), pp. 412–417. IEEE (2014)

6. Liu, Y.-C., Chen, C., Chakraborty, S.: A software defined network architecture for geobroadcast in VANETs. In: 2015 IEEE International Conference on Communications (ICC), pp. 6559–6564. IEEE (2015)

7. Khan, A.U., Ratha, B.K.: Time series prediction QoS routing in software defined vehicular ad-hoc network. In: 2015 International Conference on Man and Machine Interfacing (MAMI), pp. 1–6. IEEE (2015)

8. Jinyao, Y., Hailong, Z., Qianjun, S., Bo, L., Xiao, G.: HiQoS: an SDN-based multipath QoS solution. China Commun. **12**(5), 123–133 (2015)

9. Truong, N.B., Lee, G.M., Ghamri-Doudane, Y.: Software defined networking based vehicular adhoc network with fog computing. In: 2015 IFIP/IEEE International Symposium on Integrated Network Management (IM), pp. 1202–1207. IEEE (2015)

10. Dong, B., Wu, W., Yang, Z., Li, J.: Software defined networking based on demand routing protocol in vehicle ad hoc networks. In: 2016 12th International Conference on Mobile Ad-Hoc and Sensor Networks (MSN), pp. 207–213. IEEE (2016)

11. Kazmi, A., Khan, M.A., Akram, M.U.: DeVANET: decentralized software-defined VANET architecture. In: 2016 IEEE International Conference on Cloud Engineering Workshop (IC2EW), pp. 42–47. IEEE (2016)

12. Liu, J., Wan, J., Zeng, B., Wang, Q., Song, H., Qiu, M.: A scalable and quick response software defined vehicular network assisted by mobile edge computing. IEEE Commun. Mag. **55**(7), 94–100 (2017)

13. Lin, D., Kang, J., Squicciarini, A., Wu, Y., Gurung, S., Tonguz, O.: MoZo: a moving zone based routing protocol using pure V2 V communication in VANETs. IEEE Trans. Mob. Comput. **16**(5), 1357–1370 (2017)

14. Li, P., Zhang, T., Huang, C., Chen, X., Fu, B.: RSU-assisted geocast in vehicular ad hoc networks. IEEE Wirel. Commun. **24**(1), 53–59 (2017)

15. Luo, G., Jia, S., Liu, Z., Zhu, K., Zhang, L.: sdnMAC: a software defined networking based mac protocol in VANETs. In: 2016 IEEE/ACM 24th International Symposium on Quality of Service (IWQoS), pp. 1–2. IEEE (2016)

16. Liu, K., Ng, J.K., Lee, V.C., Son, S.H., Stojmenovic, I.: Cooperative data scheduling in hybrid vehicular ad hoc networks: VANET as a software defined network. IEEE/ACM Trans. Netw. **24**(17), 1759–1773 (2016)

17. Wang, X., Wang, C., Zhang, J., Zhou, M., Jiang, C.: Improved rule installation for real-time query service in software-defined internet of vehicles. IEEE Trans. Intell. Transp. Syst. **18** (2), 225–235 (2017)
18. Hussein, A., Elhajj, I.H., Chehab, A., Kayssi, A.: SDN VANETs in 5G: an architecture for resilient security services. In: 2017 Fourth International Conference on Software Defined Systems (SDS), pp. 67–74. IEEE (2017)
19. He, X., Ren, Z., Shi, C., Fang, J.: A novel load balancing strategy of software defined cloud/fog networking in the internet of vehicles. China Commun. **13**(2), 140–149 (2016)
20. Quan, W., Liu, Y., Zhang, H., Yu, S.: Enhancing crowd collaborations for software defined vehicular networks. IEEE Commun. Mag. **55**(8), 80–86 (2017)

P-TORA: A TORA Modification Under TCP E2E-NewReno Model

Radhika Patel[✉], Bimal Patel, Sandip Patel, and Amit Parmar

Charusat University, Anand, Gujarat, India
radhipatel999@gmail.com,
{bimalpatel.it, amitparmar.it}@charusat.ac.in,
sandippatel872@gmail.com

Abstract. Mobile Ad-hoc network, generally recognized as MANET is a non-wired, self-reliant and multi-hop network comprising of portable nodes that acts like a router in the network-system. It is a dynamic network having no central control. Evaluating the performance of MANET routing protocol is a present research topic. Reactive type of MANET routing protocol is popularly used nowadays because of the amenities provided by them. TORA (Temporally Ordered Routing Algorithm) is on-demand (Reactive) protocol. It is highly adaptive, multihop and the best for dense networks. This paper describes MANET along with the detailed study of TORA and the Proposed TORA protocol with some modifications in Original TORA. The modifications are done using TCP E2E New Reno operating model with the intention to enhance the performance of Original TORA. The new protocol was born and the name given is P-TORA. NS2 (Network Simulator 2) is a simulation tool used for measuring the performance of TORA and P-TORA in the MANET.

Keywords: Mobile Adhoc networks · Reactive routing · Proactive routing
Hybrid protocols · TORA · TCP E2E New Reno · P-TORA
Energy consumption · PDR · NS2

1 Introduction

Mobile Ad Hoc network is a non-wired (wireless) network having no specific infrastructure. In MANET, each and every node plays a role of router without depending on any other mechanism and any centralized control. Design, deployment as well as performance of MANET are affected by the factors such as multicasting, medium access scheme, management of energy consumption, route self-discovery, scalability and security [1] (Fig. 1).

In comparison of all other networks, MANETs are preferred because of its easy establishment, high scalability factor, and self-governed nodes. MANETs are to be improved in case of physical security, and authorization service [10]. Moreover, malicious attacks are slight difficult to handle in MANET. The main challenge of wireless Adhoc network is routing. This is because of the dynamic nature of this type of networks [11].

© Springer Nature Singapore Pte Ltd. 2019
P. K. Singh et al. (Eds.): FTNCT 2018, CCIS 958, pp. 338–349, 2019.
https://doi.org/10.1007/978-981-13-3804-5_25

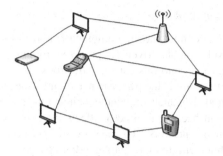

Fig. 1. MANET network

There needs some set of rules for successful communication between all the nodes of MANET. Routing protocols plays a significant and important role in the process of communication in MANET [2] (Fig. 2).

Routing protocols are divided into 3 categories depending on their working mechanism [12]. These are:

(a) Reactive type of routing protocols
(b) Proactive type of routing protocols
(c) Hybrid type of routing protocols.

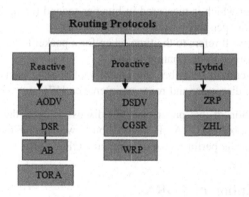

Fig. 2. Classification of routing protocols [2].

1. Reactive type of routing protocols:

These type of protocols do not store any type of topological information about any of the nodes of the network. They obtain and exchange necessary and significant information as and when required [3]. Examples of these type of protocols are AODV, DSR, TORA, ABR etc.

2. Proactive type of routing protocols:

These type of protocols stores and maintains topological information of all or at least neighboring nodes in the tabular format [2]. At some fix instance of time, the information is exchanged between nodes. Examples of these routing protocols are DSDV, CGSR, WRP, etc.

3. Hybrid type of routing protocols:

These type of protocols are those having combined features of on demand routing i.e. reactive protocols as well as table-driven i.e. proactive routing protocols. The protocol namely ZRP and ZHLS falls into this category of protocols.

It is very essential to examine the performance of any type of protocols in MANET and enhance it if required. The analyzing and enhancing the performance parameters of any protocol is important because it directly affects the communication and transmission of information in the network. To measure the performance, the performance factors such as throughput, end-to-end delay, goodput, packet delivery fraction, routing overhead, jitter etc. is taken into consideration.

Reactive routing protocols are more focused and worked upon because of their capability to maintain routing overhead, which is caused due to mobile nodes in the network. In evaluation with other reactive routing protocols, TORA is highly adaptive, well scalable, and best suited for operation in multihop and high mobility environment [4].

Any routing protocols are analyzed by update information type [16] and the below described performance metrics.

- **Packet Delivery Fraction:** The ratio of total data packets successfully received to total ones sent by sources [22].
- **Throughput:** In the given time period, the amount of successfully moved data is called throughput which is measured in bits per second (bps), megabits per second (Mbps) or gigabits per second (Gbps) [19].
- **End to end delay:** It refers to the time taken for a packet to be transmitted across a network from source to destination [13].
- **Routing Overhead:** It describes the quantity of routing packets required for the process of route discovery and route maintenance [17].

In the next section of this paper, we will discuss in brief the working of TORA along with the proposed TORA (P-TORA) built with some modification that has helped in enhancing the performance of original TORA.

2   Brief Description of TORA

TORA - Temporally Ordered Routing Algorithm

TORA, an On-demand routing algorithm is working on the theory of DAG, i.e. Directed Acyclic Graph. Temporally Ordered Routing Algorithm (TORA) is extremely adaptive, well scalable protocol, suitable for high mobile, highly dense and more traffic oriented network [4]. It utilizes minimum time in route establishment from source to destination. IMEP (Internet Manet Encapsulation Protocol) plays important role in TORA for broadcast delivery, link status mechanism as well as message aggregation [4].

- Mechanism of TORA

In one of the mostly known protocol AODV, the routes are constructed on request and destination sequence numbers are used for the discovery of the latest route to end node [18, 20, 21] whereas TORA at initial stage recognizes some route between start (source) node and end (destination) node. The routing information is retained amongst every adjacent nodes in the network. If there is occurrence of any topological error/change, control messages gets localized to near neighboring nodes.

Working of TORA involves following tasks [5, 8].

- Route Making
- Route Preservation
- Route Deletion
- Making of route by TORA.

Two packets namely UPD (update) and QRY (query) packets are used for the route making task.

Step 1: Location and Height level are set to 0 node so that of other nodes are set to be NULL [5, 8].

Step 2: Qry packet containing destination ID is broadcasted by the source node [5, 8]. Steps 1 and 2 are depicted in the following Fig. 3.

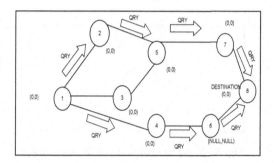

Fig. 3. Route creation procedure of TORA [5].

Step 3: A node with height not equal to NULL and the one having the height of particular node will respond back with the UPD packet [5, 8].

Step 4: The height of all the nodes taking this UPD packet will increment to more than the one height of UPD creating node [5, 8] (Fig. 4).

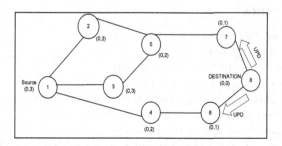

Fig. 4. Formation of DAG in TORA [5].

According to the above figure, update (UPD) packet is broadcasted by node 8 to the every node [5]. Directed Acyclic Graph (DAG) formation takes place here [5]. Arrow indicates the route wherein update (UPD) packet is obtained [5]. For instance, node 6 acknowledges the update packet and update its height as 1 (because the height parameter of received update packet was 0) [5].

- Route Preservation by TORA

Upstream link is the node with higher height whereas downstream link is the node with lower height [5]. For instance, in the above figure, node 6 and node 7 are downstream connection for node 8 whereas node 8 is the upstream linkage for node 6 and node 7. DAG is destroyed when any node in the network moves from its location [5]. At this stage, maintenance phase is carried out for the re-establishment of DAG for same end node again [5].

As soon as the last downstream connection fails, it gives rise to the new location level [5]. All neighboring nodes gives born to the new reference level and links are modified according to the changes made while modifying fresh reference level [5]. This is explained clearly in the following Fig. 5.

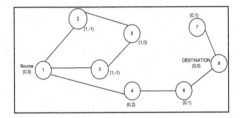

Fig. 5. Route re-establishment in TORA [5].

- Route Deletion by TORA

TORA initiates route erasure phase by broadcasting CLR packet and thereby removing all inappropriate routes. If there is separation in the network, node noticing the network separation delivers the CLR packet [5]. The statistics of all the neighboring nodes is fixed to NULL when the nodes in the network receives Clear (CLR) packet. The new route is created by route creation process from the last node that receives Clear (CLR) packet. For example (Fig. 6),

Advantages of TORA

- It provides loop free routes to the destination [6].
- It emphasis on multipath routing.
- TORA performs best for dense networks [6].
- The possibility of congestion is reduced.
- TORA is designed in such a way that it reduces routing overhead in the network [6].
- TORA maintains multiple routes to the destination.
- It has the capability of erasing invalid routes.
- The performance of TORA in high mobility environment is better than the protocols like AODV and DSR.

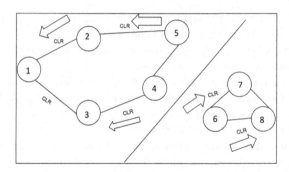

Fig. 6. Route erasure in TORA [5].

Disadvantages of TORA

- TORA is dependent on synchronized clocks for communication in the network [7].
- TORA sometimes creates invalid temporary nodes.
- One of the disadvantages of TORA is that it is dependent on lower layers for some of the functionalities.
- With the increase in mobility of nodes, the performance of TORA degrades eventually.
- When the amount of traffic increases in the network, the protocol may not work efficiently.

3 Overview of P-TORA (Proposed-TORA)

It is seen that TORA is capable of providing number of different and unique routes between start (source) and end (destination) node. TORA selects routes with the shortest hopes i.e. HHR (hop by hop retransmission) for choosing multiple paths between source and destination nodes and for easy, reliable and fast retransmission of packets/information in the network. This may cause some nodes to carry heavy loads as a result of which the performance of TORA degrades in terms of PDR, throughput, PDF etc.

In order to improve the performance of TORA, retransmission methodology needs to be changed and analysis needs to be carried out. The paper in the later part introduces P-TORA (Proposed TORA) wherein one of the concept of EER [27] (End-to-End Retransmission) methodology is utilized for packets/information transmission in the entire network. In EER (also known as three way handshaking model of TCP) methodology, the role of TCP (transport protocol) plays significant role in enhancing the performance of the protocol.

4 Operation of P-TORA (Proposed TORA)

The main idea of P-TORA is to introduce TCP E2E NewReno [26] operating model in the communication process of original TORA and build the new protocol with this modification. Let us now describe the TCP E2E NewReno operating model.

TCP E2E NewReno [26] model is capable of managing a loss/damage of multiple number of packets without altering the structure of TCP message. Here TCP message is taken a good care of because it is the one, which is responsible for the transport of messages/information/packets in the network.

There are two phases/algorithms/concepts in this operating model namely, Fast Retransmit and Fast Recovery phase [26]. These two phases/algorithms/concepts are worked upon because they doesn't wait for time out even if it doesn't achieves ACK (acknowledgment) for any packet/information/segments.

The protocol enters in the Fast Retransmit phase when it learns that it hasn't achieved the acknowledgment of more than the pre-defined minimum number of packets/segments. After getting knowledge about it, it will fastly try to resend the unacknowledged packets/segment.

The protocol enters in the Fast Recovery phase when the unacknowledged packets/segments are resend by the sender and receiver has received it. It will immediately recover the information from that packets.

The main idea is that if the sender evokes the number of the last segment sent before entering the Fast Retransmit phase.

- Then it can contract with a condition when a "fresh" ACK (which is not **duplicate ACK**) does not cover the latest evoked segment (**"partial ACK"**).
- This is a state when more packets were misplaced before arriving the Fast Retransmit phase.
- After noticing such condition the sender will resend the new misplaced packet also and will remain at the Fast Recovery stage.
- The sender will finish the Fast Recovery stage when it achieves/receives ACK that covers last segment sent before the Fast Retransmit phase.

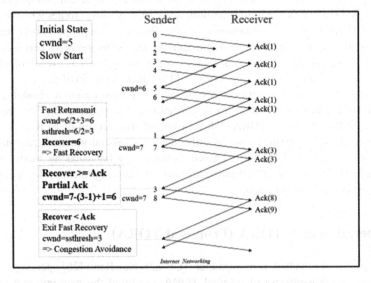

Fig. 7. Working of TCP E2E NewReno model in P-TORA.

As seen in the Fig. 7, the TCP E2E NewReno model works as described below.

- Set SSTHRESH (Threshold) to max (FlightSize/2, 2 * Maximum Segment Size (MSS)).
- Store it to "Recovery" variable, the highest sequence number transmitted.
- Resend the misplaced packet/segment and set cwnd (congestion window) to SSTHRESH + 3 * MSS.
- The congestion window is enlarged by the number of segments (three) that were sent and buffered by the receiver.
- For each extra added replicate ACK achieved, increase cwnd by MSS.
- When a partial ACK is obtained, resend the first unacknowledged packet/message/segment.
- Reduce the cwnd (congestion window) by the aggregate of new approved packet/message/segment, then increase back one MSS.
- send a fresh packet/segment if permitted by the updated value of Congestion window, cwnd.

Thus, the congestion window (cwnd) reveals the extra segment that has left the network. This methodology of the model introduced in the P-TORA will help it to transmit the more number of packets/information/segments compared to original TORA. This will in turn help in increasing packet delivery ratio and throughput of the protocol. Thus, the performance of the protocol will be enhanced.

5 Simulation Environment and Experimental Results

Simulations are concluded with network simulator NS-2.35. It is the simulator used in simulating different kind of possible scenarios [9]. NS2.35 is used for determining performance of some QoS parameters in our research. For our current analyses, the following parameters are measured as described in the following Table 1 [6, 14].

Table 1. Simulation parameters

Parameters	Specifications
Simulator	NS 2.35
Routing protocol	TORA, P-TORA
OS	Windows 7, 32-bit
Type of mobility model	Random Waypoint model
Type of MAC layer	802.11/MAC
Transmission range	$(1500 * 1500)\ m^2$
Type of traffic	Constant Bit Rate (TCP)
Total time of simulation	100 s
Pause time	0−600 (section of 100 s)
Packet length	64,512 bytes
Total no. of nodes	70

We have talked over the performance study of TORA and P-TORA for two performance parameters.

Simulation of the QoS parameter such as energy consumption and packet delivery ratio are discussed having 10 Constant Bit Rate sources [15]. The simulation environment has been organized as presented in table above.

a. *Packet Delivery Ratio Analysis*

The Fig. 8 shows a comparative analysis of PDR between TORA and P-TORA. The graph in the Fig. 8 shows that the PDR obtained for 70 nodes with P-TORA is comparatively better than original TORA.

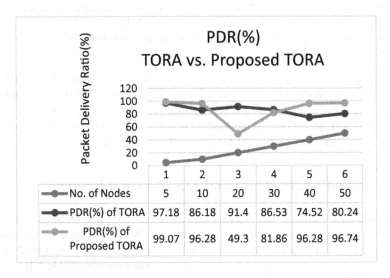

	1	2	3	4	5	6
No. of Nodes	5	10	20	30	40	50
PDR(%) of TORA	97.18	86.18	91.4	86.53	74.52	80.24
PDR(%) of Proposed TORA	99.07	96.28	49.3	81.86	96.28	96.74

Fig. 8. Packet delivery ratio (TORA) vs. packet delivery ratio (P-TORA)

b. *Energy Consumption analysis*

Below Fig. 9 shows the graph for Average Energy Consumption of Original TORA vs. Average Energy Consumption (P-TORA). It is visualized from the graph that an energy consumed by P-TORA is less in comparison with that consumed by Original TORA. It is but obvious that we have obtained enhanced results because of the TCP E2E NewReno model being introduced in the P-TORA.

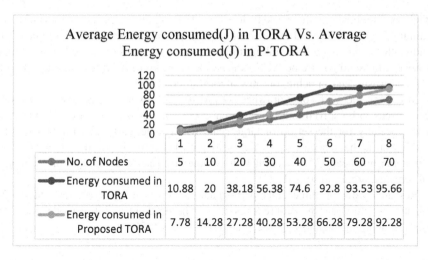

Average Energy consumed(J) in TORA Vs. Average Energy consumed(J) in P-TORA

	1	2	3	4	5	6	7	8
No. of Nodes	5	10	20	30	40	50	60	70
Energy consumed in TORA	10.88	20	38.18	56.38	74.6	92.8	93.53	95.66
Energy consumed in Proposed TORA	7.78	14.28	27.28	40.28	53.28	66.28	79.28	92.28

Fig. 9. Average energy consumed in (TORA) vs. (P-TORA)

6 Conclusion

Since a decade, MANET has increasing and speedy growth in the research studies. This is a non-wired network with multihop routing. MANET has its application in military and in surveillance of security. The network topology in the MANET alters with time. This is the reason why there is need for designing and deployment in the existing MANET routing protocol. In the present work, we have analyzed MANET reactive routing protocol named TORA. On analyzing we found that TORA degrades its performance due to some reasons in some circumstances. As a result of which a new concept was introduced in Original TORA and a new protocol named P-TORA was build.

In Proposed TORA, the TCP E2E NewReno operating model was utilized which gave a drastic increment in the performance metrics compared to original TORA. Comparison Original TORA and Proposed TORA was analyzed taking Packet Delivery Ratio and Energy consumption into consideration using the NS2 simulation tool.

This work concluded that the performance of Proposed TORA (P-TORA) gives better results than Original TORA. Packet Delivery Ratio of Proposed TORA was more than that of Original TORA for 5–70 nodes respectively. Moreover, it is necessary to analyze the energy consumed by the protocol in the network. So, we analyzed and improved the energy consumption of Original TORA.

7 Future Work

This paper exposes the working and features of Temporally Ordered Routing Algorithm (TORA) in wireless MANET network. In wireless networks, some features are required to be added in a good TCP algorithm [24] as TCP plays vital role in routing which are diminishing the packets loss rate [24], reducing packet retransmissions, attaining high addition and compatibility [24], providing efficient estimation of the bandwidth for achieving high linking throughput, anticipation of multiple transmission by breaks, Lessening extreme ACKs and evade inserting rush surges into the networks [24], and to succeed in achieving low algorithm complexity [24].

Moreover, there are some drawbacks of MANET network and its routing protocols which needs to be solved and are research issues such as lacks of effective analytical tools especially for the set-up of large scale wireless network [23], Finding out and blocking an authenticated user, which start miss behaving inside the network, Communication overhead [23], Computation complexity, Energy consumption, Scalability still remains largely unsolved [23].

Research work on three other performance metrics i.e. Network load, MOS [25] and jitter would show the different results for the different mobility models and will assists in attaining faultless and accurate conclusions [25].

References

1. Malhotra, R., Gupta, V., Bansal, R.K.: Simulation & performance analysis of wired and wireless computer networks. Global J. Comput. Sci. Technol. 11(3) (2011)
2. Hmalik, M., Awais, Q., Jamil, M., Dhyani, A.: Performance analysis of proactive and reactive protocols in mobile ad-hoc networking: a simulation based analysis. In: 2014 International Conference on Robotics and Emerging Allied Technologies in Engineering (iCREATE), pp. 25–31. IEEE, April 2014
3. Abusalah, L., Khokhar, A., Guizani, M.: A survey of secure mobile ad hoc routing protocols. IEEE Commun. Surv. Tutor. 10(4), 78–93 (2008)
4. Yu, F., Li, Y., Fang, F., Chen, Q.: A new TORA-based energy aware routing protocol in mobile ad hoc networks. In: 2007 3rd IEEE/IFIP International Conference in Central Asia on Internet, ICI 2007, pp. 1–4. IEEE, September 2007
5. Kaur, A., Mittal, M.: Influence of link sensing mechanism of IMEP on the performance of TORA under different mobility models. In: 2014 International Conference on Parallel, Distributed and Grid Computing (PDGC), pp. 16–21. IEEE, December 2014
6. Gupta, A.K., Sadawarti, H., Verma, A.K.: Performance analysis of AODV, DSR & TORA routing protocols. Int. J. Eng. Technol. 2(2), 226 (2010)
7. Kuppusamy, P., Thirunavukkarasu, K., Kalaavathi, B.: A study and comparison of OLSR, AODV and TORA routing protocols in ad hoc networks. In: 2011 3rd International Conference on Electronics Computer Technology (ICECT), vol. 5, pp. 143–147. IEEE, April 2011
8. Lim, K.H., Datta, A.: An in-depth analysis of the effects of IMEP on TORA protocol. In: 2012 IEEE Wireless Communications and Networking Conference (WCNC), pp. 3051–3056. IEEE, April 2012
9. Yadav, M., Gupta, S.K., Saket, R.K.: Multi-hop wireless ad-hoc network routing protocols-a comparative study of DSDV, TORA, DSR and AODV. In: 2015 International Conference on Electrical, Electronics, Signals, Communication and Optimization (EESCO), pp. 1–5. IEEE, January 2015
10. Yadav, M., Uparosiya, N.: Survey on MANET: routing protocols, advantages, problems and security. Int. J. Innov. Comput. Sci. Eng. 1(2), 12–17 (2014)
11. Sumyla, D.: Mobile Ad-hoc Networks (MANETS) (2006)

12. Raju, V.K., Kumar, K.V.: A simple and efficient mechanism to detect and avoid wormhole attacks in mobile ad hoc networks. In: 2012 International Conference on Computing Sciences (ICCS), pp. 271–275. IEEE, September 2012
13. El Miloud, A.R., Ghoumid, K., Ameziane, K., El Mrabet, O.: The improvement of end to end delays in network management system using networkcoding. Int. J. Comput. Netw. Commun. 5(6), 65 (2013)
14. Awerbuch, B., Mishra, A., Hopkins, J.: Ad hoc on demand distance vector (AODV) routing protocol. Johns Hopkins university, US
15. Katheeth, Z.D., Raman, K.K.: Performance evaluation with throughput and packet delivery ratio for mobile ad-hoc networks. Int. J. Adv. Res. Comput. Commun. Eng. 3(5), 6416–6419 (2014)
16. Wang, Z., Li, Z., Zhu, X.: Routing algorithms analysis for ODMA-WiFi systems. In: 2014 5th IEEE International Conference on Software Engineering and Service Science (ICSESS), pp. 1122–1125. IEEE, June 2014
17. Cheng, Y.M., Niu, J., Sun, T.J.: Study on performance comparison of OLSR and AODV routing protocols. In: Applied Mechanics and Materials, vol. 672, pp. 1977–1980. Trans Tech Publications (2014)
18. Loo, J.H., Mauri, J.L., Ortiz, J.: Mobile Ad Hoc Networks: Current Status and Future Trends. CRC Press, Boca Raton (2011)
19. Rajic, M.: Analytical testing for IEEE802.11b
20. Abdelfattah, E.: Mobile ad-hoc routing protocols: evaluation of performance. University of Bridgeport, May 2003
21. Meghanathan, N., Nagamalai, D., Chaki, N. (eds.): Advances in Computing and Information Technology: Proceedings of the Second International Conference on Advances in Computing and Information Technology (ACITY) July 13–15, 2012, Chennai, India - Volume 1. Springer, Heidelberg (2012). https://doi.org/10.1007/978-3-642-31513-8
22. Wang, J., Mikami, T., Kanamori, K., Kodama, E., Takada, T.: Improving packet delivery fraction of ad hoc network with XORs-based network coding CDS. IAENG Int. J. Comput. Sci. 38(3), 275–282 (2011)
23. Sarwar, Y., Ali, M.A.: Security issues regarding MANET (Mobile Ad Hoc Networks): challenges and solutions (2011)
24. Al-Jubari, A.M., Othman, M., Ali, B.M., Hamid, N.A.W.A.: TCP performance in multi-hop wireless ad hoc networks: challenges and solution. EURASIP J. Wirel. Commun. Netw. 2011(1), 198 (2011)
25. Kaur, R., Kumar, R.: Comparison study of routing protocol by varying mobility and traffic (CBR, VBR and TCP) using random walk & random way point models. Int. J. Eng. Trends Technol. (IJETT) 7(4), 177–183 (2014)
26. Balakrishnan, H., Padmanabhan, V.N., Seshan, S., Katz, R.H.: A comparison of mechanisms for improving TCP performance over wireless links. IEEE/ACM Trans. Netw. 5(6), 756–769 (1997)
27. Banerjee, S., Misra, A.: Minimum energy paths for reliable communication in multi-hop wireless networks. In: Proceedings of the 3rd ACM International Symposium on Mobile Ad Hoc Networking & Computing, pp. 146–156. ACM, June 2002

A Hybrid Approach for Requirements Prioritization Using Logarithmic Fuzzy Trapezoidal Approach (LFTA) and Artificial Neural Network (ANN)

Yash Veer Singh[1(✉)], Bijendra Kumar[1], Satish Chand[2], and Deepak Sharma[1]

[1] Computer Engineering, NSIT (University of Delhi), New Delhi 110078, India
yashveersingh85@gmail.com, bizender@gmail.com,
deepak.btg@gmail.com
[2] School of Computer and System Science, JNU, New Delhi 110003, India
schand20@gmail.com

Abstract. Requirements prioritization (RP) is a crucial phase of requirements engineering (RE) to rank the requirements as per their priority weight in software development process. The existing technique like FAHP (Fuzzy analytical hierarchy process) is a very suitable methodology for requirements prioritization used in the fuzzy background suffers from a number of limitations like FAHP technique does not grant the accurate priority as per the client hope, create many conflicts in priority vectors and may outcome in dissimilar conclusion which are unacceptable for a fuzzy pair-wise comparison matrix. Fuzzy preference approach (FPA) and extent analysis (EA) based nonlinear techniques are efficient but create many issues like ambiguity, time complexity, scalability, provides negative degree of membership function, inconsistency and generates many non uniqueness optimal solution in fuzzy environment. In this research a hybrid approach for requirements prioritization using 'LFTA with ANN' proposed to overcome these issues providing the most client fulfillment with all technical characteristics. The case study performed on MATLAB software and result observed for a real life example 'college selection' with three selection criteria's that illustrates the decision making result for requirements prioritization is better than previous techniques with higher priority. The proposed hybrid approach is oriented to resolve the classical gaps and meet up the client fulfillment of decision making in real applications. A hybrid approach is examined on real-life assignment for students ('selection of best college' based on three criteria's), with existent colleges and college selection criteria's are discussed in the fuzzy AHP.

Keywords: FAHP · Requirements prioritization · FPA · LFTA
Extent Analysis (EA) · ANN · College selection

1 Introduction

Requirement Prioritization (RP) is a crucial phase of requirement engineering (RE) in software development life cycle (SDLC). This phase demonstrate the identification of each requirement, like requirement gathering and elicitation, analysis, their

© Springer Nature Singapore Pte Ltd. 2019
P. K. Singh et al. (Eds.): FTNCT 2018, CCIS 958, pp. 350–364, 2019.
https://doi.org/10.1007/978-981-13-3804-5_26

documentation, validation of requirements and management. Requirement engineering (RE) consists of 'requirement prioritization' which is used to order the requirements as per their priority of importance [1–5]. When a project has not sufficient resources, too high client expectations and hard execution plan, its most important aspects must be arranged beforehand. So, requirement prioritization is very important for choosing the accurate set of requirements and takes so many decisions in project release [6, 7]. Therefore, a number of researchers is connected in the practice for developing the accurate set of weight priority in requirement prioritization [8]. As per existing studies, previous prioritization approaches dealing with ambiguity, fuzziness and uncertainty in requirement prioritization of decision, when different stakeholders have different ideas of requirements [9]. In regular as per the time passes; we create various choices, like selection of best faculty, the best college, purchasing a new DVD-player, new mobile phone, veg. food, and so on. Generally, when we consider only one criteria then it is very easy to take decisions which requirement is best for example, which one is the best college, faculty, which is the best brand etc. Indeed, while we includes more than one criteria decisions, then choices can be hard to make. While it is having tens, hundreds or even a large number of multiple criteria, then MCDM (multi-criteria decision-making) becomes much more typical work in requirements engineering. This research work generates the ranking of requirements based on multiple criteria by using a novel hybrid approach 'LFTA with ANN' to resolve conflicts regarding which one requirement must be executed first as per their priority. In this research work we examined a case study on 'college selection problem' for the students to select the best college to take their admission based on three criteria. In this proposed work, a novel hybrid approach LFTA with ANN is presented to overcome the limitations of Extent Analysis (EA) or Fuzzy Preference Approach (FPA) and FAHP. Celik et al. [10] examined a 'ship registry selection problem' with the extent analysis (EA) approach that has been revealed to be unacceptable, undesirable, and may produces result in the form of a wrong decision being made. Therefore, the EA (extent analysis) or FPA (fuzzy preference approach) should be eliminated. Hence, we proposed a novel hybrid approach 'LFTA with ANN' technique to reexamine the real life problem i.e. college selection problem for students to decide best college based on their multiple criteria. Tables 1, 2, 3, 4, 5, 6 and 7 revealed the fuzzy pair-wise comparison matrices taken for 'college selection problem'.

2 Related Work

Golmohammadi has introduced a fuzzy MCDM (multi-criteria decision-making) approach with ANN. This approach is applied to take and speak to the chiefs' inclinations. The structure of the artificial neural network (ANN) is created to set up the research model. This research model can employ chronicled data and refresh the database for selection of requirements and for future choices based on multiple criteria. Reproduction of the experts' choices is shown in brief and the execution plan of the research model is expressed by a contextual analysis [11, 12]. Nguyen et al. has expressed an integrated multi-criteria decision making (MCDM) framework consisting of fuzzy analytical hierarchy process (FAHP) and fuzzy ARAS approaches for examining and choosing conveyors. The proposed research technique has its distinctive advantages by combining

IVIF analytical hierarchy process (AHP) and IVIF ARAS for the first time [13, 14]. Büyüközkan has merged 'Interval Valued Intuitionistic Fuzzy (IVIF)' and Analytic Hierarchy Process (AHP) first time to estimate the multiple criteria weights for requirements prioritization and IVIF with Additive Ratio Assessment (ARAS) technique for substitute evaluation procedure. This technique also examines the selection of a best supplier in a real case study from Turkey to demonstrate the validity of this technique [15]. Gulzar has established a new fuzzy system that highlights for mapping requirements attributes to the linguistic variable estimation for client fulfillment by using applying fuzzy logic (FL). This research system sorts out the conflicts ease of use prerequisites properties. For implementation, we have applied MATLAB Fuzzy Logic Tool box. This proposed system is moved out for helping the prerequisite expert in taking better selections via robotizing the entire procedure of distinguishing and settling ease of use necessities clashes. The important responsibility of the proposed framework consists of deciding the numerical incentive for each characteristic considering their individual significance in various quantitative and subjective assessment principles. On the basis of numerical value, conflicts and their separate severities are recognized [16]. The application of FAHP for RP (requirement prioritization) require scientific approaches for originating the priority weights generated through fuzzy pair-wise comparison matrices with EA (extent analysis) [3] and FPA (fuzzy preference approach) is depend on non-linear technique [4]. The technologies generated using fuzzy priority weights originating by fuzzy pair-wise comparison condition usually integrates the linear goal programming (LGP) technique [17], geometric mean method [1, 18] and proposed least-squares methods (LSM) [19], and Lambda–Max methods [20, 21]. The techniques for deriving crisp-weights generated by fuzzy pair-wise comparison matrices consists of the extent analysis EA [10] and FPP (fuzzy preference programming). Since fuzzy priority weights are incapable to calculate simply crisp ones, a number of research thoughts illustrates that vast common of FAHP (fuzzy analytical hierarchy process) application uses a simple extent analysis (EA) approach proposed [10] for FAHP (fuzzy AHP) weight derivation. However, such an EA (extent analysis) technique described [17] to be undesirable and unacceptable, and the priorities weights resulting by EA (extent analysis) do not show the relative weight of decision criteria and alternatives. It has been observed to a considerably a huge number of mishandlings in the previous existing research [10, 22–25]. Incorrectly, it's utilize as a weight derivation approach should be discarded [1, 26].

Fuzzy Analytical Hierarchical Process (FAHP)

A trapezoidal fuzzy number deals with various universal conditions [27]. In this test, the views of the quantities which are included in the MCDM (multi-criteria decision making process) are represented by linguistic variables that have been express in trapezoidal fuzzy numbers.

A trapezoidal fuzzy number designated as $F\_S = (a, b, c, d)$, are represented by the following membership function:

$$\mu_{Fs}(x) = \begin{cases} \frac{x-a}{b-a} & a \leq x \leq b \\ 1 & b \leq x \leq c \\ \frac{d-x}{d-c} & c \leq x \leq d \end{cases} \tag{1}$$

Here (b, c) are termed a mode interval $\widetilde{F}\_s$ while parameters 'a' and 'd' represents lower and upper bound on $\widetilde{F}\_s$ which limit the possible evaluations in Fig. 1.

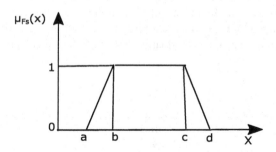

Fig. 1. Fuzzy trapezoidal degree of membership function.

The Fuzzy Priority Approach (FPA) or Extent Analysis (EA) Based Nonlinear Priority Technique

This can be equivalently states as:

$$\text{Subject to}\begin{cases} -E_i + a_{ij}E_j + \beta(b_{ij} - a_{ij})E_j \leq 0, i = 1,\ldots, n-1; j = i+1,\ldots, n, \\ E_i - c_{ij}E_j + \beta(C_{ij} - b_{ij})E_j \leq 0, i = 1,\ldots, n-1; j = i+1,\ldots, n \\ \sum_{i=1}^{n} E_i = 1, \\ E_i \geq 0, \quad i-1,\ldots, n. \end{cases} \quad (2)$$

For better understanding, we mention to the technique that is used in Eq. (2) for the fuzzy AHP priority observation as FPP based nonlinear priority technique. After review this technique, we conclude these following research points:

1. The negative values of membership degree indicate no meaning or no decision.
2. Equation (2) provides several optimized solutions when there occurs strong lack of consistency among fuzzy decisions.
3. The priority weight vectors are computed by lower or upper triangular components are same in fuzzy pair-wise comparison matrix. They are significantly different.

3 Proposed Hybrid Model (LFTA with ANN)

The Fig. 2 shows the proposed requirements prioritization model established to rank the requirements as per their order of weight priority in multi-criteria decision making (MCDM) for college selection (CS) based on three criteria (faculty profile, college infrastructure and technical, cultural activity). This model is start with the experts working together with the database. After that, decision makers (DM) obtain their requirement selection criteria for prioritization. The multiple criteria of requirements as a component of data are entered. In the step of data entry, the data are observed and sorted out by an approach 'LFTA with ANN'. The data information goes as fuzzy pair-wise comparison examinations into a pre-assembled MATLAB programming. Additionally, the prepared ANN (artificial neural network) examines the correctness and impropriety of decision makers. This part exhibits the intelligent MCDS (multi-criteria decision support) system. In the event that if the outcomes are suitable then the selections are affirmed. On the other hand if the results of the decision making box are inappropriate then passage data information must be reconsidered and will be reappear to the cycle.

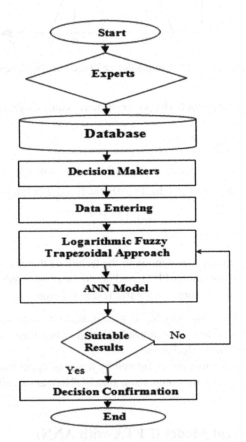

Fig. 2. Proposed hybrid model 'LFTA with ANN'.

A. **Expert Model (Collection of information):** It can be chosen by decision makers or by the students to collect all the true information about the college like faculty profile, infrastructure, technical/cultural activity, research and the placement of the students at the higher package.

B. **Database Model (To store information):** This phase is responsible for integration, storage and the determinations of all the information related to college produced by the experts or students for making good decisions.

C. **Decision Makers Model (Most favorable decision):** College selection process is done through the students or decision makers. In this model, they should be consistently required to choose the choice of gear. In this paper, we have attempted to utilize their remarks to outline the LFPP framework.

D. **Data Entering Model (proposed LFTA with ANN model)**
The input information is passed created by DM analysis.

i. LFTA (Logarithmic Fuzzy Trapezoidal Approach) Model

The Proposed research work resolves the above issues of Extent Analysis (EA) in Requirement prioritization with Logarithmic Fuzzy Trapezoidal Approach (LFTA) as shown in Fig. 3.

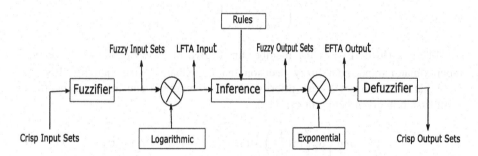

Fig. 3. Block diagram of approach 'LFTA'

The steps of the proposed approach are:

(1) Provide positive degree (β) of membership function (i.e. between 0 & 1) to make strong consistency among the fuzzy decision making.

(2) Providing a unique regularized optimal priority vector for fuzzy decisions to reduce the inconsistency.

(3) The priority weight vectors generating from upper/lower triangular elements of the fuzzy pair-wise comparison matrix are equal.

Suppose decision maker (DM) gives fuzzy decisions instead of accurate decisions for pair-wise comparison matrix, then it can be decided that criterion i is between a_{ij} and d_{ij} as important as standard j with b_{ij} and c_{ij} being the most likely times. A fuzzy trapezoidal pair-wise comparison matrix can be represented:

$$J = \begin{bmatrix} (1,1,1,1) & (a_{12},b_{12},c_{12},d_{12}) & (a_{13},b_{13},c_{13},d_{13}) & (a_{14},b_{14},c_{14},d_{14}) \\ (a_{21},b_{21},c_{21},d_{21}) & (1,1,1,1) & (a_{23},b_{23},c_{23},d_{23}) & (a_{24},b_{24},c_{24},d_{24}) \\ \cdots & \cdots & \cdots & \cdots \\ (a_{n1},b_{n1},c_{n1},d_{n1}) & (a_{n2},b_{n2},c_{n2},d_{n2}) & (a_{n3},b_{n3},c_{n3},d_{n3}) & (1,1,1,1) \end{bmatrix}$$

$$(3)$$

Here use the fuzzy pair-wise comparison matrix in (3), after that we take logarithmic of the following equation. The logarithmic of a trapezoidal fuzzy decision $\tilde{a}$ ij is seemed as close to triangular fuzzy number, which membership degree can accordingly be expressed as:

$$\ln \tilde{a}_{ij} = \left(\ln a_{ij}, \ln b_{ij}, \ln c_{ij}, \ln d_{ij} \right), \quad i,j = 1, \ldots n. \tag{4}$$

$$\mu_{ij}\left(\ln \left(\frac{E_i}{E_j} \right) \right) = \begin{cases} \frac{\ln(E_i/E_j) - \ln(a_{ij})}{\ln(b_{ij}) - \ln(a_{ij})}, & \ln \left(\frac{Ei}{Ej} \right) \leq b_{ij}, \\ \ln(1) = 0, & b_{ij} \leq \ln \left(\frac{Ei}{Ej} \right) \leq c_{ij}, \\ \frac{\ln(d_{ij}) - \ln(E_i/E_j)}{\ln(d_{ij}) - \ln(c_{ij})}, & \ln \left(\frac{Ei}{Ej} \right) \geq c_{ij}, \end{cases} \tag{5}$$

Where $\mu_{ij}(\ln(Ei/Ej))$ is the membership degree of $\ln(Ei/Ej)$ that fairly accurate (approximate) trapezoidal fuzzy decision $\ln \tilde{a}\_ij = (\ln a_{ij}, \ln b_{ij}, \ln c_{ij}, \ln d_{ij})$. It's very clear that expect to get a crisp priority vector to minimum and maximize degree of membership is given below in Eq. (14).

$$\beta = \min \left\{ \mu_{ij}\left(\ln \left(\frac{E_i}{E_j} \right) \right) | i = 1 \ldots n - 1; j = i + 1 \ldots n \right\} \tag{6}$$

Finally the resulting model can be created for maximizing the degree of membership β

$$\text{Subject to} \begin{cases} \mu_{ij} \ln \left(\frac{Ei}{Ej} \right) \geq \beta, i = 1, \ldots, n - 1; j = i + 1, \ldots, n, \\ E_i \geq 0, i = 1, \ldots, n. \end{cases} \tag{7}$$

$$\text{For maximize degree of membership } (1 - \beta) \tag{8}$$

$$\text{Subject to} \begin{cases} -\ln E_i + E_j + \beta \ln \left(b_{ij}/a_{ij} \right) \geq \ln \left(a_{ij} \right), i = 1, \ldots, n - 1; j = i + 1, \ldots, n \\ \ln E_i - E_j + \beta \ln \left(d_{ij}/c_{ij} \right) \geq - \ln \left(d_{ij} \right), i = 1, \ldots, n - 1; j = i + 1, \ldots, n \\ E_i \geq 0, i = 1, \ldots, n. \end{cases}$$

$$(9)$$

Usually, there is no guarantee that Eq. (9) will every time provide a positive value for membership degree β. One of the main reason s behind producing a negative value for β, means it has no weights which can meet for all fuzzy decisions within their support interval. This means that, there is not all be short of equalities $lnE_i - lnE_j - \beta \ln(b_{ij}/a_{ij}) \geq lna_{ij}$ or $-lnE_i + lnw_j - \beta \ln(d_{ij}/c_{ij}) \geq -lnd_{ij}$ may be held at the same time.

To keep away 'β' from allowing a negative value, we set up non-negative observation of variables γ_{ij} and σ_{ij} for i = 1, ..., n − 1 and j = i + 1, ..., n such that they bring together the following lack of equalities:

$$lnE_i - lnE_j - ln(b_{ij}/a_{ij}) + \gamma_{ij} \geq lna_{ij}, i = 1,\ldots,n-1; j = i+1,\ldots n, \quad (10)$$

$$-lnE_i + lnE_j - ln(d_{ij}/c_{ij}) + \sigma_{ij} \geq -lnd_{ij}, i = 1,\ldots,n-1; j = i+1,\ldots n \quad (11)$$

It is the most desirable which values of the 'examined variables' are better and smaller. Thus recommend the following LFTA-based nonlinear priority technique for fuzzy AHP weight observation:

$$k = (1-\beta)^2 + M. \sum_{i=1}^{n-1} \sum_{j=i+1}^{n} \left(\gamma_{ij}^2 + \sigma_{ij}^2 \right) \quad (12)$$

$$\text{Subject to} \begin{cases} z_i - z_j - \beta \ln\left(\frac{b_{ij}}{a_{ij}}\right) + \gamma_{ij} \geq lna_{ij}, i = 1,\ldots,n-1; j = i+1,\ldots,n, \\ -z_i + z_j - \beta \ln\left(\frac{d_{ij}}{c_{ij}}\right) + \sigma_{ij} \geq -lnd_{ij}, i = 1,\ldots,n-1; j = i+1,\ldots,n \\ \beta, z_i \geq 0, i = 1,\cdots,n, \\ \gamma_{ij}, \sigma_{ij} \geq 0, i = 1,\ldots,n-1; j = i+1,\ldots n, \end{cases}$$

$$(13)$$

Once the equation is linear, we can understand these two models which may produce multiple optimal outcomes, which are ignored. Let $z_i^*(i = 1, \ldots, n)$ be the optimized value of Eq. (13). The standardized ranking or priorities for fuzzy pair-wise comparison matrix $J = \tilde{a}_{ij_{n*n}}$ that can be acquired:

$$E_i^* = \frac{\exp(Z_i^*)}{\sum_{i=1}^{n} \exp(Z_j^*)}, \quad i = 1,\ldots,n, \quad (14)$$

Where exp () is specifying an exponential function, namely $\exp(z_i^*) = e^{z_i^*}$ for i = 1...n. We declare in technique that utilizes Eq. (13) for the FAHP priority examination as LFTA technique and resultant priorities as LFTA priorities. With the regard of LFTA technique, we have the following statements.

Statement 1: The priorities weights resulting by a hybrid approach LFTA with ANN technique with lower triangular components of the pair-wise fuzzy comparison matrix are exactly same as findings from upper triangular components of the pair-wise fuzzy comparison matrix.

Statement 2: This proposed hybrid approach 'LFTA with ANN' produces unique optimal result in the consistent form (standardized) optimized priority weight vector for each fuzzy pair-wise comparison matrix.

ii. **Artificial neural network (ANN) model**

In common, ANN can be classified into two categories:

a. *Supervised ANN*

There is generally an eyewitness in the supervised artificial neural network (ANN) who can evaluate the result of the system and reflect their execution authenticity to the neural network (NN).

b. *Unsupervised ANN*

Unsupervised NN (neural network) have no eyewitness. At the end of the day, there is no assessment mirroring the execution legitimacy of neural network (NN). Supervised learning is significantly more flexible than unsupervised learning. Encourage forward back technique is a show up in the central of the most widely recognized learning policies in ANN [28]. As indicated by the many examinations in the writing by the writer, there is no particular legitimate standard to decide the quantity of shrouded layers. Zahari Taha and Sarkawt Rostam have likewise clearly depicted this problem in a paper. The amount of neurons: in a large portion of assets, the number of information layer neurons is equivalent to the number of sources of info; the number of yield layer neurons is equal to the number of yields. The following four relations have been represented to make a decision for the numeral of hidden layer neurons, yet it isn't expressed which one is the best technique. These four connections include

$$NHL = (IL \times OL)^{\frac{1}{2}} \tag{15}$$

$$NHL = \frac{1}{2}(IL + OL) \tag{16}$$

$$NHL = \frac{1}{2}(IL + OL) + (SL)^{\frac{1}{2}} \tag{17}$$

$$NHL = 2(IL) \tag{18}$$

In these above given four relationships, IL is represented by the total number of input layer neurons, where OL are the numbers of output layer neurons and SL is the number of sample.

E. **Decision Making Model:** Finally, the data of fuzzy learning made through LFPP and ANN is reported to the decision makers (DM). The decision makers (DM) settle on an ultimate choice by these two ways, authorization of the decision or revision.

4   Result Estimation

In this section we elucidate the result of proposed hybrid approach LFTA with ANN for below real life example. Here we test one numerical example of college selection to decide the best college for taking admission by the students to get best decision.

Example: We let's consider a real life illustration of 'college selection problem' for the students similar to 'ship registry selection problem' Celik et al. [10] which has the hierarchical configuration for the selection of requirements problem shown in Fig. 4, where C_1, C_2 and C_3 are requirements selection criteria's, each criteria has various sub-criteria, and NIT Delhi (National Institute of Technology, Delhi), NSIT (Netaji Subhas Institute of Technology), IP University (Guru Gobind Singh Indraprastha University) and DTU (Delhi Technological University) are four colleges (alternatives) for selection of best college. Celik et al. [10] represented a 'ship registry selection problem' using the EA (extent analysis) approach that has been exhibited to be unreliable, unacceptable and may generates the result in the form of an incorrect judgment being made. This undesirable priority approach assigns a zero priority weight to every of the selection multiple criteria C_2 and C_3. If zero weights of priorities for both C_2 and C_3 were right, then these two requirement selection criteria's shouldn't have been considered. Finally, assigning a zero priority weight to any requirement selection criterion or sub-criterion within the hierarchical data structure in Fig. 4 makes no meaning. So, the EA (extent analysis) should be declined. Therefore, we reinvestigate this 'college selection problem' by using the proposed hybrid approach 'LFTA technique' to create accurate outcomes of the fuzzy AHP. Tables 1, 2, 3, 4, 5, 6 and 7 exhibits the fuzzy pair-wise comparison matrices taken for 'college selection problem'.

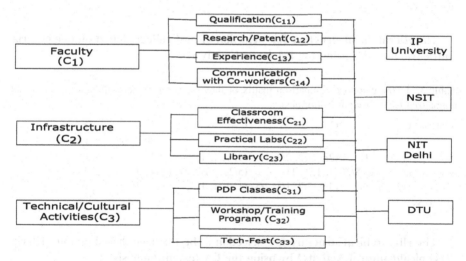

Fig. 4. Hierarchical structures for 'college selection problem'.

The Hierarchical structure for 'selection of best college' based on one criteria 'Faculty' considered:

Table 1. Fuzzy pair-wise comparison matrix for three selection criteria regarding its weights (priorities) and decision goal.

Criteria	C_1	C_2	C_3	LFTA with ANN	EA priorities [10]
C_1	(1, 1, 1, 1)	(3/2, 2, 3, 7/2)	(3/2, 2, 3, 7/2)	0.4327	1
C_2	(2/7, 1/3, 1/2, 2/3)	(1, 1, 1, 1)	(2/3, 1, 2, 5/2)	0.3321	0
C_3	(2/7, 1/3, 1/2, 2/3)	(2/5, 1/2, 1, 3/2)	(1, 1, 1, 1)	0.2352	0
$\beta = 0.561$					

Table 2. Fuzzy pair-wise comparison matrix of four sub-criteria of 'faculty (C_1)' and its normalized LFTA weights (priorities).

Criteria	C_{11}	C_{12}	C_{13}	C_{14}	LFTA with ANN	EA priorities [15]
C_{11}	(1, 1, 1, 1)	(5/2, 2, 1, 1/2)	(1, 1/2, 1/3, 1/4)	(2/3, 1/2, 1/3, 1/5)	0.1854	0.1413
C_{12}	(2, 1, 1/2, 2/5)	(1, 1, 1, 1)	(2/5, 1/2, 1/3,1/5)	(2/3, 1, 2, 5/2)	0.2618	0.1797
C_{13}	(1, 2, 3, 4)	(2/5, 1/2, 1, 3/2)	(1, 1, 1, 1)	(2/5, 1/2, 1, 2)	0.2143	0.2610
C_{14}	(5, 3, 2, 3/2)	(4, 5, 2, 4)	(1/2, 1, 1/2, 5/2)	(1, 1, 1, 1)	0.3385	0.4179
$\beta = 0.321$						

The Hierarchical structure for 'selection of best college' based on one criteria 'Infrastructure' by using the EA (extent analysis).

Table 3. Fuzzy pair-wise comparison matrix of three sub-criteria 'infrastructure (C_2)' and its normalized LFTA weights (priorities).

Criteria	C_{21}	C_{22}	C_{23}	LFTA with ANN	EA priorities [15]
C_{21}	(1, 1, 1, 1)	(2/5, 1/2, 2/3, 1)	(1, 1, 1, 1)	0.3285	0
C_{22}	(1, 3/2, 2, 5/2)	(1, 1, 1, 1)	(5/2, 3, 7/2, 9/2)	0.4076	1
C_{23}	(1, 1, 1, 1)	(2/9, 2/7, 1/3, 2/5)	(1, 1, 1, 1)	0.2639	0
$\beta = 0.591$					

The Hierarchical structure for 'selection of best college' based on one criteria 'Technical/Cultural Activity' by using the EA (extent analysis).

Table 4. Fuzzy pair-wise comparison matrix of three sub-criteria 'technical/cultural activity (C_3)' and its normalized LFTA weights (priorities).

Criteria	C_{31}	C_{32}	C_{33}	LFTA with ANN	EA priorities [15]
C_{31}	(1, 1, 1, 1)	(2/3, 1/2, 2/3, 1)	(2/5, 1/2, 1, 3/2)	0.3582	0.1461
C_{32}	(1, 3/2, 2, 3/2)	(1, 1, 1, 1)	(5/2, 1/2, 1/3, 1/5)	0.3285	0.1461
C_{33}	(2/3, 1, 2, 5)	(5, 3, 2, 2/5)	(1, 1, 1, 1)	0.3133	0.7078
$\beta = 0.621$					

Table 5. Fuzzy pair-wise comparison matrix for four colleges' alternatives regarding the sub-criteria of C_1 and their normalized weights [priorities].

	IP University	NSIT	NIT Delhi	DTU	LFTA with ANN	EA priorities [15]
A: Comparisons of four colleges (alternatives) regarding the sub-criterion C_{11}						
IPU	(1, 1, 1, 1)	(2/7, 1/5, 1/3, 2/5)	(2/9, 1/4, 2/7, 1/3)	(2/3, 1, 3/2, 2)	0.3386	0
NSIT	(5/2, 3, 5/2, 7/2)	(1, 1, 1, 1)	(3/2, 2, 5/2, 3)	(3/2, 2, 5/2, 3)	0.2953	0.5239
NIT	(3, 7/2, 4, 9/2)	(1/3, 2/5, 1/2, 2/3)	(1, 1, 1, 1)	(3/2, 2, 3, 7/2)	0.2133	0.4761
DTU	(2, 2/3, 1, 3/2)	(1/3, 2/5, 1/2, 2/3)	(7/2, 1/3, 1/2, 2/3)	(1, 1, 1, 1)	0.1528	0
$\beta = 0.23$						
B: Comparisons of four colleges (alternatives) regarding the sub-criterion C_{12}						
IPU	(1, 1, 1, 1)	(2/5, 1/2, 1, 3/2)	(2/7, 1/3, 2/5, 1/2)	(5/2, 2, 1, 1/2)	0.1753	0
NSIT	(2/3, 1, 1/2, 5/2)	(1, 1, 1, 1)	(2/5, 1/2, 3/5, 2\3)	(3/2, 2, 5/2, 3)	0.2356	0.3482
NIT	(2, 5/2, 3, 7/2)	(3/2, 5/3, 2, 5/2)	(1, 1, 1, 1)	(3/2, 2, 5/2, 3)	0.1663	0.6518
DTU	(2, 1, 1/2, 2/5)	(1/3, 2/5, 1/2, 2/3)	(1/3, 2/5, 1/2, 2/3)	(1, 1, 1, 1)	0.4228	0
$\beta = 0.14$						
C: Comparisons of four colleges (alternatives) regarding the sub-criterion C_{13}						
IPU	(1, 1, 1, 1)	(2/3, 1, 1/2, 5/2)	(2/3, 1, 3/2, 2)	(2/5, 1/2, 2/3, 1)	0.2213	0.1645
NSIT	(2/5, 1/2, 1, 3/2)	(1, 1, 1, 1)	(2/3, 1, 3/2, 2)	(2/5, 1/2, 2/3, 1)	0.2723	0.1645
NIT	(1/2, 2/3, 1, 3/2)	(1/2, 2/3, 1, 3/2)	(1, 1, 1, 1)	(2/5, 1/2, 2/3, 1)	0.1940	0.1645
DTU	(1, 3/2, 2, 5/2)	(1, 3/2, 2, 5/2)	(1, 3/2, 2, 5/2)	(1, 1, 1, 1)	0.3124	0.1645
$\beta = 0.1$						
D: Comparisons of four colleges (alternatives) regarding the sub-criterion C_{14}						
IPU	(1, 1, 1, 1)	(2/9, 1/4, 2/7, 1/2)	(2/7, 1/3, 2/5, 1/2)	(2/5, 1/2, 2/3, 1)	0.2155	0
NSIT	(2, 7/2, 4, 9/2)	(1, 1, 1, 1)	(2/3, 1, 3/2, 5/2)	(2/3, 1, 3/2, 5/2)	0.3233	0.4076
NIT	(2, 5/2, 3, 7/2)	(5/2, 2/3, 1, 3/2)	(1, 1, 1, 1)	(3/2, 2, 5/2, 3)	0.2255	0.4076
DTU	(1, 3/2, 2, 5/2)	(5/2, 2/3, 1, 3/2)	(1/3, 2/5, 1/2, 2/3)	(1, 1, 1, 1)	0.2354	0.1847
$\beta = 0.36$						

Table 6. Fuzzy pair-wise comparison matrix of four alternatives regarding the sub-criteria of C_2 and their normalized weights (priorities).

	IP University	NSIT	NIT Delhi	DTU	LFTA with ANN	EA priorities [15]
A: Comparisons of the four alternatives regarding the sub-criterion C_{21}						
IPU	(1, 1, 1, 1)	(2/3, 1, 2, 5/2)	(2/5, 1/2, 2/3, 1)	(2/5, 1/2, 2/3, 1)	0.2412	0.0717
NSIT	(2/5, 1/2, 1, 3/2)	(1, 1, 1, 1)	(1, 1, 1, 1)	(2/3, 1, 2, 5/2)	0.3185	0.2164
NIT	(1, 3/2, 2, 5/2)	(1, 1, 1, 1)	(1, 1, 1, 1)	(3/2, 2, 5/2, 3)	0.2316	0.4305
DTU	(1, 3/2, 2, 5/2)	(2/5, 1/2, 1, 3/2)	(1/3, 2/5, 1/2, 2/3)	(1, 1, 1, 1)	0.2087	0.2815
$\beta = 0.48$						
B: Comparisons of the four alternatives regarding the sub-criterion C_{22}						
IPU	(1, 1, 1, 1)	(1/3, 2/5, 1/2, 2/3)	(2, 1/2, 5/2, 3)	(1, 3/2, 2, 5/2)	0.2198	0.4199
NSIT	(1/2, 1/3, 1/4, 1/5)	(1, 1, 1, 1)	(1, 2, 3, 5)	(2/3, 1, 2, 5/2)	0.3785	0.2349
NIT	(2/7, 1/3, 2/5, 1/2)	(1/5, 1/3, 1/2, 1)	(1, 1, 1, 1)	(3/2, 2, 5/2, 3)	0.2092	0.3136
DTU	(1/3, 2/5, 1/2, 2/3)	(1/3, 2/5, 1/2, 2/3)	(1/3, 2/5, 1/2, 2/3)	(1, 1, 1, 1)	0.1919	0.0316
$\beta = 0.67$						
C: Comparisons of four colleges (alternatives) regarding the sub-criterion C_{23}						
IPU	(1, 1, 1, 1)	(1/2, 1/3, 1/4, , 1/5)	(1/2, 1/3, 1/4, 1/5)	(1/2, 1/3, 1/4, 1/5)	0.3572	0.5343
NSIT	(1/3, 2/5, 1/2, 2/3)	(1, 1, 1, 1)	(1/2, 1/3, 1/4, 1/5)	(1/2, 1/3, 1/4, 1/5)	0.2354	0.3850
NIT	(1/3, 2/5, 1/2, 2/3)	(1/3, 2/5, 1/2, 2/3)	(1, 1, 1, 1)	(1, 4, 4, 4)	0.0874	0.0401
DTU	(1, 5, 5, 4)	(1/3, 2/5, 1/2, 2/3)	(1/3, 2/5, 1/2, 2/3)	(1, 1, 1, 1)	0.3200	0.0401
$\beta = 0.33$						

Table 7. Fuzzy pair-wise comparison matrix of four colleges (alternatives) regarding the sub-criteria of C_3 and their normalized weights (priorities)

	IP University	NSIT	NIT Delhi	DTU	LFTA with ANN	EA priorities [15]
A: Comparisons of four colleges (alternatives) regarding the sub-criterion C_{31}						
IPU	(1, 1, 1, 1)	(1/3, 2/5, 1/2, 2/3)	(1/3, 2/5, 1/2, 2/3)	(2/3, 1, 2, 5/2)	0.1738	0.4313
NSIT	(1/3, 2/5, 1/2, 2/3)	(1, 1,1, 1)	(1, 1, 1, 1)	(1/3, 2/5,1/2, 2/3)	0.6690	0.2633
NIT Delhi	(1/3, 2/5, 1/2, 2/3)	(1, 1,1, 1)	(1, 1, 1, 1)	(1/3, 2/5, 1/2, 2/3)	0.0670	0.0194
DTU	(2/5, 1/2, 1, 3/2)	(1/3,2/5, 1/2, 2/3)	(1/3, 2/5, 1/2, 2/3)	(1, 1, 1, 1)	0.0902	0.2860
$\beta = 0.76$						
B: Comparisons of four colleges (alternatives) regarding the sub-criterion C_{12}						
IPU	(1, 1, 1, 1)	(2/9, 1/4, 1/3, 2/5)	(5/2, 3, 7/2, 4)	(1/3, 2/5, 1/2, 2/3)	0.2523	0.3663
NSIT	(5/2, 3, 4, 9/2)	(1, 1, 1, 1)	(1, 1, 1,1)	(1/3, 2/5, 1/2, 2/3)	0.5468	0.6363
NIT Delhi	(1/4, 2/7, 1/3, 2/5)	(1, 1, 1, 1)	(1, 1, 1, 1)	(1/3, 2/5, 1/2, 2/3)	0.0845	0
DTU	(2/5, 1/2, 1, 3/2)	(2/5, 1/2, 1, 3/2)	(2/5, 1/2, 1, 3/2)	(1, 1, 1, 1)	0.1164	0
$\beta = 0.86$						
C: Comparisons of four colleges (alternatives) regarding the sub-criterion C_{13}						
IPU	(1, 1, 1, 1)	(2/9, 1/4, 1/3, 2/5)	(2/3, 1, 2, 5/2)	(2/5, 1/2, 1, 3/2)	0.2528	0
NSIT	(5/2, 3, 4, 9/2)	(1, 1, 1, 1)	(1/3, 2/5, 1/2, 2/3)	(1/3, 2/5, 1/2, 2/3)	0.5560	0.8621
NIT Delhi	(2/5, 1/2, 1, 3/2)	(3/2, 2, 5/2, 3)	(1, 1, 1, 1)	(2/3, 1, 2, 5/2)	0.0756	0
DTU	(2/3, 1, 2, 5/2)	(3/2, 2, 5/2, 3)	(5/2, 1/2, 1, 3/2)	(1, 1, 1, 1)	0.1156	0.1379
$\beta = 0.321$						

The priority weights calculated by using the proposed hybrid approach LFTA with ANN technique are represented inside the columns under heading "LFTA with ANN weights (priorities)" at the end columns of each table. The aggregated priorities are presented in Table 8. At last from that "LFTA with ANN technique" calculates 'NSIT' is the best alternative college, whereas the EA (Extent Analysis) provides a different result that selects 'NIT Delhi' is the best alternative college. From this case study of Multiple Criteria Decision-Making (MCDM) the results provided by the proposed approach is a lot more consistent and reliable than that generated by the EA. So, we've causes to reject the outcome generated by the EA.

Table 8. Aggregation of the Global weights (priorities) achieved by LFTA with ANN methodology

	Global weights (priorities) of the four selection colleges (alternatives) regarding the judgment goal			
Weight	0.4502	0.3021	0.2477	-
IP University	0.2232	0.2570	0.1144	0.1982
NSIT	**0.2828**	**0.3186**	**0.2636**	**0.2884**
NIT Delhi	0.2164	0.1754	0.4364	0.2760
DTU	0.2776	0.2490	0.1856	0.2374

5   Conclusion

Requirement Prioritization is a most important step in the direction of making good decisions. From the literature survey it was found that none of the technique of requirements prioritization do not work well for ranking of requirements and suffers from a number of limitations like complexity, uncertainty, ambiguity and negative degree of membership function etc. To overcome these issues of MCDM for prioritizing the requirements, a novel hybrid approach is proposed based on LFTA with ANN that gives the unique normalized optimal priority weight vector and provides positive degree of membership function always because the use ANN. We applied this proposed technique on a real life example i.e. "best college selection based on three criteria" for students in the FAHP. It derives weight priorities are accurately same of the lower triangular components of pair-wise comparison matrix and the upper triangular components of pair-wise comparison matrix. In future, the complexity of the proposed hybrid approach can be improved by using genetic algorithm (GA) and PSO techniques. At last, the 'NSIT College' is best college having highest weight priority and 'NIT Delhi' is next alternative college based on defined three criteria.

References

1. Sun, C.C.: A performance evaluation model by integrating fuzzy AHP and fuzzy TOPSIS methods. Expert Syst. Appl. **37**(12), 7745–7754 (2010)
2. Sadiq, M., Jain, S.K.: Applying fuzzy preference relation for requirements prioritization in goal oriented requirements elicitation process. Int. J. Syst. Assur. Eng. Manag. **5**(4), 711–723 (2014)
3. Veerabathiran, R., Srinath, K.A.: Application of the extent analysis method on fuzzy AHP. Int. J. Eng. Sci. Technol. **4**(7), 3472–3480 (2012)
4. Wang, Y.-M., Chin, K.-S.: Fuzzy analytic hierarchy process: a logarithmic fuzzy preference programming methodology. Int. J. Approx. Reason. **52**(4), 541–553 (2011)
5. Sipahi, S., Timor, M.: The analytic hierarchy process and analytic network process: an overview of applications. Manag. Decis. **48**(5), 775–808 (2010)
6. Ahmad, S.: Negotiation in the requirements elicitation and analysis process. In: 2008 19th Australian Conference on Software Engineering. ASWEC 2008, pp. 683–689. IEEE, March 2008
7. In, H., Roy, S.: Visualization issues for software requirements negotiation. In: 2001 25th Annual International Computer Software and Applications Conference. COMPSAC 2001, pp. 10–15. IEEE (2001)
8. Kyoya, Y.: Priority assessment of software requirements from multiple perspective, vol. 1, pp. 410–415. IEEE (2004). ISBN 0-7695-2209-2
9. Karlsson, J.: Software requirements prioritizing. In: 1996 Proceedings of the Second International Conference on Requirements Engineering, pp. 110–116. IEEE, April 1996
10. Celik, M., Er, I.D., Ozok, A.F.: Application of fuzzy extended AHP methodology on shipping registry selection: the case of Turkish maritime industry. Expert Syst. Appl. **36**(1), 190–198 (2009)
11. Golmohammadi, D.: Neural network application for fuzzy multi-criteria decision making problems. Int. J. Prod. Econ. **131**(2), 490–504 (2011)

12. Dhingra, S., Savithri, G., Madan, M., Manjula, R.: Selection of prioritization technique for software requirement using Fuzzy Logic and Decision Tree. In: 2016 Online International Conference on Green Engineering and Technologies (IC-GET), pp. 1–11. IEEE, November 2016

13. Karande, A.M., Kalbande, D.R.: Selection of optimal services working on SCM strategies using fuzzy decision making methods. In: 2016 Second International Conference on Computational Intelligence & Communication Technology (CICT), pp. 455–461. IEEE, February 2016

14. Nguyen, H.T., Dawal, S.Z.M., Nukman, Y., Rifai, A.P., Aoyama, H.: An integrated MCDM model for conveyor equipment evaluation and selection in an FMC based on a fuzzy AHP and fuzzy ARAS in the presence of vagueness. PLoS ONE 11(4), e0153222 (2016)

15. Büyüközkan, G., Göçer, F.: An extention of ARAS methodology based on interval valued intuitionistic fuzzy group decision making for digital supply chain. In: 2017 IEEE International Conference on Fuzzy Systems (FUZZ-IEEE), pp. 1–6. IEEE, July 2017

16. Gulzar, K., Sang, J., Ramzan, M., Kashif, M.: Fuzzy approach to prioritize usability requirements conflicts: an experimental evaluation. IEEE Access 5, 13570–13577 (2017)

17. Wang, Y.M., Chin, K.S.: A linear goal programming priority method for fuzzy analytic hierarchy process and its applications in new product screening. Int. J. Approx. Reason. 49 (2), 451–465 (2008)

18. Jaskowski, P., Biruk, S., Bucon, R.: Assessing contractor selection criteria weights with fuzzy AHP method application in group decision environment. Autom. Constr. 19(2), 120–126 (2010)

19. Wang, Y.M., Elhag, T.M., Hua, Z.: A modified fuzzy logarithmic least squares method for fuzzy analytic hierarchy process. Fuzzy Sets Syst. 157(23), 3055–3071 (2006)

20. Calabrese, A., Costa, R., Menichini, T.: Using fuzzy AHP to manage intellectual capital assets: an application to the ICT service industry. Expert Syst. Appl. 40(9), 3747–3755 (2013)

21. Chang, D.Y.: Applications of the extent analysis method on fuzzy AHP. Eur. J. Oper. Res. 95(3), 649–655 (1996)

22. Büyüközkan, G., Berkol, Ç.: Designing a sustainable supply chain using an integrated analytic network process and goal programming approach in quality function deployment. Expert Syst. Appl. 38(11), 13731–13748 (2011)

23. Shaw, K., Shankar, R., Yadav, S.S., Thakur, L.S.: Supplier selection using fuzzy AHP and fuzzy multi-objective linear programming for developing low carbon supply chain. Expert Syst. Appl. 39(9), 8182–8192 (2012)

24. Yücel, A., Güneri, A.F.: A weighted additive fuzzy programming approach for multi-criteria supplier selection. Expert Syst. Appl. 38(5), 6281–6286 (2011)

25. Taha, R.A., Daim, T.: Multi-criteria applications in renewable energy analysis, a literature review. In: Daim, T., Oliver, T., Kim, J. (eds.) Research and technology management in the electricity industry, pp. 17–30. Springer, London (2013). https://doi.org/10.1007/978-1-4471-5097-8_2

26. Wang, J., Fan, K., Wang, W.: Integration of fuzzy AHP and FPP with TOPSIS methodology for aeroengine health assessment. Expert Syst. Appl. 37(12), 8516–8526 (2010)

27. Sadi-Nezhad, S., Damghani, K.K.: Application of a fuzzy TOPSIS method base on modified preference ratio and fuzzy distance measurement in the assessment of traffic police centers performance. Appl. Soft Comput. 10(4), 1028–1039 (2010)

28. Taha, Z., Rostam, S.: A fuzzy AHP–ANN-based decision support system for machine tool selection in a flexible manufacturing cell. J. Manuf. Technol. Manag. 57(5–8), 719–733 (2011)

Wireless Networks

Improved Computation of Change Impact Analysis in Software Using All Applicable Dependencies

Mrinaal Malhotra[✉] and Jitender Kumar Chhabra

Department of Computer Engineering, National Institute of Technology,
Kurukshetra 136119, Haryana, India
mrinaalmalhotra@gmail.com, jitenderchhabra@gmail.com

Abstract. Different types of environment and user changes necessitate changes in the source code of the software and these changes also get propagated to other entities of the software. Change Impact Analysis (CIA) is one technique which helps the developers to know about the risks involved in changing different entities of the software system. This type of analysis can be carried out by computing different dependencies present in the source code. This paper proposes a new approach to compute CIA based on 8 different types of source code dependencies, out of which 3 dependencies are being introduced for the first time in this paper. The performance of the proposed technique is evaluated over four different software and results indicate that new dependencies used by us contribute significantly in accurate computation of CIA.

Keywords: Change impact analysis · Source code dependencies
Software evolution

1 Introduction

Software has the ability to grow rapidly with time. The rapid growth of any software system can be seen as evolution. Software evolution has been a major concern of software engineering for a while now. Software engineering consists of various activities, maintenance being one of them. Software maintenance deals with post-production activities (Mens 2008). IEEE 1219 standard defines software maintenance as "the modification of a software product after delivery to correct faults, to improve performance or other attributes, or to adapt the product to a modified environment" (Moore 1998). Software maintenance is the key activity during evolution phase as growth of the system requires management even after delivery of the product. In order to manage continuously changing software system one need to understand the basic functionality and system architecture. It can be seen that modifications in one entity of the system leads to unpredictable changes in other entities of the system. Origin of these modifications can be policy constraints, functional requirements or improvement in design (Alam et al. 2015). These changes can be monitored by analyzing the different source code dependencies present in the system because if any component is dependent on any modified component then there is a scope of impact on that one too.

© Springer Nature Singapore Pte Ltd. 2019
P. K. Singh et al. (Eds.): FTNCT 2018, CCIS 958, pp. 367–381, 2019.
https://doi.org/10.1007/978-981-13-3804-5_27

In this paper we are comparing different techniques of dealing with software evolution which are based on different source code dependencies. This paper has been organized as follows. Section 2 represents the background and the previous work, which is done in the literature, related to change impact analysis which uses source code dependencies as a medium for calculating the final result. Section 3 discusses the various research issues which have not been utilized until now. Section 4 describes our proposed methodology which is demonstrated with the help of a simple example. Section 5 shows the empirical investigations performed. Section 6 describes the results and finally Sect. 7 concludes the paper.

2 Background and Related Works

Various researchers have used source code dependencies for software maintenance activities. There are several types of source code dependencies which have been used in the past for analysis of complete software system as thorough analysis is required for the continuous changing requirements of user's. Source code dependencies arise from interconnectivity between different software entities (Amarjeet and Chhabra 2018); (Amarjeet and Chhabra 2017). Different source code dependencies which have been addressed in the past are explained as follows.

Data dependencies, which is proposed by (Alzamil 2007), depicts that one variable is dependent on the other one if and only if value of the first variable is assigned to second. Control dependencies are also proposed by (Alzamil 2007). Control dependencies means the execution of some entity relates with the evaluation of some statement. There are few other dependencies which have found application in software evolution recently. These include semantic, SEA and feature dependency. Semantic dependencies, proposed by (Podgurski and Clarke 1990), show that two statements are semantically dependent on each other if the result of one statement is related with the logic or semantics of another statement. SEA dependencies are proposed by (Jász et al. 2008). Two modules f and g are SEA dependent if any part of f has to be executed before g. The last dependency is feature dependency (Lienhard et al. 2007). Feature dependencies means one behavioral unit is related to some other unit.

These dependencies have been used for various purposes until now such as Architecture recovery (Lutellier et al. 2017), code optimization (Ferrante et al. 1987), software testing (Podgurski and Clarke 1990), software re-modularization (Alzamil 2007); (Amarjeet and Chhabra 2018) change impact analysis (Sharma and Suryanarayana 2016), evaluating requirements of a system (Parashar and Chhabra 2016).

In order to deal with software evolution thorough understanding of change impact analysis (CIA) is crucial (Sun et al. 2012). CIA is a fundamental process of software maintenance and development process (Dit et al. 2014) CIA deals with predicting the effects of modifications done with one portion of the system. During the process of CIA, we need to make a change set which is calculated after studying the user's requirements (De-Lucia et al. 2008). A small change can impact lots of project's by-products such as test cases, source code components at all levels etc. (Tóth et al. 2010). During the process, the primary goal is to find out the set, estimated impact set (EIS), of affected components of the software systems that got impacted by the changes done

(Abdeen et al. 2015). The impact set deserves maintenance effort because of the modifications (Bohner and Arnold 1996). In order to judge the effectiveness of CIA technique EIS is compared with actual impact set (AIS). AIS are set of those entities which are actually affected by the modifications. There are several techniques for computing impact set. These techniques can be broadly classified as static and dynamic (Abdeen et al. 2015). Dynamic techniques relies on information collected using program execution such as execution traces, coverage information etc. but this technique can result in some false-negatives (Sun et al. 2015). The other method for pursuing the same work is static CIA technique. It has been studied that 70% techniques belong to static category (Li et al. 2012). Static techniques can be further divided into three categories. First one is structural analysis in which source code dependencies are identified and used for finding the impact set. Second one is textual analysis in which comments and identifiers are used for finding the impact set. And the last one is historical analysis in which source code components are identified which used to change together in the past. It is believed that those components which changed together in the past is most likely to change together again in the future (Sun et al. 2012).

Various CIA techniques can be employed to determine the impact set such as call graph (Ryder 1979), static slice (Horwitz et al. 1990), SEA (Jász et al. 2008). Change impact analysis can be done to different types of system including software product lines (Maâzoun et al. 2016), object-oriented systems, non-object oriented systems etc. by taking source code or text document as input (Autexier and Müller 2010). Sun and Li proposed a method in which they computed impact set with the help of method dependencies and lattice of class (Sun et al. 2011). They presented their theory on object oriented languages and used a simple java program to explain the concept. Bixin Li and Zang proposed a different approach. They introduced wave CIA which is a structural technique that utilizes the call graph (Li et al. 2013). Bogdan Dit made a tool called impact miner which uses software histories for computing the change set (Dit et al. 2014). This tool refers the co-change histories of the software system.

In this paper we are focusing on the static change impact analysis technique.

3 Research Issues in Computation of Change Impact Analysis

Above section has already established that the dependencies are a key to change impact analysis. A careful study of CIA indicates that eight different types of dependencies affect it. But most of the researchers in the literature have covered 4–5 different types. After detailed literature survey, it has been observed that three types of dependencies namely include dependency, temporal dependency and symbol dependency have not been utilized until now. All of these three significantly affect CIA, which is justified and explained below:

- **Symbol dependency** means module A of file B is related to module C of file C. (Lutillier et al. 2015) Symbol dependency plays an important role in change impact analysis. The usage of symbol dependency in change impact analysis can be explained with the help of a small example. Consider the code fragment shown in Fig. 1. According to this code fragment print function calls func() with values 15 and 2 and gets the result 22. But if line number 5 and 6 of func() is changed to

```
5.    int q;
6.    q = p/r;
```

Then output will be 23. Hence a small change can change the final result and thus symbol dependencies should be included.

```
1   #include<stdio.h>
2
3   int func(int p,int r)
4 ▾ {
5       float q;
6       q=(float)p/r;
7       q=q+15;
8       if(q<=22)
9           q++;
10      int t=q;
11      return t;
12  }
```

```
1   #include<stdio.h>
2   void print()
3 ▾ {
4       printf("the value returned is %d", func(15,2));
5   }
6 ▾ int main() {
7
8   print();
9   }
```

a)   b)

Fig. 1. Example for symbol dependency (a) function called (b) function caller

- The term temporal means related to time. **Temporal dependencies** means that the execution time of two or more source code entities are suppose to be related to each other (Cataldo et al. 2008). One entity has to be executed before or after (depending on situation) another entity. This will help us to eliminate false-positives in the impact set as those entities, which have to be executed before those entities which are present in the change set, should not be in impact set. This can improve the precision value of the resultant impact set.
- **Include dependency** means one file is contained within another file. For example c. cpp includes a.h as a header file (Lutillier et al. 2015). Now suppose in the file c.cpp a method calls another method which is provided by that header file. But if that method, which is called, is changed slightly (say its signatures or return variable's type) then the caller will not work properly and hence will cause ripple effects. So, the caller method must be included in the impact set.

From our discussion these dependencies are directly co-related with CIA but they are not included for CIA. Hence, this paper proposes a new approach of finding CIA based on 8 types of dependencies out of which 1 or more of 5 dependencies (data, control, semantic, SEA, feature and environment) have already been considered by researchers but 3 additional dependencies are being considered for the first time in this paper. The scope of our paper includes the source code of the software system as we are utilizing source code dependencies only.

Improvement in the measurement of CIA is very important as CIA is a backbone for software evolution. It is seen that software systems evolve over time. Various modifications are done in the system to cope up with changing trends of the environment. If any software is not updated properly (within a time limit) then the software becomes obsolete. In order to prevent this, regular updating of system is mandatory. And if any system is updated then CIA comes into picture as it describes the possible areas of code where the modifications can cause an effect.

Primary contribution of our work is

- This paper proposes a new computation methodology where 3 new dependencies (include, symbol and temporal) are utilized towards CIA.
- A new approach to compute CIA based on 8 different types of dependencies including above 3 dependencies is proposed in this paper.
- The new proposed approach is tested against four software of varied characteristics.
- The proposed approach is compared with another existing approach.
- The improvement in the results due to our proposed approach is demonstrated finally.

4 Proposed Methodology

The proposed methodology is explained below (Fig. 2).

4.1 Computation of Dependencies

In order to find the impacts set, all the dependencies defined in Sects. 2 and 3 has to be computed which is explained in the section below.

4.1.1 Computation of Already Defined Dependencies

- Data dependencies (DD) are computed by searching for all the def-use pairs in the software system (Alzamil 2007).
- Control dependencies (CD) are computed by finding all the conditional statements of the source code like if, if-else-if, and switch case (Alzamil 2007).
- SEA dependencies (SD) are computed by studying the execution order of all the methods of the software system (Jász et al. 2008).
- Semantic dependencies (SeD) are computed by following methods

  (a) By examining signatures of every overloaded methods in the system (Sharma and Suryanarayana 2016)
  (b) By examining constructors of each parent-child pair of classes (Sharma and Suryanarayana 2016)
  (c) By examining the each output statement and finding which of the previous statements have an impact on the output statement (Manson et al. 2005).

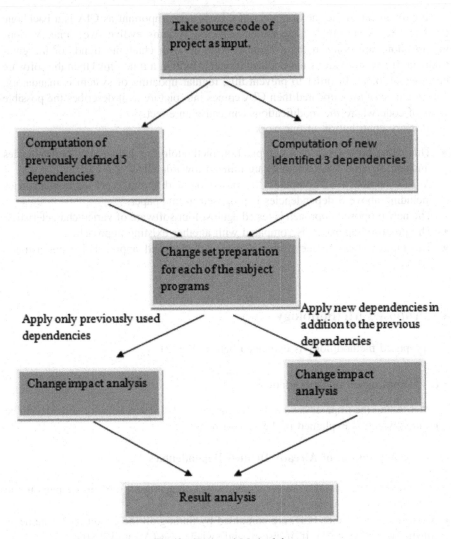

Fig. 2. Proposed Methodology

- Feature dependencies (FD) are computed by first finding the main objectives of the system then searching whose results are used in which of the other objectives (Cafeo et al. 2016).

4.1.2   Computation of Newly Identified Dependencies

- Include dependencies (ID) are computed by analyzing the preprocessor directives of each file of the source code.
- Symbol dependencies (SyD) are computed by analyzing the function calls which are going outside the file.

- Temporal dependencies (TD) are computed easily by analyzing the sequence of execution of different methods present in the system.

4.2   Integration of Dependencies

Final dependency value (Dep.) is calculated by considering all 8 dependencies (5 previous and 3 new) which are provided equal weightage and are integrated together by using the following formula

$$\text{Dep.} = \sum_{i=1}^{n} \frac{d_i}{n} \tag{1}$$

Where n is the total number of dependencies, d are the 8 type of dependencies

4.3   Preparation of Change Set

Change set is obtained by studying the bug reports and issues collected from their respective histories which are mentioned on the website (github.com) and short listing of these issues is done on the basis of their difficulty level. Change set consists of both methods and variables.

4.4   Preparation of Actual Impact Set (AIS)

Actual impact set is computed by taking each entity of change set

(a) And if it's a variable then searching the source code for entities which uses the value of changed entity directly or indirectly.
(b) And if it's a method then searching for those methods who called the changed method or whom the changed method is calling.

4.5   Computation of Estimated Impact Set (EIS)

4.5.1   Computation of EIS 1

For computing EIS 1 those 5 dependencies which are listed in Sect. 4.1.1 are utilized. EIS 1consists of both variables and methods.

4.5.2   Computation of EIS 2

Here newly identified dependencies which are listed in Sect. 4.1.2 are utilized for analyzing the impact set. Then EIS 1 is merged together with impact set calculated just now which gives us our final result. EIS 2 also consists of both method and variables.

4.6   Comparison of Accuracy of EIS 1 and EIS 2

Precision, recall and f-measure is used for comparing the accuracy. Precision describes the effect on accuracy due to false-positives and recall describes the effect due to false-negatives. Hence both are supposed to higher to attain better accuracy. F-measure is the harmonic mean of the two.

4.7 Demonstration

Consider the example for understanding the importance of adding new dependencies.
Example to explain the importance of newly identified dependencies.

```
#include<iostream.h>
#include<manage.h>
class student{
char name[30];
int age;
int rollno;
char class_name[10];
int marks[5];
public:
void display(){
}    // displays the complete info about one student
char get_section(){
}          // returns the section of student
char get_result(){   //returns the final result
}
char get_grade(float p){
}   // returns the grade by taking percentage as input.
int get_total(){
}          // returns total marks
class CLASS{

public:

    char name[];
    int size;
}
void main(){

    CLASS cl;
    int strength;
    cl.name="XIIB";
    strength=get_classsize(cl.name);
}
```

Where get_classsize is the function defined in header file manage.h. This header file
contains all the necessary function required for backend maintenance.

Suppose the following requirements are supposed to be added in the system.

The actual impact set (AIS) of these changes will be {get_classsize(), strength,
get_result(), display(), get_grade(), get_section() }

Estimated impact set 1(EIS 1) which is calculated without new dependencies:

(i)   Through data and control dependencies: get_section()
(ii) Through SEA dependencies: get_result(), get_grade()

Estimated impact set 2(EIS 2) which is calculated with new dependencies:

(i)   Through data and control dependencies: get_section(), strength
(ii) Through SEA dependencies: get_result(), get_grade(),
(iii) Through include and symbol dependencies: get_classsize(), display()

Table 1. New requirements

Sr. no	User's requirements	Changes needed
1	Updation of result	Addition of new method in student class which will change the result of student in database
2	Different criteria for grading	Change in get_grade() method of class student
3	Updation of strength of class	Addition of new method in manage.h header file which will append new information in database and also update the data member of class CLASS

It can be established that if we compare the impact set calculated from considering only those dependencies which are already used and from considering newly identified dependencies too with the old dependencies then the impact set made by considering new dependencies also is more close to the actual impact set. Hence, the accuracy of change impact analysis will increase if we add the newly identified dependencies into consideration.

5 Empirical Investigations

5.1 Subject Programs

Four open source projects are considered for conducting our research namely tokenizer (T), nloc (N), mccabe cyclomatic (M) and Go-callvis (G). Table 1 shows some information about these open source systems and information about the data sets that have been prepared for CIA. The projects have been taken from github.com (Table 2).

Table 2. Information about subject programs

Sr. no	Name	No. of methods	No. of class	Lines of code
1	Tokenizer	49	7	1094
2	Nloc	11	8	500
3	Mccabe cyclomatic	10	1	245
4	Go-callvis	13	10	548

5.2 Data Sets

Four data sets have been created during the process of CIA namely; change set which consists of those entities which are modified, AIS which is the actual impact set, EIS 1 which is the impact set made from previous 5 dependencies and EIS 2 made from considering all 8 dependencies (Table 3).

Table 3. Information about data sets

Sr. no	Name	Change set	AIS	EIS 1	EIS 2
1	Tokenizer	3	18	13	16
2	Nloc	5	19	17	21
3	Mccabe cyclomatic	4	19	10	15
4	Go-callvis	5	12	10	14

6 Results and Discussion

Thorough analysis of the source code of all the subject programs helped us to identify the 8 dependencies which are present inside the system. The detailed description of all dependencies (listed in Sect. 4.1) of each subject program is shown in Table 4.

Table 4. Detail description of dependencies of each project

Sr. no	Name	DD	CD	SD	FD	SeD	ID	SyD	TD
1	T	24	45	4	6	18	0	15	1
2	N	20	40	3	1	13	9	2	6
3	M	14	15	4	2	7	13	3	4
4	G	32	43	19	2	30	24	9	6

The total number of dependencies which are present in all the subject programs is given in Table 5.

Table 5. Number of dependencies

Sr. no	Subject Program	Already utilized	Newly identified	% of new dependencies
1	Tokenizer	95	16	14%
2	Nloc	62	16	20%
3	Mccabe cyclomatic	34	20	37%
4	Go callvis	124	39	31%

The average contribution of each type of dependency in each of the projects of both methodologies is described in Fig. 3. According to Fig. 3 the first pie depicts the percentage of each dependency if only previous 5 dependencies are considered and the second pie shows the percentage of each dependency if complete 8 dependencies are considered.

Our approach is compared with other existing approaches in Table 6. Table 6 shows the fundamental differences between our approach and the existing ones.

Table 6. Comparison between different CIA techniques

Sr. no	Name	Category	Source of input	Scope of impact set
1	Our method	Static	Source code	Methods, variables
2	Wave CIA (Li et al. 2013)	Static	Source code	Methods
3	PathImpact (Cai and Santelices 2015)	Dynamic	Execution traces	Single-method and multiple method
4	Dependencies based prediction (Abdeen et al. 2015)	Static	Change histories	Methods, Classes, visibility of members

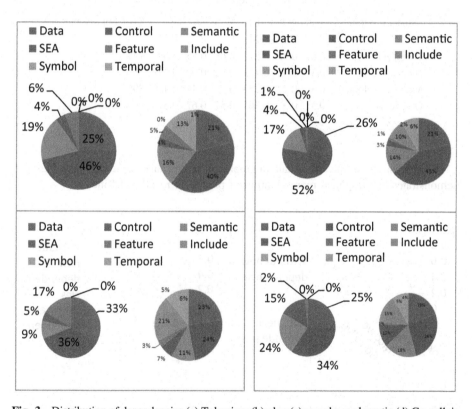

Fig. 3. Distribution of dependencies (a) Tokenizer (b) nloc (c) mccabe cyclomatic (d) Go-callvis

The resultant impact set of both methodologies can be described with the help of bar graph as shown in Fig. 4.

Precision (P), recall (R) and f-measure (F-M) is used as a metric to judge the accuracy of the method. Table 7 depicts the precision and recall values obtained after evaluating the estimated impact set for with and without new dependencies.

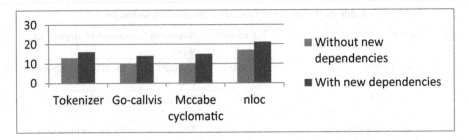

Fig. 4. Impact sets obtained from both the methodologies

Table 7. Precision and recall values

Subject program	Without new dep.			With new dep.			% of Improvement
	P	R	F-M	P	R	F-M	
Tokenizer	0.61	0.45	0.517	0.68	0.55	0.608	17%
Nloc	0.47	0.4	0.432	0.52	0.50	0.509	18%
Mccabe cyclomatic	0.3	0.22	0.253	0.53	0.44	0.480	89%
Go-callvis	0.4	0.33	0.361	0.57	0.67	0.616	70%

Representation of the above data in graphical form is easier to understand. Figure 5 demonstrates the graphical representation of precision, recall and f-measure.

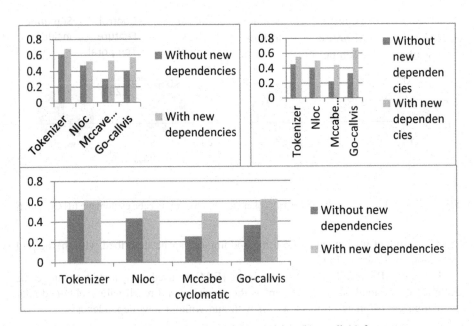

Fig. 5. Graphical representation of (a) precision (b) recall (c) f-measure

It can be inferred from the above results that

- Recall value doubles in the case of mccabe cyclomatic and Go-callvis because the number of false-negatives is much less in EIS 2 of these projects as the contribution of new dependencies (Include and Symbol) is much higher (as shown in Fig. 3) in these two projects.
- Precision values of mccabe cyclomatic and Go-callvis changes significantly in EIS 2 because the number of false-positives in these situations is much less as compared to EIS 1as the new dependencies (Temporal) are more accurate.
- Precision and recall values of Tokenizer and nloc did not change much because the number of false-positives and false-negatives did not change significantly as the contribution of new dependencies in overall result (as shown in Fig. 3) is quite less (only 14% and 20& respectively).
- The % of improvement is more in mccabe cyclomatic and Go-callvis because the contribution of new dependencies (listed in 4.1.2) is more in these cases. According to Fig. 3, the contribution of new dependencies in mccabe cyclomatic and Go-callvis is 37% and 31% respectively, which is primary reason of large improvement in overall CIA.

7 Conclusions

This paper has presented an improved method of computation of CIA which includes identification of a new set of source code dependencies. Combined values of these 8 type of dependencies has been used for the first time in this paper to find the impact set and subsequently used to compute CIA. The proposed methodology has been evaluated over four software and results have been compared with an existing approach. The obtained results clearly showed that new dependencies improved the precision and recall measures significantly.

References

Sun, X., Li, B., Li, B., Wen, W.: A comparative study of static CIA techniques. In: Proceedings of the Fourth Asia-Pacific Symposium on Internetware, pp. 23–31. ACM (2012)

Tóth, G., Hegedűs, P., Beszédes, Á., Gyimóthy, T., Jász, J.: Comparison of different impact analysis methods and programmer's opinion: an empirical study. In: Proceedings of the 8th International Conference on the Principles and Practice of Programming in Java, pp. 109–118. ACM (2010)

Abdeen, H., Bali, K., Sahraoui, H., Dufour, B.: Learning dependency-based change impact predictors using independent change histories. Inf. Softw. Technol. **67**, 220–235 (2015)

Sun, X., Li, B., Leung, H., Li, B., Zhu, J.: Static change impact analysis techniques: a comparative study. J. Syst. Softw. **109**, 137–149 (2015)

Alzamil, Z.A.: Redundant coupling detection using dynamic dependence analysis. In: International Conference on Software Engineering Advances (2007). https://doi.org/10.1109/icsea.2007.56

Mens, T.: Introduction and roadmap: history and challenges of software evolution. Software Evolution, pp. 1–11. Springer, Heidelberg (2008). https://doi.org/10.1007/978-3-540-76440-3_1

Moore, J.W.: Software engineering standards (1998)

Podgurski, A., Clarke, L.A.: A formal model of program dependences and its implications for software testing, debugging, and maintenance. IEEE Trans. Softw. Eng. 16(9), 965–979 (1990)

Sharma, T., Suryanarayana, G.: Augur: incorporating hidden dependencies and variable granularity in change impact analysis. In: IEEE 16th International Working Conference on Source Code Analysis and Manipulation (SCAM), pp. 73–78. IEEE (2016)

Jász, J., Beszédes, Á., Gyimóthy, T., Rajlich, V.: Static execute after/before as a replacement of traditional software dependencies. In: Software Maintenance ICSM, pp. 137–146. IEEE (2008)

Ferrante, J., Ottenstein, K.J., Warren, J.D.: The program dependence graph and its use in optimization. ACM Trans. Programm. Lang. Syst. (TOPLAS) 9(3), 319–349 (1987)

Lutellier, T., et al.: Measuring the impact of code dependencies on software architecture recovery techniques. IEEE Trans. Softw. Eng. 1–22 IEEE (2017)

Lienhard, A., Greevy, O., Nierstrasz, O.: Tracking objects to detect feature dependencies. In: 15th IEEE International Conference on Program Comprehension. ICPC, pp. 59–68. IEEE (2007)

Cataldo, M., Herbsleb, J.D., Carley, K.M.: Socio-technical congruence: a framework for assessing the impact of technical and work dependencies on software development productivity. In: Proceedings of the Second ACM-IEEE International Symposium on Empirical Software Engineering and Measurement, pp. 2–11. ACM (2008)

Cafeo, B.B.P., Cirilo, E., Garcia, A., Dantas, F., Lee, J.: Feature dependencies as change propagators: an exploratory study of software product lines. Inf. Softw. Technol. 69, 37–49 (2016)

Lutellier, T., et al.: Comparing software architecture recovery techniques using accurate dependencies. In: 37th IEEE International Conference on, Software Engineering (ICSE), vol. 2, pp. 69–78. IEEE (2015)

Alam, K.A., Ahmad, R., Akhunzada, A., Nasir, M.H.N.M., Khan, S.U.: Impact analysis and change propagation in service-oriented enterprises: a systematic review. Inf. Syst. 54, 43–73 (2015)

Li, B., Sun, X., Leung, H., Zhang, S.: A survey of code-based change impact analysis techniques. J Softw. Test. Verif. Reliab. 23, 613–646 (2012)

Horwitz, S., Reps, T., Binkley, D.: Interprocedural slicing using dependence graphs. ACM Trans. Programm. Lang. Syst. 12(1), 26–61 (1990)

Ryder, B.G.: Constructing the call graph of a program. IEEE Trans. Softw. Eng. 5(3), 216–226 (1979)

Dit, B., et al.: Impactminer: a tool for change impact analysis. In: Companion Proceedings of the 36th International Conference on Software Engineering, pp. 540–543. ACM (2014)

De-Lucia, A., Fasano, F., Oliveto, R.: Traceability management for impact analysis. In: Proceedings of the International Conference on Software Maintenance, pp. 21–30. IEEE (2008)

Maâzoun, J., Bouassida, N., Ben-Abdallah, H.: Change impact analysis for software product lines. J. King Saud Univ. -Comput. Inf. Sci. 28(4), 364–380 (2016)

Autexier, S., Müller, N: Semantics-based change impact analysis for heterogeneous collections of documents. In: Proceedings of the 10th ACM Symposium on Document Engineering, pp. 97–106. ACM (2010)

Bohner, S., Arnold, R.: Software Change Impact Analysis. IEEE Computer Society Press, Los Alamitos (1996)

Manson, J., Pugh, W., Adve, S.V.: The Java memory model, vol. 40, no. 1. ACM (2005)

Sun, X., Li, B., Zhang, S., Tao, C., Chen, X., Wen, W.: Using lattice of class and method dependence for change impact analysis of object oriented programs. In: Proceedings of the 2011 ACM Symposium on Applied Computing, pp. 1439–1444. ACM (2011)

Li, B., Zhang, Q., Sun, X., Leung, H.: WAVE-CIA: a novel CIA approach based on call graph mining. In: Proceedings of the 28th Annual ACM Symposium on Applied Computing, pp. 1000–1005. ACM (2013)

Cai, H., Santelices, R.: A comprehensive study of the predictive accuracy of dynamic change-impact analysis. J. Syst. Softw. **103**, 248–265 (2015)

Amarjeet, Chhabra, J.K.: FP-ABC: fuzzy pareto-dominance driven artificial bee colony algorithm for many objective software clustering. Comput. Lang. Syst. Struct. **51**, 1–21 (2018)

Amarjeet, Chhabra, J.K.: Harmony search based remodularization for object-oriented software systems. Comput. Lang. Syst. Struct. **47**(2), 153–169 (2017)

Parashar, A., Chhabra, J.K.: Mining software change data stream to predict changeability of classes of object-oriented software system. Evolv. Syst. **7**(2), 117–128 (2016)

Self-optimization in LTE: An Approach to Reduce Call Drops in Mobile Network

Divya Mishra[✉] and Anuranjan Mishra[✉]

Noida International University, G.B. Nagar, Noida, U.P., India
divya_rbl2@yahoo.com, amc290@gmail.com

Abstract. Unwanted terminations of an on-going wireless conversation become the biggest issue of the whole world. Call drop degrades the voice call quality and impacted the quality of service of the network. Researchers, industries, and telecom- vendors are bothered to improve the call quality in existing telecom infrastructure and already proposed many valuable solutions which have own pros and cons but still there is no optimized reliable solution to reduce call drop has been deployed till now. This research paper focuses on some background reasons for call drop in existing wireless infrastructure and proposed the self-optimization concept to handle the overall network issue automatically in perspective of call drops minimization in mobile networks. This Research paper proposed some robust functionality of self-optimizing network such as automatic neighbor list optimization, mobility load balancing optimization and handover optimization approach used to improve voice call quality and make a self-automated mobile network that would be fruitful to reduce call drop rate.

Keywords: Call drop · Long term evolution · Self-optimization network
Automatic neighbor list optimization · Handover optimization
Mobility Robustness Optimization

1 Introduction

In today's world cellular phone became a most important accessory and status symbol of human life, but generally, this status symbol does not work at that moment whenever we required and we faced to our important conversation terminated, this phenomenon is called call drop. There are many recommended techniques proposed by scholars [1] to degrade the call drop ratio but there is no reliable and cost-effective optimized solution has been deployed till now even changing the service provider time to time, based on their complementary offers, but this is not a permanent solution for all in perspective of call drop because these complementary offers can add extra cost in our monthly billing cycle.

Nowadays cell phone subscribers are increasing day by day for using voice calling and different smart phone features like Wi-Fi calling, internet surfing, WhatsApp, social media, downloading-uploading, GPRS etc. provided by telecom service providers on the basis of their value-added offers but the existed cell phone infrastructure is not improving very fast as subscriber rate. The result is all of us suffering from the low

© Springer Nature Singapore Pte Ltd. 2019
P. K. Singh et al. (Eds.): FTNCT 2018, CCIS 958, pp. 382–395, 2019.
https://doi.org/10.1007/978-981-13-3804-5_28

quality of services and bad moving experience with our smart phone. Even some subscribers are bothered for strong coverage and some subscribers are getting bothered for improving voice call quality that is based on area to area.

According to TRAI (Telecom Regulatory Authority of India)-2017 survey [1], around 62% of mobile subscribers are grappling with the issue of frequent call disconnection or unexpected call drop. The initiative has been taken by Indian Government using IVR (Interactive Voice Response) system at many locations such as Delhi, Mumbai, Punjab, Uttarakhand and Goa to find out the feedback of mobile subscriber directly about voice call quality. The resultant feedback is shared with telecom operators to understand the problem and taking appropriate beneficial actions to improve the voice quality in particular areas.

Call drop is any unexpected termination of a wireless mobile call. This is the situation when in middle of an important conversation; an ongoing conversation is broken down. According to TRAI call drop ratio should be less than or equal to 2% i.e., in 100 calls only 2 calls or lesser can drop. According to survey of telecom department [1], more than 112-crore mobile connections are in living stage, that means subscriber pace is increasing day by day but unfortunately the telecom infrastructure is not expanding and modified with robust technology, that would be able to handle the overloaded cells and provide better reliability to roam anywhere with our smart phone.

Call drop is impacting rural and urban subscribers both where people are running from one place to another place to get some signals to maintain their ongoing call or getting good coverage area. In some areas drive test has also conducted by TRAI [1] to find out the reasons of calls drop but only for collecting live data as a theoretical fact. That is not a permanent solution to this issue. Call drop does not only degrade the performance, it also adds cost to monthly billing cycle. There are various reasons for unexpected call termination few of them are like weak signals, coverage area, lack of improved LTE based towers, users press wrong button because of not having enough knowledge to operate the mobile phone, weak battery, Ping-Pong handovers etc.

Our research paper proposed the self-optimization concepts that can be implemented with LTE technology to handle all the call drop related factors automatically. This is the plug and plays concept worked together with self-planning and self-healing, can be deployed in individual eNodeB, OAM or in both bringing proactive defense feature against unauthorized access. So that self-optimizing mechanism can be combined with Wi-Fi port, called Wi-Fi SON [23]. Self-optimizing network degrades the operational cost and capital expenditure by reducing the manual work and improves the quality of experience and quality of service. It works even under the conflicts situations whenever cells are overloaded or radio traffic would be unbalanced.

Self-optimizing concept is basically developed by 3GPP and NGMN but now there are many vendors who are continuously doing the research in this field to enhance and improve the self-optimizing network that can fight with implementation challenges of optimizing algorithm in real platform such as Nokia Siemens, Cisco System, NEC Corporation etc. has done the great job to establish self-optimizing concept in multi-vendor environment [11]. According to a report of SNS Research [24], the revenue of Self-optimizing network is expected to increase more than $5 billion by the end of 2020. So hopefully this concept would be adopted worldwide and helpful to make green telecommunication infra.

2 Related Work

TRAI [1] conducted the independent drive test to monitor the different network performance in various locations and arranged surveys to dig out the factors responsible for call drop. Most of the calls could be dropped due to reasons of electromagnetic effects, irregular user behavior, and abnormal network response. Lin and Balapuwaduge [18] proposed the queuing priority channel assignment in their research paper which could be helpful to reduce call drop, in this algorithm priority has been given to ongoing call rather than new introducing call. Queues are also introduced to buffer the secondary call to entertain later. The drawback of this scheme is the high consumption of bandwidth.

The prioritization scheme could be getting a better result with combining another scheme for example measurement based prioritization scheme, guard channel prioritization scheme, queue handoff calls, call admission control protocol and use auxiliary station [1]. Although many telecom operators used TDMA based dynamic channel allocation in a situation of overloaded cells [1, 13]. A Research paper [15] proposed the bandwidth degradation scheme where bandwidth allocation to various subscribers is adjusted dynamically as required to optimize the utilization of bandwidth for other calls.

Author of [25] proposed the adaptive bandwidth reservation scheme to reserve the bandwidth in all neighboring cell to reuse by another subscriber at the time of handoff. In [26] Lobinger and Stefanski done a great job in the coordination of load balancing algorithm and handover optimizing algorithm in LTE network. These algorithms are the part of self-organizing network and bring the call drop degradation in the mobile network.

3 Background Reasons for Call Drop

Call drop ratio is an important key factor to measure mobile network performance. Unexpected call drop can stop many urgent works of mobile subscribers and reduce the trust on telecom service providers. There are many factors [1] responsible for unwanted call drop such as:

3.1 Network Congestion

While new customers are added rapidly by telecom service provider, less focus on scaling up of infrastructure is being made hence making existing infrastructure operating at threshold level and leading to call drops in terms of reduction of customer experience.

3.2 High Call Volumes

Call volumes grow phenomenally during festival occasion or any events during which high call volumes are made can add more congestion into the network and may result in call drop as an existing system will be overrunning.

3.3   Cells Overlap

Cells overlap is also a contributing factor for Call drop. This usually happens because various cells of different coverage areas overlap with each other and impact smooth call handover when users move from one cell to adjacent cell.

3.4   Weak Signals

There are some areas where signal strength is not strong (intensity of the connection between mobile and network) e.g. tunnels, high mountains, in-building areas. Impacted users more often to buy and install the boosters which are not frequency band specific to telecom service providers and boost up the complete GSM band of all service providers. The resultant feedback is radio interference in others signals. As per TRAI [1], in Delhi, more than 250 illegal boosters are installed in present.

3.5   User Is Roaming

When a mobile user is roaming with high speed from one place to another place then call passes through various cells having strong or weak signal strength can interrupt the call where bad signal/coverage is found.

3.6   Hardware Related Issues

Hardware related issue is a major concern in the mobile network. It can happen because of legacy technology is using by network providers, hardware compatibility between UE and towers, users having no enough understanding to operate mobile phone and weak battery etc.

3.7   Call Handover

Call handover is a situation when a user leaves his source cell coverage and enters in new cell coverage during an on-going call. For successful handover, the call should be transfer to a new cell but unfortunately, if the traffic channel is not free of destination cell, the call would be dropped.

4   Self-optimization in LTE

Self-optimization process controls and optimizes all the network parameters according to the network environment as required automatically and continuously with less human intervention and efforts and offers more reliability at any time and in any place. Self-optimization is one of the key pillars of LTE-SON (Self Organizing Network) developed by 3GPP and NGMN (Next Generation Mobile Network). SON has been identified within 3GPP release 8, 9 and 10 and its first installation has been done in Japan and USA in 2009/10.

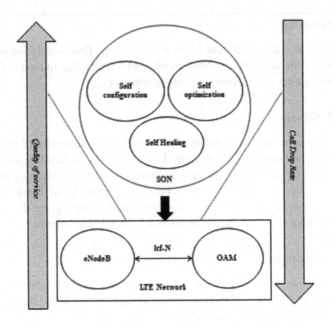

Fig. 1. SON functionality with LTE

As Fig. 1 depicted, the SON is based on three robust automated functionality i.e. self-configuration, self-optimization and self-healing to optimize the network resources automatically without human intervention. Self-configuration is a pre-operational stage where newly installed eNodeBs are configured by automatic procedures to find basic parameters and download required software for operation. Self-Configuration is also used in automatic failure recovery mechanism also called cell outage case [2].

Self-optimization is an operational stage where SON functions optimized all the network resources without any human effort using different robust algorithms such as Coverage and Capacity Optimization, Energy Savings, Interference Reduction, Mobility Robustness Optimization, Mobility Load balancing optimization and RACH Optimization algorithm. It sets the network parameters according to requirement automatically [7].

The third functionality is self-healing function which works in operational stage, is used to detect and rectify the network fault without any delay. The network fault can be related to corresponding software or hardware equipment which could be solved automatically by triggering appropriate recovery actions. For example, Cell outage detection and Cell Outage Recovery [2].

In perspective of call drop issue there are some robust optimizing algorithms of self-organizing network released by 3GPP which could be useful to control the factors that impacted the ongoing conversation. There are some important key optimizations of self-optimizing network which are used to minimize call drop issue are given below:

1. Mobility Robustness Optimization (MRO)
2. Mobility Load Balancing optimization
3. Automatic neighbor list optimization

4.1 Mobility Robustness Optimization (MRO)/Handover Optimization

Handover is a very important situation handled by the mobile network where one UE moves from one cell coverage area to another cell coverage area during an on-going call. If there is any failure occurs to handed over the call successfully to another eNodeB, the on-going conversation may drop out and this is one of the key factors to lead customer dissatisfaction and to move on another reliable telecom network which keeps robust optimisation feature to handle the on-going call automatically.

A manual adjustment of handover parameters is a time-consuming task in 2G and 3G system. So MRO function of self-optimisation network reduces the manual work of operators and increases the reliability during handover process and reducing operational expenditure. MRO function purpose is to find out the problem and then update the mobility parameter according to the issue. In sometimes, the radio resource management algorithm in one eNodeB is unable to solve the issue like [2]:

A. Detect and remove useless neighbor.
B. Detect knotty settings of call selection and reselection.
C. Reduce handover after initial radio resource control protocol connection established.

The objective of this handover optimisation approach is to minimize the risk of ping-pong handover. For this purpose it adjusts the mobility parameters automatically at that time where radio resource management concept failed according to above cases and expected results should be as given below:

A. Useless neighbors are identified and removed.
B. Identify knotty settings of call selection and reselection.
C. Reduced immediate handovers after initial radio resource control protocol connection established.

As shown in Fig. 2, there are three types of mobility problem can occur:

1. Too late handover
2. Too early handover
3. Handover to the wrong cell

- In too late handover, radio link failed before handover completed and UE tries to re-establish its link with source cell.
- In too early handover, radio link of target cell failed immediately after a handover has been completed and the UE tries to re-establish its radio link with source cell.
- In to the wrong cell handover phenomenon, radio link of the target cell failed after a handover completed and UE tries to re-establish its radio link with a cell which is not a source nor the target.

The above-said occurrence can be measured by establishing the three relationship counters between each pair of cells for monitoring their pair relationship problem. One is the too early counter that described the situation where handover is performed too early between this pair of cells. The second one is called too late counter which

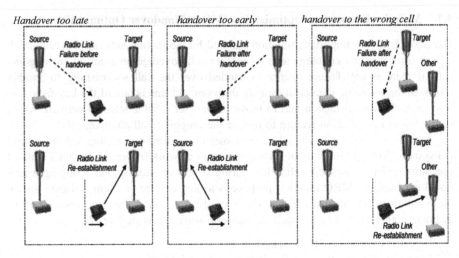

Fig. 2. Handovers too late, too early and to the wrong cell

described the handover should be earlier between this pair of cells and the third one is called to wrong counter which described the radio link of the UE should be established with a right cell after failure the radio link of target cell if handover is completed. The eNodeBs collects the counters of each pair of cells redirect it to a centralized operation and maintenance (OAM). Finally, OAM is carrying the responsibility to adjust the parameters based on their counter information. some scenarios are given below to demonstrate how to employ the above-said counters [2]:

1. Speedy handover among three cells

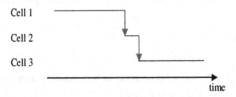

Fig. 3. Speedy handover

The Fig. 3 demonstrates that after the handover between cell 1 and cell 2 the UE performs the handover to cell 3 before long. It shows that it is better to handover directly from cell 1 to cell 3. It argues that the handover:

- Between cell 1 and cell 2 is too Early
- Between cell 1 and cell 3 is too late

2. Failure of radio link before time after established the radio link

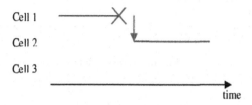

Fig. 4. Failure of radio link before time after established the radio link

The Fig. 4 demonstrates that in cell 1 the radio link failure soon and UE re-established the radio link with cell 2. It shows that it is better to handover between cell 1 and cell 2 should be as soon as possible before radio link failure. It argues that the handover:

- Between cell 1 and cell 2 is too late

3. After handover, radio link failure before long

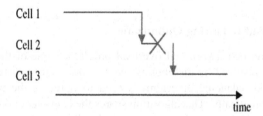

Fig. 5. After handover, radio link failure before long

The Fig. 5 demonstrates that after the handover between cell 1 and cell 2, radio link failure before long and UE re-established the new radio link with cell 3. It shows that cell 3 is the perfect neighbor cell for cell 1. So it is better to handover between cell 1 to cell 3. It argues that the handover:

- Between cell 1 and cell 2 is too Early
- Between cell 1 and cell 3 is too late

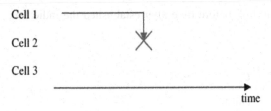

Fig. 6. Access failure

4. Access failure

The Fig. 6 demonstrates, UE was unsuccessful to entrée to cell 2 during handover between cell1 and cell 2, it shows that the handover executed too early. It argues that the handover:

- Between cell 1 and cell 2 is too Early

MRO features optimize the network resources efficiently and reduce the calls drop problem during the handover process.

This approach brings some benefits for subscribers and telecom vendors also:

- Improved operational efficiency
- Fast adoption to network changes
- Improved key performance indicators
- Increase successful handovers

4.2   Mobility Load Balancing Optimization

Network congestion or network cell overload problem is one of the reasons for call drop. So it can be resolved by distributing the network load to spare resources. LTE-SON mobility load balancing algorithm is used to optimize the network resources efficiently and automatically. This algorithm shares the overload of one cell to neighbor cell. The objective of this algorithm is to give the direction to unequal traffic in the mobile network and reduces the numbers of unsuccessful handovers [21]. The load can radio load, network load or even processing load. As shown in Fig. 7, using this algorithm traffic load of overloaded cell can be reduced by choosing the best neighbor

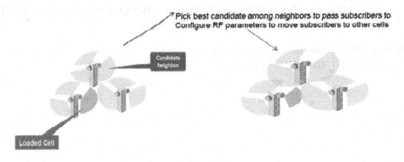

Fig. 7. Load balancing optimisation

cell that has free carrier signal to hold on the on-going call seamlessly. Algorithm picks the best candidate cell among neighbor cells to pass subscribers to move to other cells.

In this process common pilot channel (CPICH) on loaded cell should be decreased and CPICH on neighbor cell would be increased because of UE (user equipment) move to candidate cell. Mobility Load Balancing (MLB) can be possible between inter and intra cell environment. For that reason CPICH is used to measure the signal quality for handover if handover is between LTE and WCDMA cells. In Fig. 8, SON Load balancing algorithm effects on congested cell has been shown. Red Line shows the loaded cells and blue lines shows the unloaded cells. This approach reduced the power load by 20% as shown in graph.

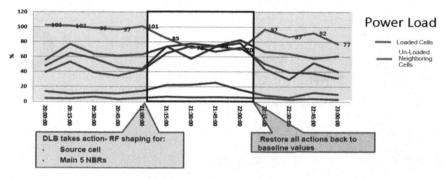

Fig. 8. SON LB effects on congested cells (Color figure online)

To implement the load balancing approach there are some actions to be processed:

a. Every cell is measured for load information and this information is shared between eNodeBs over X2 interface.
b. The overloaded cell will be identified and distribute its load to adjacent cells.
c. Handover or cell reselection parameters are adjusted in both cells to activate the load balancing and at the same time reduce the Ping-Pong effect. Because Ping-Pong handover increases the number of dropped calls and degrades the quality of services.

This approach brings some benefits for subscribers and telecom vendors also:

• Capital expenditure saving
• Improved quality of service
• Increased revenue
• Decrease call drop rate in multivendor environment

4.3 Automatic Neighbor List Optimization/Automatic Neighbor Relation (ANR)

Automatic Neighbor Relation function is installed in eNodeB and having full control on conceptual NRT (Neighbor Relation Table) to maintain the Automatic Neighbor

Relation from other cells. This function raises the successful handover and reduces the calls drop by updating the neighbor relation using X2 interface between two cells. ANR function creates, configures and updates the neighboring list in newly deployed eNo-deB in both directions as shown in Fig. 9, which is used by UE during handovers. This function optimizes the list configuration during operation. This is only plug and play concept, reduces the complexity of legacy system where manual work is performed by one operator to maintain thousands of relations manually. This function increases the real-time experience when a user moves from one cell to another cell because of automatically find out the best neighbor cell for handling on-going calls.

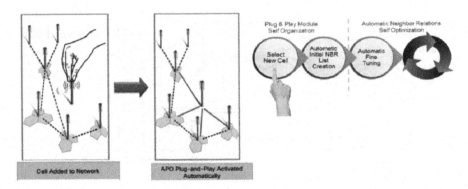

Fig. 9. Neighbour list optimization

At the time of handover, the source eNodeB needs the neighboring eNodeB information i.e. PCI (Physical Cell Identity) and CGID (Cell Global Identity). There are 504 different PCIs presents in LTE [8].

ANR function contains three sub-functions.

1. NRT Management function
2. Neighbor Removal Function
3. Neighbor Detection Function

The NRT management function is also divided into three properties i.e. no remove, no handover and no X2. This function manages the neighbor relation table (NRT) by selecting the particular properties.

The neighbor removal function removes unused and outdated neighbor relation. And neighbor detection function finds the measurement report by RRC (Radio Resource Control) to find out the new neighbor.

ANR function is a first and most important function of SON concept in 3GPP release used to optimize the neighbor relations efficiently to offers the seamless handover without any call termination. As shown in Fig. 10, graph shows the 12% calls dropped reduction is possible with self-optimizing approach.

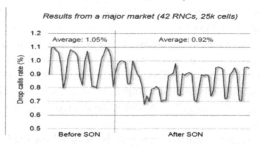

Fig. 10. Neighbour list optimization result

This approach brings some benefits for subscribers and telecom vendors also:

- It will minimize the manual handling of neighbor relations.
- Optimizing the neighbor list automatically.
- Improve the key performance indicators.
- Improved operational efficiency.
- Dynamic adaptation to network changes.
- Network topology improvement.
- Degrades calls drop rate.

5 Conclusion and Future Work

Many researchers, telecom vendors, and even telecom government authority tried to resolve the call drop problem in existing network technology with an optimized utilization of network resources but still, no reliable and optimized future-proof solution has discovered which improved the telephonic conversation quality as expected. Unexpected call termination problem has become complex with a rapid growth of wireless technology and urgent requirement of network resources for new mobile connection. The new added smart phone connection required robust automated technology for strong coverage signals in splitting cells coverage area (macro, micro, pico and femto cells) with high quality of service at low cost without any intervention which would be also compatible with coexisting wireless technology (2G, 3G, 4G, 5G and even GPRS).

This research paper proposed the self-optimizing network approach in a multivendor heterogeneous network environment with LTE infrastructure. Self-optimizing network is a part of LTE but it is compatible with legacy GSM technologies also. Some authors depicted it as a cost-effective model in telecom industry because it reduces the operational expenditure and capital expenditure both with the optimized utilization of network resources with low man-power. Radio traffic on cells and numbers of unsuccessful handovers are decreased by implementing SON functions in a mobile network. SON reduced the manual work and increased the operational efficiency by the various algorithm functions such as handover optimization, mobility load balancing and automatic neighbor relation function. SON can increase the revenue of telecom operators with upcoming technology because total revenue depends on network operational efficiency.

Despite widespread intensive research, Self-optimizing network (SON) has many challenges remain to investigate and improve in R&D of SON algorithm to make it more suitable and cost-effective in existing and upcoming telecom infrastructure. SON algorithm implementation complexity and its dedicated backhaul interface between eNodeBs and configuration server need more research work in real implementation platform.

Our future research work will be focused on implementation challenges of self-optimizing network with upcoming 5G technology without any dedicated backhaul complexity where newly added eNodeB will boot up in UE mode first then connect to a neighbor eNodeB in operation state.

References

1. Telecom Regulatory Authority of India: Technical Paper on Call Drop in Cellular Networks (2016). http://www.trai.gov.in/web-123/Call-Drop/Call_Drop.pdf
2. Feng, S., Seidel, E.: Self-organizing networks (SON) in 3GPP long term evolution. Nomor Research GmbH, Munich, Germany, 20 May 2008
3. NGMN Alliance: Next generation mobile networks use cases related to self organising network, overall description, 31 May 2007
4. Nohrborg, M.: Self-organizing network (2017). http://www.3gpp.org/technologies/keywords-acronyms/105-son
5. Cisco: SON and the LTE Challenge: How to Get More for Less White Paper (2015). https://www.cisco.com/c/en/us/solutions/collateral/service-provider/son-architecture/white-paper-c11-733194.pdf
6. Hämäläinen, S., Sanneck, H., Sartori, C.: LTE Self-Organizing Networks (SON). ISBN 9781119970675
7. Nokia Siemens Networks: Self-Organizing Network (SON) Introducing the Nokia Siemens Networks SON Suite – an efficient, future-proof platform for SON. http://cwi.unik.no/images/c/c3/SON_white_paper_NSN.pdf
8. Dahlén, A., Johansson, A., Gunnarsson, F., Moe, J., Rimhagen, T., Kallin, H.: Evaluations of LTE automatic neighbor relations (2011). 978-1-4244-8331-0/11/$26.00 ©2011 IEEE9
9. Sauter, M.: From GSM to LTE an Introduction to Mobile Networks and Mobile Broadband. Wireless Moves, Germany. ISBN 978-0-470-66711-8
10. 3GPP: Evolved Universal Terrestrial Radio Access (E-UTRA) and Evolved Universal Terrestrial Radio Access (E-UTRAN); Overall description; Stage 2, 3rd Generation Partnership Project (3GPP), TS 36.300, September 2008. http://www.3gpp.org/ftp/Specs/html-info/36300.htm
11. NEC Corporation: Self Organizing Network: "NEC's proposals for next-generation radio network management". White paper, February 2009
12. Balapuwaduge, I.A.M., Jiao, L., Pla, V.: Channel assembling with priority-based queues in cognitive radio networks: strategies and performance evaluation. IEEE Trans. Wireless Commun. 13, 630–645 (2014)
13. Li, X.J., Chong, P.H.J.: A dynamic channel assignment scheme for TDMA-based multihop cellular networks. IEEE Trans. Wireless Commun. 7 (2008)

14. Nokia buys Eden Rock for self-organizing networks (German). http://www.zdnet.de/88235891/nokia-kauft-eden-rock-fuer-self-organizing-networks/
15. Monica, C.H., Bhavani, K.V.L.: A bandwidth degradation technique to reduce call dropping probability in mobile network systems. Telkomnika Indones. J. Electr. Eng. **16**, 303–307 (2015)
16. Shiokawa, S., Ishizaka, M.: Call admission scheme based on estimation of call dropping probability in wireless network (2002). 0-7803-7589-0/02/$17.00 ©2002 IEEE
17. Khara, S., Saha, S., Mukhopadhyay, A.K., Ghosh, C.K.: Call dropping analysis in a UMTS/WLAN integrated cell. Int. J. Inf. Technol. Knowl. Manag. **2**, 411–415 (2010)
18. Lin, Y.-B., Mohan, S., Noerpel, A.: Queuing priority channel assignment strategies for pcs handoff and initial access. IEEE Trans. Veh. Technol. **43**, 704–712 (1994)
19. Iraqi, Y., Boutaba, R.: Handoff and call dropping probabilities in wireless cellular networks. In: International Conference on Wireless Networks, Communications and Mobile Computing (2005)
20. Döttling, M., Viering, I.: Challenges in mobile network operation: towards self-optimizing networks (2009). 978-1-4244-2354-5/09/$25.00 ©2009 IEEE
21. Hu, H., Zhang, J., Zheng, X., Yang, Y., Wu, P.: Self-configuration and self-optimization for LTE networks. IEEE Commun. Mag. **48**, 94–100 (2010)
22. Moysen, J., Giupponi, L.: From 4G to 5G: self-organized network management meets machine learning. arXiv:1707.09300v1 [cs.NI], 28 July 2017
23. Gacanin, H., Ligata, A.: Wi-Fi self-organizing networks: challenges and use cases. IEEE Commun. Mag. **55**, 158–164 (2017)
24. SNS Research: https://www.vanillaplus.com/2016/11/28/23993-son-revenue-expected-to-grow-to-more-than-5bn-by-end-of-2020-says-sns/
25. Oliveira, C., Kim, J.B., Suda, T.: An adaptive bandwidth reservation scheme for high-speed multimedia wireless networks. IEEE J. Sel. Areas Commun. **16**, 858–874 (1998)
26. Lobinger, A., Stefanski, S., Jansen, T.: Coordinating handover parameter optimization and load balancing in LTE self-optimizing networks. In: 73rd IEEE Vehicular Technology Conference (VTC Spring) (2011)
27. The Big Difference in Cell Phone Technology: CDMA vs. GSM. http://www.mindmygadget.com/the-big-difference-in-cell-phone-technology-cdma-vs-gsm/
28. 1G. https://en.wikipedia.org/wiki/1G
29. 2G. https://en.wikipedia.org/wiki/2G

Performance Analysis of CBR and VBR Applications on Different Multicast Routing Protocols Over MANET

Dinesh Chander[✉] and Rajneesh Kumar

CSE Department, M. M (Deemed to be University), Mullana, Ambala, India
me.dinesh17@gmail.com,
drrajneeshgujral@mmumullana.org

Abstract. MANET has become one of the most economical means of group communication where other means of communications are either not feasible or very expensive. Traffic pattern plays a key role in achieving the quality of service (QoS) in various applications of the MANET. In this paper, Constant Bit Rate (CBR) and Variable Bit Rate (VBR) traffic patterns with varying density of nodes are considered to observe the performance of Multicast MAODV, PUMA, and ODMRP in terms of QoS parameters such as end-to-end (E2E) delay, routing load and packet delivery ratio (PDR) to propose and design the new multicast routing protocols in future. From the analysis, it is observed that it is difficult to rank the multicast protocols on the basis of performance under CBR and VBR, but the overall performance of ODMRP multicast protocols is more optimized than PUMA and MAODV under CBR than VBR.

Keywords: MANET · QoS · MAODV · PUMA · ODMRP · CBR
VBR

1 Introduction

A MANET is a collection of wireless battery operated autonomous mobile nodes created under a situation where other means of communication is not feasible to deploy [1]. MANET offers quick deployment of the communication system without setup of any central administration like in wired or other wireless communication networks. Every node in MANET performs as a router to forward and receive the data packets [2]. Major applications of MANETs include battlefields, military operations, rescue operation, emergency services, education, entertainment, and search operation that needs a high degree of QoS [16]. A typical MANET diagram is shown in Fig. 1 with three mobile nodes and their respective transmission range.

Generally, the MANET's applications are categorized in real-time and non real-time applications. The real-time application refers the stringent time constraints on the data traffic while non real-time applications are not so strict in terms of time [3]. Applications like multimedia, teleconferencing perform better with VBR while other applications like voice, interactive video-conferencing, text exchange require CBR traffic for a better outcome [4]. VBR is suitable for bursty data applications while CBR

© Springer Nature Singapore Pte Ltd. 2019
P. K. Singh et al. (Eds.): FTNCT 2018, CCIS 958, pp. 396–411, 2019.
https://doi.org/10.1007/978-981-13-3804-5_29

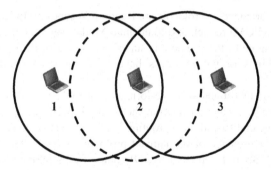

Fig. 1. Mobile ad-hoc network with three nodes

is suitable for timing sensitive applications. On the basis of topology used, multicast routing protocols are categorized into three classes: (1) Tree-based (2) Mesh-based (3) Hybrid. In tree-based multicast routing protocols, a single path exist in between a sender and receiver pair and found to be efficient multicast in terms of packet forwarding and bandwidth consumption. In mesh-based multicast routing protocols, more than one path may exist between a source-destination pair and considered to be more robust due to availability of alternate paths between a pair. Further on the basis of route information, multicast routing protocols can be classified as proactive/table-driven and reactive/on-demand schemes [6, 7]. In the proactive/table-driven approach, each node keeps the route information in the form of the routing table all the time and this table is periodically updated and exchanged by the group members to keep the route information updated [8]. In case reactive/on-demand approach, a route is formed only when it is required. The overall network performance also affected by mobility models like Random Waypoint Model, Reference Point Group Mobility (RPGM) model, and Manhattan Model [9, 14]. In this paper, we evaluate the behavior of mesh-based and tree-based multicast routing protocols in term of QoS parameters under VBR, CBR traffic patterns and varying density of senders.

The organization of the paper is the following: Sect. 2 gives brief overviews about literature survey in this direction; Sect. 3 presents the overview of multicast routing protocols; Sect. 4 presents the types of various traffic patterns; Sect. 5 presents the various mobility models; step by step algorithm is given in Sect. 6; performance analysis is discussed in Sect. 7 and finally the conclusion and future scope discussed in Sect. 8.

2 Literature Survey

Traffic behavior in MANET plays a vital role to achieve the QoS in terms of improved network performance [5]. Many authors have analyzed the behavior of broadcast algorithms under various traffic pattern, but very few attempts have been found in multicast routing protocols.

Manoharan and Ilavarasan [9] studied the impact of models over MAODV, ODMRP, and ADMR multicast routing protocols. There are certain mobility models that affect the performance of protocols are Random Waypoint Model, Reference Point Group Mobility (RPGM) model, and Manhattan Model were under consideration. The results show that none of the protocol is superior in terms of performance as different performance rankings of the protocols have been observed on different mobility patterns.

Mali et al. [10] investigated the performance of DSDV, AODV, and DSR under CBR and TCP traffic pattern to observe the network performance in terms of PDR, normalized average end-to-end delay, routing load, and average jitter. The result shows that the overall performance of on demand protocols is better than table driven protocols. With the CBR traffic pattern, AODV outperforms DSR in terms of PDR and average end-to-end delay. Whereas, in case of TCP, DSR performs better than other protocols in terms of PDR.

Pal et al. [11] presented the analysis of DSR and AODV routing protocols under Exponential traffic model and Pareto traffic model to observe the Packet Delivery Fraction, Normalized routing load, and throughput. The results exhibit that Normalized routing load of DSR and AODV is higher with Exponential traffic model and Pareto traffic model as compared to CBR model. The throughput of AODV is observed to be higher than other routing protocols in both models.

Wahed et al. [12] analyze the impact of traffic patterns and mobility models on few reactive as well as proactive protocols. Network performance of AODV, DSDV, and OLSR under CBR and TCP (TCP-Reno, TCP-Vegas, TCP-Newreno, and TCP-Sack) with different mobility models were observed in terms of average throughput, PDR, and end-to-end delay. The results depict that the overall performance of AODV protocol is better than other two. In a nutshell, all protocols performed better with the TCP traffic pattern than CBR pattern.

Ahmed et al. [13] presented the analysis of AODV, DSR, and INTANTSENSE routing protocols under FTP, CBR and POISSON traffic patterns in Zigbee personal area networks. In case of CBR, AODV presented higher throughput than other protocols and less control overhead in case of DSR. In case of FTP, AODV presents lowest delay and data loss, while better throughput with DSR and lowest overhead with INTANTSENSE. With POISSON pattern, all protocols show a high data loss, but DSR observed with a minimum of all.

Tripathi et al. [14] also investigated the overall performance of AODV, WRP, and DSR routing protocols under RPGM with CBR and FTP traffic models. The evaluation of protocols carried out to observe throughput, PDR, and end-to-end delay metrics. Simulation results show that the AODV performs considerably better than other protocols on all metrics. It also observed that all protocols produced optimized results under CBR traffic and RPGM model.

Kumari et al. [15] observed the performance of Optimized Link State Routing (OLSR) and Destination Sequenced Distance Vector (DSDV) protocols by using VBR and CBR traffic patterns under various mobility models. The analysis of these protocols was carried out to observe the QoS parameters like throughput, packet drop, and delay. Finally, they concluded that the OLSR outperforms DSDV in terms of QoS when the node density keeps growing.

Rani et al. [26] observed the behavior of AODV and DSR routing protocols under three traffic patterns: FTP, FTP/GENERIC, and TELNET to get the insight of in terms of performance metrics such as PDR and average throughput. The simulation results depict that the overall performance of AODV is better than DSR.

From literature survey, it is clear that very few attempts have been made to analyze the behavior of multicast routing protocols under various traffic patterns and mobility models. Therefore, our motive is to study the behavior of MAODV, ODMRP, and PUMA under CBR and VBR traffic patterns in terms of QoS parameters.

3   Overview of Multicast Routing Protocols

As per the network topology, multicast routing protocols in MANET are broadly categorized as Tree-based and Mesh-based [28]. Tree-based protocols are found to be highly efficient in terms of packet forwarding and bandwidth consumption, but at the same time, it exhibits poor robustness due to a single path between two nodes. Whereas, mesh-based multicast protocol exhibit robustness due to the availability of alternate paths between the source and destination.

3.1   Multicast Ad-hoc On-demand Distance Vector Routing (MAODV)

MAODV is a tree-based multicast protocol that creates a shared tree to communicate with multiple senders and receivers during a multicast session [17]. In order to establish a path, MAODV uses route request (RREQ) message and route reply (RREP) message at the time of route demand. When a node wants to be the part of multicast group for communication it broadcast the RREQ packet. Only the nodes belong to the multicast tree will reply with RREP packet. In MAODV, the first node of the multicast group treated as the group leader, and it remains the leader until it leaves the group [18]. The main responsibility of the group leader is to periodically broadcast group sequence number to the entire group through HELLO message (Fig. 2).

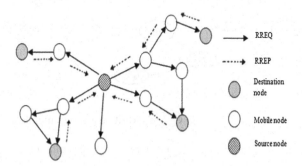

Fig. 2. Route discovery in MAODV multicast protocol

The RREP packet unicast by group member nodes contains the distance from the group leader and the latest sequence number of the multicast group. This protocol is the loop-free protocol and best suitable if the number of multicast session is very high.

3.2   Protocol for Unified Multicasting Thorough Announcement (PUMA)

PUMA is a mesh-based multicast protocol and considered as robust one in terms of availability of a route to destinations. PUMA is independent of any unicast routing protocols for its fundamental routing operations. PUMA is also one of the best suitable multicast algorithms for video streaming applications. A single control packet, Multicast Announcement (MA), is used by PUMA for creating and maintaining the mesh structure, electing the core node, forwarding the data packets. This election algorithm is just like building a spanning tree for a given graph to find the shortest path without forming any loop between group leader and members [19]. PUMA uses a single Multicast Announcement (MA) control packet that consists of Group ID, Core ID, the parent node and Distance to the core of managing and maintenance of the multicast group [20].

3.3   On-demand Multicast Routing Protocol (ODMRP)

ODMRP is a mesh-based multicast routing protocol developed by WAM Laboratory at UCLA [21]. In ODMRP multiple paths may exist between the nodes due to mesh formation, that helps in searching the most optimized route [22]. Similar to MAODV, ODMRP also uses two-phase for the route formation i.e. join-query and join-reply. When an intermediate node receives the join-reply packet, it checks for its ID in the routing table as a next node ID. If it is there, it considers itself in the route between source and destination and become the member of the forwarding group. Figure 3, represents the concept of forwarding group in ODMRP routing protocol.

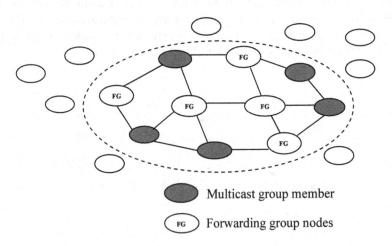

Fig. 3.   Forwarding nodes in ODMRP

ODMRP use soft-state approach for the maintenance of a multicast group and it does not use any explicit control packet to join or leave the multicast group [23]. Therefore, ODMRP is considered as a robust multicast protocol due to the multiple routes for the receiver and it also induces less control overhead in group communication [24].

4 Traffic Patterns

Traffic Patterns Play an Important Role in the Overall Performance of Multicast Routing in MANET. Some Important Traffic Patterns Are Discussed Here

(i) **Constant Bit Rate (CBR):** The constant bit rate (CBR) is the most common type of traffic used wireless networks. In CBR, the generator generates the data packets of fixed size at the constant rate with parameters that can change the time interval between packets [11]. CBR traffics are suitable for applications that require a constant bit stream, such as video-conferencing, and uncompressed Audio/Video distribution. Following format and parameters are used CBR during simulation:
CBR <source> <destination> <data to send> <data size> <interval> <start-time> <end-time>

(ii) **Variable Bit Rate (VBR):** In variable bit rate, packet size and transmission rate both vary as per the requirement of multimedia/video scenario [25]. It has the interval of ON/OFF states, ON state refers the data being generated and OFF state refers that data traffic is not being generated during a certain period of time.

(iii) **PARETO:** It is a kind of ON/OFF traffic pattern. The parameters that are required to configure are packet size, ON time, OFF time, and rate of transmission. It is well suited for video, multimedia, and voice traffic data sources [11].

5 Mobility Models

Mobility models in wireless communication represent the movement pattern of mobile nodes along with their location, velocity, and acceleration change overtime period [27]. Some most widely used mobility models are discussed here.

(i) **Random Waypoint Mobility Model (RWPMM):** It is one of the most extensively used mobility models in which mobile nodes randomly chosen within a fixed location, move linearly to a predefined location with random speed. The speed of a node is a predefined from a given limit of maximum and minimum speed. This model uses pause time to change the direction or speed [14].

(ii) **Random Walk Mobility Model (RWMM):** RWMM was first described mathematically by Einstein in 1926. A mobile node in this model can take any direction from predefined range 0 to 2π and speed from 0 to v_{max}. The Pause time of Random walk mobility model is zero. This is a memory-less model as it does not retain any previous information to take a future decision.

(iii) **Reference Point Group Mobility (RPGM):** In this model, each communication group has a group leader (logical center) that defines and monitor the group's motion. The logical center of the group performs the calculation of group motion. Each individual node can move about the predefined reference points under the control of group movement [9]. RPGM has found useful in the military battlefield and rescue communication.

(iv) **Gauss-Markov Mobility Model:** In this model the velocity of a node correlated over the varying time. The movement of the node is dependent on the current direction and velocity. This model overcomes the issue of sudden and sharp change present in random-based mobility models.

(v) **Random Direction:** It is very similar to Random walk mobility model in terms of random movement. Nodes take a pause after reaching at simulation boundary, again choose the other direction of movement in between 0 to 180°. It overcomes the issue of over clustering in some part of the simulation area present in RWPMM.

6 Algorithm Setup

Here, the whole process i.e. from multicast group formed to start of communication is given in the form of an algorithm. The given algorithm will be executed for MAODV, PUMA, and ODMRP.

Step 1. Initialize *MANET (M), Node_density (N),* *Sender_density, Wireless _Terrain, Group_Size,* *Propagation_Model, Node_Speed, IFQ_length* all required parameters. Step 2. Define group formation event 　　// *Group Join Event* 　　*For each N_i* 　　*N_i->Message_Send(JOIN)* 　　*End* 　　// *Group Leave Event* 　　*For each N_i* 　　*N_i->Message_Send(LEAVE)* 　　*End* *Step3.* Group initialization Phase 　　// *Call group Join Event* 　　*For each N_i* 　　*N_i ->Message_Send(JOIN)* 　　*End* 　　// *Call group Leave Event* 　　*For each N_i* 　　*N_i ->Message_Send(LEAVE)* 　　*End* Step 4. Join/Leave event Call 　　*Message_Send (Event)* 　　*{* 　　*Select Event* 　　*Case: GROUP_JOIN*	*N_i ->JOIN=TRUE* 　　*N_i ->GROUP_ID=Mg->ID* 　　*//Generate multicast group ID* 　　*}* 　　*Case: GROUP_LEAVE* 　　*N_i ->JOIN=FALSE* 　　*N_i ->GROUP_ID=NULL* 　　　　// *Set group id of node= null* 　　　　*End select* Step 5. Multicast group formation 　　*Create_Multicast_Group()* 　　*{* 　　*If Exists (M) then Mg=create_group()* 　　// *if MANET exist then start group formation* 　　*Mg->ID=getMAXID()* 　　// *assign max ID to multicast group* 　　*}* Step 6. Traffic initialization 　　*Genearate_Traffic_APP()* 　　*{* 　　*Set Interval_Time ()* 　　*Set Traffic Type =CBR/VBR* 　　*Set Packet Size =512 Bytes* 　　*}* Step 7. Group Communication Phase 　　*Data_communication= True* Step 8. Stop

The successful execution of above algorithm will results in the formation multicast group in MANET as shown in Fig. 4.

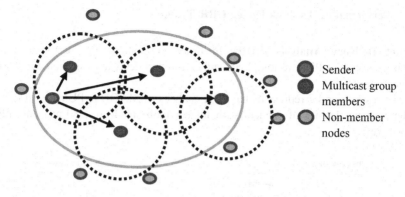

Fig. 4. Formation of multicast group in MANET

7 Performance Analysis

Performance analysis of MAODV, PUMA, and ODMRP multicast protocols have been carried out under the CBR and VBR traffic pattern as the majority of MANET's application usages these two traffic patterns. The simulation is performed using NS 2.35 simulator to observe the QoS parameters. Following are the simulation parameters (Table 1):

Table 1. Simulation parameters

Simulation parameters	
Node (s)	50
Sender Density	1, 2, 4, 6
Receiver Density	Max. possible rev = 29 (w.r.t sender density)
MAC Protocol	802.11
Antenna Type	Omni directional
Terrain	1001 × 1001
Ad Hoc Multicast Routing Protocol	MAODV, PUMA, ODMRP
Simulation Time	50 s
Group Size	1
Propagation Model	TwoRayGround
Simulator	NS-2
Node's Speed	40 m/s, 80 m/s, 120 m/s
Queue Type	DropTrail/Priority Queue
Traffic Type	Constant Bit Rate (CBR)
	Interval: 0.15 ms
	Packet Size: 1024 Bytes
	Variable Bit Rate (VBR)
	Burst Time: 0.15 ms
	Packet Size: 1024 Bytes
IFQ Length	50

7.1   Performance Analysis Under CBR Traffic

Packet Delivery Analysis (PDR): In order to evaluate the performance, QoS parameters such as PDR, routing load, and end-to-end delay are considered under CBR traffic.

Figures 5, 6 and 7 represents the PDR analysis of MAODV, PUMA and ODMRP under varying density of senders with node's mobility 40 ms, 80 ms, and 120 ms respectively.

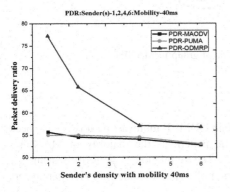

Fig. 5. PDR analysis under CBR traffic with node's speed 40 ms

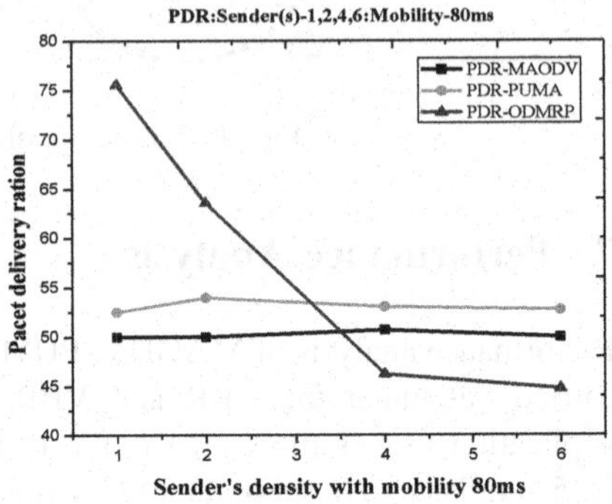

Fig. 6. PDR analysis under CBR traffic with node's speed 80 ms

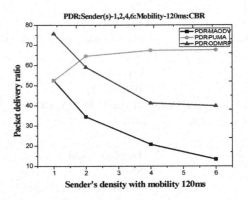

Fig. 7. PDR analysis under CBR traffic with node's speed 120 ms

From the above figures, it is clear that at low density of senders, ODMRP outperforms PUMA and MAODV in terms of PDR. But with the increase in senders density and mobility, ODMRP gradually increases the control overhead and shows reduced PDR. PUMA performs much better in terms of PDR with increasing senders and mobility of nodes due to low control overhead.

Routing Load Analysis: Figures 8, 9 and 10 represents the routing load analysis of MAODV, PUMA and ODMRP under varying senders and the mobility of nodes 40 ms, 80 ms, and 120 ms respectively.

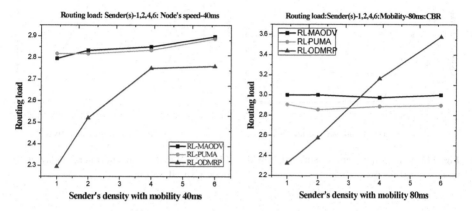

Fig. 8. Variation in routing load under CBR with node's mobility 40 ms

Fig. 9. Variation in routing load under CBR with node's mobility 80 ms

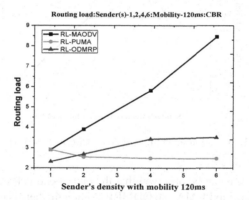

Fig. 10. Variation in routing load under CBR with node's speed 120 ms

From the figures, it is clear that the routing load of ODMRP is less as compared to PUMA and MAODV with low mobility and sender's density. But with the increase of mobility and sender's density, PUMA outperforms ODMRP and MAODV due to its ability to control all tree operations with a single control packet.

End-to-End Delay: Figures 11, 12 and 13 represents the end-to-end delay of MAODV, PUMA and ODMRP under varying senders and the mobility of nodes 40 ms, 80 ms, and 120 ms respectively.

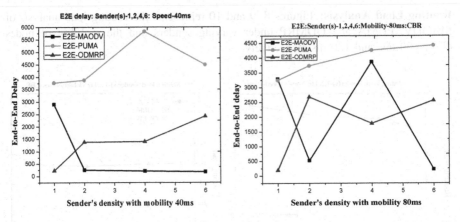

Fig. 11. Variation in end-to-end delay with node's speed 40 ms

Fig. 12. Variation in end-to-end delay with node's speed 80 ms

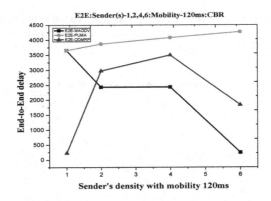

Fig. 13. Variation in end-to-end delay with node's speed 120 ms

From the figures, it can be observed that the end-to-end delay of ODMRP is more consistent as compared to PUMA and ODMRP. Although, there is no multicast protocol that can be considered as best under varying sender nodes and mobility, the overall performance of ODMRP is much more optimized than PUMA and MAODV under CBR traffic and increasing mobility. In nutshell, ODMRP exhibits sound scalability support in the mobile ad-hoc network as compared to PUMA and MAODV with CBR traffic.

7.2 Performance Analysis Under VBR Traffic

Packet Delivery Ratio (PDR): Figures 14, 15 and 16 represents the performance analysis of MAODV, PUMA, and ODMRP multicast routing protocols in terms of PDR under VBR traffic with varying sender(s) density (1, 2, 4, 6) and node's mobility 40 ms, 80 ms, and 120 ms respectively.

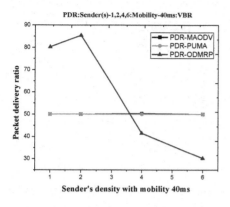

Fig. 14. PDR variation under varying sender(s) density with node's mobility 40 ms

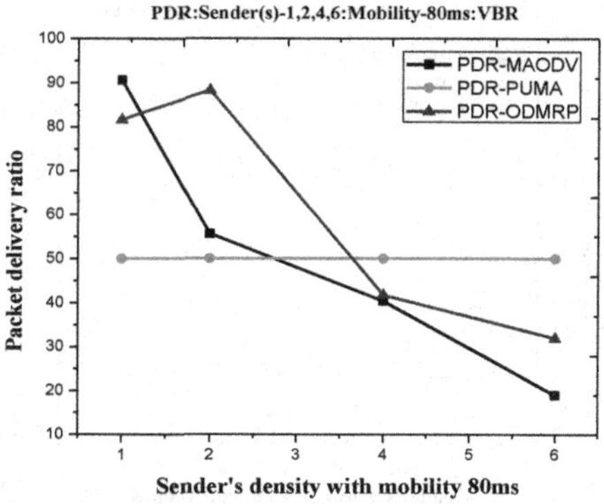

Fig. 15. PDR variation under varying sender (s) density with node's mobility 80 ms

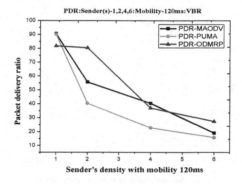

Fig. 16. PDR variation under VBR traffic and varying sender(s) density with node's mobility 120 ms

From figures, it is observed that under VBR traffic ODMRP has a better PDR at low density of senders and node's mobility, but with the increases of mobility and sender's density, PUMA has shown more consistent PDR than MAODV and ODMRP.

Routing Load Analysis: Figures 17, 18 and 19 represents the routing load analysis of MAODV, PUMA and ODMRP under varying density of senders and node's mobility 40 ms, 80 ms, and 120 ms respectively.

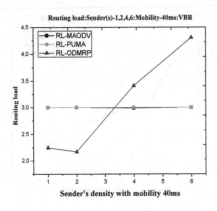

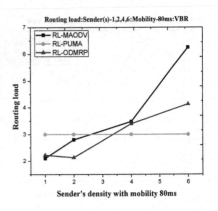

Fig. 17. Variation in routing load under VBR and varying density of sender(s) with node's speed 40 ms

Fig. 18. Variation in routing load under VBR and varying density of sender(s) with node's speed 80 ms

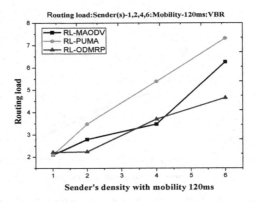

Fig. 19. Variation in routing load under VBR and varying density of sender(s) with node's speed 120 ms

From routing load analysis, it is observed that the routing load of ODMRP is more consistent than PUMA and MAODV under VBR traffic. Performance of MAODV is not so optimized due to periodic flooding by the group leader.

End-to-End Delay: Figures 20, 21 and 22 represents the end-to-end delay analysis of MAODV, PUMA and ODMRP under varying density of senders and node's mobility 40 ms, 80 ms, and 120 ms respectively.

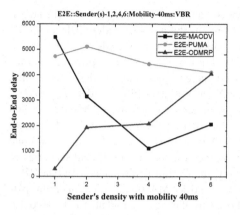

Fig. 20. Variation in end-to-end delay under varying sender(s) and node's speed 40 ms

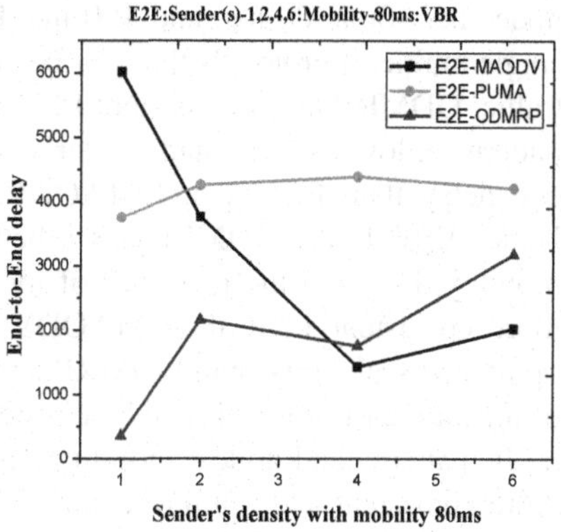

Fig. 21. Variation in end-to-end delay under varying sender(s) and node's speed 80 ms

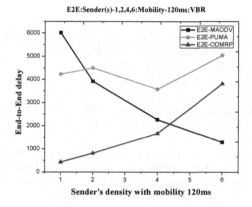

Fig. 22. Variation in end-to-end delay under varying sender(s) and node's speed 120 ms

From Figs. 20, 21 and 22, it is noticed that with at low density of senders ODMRP has a better end-to-end delay than PUMA and ODMRP. With the increase of sender's density, end-to-end delay of ODMRP is increased that indicates its resistance towards scalability. MAODV have shown better scalability under VBR traffic than PUMA and ODMRP.

8   Conclusion and Future Scope

In this work, performance analysis of MAODV, PUMA, and ODMRP is presented to analyze QoS parameters such as PDR, end-to-end delay, and routing load under CBR and VBR traffic patterns with varying density of sender's node and varying mobility of nodes i.e. 40ma, 80 ms, and 120 ms. From the analysis, it is found that there are no single multicast protocols that can be considered as the best one under CBR and VBR traffic. ODMRP has a consistent PDR and routing load in both CBR and VBR traffic patterns at low mobility and sender's density. Further, ODMRP has optimized end-to-end delay than PUMA and MAODVA with increasing senders under CBR traffic. Under VBR traffic ODMRP has a better PDR at low density of senders and node's mobility, but with the increases of mobility and sender's density, PUMA has shown more consistent PDR than MAODV and ODMRP. However, MAODV has more optimized scalability than ODMRP and PUMA under VBR traffic. In a nutshell, none of the multicast protocols can be considered as the best one under different scenarios of traffic patterns and node's mobility. However, the overall performance of ODMRP is more consistent and optimized than MAODV and PUMA under different traffic patterns and node's mobility and can be chosen as the best candidate to be used for multicast out of these three protocols. In future, analyses of other multicast routing protocols under more traffic patterns and various mobility models can be carried out to observe the performance to design the new multicast routing protocols.

References

1. Patil, G.M., Kumar, A., Shaligram, A.D.: Performance analysis and comparison of MANET routing protocols in selected traffic patterns for scalable network. Int. J. Comput. Sci. Inf. Technol. Secur. (IJCSITS) **6**(3), 109–117 (2016)
2. Chander, D., Kumar, R.: IDS enabled MAODV for secure group communication over MANET. Int. J. Comput. Sci. Inf. Secur. **14**(10), 648 (2016)
3. Sharma, P., Kaul, A., Garg, M.L.: Performance evaluation of CBR and VBR applications on different routing protocols in VANETs. Int. J. Recent Trends Eng. Technol. **11**(1), 566 (2014)
4. Al-Sharafi, A.M., Alrimi, B.A.: Throughput comparison of AOMDV and OLSR ad hoc routing protocols using VBR and CBR traffic models. In: 2013 International Conference on Advanced Computer Science Applications and Technologies (ACSAT), pp. 466–469. IEEE (2013)
5. Chander, D., Kumar, R.: A survey of issues in supporting QoS based multicast routing protocols over MANETs. Int. J. Comput. Appl. **112**(13), 1–5 (2015)
6. Yadav, A.K., Tripathi, S.: QMRPRNS: design of QoS multicast routing protocol using reliable node selection scheme for MANETs. Peer-to-Peer Netw. Appl. **10**(4), 897–909 (2017)
7. Qabajeh, M.M., Abdalla, A.H., Khalifa, O.O., Qabajeh, L.K.: A survey on scalable multicasting in mobile ad hoc networks. Wireless Pers. Commun. **80**(1), 369–393 (2015)
8. Shivahare, B.D., Wahi, C., Shivhare, S.: Comparison of proactive and reactive routing protocols in mobile adhoc network using routing protocol property. Int. J. Emerg. Technol. Adv. Eng. **2**(3), 356–359 (2012)
9. Manoharan, R., Ilavarasan, E.: Impact of mobility on the performance of multicast routing protocols in MANET. 1005.1742 (2010)
10. Mali, B.R., Barwar, N.C.: Effect of mobility on performance of MANET routing protocols under different traffic patterns. Int. J. Comput. Appl. **1**, 978–993 (2011)

11. Pal, A., Singh, J.P., Dutta, P., Basu, P., Basu, D.: A study on the effect of traffic patterns on routing protocols in ad-hoc network following RPGM mobility model. In: 2011 International Conference on Signal Processing, Communication, Computing and Networking Technologies (ICSCCN), pp. 233–237. IEEE (2011)

12. Wahed, M., Al-Mahdi, H., Mahmoud, T.M., Shaban, H.: The effect of mobility models and traffic patterns on the performance of routing protocols in MANETs. Int. J. Comput. Appl. **101**(9), 52–58 (2014)

13. Ahmed, E.S., Altahir, I.K., Mohammed, A.A., Salih, A.D.: Performance analysis of traffic patterns over MANET routing protocols in zigbee personal area network. Int. J. Comput. Sci. Telecommun. **6**(1), 13–19 (2015)

14. Tripathi, S., Kumar, A., Patel, S.K.: Impact of mobility speed on different traffic patterns in MANET. J. Netw. Commun. Emerg. Technol. (JNCET) **6**(8), 19–23 (2016)

15. Kumari, A., Gandotra, N., Gupta, S.C., Upadhyay, S.: Performance evaluation and analysis of QoS routing using OLSR and DSDV protocol in MANETs under different scenario using NS-2. J. Int. Acad. Phys. Sci. **17**(4), 419–432 (2013)

16. Singla, S., Jain, S.: Performance comparison of routing protocols of MANET in real world scenario using NS3. Int. J. Comput. Appl. **99**(14), 17–23 (2014)

17. Shrestha, R., Han, K.H., Choi, D.Y., Han, S.J.: A novel cross layer intrusion detection system in MANET. In: 2010 24th IEEE International Conference on Advanced Information Networking and Applications (AINA), 20 April, pp. 647–654. IEEE (2010)

18. Wang, Z., Liang, Y., Wang, L.: Multicast in mobile ad hoc networks. In: Li, D. (ed.) CCTA 2007. TIFIP, vol. 258, pp. 151–164. Springer, Boston, MA (2008). https://doi.org/10.1007/978-0-387-77251-6_17

19. Sumathy, S., Yuvaraj, B., Harsha, E.S.: Analysis of multicast routing protocols: PUMA and ODMRP. Int. J. Mod. Eng. Res. (IJMER) **2**(6), 4613–4621 (2012)

20. Vellore, P., Gillard, P., Venkatesan, R.: Reliability and overhead analysis of multicast BitTorrent enabled ad hoc network routing. In: 2010 IEEE International Conference on Communications (ICC), 23 May 2010, pp. 1–6. IEEE (2010)

21. Kharraz, M.A., Sarbazi-Azad, H., Zomaya, A.Y.: On-demand multicast routing protocol with efficient route discovery. J. Netw. Comput. Appl. **35**(3), 942–950 (2012)

22. Manoharan, R., Ilavarasan, E.: Impact of mobility on the performance of multicast routing protocols in MANET, 11 May. arXiv preprint arXiv:1005.1742 (2010)

23. Rangarajan, J., Baskaran, K.: Performance analysis of multicast protocols: ODMRP, PUMA and OBAMP. Int. J. Comput. Sci. Commun. **2**(2), 577–581 (2011)

24. Saghir, M., Wan, T.C., Budiarto, R.: Load balancing QoS multicast routing protocol in mobile ad hoc networks. In: Cho, K., Jacquet, P. (eds.) AINTEC 2005. LNCS, vol. 3837, pp. 83–97. Springer, Heidelberg (2005). https://doi.org/10.1007/11599593_7

25. Xu, Y., Elayoubi, S.E., Altman, E., El-Azouzi, R., Yu, Y.: Flow-level QoE of video streaming in wireless networks. IEEE Trans. Mob. Comput. **15**(11), 2762–2780 (2016)

26. Rani, M., Singla, R.: Impact of FTP, FTP/GENERIC and TELNET traffic pattern on the performance of routing protocols (AODV, DSR) in MANET. Int. J. Innov. Res. Comput. Commun. Eng. **4**(5), 9939–9947 (2016)

27. Bai, F., Helmy, A.: A survey of mobility models. Wireless Adhoc Networks. University of Southern California, USA, vol. 206, p. 147 (2004)

28. Chopra, A., Gujral, R.: QoS enabled communication support over multicast ad hoc network: an overview. Amit Chopra Int. J. Eng. Res. Appl. **5**(1), 01–06 (2015)

Modified Trust Value Based Approach to Secure Wireless Sensor Networks

Pardeep Kaur[(⊠)] and Sandeep Kad

Department of Computer Science and Engineering,
Amritsar College of Engineering and Technology, Amritsar, Punjab, India
parichahal23@gmail.com, sandeepkad@acetamritsar.org

Abstract. The unattended nature of the WSN makes the nodes susceptible to various attacks. Among many of the possible attacks, ones that are focused on draining nodes' energy are most dangerous since they leave the network dead. This paper proposes a scheme to detect the aggressive behavior of nodes by using the packet- forwarding behavior of the nodes. Trust value is lessened if in any case there is a difference between the number of packets forwarded by the sensor hub during data transmission is discovered abnormal. In this way, after a certain number of rounds, nodes which are acting as aggressive will be removed. For transmitting the information over the system effectively when the abnormal hub is to be expelled from existing path would require second way promptly accessible, to take care of this issue in this method two nearest neighboring hubs are chosen to shape two ways. The rendition of the system is analyzed on the basis of remaining energy, packet forwarding ratio, and throughput.

Keywords: Energy efficient routing · Wireless Sensor Network
PDORP · Packet forwarding ratio · DSR · Trust value

1 Introduction

Recent days due to advances in the Wireless Sensor Networks, they are popular in various modern applications such as industrial checking and control, machine health observing etc. as they are much cheaper to deploy than Wired networks. Wireless Sensor Networks (WSNs) consist of self-sufficient specific transducers with a correspondence framework intended to detect and capture the physical and environmental parameters, such as temperature, vibration, motion or pollutants, sound, wind direction, humidity at different locations over a time or over a space at diverse location [1, 2]. WSNs are highly distributed and comprise of few to a large number of little and lightweight sensor hubs are arranged to frame a system with the end goal that every sensor hub can transmit and get information bundles messages over remote connections. WSN comprises of the following basic components: 1. A get together of Distributed or restricted sensor, 2. An interconnecting system, 3. The main point for data grouping, 4. An arrangement of processing assets at the essential point to deal with the information gathered from all the sensor hubs. These are systems of regularly little, battery controlled, Wireless gadgets and groups on-board handling, correspondence, detecting abilities [3]. Following is the Fig. 1 portraying the fundamental structure of remote Sensor Network.

© Springer Nature Singapore Pte Ltd. 2019
P. K. Singh et al. (Eds.): FTNCT 2018, CCIS 958, pp. 412–424, 2019.
https://doi.org/10.1007/978-981-13-3804-5_30

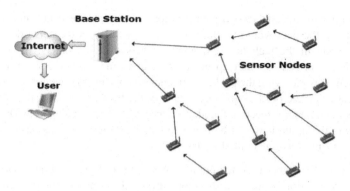

Fig. 1. Basic structure of Wireless Sensor Network [3]

Sensor nodes are tiny computers which can compute, sense, store and transmit the data. Sensors are the fundamental building blocks of WSN and might change in the measure from that of the dust grain to the extent of the shoe box. Sensor hubs contain onboard sensor, storage (Limited storage), low power processor (Limited processing), radio transceiver (Low-power, low data rate, limited range), and power supply (battery or Embedded form of power gathering e.g. solar cells) and convert physical parameters e.g. heat, light, motion, vibration into electrical signals. Mostly sensor hubs are self-powered and frequent replacement of batteries is not possible, therefore they have a strict power consumption restriction [3–5]. Energy utilization in a sensor hub could be expected to either "supportive" or "inefficient" sources. Supportive power utilization can be because of transmitting or accepting information, handling query demands, and sending inquiries and information to neighboring hubs. Inefficient power usage can be because of at least one of the accompanying realities. Idle listening is one of the major sources of power wastage (where handset is active yet no information transmit or got by sensor) and another major cause for power dissipation is collision (When a hub gets more than one packet in the meantime, these packets are named collided), even when they coincide only to some extent [6]. The ultimate challenges of sensor hubs are the maximization of network lifetime and energy conservation [7]. Due to the deployment of WSN in remote zones they are powerless against various security dangers like the attackers can easily insert malicious message into network and also WSN more likely to be influenced by denial of service attack in which attacker tries to deplete assets accessible to the victim hub by sending additional pointless packets leads in early passing of the hub influencing the lifetime of system [8, 9].

The main contributions of this paper are as follows:

- The communication distance among the nodes is decreased by choosing neighboring nodes with minimum distance while formulating the transmission path with the intention that smaller amount of power gets expended.
- Two neighboring nodes are chosen in the way of destination resulting in two paths from source to destination because if the node in path has been detected successfully as the aggressive node then the elimination of such a node from the existing

path would necessitate second path promptly accessible for data transmission else re-building the path would produce unwelcomed delay in the network.

- If any node in the path has sent more packets than the others, its energy consumption is bound to shoot up but at the same time, energy consumption of the node which is receiving the packets will also go up. Thus if the energy consumption levels are checked out for the fitness value of the trust of the node, this might result in the detection of receiving node as an attacker which must be avoided. To resolving this issue It would be better to calculate the trust value according to the number of packets transmitted by the nodes.

The rest of this paper is sorted out as follows: Sect. 2 gives a brief presentation of related work. Section 3 provides the motivation behind proposing the scheme. Section 4 introduces the proposed work. Section 5 indicates simulation results and execution assessment. At long last, this paper is concluded in Sect. 6.

2 Literature Survey

Genetic Algorithm (GA) [10] was introduced for finding the most limited way in steering. Variable-length chromosomes have been utilized. Their components speak to hubs incorporated into a way between an assigned match of the source and goal hubs. By using crossover partial- routes are exchanged and mutation present new incomplete routes. To manage all the infeasible chromosomes a new repair function is introduced. This paper additionally builds up a populace measuring condition that guarantees an answer to wanted quality for the proposed GA. The proposed calculation can look through the arrangement space viably and expediently contrasted and other surviving calculations. It makes the connections among the extent of the populace, the nature of the arrangement, the cardinality of letters in order. The populace measuring condition has all the earmarks of being a moderate instrument to decide a populace estimate in the steering issue.

In Power-Efficient Gathering in Sensor Information Systems (PEGASIS) [11] protocol, a strategic distance is maintained from the supposition of direct correspondence and decreases the generally expansive overhead of the LEACH convention. In PEGASIS, the hubs shape a sequence, and every hub saves the location of an upstream and a downstream hub in its directing table. The information accumulation procedure is started at the most distant end of the sequence. Each middle of the road hub totals the gathered information with its nearby information before sending the outcome to its neighbor. The farthest hub in the sequence is in charge of transferring data to the sink hub.

Lee [12] investigated that TDMA spaces alongside scheduling algorithms enhance the system lifetime. This made every one of the hubs be functional amid just their apportioned time. The proposed ACO calculation (Three Pheromones ACO, TPACO) which utilizes three sorts of pheromones to discover the arrangement proficiently, while traditional ACO calculations utilize just a single kind of pheromone. One is the neighborhood pheromone, which enables a subterranean insect to arrange a scope set with lesser sensors; the others are the global pheromones. One global pheromone is utilized for the advancement of the quantity of desired dynamic sensors per PoI, and the second global pheromone is utilized to frame a set of hubs that have the same number of hubs as an insect has chosen the count of dynamic hubs by utilizing the previous pheromone. They demonstrated that TPACO calculation can unravel the EEC (Efficient-Energy Coverage) issue with a more reasonable approach and enhances the lifetime of the system by finding the ideal cover set of sensors in each time slot.

Jain [13] built up another fuzzy graph based displaying technique for remote hub organize that considers the dynamic idea of the system, unstable parts of radio connections and physical layer vulnerability. Fuzzy neighborhoods are developed by the fuzzy graph which is utilized to distinguish all the forthcoming part hubs of a group. To calculate the ideal centrality of a cluster another centrality metric to be specific fuzzy k-hop centrality is characterized. The new centrality metric thinks about the leftover vitality of individual hubs, connect excellence, hop space among the forthcoming cluster head and particular part hubs to guarantee improved group leader choice and bunch value. This method Fuzzy logic and ACO based OD-PPRP directing has enhanced system lifespan, less communication hindrance, improved parcel conveyance proportion and a decline in operating cost than other steering conventions like EARQ, EEABR, and EAODV.

Yadav [14] exhibited Newton divided difference interpolation for interface expectation strategy. This joins the impact of ideal transmit control and received signal strength based connection accessibility appraisal with AODV steering convention utilizing cross-layer approach. The proposed strategy introduced to utilize ideal transmission control for transferring the information to the neighbor to build the battery life of ad-hoc hubs and got received signal strength based connection expectation to expand the accessibility of the connections. The outcomes demonstrate that there is a huge diminishment in packet loss and end-to-end postpone parameters and change in information parcel conveyance proportion for AODV with connecting expectation.

Gopal [15] exhibit a hybrid system by consolidating the Virtual Circle Combined Straight Routing (VCCSR) and Virtual Grid-based Dynamic Route Adjustment (VGDRA) methods for elongating the lifetime of virtual remote sensor Network. This strategy gives sink versatility and proficient in finding an ideal way as indicated by the position of the sink. In this strategy, the VCCSR steering tradition is utilized for the arrangement of nodes for cluster formation and assembling the information by making a dynamic tree structure. Then again the VGDRA is utilized to parcel the sensors into cells and setting up a course to forward the information to sink. The strategy has indicated preferred outcomes over VCCSR and VGDRA in the terms of energy efficiency, normal postpone time and system lifetime for expansive WSNs.

Mohamed [16] analyzed that by using genetic algorithm the directing definition decreases the deferral and vitality utilization. Their work assesses the vitality utilization and outline systems are tended to with expanded adaptability in WSN interchanges. They utilized stream rate task strategies and MOPT-based steering for WSNs. The primary strategy utilizes Karush-Kuhn-Tucker (KKT) circumstances to locate the ideal arrangement, while the second one depends on hereditary calculations (GA). Another plan is presented mutually limit the vitality and the postponement. The strategy proposed causes arrange originators to address plan methodology proficiently and increment the adaptability in the vitality defer tradeoff for correspondences in WSN.

Tarasia [17] proposed an algorithm in which the progressive structure is built and stretched out for finish scope region to fulfill the network and a similar structure is additionally reached out to accomplish full scope in WSN. In this approach, a tree is developed by utilizing a directing component with sleep schedules, to such an extent that every single transitional hub which is partaking in steering is in dynamic mode, and whatever remains of the hubs are probably going to be in rest mode. To guarantee reasonable vitality utilization among the hubs, recreations of tree happens intermittently. To satisfy the scope prerequisite, the leaf hubs are separated again into two sections, i.e., the leaf hubs that are dynamic, however not taking an interest in steering, and the leaf hubs that are totally in rest mode. In this way, while the steering tree is remade, the leaf hubs which are totally in rest mode in the past round, have more opportunity to be in the dynamic mode in the following round, thus the lifetime of the system gets extended.

3 Motivation

The nodes with lesser batteries characterize Wireless Sensor Networks. If illegitimate hub focuses on draining the power of the nodes, then the life span of the network would become much less. In this case, replacing the nodes is the only way out which is a costly affair. This paper has focused on the discovery of node, which becomes aggressive during information transfer phase by sending extra number of packets than genuine nodes. This node will consume power of the nodes participating in the data transfer. The existing PDORP scheme detects such node by computing the trust values based on abnormal energy consumption of the nodes. By the time difference in the energy levels of the nodes get to an abnormal level, the attacker node would have launched the attack successfully. Thus, the existing scheme might not be much energy efficient in detection of such malicious node. Thus, it motivates us to propose a scheme to detect these kind of nodes in an energy efficient way.

4 Proposed Work

The authors in the scheme "Energy Efficient Direction Based PDORP Routing Protocol for WSN" has focused on detecting the nodes, which are aggressive while forwarding the data packets. For this, the energy consumed by each node is taken as basic criteria to detect any abnormality.

The proposed technique, however, considers the packet-forwarding behavior of the nodes considering their aggressive behavior as the criteria to detect the abnormality. Now, if the node has been detected successfully as the aggressive node then the removal of such a node from the existing path would require second path readily available for data transmission else re-building the path would produce an unwelcome delay in the network. Thus, there must be more than one paths stored in the cache memory for the immediate availability of the second path.

When the source hub has some data to transmit to the destination hub, it will use the GPS routing to formulate a path. It will first look for the neighbors in the communication range. All the neighbors whose x as well as y coordinates are in the direction towards the destination node are considered. From all these neighbors, the two nodes will be selected that will be closest to the destination node thus resulting in two paths from source to destination. The source hub would transmit data to the destination using the first path. After the first round, the number of packets forwarded by each node would be checked in order to find out the fitness value of the trust of each node. If any node has forwarded the greater number of packets than the others, then its trust value would be reduced. After the end of second round, if the same node is found to behave aggressively then its trust value would be reduced to zero and source node would fetch the second path from its cache memory to forward the data (Fig. 2).

Algorithm 1

Suppose N is the no. of nodes in the network and N_{ei} be Neighbor set of each node.

1. for i = 1:N
2.   for j = 1:N_{ei}
3.   if x(i) < x(j) && y(i) < y(j) && x(d) > x(j) && y(d) > y(j)
4.   Consider node for path selection.
5.   End if.
6.   Choose the shortest node and complete path formation.
7.   End for.
8. End for.
9. Send data over the path.
10. Compute no. of packets forwarded.
11. Compute trust :

11.1. $A = \dfrac{\sum no.\,of\ packets\ forwarded}{no.\,of\ nodes\ in\ path}$

11.2. $ga = 1 - \dfrac{(no.\,of\ packets\ forwarded)}{A}$

11.3. if ga > 0

11.4.   trust = trust + Rand ()

11.5. else

11.6.   trust = trust - Rand ()

11.7. End if

12.   if trust value > 0

12.1.   Repeat steps 9 to 11.6

12.2. else

12.3.   Choose new path to send data

12.4. End if

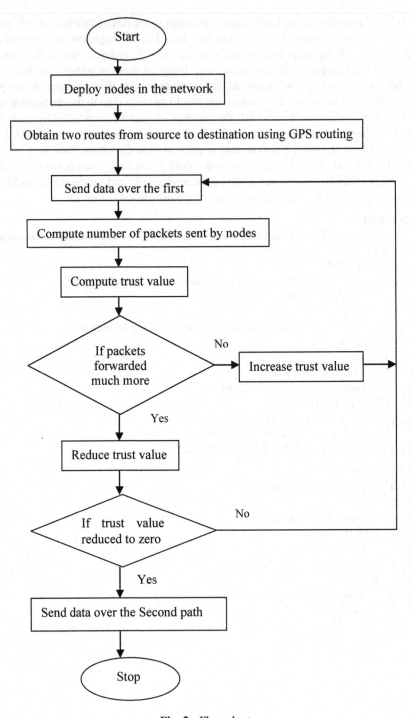

Fig. 2. Flow chart

5 Results

The proposed scheme was implemented in NS2.35. The language used to construct the system and implement the method was tool command language and awkward scripts. The simulation parameters used have been described in Table 1 below:

Table 1. Simulation parameters

Parameter	Value
Channel	Wireless
Number of nodes	60
Simulation tool	NS2.35
Initial energy	30 Joules
Mac	802.11
Propagation	Two ray ground
Sensing region	1150 m * 1100 m
Antenna	Omni directional
Routing protocol	DSR

Analysis of Experimental Outcomes

The examination of the proposed strategy to PDORP technique and interpretation of the framework was analyzed in perspective of three parameters

1. **Throughput:** It is defined as a measure of information got at the base station from the group heads. It is measured in Kbps.
2. **Remaining Energy:** This parameter indicates the lifespan of the system. More is the remaining power, better is the network's lifetime.
3. **Packet Forwarding Ratio:** This is the ratio of the count of packets forwarded by the hubs to the count of packets received by them. This is an important factor in determining the aggressive nature of the node.

Figure 3 illustrates the value of throughput. The amount of data received at the destination is approx. 1400 Kbps. During the first round, the value of throughput increased to 524 Kbps, during the second round, its value was increased by further 536 Kbps. These two rounds indicate the aggressive forwarding of the data packets in the network, which increases the throughput. During the last round, when the attacker has been detected, the throughput increased by 350 Kbps. Thus, the aggressive forwarding gets reduced. In addition, it is clearly indicated by the results that proposed trust value based technique outperforms than PDORP.

Figure 4 represents the percentage of packets forwarded by the nodes in the network. Since this work was focused on aggressive data forwarding node, the evaluation

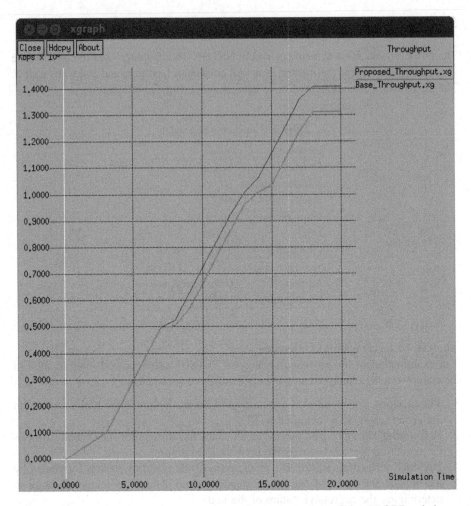

Fig. 3. Comparison of throughput of the proposed strategy - red to existing PDORP technique - green. (Color figure online)

of this parameter was necessary, as this would allow us to measure the impact of attacker node in the network. The value of PFR was around 2.5 two times through the entire simulation. This represents the run of simulation for two rounds during which the trust value of the nodes is being computed. This indicates aggressive nodes are present in the path as the number of packets forwarded are much more. The third time, the trust value of the malicious node reduces to zero and is removed from the path over which data is being forwarded. Consequently, the value of PDR reduces down indicating no more aggressive data forwarding is happening in the network. Figure 4 clearly

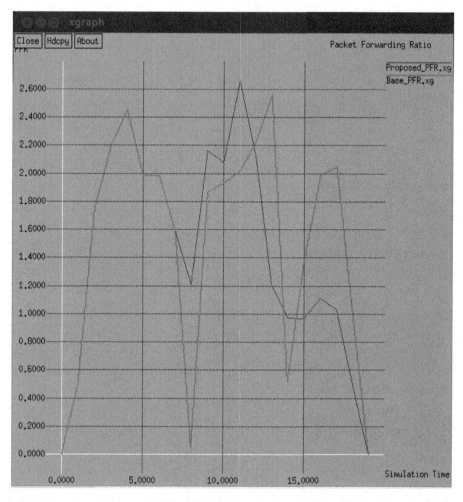

Fig. 4. Comparison of packet forwarding ration(PFR) of the proposed approach - red to existing PDORP technique - green. (Color figure online)

demonstrates that proposed scheme is more effective than PDORP in discovering the malicious node in the network.

Figure 5 shows the variation of remaining energy in the network versus simulation time. Initially, the network was supplied with the initial average energy of 30 J and remaining energy in the network was approx. 21 J. Figure 5 illustrates that the energy consumption of existing PDORP method is slightly higher than the Proposed method. Hence proposed method is performing better than the existing method in case of energy conservation of the system and improving the lifespan of system.

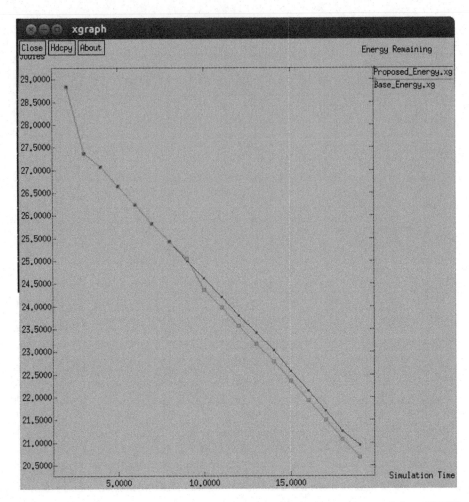

Fig. 5. Comparison of remaining energy of proposed strategy - red to existing PDORP technique - green. (Color figure online)

6   Conclusion

The focus of this study was to use trust value of the nodes calculated based on their packet forwarding nature, to check if a node is aggressive or not. The value of PFR obtained went up to 2.4 for the first time, 2.6 for the second time. Consequently, for the third time, the value was reduced. Likewise, the value of throughput increased more during the initial two rounds and it reduced to lower levels for the third round after successful detection of the malevolent node. The proposed schemes require a run of two rounds to reduce the trust rate of the malicious hub to zero and thereby eradicate it in the successive rounds. Thus, more rate of PFR in initial two rounds of simulation means more power will be consumed for a minimum of two rounds only, (since energy is proportional to the number of packet transmissions). Since, after the second round the value of PFR reduces, this would mean that network's energy consumption would occur in a normal way. This indicates successful detection of the aggressive node from the network without much wastage of network resources.

References

1. Akyildiz, I.F., Su, W., Sankarasubramaniam, Y., Cayirci, E.: A survey on sensor networks. IEEE Commun. Mag. **40**(8), 102–114 (2002). https://doi.org/10.1109/MCOM.2002. 1024422
2. Chen, M., Gonzalez, S., Vasilakos, A., Cao, H., Leung, C.M.: Body area networks: a survey. Mob. Netw. Appl. **16**(2), 171–193 (2011). https://doi.org/10.1007/s11036-010-0260-8
3. Garg, V.: Wireless Communication and Networking. Elsevier Inc., Amsterdam (2007)
4. Wu, M., Collier, M.: TSEP: a localised algorithm for extending the lifetime of sensor networks. In: Proceedings of the IEEE Wireless Advanced (WiAD), pp. 289–294 (2011). https://doi.org/10.1109/wiad.2011.5983271
5. Lindsey, S., Raghavendra, C., Sivalingam, K.M.: Data gathering algorithms in sensor networks using energy metrics. IEEE Trans. Parallel Distrib. Syst. **13**(9), 924–935 (2002). https://doi.org/10.1109/TPDS.2002.1036066
6. Tian, D., Georganas, N.D.: Energy efficient routing with guaranteed delivery in wireless sensor networks. In: IEEE Wireless Communication Networking, WCN, vol. 3, pp. 1923–1929. IEEE (2003). https://doi.org/10.1109/wcnc.2003.1200681
7. Saravanakumar, R., Susila, S.G., Raja, J.: An energy-efficient cluster based node scheduling protocol for wireless sensor networks. In: 2010 IEEE International Conference on Computational Intelligence and Computing Research (ICCIC), vol. 1–5, pp. 28–29, December 2010
8. Karlof, C., Wagner, D.: Secure routing in wireless sensor networks: attacks and countermeasures. In: IEEE International Workshop on Sensor Network Protocols and Applications (2003). http://10.0.4.85/SNPA.2003.1203362
9. Nagarathna, K., Kiran, Y.B., Mallapur, J.D., Hiremath, S.: Trust-based secured routing in wireless multimedia sensor networks. In: International Conference on Computational Intelligence, Communication Systems and Networks (CICSyN) (2012). https://doi.org/10. 1109/cicsyn.2012.20
10. Ahn, C.W., Ramakrishna, R.S.: A genetic algorithm for shortest path routing problem and the sizing of populations. IEEE Trans. Evol. Comput. **6**(6), 566–579 (2002). https://doi.org/ 10.1109/tevc.2002.804323
11. Lindsey, S., Raghavendra, C.S.: PEGASIS: power-efficient gathering in sensor information systems. In: IEEE Aerospace Conference, pp. 1125–1130. IEEE (2002). https://doi.org/10. 1109/aero.2002.1035242
12. Lee, J., Choi, B., Lee, J.: Energy efficient coverage of wireless sensor networks using Ant colony optimization with three types of pheromones. IEEE Trans. Ind. Inf. **7**, 419–427 (2011). https://doi.org/10.1109/tii.2011.2158836
13. Jain, A., Ramana Reddy, B.V.: A novel method of modeling wireless sensor network using fuzzy graph and energy efficient fuzzy based k-hop clustering algorithm. Wirel. Pers. Commun. **82**(1), 157–181 (2015)
14. Yadav, A., Singh, Y.N., Singh, R.: Cross-layer design for power control and link availability in mobile adhoc networks. Int. J. Comput. Netw. Commun. (IJCNC) **7**(3), 127–143 (2015). https://doi.org/10.5121/ijcnc.2015.7310

15. Gopal, D., Suriyakala, C.D.: Performance evaluation of hybrid energy efficient cluster based routing scheme for mobile sink based WSN. In: IEEE Conference on Control, Instrumentation, Communication and Computational Technologies (ICCICCT) (2015). https://doi.org/10.1109/iccicct.2015.7475342

16. Mohamed, E., Ahmed, M., Abderrazak, A., Elfouly, T.M.: Routing and flow rate assignment using multi-objective optimization in wireless sensor networks. In: IEEE Conference on Wireless Communications and Networking Conference (WCNC 2015), pp. 1368–1373 (2015). https://doi.org/10.1109/wcnc.2015.7127668

17. Tarasia, N., Lenka, M., Swain, A.: Energy efficient extended coverage in wireless sensor networks. In: IEEE International Conference on Advanced Information Networking and Applications, AINA 2015, Gwangiu, pp. 247 – 254 (2015). https://doi.org/10.1109/aina.2015.192

PF-AID-2KAP: Pairing-Free Authenticated Identity-Based Two-Party Key Agreement Protocol for Resource-Constrained Devices

Mahender Kumar[✉] and P. C. Saxena

School of Computer and Systems Sciences,
Jawharlal Nehru University, New Delhi, India
mahendjnu1989@gmail.com, pcsaxena@jnu.ac.in

Abstract. An adequate construction of shared session key for wireless-resource constrained devices is a challenging task than conventional wired, memory and power-rich devices. Since several two-party key establishment schemes have been proposed but they are not suitable for resource-constrained devices. It has been seen that pairing operations on elliptic curves are computationally more costly than scalar multiplication and addition operations on the elliptic curve. In this article, we proposed pairing-free two-party authenticated ID-based key agreement protocol (PF-AID-2KAP) for such resource constrained devices. Under the assumption to solve ECDLP and CDHP problems, the propose PF-AID-2KAP scheme is provably secure. Further, we show that the key agreement scheme is resilience to following adversarial attacks: perfect forward secrecy, MITM attack, key control, known session key security. As compared to other schemes, our proposed system have less running time, less bandwidth cost and takes less number message exchange during communication.

Keywords: Identity based cryptosystem · Elliptic curve cryptosystem
Key agreement protocol · Resource- constrained devices

1 Introduction

Today, the exponential growth of wireless-electronic technology, for example, mobile phones, personal computer, personal digital assistant (PDA), etc., made people's daily life interesting, efficient and convenient [1, 2]. The secure communication between two resource-constrained devices, having less memory space and less battery power requires lightweight cryptosystem [3, 4]. For instance, one device wants to make private conversation with the second device in the same network; both parties must ensure the authenticity of identity with other for confidential communication. It can be implemented with conventional public key cryptography [5].

In the conventional communication system, public key cryptography was the essential techniques for providing the security requirements [5]. In public key cryptography, user computes the pair of public and private key in which the private key is used for signature and decryption purpose, and the public key is published publically for encryption and signature verification. Both keys are mathematically interconnected to each other in such a way that public key can be efficiently computed from private

© Springer Nature Singapore Pte Ltd. 2019
P. K. Singh et al. (Eds.): FTNCT 2018, CCIS 958, pp. 425–440, 2019.
https://doi.org/10.1007/978-981-13-3804-5_31

key, but it is hard to generate the private key if public key is given. Since wireless-low power devices are restricted to high computational, and memory overhead, so traditional public-key cryptosystem based on RSA cannot deploy in low power devices as they are the computationally rich operation, for example, modular exponentiation [4].

Compared with RSA based-public key cryptosystem, elliptic curve cryptosystem (ECC) has significant advantages, for example, faster computation and more secure on small key sizes [6]. It shows that ECC-based authentication has remarkable benefits in low power devices than other cryptosystems [7]. However, the ECC requires the public key infrastructure (PKI) managed by the trusted third party known as the certification authority (CA). CA computes the digital certificate for every device that binds the device public key with his/her unique identity. This system is beneficial for a small network, but in practice, if the network size grows it suffers from the certificate management overhead.

In order to address the such issues associated with PKC, Shamir [8], gives the identity-based cryptosystem (IBC) in 1984. In this approach, author supposed the device's unique identity such as phone number, SSN, email address, postal address, etc., as the public key and the trusted authority is known as the private key generator (PKG) authenticates the device and compute the private key corresponding to device's unique identity. Till 2001, this scheme was used for the signature and verification purposes only. Later, Boneh and Franklin [9] was the first to implement the fully functional identity-based encryption scheme using bilinear pairing and after that several identity-based signature and encryption schemes [10–14] have discussed.

Several authenticated two-parties identity-based key agreement schemes that exploit the advantages of IBC have addressed in [15–24]. However, these protocols are based on bilinear pairing, and integer factorization and some of the protocols are susceptible to the security attacks, for example, man-in-the-middle (MITM) attack, perfect forward security, known session key attack and key control attack. Additionally, it has been seen that pairing operations are around 20 times slower than the operations on elliptic curves [25]. In this article, we proposed two-party authenticated ID-based key establishment protocol based on ECC (PF-AID-2KAP). Our proposed scheme is considered as provable secure against discrete logarithm problem on the elliptic curve (ECDLP) and computational Diffie-Hellman problem. Further, we show that proposed key agreement scheme is secure against MITM attacks, perfect forward security, known session key attack and key control attacks. Additionally, the proposed system performs better as compared to the other related schemes.

The rest of the paper is arranged as follows: mathematical background includes elliptic curve cryptography, bilinear map, resource-constrained devices, identity-based encryption, and mathematical complexity are given in Sect. 2. The definitions and security notions of our proposed key establishment protocol are discussed in Sect. 3. Sections 4 gives the construction of the proposed scheme. Security analysis and computation comparison of our scheme against with existing systems are analyzed in Sect. 5. Finally, the conclusion is given in Sect. 6.

2 Background

2.1 Elliptic Curve Cryptography

Koblitz [25] and Miller [26] introduce an extension of Public Key Cryptosystem called the elliptic curve cryptosystem (ECC) which security is defined over the elliptic curve. To have an ability to improve computation efficiency and complexity of traditional cryptosystem, concerning the parameters (such as having smaller key size, smaller system parameter, lower bandwidth and power requirements, and tiny hardware requirements), ECC is recommendable in the area of the sensor network and ad-hoc wireless network.

Consider two integers, x and $y \in F_P$, an equation $E : y^2 = (x^3 + mx + n) mod p$ and condition $C : 4m^2 + 27n^2 \neq 0$. Formally, if the set of points (x, y) satisfied the equation E and formed an abelian group with points 0 is considered its identity element, then it is known as the elliptic curve. The condition C on above equation support that the equation E consists of the finite abelian group defined over the set of points $E_P(m, n)$ on the elliptic curve. A sample of elliptic curve is shown in Fig. 1(a) for m = −1 and n = 0 and in Fig. 1(b) for m = −1 and n = 1.

Consider the two points on elliptic curve E are $P = (x_P, y_P)$ and $Q = (x_Q, y_Q)$, the third points which are obtained by performing addition of A and B on the elliptic curve is $R = (x_R, y_R)$. The addition of two points on elliptic curve is represented as P + Q = R.

$$x_R = \left(\mu^2 - x_P - x_Q \right) mod p$$

$$y_R = (\mu(x_P - x_Q) - y_P) mod p$$

Where,

and $$\mu = \begin{cases} \left(\frac{y_Q - y_P}{x_Q - x_P} \right) mod p, & \text{if } P \neq Q \\ \left(\frac{3x_P^2 + m}{2y_P} \right) mod p, & \text{if } P = Q \end{cases}$$

Adding points: The addition of two points of the elliptic curve is computed as $R = P + Q$ with the help of equation defined above, where two points are different.

Doubles points: The double points of elliptic curve is computed as $R = P + P = 2P$ with the help of equation defined above, where two points are same.

Scalar multination points: The scalar multiplication on the elliptic curve is computed as $R = nP = P + P + ... + P(n \ times)$ with the help of adding points.

Private and Public Key. Scalar multiplication on elliptic curve plays the central role in cryptography to compute the pair of the public and private key. Consider user calculates the pair of private and public key, he chooses a random number n from a finite field, kept a secret to him, act as a private key, and he picks a point on elliptic curve E, say P, which published publically. User then perform the scalar multiplication to get the points R on elliptic curve, such that R = nP is act as a public key. Table 1 gives the comparison of security level achieved by the Digital Signature Standard (DSS), RSA and ECC scheme and reader may observed that as compared with the public key cryptographic based on RSA and DSS, ECC provide same level of security with small key size.

Table 1. NIST guidelines for public key size.

Security level (bits)	Public key size (in bits)			Ratio
	DSS	RSA	ECC	ECC:RSA
80	1024	1024	160–223	1:6
112	2048	2048	224–255	1:9
128	3072	3072	256–383	1:12
192	7680	7680	384–511	1:20
256	15380	15380	512+	1:30

The security of ECC is equivalent to solve the discrete logarithm problem on Elliptic Curve (ECDLP) and Computational Diffie-Hellman problem (CDHP). The ECDLP [25] is described as: given P, $Q = xP \in E_p(a, b)$ where $x \in Z_q$, it is computationally difficult to compute x. Those readers who are not familiar with traditional public key cryptosystem; the ECC-based addition operation and ECC-based multiplication operation is equivalent to modular multiplication and modular exponentiations respectively. Computational Diffie-Hellman Problem [27] state that given x, $y \in Z_q$, and $<X, xX, yX> \in G_1$, it is computationally hard to find xyX.

2.2   Bilinear Mapping

Assume G_1 be an additive group and G_2 be multiplicative group are two group with same order q, and let $P \in G_1$ denotes the generator of group G_1. The mapping between the two groups denoted as e: $G_1 \times G_1 \rightarrow G_2$ which meets the following requirements:

1. *Bilinearity*: For any two points P and $Q \in G_1$, and a and $b \in Z_q$, the pairing operations is defines as:

$$e(aP, bQ) = e(P, Q)^{ab}$$

2. *Non-Degeneracy*: For any points $P \in G_1$, such that $e(P, P) \neq 1$, that means the generator of G_2 cannot be the identity element.
3. *Computability*: For any two points P and $Q \in G_1$, there exists an algorithm which computes e(P, Q) easily.

A mapping function that satisfying the above three conditions is known as admissible bilinear map. The security of pairing function is equivalent to solve the Bilinear Diffie-Hellman (BDH) Problem. The BDH problem [9] in $\langle P, Q, R, S, G_1, G_2 \rangle$

is described as: given four points $P, Q, R, S \in G_1$ and $a, b, c \in Z_q$, where $Q = aP$, $R = bP$ and $S = cP$. It is hard to compute the $e(P, P)^{abc} \in G_2$.

Now, we are ready to define the lightweight form of ECC and PBC. In our following implementations, we assume the TinyPBC library, which has an efficient implementation over binary fields F_2^m with 80-bit security [28] and achieves 1024-bit RSA level security for pairing-based cryptosystem, This library is written in C language running on operating system, TinyOS and MICAs sensor user. MICA sensor user is one of the most generic sensor platform used in industry as well as in academic for research purpose. The configuration of MICA is 128 KB ROM, 4 KB RAM, and microcontroller of 8-bit/7.3828-MHz ATmega128L.

2.3 Resource Constrained Devices

In the very initial years of the last decade, many researchers had predicted that billions of isolated computing devices would be connected and aggregated with the computer network in future Internet of Things (IoT) [29]. These computing devices are nothing but the sensors node that senses the nearby surrounding, process the inputted data and transmit it to other sensor node or the controlling device. Because of the low computational and storage capabilities, and run on limited battery, these sensor nodes are also known as the resource constrained devices [3]. Due to this issues, it is severe to have substantial security measure for resource-constrained devices. Consequently, they are subjected to adversarial attacks. One way is to provide the security is to adopt the encryption and decryption, but they require more computational and memory. Thus, they use a lightweight algorithm that comfortable for resource-constrained environments [30].

2.4 Identity-Based Encryption

The basic idea of IBE is to considered the user's unique identification as the user's public key and the trusted third party known as a private key generator (PKG) issues the private key. IBE consists of following four algorithms (Setup, Encryption, Extract, and Decryption), defined as follows:

- *Setup*: The PKG computed the pair of master key s and public parameters, *param*. PKG kept *s* secret and published *param*.
- *Encryption:* Sender encrypts the message M using the receiver's identity as public key gives ciphertext C to receiver.
- *Private Key Extraction*: Receiver first request to PKG to issue private key S_{IDB} against his identity ID_B. PKG validate the receiver's identity and computes the private key as $S_{IDB} = sH_1(ID_B)$ using his secret key s and issue to the receiver on secure channel.
- *Decryption*: Now, receiver decrypts the encrypted message C with their private key S_{IDB}.

With taking the advantage of ECC and IBE, we give the overview of key agreement protocol in next section.

3   Pairing Free-Authenticated Identity-Based 2-Party Key Agreements Protocol

This section gives the overview accommodating the PF-AID-2KAP to resource constrained devices which is unable to perform online computation.

3.1   Overview

The key agreement scheme for heterogeneous wireless-devices is designed to provide the two-party session key for secure communication over an unsecured wireless link. The proposed scheme is completed in three phase between the devices and trusted device, known as the Base device (BD) in which devices denotes the resource-constrained wireless devices, and BD denotes the one device in a single network or manufacturer. The responsible of BD is to compute the long-term private key using IBC technique and passes to the corresponding devices in the network or installed at the time of device manufacturing. The three phases are defined in Sect. 3.2. In this way, we exploit the advantages of the IBE that provides the mutual authentication between two entities and ECC (whose operations are based on TinyPBC library) that contains the lightweight cryptographic way to establish the secure key agreement protocol.

3.2   Definition

The proposed PF-AID-2KAP involves three algorithms: Setup, Key generation, and Key agreement. They are defined as:

1. Setup: This phase is completed on BD. Given some security parameter, the BD selects master key s on its choice and sets the public parameters, *param,* where master key is secret to BD and *param* is available on public domain
2. Key generation: This phase is run on BD side in which BD issues the long-term private key S_{IDX} against all devices identity in the network. The long-term private key is securely sends to corresponding device or installed at the time of device manufacturing.
3. Key agreement: This phase is run between the two devices in which they used their long-term private key, other's identities and public parameter to establish an authenticated session key S_k.

The very first two phases of above scheme, i.e., Setup and key generation are considered as the offline phase as it pre-computes the public parameter and pre-installed the long-term private key to the devices. The third phase i.e., key agreement is considered as the online as it allows two devices in the same network to establish an on demand secure authenticated key agreement whenever they want.

3.3   Security Notion

In this section, we gives key agreement security requirements:

- **Provable secure:** Under the assumption of solving ECDLP and CDHP problem is hard, the proposed scheme is provably secure.

- **Mutual authentication**: It make sure that two device must prove their identities to each other before generating the session key.
- **Perfect forward secrecy**: A key agreement scheme is known as perfect forward secrecy or forward secrecy, if any adversary A is able to compromise the device long term private key but could not compromise session keys that have been established previously.
- **Man-in-the-middle attack**: Any adversary cannot intercept the communication between the two devices.
- **Known session key attack**: A key agreement scheme is said to secure against the known session key attacks, if any adversary A is able to compromise the previously established session keys but could not compute the current session key.
- **No key control**: It make sure that device cannot compute the session key before proving his identity.

4   Construction

Here, we construct the pairing-free authenticated key agreement protocol. Suppose two devices, namely A and B are resource constrained devices for example IoT sensors, mobiles etc. To make secure conversation between them, they need a shared session key S_k. Notations and abbreviations are given in Table 2.

According to the framework given in Sect. 3, our proposed key protocol consists of three phases: Setup, Key generation and key agreement protocol and defined as:

1. Setup: On given security parameter k, BD performs following operations:

   - Select a random $s \in Z_P$, known his secret key and computes the public key $P_{Pub} = sP$.
   - Select two one-way hash function

$$H_1 : \{0, 1\}^n X \ G_1 \rightarrow Z_p.$$

$$H_2 : \{0, 1\}^* \rightarrow Z_p$$

   - Published the parameter $param = \{P, P_{Pub}, G, H_1, H_2\}$ and keep master key s secret.

2. Key Extract: Given system parameter $param$, master key s, and devices identifier ID_A and ID_B as input and BD outputs the identity-based long-term private key S_A and S_B as follows:

   - Pick two random number r_A and $r_B \in Z_P$, and computes:

$$R_A = r_A P, \qquad Q_A = H_1(ID_A \| R_A)$$

$$R_B = r_B P, \qquad Q_B = H_1(ID_B \| R_B)$$

Table 2. Abbreviations and notations

Abbreviations/Notations	Meaning
$k \in Z^+$	Security parameter
G_1	Additive cyclic group on elliptic curve
G_2	Multiplicative cyclic groups on elliptic curve
q, P	Order and generator of G_1
$e: G_1 \times G_1 \rightarrow G_2$	Bilinear mapping
s, P_{Pub}	Master secret key and public key of BD
$ID_X \in \{0,1\}^n$	Unique identification of device X
S_{IDX}	Long-term private key of device X
$r_X \in Z_q^*$	BD's chosen random number for device X
$a, b \in Z_q^*$	Random number chosen by device A and B
$a^X, b^X \in Z_q^*$	Random number chosen by adversary against device A and B
$H_1 : \{0,1\}^* \times G_1 \rightarrow Z_q^*$	Hash function that takes a string of any length and point on G_1 as input and gives a finite field of any length
$H_2 : \{0,1\}^* \rightarrow Z_q^*$	Hash function that takes a string of any length as input and gives a finite field of any length
S_k	Secret session key
BD	Base device
PKC	Public key cryptosystem
IBC/E/S	Identity-based cryptosystem/Encryption/Signature
MITM	Man-in-the-middle attack
PF-AID-2KAP	Pairing-free Authenticated Identity-based key agreement protocol

- Now, BD computes private key for A and B as follows:

$$S_A = r_A s Q_A$$

$$S_B = r_B s Q_B$$

Where, $\{S_A, R_A\}$ and $\{S_B, R_B\}$ are considered as the A's and B's private key respectively and send via a secure channel or preloaded at the time of device installation.

Meanwhile, device i can validates their private key with the following equation:

$$e(S_i P, P)? = e(H_1(ID_i \| R_i) P_{Pub}, R_i)$$

where $i \in \{A, B\}$.

3. Key Agreement: Now, two device establish an authenticated session key S_k (shown in Fig. 1) as follows:

  - A pick $a \in Z_P$ and compute $T_A = a R_A$ and sends ID_A, R_A and T_A to device B.
  - B pick $b \in Z_P$ and compute $T_B = b R_B$ and sends ID_B, R_B and T_B to device A.

- Using his private key S_A, A compute $K_{A|B} = S_A a H_1(ID_B||R_B)T_B$ and compute $S_k = H_2(ID_A, ID_B, R_A, R_B, T_A, T_B, K_{A|B})$.
- Using his private key S_B, device B compute $K_{B|A} = S_B b H_1(ID_A||R_A)T_A$ and compute

$$S_k = H_2(ID_A, ID_B, R_A, R_B, T_A, T_B, K_{B|A})$$

This completes the establishment of secret session key S_k between two devices.

Device A		Device B
Pick $a \in Z_p$	$\{ID_A, R_A, T_A\}$	Pick $b \in Z_p$
$T_A = aR_A$	$\xrightarrow{\hspace{2cm}}$	$T_B = bR_B$
	$\{ID_B, R_B, T_B\}$	
	$\xleftarrow{\hspace{2cm}}$	
$K_{A|B} = S_A H_1(ID_B||R_B)T_B$		$K_{B|A} = S_B H_1(ID_A||R_A)T_A$
$S_k = H_2(ID_A, ID_B, R_A, R_B, T_A, T_B, K_{A|B})$		$S_k = H_2(ID_A, ID_B, R_A, R_B, T_A, T_B, K_{B|A})$

Fig. 1. Proposed two party authenticated identity-based key agreement protocol.

5 Protocol Analysis

Here, we give the security analysis and efficiency comparison with other related scheme.

5.1 Security Analysis

Theorem 1: The proposed key agreement protocol is correct.

Proof: The common secret key are agree because:

$$\begin{aligned}
K_{A|B} &= S_A a H_1(ID_B||R_B)T_B \\
&= r_A s Q_A a H_1(ID_B||R_B)T_B \\
&= r_A s H_1(ID_A||R_A)a H_1(ID_B||R_B)T_B \\
&= r_A s H_1(ID_A||R_A)a H_1(ID_B||R_B)br_B P \\
&= br_B s H_1(ID_B||R_B)H_1(ID_A||R_A)ar_A P \\
&= b S_B H_1(ID_A||R_A)T_A \\
&= K_{B|A} = K_{AB}
\end{aligned}$$

This set of equalities verifies the correctness of shared session key S_k.

Theorem 2: Assuming the H_1 and H_2 are two random oracle model and ECDLP and CDH problem are difficult to compute, our proposed is a secure key agreements protocol.

Proof: The security proof of our proposed is proved as similar to Theorem 2 in Wang et al. [15].

Theorem 3: The proposed pairing-free authenticated Identity-based two-party key agreement protocol achieves mutual authentication.

Proof: In our proposed identity-based key agreement scheme, device issues his long-term private key from BD such that BD compute using his master key s and a random variable r_i. Then, two device can come-up with the common key agreement using their long-term private key, identity and random chosen integer. Although, session key includes the private key of first device and identification of another device. Only those devices who registered/authenticated with BD can establish a session shared key. Therefore, the proposed provides device authenticity.

Theorem 4: The proposed pairing-free authenticated Identity-based two-party key agreement protocol is secure against man-in-the-middle attack.

Proof: Suppose an adversary and his assistant X impersonate between two devices, A and B. Suppose adversary attack on the public channel and obtains some information $\{R_A, R_B, T_A, T_B ID_1, \ldots ID_n\}$. Attacker chooses two random number a^x, b^x, r_A^x and $r_B^x \in Z_P$ and computes the parameters $R_A^x = r_A^x P$, $R_B^x = r_B^x P$, $T_A^x = a^x R_A^x$ and $T_B^x = b^x R_B^x$ and passed them to A and B respectively.

1. On given received parameter $\left(R_A^x, T_A^x\right)$, A computes $K_{A|B} = S_A a H_1(ID_B \| R_B^x) T_B^x$.
2. On given received parameter $\left(R_A^x, T_A^x\right)$, B computes $K_{B|A} = S_B b H_1(ID_A \| R_A^x) T_A^x$.
3. On given received parameter, assistant X pick $x \in Z_P$ computes

$$K_{X|B} = x H_1(ID_A \| R_A^x) H_1(ID_B \| R_B) T_B$$

$$K_{X|A} = x H_1(ID_B \| R_B^x) H_1(ID_A \| R_A) T_A$$

Now, we show that the session key established between the attacker X and any device in the network is not equal. Since, for session key between attacker X and device A, we have

$$K_{A|B} = S_A a H_1(ID_B||R_B^x)T_B^x$$
$$= sr_A H_1(ID_A||R_A)aH_1(ID_B||R_B^x)T_B^x$$
$$= sr_A H_1(ID_A||R_A)aH_1(ID_B||R_B^x)r_B^x b^x P$$
$$= b^x sr_B^x H_1(ID_A||R_A)H_1(ID_B||R_B^x)ar_A P$$
$$= b^x sr_B^x H_1(ID_A||R_A)H_1(ID_B||R_B^x)T_A$$
$$\text{Or} \quad = ab^x r_A r_B^x H_1(ID_A||R_A)H_1(ID_B||R_B^x)sP$$
$$= ab^x r_A r_B^x H_1(ID_A||R_A)H_1(ID_B||R_B^x)P_{Pub}$$
$$\neq K_{X|A}$$

Similarly, for session key between attacker X and device B, we have

$$K_{B|A} = S_B b H_1(ID_A||R_A^x)T_A^x$$
$$= sr_B H_1(ID_B||R_B)bH_1(ID_A||R_A^x)T_A^x$$
$$= sr_B H_1(ID_B||R_B)bH_1(ID_A||R_A^x)a^x r_A^x P$$
$$= a^x sr_A^x H_1(ID_B||R_B)H_1(ID_A||R_A^x)br_B P$$
$$= a^x sr_A^x H_1(ID_B||R_B)H_1(ID_A||R_A^x)T_B$$
$$\text{Or} \quad = a^x br_A^x r_B H_1(ID_B||R_B)H_1(ID_A||R_A^x)sP$$
$$= a^x br_A^x r_B H_1(ID_B||R_B)H_1(ID_A||R_A^x)P_{Pub}$$
$$\neq K_{X|B}$$

To achieve the equality, the attack should have to compute the value of either master key s or random a, b, r_A and r_B, that is similar solve the ECDLP problem. Therefore, our proposed scheme is secure against main-in-the-middle attack.

Theorem 5: The proposed pairing-free authenticated Identity-based two-party key agreement protocol is provable perfect secure.

Proof: In our scheme, the use of pre-image and uniformly distributed cryptographic hash function H_2 preserves perfect forward secrecy. The result of hash function H_2 gives the shared session key $S_k = H_2(ID_A, ID_B, R_A, R_B, T_A, T_B, K_{A|B}) = H_2(ID_A, ID_B, R_A, R_B, T_A, T_B, K_{B|A})$, where public parameter $T_A, and\ T_B$ computed with device A's and B's random chosen secret value a and b respectively. If adversary A compromised the private key S_A and S_B of both device, he must require to compute the secret value a and b of both device which is equivalent to solve the ECDLP and CDHP problem. Thus, assuming the ECDLP, CDHP and given private key of both device, our proposed scheme is secure against perfect forward secrecy attack.

Theorem 6: The proposed pairing-free authenticated Identity-based two-party key agreement protocol is resilience to key control attack.

Proof: In our proposed protocol, session Key S_k is the hash of $H_2(ID_A, ID_B, R_A, R_B, T_A, T_B, K_{A|B})$ or $H_2(ID_A, ID_B, R_A, R_B, T_A, T_B, K_{B|A})$, where $K_{A|B} = S_A H_1(ID_B||R_B)T_B$ and $K_{B|A} = S_B H_1(ID_A||R_A)T_A$, and a and b are random chosen number chosen by A and

B respectively. Thus, neither A nor B could not pre-compute the session key S_k. Therefore, it proves that our protocol does not have control on key.

Theorem 7: The proposed pairing-free authenticated Identity-based two-party key agreement protocol is secure against known session key attack.

Proof: Given list of past session keys, adversary cannot obtain the current session keys in key agreement protocol. Our protocol uses pre-image and uniformly distributed cryptographic hash function H_2, which inputs the identity, public parameter and secret key of both device and outputs is uniformly distributed session key S_k. Since the result of hash function is uniformly distributed in $\{0, 1\}^k$, the probability that two session key has relation is $1/2^k$ which is very negligible. Assuming the pre-image and uniformly distributed cryptographic hash function H_2, we achieve the known session key resilience scheme.

Table 3. Notation and execution time of pairing-related operations on MICAs [28].

Operations	Notation	Execution cost (sec)
Hash-to-point	T_H	0.89
Point compression	T_{PC}	0.38
Point decompression	T_{PD}	0.38
Scalar point multiplication (original)	TEM_{orig}	7.75
Scalar point multiplication (optimized)	TEM_{opt}	2.45
Pairing	T_P	5.32

Table 4. Computational and execution cost comparison our proposed scheme with other related schemes.

Schemes	Computational cost	Execution cost (sec)
He et al. [19]	$5TEM_{op}$	12.45
Tseng et al. [20]	$3T_P + 8TEM_{op}$	35.52
Islam et al. [21]	$8TEM_{op}$	19.60
Tseng et al. [22]	$8TEM_{op}$	19.60
Our Scheme	$2TEM_{op}$	4.90

5.2 Efficiency Comparison

Here, we give comparison, in term of computational cost (in operations), execution cost (in msec) and bandwidth cost (in Bytes), of our key agreement protocol with other related schemes He et al. [19], Tseng et al. [20], Islam et al. [21] and Tseng et al. [22]. It takes 0.89 s, 0.38 s, 0.38 s, 7.75 s, 2.45 s and 5.32 s to complete hash-to-point T_H, point compression T_{PC}, point decompression T_{PD}, scalar point multiplication before optimization TEM_{orig}, scalar point multiplication after optimization TEM_{opt} and pairing operation T_P on elliptic curve as shown in Table 3.

Table 5. Bandwidth cost comparison of our proposed scheme with other related schemes.

Schemes	Bandwidth (Bytes)	#Round
He et al. [19]	(3 * 80 + 16)/8 = 32	3
Tseng et al. [20]	(4 * 80 + 16)/8 = 42	3
Islam et al. [21]	(4 * 80 + 16)/8 = 42	2
Tseng et al. [22]	(3 * 80 + 16)/8 = 32	3
Our scheme	(2 * 80 + 16)/8 = 22	2

As compare with the computation time of ECC-based scalar multiplication, pairing-based scalar multiplication, and modular exponentiation, the computation cost of hash function operation is very less. Thus, we could ignore the computation cost of hash function operation. Thus, we consider only pairing operations, pairing-based scalar multiplication, ECC-based scalar multiplication and modular exponentiation. We then show the efficiency of our scheme with related schemes in terms of computational cost (running in sec), Bandwidth cost (Bytes) and number message exchange in Tables 4 and 5.

In Table 4, reader can see that proposed scheme takes only two multiplication operation on elliptic curve executed in (2 * 2.45) = 4.90 s while He et al. [19], Tseng et al. [20], Islam et al. [21] and Tseng et al. [22] take 12.45 s, 35.52 s, 19.60 s and 19.60 s respectively to complete the key agreement process. That means, our proposed scheme is 39.35%, 13.80%, 25%, and 25% of He et al. [19], Tseng et al. [20], Islam et al. [21] and Tseng et al. [22] respectively, in terms of computational running time.

We assume the size of device identity be 16 bit and order of elliptic curve group be 80 bit. From Table 5, we show that proposed scheme consumes only (2 * 80 + 16)/8 = 22 bytes while He et al. [19], Tseng et al. [20], Islam et al. [21] and Tseng et al. [22] consumes (3 * 80 + 16)/8 = 32 bytes, (4 * 80 + 16)/8 = 42 bytes, (4 * 80 + 16)/8 = 42 bytes and (3 * 80 + 16)/8 = 32 bytes respectively, of channel bandwidth during the key establishment completion. That means, our proposed scheme is 68.75%, 52.38%, 52.38% and 68.75% of He et al. [19], Tseng et al. [20], Islam et al. [21] and

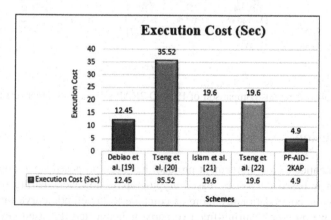

Fig. 2. Execution cost (sec) comparison of PF-AID-2KAP scheme with other related schemes.

Tseng et al. [22] respectively, in terms of bandwidth requirement. Additionally, we protocol completes in two round while other takes three rounds except Islam et al. protocol [21] which takes 2 round. Figures 2, 3 and 4 represents the graphic view comparison of Execution cost, Bandwidth cost and number of rounds.

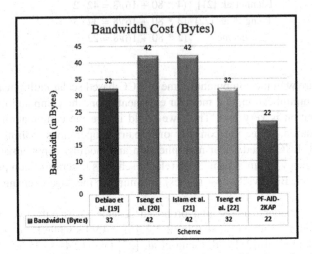

Fig. 3. Bandwidth comparison of PF-AID-2KAP scheme with other related schemes.

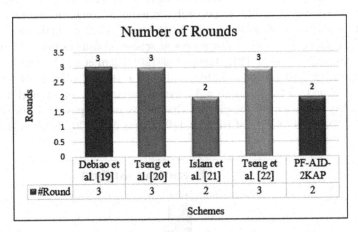

Fig. 4. Number of rounds comparison of PF-AID-2KAP scheme with other related schemes.

6   Conclusion

Several authenticated key agreement protocol has been proposed since now. But their construction is based on pairing based cryptography. however, pairing operation on elliptic curve is computationally more as compare to the elliptic curve operations. In this article, we proposed pairing-free two party authenticated ID-based key agreement protocol whose security is based on solving the ECDLP and CDHP. Further, we demonstrate that our proposed scheme is secure against man-in-middle-attack, perfect forward secrecy, no key control, and Known session key security. The performance of proposed key agreement protocol found better in terms of computational cost, bandwidth cost and number of rounds as compare to the other related schemes.

Acknowledgements. This research work has been partially supported by the Council of Scientific and Industrial Research, a research and development organization in India, with sanctioned no. 09/263(1052)/2015 EMR-I and the UPE-II grant received from JNU. Additionally, the author would like to sincere thanks to the anonymous reviewers for their fruitful comments.

References

1. Al-Fuqaha, A., Guizani, M., Mohammadi, M., Aledhari, M., Ayyash, M.: Internet of Things: a survey on enabling technologies, protocols, and applications. IEEE Commun. Surv. Tutorials **17**(4), 2347–2376 (2015)
2. Botta, A., De Donato, W., Persico, V., Pescapé, A.: Integration of cloud computing and Internet of Things: a survey. Future Gener. Comput. Syst. **56**, 684–700 (2016)
3. Sheng, Z., Wang, H., Yin, C., Hu, X., Yang, S., Leung, V.C.M.: Lightweight management of resource-constrained sensor devices in Internet of Things. IEEE Internet Things J. **2**(5), 402–411 (2015)
4. Oliveira, L.B., Aranha, D.F., Morais, E., Daguano, F., López, J., Dahab, R.: Tinytate: computing the tate pairing in resource-constrained sensor nodes. In: Sixth IEEE International Symposium on Network Computing and Applications, NCA 2007, pp. 318–323 (2007)
5. Rivest, R.L., Shamir, A., Adleman, L.: A method for obtaining digital signatures and public-key cryptosystems. Commun. ACM **21**(2), 120–126 (1978)
6. Vanstone, S.A.: Elliptic curve cryptosystem—the answer to strong, fast public-key cryptography for securing constrained environments. Inf. Secur. Tech. Rep. **2**(2), 78–87 (1997)
7. Szczechowiak, P., Oliveira, L.B., Scott, M., Collier, M., Dahab, R.: NanoECC: testing the limits of elliptic curve cryptography in sensor networks. In: Verdone, R. (ed.) Wireless Sensor Networks. EWSN 2008. LNCS, vol. 4913, pp. 305–320. Springer, Heidelberg (2008). https://doi.org/10.1007/978-3-540-77690-1_19
8. Shamir, A.: Identity-based cryptosystems and signature schemes. In: Blakley, G.R., Chaum, D. (eds.) CRYPTO 1984. LNCS, vol. 196, pp. 47–53. Springer, Heidelberg (1985). https://doi.org/10.1007/3-540-39568-7_5
9. Boneh, D., Franklin, M.: Identity-based encryption from the Weil pairing. In: Kilian, J. (ed.) CRYPTO 2001. LNCS, vol. 2139, pp. 213–229. Springer, Heidelberg (2001). https://doi.org/10.1007/3-540-44647-8_13
10. Choon, J.C., Hee Cheon, J.: An identity-based signature from gap diffie-hellman groups. In: Desmedt, Y.G. (ed.) PKC 2003. LNCS, vol. 2567, pp. 18–30. Springer, Heidelberg (2003). https://doi.org/10.1007/3-540-36288-6_2
11. Chatterjee, S., Sarkar, P.: Identity-Based Encryption. Springer, Heidelberg (2011). https://doi.org/10.1007/978-1-4419-9383-0
12. Kumar, M., Katti, C.P., Saxena, P.C.: A secure anonymous e-voting system using identity-based blind signature scheme. In: Shyamasundar, Rudrapatna K., Singh, V., Vaidya, J. (eds.) ICISS 2017. LNCS, vol. 10717, pp. 29–49. Springer, Cham (2017). https://doi.org/10.1007/978-3-319-72598-7_3

13. Boneh, D., Lynn, B., Shacham, H.: Short signatures from the weil pairing. In: Boyd, C. (ed.) ASIACRYPT 2001. LNCS, vol. 2248, pp. 514–532. Springer, Heidelberg (2001). https://doi.org/10.1007/3-540-45682-1_30

14. Kumar, M., Katti, C.P., Saxena, P.C.: An untraceable identity-based blind signature scheme without pairing for e-cash payment system. In: Kumar, N., Thakre, A. (eds.) UBICNET 2017. LNICST, vol. 218, pp. 67–78. Springer, Cham (2018). https://doi.org/10.1007/978-3-319-73423-1_7

15. Wang, S., Cao, Z., Choo, K.-K.R., Wang, L.: An improved identity-based key agreement protocol and its security proof. Inf. Sci. (Ny) **179**(3), 307–318 (2009)

16. Chen, L., Cheng, Z., Smart, N.P.: Identity-based key agreement protocols from pairings. Int. J. Inf. Secur. **6**(4), 213–241 (2007)

17. Kumar, M., Katti, C.P., Saxena, P.C.: An ID-based authenticated key exchange protocol. Int. J. Adv. Stud. Comput. Sci. Eng. **4**(5), 11 (2015)

18. Hölbl, M., Welzer, T., Brumen, B.: An improved two-party identity-based authenticated key agreement protocol using pairings. J. Comput. Syst. Sci. **78**(1), 142–150 (2012)

19. He, D., Chen, J., Hu, J.: A pairing-free certificateless authenticated key agreement protocol. Int. J. Commun. Syst **25**(2), 221–230 (2012)

20. Tseng, Y.-M., Huang, S.-S., Tsai, T.-T., Tseng, L.: A novel ID-Based authentication and key exchange protocol resistant to ephemeral-secret-leakage attacks for mobile devices. Int. J. Distrib. Sens. Netw. **11**(5), 898716 (2015)

21. Islam, S.K.H., Biswas, G.P.: A pairing-free identity-based two-party authenticated key agreement protocol for secure and efficient communication. J. King Saud Univ. Inf. Sci. **29**, 63–73 (2015)

22. Tseng, Y., Huang, S., You, M.: Strongly secure ID-based authenticated key agreement protocol for mobile multi-server environments. Int. J. Commun. Syst. 30(11) (2017)

23. Cao, X., Kou, W., Yu, Y., Sun, R.: Identity-based authenticated key agreement protocols without bilinear pairings. IEICE Trans. Fundam. Electron. Commun. Comput. Sci. **91**(12), 3833–3836 (2008)

24. Cao, X., Kou, W., Du, X.: A pairing-free identity-based authenticated key agreement protocol with minimal message exchanges. Inf. Sci. (Ny) **180**(15), 2895–2903 (2010)

25. Koblitz, N.: Elliptic curve cryptosystems. Math. Comput. **48**(177), 203–209 (1987)

26. Miller, V.S.: Use of elliptic curves in cryptography. In: Williams, H.C. (ed.) CRYPTO 1985. LNCS, vol. 218, pp. 417–426. Springer, Heidelberg (1986). https://doi.org/10.1007/3-540-39799-X_31

27. Shparlinski, I.: Computational diffie-hellman problem. In: van Tilborg, H.C.A., Jajodia, S. (eds.) Encyclopedia of Cryptography and Security, pp. 240–244. Springer, Heidelberg (2011). https://doi.org/10.1007/978-1-4419-5906-5

28. Xiong, X., Wong, D.S., Deng, X.: TinyPairing: a fast and lightweight pairing-based cryptographic library for wireless sensor networks. In: 2010 IEEE Wireless Communications and Networking Conference (WCNC), pp. 1–6 (2010)

29. Messer, A., et al.: Towards a distributed platform for resource-constrained devices. In: Proceedings of the 22nd International Conference on Distributed Computing Systems, pp. 43–51 (2002)

30. Sehgal, A., Perelman, V., Kuryla, S., Schonwalder, J.: Management of resource constrained devices in the Internet of Things. IEEE Commun. Mag. 50(12) (2012)

Monitoring of Network to Analyze the Traffic and Analysis of Audit Trails Using Process Mining

Ved Prakash Mishra[1]([✉]), Balvinder Shukla[2], and Abhay Bansal[2]

[1] Department of Computer Science and Engineering,
Amity University, Dubai, UAE
mishra.ved@gmail.com, vmishra@amityuniversity.ae
[2] Amity University, Noida, India

Abstract. Monitoring of network is an essential part of the current digital world to analyze the traffic in the organizational networks to detect the intrusions and cyber-attacks. For Intrusion detection system, many approaches have been used till now, but network administrators are still facing the problems due to false alarms. In this manuscript, we have monitored the organization network in real time for the analysis. We have also compared the different data mining approaches being used for intrusion detection method and malicious activities detection in the database using log mining approach. A model is proposed using process mining approach to detect the malicious transaction automatically in the database. The process mining approach can help to reduce the false positive alarms as compared to the current intrusion detection and prevention systems. To implement the process mining concept, audit trails for road traffic fine management process was collected and it has been analyzed to generate the processes using PRoM tool.

Keywords: Process mining · Log events · Data mining · Network monitoring
Intrusion detection · Security

1 Introduction

Managing any educational and corporate network is becoming harder as the amount of data in the organizational networks are growing day by day due to the more data. Since, world is moving towards the digital age, networks are becoming larger and more complex. When we talk about network management, it includes not only the component that transports information in the network, but also systems that generate the traffic in the network. What is the use of a computer network if there are no systems in the network to provide service to the users? The system could be client host, or database servers or file servers, or mail servers. In the client/server environment, the network control is no longer centralized, but distributed. In general, network management is a service that employs a variety of tools, applications, and devices to assist human

© Springer Nature Singapore Pte Ltd. 2019
P. K. Singh et al. (Eds.): FTNCT 2018, CCIS 958, pp. 441–451, 2019.
https://doi.org/10.1007/978-981-13-3804-5_32

network managers in monitoring and maintaining networks. Now, network management is becoming tough due to the different types of attacks. Since, most of the internet users are using the smart devices like smart phone and gadgets, Browser-based attacks are becoming more popular now. The goal of network management is to ensure that the users of a network receive the information technology services with quality of service that they expect. From a business administration point of view, network management involves strategic and tactical planning of the engineering, operations, and maintenance of a network and network services for current and future needs at minimum overall cost. A well established and secure communication among the various groups is necessary to perform these functions. Figure 1 shows different network management model which is currently in use.

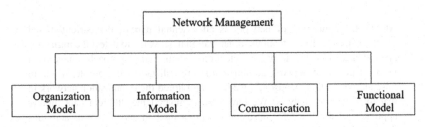

Fig. 1. Network management model

1.1 Introduction to Analyzer

This analyzer operates in agent - manager relationship. The Analyzer application is regarded as the manager, and it can communicate with any device that supports Simple Network Management Protocol (SNMP) and Remote Monitoring (RMON). SNMP is a basic protocol that allows different devices on a network to communicate.

2 Monitoring the Network in Real Time

When we launch Analyzer, the two main windows will display. The Summary View window provides a list of all of the monitored devices and their status information. The other window, Map View, shows the devices as icons and displays their up/down status. Summary View uses to see the Flow Index, alarms, and other statistics about the devices in our network. When new devices are discovered and added to the Summary View, no message is logged to the system log file. The Event Log table contains the following fields: Index, Time and Description. If Discovery is enabled, Analyzer will attempt to contact each device in the Seed IP addresses list (which we specified during installation or later in the RMON Discovery window) and use the list of default community names. Each name in the list is tried until a response is received from the device or the list of names is exhausted. As soon as Analyzer receives a response from a device using a given read community name, that name will be used for all further communication. The log file can be found in <Install Directory>\Log\Discvr.log. We can open the text file with Notepad or with another similar application. Figure 2 shows the port summary where information about each port which is being currently used in the network is available. In the port summary widow, each port is visible in any or combination of following three colors: red, yellow and green. Red color port shows that the flow index is good, yellow color shows that the flow index of that port is fair and green color shows that the flow index for the port is poor. This window also shows the total number of devices currently available in the network and arrow show that whether link is up or down for that port or device. Figure 3 shows that the top servers which are being used currently in the network.

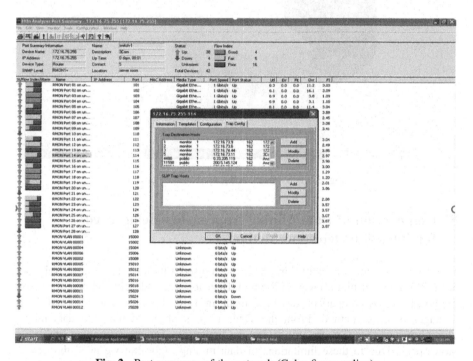

Fig. 2. Port summary of the network (Color figure online)

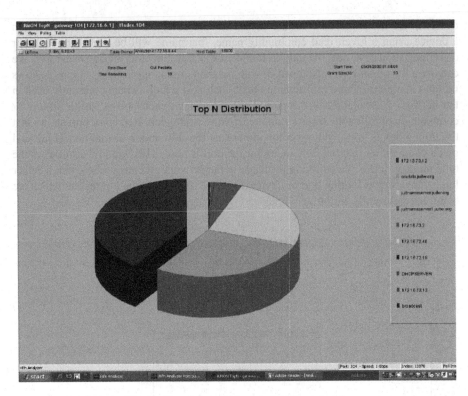

Fig. 3. Top servers being used in the network

3 Comparison of Data Mining Approaches Being Used for Intrusion Detection Method

Following data mining algorithms have been used till now: K-Nearest Neighbor, Support vector machine, Bayesian Method, Decision tree and Artificial neural network method [1–4]. A comparison has been made in Table 1 with advantages and disadvantages of each method. From the Table 1, it is observed that, the data mining algorithms used for IDS are still having the limitation. The most common problem is slow speed. Due to these limitations of data mining algorithm we need the process mining approach which can work in real time to detect the intrusions [5–7].

Table 1. Data mining algorithms used in intrusion detection: a comparison

Algorithm name	Method	Advantage	Disadvantage
K-nearest neighbor	1. This is instance based learning to classify objects based on closest training examples in the feature space	1. Use the local information and because of this it may be adaptive in behavior	1. When we need to classify the test tuple, it's very slow
	2. By majority vote of its neighbors, an object classified and most common amongst its K-nearest neighbors, object being assigned to the class		2. Storage problem (need large storage)
	3. To find the locally optimal hypothesis function, uses the similarity based search	2. Can be used for parallel implementation	
Support vector machine	1. It makes the set of hyper planes which can be used for regression, classification etc.	1. Less chances of over fitting in comparison to other algorithms	1. Testing speed is slow
	2. Through linear programming, support vector machine algorithm maps the real valued feature vector to higher dimension feature space	2. More accurate	2. Kernel choice is difficult
Bayesian method	1. Bayesian method encodes the probabilistic relationships in variable of interest	1. In large database accuracy and speed is more	1. Probability data is not available easily
	2. This is generally used with the combination of statistical schemes for intrusion detection	2. Computation is simple in comparison to others	2. The main disadvantage of Bayesian method is that the results are similar to those derived from threshold-based systems, while considerably higher computational effort is required
Decision tree	1. Mainly used for the classification in data mining	1. This algorithm is able to handle all types of data	1. Algorithms are unstable
	2. It uses the value of its attributes for the classification of data. Initially decision tree constructed from pre-defined data	2. No need of any particular domain knowledge for construction	2. Need of categorical output attribute
	3. Firstly it selects the attributes and then it divides the data items into classes		

(*continued*)

Table 1. (*continued*)

Algorithm name	Method	Advantage	Disadvantage
Artificial neural network	1. This algorithm is adaptive in nature and change the structure on the basis of internal and external information pass through the network/system during initial phase	1. High tolerance to noisy data	1. Over fitting
		2. It has high degree of accuracy to recognize known suspicious events	2. More computation is required
	2. It measure how far the particular solution is from optimal solution. The concept is used in ANN is called Cost function	3. It has the ability to learn the characteristics of misuse attacks and identify instances, which have been observed before by the network	3. Black box in nature
		4. It is used to learn complex nonlinear input-output relationships	

3.1   Limitations of Intrusion Detection Methods for Database

Query optimization is the essential part for database query completion process. Query completion process is having four stages like parsing, cost-based optimization, simplification and plan preparation. For database security and monitoring of information system, detection of intrusion can be a passive approach i.e. whenever security violation is detected then only alarms will be generated. Weighted sequence mining, CANDID, using positive tainting & syntax aware evaluation and RBAC are the major approaches which have been used for the intrusion detection in database. In all the above methods are having some limitation like:

- In RBAC method, updating and maintaining of large number of user profiles is not an easy task.
- In weighted sequence mining, handling the attributes at deferent level in not possible in efficient manner.
- The major limitation of Using positive tainting & Syntax aware evaluation is the efficiency.
- In CANDID method, automatic detection of SQL injection attack is still challenging task.

Log mining approach has been also proposed and being used but still this method is having limitation like it's not able to handle the large data [8–11]. Processing power is also having less than the required. Data dependencies rule capability is also limited.

4   Process Mining Approach for Intrusion Detection System

The purpose of process mining is to determine new procedures, monitor and improve existing procedures using the information received after examination of event logs [12–14]. It is useful to detect the intrusions in effective manner (Fig. 4).

Fig. 4. Process analytics and mining fields [20]

As prior methods and algorithm used in data mining approaches are not able to detect the intrusions in effective manner. There are three steps in process mining: process discovery, process conformance and process enhancement [15–17]. Process analytics and mining combines many fields together like process modeling, data integration, visualization, optimization and machine learning, data analytics and mining, domain knowledge and business process management. Using process mining approach system continuously monitors the network and discover the various processes for analysis. After analysis if there is any difficulties, unusual pattern or problem in processes is found, it can enhance the processes automatically [18–21].

5 Proposed Model

Using Fig. 5(a), system can get the information whether IDS need to check the intrusions or attack in real time or not. Traffic in real time i.e. data rate in real time will be taken from the network monitoring software and if any unusual traffic will be found then this system will automatically activate the IDS to detect the suspicious activity in real time as proposed in Fig. 5(b). To detect the suspicious activity or network attack, especially the DDoS attack in real time we need a strong system which can work with the help of audit trails. For this we can use the approach of process mining to create the process automatically using the log events in real time if there is any unusual traffic is found. When this system will experience any unusual traffic, profile detector generator will be active, and it will detect the profile. For the automatically detected profile, the stored process will be accessed. The accessed profile will be compared using delta analysis with the process is being created with real time audit trails. If any mismatch is found, this system will give the alarm and current user will be stopped to access the network until the verification process is not being completed.

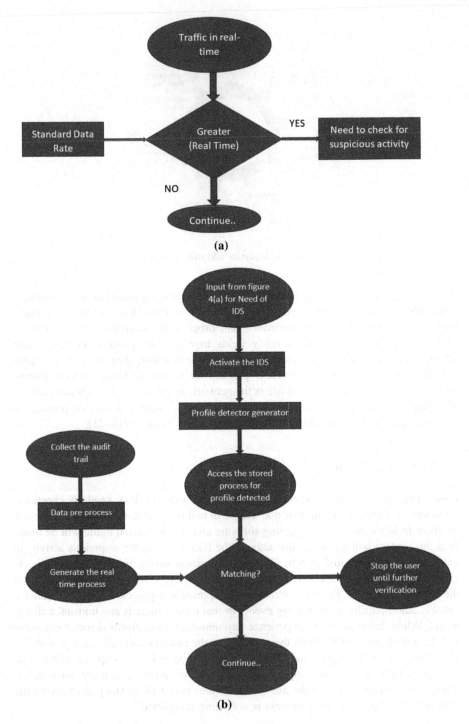

Fig. 5. (a): Process to check the need of Active IDS (b): IDS to detect the suspicious activity in Real-Time

6 Result and Discussion

Audit trails for road traffic management system was collected from 2000 to 2013 and analyzed to create the processes using PRoM tool. Figure 6 shows that sample of audit trails. PRoM tool accepts the log event file in XES format. Figure 7 shows the log visualizer for road traffic management process where two graphs are available: Event per case and event classes per case. In event per case graph, for single process 150370 cases, 561470 events are shown and in event classes per case, 11 event classes, with one event type and 149 originators are available.

```
Road_Traffic_Fine_Management_Process - Notepad
File Edit Format View Help
value="0.499"/>          <float key="Insert Fine Notification" value="0.499"/>          <float key="Send for Credit
Collection" value="0.488"/>          <float key="Create Fine" value="0.0"/>          <float key="Send Fine"
value="0.462"/>          </float>          <float key="meta_general:different_classified_average" value="3.681"/>          <int
key="meta_general:different_traces" value="231">          <int key="Create Fine;Send Fine;Insert Fine Notification;Add
penalty;Payment;Payment;Payment;Payment;Payment" value="4"/>          <int key="Create Fine;Send Fine;Payment;Insert Fine Notification;Add
penalty;Payment" value="56"/>          <int key="Create Fine;Send Fine;Insert Date Appeal to Prefecture;Insert Fine Notification;Send
Appeal to Prefecture;Add penalty;Receive Result Appeal from Prefecture;Notify Result Appeal to Offender;Payment;Payment" value="1"/>
<int key="Create Fine;Send Fine;Insert Fine Notification;Insert Date Appeal to Prefecture;Add penalty;Send Appeal to Prefecture;Receive Result Appeal from
Prefecture;Notify Result Appeal to Offender;Payment" value="139"/>          <int key="Create Fine;Send Fine;Insert Fine Notification;Add
penalty;Payment;Payment;Payment;Payment" value="13"/>          <int key="Create Fine;Send Fine;Insert Fine Notification;Add
penalty;Payment" value="9520"/>          <int key="Create Fine;Send Fine;Insert Fine Notification;Appeal to Judge;Add penalty;Insert Date
Appeal to Prefecture;Send Appeal to Prefecture" value="1"/>          <int key="Create Fine;Send Fine;Insert Fine Notification;Add
penalty;Insert Date Appeal to Prefecture;Receive Result Appeal from Prefecture;Notify Result Appeal to Offender;Appeal to Judge;Send Appeal to Prefecture"
value="1"/>          <int key="Create Fine;Send Fine;Insert Fine Notification;Add penalty;Insert Date Appeal to Prefecture;Send Appeal to
Prefecture;Receive Result Appeal from Prefecture;Notify Result Appeal to Offender;Appeal to Judge" value="12"/>          <int key="Create
Fine;Send Fine;Insert Fine Notification;Appeal to Judge;Add penalty;Insert Date Appeal to Prefecture;Send Appeal to Prefecture;Payment" value="1"/>
          <int key="Create Fine;Send Fine;Insert Fine Notification;Add penalty;Appeal to Judge;Payment;Payment" value="1"/>
<int key="Create Fine;Send Fine;Insert Fine Notification;Insert Date Appeal to Prefecture;Send Appeal to Prefecture;Add penalty;Receive Result Appeal from
Prefecture;Appeal to Judge;Notify Result Appeal to Offender;Payment" value="1"/>          <int key="Create Fine;Send Fine;Insert Fine
Notification;Insert Date Appeal to Prefecture;Appeal to Judge;Send Appeal to Prefecture;Add penalty;Payment;Payment;Payment;Payment;Payment" value="1"/>
          <int key="Create Fine;Send Fine;Insert Fine Notification;Add penalty;Insert Date Appeal to Prefecture;Send Appeal to
Prefecture;Receive Result Appeal from Prefecture;Appeal to Judge;Notify Result Appeal to Offender" value="1"/>          <int key="Create
Fine;Send Fine;Insert Fine Notification;Add penalty;Receive Result Appeal from Prefecture;Notify Result Appeal to Offender" value="2"/>
<int key="Create Fine;Send Fine;Insert Fine Notification;Insert Date Appeal to Prefecture;Appeal to Judge;Add penalty;Send Appeal to Prefecture;Receive
Result Appeal from Prefecture;Notify Result Appeal to Offender" value="1"/>          <int key="Create Fine;Send Fine;Insert Fine
Notification;Add penalty;Appeal to Judge" value="32"/>          <int key="Create Fine;Send Fine;Insert Fine Notification;Insert Date Appeal
to Prefecture;Add penalty;Send Appeal to Prefecture;Receive Result Appeal from Prefecture;Payment" value="15"/>          <int key="Create
Fine;Send Fine;Insert Date Appeal to Prefecture;Insert Fine Notification;Add penalty;Payment" value="3"/>          <int key="Create
Fine;Insert Date Appeal to Prefecture;Send Appeal to Prefecture;Send Fine;Insert Fine Notification;Payment;Add penalty;Payment" value="1"/>
     <int key="Create Fine;Send Fine;Insert Fine Notification;Insert Date Appeal to Prefecture;Send Appeal to Prefecture;Add penalty;Receive Result
Appeal from Prefecture;Notify Result Appeal to Offender" value="13"/>          <int key="Create Fine;Send Fine;Insert Fine
```


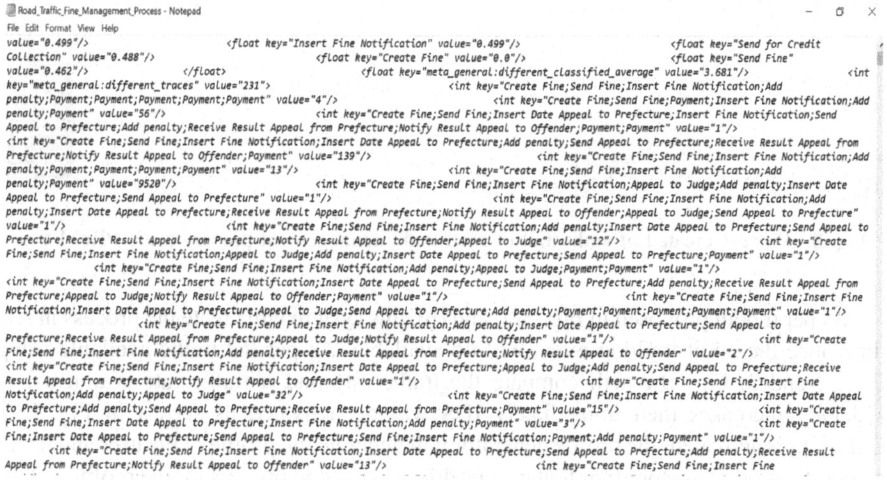

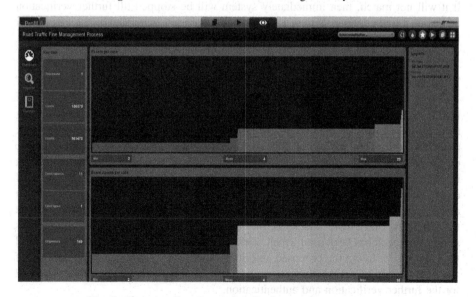

Fig. 6. Audit trails for road traffic management system

Fig. 7. Log visualizer for road traffic fine management process

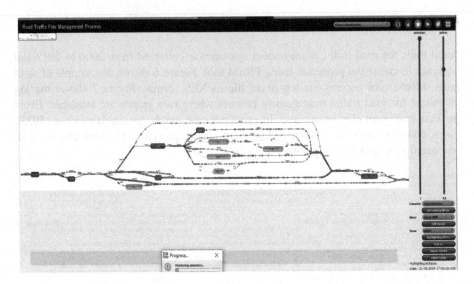

Fig. 8. Process created of audit trail of road traffic management process using PRoM tool

As per model proposed in Fig. 5(a) and (b), this system will create the process in real time once the audit trail/log event will be available. As per the traffic available using Figs. 2 and 3, Fig. 5(a) will compare the traffic rate and if traffic rate is unusual or suddenly increases then immediately IDS will be activated as shown in Fig. 5(b). Once IDS is activated, the profile generator will generate the profile of the user and it will access the processes stored for that user profile. This stored process for the profile will be compared with the process generated in real time as per the system proposed in Fig. 5(b). If it will not match, then immediately system will be stopped till further verification otherwise it will continue. Figure 8 shows that the process generated by the PRoM tool for the analysis. To generate this process inductive visual miner is being used.

7   Conclusion and Future Scope

In this manuscript, monitoring of network in real time is discussed and shown. Using real time monitoring of the network, traffic can be monitored easily with the network analyzer and this will help to analyze the unusual traffic. During DDoS attacks, traffic on the network can be more and in this situation this system will work in an efficient manner. A comparison of data mining algorithm has been done and limitation of algorithms used in IDS for the database are also discussed. Current IDS are still not able to detect the intrusion in real time. The proposed method may be helpful to detect the intrusions and DDoS attacks in real time. In the proposed method, the process mining approach has been used which works with audit trails and this may work on real time as well. In future the proposed algorithm can be used in the real-time network of any organization to get the accurate result. In future this method can also be extended for the further verification and authentication.

References

1. Salama, S.E., Marie, M.I., El-Fangary, L.M., Helmy, Y.K.: Web server logs preprocessing for web intrusion detection. Comput. Inf. Sci. **4**(4), 123–133 (2011). Canadian Center of Science & Education
2. Vijayarani, S., Maria, S.S.: Intrusion detection system - a study. IJSPTM **4**(1), 31–44 (2015)
3. Hassan, M.Md.: Current studies on intrusion detection system, genetic algorithm and fuzzy logic. Int. J. Distrib. Parallel Syst. (IJDPS) **4**(2), 35–47 (2013)
4. Patel, R., Thakkar, A., Ganatra, A.: A survey and comparative analysis of data mining techniques for network intrusion detection systems. IJSCE **2**(1), 265–271 (2012). ISSN: 2231-2307
5. Adebowale, A., Idowu, S.A., Amarachi, A.: Comparative study of selected data mining algorithms used for intrusion detection. IJSCE **3**(3), 237–241 (2013). ISSN: 2231-2307
6. Mukkamala, S., Janoski, G., Sung, A.: Intrusion detection using neural networks and support vector machines. In: International Joint Conference on Neural Networks (IJCNN), vol. 2, pp. 1702–1707. IEEE (2002)
7. Mishra, V.P., Shukla, B.: Process mining in intrusion detection-the need of current digital world. In: Singh, D., Raman, B., Luhach, A.K., Lingras, P. (eds.) Advanced Informatics for Computing Research. CCIS, vol. 712, pp. 238–246. Springer, Singapore (2017). https://doi.org/10.1007/978-981-10-5780-9_22
8. Van der Aalst, W.M.P., De Medeiros, A.K.A.: Process mining and security: detecting anomalous process executions and checking process conformance. Electron. Notes Theor. Comput. Sci. **121**(4), 3–21 (2005)
9. Pathan, A.C., Potey, M.A.: Detection of malicious transaction in database using log mining approach. ICESC **2014**, 262–265 (2014)
10. Park, S., Kang, Y.S.: A study of process mining-based business process innovation. Procedia Comput. Sci. **91**, 734–743 (2016). Elsevier, Science Direct
11. Ambre, A., Shekokar, N.: Insider threat detection using log analysis and event correlation. Procedia Comput. Sci. **45**, 436–445 (2015)
12. Mishra, V.P., Shukla, B.: Development of simulator for intrusion detection system to detect and alarm the DDoS attacks. In: IEEE International Conference on Infocom Technologies and Unmanned Systems (ICTUS 2017) (Trends and Future Directions), 10–12 December 2017
13. Lee, W., Stolfo, S., Mok, K.: A data mining framework for building intrusion detection model. In: Proceedings of IEEE Symposium Security and Privacy, pp. 120–132 (1999)
14. Van der Aalst, W.M.P.: Process Mining: Discovery, Conformance and Enhancement of Business Processes. Springer, New York (2011)
15. Weijters, A.J.M.M., Van der Aalst, W.M.P., Alves de Medeiros, A.K.: Process mining with the heuristics miner algorithm. In: BETA Working Paper Series, WP 166, Eindhoven University of Technology, Eindhoven, pp. 1–30 (2006)
16. Weijters, A.J.M.M., Van der Aalst, W.M.P.: Process mining discovering workflow models from event-based data. In: Proceedings of the 13th Belgium, Citeseer (2001)
17. Corney, M., Mohay, G., Clack, A.: Detection of anomalies from user profiles generated from system logs. In: AISC 2011, Perth Australia, CRPIT Volume 116- Information Security 2011, pp. 23–31(2011)
18. Bae, J., Liu, L., Caverlee, J., Rouse, W.B.: Process mining, discovery, and integration using distance measures. In: IEEE International Conference on Web Services (ICWS 2006) (2006)
19. Mishra, V.P., Yogeshwaran, S.: Detecting attacks using big data with process mining. Int. J. Syst. Model. Simul. **2**(2), 5–7 (2017)
20. www.eckerson.com
21. www.processmining.org

DV-HOP Based Hybrid Range-Free Localization Methods for Wireless Sensor Networks

Ananya Dwivedi[✉] and P. Raghu Vamsi

Department of Computer Science and Engineering,
Jaypee Institute of Information Technology, Noida, India
ananyadwivedi1995@gmail.com, prvonline@yahoo.co.in

Abstract. Localization in a Wireless Sensor Network (WSN) is the process of discovering location by a location unaware node with the help of known locations of reference nodes. Among the available localization techniques, a category of localization technique called range-free localization has received considerable attention in the WSN research due to low processing, memory, and energy overheads. However, each localization method has its own advantages and limitations in the view of performance. To this end, this paper analyses four well-known range-free localization methods such as Distance Vector Hop (DV-HOP), 2D-Hyperbolic (2DH), Weighted Centroid Localization (WCL) and Concentric Anchor Based (CAB) localization with respect to their performance. With the experience gained from the analysis, this paper then proposes and analyses the performance of DV-HOP based hybrid localization methods for WSNs. The simulation results from MATLAB shown that the DV-HOP with 2DH resulting into high localization accuracy as compared to other methods.

Keywords: 2D-Hyperbolic · Concentric anchor based method
DV-HOP · Localization · Sensor nodes · Wireless Sensor Networks
WCL

1 Introduction

Wireless Sensor Networks (WSNs) are widely used in reporting of events in the hostile and remote environments [1]. These networks are termed as distributed networks that work without the presence of a centralized control. WSNs are composed of several tiny, low cost, limited energy sensing and communication devices (or sensor nodes (SNs)) and they communicate among them via wireless links. Location information is a vital requirement in various applications such as environmental monitoring, area monitoring, medical and health-care monitoring, traffic control etc., where decisions need to be taken based on location of event. For this, when SNs are deployed in the network, they have to calculate their location data. In conventional wireless networks, it is done by using Global Positioning Systems (GPSs), however, use of GPS may lead to fast energy drain in SNs.

An alternative approach used to evaluate location data is by implementing localization algorithms. Localization in Wireless Sensor Network (WSN) is the process of

© Springer Nature Singapore Pte Ltd. 2019
P. K. Singh et al. (Eds.): FTNCT 2018, CCIS 958, pp. 452–463, 2019.
https://doi.org/10.1007/978-981-13-3804-5_33

discovering location by a location unaware node with the help of known locations of reference nodes. WSNs require self-localization capability because sensor data without location information is not useful for necessary action. For this reason, effective localization and positioning of SNs received significant attention, and a many algorithms have been proposed by the researchers in the literature. Most of the research on localization in WSNs assumes that the beacon nodes are equipped with GPS receivers. Beacon locations are then used to determine the positions of normal SNs. Equipping a GPS receiver at SNs may not be feasible due to the limitations of energy resource. GPS based methods are said to be absolute localization methods which acquire the global coordinate in network environment. On the other hand, in relative localization all nodes in the network estimate the range between themselves and their neighboring node [2, 21–23].

There exist several localization methods available in the literature. They are broadly classified as Range-Based (RBL) and Range-Free Localization (RFL) methods [3]. Range based method uses angle estimation or absolute point-to-point distance estimation location calculation. Range-based schemes are angle-estimation-based techniques and distance-estimation. Important techniques used in range-based localization are Angle of Arrival (AOA), Time of Arrival (TOA), Received Signal Strength Indication (RSSI), and Time Difference of Arrival (TDOA). Requirement of additional hardware and high energy consumption are the bottleneck for these methods [3]. On the other hand, in range free localization algorithms the position estimation of unknown nodes is obtained not by any measurement technique. Location of unknown node is obtained by the connectivity information of network nodes. In this localization technique, no need to calculate the angle or any distance measurement between the nodes. Location estimation depends upon the connectivity of the nodes. Connectivity has a limited range of communication in the network. Examples of this category are DV-HOP, Concentric Anchor Based (CAB), Centroid, Weighted Centroid (WCL), 2D-Hyperbolic (2DH) and others [3–14, 21–23]. Range-free localization has received considerable attention in the WSN research due to low processing, memory, and energy overheads. To achieve localization accuracy using range-free localization algorithms, this paper proposes and analyzes DV-HOP based hybrid localization method. Details of the contributions in this paper are

1. Performance of four well-known range-free localization methods such as DV-HOP, 2DH, WCL, and CAB localization with respect to their advantages and limitations.
2. With the experience gained from the analysis, Hybrid Range-Free Localization methods with DV-HOP for WSNs are proposed.
3. The performance of the proposed method is evaluated using MATLAB and found that DV-HOP with 2DH results into high localization accuracy as compared to other methods.

Rest of the paper is organized as follows. Section 2 presents the brief literature survey on localization algorithms and then analyses the four well-known range-free localization methods DV-HOP, 2DH, WCL, and CAB with respect to their advantages and limitations using MATLAB simulations. Section 3 describes the proposed hybrid range-free localization method. The performance of the proposed method is evaluated in Sect. 4 using the simulation study. Finally, Sect. 5 concludes the paper with future work.

2 Related Work

The first part of this section presents a brief literature survey on localization algorithms and the next part presents the performance of DV-HOP, 2DH, WCL, and CAB methods.

2.1 Literature Survey

Figure 1 depicts non exhaustive list of localization methods available in the literature. The descriptions of these algorithms are as follows

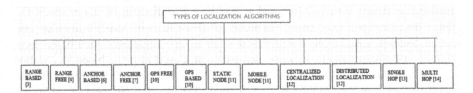

Fig. 1. Types of localization algorithms

- *Range based localization* [3] – Range based localization calculation utilizes different estimation systems for finding the separation between an anchor node and an unknown node. Some examples are Time of Arrival, Time difference of Arrival, etc., are used to estimate the distance. Although RBL methods are more accurate than RFL methods, the distance estimation with topology maintenance and localization in a global coordinate system is not attempted.
- *Range free localization* [4] – In these algorithms, the location information of unknown nodes are found without any measurement technique. Location of an unknown node is obtained by the connectivity information of the network. Location data is obtained based on the availability of the nodes.
- *Anchor Based Localization* [6] – In this approach, location of few anchor nodes is known to the network. In order to find the location information of other nodes, these anchor nodes are used. Location unaware nodes are localized with the help of these localize nodes.
- *Anchor-Free Localization* [7] – These algorithms compute relative positions of nodes instead of absolute position computation.
- *GPS Free Localization* [10] – These methods calculate the relative distance between the nodes without GPS.
- *GPS based Localization* [10] – In these methods, a GPS device is equipped with each node in the network. Due to the presence of GPS the localization accuracy is very high. Equipping GPS device in each SN is a costly effort.
- *Static Node Localization* [11] – Static Localization deals with localizing SNs in a static WSN.

- **Mobile Node Localization** [11] – Oppose to the static node localization, SNs are mobile in WSN. Mobile anchors nodes are responsible for disseminating location information such that unknown nodes calculates their location periodically.
- **Centralized Localization** [12] – In centralized localization method, one node act as a "sink node", which is responsible for computing locations of all nodes in the network. The advantage of this method, energy consumption of high configuration sink node is less as compared to the distributed system.
- **Distributed Localization** [12] – In these methods, nodes calculates and estimates their positions individually with the help of neighboring nodes.
- **Single Hop Localization** [13] – In these methods, location data is communicated and computed between anchor nodes and unknown nodes via a single hop.
- **Multi Hop Localization** [14] – In multi-hop localization methods, location computation and communication happens between two nodes is carried out through the number of intermediate nodes. The role of the intermediate nodes is to relay information from on hop to another.

From the above mentioned localization methods, next subsection presents a study on RFL methods.

2.2   Performance Analysis of DV-HOP, 2DH, WCL and CAB Range-Free Localization Methods

This section first briefly describes DV-HOP, 2DH, WCL, and CAB range-free localization methods and then shows the localization accuracy of these methods using the results obtained from MATLAB simulations.

- **Distance Vector-HOP Localization** [15–17]: In this method, Unknown Nodes (UNs) calculate their location information with the help of location information and the hop count received from Anchor Nodes (ANs). ANs are equipped with GPS devices and periodically broadcasts a beacon contains identity, location information, and hop limit. All UNs in the vicinity of AN check for hop limit. Beacon will be forwarded further by increasing the hop count by 1 if the UNs hop count is less than the hop limit. Else the beacon will be discarded. This way of forwarding message helps to maintain minimum hop count with every AN in the network. UNs calculate hop size (Hopsize) between two ANs i and j with locations (x_i, y_i) and (x_j, y_j) as follows

$$HopSize = \sum_{i \neq j} \frac{\sqrt{(x_i - x_j)^2 + (y_i - y_j)^2}}{Hop_{i,j}} \tag{1}$$

With this UNs estimates their distance from AN by multiplying HopSize and HopCount. With this distance value, UNs calculate position by applying triangulation or multiliteration.

- **Two Dimensional Hyperbolic Localization** [18]: In this method, each UN calculate HopSize with similar procedure followed in DV-HOP method. With the HopSize, in 2DH arrange HopSize is calculated

$$HopSize_{avg} = \frac{HopSize_i}{n} \qquad (2)$$

Where n is the number of ANs, $HopSize_i$ is evaluated using Eq. (1). This $HopSize_{avg}$ is transmitted in the network. UNs evaluate distance with this value by multiplying it using the number of hops between them. UNs use 2DH method to calculate locations instead of triangulation.

- **Weighted Centroid Localization** [19]: WCL is an enhancement of centroid localization method. In this, the coordinates of UN remains at the centroid of the polygon constructed by ANs. Let a UN calculates its location (x, y) from the locations of ANs as

$$(x, y) = \left(\frac{1}{n} \sum_{i=1}^{n} x_i, \frac{1}{n} \sum_{i=1}^{n} y_i \right) \qquad (3)$$

Further, distance between UN and ANs is considered as weight and this value is being multiplied by ANs coordinates and then divides by the sum of the weights to get the location information. Let W(i) is the weight value between k anchor nodes using these weight values the location is calculated as follows

$$(x, y) = \left(\frac{\sum_{i=1}^{k} W(i) * x_i}{\sum_{i=1}^{k} W(i)}, \frac{\sum_{i=1}^{k} W(i) * y_i}{\sum_{i=1}^{k} W(i)} \right) \qquad (4)$$

- **Concentric Anchor Based Localization** [20]: In this method, each AN periodically broadcasts beacons by varying power levels. Each beacon consists of information such as the anchor's location data, its power level, and the maximum distance that the beacon can transmitted. Nodes observe and record the beacons from the ANs. Nodes then determine within which annular ring they are located using the information received beacons.

The performance of these algorithms has been evaluated using MATLAB. A $500 \times 500 \ m^2$ network is considered in which 1500 nodes are randomly deployed. The number of beacon nodes is varied from 100 to 500. Each node has 50 m communication range. The results presented here are the average of 10 simulation runs.

Localization error resulted by these algorithms has been verified in two scenarios such as (1) by varying the number of beacon nodes, and (2) by varying communication range of network nodes.

Figure 2(a) shows the localization error in case of increasing number of BN in the network. It is observed from the figure that a CAB method has very low localization

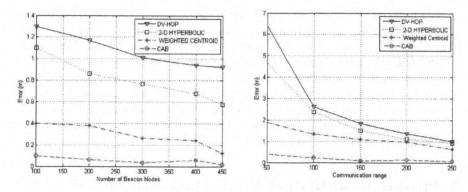

Fig. 2. (a) Number of beacon nodes vs. localization error; (b) communication range vs. localization error

error as compared to other RFL methods. It is because CAB can be used to locate nodes in the network.

Figure 2(b) shows the localization error in the case of increasing the communication range of nodes in the network. As the communication range increases the number of UNs fall under a BN increases. It is observed from the figure that the CAB method is performing well in varying communication range as compared with other methods.

The localization error is dropped suddenly in the DV-Hop method is due to UNs are able to identify BNs. However, as the communication range increases to 200, DV-HOP, weighted centroid, and 2D-Hyperbolic methods resulted into almost same localization accuracy. Among all communication ranges, CAB method outperforms the other RFL methods.

In addition, some more observations from the simulation results of the four RFL algorithms are

- Node distribution plays a major role in achieving localization accuracy in DV-Hop localization method. In addition, the number of ANs placed in the network also affects the localization performance such as localization error and localization coverage. Further, DV-Hop method is best suited for isotropic environments and hence some specialized methods are required to improve the localization accuracy in any network environment.
- Localization accuracy of DV-Hop method is affected by the distance between the ANs and UNs.
- CAB has many advantages as compared to other range free approaches such as (1) CAB is cost effective as it does not require specialized range-determining hardware in the sensor nodes, (2) CAB is distributed and energy efficient, and (3) CAB is simple to implement.
- Centroid and WCL methods are showing low localization error than DV-Hop method in high density of the ANs.

UN locations are estimated using location data received from three neighboring ANs. To increase the estimated position accuracy, it is essential to minimize the region of overlapping by choosing the three farthest ANs. This is done by calculating all the possible triangular areas that are made up of the ANs heard and by choosing the three ANs which form the large triangle. In these methods, a UN has a great impact of its nearest AN. Further, these methods will only calculate the coordinates of UN which is directly connected to AN. Therefore, improvements to this method are still required. To this end, in the next section hybrid range free localization methods based on DV-HOP method have been proposed and verified.

3 Proposed DV-HOP Based Hybrid Localization Methods

This section first presents the network model and assumptions considered in the study. Then, proposed hybrid range free localization method is described.

3.1 Network Model and Assumptions

The system model considered for the study is as follows.

1. A set of N homogeneous sensor nodes is randomly deployed in a $M X M$ m^2 network area.
2. Nodes are static in the network.
3. Each node in the network has a fixed communication range.
4. Communication between each node is symmetric.
5. Only anchor nodes are equipped with GPS.
6. Anchor nodes send out a beacon consists of identity, and location information to initiate the localization process.

3.2 Proposed DV-HOP Based Hybrid Localization Methods

Algorithm 1 and Fig. 3 shows the proposed DV-HOP based hybrid localization method. In order to reduce the positioning error of DV-HOP localization algorithm, a hybrid algorithm using 2D hyperbolic, WCL, and CAB is proposed. Similar to DV-HOP, in the proposed algorithm ANs periodically broadcast beacons consisting of location data and hop limit. Normal nodes receive the beacon packets and save the beacon information that has small hop count. Then, each node calculates the average hop count using Eq. (1). Nodes drop the beacon they receive beacons with higher hop limit. Once average hop count is calculated, each node runs the 2D hyperbolic, WCL, and CAB sequentially with DV-HOP localization to reduce the position error. This process will be repeated till position error is reduced. The simulation analysis of the proposed method is presented in the next section.

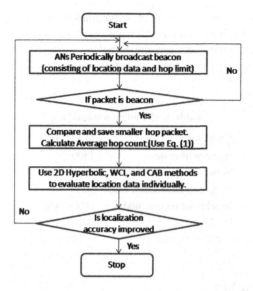

Fig. 3. Flow chart of the proposed hybrid localization algorithm

Algorithm 1. DV-HOP based hybrid localization method	
Input	Location data from anchor nodes (ANs), and hop count from neighbor nodes
Output	Location estimation by unknown nodes (UNs)
Step 1	ANs periodically broadcast beacons consist of identity location data, and hop limit.
Step 2	UNs when receive the beacon record the anchor identity, location data, and hop count.
Step 3	UNs calculate the HopSize using Eq. (1). Forward the beacon further if the hop limit prescribed by AN is not reached. Otherwise, drop the beacon.
Step 4	Once HopSize is calculated, UNs use 2D Hyperbolic, WCL, and CAB methods to evaluate location data individually.
Step 5	With AN beacons, UNs repeat Step 2 to 4 till localization accuracy is improved.

4 Simulation Study

This section first presents the simulation setup and followed by simulation results.

4.1 Simulation Setup

A static WSN deployed in M × N meters area with n sensor nodes is considered. Two categories of nodes are considered. They are Beacon Nodes (BNs) and UNs. Each node including BN is having a fixed communication range. It is assumed that each BN periodically broadcasts a beacon message consisting of node identity, location data, and timestamp. UNs make use of this information to run the RFL methods to compute their location data. Table 1 shows the simulation parameters considered for the study. The proposed algorithm has been evaluated for position accuracy. Localization accuracy is measured by the difference between the actual locations of nodes to the estimated location. The results presented in the next section are the average of 10 simulation runs.

Table 1. Simulation parameters

Simulator	MATLAB
Number of nodes	1500
Network area	500×500 m^2
Node communication range	50 m
Number of beacon nodes	100 to 450
Deployment	Random
Simulation runs	10

4.2   Simulation Results

Three scenarios are considered to evaluate the localization accuracy of the proposed hybrid localization method. In the first scenario, localization error is tested with increasing number of BNs. In the second scenario, localization error is tested with increasing communication range. Finally in the third scenario, localization error is observed with increasing number of UNs.

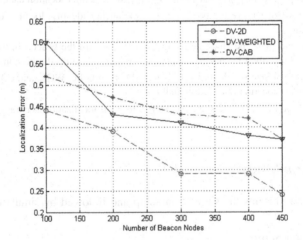

Fig. 4. Number of beacons vs. localization error

Figure 4 shows the first scenario, in which the number of BNs varied from 100 to 450, and the localization accuracy of DV-Hop with 2D-Hyperbolic, Weighted centroid and CAB localization methods is measured. It is observed from the figure that the DV-Hop with 2D method has very low localization error as compared to other methods. It is because DV-Hop with 2D hyperbolic localization combination can be used to locate nodes in the network.

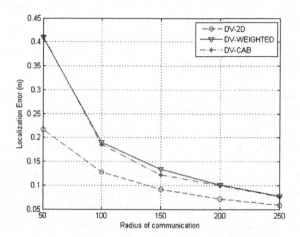

Fig. 5. Communication range vs. localization error

Figure 5 plots second scenario i.e., the localization error of the proposed method with respect to increase in communication range. It is observed that the DV-hop with WCL and CAB shows similar localization error across varying communication range. On the other hand, DV-hop with 2D hyperbolic localization shows low localization error as compared to other methods. It is due to the reason that the proposed method utilizes the advantage of 2D hyperbolic to minimize the error.

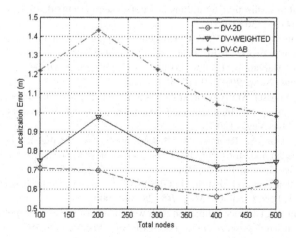

Fig. 6. Increasing number of nodes vs. Localization error

Figure 6 plots third scenario i.e., the localization error of the proposed method with respect to increase in number of nodes. The node count is varied from 100 to 500 while keeping total anchors and communication range as constant. It is observed from the figure that DV-Hop with 2D hyperbolic is resulting into low localization error as compared to other RFL method combinations.

5   Conclusion and Future Work

This paper proposed DV-Hop based hybrid range free location methods for WSNs. First, the existing range free localization methods are analyzed using a simulation study. In this study, it is observed that each method have several limitations under different network scenarios. To overcome them, hybrid range free localization methods are proposed. The proposed methods are analyzed by conducting a simulation study. It is observed from the simulation results that even though CAB algorithm performs better independently, when it combines with DV-Hop its performance was significantly degraded. Finally, it was observed that DV-Hop with 2D hyperbolic method show significant improvement in position accuracy as compared to other methods. In future, we attempt to extend it to 3 dimensional localizations of sensor nodes.

References

1. Akyildiz, I.F., Su, W., Sankarasubramaniam, Y., Cayirci, E.: Wireless sensor networks: a survey. Comput. Netw. 38(4), 393–422 (2002)
2. Ghayvat, H., Mukhopadhyay, S., Gui, X., Suryadevara, N.: WSN-and IOT-based smart homes and their extension to smart buildings. Sensors 15(5), 10350–10379 (2015)
3. Adnan, T., Datta, S., MacLean, S.: Efficient and accurate range-based sensor network localization. Proc. Comput. Sci. 10, 405–413 (2012)
4. Han, G., et al.: Localization algorithms of wireless sensor networks: a survey. Telecommun. Syst. 52(4),2419–2436 (2013)
5. Vivekanandan, V., Wong, V.W.S.: Concentric anchor beacon localization algorithm for wireless sensor networks. IEEE Trans. veh. Technol. 56(5) 2733–2744 (2007)
6. Alrajeh, N.A., Maryam B., Bilal S.: Localization techniques in wireless sensor networks. Int. J. Distrib. Sens. Netw. 9(6) 1–9 (2013)
7. Youssef, A., Youssef, M.: A taxonomy of localization schemes for wireless sensor networks. In: Proceedings of the International Conference on Wireless Networks (ICWN 2007), pp. 444–450, Las Vegas (2007)
8. Qureshi, S., Asar, A., Rehman, A., Baseer, A.: Swarm intelligence based detection of malicious beacon node for secure localization in wireless sensor networks. J. Emerg. Trends Eng. Appl. Sci. 2(4), 664–672 (2011)
9. Bulusu, N., Heidemann, J., Estrin, D.: GPS-less low-cost outdoor localization for very small devices. IEEE Pers. Commun. Mag. 7(5) 28–34 (2000)
10. Kim, E., Kim, K.: Distance estimation with weighted least squares for mobile beacon-based localization in wireless sensor networks. IEEE Sig. Process. Lett. 7(6), 559–562 (2010)
11. Langendoen, K., Reijers, N.: Distributed localization in wireless sensor networks: a quantitative comparison. Comput. Netw. 43(4), 499–518 (2003)

12. Humphrey, D., Thuraiappah, S., Mark, H.: Improved first responder localization for single-hop and multi-hop networks. In: Proceedings of Position Location and Navigation Symposium (PLANS), pp 498–504, IEEE/ION (2010)
13. Zaidi, S., et al.: Accurate range-free localization in multi-hop wireless sensor networks. IEEE Trans. Commun. **64**(9), 3886–3900 (2016)
14. Pal, A.: Localization algorithms in wireless sensor networks: current approaches and future challenges. Netw. Protoc. Algorithms **2**(1), 45–73 (2010)
15. Gayan, S., Dileeka, D.: Improved DV-hop algorithm through anchor position re-estimation. In: Proceedings of 2014 IEEE Asia Pacific Conference on Wireless and Mobile Computing, pp. 126–131. IEEE (2014)
16. Chen, K., et al. An improved DV-hop localization algorithm for wireless sensor networks. In: IET International Conference on Wireless Sensor Networks, pp 255–259, IET (2010)
17. Tomic, S., Mezei, I: Improved DV-hop localization algorithm for wireless sensor networks. In: Proceedings of IEEE 10th Jubilee International Symposium on Intelligent Systems and Informatics (SISY), pp. 389–394. IEEE (2012)
18. Zhang, B., Minning, J., Lianhai, S.: A weighted centroid localization algorithm based on DV-hop for wireless sensor network. In: 8th International Conference on Wireless Communications, Networking and Mobile Computing (WiCOM), pp 1–5. IEEE (2012)
19. Müller, C., Alves, D.I., Uchôa-Filho, B.F., Machado, R., de Oliveira, L.L., Martins, J.B.S.: Improved solution for node location multi-literation algorithms in wireless sensor networks. Electron. Lett. **52**(13), 1179–1181 (2016)
20. Jo, C., Lee, C.: Multi-literation method based on the variance of estimated distance in range-free localization. Electron. Lett. **52**(13), 1078–1080 (2016)
21. Vamsi, P.R., Krishna K.: Detecting sybil attacks in wireless sensor networks using sequential analysis. Int. J. Smart Sens. Intell. Syst. **9**(2), 651–680 (2016)
22. Ananya, D., Raghu Vamsi, P.: Performance analysis of range free localization methods for wireless sensor networks. In: Proceedings of 4th International Conference on Signal Processing, Computing and Control (ISPCC), pp 1–6, Waknagat (2017)
23. Benkouider, Y.K., Keche, M.: Mobile localization and tracking with LOS and NLOS identification in wireless sensor networks. Int. J. Smart Sens. Intell. Syst. **9**(2), 1054–1072 (2016)

Analysis of Enhanced Hybrid Approach Using Greedy Perimeter Stateless Routing in VANET

Ashish Kr. Luhach[1(⊠)], Isha[2], Neha[2], and X. Z. Gao[3]

[1] Maharshi Dayanand University, Rohtak, Haryana, India
ashishluhach@acm.org
[2] Lovely Professional University, Phagwara, India
[3] University of Eastern Finland, Kuopio, Finland

Abstract. With the advent in VANET (Vehicular Adhoc Network) technology, the need of innovation in social issues is demanding at high pace. VANET correspondence as of late turned into an undeniably prominent research point in the zone of wireless networking. Routing in VANET is an essential subject. Position based routing protocols are more reasonable for VANET when contrasted with every other protocol. GPSR is a standout amongst most appropriate routing protocol that works as position based. Here a hybrid PHRHLS (A Movement Prediction based Joint Routing and Hierarchal Location Based Service) approach collaborating HLS area advantage and GPSR protocol is utilized. In this GPSR protocol has been improved and our model gives enhanced outcome regarding parcel average latency and packet delivery ratio (PDR).

Keywords: VANET · RSU · Routing protocols · GPSR

1 Introduction

VANET is one of the applicative branches of MANET. VANET has a place with wireless communication network in which correspondence among means of transportations happens. Here automobile go about as hubs in system. The message categories are Vehicle to Infrastructure (V2I), Vehicle to Vehicle (V2V), and Vehicle to Roadside (V2R). VANET is designated as the most crucial division of intelligent transportation system (ITS) wherein automobile are outfitted through various small area and several medium-extend remote communication. A VANET transform all associated automobile into a remote switch or hub enabling means of transportation to interface plus thus make system with a broad diversity. Essential VANET objective is to build street wellbeing, enhancing transportation framework and expanding vehicle security. To carry out this, automobile go about as sensors as well as interchange threatening that empower the drivers to respond ahead of schedule to strange and conceivably risky circumstances like accidents, congested roads. Rather than wellbeing applications it likewise gives comfort applications to street clients. For instance web access, internet business and interactive media applications. Through web access clients can download song, fire messages and take part in recreations. Different applications which were produced in mutual attempt of different administration and vehicle maker several of them are ADASE2, CAMP.

© Springer Nature Singapore Pte Ltd. 2019
P. K. Singh et al. (Eds.): FTNCT 2018, CCIS 958, pp. 464–471, 2019.
https://doi.org/10.1007/978-981-13-3804-5_34

In Fig. 1, VANET architecture is shown along with its communication types.

Vehicle to Vehicle (V2V) – Considering this Vehicle to Vehicle communication as appropriate for the favor of small collection vehicular system. It gives immediate security, quick and trustworthy. It needn't bother with any roadside foundation. It isn't extremely helpful in the event of meagerly associated system or little thickness vehicular system. In V2V cautioning significances be communicated from automobile to automobile.

Vehicle to Roadside (V2R) – Vehicle to Roadside gives correspondence amongst automobile and the wayside entities. It composes utilization of prior system framework, for example, remote access hub. In V2R cautioning communication are send to wayside entities and afterward from that wayside entities cautioning communication send to the automobile.

Vehicle to Infrastructure (V2I) – In VANET, Vehicle to infrastructure communication gives long operating vehicular systems.

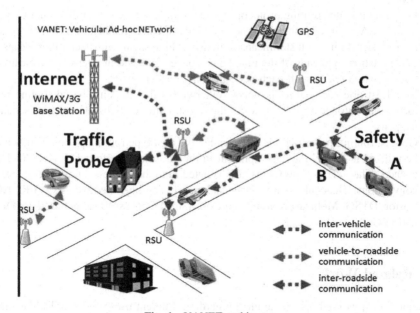

Fig. 1. VANET architecture

2 Routing Protocols in VANET

The existing routing protocols in VANET are classified into numerous groups such as Position based routing, Topology based routing, Geographic routing, Geocast routing, Cluster based routing, and Broadcast routing.

- Topology based routing do package sending through utilizes the connections be present in the system. Different sort of routing based on topology are Reactive, Proactive, and Hybrid. Proactive protocols are generally based on table driven routing e.g. OLSR, FSR, and TBRPF. Receptive protocols are examples of routing protocols that are on demand and may diminish operating cost originated by proactive type routing protocols. It utilizes way toward flooding e.g. DSR, AODV, and TORA. Hybrid protocols will try to minimize manage operating cost of proactive type routing protocol and it is blend of receptive and proactive routing protocols e.g. HARP and ZRP.
- In position based routing protocols each hub be familiar with it's neighbor by utilizing GPS data. It doesn't keep up any direction-finding chart. These protocols need learning as regards neighbor hubs and target hubs to propel small package effectively. Hi post or reference point post is utilized to refresh the data. A supply hub utilizes hi post to discover area of the neighbors. Situation data of all hubs and automobiles are distinguished by region services. Different position categorized routing protocols are GSR, GPSR, A-STAR, BMFR, GYTAR, BMAR, and AMAR.
- In Cluster oriented routing protocols, means of transportation near every node frame a cluster. Accordingly, there can be two kinds of correspondences intra-cluster and inter-cluster. In intra-cluster means of transportation speak with each other means of transportation by means of the immediate connections and in inter-cluster means of transportation speak with each node utilizing cluster leader.
- Broadcast oriented routing protocols otherwise called flooding based routing protocols that broadcast data toward the most extreme hubs while a mischance happens.
- Geocast routing protocols otherwise called the area type routing protocols that may be utilized to propel messages present in the chose zone referred as Zone of Relevance. The referred protocols are isolated into beaconless and beacon based conventions. Beaconless are Cached Geocast, Abiding Geocast, ROVER, DG-Castor, DTSG, Mobicast routing, and Constrained Geocast. Beacon based are DRG and IVG.

3 Related Work

Authors in [1] worked upon examined regarding different uses of VANETs like smart transportation appliances, ease functions, crash shirking, agreeable driving, traffic enhancements, instalment services and area based services every one of these functions enable vehicle drivers, to stay away from blockage on street, and keep up security and any more. At that point in the given paper, they talked on the subject of the advantages as well as disadvantage of different routing protocols.

Authors in [2] evaluated different place based routing protocols specifically GSR, GPSR, A-STAR, BMFR, AMAR, GYTAR and BMAR. Routing protocols based on position utilizes the GPS data to pick following sending step. The referred protocols have need of learning regarding neighbor hubs along with goal hubs to forward the packets effectively. Hi post or beacon post are utilized to refresh data. A supply hub utilizes hi communication to discover area of the neighbors. The situation data of every single one hub and automobiles are distinguished by their location services. The authors simulated protocols EBGR, GyTAR, B-MFR on two parameter bundle conveyance proportion and end-to-end defer.

Authors in [3] matched up to execution factors related to three distinctive VANET based routing protocols which are DSDV, DSR, and AODV. In adhoc network, on request distance vector routing protocol is used to set up a path while information packet remit by the hub it keeps up directing table moreover inside assured time stage if hub isn't utilized then it gets erased from the existing table. On the other hand, in destination sequenced based distance vector it utilizes the bellman ford algorithm where each hub keeps up a routing table. It utilizes two way sorted renew packages incremental packets and full dump. In dynamic source based routing the source hub remit RREQ package through assistance of different hubs to a specific target moreover while package achieves target then it remits RREP bundle to goal. At that point in this, they thought about every one of these protocol on different parameters which demonstrate no protocol carry out fit.

Authors in [4] has worked upon the two blends first one is GPSR having grid location service (GLS) known as HRGLS hybrid routing and grid location service furthermore second one works with hierarchical location service referred as HRHLS hybrid routing and hierarchical location service. This research works for directing packet GPSR utilized locality data. Further, to locate correct target place, package is remit to the old target location and as of that previous location nearby area ask for send to get back the correct place. Here the GLS and HLS calculations are adjusted by HRGLS and HRHLS where previous place is utilized to onward information bundle At that point middle hub send location appeal to locate the new target.

Authors in [5] examined planned routing method that is blending of Hierarchical location service and geographic routing protocol greedy perimeter stateless routing. All routing packets are dealt with by the GPSR protocol and hierarchical place service. Further benefit is utilized to discover object location. Major issue that emerges here is place operating cost considering the resource and object are far away. Thus mix of HLS service and GPSR protocol will diminish operating cost and enhance system exhibitions.

Authors in [5] projected a hybrid approach where, mixture of HLS location based service and GPSR protocol is used. With the help of predictable position, location based service and movement prediction based joint routing, route to destination is originated. Therefore, to accomplish expected object place unit with assistance of middle hubs, it utilizes older route yet it carries a downside that if moderate hub have been displaced or changing their current speed then it can't utilize older route to come to evaluated cell for spreading and at whatever point packet comes to at halfway hubs these hubs needs to check the course to the object causes moderate information exchange issue. They additionally clarified proposed modifications in algorithm in these two algorithm may be utilized initially Location based services HLS where two functions are utilized Predictposn and Poslookup. Secondly, the GPSR protocol wherein two functions are forward packet and GPSRemit The issue may be settled by picking vehicles having comparative speed to source hub working as transitional hubs.

4 Problem Definitions and Objective

In vehicular ad hoc network, the vehicles exchange information with every one utilizing dedicated short range communication (DSRC). Data that is traded among vehicles is typically identified with traffic related monitoring services, visitor directing data, common risks and so forth. The vehicles move indiscriminately speeds when contrasted with the hubs in portable specially appointed systems where versatility of hubs is generally less. The data must be agreed to the target automobile precisely without influencing it i.e. that ought not rely on the speed of the automobiles. At whatever point the target automobile moves starting with one place then onto the next, the supply automobile needs to communicate the path appeal keeping in mind the end target to discover a appropriate route to target. Hence, there emerges requirement for routing protocol which have to be intended for the vehicular ad hoc systems so as to directing operating cost is limited. In the existing research work the authors proposed a technique so as to discover a route amongst source and goal vehicle utilizing hierarchical location service and hybrid routing that makes utilization of the greedy perimeter stateless routing along with location services and mobility guess. As indicated by PHRHLS, at whatsoever point the source hub needs to transfer information to goal automobile. GPSR protocol may refer the location services with a specific end object to locate the crisp route to the end. It gauges the new region of the object utilizing movement angle and speed i.e. track of automobile. Subsequently starting place advances the information significance toward the hubs with the aim of has past track to the goal and when information achieves the transitional hub which is situated close to the assessed position of the goal at that point path request message is communicated to discover correct place of the object. The weakness in the given approach is that intermediary vehicular hubs may have changed the speed i.e. may turn out to be slower or speedier. Therefore sending the information through the middle hub before communicating the route request message might cause issue if moderate hubs have shifted their speed constraint so the accompanying purpose have to meet up to beat the issue of time-consuming information transmit.

5 Research Methodology

The entire system can be organized into specific cells. It is expected that automobiles in a specific cell will approach street side entity. The street side entities will follow the speed of the automobiles traveling in its area. As the automobile be in motion at more prominent velocity in vehicular ad hoc networks, connection splintering among those circumstances is normal. Keeping in view the ultimate goal to diminish system overhead that is caused by connection breakage, utilization of idea for choosing way from source and to goal automobile comprising of hubs that are moving generally at an indistinguishable speed from source vehicle with the goal that connection splintering may be narrowed. Each time source hub needs to transfer information to goal automobile, source hub will send inquiry reminder to street side unit alongside its speed. Street area entity on accepting question give answer reverse to supply automobile with automobiles traveling at moderately similar rate as the resource automobile. The supply automobile will drive information to the goal utilizing the data gave by the street side units.

6 Proposed Algorithm

Procedure 1

1. Start to send data packet from vehicle s to vehicle d.
2. Request send to RSU unit within the cell where vehicles is located.
3. If RSU has information of vehicle d then receive the data packet from vehicle s otherwise follow Procedure 2.
4. Send the data packet received from vehicle s to vehicle d using intermediate RSUs.
5. Finally the packet received by RSU of the destination vehicle's cell zone RSU.
6. Locate the actual position of vehicle d using HLS and then transfer the data packet.
7. Update the actual position and speed of the vehicle d to source cell RSU.

Procedure 2

1. Request neighbor vehicle for speed update and request for further update of other vehicles in the network.
2. Accept the request for path creation from those neighbors whose speed is relative to the source vehicle node s.
3. When path created, start to send the data packet to the neighbor's vehicles.
4. Update the destination position and speed to cell zone RSU for further successful communication setup via intermediate RSUs.

7 Performance Evaluations

The simulation parameters that have been taken are listed below (Table 1).

Table 1. Simulation parameters

S. No	Parameter	Value
1	No. of lanes	4
2	Transmission range	250 m
3	Wireless medium	IEEE 802.11
4	Simulation time	100 s
5	Grid Size	4 × 4

In this graph the red line represents the old delay and green line represents the new delay. This graph shows the RGPSR have less delay as compared to the GPSR. The enhanced protocol gives better result in terms of delay as compared to previous protocol (Fig. 2).

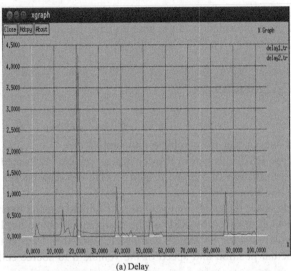

(a) Delay

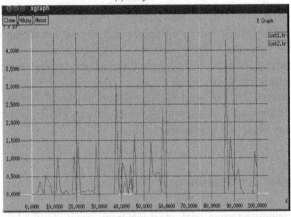

(b) Packet loss

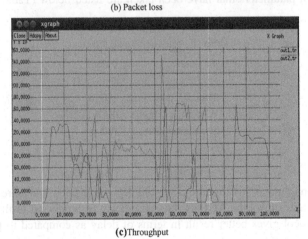

(c)Throughput

Fig. 2. (a)–(c) The performance of enhanced protocol (Color figure online)

8 Conclusion

The framework is better as far as execution measures when contrasted with the current framework. The framework gives more proficient way to broadcasting route request message when contrasted with the current framework. To decrease the overhead originated by connection breakage we capture relative velocity of automobiles as for source hub as the middle of the road hubs and discover the way from source to goal. This will offer the more solid way when contrasted with past one. This work tends to expand packet delivery ratio and works on minimizing the average latency when contrasted with the current framework. This planned and proposed approach offers better performance as compared to literature.

References

1. Singh, S., Agrawal, S.: VANET routing protocols: issues and challenges. In: 2014 Recent Advances in Engineering and Computational Sciences (RAECS), pp. 1–5. IEEE, March 2014
2. Raw, R.S., Das, S.: Performance comparison of position based routing protocols in vehicle-to-vehicle (V2V) communication. Int. J. Eng. Sci. Technol. 3(1), 435–444 (2011)
3. Monika, S.B., Singh, A.: Border-node based movement aware routing protocol. Int. J. Comput. Sci. Inf. 1(4), 121–124 (2012). ISSN (PRINT): 2231-5292
4. Rani, P., Sharma, N., Singh, P.K.: Performance comparison of VANET routing protocols. In: 2011 7th International Conference on Wireless Communications, Networking and Mobile Computing (WiCOM), pp. 1–4. IEEE, September 2011
5. Karp, B., Kung, H.T.: GPSR: Greedy perimeter stateless routing for wireless networks. In: Proceedings of the 6th Annual International Conference on Mobile Computing and Networking, pp. 243–254. ACM, August 2000
6. Hu, L., Ding, Z., Shi, H.: An improved GPSR routing strategy in VANET. In: 2012 8th International Conference on Wireless Communications, Networking and Mobile Computing (WiCOM), pp. 1–4. IEEE, September 2012
7. Xiang, Y., Liu, Z., Liu, R., Sun, W., Wang, W.: GeoSVR: a map-based stateless VANET routing. Ad Hoc Netw. 11(7), 2125–2135 (2013)
8. Lin, Q., Li, C., Wang, X., Zhu, L.: A three-dimensional scenario oriented routing protocol in vehicular ad hoc networks. In: 2013 IEEE 77th Vehicular Technology Conference (VTC Spring), pp. 1–5. IEEE, June 2013
9. Ayaida, M., Barhoumi, M., Fouchal, H., Ghamri-Doudane, Y., Afilal, L.: HHLS: a hybrid routing technique for VANETs. In: Global Communications Conference (GLOBECOM), 2012 IEEE, pp. 44–48. IEEE, December 2012
10. Ayaida, M., Barhoumi, M., Fouchal, H., Ghamri-Doudane, Y., Afilal, L.: Joint routing and location-based service in VANETs. J. Parallel Distrib. Comput. 74(2), 2077–2087 (2014)
11. Ayaida, M., Fouchal, H., Afilal, L., Ghamri-Doudane, Y.: A comparison of reactive, grid and hierarchical location-based services for vanets. In: Vehicular Technology Conference (VTC Fall), 2012 IEEE, pp. 1–5. IEEE, September 2012
12. Ayaida, M., Barhoumi, M., Fouchal, H., Ghamri-Doudane, Y., Afilal, L.: PHRHLS: A movement-prediction-based joint routing and hierarchical location service for VANETs. In: 2013 IEEE International Conference on Communications (ICC), pp. 1424–1428. IEEE, June 2013
13. Neha, Isha: Analysis of hybrid GPSR and location based routing protocol in VANET. Int. J. Comput. Sci. Inf. Technol. (2015)

Power Consumption Analysis in Multi-hop Networks of Mobile Environments

Fahmina Taranum[1,3](✉), Khaleel Ur Rahman Khan[2,4],
and Muhammed Aleemuddin[1,3]

[1] Computer Science and Engineering, Osmania University, Hyderabad, India
aleem93.md@gmail.com
[2] Computer Science and Engineering, J.N.T.U.H., Hyderabad, India
khaleelrkhan@gmail.com
[3] Muffakham Jah College of Engineering and Technology, Hyderabad, India
ftaranum@mjcollege.ac.in
[4] ACE Engineering College, Hyderabad, India

Abstract. The recent advances in cellular technologies have led to the introduction of 4G, LTE and 5G wireless services, with the usage of OFDM which is complex in computation but can easily be taken care of. The paper made an attempt to highlight the characteristics of two standards of IEEE to keep an open option for selecting devices. The proposed system utilizes the concept of multihop relay and has handled power consumption at the mobile station for battery utilization under high mobile environment. An attempt is made to calculate the power utilization at all the nodes to analyze the power consumed at the base, mobile and relay node in IEEE standard 802.11 and 802.16. Different energy and battery models were used for enhancing the performance. To increase the spectrum of the signal CDMA is used in between RN and BS and OFDMA is used in between BS and MS. The objective is to check for an optimal solution in between two standards of IEEE 802.11 and 802.16 if any one of it is to be selected.

Keywords: Multi-hop · Duracell-AA · AAA
Code division multiple access (CDMA)
Orthogonal frequency division multiple access (OFDMA) · Relay node (RN)
Mobile station (MS) · Base station (BS)

1 Introduction

The major challenges in current technological advancement is to make old technology based devices compatible with new ones and managing disconnectivity, power optimization, minimizing the battery usage along with maximizing features at the MS. As the mobile stations moves with high speed, the battery utilization is wasted, to overcome this; many attempts were made to reduce the power consumption when MSs communicate with the BSs. The scenarios are designed by using 802.11, 802.16 with and without relay node and added with more features of battery model, energy models and different modulation techniques have been applied to increase the signal capturing facility. The concept of selecting a station type as that of base and subscriber type is

© Springer Nature Singapore Pte Ltd. 2019
P. K. Singh et al. (Eds.): FTNCT 2018, CCIS 958, pp. 472–483, 2019.
https://doi.org/10.1007/978-981-13-3804-5_35

available only in IEEE 802.16 but not in 802.11, still the scenario can be designed as that of destination and source with CBR connecting the source and destination node in IEEE 802.11. The provision to enable OFDMA at the MAC layer is available in IEEE 802.16 only. Therefore the OFDMA burst received and forwarded to MAC is analyzed only in IEEE 802.16. To model the PHY layer certain characteristics need to be incorporated at the source and the destination end like modulation, coding, noise, interference and antenna gains. In QualNet 7.4, a MAC Layer interface consists of Ranging type as normal or CDMA, normal type represent OFDMA modulation by default. The PHY component caters to signal transmission, reception and reflects the effects of the MAC, distortions and interference. As far as latest network scenarios and technology development are concerned, power optimization should be the foremost concern for NGN (Next Generation Networks) when battery discharges while experiencing high mobile environment. Minimizing the battery usage for enhancing the network performance as well as maximizing the proper utilization is a big challenge. Two ray pathloss model with −111dBm propagation limit and signal propagation speed of 3E8 are used for all the architectures in consideration. At the network layer, the details of AODV route request and reply can be generated for 100 buffered packets of size 512 bytes transmitted with maximum velocity of 10 m/s.

The rest of the paper is organized as follows: Sect. 2 provides a brief description of related work, Sect. 3 describes about topologies or architectures designed and analyzed, Sect. 4 discusses the result analysis of power consumption, energy models and its statistical analysis. Section 5 portrays conclusion and future research scope.

2   Related Work

The related work surveyed is summarized as follows:

The main aim of the proposal is to reduce power consumption for which concepts from the different papers were explored, Surveyed and adapted- Paper [1] is about the routing algorithms, energy models, battery model and propagation model. The different energy models discussed include user defined, Mica motes, Micaz and Generic collaborated with linear battery model and two ray propagation model. [2] Suggested considering both the total transmission energy consumption of routes and the residual power of the nodes for designing the system with minimum total transmission power above some threshold. Realistic consumption model [3] is used for calculation of energy cost, using channel quality as parameter for ensuring successful delivery of packet. Efficiency of protocols is evaluated [4] for energy consumption indicating their usage of node's energy, taking into consideration nodes density and mobility. A new approach for optimizing power consumption in MANETs has been proposed and implemented [5] by introducing a threshold value on each node and transmitting the equal length of packet on the route. [6] specifies using the multi-hop relay networks to improvise the range of the existent cells and analyze the power saving obtained, but still none of the above have taken up the issue of high mobile environments, such as those experienced while moving in high speed trains, and analyzed networks accordingly. Hence, this paper takes up this task and analyzes as well as compares the performance of the existent topologies with the multi-hop relay topologies. Paper [7] discusses the upshot of power optimization in Mobile stations. Different levels of power were taken as input using user defined energy model at different nodes depending on their requirement.

3 Architectures

Qualnet is used to design the architectures with *.cpp, *.pcm, *.utl and *.h files to obtain the required functionality in collaboration with visual studio c++, which helps in generating *.stat and *.config files. The parameters used for designing this continental network topologies with high mobile environment is depicted in Table 1. 3D view of the network with BS, SS, internet and point to point links is shown in Fig. 1. The network consist of one base station, one relay station, three mobile stations, two subnets, CBR (constant bit rate) and point to point links, with random wave point flags as shown in Fig. 2.

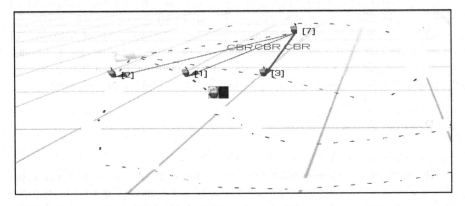

Fig. 1. 3D view of BS, SS, subnet and CBR

Node 7 is acting as base station and node 1, 2 and 3 are acting as subscriber stations which moves along the random path set using random waypoint model denoted by red flags as shown in Figs. 2 and 3. Node 7 is connected to mobile nodes using a subnet and the traffic is regulated from base to subscriber station using CBR (represented by Green line). The relay node acts as a caching node, which is an intermediate node connecting a source and destination node in wireless network used to store and transmit the data. The shaded circles around the node 1, 3 and 7 are the transmitting regions. The light green arrow head shows the direction of packet transmission in between node 1 to node 7. The blue dotted line shows the connectivity of node 1, 2, 3 to the subnet 192.0.3.1. Three CBR links are used to connect one source and three destination nodes for transmitting data using AODV routing protocol. A relay node is being added in between base and mobile stations connected by a subnet 190.0.3.2 while the relay and base are connected with a subnet 190.0.3.1 as shown in Fig. 2. As node 2 is far apart from the base station it receives fewer packets. The reason for taking less number of nodes in the scenario is to ease out the comparison parameters used to measure the performance metrics. The nodes 1, 2, 3, 7 & 8 are with addresses 190.0.2.2, 190.0.2.1, 190.0.2.4 and 190.0.3.2 and 190.0.2.5 respectively. The mobile nodes moves along the path of random wavepoint model and the nodes at the shortest distance to mobile station get good reception and throughput, which be interpreted from node 1 and 3. The base station and relay are connected with same subnet and all mobile stations and relay are connected by another subnet.

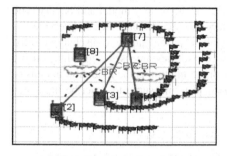

Fig. 2. Architecture with relay node   **Fig. 3.** Network transmission

The Fading model used is Ricean fading model as it supports scenarios in which the sight signal is dominant signal seen at the receiver and for line of sight communication. A fading model calculates the effect of changes in characteristics of the propagation

Table 1. Network parameters used in the scenario

Parameter	Value
Qualnet version	7.4
Terrain size	1500 * 1500 m
Physical layer	802.11b Radio/802.16 Radio
Mobility model	Random waypoint
Fading model	Ricean
Traffic type	CBR
Network layer	IPv4
Routing protocol	AODV
Simulation time	60 s and 15 min
Frequencies	2.4 GHz
No of channels	2
Gaussian component file	default.SR10000.fading
Battery model	Service life Estimator/Residue model
Max transmission power at PHY layer, power transmission	50 dBm, 802.16 = 20 dBm, 802.11 = 15 dBm
Energy model	User-specified
MAC interface ranging type	CDMA or normal

path on the signal strength. The units of time and average interference are in seconds and dBm respectively.

The designed scenarios include IEEE 802.16 and 802.11 with relay, energy model, battery model and CDMA. A default Gaussian Components file, default fading can be found in INSTALL_DIR/scenarios/default. A segment of this file is SAMPLING-RATE = 1000 BASE-DOPPLER-FREQUENCY = 30 NUMBER-OF-GAUSSIAN-COMPONENTS = 16384 used to construct a zero means and unit variance Gaussian random process. The input parameter must be configured initially for a given battery type from a battery manufacturer. The categories of the battery model and battery type used are depicted in Table 2. Service life battery model estimates the total service life of the battery model which calculates the time taken for the battery to discharge to zero from start time of simulation. Different types of batteries are used depending on the usage of battery power at the nodes. Path loss or attenuation is the reduction in density of a signal when it propagates through medium. It is measured to describe the atten-

Table 2. Battery types used at the nodes

Battery model	Service life estimator	Residual life estimator
Battery charge monitoring interval	60 s	60 s
Battery type	MS-Duracell AAA, RN-Duracell AA, BS-Duracell AA	MS-Duracell AAA(MN-2400), BS-Duracell AA(MX-1500)

uation between receiver and transmitter antenna at the PHY layer as a function of distance or other parameters as shown in Tables 6 and 7.

PCM file contain each entry in time interval of one second to represent a unit load applied when the battery will be drained by X. PCM are used by Service life estimator model. The amount of battery drained is more in Duracell AAA, as Duracell AA has more power and stores more energy i.e. ten times long lasting power than Duracell AAA. The voltage of all the Duracell battery models is 1.5 V. The Duracell batteries are made of Alkaline-Manganese Dioxide. Residual life estimator uses *.utl files to provide values to load table files for each battery types. The scenario value column of Table 3 depicts the assumption made for user defined energy model, which is a configurable permitting user to specify the energy consumption parameters of the radio in different power modes. The configurable parameters include the power supply voltage of the radio's hardware, electrical current load consumed in *Transmit, Receive, Idle*, and *Sleep* modes. The battery model captures the characteristics of real life batteries and can be used to predict their behavior under various conditions of charge or discharge. The three Battery models that are supported by Qualnet are Service life time, Linear and Residue model works with the parameters like system architectures, power management policies, and transmission power control. The current and voltage are set high at the BS as it acts as a short range transceiver. The modulation technique used in between BS and Relay is CDMA for wide spreading range of signal. The amount of default current consumed and scenarios values considered are listed out in Table 3. The algorithm used to calculate the power consumption of all the nodes in the designed scenario for transmit, receive, idle and sleep mode are defined at the physical layer using steps defined in program code 1. It can be noted that the sleep current load for all nodes is set to zero. Sleep is enabled if there is a period of inactivity. The reason for selecting user defined model of energy is to assign required amount of current according to users need. The formulae listed below are used in pseudo code to measure the amount of current used at the nodes. The energy consumed by transmitting (E_{tx}) id the length of the packet with the preamble times the packet rates (i.e. Energy = Power * Time). The user defined

Table 3. Energy model used-user defined

GUI parameter	Parameter	Default value	Scenario value
Transmit current load	ENERGY-TX-CURRENT-LOAD	280 mA	BS = 250 mA SS = 220 mA RN = 230 mA
Reception load	ENERGY-RX-CURRENT-LOAD	204 mA	BS = 220 mA SS = 200 mA RN = 210 mA
Idle current load	ENERGY-IDLE-CURRENT-LOAD	174 mA	BS = 180 mA SS = 150 mA RN = 160 mA
Sleep current load	ENERGY-SLEEP-CURRENT-LOAD	14 mA	SS = 0 mA
Supply voltage of the interface	ENERGY-OPERATIONAL-VOLTAGE	3 V	BS = 5 V SS = 3 V RN = 3.5 V

radio energy model allows the user to specify the energy consumption of the radio in different power modes according to user requirement.

Formulae

The following formulae are used in the energy.cpp files for calculating different energies

$$\text{Transmission Energy Consumed } (E_{tx}) = \text{Transmitting Current} * \text{Voltage} * \text{Time} \quad (1)$$

$$\text{Receiving Energy Consumed } (E_{rx}) = \text{Receiving Current} * \text{Voltage} * \text{Time} \quad (2)$$

$$\text{Idle Energy Consumed } (E_{idle}) = \text{Idle Current (mA)} * \text{Voltage} * \text{Time} \quad (3)$$

$$\text{Sleep Energy Consumed } (E_{sleep}) = \text{Sleep Current} * \text{Voltage} * \text{Time} \quad (4)$$

$$\text{Total energy consumed} = E_{tx} + E_{rx} + E_{idle} + E_{sleep} \quad (5)$$

$$\text{Power consumption at Mobile station} = E_{tx} + E_{rx} + E_{idle} + E_{sleep} \, (\text{all MS}) \quad (6)$$

$$\text{Power consumption at Base station} = E_{tx} + E_{rx} + E_{idle} + E_{sleep} \ (\text{all BS}) \qquad (7)$$

$$\text{Power consumption at Relay station} = E_{tx} + E_{rx} + E_{idle} + E_{sleep} \ (\text{all RS}) \qquad (8)$$

$$\text{Power in dBm is converted to mW} \qquad (9)$$

$$\text{One dBm} = (\text{double})10.0 * (\log(mW)/\log(10.0)) \qquad (10)$$

Step 1: Initialize the variables:-Duration, actDuration, load, totalIdlePower,
totalTxPower, Sleep_load to 0, now=getNodeTime();

Step 2: Equation to generate values for the variable:
Duration = (now-lastUpdate) / seconds;
actDuration = (now-starttime) / seconds;
Sleep_load = sleep - currentload;
Get no. of configured and active antennas elements from physical layer
inActiveAntennas = numConfigAntennas-numActiveAntennas;
loadTable = load * (actDuration*numActiveAntennas)

Step 3: Check the state of the battery and do the following updations.
If (battery is alive) then
decrement the battery charge for currently active antennas
load = load- (load * (no. of active antenna))
else
now = deadtime of battery;
actDuration = (now- starttime) / second
if (actDuratio n< 0) then exit
else go to step 4

Step 4: For the state from which PHYSICAL is exiting referred as (prevstatus)
If prevstatus = IDLE then
totalIdlePower = totalIdlePower + loadTable + (sleep_load * actDuration *
inActiveAntennas);
If prevstatus = TRANSMITTING then
totalTxPower = totalTxPower + loadTable + (sleep_load *actDuration*
inActiveAntennas);
If prevstatus = RECEIVING then
totalRxPower = totalRxPower+ loadTable + sleep_load * actDuration *
inActiveAntennas);
If prevstatus=TRX_OFF then
totalSleepPower = powStats. TotalSleepPower + loadTable + (sleep_load *
actDuration* inActiveAntennas));

Step 5: Printing the output generated
txPower_mW = txPower_mW/numConfigAntennas;
txPower_dBm = (double) 10.0 * (log(txPower_mW) / log(10.0));
Energy consumed in Transmit mode=E_t =(totalTxPower *volt) / 3600.0
Energy consumed in Receive mode =E_r= (totalRxPower*volt) / 3600.0
Energy consumed in Idle mode = E_i =(totalIdlePower*volt) / 3600.0
Energy consumed in Sleep mode =E_s= (totalSleepPower*volt) / 3600.0
Total Energy =$E_t + E_r + E_i + E_s$
End;

Program code *1: Physical Layer _Energy Model.cpp file*

The total current consumed at all the mobile stations is calculated separately using energy consumed in all modes of mobile nodes and compared with the power utilization of the base and the relay node. Program code 1 defined above is used to calculate the energy consumed by taking input from the properties of physical layer such as number of configured antennas, packet size, transmission range, transmission power, data rate and time to live. Network diameter for hops is 35 m with TTL 1, 2, 7 (for start, increment and threshold) are considered for both the standards. Transmission power is constant 15 dBm in case of 802.11 irrespective of transmitting 1 Mbps to 11 Mbps while 802.16 are fixed to 20 dBm. An analysis of two battery models are made to estimate the total service life of the battery (i.e. the time it takes the battery charge to reach zero from the start of simulation) and the remaining service life of the battery at any time in the simulation using service life model and Residual life estimator.

4 Results Generated and Analysis

The results at the physical layer for all the nodes with the standard IEEE 802.11 and 802.16 are shown in Figs. 4, 5, 6, 7 and Figs. 8, 9, 10 respectively. The average energy consumed in IEEE 802.16 is less when compared to 802.11, therefore while selecting the technology it is better to go with 802.16 for resolving the issues of power con-

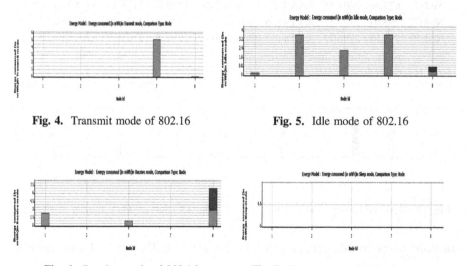

Fig. 4. Transmit mode of 802.16

Fig. 5. Idle mode of 802.16

Fig. 6. Receive mode of 802.16

Fig. 7. Sleep mode of 802.16 and 802.11

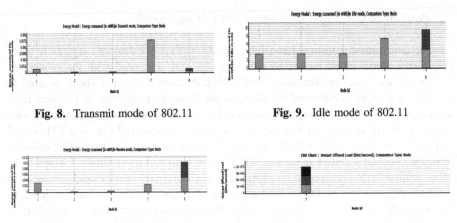

Fig. 8. Transmit mode of 802.11   **Fig. 9.** Idle mode of 802.11

Fig. 10. Receive mode of 802.11   **Fig. 11.** Unicast load at application layer

Table 4. Battery model and types used in IEEE standards for 60 s

	Residual life estimator			Service life estimator		
	802.11	802.16	Battery type	802.11	802.16	Battery type
Node1	2627.11	2648.63	AAA Duracell-MN-2400	1179.29	1182.2	AAA Duracell
Node2	2627.37	2629.83	AAA Duracell-MN-2400	1179.3	1179.45	AAA Duracell
Node3	2627.36	2604.55	AAA Duracell-MN-2400	1179.3	1178.28	AAA Duracell
Node7	2798.01	2797.55	AA Duracell-MX-1500	2775.28	2770.49	AA Duracell
Node8	2795.68	2796.73	AA Duracell-MX-1500	2754.7	2763.59	AA Duracell

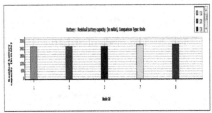
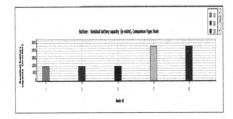

Fig. 12. Residual battery model of 802.11   **Fig. 13.** Service life estimator of 802.11

sumption of the mobile devices in mobile environment. The unicast load is same in

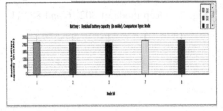
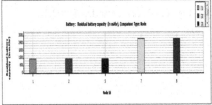

Fig. 14. Residual battery model of 802.16   **Fig. 15.** Service life estimator of 802.16

both the standards and is represented in Fig. 11.

The actual capacity of the battery decreases when the discharge current increases. With efficiency of 100% the battery last for one hour. The capacity of the battery for all the nodes of IEEE 802.11 and 802.16 are depicted in Figs. 12, 13 and Figs. 14, 15 respectively. It may be noted from graphs that there is negligible difference in the IEEE standards. The residual and service life of the battery remains almost same for base and relay stations but the value of service life estimators at the mobile stations is almost half when compared to residual model.

The comparsion of residual and service life estimator is shown in Table 4. It may be noted that the total power consumption calculated using program code 1 in 802.11 is more at the mobile nodes and the relay node when compared to IEEE 802.16 as shown in Table 5.

The analysis in Table 6 shows the signal arrival power at the mobile stations, base station and relay station.

The analysis shows that the time spent in transmission at the base node is quite high when compared to all the mobile nodes. Average path loss is high for a node involved in greater transmission. The rate of signal transmission, utilization and average signal power are more at the base station for non relay. The average signal power required is high at the relay node when compared to other nodes in the architecture. The physical layer utilization is high in relay node when compared to base node. Therefore the optimal selection is to be based on the results depicted in Tables 6 and 7.

Table 5. Comparison of power consumption

Total power

	BS	MS	Relay
802.11	7.5027	11.2520	9.6276
802.16	8.903	9.7111	7.923

Table 6. Results generated at physical layer of 802.11

Simulation time-60 s, Scenario 802.11					
Node Id	1	2	3	7	8
Avg. transmitting delay	.000000458	.000000464	.000000627	.000000632	.000000639
Utilization	0.00006	0.000053	0.0001345	0.001393	.001171
Avg. signal power	−75.193	−75.427	−77.56	−77.807	.538916
Avg. interference	−90.97	−90.97	−90.97	−90.97	−90.970077
Avg. path loss	86.72	86.76	89.526	89.587	75.306

The analysis of IEEE 802.16 standard used in the physical layer of the devices is shown in Table 7. The entire signals received are forwarded to MAC and are locked by physical layer. The value 0 in node 2 indicates that node 2 is not reachable. The Average interference and the noise ratio remain same in both IEEE scenarios. The time spent in transmission at the base node is quite high when compared to all the mobile nodes. The rate of signal transmitted, utilization and average signal power is more at the base station.

Table 7. Results generated at physical layer of 802.16

Simulation time-60 s, Scenario 802.16					
Node Id	1	2	3	7	8
Signal transmitted	753	0	537	3000	743
Signal received & forwarded to MAC	2968	0	2109	2770	2997
OFDMA received & forwarded to MAC	6042	0	4284	2770	6107
AVG path loss	95.83	0	102.2	94.06	94.229
Signal arrival (Power)	2.02E−08	0.00E+00	7.78E−10	4.81E−09	3.46E−08

5   Conclusions

The final analysis confirms that 802.16 outperforms in less energy consumption when compared to 802.11 with AODV routing protocol and hence can be selected for high mobile subscriber stations. Node 7 is base station which uses its energy for transmit, idle but not for receive mode. As the sleep duration is explicitly set to 0 for all nodes, none of the nodes consume any energy in this mode. The closer the placement of node the better is the transmission.

The power consumed at mobile station in 802.16 = .1797 mA for no relay node
The power consumed at mobile station in 802.16 = 11.37 mA for relay node

The ratio of energy consumed for service life and residue model using AODV-IEEE 802.16 for mobile nodes using simulation time of 15 s is 3155:3461.09 mAh and for the base station it is almost double in both cases.

Therefore it is proved that there is reduction of energy consumed at the base station. The amount of energy consumed at the mobile station is marginally more than the base, but is less for other scenarios designed with predefined energy models. Further, the concept of caching at the relay node increases the possibility of spreading the data but requires more energy to redirect the data to additional nodes. The future enhancement is to reduce energy requirement at the mobile nodes. Power aware routing algorithms or DYMO has been proved to save more energy when compared to AODV. Hence, an extension to this work would be to redesign the architecture using DYMO or other power aware routing algorithm to further reduce the power consumption.

References

1. Soni, B., Fatima, M.: Overview of energy consumption and propagation in MANET Int. J. Innovative Res. Sci. Technol. **6**(7) (2017)
2. Fotino, M., Marano, S.: EE-OLSR: energy efficient OLSR routing protocol for mobile adhoc networks. IEEE Trans., 1–7 (2008)

3. Kanjanarot, J., Sitthi, K., Saivichit, C.: Energy-based route discovery mechanism in mobile ad hoc networks. In: ICA0T2006 (2006)
4. Kumar, A., Rafiq, M.Q., Bansal, K.: Performance evaluation of energy consumption in MANET. Int. J. Comput. Appl. **42**(2), 7–12 (2012)
5. Gopinath, S., Rajaram, A., Suresh Kumar, N.: Improving minimum energy consumption in ad hoc networks under different scenarios. Int. J. Adv. Innovative Res. (IJAIR) **1**(4), 40–46 (2012)
6. Chandwani, G., Datta, S.N., Chakrabarti, S.: Relay assisted cellular system for energy minimization. In: Annual IEEE Indian Conference (INDICON) (2010)
7. Jain, A.: Improving minimum energy consumption in ad hoc networks under different scenarios. In: 2012 1st International Conference on Emerging Technology Trends in Electronics, Communication and Networking. IEEE (2012). https://doi.org/10.1109/ET2ECN.2012.6470043

Anonymity Preserving Authentication and Key Agreement Scheme for Wireless Sensor Networks

Deepti Singh[1]([✉]), Samayveer Singh[2], Bijendra Kumar[1],
and Satish Chand[3]

[1] Department of Computer Engineering, Netaji Subhas Institute of Technology,
New Delhi, India
deepti19singh@gmail.com, bizender@gmail.com
[2] Department of Computer Science Engineering, Bennett University,
Greater Noida, UP, India
samayveersingh@gmail.com
[3] School of Computer and System Sciences, Jawaharlal Nehru University,
New Delhi, India
schand86@hotmail.com

Abstract. The main purpose of our paper is to design efficient smartcard based authentication and session key agreement scheme for wireless sensor networks. Our scheme uses registration phase for both user and sensor nodes. We analyze security and simulation results using AVISPA shows that our scheme is secure against attacks.

Keywords: Wireless sensor network · Authentication · Hash function
Smart card · Formal verification · AVISPA

1 Introduction

Wireless sensor networks (WSNs) consists of small sensor devices. These nodes are deployed randomly over the target region [5, 13]. In WSNs all the sensor node sense the environment and send the necessary information to Base station. The user then access the data from Base station. As the communication network is wireless and not secure any intruder can attack very easily and get/modify the information. Because of its imminence and delicacy the significant information in transit must be protected by a secure channel between user and sensor node. For secure channel we require authentication and key agreement mechanism to allow user and sensor node to mutually authenticate each other. And the communicating entities develop some common session key to protect the information from various attacks.

However, it is not easy to directly utilize internet security protocols because of resource-constrained sensor node. For secure communication over an unreliable channel, mutual authentication and key agreement between the entities is important. To improve security, two-factor (2FA) and three-factor authentication (3FA) scheme have been proposed in WSNs. In 2FA scheme, smart card and password are used to prove

© Springer Nature Singapore Pte Ltd. 2019
P. K. Singh et al. (Eds.): FTNCT 2018, CCIS 958, pp. 484–495, 2019.
https://doi.org/10.1007/978-981-13-3804-5_36

user's identity. Therefore, 2FA is less secure. The 3FA scheme consists of smartcard, password and biometric as credentials. 3FA is more secure then 2FA because biometric can neither be forgotten nor can be easily guessed. Below we have also discussed energy model, network model and desired security features in authentication scheme of Wireless sensor networks.

1.1 Energy Model

In WSNs, sensor nodes are of low battery and they can neither be recharged nor replaced easily. Therefore, there is a need to save the battery of sensor nodes. The sensor node consists of transceiver unit, receiving unit, memory and power source. The transceiver and receiving unit is responsible for sending and receiving the message. As we know communication, overhead of sensor nodes depends on three factors that is transmitted, received message and distance between the communicating components. Base station has high energy compared to sensor node.

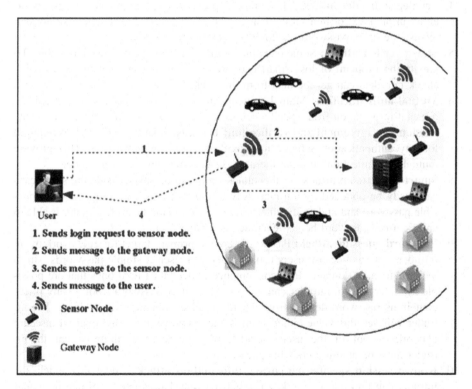

Fig. 1. Network model

1.2   Network Model

The model discussed in [1] is given in Fig. 1 that includes gateway node (GWN), user (U_i) and sensor node (Sj). Sensor node and user mutual authenticate each other and then the sensed information is send to user.

1.3   Security Feature

1. **User Anonymity:** Privacy is very important factor in today's era. if any intruder collects all the transmitted message between the communicating parties during the scheme execution. In this attack, intruder tries to get the identity of user with the help of gathered messages.
2. **User Untraceability:** In this attack intruder gets message from different sessions and check if they belong to same session.
3. **Impersonation attack:** Under this attack, if any intruder captures the communicating message of the previous sessions. Then it modifies the login request to access the information not meant for them.
4. **Privileged Insider attack:** This attack is possible when user sends the password either in plaintext or in a format that can be easily guessed. The administrator can misuse the users password resulting in users impersonation.
5. **Stolen verifier attack:** Some relevant information are stored in database table. To handle the problem of loss smart card we need such types of table. Under this attack intruders can get the data from this table
6. **Mutual authentication:** Mutual authentication is required because user want the relevant information from specific sensor node that acts as information provider.
7. **Session key agreement and verification:** The session key generation is is required for any authentication scheme to provide secure communication. This provide mutual authentication between the user, sensor node and gateway node.
8. **Smart card stolen attack:** In this attack, information saved inside the smart card can easily be obtained by intruder. Any intruder or attacker can guess some possible password and update it in the storage space of smart card.If intruder is able to enter correct password he can even act as a valid user.
9. **Password guessing attack:** Passwords are the primary target for guesswork by an intruder. It is because users usually   tend to   select simple passwords   from their acquainted domain for convenience rather than hard ones that are possible to   forget. An intruder can guess   a   user password from   any price-containing password despite from where intruder   obtains   this value.   The intruder will get this value either from some message traveling over an insecure network or out of the user's smart card. The necessary thing is that the intruder must be able to verify his guess.
10. **Known session specific temporary information attack:** Under this attack, the intruder can find the session key if other relevant data is known of that particular session.

Table 1. Notations used in this paper

Symbol	Description
GWN	Gateway node
SMi	Smart card number (unique)
UIDi	Identity of user
Ti	Timestamp
IDsnj	Identity of sensor node
ΔT	Transmission delay
PWi	Password of user
MKsnj	Secret key of sensor node
Bi	Biometric template
SK	Session key
Ru	Random nonce generated by user
Rbs	Random nonce generated by base station
h(.)	One way hash function
Rsnj	Random nonce generated by sensor node
⊕	XOR operation
‖	Concatenation of message

2 Literature Review

To improve functionalities and security in WSNs, various user authentication schemes has been discussed in the literature. Watro et al. [2] proposed a user authentication protocol that uses RSA and Diffie-Hellman that is known as TinyPK but later it had been found that it suffers from man-in-the middle attack. In the year 2009, Xu et al. [3] again proposed the protocol based on RSA, as all keys of sensor node and user is stored there which leads to high memory overhead. Yeh et al. [15] propose an elliptic curve based protocol. Wong et al. [5] proposed an authentication protocol that uses hash function and passwords but it is vulnerable to same login-id and stolen-verifier attack. Tseng et al. [16] proposed a authentication scheme that is based on dynamic identity. Vaidya et al. [6] found that authentication scheme [16] suffers from replay and main-in-the middle attack and it suggested an improved 2FA in WSNs. Das's proposed an improved protocol base on passwords. Later in 2010, Khan et al. [7] found that it is vulnerable to privileged insider attack. Holbl et al. [9] claimed that Das et al. [8] is not perfect and they propose two enhanced protocol. Fan et al. [13] proposed an authentication scheme for two tiered WSNs and it is resistant to Denial-of-Service attack. Turkanovic et al. [1] is an energy efficient user authentication protocol based on hash function that provides high security and low computational overhead. However Biswas et al. [10] found that Turkanovic et al. suffers from various attacks like impersonation attack, offline password guessing attack, offline identity guessing attack and is not suitable for practical application. Farash et al. [11] also found that Turkanovic et al. is prone to smartcard loss attack, session key disclosure etc. Chang et al. [14] revealed that Turkanovic et al. is suspectible stolen smart card attack, stolen verifier attack and spoofing attack. Then they found two protocols P1 and P2. P1 is based on hash function while P2 employs Elliptic Curve Cryptography. We solve the problem of attacks by suggesting a new secure scheme. The security of our scheme is demonstrated by formal verification using AVISPA tool.

The remainder of the paper is organized as follows. Section 2 discussed literature survey. In Sect. 3, we present a novel three-factor authentication using smart card, which is efficient and provides mutual authentication. In Sect. 4 AVISPA tool is used for formal security verification of our authentication scheme. Finally, Sect. 5 concludes the work.

3 Proposed Scheme

In this section, we propose an user authentication scheme for WSNs environment. Here we will check for authorized user and the sensors before the message transmission starts. The list of notation used throughout this paper is given in Table 1. Our scheme consists of (1) sensor registration phase; (2) user registration phase; (3) login phase; (4) authentication and key agreement phase.

3.1 Sensor Node Registration Phase

Initially GWN deploy sensor node (SNj) and their identity and master key in memory of sensor node and assume that intruder cannot extract data from sensors' memory. The following steps are executed to registration SNj:

Step 1: Sensor node computes:
$A1 = SNj \oplus h(Rsn||T1)$ and
$A2 = h(SNj ||Xbs||Rsn||T1)$ and sends $< A1, A2, T1 >$.
Step 2: BS checks if $|T2 - T1| \leq \Delta T$ is correct. Then GWN authenticates sensor node and stores its identity in the database.
Step 3: Then GWN sends an acknowledgement message to the sensor node.

3.2 User Registration Phase

In user registration phase, user register itself to base station and base station provides smartcard to him. The following steps are executed to register user with the base station.

Step 1: User send its identity UIDi and password PWi along with random nonce to GWN in the encrypted form as
$B1 = h(UIDi||T3)$,
$B2 = h(PWi||Rc)$ through a secure channel.
Step 2: Let T3 be time a which GWN receives registration request. GWN computes
$C1 = h(UIDi||Rgwn)$,
$C2 = h(SMi ||Rgwn)$ and store $< C1, C2, SMi. Bi >$ in the smart card.
Step 3: User inserts smartcard in card reader. User inserts its identity, password and biometric template. Then smart card stores
$D1 = h(UIDi||PWi||Bi)$,
$D2 = C1 \oplus h(UIDi||PWi)$,
$D3 = C2 \oplus h(UIDi \oplus PWi)$. Smartcard then update its value $< D1, D2, D3, SMi >$.

3.3   Login Phase

In login phase user needs to enter its secret value like identity, password etc.; they are first verified and then login information is sent to GWN.

Step 1: User inserts the smart card and input the biometric template. It it is verified then user inputs its identity and password. Smartcard then compare the value of D1,if it is correct then move to step 2.

Step 2: After verifying user, smartcard computes

$E1 = UIDi \oplus h(C2||T4),$

$E2 = Rc \oplus h(C1||T4),$

$E3 = h(C1||Ru||T4),$

$E4 = SMi \oplus h(T4).$

Step 3: The smartcard the calculates

$E5 = SNj \oplus h(UIDi||Ru||T4)$ and sends $< E1, E2, E3, E4, E5 >$ to GWN through an unsecured channel.

3.4   Authentication and Key Agreement Phase

In the authentication and key agreement phase phase, mutual authentication is established and a key for that particular session is generated between user, gateway node and sensor node.

Step 1: In order to proof user's and GWN authenticity to sensor node, GWN computes

$E6 = h(UIDi||SNj||Ru||MKsnj||T5),$

$E7 = UIDi \oplus h(MKsnjj||T5),$

$E8 = Ru \oplus h(UIDi||SKsnj)$ And then sends $< E6, E7, E8, T5 >$ to sensor node.

Step 2: Sensor node checks if $|T6 - T5| \leq \Delta T$ and verify the value of E6. Then the authenticity of user and gateway node is verified. Then sensor node computes session key

$SKsnj = h(UIDi||SNj||Ru||Rsnj),$

$E9 = h(SK||MKsnj||Rsnj||T6),$

$E10 = Ru \cup Rsnj.$ Then sensor node sends $< E9. E10, T6 >$ to gateway node.

Step 3: GWN checks the value of E9 and $|T7 - T6| \leq \Delta T$. If it holds, GWN computes

$MKgwn = h(UIDi||IDsnj||Ru||Rsnj),$

$E11 = h(SKgwn||UIDi||C1||Rsnj).$ GWN then sends $< E11. E10 >$ to user.

Step 4: User compares the value of E11. If it is equal then calculates

$SKu = h(UIDi||SNj||Ru||Rsnj).$

Now the session key is established user, sensor node and gateway node $SKu = SKsnj = SKgwn$ after performing mutual authentication.

4 Security Analysis Using AVISPA Tool

AVISPA (Automated Validation of Internet Security Protocols and Applications) is widely accepted tool for formal verification to check if a given security scheme is safe or not safe.

The code is written in HLPSL language that is converted to IF format by using hlpsl2if translator. The hlpsl2if generates a specification in IF format. It is a lower level then HLPSL and it can be easily understand by AVISPA tool. It can implements four back-ends. These back-ends are called On-the-Fly Model-Checker(OFMC), Constraint Logic based attack searcher (Cl-AtSe),SAT-based model checker (SATMC) and Tree Automata based on Automatic Approximations for the analysis of security protocols (TA4SP). The OUTPUT FORMAT (OF) is generated based on these back-ends. The result is generated in OF format that gives the information regarding the safety of scheme or under what condition the output is obtained.

The simulation result of our scheme using and CL-AtSe and OFMC are shown in Figs. 2 and 3 respectively. The intruder has been provided public data in session and it can cooperate with other role of scheme. Its goal is to find attacks, compromise the legitimacy of entities, etc. This verifies whether the security goal can be achieved or not. It is clear from the Figs. 2 and 3 our authentication scheme is safe against active and passive attacks.

```
SUMMARY
 SAFE

DETAILS
 BOUNDED_NUMBER_OF_SESSIONS
 TYPED_MODEL

PROTOCOL
 /home/deepti/avispa-1.1/testsuite/results/paper.if

GOAL
 As Specified

BACKEND
 CL-AtSe

STATISTICS

 Analysed  : 0 states
 Reachable : 0 states
 Translation: 0.36 seconds
 Computation: 0.00 seconds
```

Fig. 2. HLPSL Result-1 for CL-AtSe

```
% OFMC
% Version of 2006/02/13
SUMMARY
  SAFE
DETAILS
  BOUNDED_NUMBER_OF_SESSIONS
PROTOCOL
  /home/deepti/avispa-1.1/testsuite/results/paper.if
GOAL
  as_specified
BACKEND
  OFMC
COMMENTS
STATISTICS
  parseTime: 0.00s
  searchTime: 1.2s
  visitedNodes: 40 nodes
  depth: 6 plies
```

Fig. 3. HLPSL Result-2 for OFMC

5 Informal Security Analysis

We will also analyze different type of attacks for security analysis of our proposed scheme.

User Anonymity: Suppose any intruder access the login and authentication information. But these values are protected by hash function and Random nonce Ru and Rbs. As these values are different during two login message. Hence intruder cannot find any relationship between them. Hence, our scheme preserves user anonymity.

User Untraceability: To trace a user, intruder captures the message involved in different sessions to check whether the fields belong to same user. However, it cannot trace each message involved different values. As message of each session are also different. Hence, our scheme resist user untraceability.

Impersonation Attack: To impersonate user or base station, the intruder needs to know the identity of user $UIDi$ and the value of $h(UIDi||Rbs)$ that is not possible. For this, the intruder needs to know the correct password and the biometric information.

Mutual Authentication: As public messages are passing through the unreliable channel, therefore mutual authentication is essential between the participants. During the execution of our scheme, each participant authenticates each other with the help of message passing.

Session Key Agreement: If authentication is successful, then session key is established between user and sensor node. If random nonces are secret, then only our session key is secret. As we can see these values are well protected. Even if an adversary gets the session key he/she will not be able to past or future session key as random nonce are different in each session. Hence our scheme achieves session key agreement.

Smart Card Stolen Attack: In this attack, an adversary attempts to retrieve user and base station confidential information. As each information is stored in an encrypted form so its very difficult to guess user identity and password. Therefore our scheme resist smart card stolen attack.

Password Guessing Attack: As our message through which communication takes place does not contain password. Therefore extracting password from public message is difficult in our scheme.

Known Session Specific Temporary Information Attack: In this attack, even if attacker knows the random nonce of user or base station or sensor node and try to calculate session key. The session key not only depend on random nonce but also depend on identity of user and sensor node. But it is very difficult to get the identity. Hence, our scheme is secure against these attack.

6   Performance Analysis

This section compares our scheme with performance of other schemes based on their communicational and computational overhead. Since sensor nodes are restricted with respect to its capacity, computational and communicational capabilities, energy etc.; therefore proper attention needs to be given to computational cost of security schemes for WSNs. As discussed in Sect. 1.3 we have found that our scheme is secured against these attacks.

6.1   Comparison of Computation Cost

In Table 2, we have found and also compared the computation cost of our scheme with other related scheme, like Turkanovic et al.'s [1], Das et al.'s [8], Holbl et al.'s [9] and Farash et al.'s [11]. We have considered the computation cost for user, gateway node and sensor node. We have only considered the hash function in the computation cost.. From this table, it is clear that our scheme is better as compared to other schemes. We have used T_h for hash computation and have assumed its value as 0.0004 ms as given by experimental analysis done in this paper [1]. In our scheme, the computation cost during the different phases for User, gateway node and sensor node are $12T_h$, $15T_h$, and $5T_h$ respectively. As hash function is very efficient sensor node does not require much computation cost. We have summarized the computational cost and running time of our scheme and other schemes [1, 8, 9, 11] in Table 2. From the table we can say, that our scheme is suitable for wireless sensor network.

Table 2. Computation cost and running time.

	Computation cost for user	Computation cost for GWN	Computation cost for sensor node	Total cost	Running time (in ms)
Turkanovic et al.'s [1]	$7T_h$	$5T_h$	$7T_h$	$19T_h$	0.0076
Das et al.'s [8]	$5T_h$	-	$5T_h$	$10T_h$	0.0040
Holbl et al.'s [9]	$4T_h$	$7T_h$	$3T_h$	$14T_h$	0.0056
Farash et al.'s [11]	$11T_h$	$7T_h$	$14T_h$	$32T_h$	0.0128
Ours	$12T_h$	$15T_h$	$5T_h$	$32T_h$	0.0128

6.2 Comparison of Communication Cost

We have compared the communication cost of our scheme with other related scheme, such as Turkanovic et al.'s [1], Das et al.'s [8], Holbl et al.'s [9] and Farash et al.'s [11]. This cost depends on length of the messages during the communication. For efficient message transmission, the communication cost should be as small as possible. In our scheme, the total communication cost for user, gateway node and sensor nodes of all is 3968 bits. The communication cost of our scheme and other discussed scheme is given in the Table 3. From this table we can say that our scheme achieves better performance as compared to other discussed scheme.

Table 3. Communication cost of our scheme and others

	Communication cost for user (in bits)	Communication cost for GWN (in bits)	Communication cost for sensor node (in bits)	Total cost (in bits)
Turkanovic et al.'s [1]	3200	1408	1772	6380
Das et al.'s [8]	0	768	768	1436
Holbl et al.'s [9]	0	768	768	1436
Farash et al.'s [11]	2816	1152	1664	5632
Ours	1024	1280	1664	3968

7 Conclusion

In this paper, we contributed an efficient three-factor user authentication scheme by reducing the consumption of energy for sensor nodes. We simulated our scheme using AVISPA tool for security verification and the results shows that our scheme is secure against active and passive attacks. The mutual authentication and session key is also established in our scheme. The performance analysis shows that our scheme is efficient as compared to the other discussed scheme with respect to communication cost, computation cost and running time. Our scheme also achieves better login phase, very secure session key, strong security protection etc. The overall efficiencies, security and functionalities justify that our scheme is suited for Wireless sensor networks.

References

1. Turkanovic, M., Brumen, B., Hölbl, M.: A novel user authentication and key agreement scheme for heterogeneous ad hoc wireless sensor networks, based on the internet of things notion. Ad Hoc Netw. **20**, 96–112 (2014)
2. Watro, R., Kong, D., Cuti, S.-F., Gardiner, C., Lynn, C., Kruus, P.: Tinypk: securing sensor networks with public key technology. In: Proceedings of the 2nd ACM Workshop on Security of Ad Hoc and Sensor Networks, pp. 59–64 (2004)
3. Xu, J., Zhu, W.-T., Feng, D.-G.: An improved smart card based password authentication scheme with provable security. Comput. Stand. Interface **31**, 723–728 (2009)
4. Singh, S., Chand, S., Kumar, B.: Heterogeneous HEED protocol for wireless sensor networks. Wirel. Pers. Commun. **77**, 2117–2139 (2014)
5. Wong, K., Zheng, Y., Cao, J., Wang, S.: A dynamic user authentication scheme for wireless sensor networks. In: Proceedings of the IEEE International Conference on Sensor Networks, Ubiquitous, and Trust worthy Computing, vol. 1, pp. 8–17 (2006)
6. Vaidya, B., Silva, J.S., Rodrigues, J.J.: Robust dynamic user authentication scheme for wireless sensor networks. In: Proceedings of the 5th ACM Symposium on QoS and Security for Wireless and Mobile Networks, pp. 88–91 (2009)
7. Khan, M.K., Alghathbar, K.: Cryptanalysis and security improvements of two-factor user authentication in wireless sensor networks. Sensors **10**, 2450–2459 (2010)
8. Das, A.K., Sharma, P., Chatterjee, S., Sing, J.K.: A dynamic password based user authentication scheme for hierarchical wireless sensor networks. J. Netw. Comput. Appl. **35** (5), 1646–1656 (2012)
9. Turkanovic, M., Hölbl, M.: An improved dynamic password-based user authentication scheme for hierarchical wireless sensor networks. Elektronika Ir Elektrotechnika **19**(6), 109–116 (2013)
10. Amin, R., Biswas, G.P.: A secure light weight scheme for user authentication and key agreement in multi-gateway based wireless sensor networks. Ad Hoc Netw. **36**, 58–80 (2016)
11. Farash, M.S., Turkanovic, M., Kumari, S., Hölbl, M.: An efficient user authentication and key agreement scheme for heterogeneous wireless sensor network tailored for the internet of things environment. AdHoc Netw. **36**, 152–176 (2016)
12. Manju, Chand, S., Kumar, B.: Selective α-coverage based heuristic in wireless sensor networks. Wirel. Pers. Commun. **97**(1), 1623–1636 (2017)
13. Fan, R., di Ping, L., Fu, J.-Q., Pan, X.-Z.: A secure and efficient user authentication protocol for two-tiered wireless sensor networks. In: Proceedings of the Second Pacific-Asia Conference on Circuits, Communications and System (PACCS 2010), vol. 1, pp. 425–428 (2010)
14. Chang, C.C., Le, H.D.: A provably secure, efficient and flexible authentication scheme for ad hoc wireless sensor networks. IEEE Trans. Wirel. Commun. **15**(1), 357–366 (2016)

15. Yeh, H.-L., Chen, T.-H., Liu, P.-C., Kim, T.-H., Wei, H.-W.: A secured authentication protocol for wireless sensor networks using elliptic curves cryptography. Sensors **11**(5), 4767–4779 (2011)
16. Tseng, H.-R., Jan, R.-H., Yang, W.: An improved dynamic user authentication scheme for wireless sensor networks. In: Proceedings of the Global Telecommunications Conference (GLOBECOM 2007), vol. 1276, pp. 986–990 (2007)
17. Singh, S., Chand, S., Kumar, B.: Multilevel heterogeneous network model for wireless sensor networks. Telecommun. Syst. **64**(2), 259–277 (2016)

Performance Investigation of Energy Efficient HetSEP for Prolonging Lifetime in WSNs

Samayveer Singh[1](✉) and Pradeep Kumar Singh[2](✉)

[1] Department of Computer Science Engineering, Bennett University,
Greater Noida, UP, India
samayveersingh@gmail.com
[2] Department of Computer Science and Engineering,
Jaypee University of Information Technology, Waknaghat, HP, India
pradeep_84cs@yahoo.com

Abstract. In this work, we investigate the performance of heterogeneous stable election protocol (HetSEP) for prolonging the network lifetime. An order-5 heterogeneous energy network model is proposed in this work that can defines the order-1, order-2, order-3, order-4, and order-5 heterogeneity. We consider the SEP protocol to calculate the lifetime of the network and consequently describe its accomplishments as HetSEP-1, HetSEP-2, HetSEP-3, HetSEP-4, and HetSEP-5. The SEP protocol is HetSEP-1 in which all the sensor nodes have same amount of energy. The HetSEP-2, HetSEP-3, HetSEP-4, and HetSEP-5, contain two, three, four, and five orders of energy, respectively. The network lifetime increases as increasing the order of heterogeneity. The HetSEP-2, HetSEP-3, HetSEP-4, & HetSEP-5, prolong the lifetime of the network 100.39%, 126.12%, 186.56%, & 285.67%, in respect to the increase the energy of the network by 65.0%, 72.58%, 107.10%, & 208.40% with respect to the HetSEP-1.

Keywords: Network lifetime · Heterogeneity · Round
Stable election protocol

1 Introduction

Now a day, a wireless sensor networks (WSN) have turn out to be an attractive technology, where WSNs deployed easily without increasing the cost of the network in terms of communication infrastructures. These networks become popular because it takes very less time in installation where we want to perform monitoring task in the environment. Sensor networks are a network of network that includes a low size, low battery power, low memory, and low complex devices, known as sensor nodes. A WSN consists of thousands of thousand of sensor nodes installed with different communication, sensing, storing and computing abilities. In the monitoring environment, every sensor has the facility to capture the object in the monitoring environment of an activity and these sensor nodes perform calculation, and computations of the received data from the monitoring environment. Each node create communicates between the sensor nodes and its peers for collecting the monitored data and forward the sensed data to the base station (BS) with the help of other sensor nodes. A lot of

© Springer Nature Singapore Pte Ltd. 2019
P. K. Singh et al. (Eds.): FTNCT 2018, CCIS 958, pp. 496–509, 2019.
https://doi.org/10.1007/978-981-13-3804-5_37

protocol are exits for data collection from the monitoring environment, and these are energy aware for prolong the lifetime of the network because the substitution of the battery power of the nodes is a extremely complicated practice, once upon a time these sensor nodes have been installed in the monitoring environment. Sensor networks can efficiently utilized the battery power of sensor nodes by considering the different protocols for increasing the lifetime of wireless sensor networks [1]. There are two possible ways to deploy the sensor nodes in the monitoring area namely deterministically or randomly. The deployment of the sensor nodes in the deterministic fashion are additional favorable in different applications such as physically accessibility of the nodes are easy or nodes are placed manually in the monitoring locations. Example are as follows for the deterministic fashion deployment the line in sand for target tracking, city sense for urban monitoring, soil monitoring, etc. Another way of sensor node deployment is the random deployment where sensor nodes are not physically inaccessible in the monitoring area, for example, Mines, bird observation on Great Duck Island etc. In random deployment environment, the nodes are jumped down through an aircraft.

Longevity of the network for prolonging the lifetime of networks is the most important issue in wireless sensor networks, which is directly or indirectly influenced by the energy of network. There are two possible ways to increasing the lifetime of wireless sensor networks, firstly add some extra node in the monitoring environment, and secondly, increase the energy of the existing sensor nodes. Adding some extra node in the monitoring environment is the ten times costlier to increasing the energy of the exiting nodes. Therefore, increasing the energy of the existing nodes is the best way to increasing the lifetime of the networks. The categorizing the sensor nodes into groups are an efficient way for utilizing the network energy called clusters where each cluster has a master sensor node and it is also called the cluster head. This type of nodes has several member nodes and usually called member of the cluster. The cluster head generally performs the data fusion and data aggregation in order to have longer lifetime, the network should have good amount of energy. The wireless sensor networks with different energy levels are called heterogeneous WSNs [2]. In this paper, we propose a 5-order heterogeneous network model for wireless sensor networks to increasing the network lifetime. This model is capable to define order-1, order-2, order-3, order-4, and order-5 heterogeneity. The order-1 describes single type of nodes in a network in term of energy i.e., homogeneous network. The order-2, order-3, order-4, and order-5 describe two types, three types, four types, and five type sensor nodes, respectively. The election of cluster heads probabilities are weighted by the initial energy of a sensor relative to that of other sensors in the network.

The rest of the paper is organized as follows. Section 2 discusses the literature review based on clustering. Section 3 discusses the proposed heterogeneity network model for five order of heterogeneity. In Sect. 4, experimental results are discussed and finally in Sect. 5, the paper is concluded.

2 Related Work

Now a day's WSNs have attracted several researchers due to their potential applications and challenges. Fruitful applications of the WSNs are as military, environmental, health, scientific exploration, area monitoring and structural health monitoring applications, etc. At the same point of time, WSNs have numerous challenges like efficient use of energy, fault-tolerance, connectivity, simplicity, coverage, robustness, scalability, security, etc. The main challenges in wireless networks are related to the improvement in network lifetime for longevity of the sensor networks. The lifetime of the network is an essentially related to the efficient use of energy of the network. Accordingly, lot of protocols have been developed for increasing the lifetime of wireless sensor networks by considering different deployment techniques, and heterogeneous networks models. Papers [6, 10] discuss an extremely first protocol for prolonging the lifetime in WSNs by Heinzelman et al. in 2000, and this protocol is known as low energy adaptive clustering hierarchy (LEACH) protocol. In this protocol, sensor nodes are divided into several groups called as cluster, and a cluster node in each cluster called cluster head that collects the information from its cluster members and sends that to the base station (BS), and all sensors don't send the data directly to the BS. They send their data through cluster heads that is why this protocol is called hierarchical protocol. In this protocol, the cluster heads may not be dispersed uniformly. The solution of this problem has been given in LEACH-C and fixed LEACH [10], by dispersing the cluster heads all over the network so that it can produce better performance in terms of network lifetime and energy consumption.

From the past few decades researcher mainly focuses on the homogeneous network technologies but recently researchers are shifted to the heterogeneous network technology because it become more popular due to its better performance. It has been proved by the researchers that lifetime in case of heterogeneous networks is large as compare to the homogeneous networks. Due to that region many researchers are shifted to heterogeneous networks and some works has been done the heterogeneous networks models. In paper [11], stable election protocol (SEP) is proposed by Smaragdakis et al. for heterogeneous networks, and it is an extension of LEACH and a very first protocol in the field of energy heterogeneity. The selection of cluster head in SEP is based on weighted election probability that can be calculated by the remaining energy of the nodes and node initial energy. SEP considers two level of heterogeneity, which contains two type of nodes namely normal and advance nodes. In this protocol, advanced node energy is higher than that of the normal nodes. In paper [13], a distributed energy efficient clustering (DEEC) protocol is discussed by Qing et al. using 2-level and multilevel heterogeneity. The 2-level heterogeneity network model is precisely identical as discussed in [12] and multilevel heterogeneous model, the energy of each node is arbitrarily to be paid from a given energy interval. Therefore, in this network levels of energy can be infinite due to random allocation of the energy. This model is hardly of any use because each node has different amount energy level and designing of such type of nodes may not be practically feasible. In paper [12], an EEHC protocol for heterogeneous WSNs is discussed by Mao et al. and it considers 3-levels of heterogeneity is discussed by using 3 types of nodes namely: normal nodes, advanced nodes, and super nodes. Advanced node energy is higher than normal node energy and the super node energy is higher than advanced node energy. The selection of cluster head is based on the weighted election probability so that the sensor nodes energy is efficiently utilized. In [14] authors discuss a balanced energy efficient network integrated super heterogeneous (BEENISH) protocol to compute lifetime of the network on the basis of its average energy and its residual energy of nodes. In [15–22] authors discuss a modified HEED protocol for heterogeneous WSNs. It describes 1-level heterogeneity, 2-level heterogeneity, and 3-level heterogeneity by considering level or order of energies. It considers one additional parameter for fuzzy clustering called distance between the sensor node and the cluster head to determine the cluster heads.

In paper [20] a novel energy-efficient clustering protocol (NEECP) for increasing the network lifetime in wireless sensor networks is proposed. It selects the cluster heads in an effective way with an adjustable sensing range and performs data aggregation using chaining approach. It also avoids transmission of redundant data by using a redundancy check function for improving the network lifetime. It is implemented by considering the data with aggregation and without aggregation. In paper [21, 22] a 3-level heterogeneous network model for WSNs to enhance the network lifetime, which is characterized by a single parameter is proposed. Depending upon the value of the model parameter, it can describe 1-level, 2-level, and 3-level heterogeneity. The proposed heterogeneous network model also helps to select effective active sensor nodes for scheduling and compute the network lifetime by implementing two protocols for our network model, which include ALBP and ADEEPS. The ALBP and ADEEPS protocols are implemented for the existing 1-level, 2-level, and 3-level heterogeneous network models, and for the proposed 3-level heterogeneous network model, the ALBP implementations. The simulation results indicate that heterogeneous protocols prolong the network lifetime as compared to the homogeneous protocols. Furthermore, as the level of heterogeneity increases, the lifetime of the network also increases.

Paper [23] discusses a cluster based approach is proposed to increase the network lifetime and throughput of the heterogeneous wireless sensor networks. This approach combined the direct data transmission to base station with the cluster head transmission of data in wireless sensor networks. It uses the twice energy for advanced nodes in comparison to normal nodes. It is observed that results are found good with the use of 10% of advanced nodes along with normal nodes in the network in this approach. However, on further increasing the advanced node deployment beyond deployment 30%, network lifetime and throughput of network start degrading. So, the proposed solution with 10% advanced node may be considered as the best suitable and acceptable solution for better network throughput and life time in WSNs. This paper [24] gives a new reputation based OR metric and some rules, in which the next hop selection is based on its reputation. This metric considers the reputation level as a primary selection parameter for next-hop. A new OR metric relies on energy efficiency and packet delivery ratio of next-hop. This OR protocol selects all middle position neighbors as next-hop and potential forwarder will be decided on the basis of new OR metric. Energy consumption is considered to be dynamic. It has been compared with Middle Position Dynamic Energy Opportunistic Routing (MDOR), and Trust and Location Aware Routing Protocol (TLAR). Paper [25] discusses a data aggregation approach for analyzing in wireless sensor network. This approach minimizes the traffic between the clusters and the sensor nodes by removing the duplicate data at the cluster heads.

In this work, we discuss an order-5 energy network model for increasing the lifetime of a wireless sensor networks. We consider SEP implementations for performance evaluation of the proposed model and accordingly the implementation of SEP is denoted as HetSEP-1, HetSEP-2, HetSEP-3, HetSEP-4, and HetSEP-5. The variants of HetSEP-1, HetSEP-2, HetSEP-3, HetSEP-4, and HetSEP-5 are one, two, three, four, and five order of nodes, respectively. The heterogeneity is beneficial in networks because increasing the network energy by adding more sensors is much costlier than by increasing the energy of some of the nodes. In next section, we will discuss network assumptions and propose our heterogeneous network model.

3 Proposed Method

We assume the following for the WSNs.

- All the nodes have similar abilities such as its memory, processing power, communication range and having equal significance.
- Sink is stationary in our networks and situated in middle in the networks.
- Sensor nodes have capabilities of data fusion and aggregation.
- The categorization of sensor and their energies depends on the order of heterogeneity.
- All the sensor nodes are randomly deployed.
- All the nodes have same capability such as link, memory, sensing range and microprocessor except energy.

We propose an order-5 heterogeneity or non homogeneous network energy model i.e., capable to describe the order-1, order-2, order-3, order-4, and order-5 heterogeneity. Let N be the total number of nodes in the network. The numbers of nodes for all five order of heterogeneity in the network are denoted as N_1, N_2, N_3, N_4, N_5 and they necessity assure the inequality $N_5 < N_4 < N_3 < N_2 < N_1$. The sum of energy/battery power of the heterogeneous networks is denoted by E_{total} and given by

$$E_{total} = E_0 * \beta * N + E_1 * \beta^2 * N + E_2 * \beta^3 * N + E_3 * \beta^4 * N + E_4 * \beta^5 * N \quad (1)$$

where, β is a parameter and E_0, E_1, E_2, E_3 and E_4 are the energies of order-1, order-2, order-3, order-4, and order-5 nodes that necessity assure the inequality $E_4 > E_3 > E_2 > E_1 > E_0$. The battery power of order-i sensor nodes is related to the battery power of order-1 sensors is give by

$$E_j = E_0 + \mu_j \quad (2)$$

Using (1), (2) can be written as

$$E_{total} = E_0 * \beta * N + (E_0 + \mu_1) * \beta^2 * N + (E_0 + \mu_2) * \beta^3 * N + (E_0 + \mu_3) * \beta^4 \\ * N + (E_0 + \mu_4) * \beta^5 * N$$

$\mu_1, \mu_2, \mu_3,$ and μ_4 are the new model parameters. E_{total} can be simplified as follows:

$$E_{total} = N * \left(E_0 * \left(\beta + \beta^2 + \beta^3 + \beta^4 + \beta^5\right) + \left(\beta^2 * \mu_1 + \beta^3 * \mu_2 + \beta^4 * \mu_3 + \beta^5 * \mu_4\right)\right)$$
$$(3)$$

Order-1 Heterogeneity: For $\mu_1 = \mu_2 = \mu_3 = \mu_4 = 0$, the model defined in (3) described one non zero term or one type of nodes (order-1) i.e., called order-1 heterogeneity. The total network energy of order-1 is as follows:

$$E_{order-1} = E_0 * \left(\beta + \beta^2 + \beta^3 + \beta^4 + \beta^5\right)$$

The total no. of sensor nodes in order-1 heterogeneity is defined as

$$N_1 = N * \left(\beta + \beta^2 + \beta^3 + \beta^4 + \beta^5\right)$$

With the following condition

$$\beta + \beta^2 + \beta^3 + \beta^4 + \beta^5 = 1.$$

Order-2 Heterogeneity: For $\mu_2 = \mu_3 = \mu_4 = 0$, the model defined in (3) contains two non zero. It defines order-2 heterogeneity and contains order-1 and order-2 nodes. The total network energy of order-2 is as follows:

$$E_{order-2} = E_0 * \left(\beta + \beta^2 + \beta^3 + \beta^4 + \beta^5\right) + \beta^2 * \mu_1$$

The total no. of order-1 and order-2 nodes in order-2 heterogeneity, denoted by N_1 and N_2, respectively, are given as

$$N_1 = N * \left(\beta + \beta^2 + \beta^3 + \beta^4 + \beta^5\right),$$
$$\text{and } N_2 = N * \beta^2 * \mu_1$$

With the following conditions

$$\left(\beta + \beta^2 + \beta^3 + \beta^4 + \beta^5\right) * 100 = N_1 \text{ and, } \beta^2 * \mu_1 = N - N_1.$$

Order-3 Heterogeneity: For $\mu_3 = \mu_4 = 0$, the model defined in (3) contains three non zero terms and define three types of nodes as called order-1, order-2, and, order-3 nodes. The total network energy of 3-order is as follows:

$$E_{order-3} = E_0 * \left(\beta + \beta^2 + \beta^3 + \beta^4 + \beta^5\right) + \beta^2 * \mu_1 + \beta^3 * \mu_2$$

The total no. of order-1, order-2 and order-3 nodes in 3-order heterogeneity, denoted by N_1, N_2 and N_3, are respectively, given as

$$N_1 = N * \left(\beta + \beta^2 + \beta^3 + \beta^4 + \beta^5\right), N_2 = N * \beta^2 * \mu_1, \text{and } N_3 = N * \beta^3 * \mu_2.$$

With the following conditions

$$\left(\beta + \beta^2 + \beta^3 + \beta^4 + \beta^5\right) * 100 = N_1, \text{and } \beta^2 * \mu_1 + \beta^3 * \mu_2 = N - N_1.$$

Order-4 Heterogeneity: For $\mu_4 = 0$, the model defined in (3) contains four non zero terms and define four types of nodes as order-1, order-2, order-3, and order-4 nodes. The total network energy of order-4 heterogeneity is as follows:

$$E_{tire-4} = \left(E_0 * \left(\beta + \beta^2 + \beta^3 + \beta^4 + \beta^5\right) + \left(\beta^2 * \mu_1 + \beta^3 * \mu_2 + \beta^4 * \mu_3\right)\right)$$

The total no. of order-1, order-2, order-3, and order-4 nodes in *order-4* heterogeneity denoted by N_1, N_2, N_3, and N_4, are respectively, given as

$$N_1 = N * \left(\beta + \beta^2 + \beta^3 + \beta^4 + \beta^5\right),$$
$$N_2 = N * \beta^2 * \mu_1,$$
$$N_3 = N * \beta^3 * \mu_2, \text{and}$$
$$N_4 = N * \beta^4 * \mu_3.$$

With the following conditions

$$\left(\beta + \beta^2 + \beta^3 + \beta^4 + \beta^5\right) * 100 = N_1, \text{and}$$
$$\beta^2 * \mu_1 + \beta^3 * \mu_2 + \beta^4 * \mu_3 = N - N_1.$$

Order-5 Heterogeneity: the model defined in (3) contains all non zero terms and define five order heterogeneity. The five typ of are as order-1, order-2, order-3, order-4, and order-5 nodes. The total network energy of order-5 heterogeneity is as follows:

$$E_{tire-5} = \left(E_0 * \left(\beta + \beta^2 + \beta^3 + \beta^4 + \beta^5\right) + \left(\beta^2 * \mu_1 + \beta^3 * \mu_2 + \beta^4 * \mu_3 + \beta^5 * \mu_4\right)\right)$$

The total no. of order-1, order-2, order-3, order-4, and order-5 nodes in order-5 heterogeneity denoted by N_1, N_2, N_3, N_4, and N_5, are respectively, given as

$$N_1 = N * \left(\beta + \beta^2 + \beta^3 + \beta^4 + \beta^5\right),$$
$$N_2 = N * \beta^2 * \mu_1,$$
$$N_3 = N * \beta^3 * \mu_2,$$
$$N_4 = N * \beta^4 * \mu_3, \text{ and}$$
$$N_5 = N * \beta^5 * \mu_4$$

With the following conditions

$$\left(\beta + \beta^2 + \beta^3 + \beta^4 + \beta^5\right) * 100 = N_1, \text{ and}$$
$$\beta^2 * \mu_1 + \beta^3 * \mu_2 + \beta^4 * \mu_3 + \beta^5 * \mu_4 = N - N_1.$$

The selection of master node or cluster head is depends on the probability of nodes. We determine the probability of order-5 heterogeneity nodes i.e., order-1, order-2, order-3, order-4, and order-5 nodes as follows:

$$\left.\begin{aligned}
P_{order-1} &= \frac{P_{opt}}{\left(\left(\beta + \beta^2 + \beta^3 + \beta^4 + \beta^5\right) + \left(\beta^2 * \mu_1 + \beta^3 * \mu_2 + \beta^4 * \mu_3 + \beta^5 * \mu_4\right)\right)} \\
P_{order-2} &= \frac{P_{opt} * (\mu_1)}{\left(\left(\beta + \beta^2 + \beta^3 + \beta^4 + \beta^5\right) + \left(\beta^2 * \mu_1 + \beta^3 * \mu_2 + \beta^4 * \mu_3 + \beta^5 * \mu_4\right)\right)} \\
P_{order-3} &= \frac{P_{opt} * (\mu_2)}{\left(\left(\beta + \beta^2 + \beta^3 + \beta^4 + \beta^5\right) + \left(\beta^2 * \mu_1 + \beta^3 * \mu_2 + \beta^4 * \mu_3 + \beta^5 * \mu_4\right)\right)} \\
P_{order-4} &= \frac{P_{opt} * (\mu_3)}{\left(\left(\beta + \beta^2 + \beta^3 + \beta^4 + \beta^5\right) + \left(\beta^2 * \mu_1 + \beta^3 * \mu_2 + \beta^4 * \mu_3 + \beta^5 * \mu_4\right)\right)} \\
P_{order-5} &= \frac{P_{opt} * (\mu_4)}{\left(\left(\beta + \beta^2 + \beta^3 + \beta^4 + \beta^5\right) + \left(\beta^2 * \mu_1 + \beta^3 * \mu_2 + \beta^4 * \mu_3 + \beta^5 * \mu_4\right)\right)}
\end{aligned}\right\} \quad (4)$$

In Eq. (1), replace the value of P_{opt} by the weighted probability for the threshold i.e., applied to select the master node in each and every round. The threshold of order-1, order-2, order-3, order-4, and order-5 nodes are define as $T(s_{order-1})$, $T(s_{order-2})$, $T(s_{order-3})$, $T(s_{order-4})$, and $T(s_{order-5})$, respectively, as in (5).

$$T(s_{order-1}) = \begin{cases} \dfrac{p_{order-1}}{1-p_{order-1}\cdot\left(r \bmod \frac{1}{p_{order-1}}\right)} & \text{if } s_{order-1}G^1 \\ 0 & \textit{Otherwise} \end{cases}$$

$$T(s_{order-2}) = \begin{cases} \dfrac{p_{order-2}}{1-p_{order-2}\cdot\left(r \bmod \frac{1}{p_{order-2}}\right)} & \text{if } s_{order-2}G^2 \\ 0 & \textit{Otherwise} \end{cases}$$

$$T(s_{order-3}) = \begin{cases} \dfrac{p_{order-3}}{1-p_{order-3}\cdot\left(r \bmod \frac{1}{p_{order-3}}\right)} & \text{if } s_{order-3}G^3 \\ 0 & \textit{Otherwise} \end{cases} \qquad (5)$$

$$T(s_{order-4}) = \begin{cases} \dfrac{p_{order-4}}{1-p_{order-4}\cdot\left(r \bmod \frac{1}{p_{order-4}}\right)} & \text{if } s_{order-4}G^4 \\ 0 & \textit{Otherwise} \end{cases}$$

$$T(s_{order-5}) = \begin{cases} \dfrac{p_{order-5}}{1-p_{order-5}\cdot\left(r \bmod \frac{1}{p_{order-5}}\right)} & \text{if } s_{order-4}G^5 \\ 0 & \textit{Otherwise} \end{cases}$$

where, r is the current round, $G^1, G^2, G^3, G^4,$ and G^5, are the set of order-1, order-2, order-3, order-4, and, order-5 nodes that have not yet turn into master node in last $\left\{\frac{1}{p_{order-1}}, \frac{1}{p_{order-2}}, \frac{1}{p_{order-3}}, \frac{1}{p_{order-4}} \text{and} \frac{1}{p_{order-5}}\right\}$ rounds, and $T(s_{order-1})$, $T(s_{order-2})$, $T(s_{order-3})$, $T(s_{order-4})$, and $T(s_{order-5})$ are the thresholds applied to the population of order-1, order-2, order-3, order-4, and order-5 nodes, respectively.

In the next section, we will discuss the simulation of the exiting SEP i.e., HetSEP-1, HetSEP-2, HetSEP-3, HetSEP-4, and HetSEP-5 protocols.

4 Simulation Results

In this section, we present the simulation results for our proposed heterogeneous network model by considering SEP protocol and the implementation of SEP protocol over our proposed model is called HetSEP. Section 3 has discussed a proposed model and it can define order-1 (original SEP), order-2, order-3, order-4, and order-5 heterogeneity of the WSNs. On the bases of heterogeneity, we call the implementations as HetSEP-1, HetSEP-2, HetSEP-3, HetSEP-4, and HetSEP-5 heterogeneity. In this work, we compute the network lifetime, no. of alive nodes, no. of dead nodes, no. of packets sent at the sink and total energy consumption for the proposed heterogeneous network model. In this work, we have randomly deployed 100 no. of nodes in an area of size 100 M × 100 M. The energy dissipation model is used in this work as same given in [2, 6, 10]. Table 1 shows the input parameters which are used in our simulations.

For different order of heterogeneity, the proposed model has characterized by different parameters $\beta, \mu_1, \mu_2, \mu_3$ and μ_4. For order-1 heterogeneity (HetSEP-1), we assume the total no. of sensor nodes are 100 with initial energy 0.5 J. For order-1 heterogeneity (HetSEP-2), we compute the no. of order-1 and order-2 nodes are 75 and 25 and the energies of order-1 & order 2 are as 0.5 J and 1.80 J, respectively. For order-3 heterogeneity (HetSEP-3), we compute the no. of order-1, order-2, and order-3 nodes are 70, 20 and 10 and the energies are 0.5 J, 1.64 J and 1.85 J, respectively. For order-3 heterogeneity (HetSEP-4), the no. of order-1, order-2, order-3, and order-4 nodes are 65, 20, 10 & 5 and the energies are 0.5 J, 1.75 J, 2.06 J & 2.45 J, respectively. For order-5 (HetSEP-5), we compute the no. of order-1, order-2, order-3, order-4, and order-5 nodes are 60, 15, 12, 8 & 5, and the energies are 0.5 J, 1.54 J, 2.69 J, 4.34 J & 6.82 J, respectively.

Table 1. Simulation parameters

Heterogeneity	No. of Nodes	β	μ_1	μ_2	μ_3	μ_4	E_0	E_1	E_2	E_3	E_4	E_{total}	Lifetime
Order-1	100	NA	NA	NA	NA	NA	0.5	NA	NA	NA	NA	50.00	1815
Order-2	75 + 25	0.44	1.31	NA	NA	NA	0.5	1.80	NA	NA	NA	82.50	3637
Order-3	70 + 20 + 10	0.42	1.14	1.35	NA	NA	0.5	1.64	1.85	NA	NA	86.29	5201
Order-4	65 + 20 + 10 + 5	0.40	1.25	1.56	1.95	NA	0.5	1.75	2.06	2.45	NA	103.55	4104
Order-5	60 + 15 + 12 + 8 + 5	0.38	1.04	2.19	3.84	6.31	0.5	1.54	2.69	4.34	6.82	154.20	7000

NA- not applicable

In Fig. 1, we have work out for different orders of heterogeneity by considering the no. of alive nodes with respect to the number of rounds. It is evident from the analysis of simulation of results, as the order of heterogeneity increases, the network lifetime of the network increases. It is also clear from the Fig. 1 that the last sensor nodes dead come about in 1815th, 3637th, 5204th, 4104th and 7000th no. of rounds for all five variants of HetSEP protocols, respectively. The HetSEP-5 performs the better than among all others in terms of no. of alive sensor nodes. We also computed the no. of dead nodes in Fig. 2 for different orders of heterogeneity with respect to the number of rounds.

In Fig. 2, the first nodes dead become 402th, 662th, 843th, 1020th, and 1602th in no. of rounds for HetSEP-1, HetSEP-2, HetSEP-3, HetSEP-4, and HetSEP-5, respectively.

In Fig. 3, we have computed the no. of packets delivered to the sink with respect to the no. of rounds for different orders of heterogeneity. The no. of packets transferred to the sink in HetSEP-1, HetSEP-2, HetSEP-3, HetSEP-4, and HetSEP-5, has been obtained as 1.51×10^4, 2.51×10^4, 2.72×10^4, 3.33×10^4 and 4.73×10^4, respectively, with respect to the no. of rounds. It is also evident that the HetSEP-5 has more no. of data packets delivered to the sink than the HetSEP-1, HetSEP-2, HetSEP-3, and HetSEP-4. In this work, we have also computed the total energy consumption with respect to the number of rounds as shown in Fig. 4. The five order of heterogeneity (HetSEP-5) performs better among all orders of heterogeneity of the HetSEP variants. However, the rate of energy consumption is much slower in case the HetSEP-5 (five order of heterogeneity) than the all other orders of heterogeneity. The HetSEP-2, HetSEP-3, HetSEP-4, and HetSEP-5, increase the network lifetime 100.39%, 126.12%, 186.56%, and 285.67%, corresponding to the increase in the network energy by 65.0%, 72.58%, 107.10%, and 208.40% with respect to the HetSEP-1.

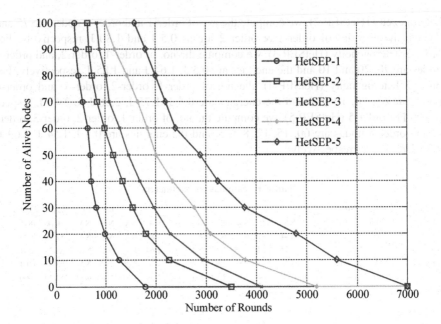

Fig. 1. No. of nodes alive vs. number of rounds

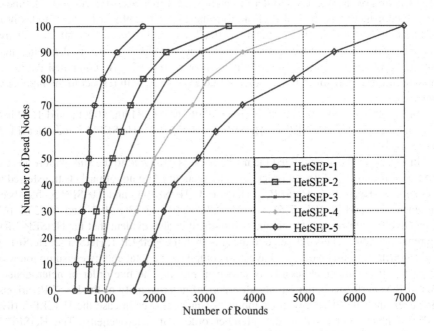

Fig. 2. No. of dead nodes vs. number of rounds

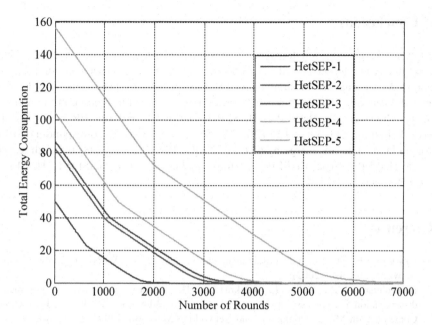

Fig. 3. Total energy consumption vs. number of rounds

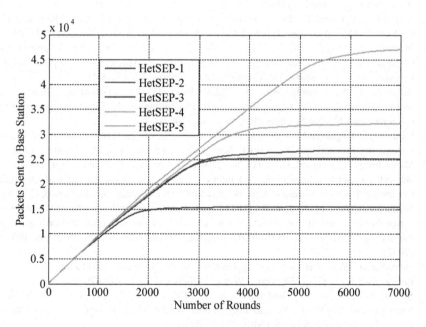

Fig. 4. No. of packets sent to the sink vs. number of rounds

5 Conclusions

In this work, an order-5 heterogeneity network model has been proposed for WSNs, namely: order-1, order-2, order-3, order-4, and order-5 heterogeneity in terms of energy. As the analysis of simulation of results, prolonging heterogeneity order prolongs the network lifetime in much proportion as compared to prolong in the network energy. However, the HetSEP-2, HetSEP-3, HetSEP-4, and HetSEP-5, prolong the network lifetime 100.39%, 126.12%, 186.56%, and 285.67% corresponding to the prolong in the network energy by 65.0%, 72.58%, 107.10%, and 208.40% with respect to the HetSEP-1. The HetSEP-5 performs better than the HetSEP-1, HetSEP-2, HetSEP-3, and HetSEP-4.

References

1. Akyildiz, I.F., Su, W., Sankarasubramaniam, Y., Cayirci, E.: WSNs: a survey. Comput. Netw. **38**, 393–422 (2002)
2. Heinzelman, W.R., Kulik, J., Balakrishnan, H.: Adaptive protocols for information dissemination in wireless sensor networks. In: Proceedings of ACM/IEEE International Conference on Mobile Computing and Networking MobiCom 1999, Seattle, WA (1999)
3. Intanagonwiwat, C., Govindan, R., Estrin, D.: Directed diffusion: a scalable and robust communication paradigm for sensor networks. In: Proceedings of ACM MobiCom 2000, Boston, MA, pp. 56–67 (2000)
4. Braginsky, D., Estrin, D.: Rumor routing algorithm for sensor networks. In: Proceedings of the First Workshop on Sensor Networks and Applications (WSNA), Atlanta, GA (2002)
5. Madiraju, S., Mallanda, C., Kannan, R., Durresi, A., Iyengar, S.S.: EBRP: energy band based routing protocol for wireless sensor networks. Department of Computer Science, Louisiana State University, 298 Coates Hall, LA 70803, USA (2004)
6. Heinzelman, W., Chandrakasan, A., Balakrishnan, H.: Energy-efficient communication protocol for wireless microsensor networks. In: Proceedings of the 33rd Hawaii International Conference on System Sciences (HICSS 2000) (2000)
7. Lindsey, S., Raghavendra, C.S.: PEGASIS: power efficient gathering in sensor information systems. In: Proceedings of the IEEE Aerospace Conference, Big Sky, Montana (2002)
8. Manjeshwar, A., Agarwal, D.P.: TEEN: a protocol for enhanced efficiency in wireless sensor networks. In: Proceedings of the 1st International Workshop on Parallel and Distributed Computing Issues in Wireless Networks and Mobile Computing, San Francisco, CA (2001)
9. Manjeshwar, A., Agarwal, D.P.: APTEEN: a hybrid protocol for efficient routing and comprehensive information retrieval in wireless sensor networks. In: Proceedings of the International Parallel and Distributed Processing Symposium, IPDPS 2002, pp. 195–202 (2002)
10. Heinzelman, W.B., et al.: An application-specific protocol architecture for wireless microsensor networks. IEEE Trans. Wireless Commun. **1**(4), 660–670 (2002)
11. Smaragdakis, G., Matta, I., and Bestavros, A.: SEP: a stable election protocol for clustered heterogeneous WSNs. In: Second International Workshop on Sensor and Actor Network Protocols and Applications (SANPA 2004) (2004)
12. Kumar, D., Aseri, T.C., Patel, R.B.: EEHC: energy efficient heterogeneous clustered scheme for WSNs. Comput. Commun. **32**, 662–667 (2009)

13. Qing, L., Zhu, Q., Wang, M.: Design of a distributed energy efficient clustering algorithm for heterogeneous WSNs. Comput. Commun. **29**, 2230–2237 (2006)
14. Qureshi, T.N., et al.: BEENISH: balanced energy efficient network integrated super heterogeneous protocol for wireless sensor networks. In: International Workshop on Body Area Sensor Networks (BASNet-2013) (2013). Procedia Comput. Sci. **00**, 1–6
15. Chand, S., Singh, S., Kumar, B.: Heterogeneous HEED protocol for wireless sensor networks. Wirel. Pers. Commun. **77**(3), 2117–2139 (2014)
16. Singh, S., Malik, A.: hetDEEC: heterogeneous DEEC protocol for prolonging lifetime in wireless sensor networks. J. Inf. Optim. Sci. **38**(5), 699–720 (2017)
17. Singh, S., Malik, A., Kumar, R.: Energy efficient heterogeneous DEEC protocol for enhancing lifetime in WSNs. Int. J. Eng. Sci. Technol. **20**(1), 345–353 (2017)
18. Singh, S.: Energy efficient multilevel network model for heterogeneous WSNs. Int. J. Eng. Sci. Technol. **20**(1), 105–115 (2017)
19. Singh, S., Chand, S., Kumar, B.: Multilevel heterogeneous network model for wireless sensor networks. Telecommun. Syst. **64**(2), 259–277 (2016)
20. Singh, S., Chand, S., Kumar, R., Malik, A., Kumar, B.: NEECP: a novel energy efficient clustering protocol for prolonging lifetime of WSNs. IET Wirel. Sens. Syst. **6**(5), 151–157 (2016)
21. Singh, S., Malik, A.: Energy efficient scheduling protocols for heterogeneous WSNs. Int. J. Forensic Comput. Sci. **11**(1), 8–29 (2016)
22. Chand, S., Singh, S., Kumar, B.: hetADEEPS: ADEEPS for heterogeneous wireless sensor networks. Int. J. Future Gener. Commun. Netw. **6**(5), 21–32 (2013)
23. Kumar, H., Singh, P.K.: Node energy based approach to improve network lifetime and throughput in wireless sensor networks. J. Telecommun., Electron. Comput. Eng. **9**(3), 83–88 (2017)
24. Kumar, N., Singh, Y., Singh, P.K.: Reputation-based energy efficient opportunistic routing for wireless sensor networks. J. Telecommun., Electron. Comput. Eng. **9**(3), 29–33 (2017)
25. Kumar, H., Singh, P.K.: Analyzing data aggregation in wireless sensor network. In: Proceedings of the INDIACom-2017, 01–03 March 2017, pp. 4024–4029 (2017)

Author Index

Printed in the United States
By Bookmasters